THE BOUNDARIES OF

Desire

THE
BOUNDARIES OF

Desire

A CENTURY OF BAD LAWS,
GOOD SEX, AND CHANGING IDENTITIES

•

ERIC BERKOWITZ

COUNTERPOINT | BERKELEY, CALIFORNIA

LIBRARY OF CONGRESS CATALOGING-IN-PUBLICATION DATA
Berkowitz, Eric.
The Boundaries of Desire: Bad Laws, Good Sex, and Changing Identities / Eric Berkowitz.
pages cm
ISBN 978-1-61902-529-5 (hardback)
1. Sex—Social aspects. 2. Sex customs—History. I. Title.
HQ21.B547 2015
306.7—dc23
2015005123

COUNTERPOINT
2560 Ninth Street, Suite 318
Berkeley, CA 94710
www.counterpointpress.com

Printed in the United States of America

Distributed by Publishers Group West

10 9 8 7 6 5 4 3 2 1

AS ALWAYS, FOR JENNIFER

CONTENTS

INTRODUCTION

Some aspects of existence, such as the speed of light, don't change. Others, such as our bodies, are in continual transformation. Still others remain constant but are subject to ever-changing perceptions. Sex falls into this last category. The act of reproduction and all its variants have been practiced in roughly the same ways since the beginning, but our views about the meaning and consequences of sex are in perpetual flux. Those beliefs determine the way we judge and punish the sex of others.

Lawmakers have always set boundaries on how people take their sexual pleasures. At any given point in time, everywhere, some forms of sex have been encouraged while others have been punished without mercy. Today's sacred truths often become tomorrow's hateful prejudices, and vice versa. Jump forward or backward a few decades, cross a border, or traverse social classes and the harmless fun of one culture becomes the gravest crime in another. Because the sexual urge burns at the intersection of existence, identity, and power, it has always carried outsize significance. Whom we make love to, how we do it, and why are among the law's central concerns. "The personal is political" was a common feminist refrain in the 1960s and 1970s. Sex—the quintessentially personal activity—has always been political.

Over the past hundred-plus years, nearly every aspect of Western sexual morality has been turned on its head. With the expansion of women's rights and gay rights, the decriminalization of birth control and abortion, and effective treatments for most venereal infections, sex is now less risky for more people than ever before. In many ways, the law in the US and much of Europe has kept pace with these changes. No longer are adultery, fornication, or homosexuality treated as crimes, and while those who have sex with people of a different race still face social stigma, they cannot be driven from their homes or put in jail. Even within the home, the rules have transformed. Men recently lost the right to rape their wives and broad domestic violence laws have given women and children unprecedented protection from sexual aggression in the very place where it happens most often. At the same time, sexually oriented reading or viewing material— whether health information, explicit pornography, or auto-parts advertisements featuring under clad women—are omnipresent, and controls on their dissemination have never been more easily circumvented.

Yet none of this has gone down easily, and as the twenty-first century finds its stride, Western society is still struggling to digest the post– Second World War sexual revolution. The compulsion to control the sex lives of others remains as powerful as the yearning for sex itself, and with each unfastening of sexual restrictions have come other, sometimes fearsome restraints. While sex can be more safely pursued now than in previous centuries, and a rewarding sex life has become an essential condition for personal fulfillment, the age-old dread of sexual desire—as destructive of both the individual soul and the well-being of society—has not diminished. "Sex is always something we can't control—we have to defend against it. . . . Why? Because sex is really penetrating inside everyone." This quote comes from a scholar explaining the strict separation of sexes among Orthodox Jews, but it also captures an enduring principle of secular sex law. At both the left and right ends of the political spectrum, the view persists that sex is uncontrollable and dangerous.

Sexual transgressions are seen as harmful both to the victims and, by extension, to everyone else. One's activities in the outside world can draw mixed opinions, but those who have forbidden sex often find they have no allies. That is why charges of sexual misbehavior are so commonly used to neutralize enemies and troublemakers. The black boxing champion Jack Johnson's victories over white opponents caused riots, but sex trafficking charges drove him out of the US in 1913. Martin Luther King Jr. was one of the FBI's main political targets, but when the bureau failed to link him to criminal or communist conspiracies, it turned to sex: in 1964, with evidence of King's rather unremarkable adulterous affairs in hand, the FBI wrote to him threatening to expose his "evil," "filthy," "psychotic," "animal," and "hideous" "orgies." Telling King he was now "finished," the letter counseled suicide: "King, there is only one thing left for you to do. You know what it is." In 2010, Julian Assange became a hero to some and a villain to many others when his WikiLeaks website published reams of classified US documents. However, it was not his political subversion that forced him to take refuge in the Ecuadoran embassy in London—it was the risk of extradition to Sweden on the thinnest possible sex-crime charges.

The sex smear has become a reflexive device to discredit people, even the long dead. In 2013, during a bone-dry conference discussion on the government-deficit theories of the British economist John Maynard Keynes (1883–1946), Harvard historian Niall Ferguson—no fan of Keynesian economics—dismissed Keynes as a childless gay man who couldn't satisfy his wife and who had no concern for the impact of his theories on posterity. (This charge had already been a staple of conservative academic thought for decades.) Economics is indeed a "dismal science," but when it gets too dreary, even highbrow academics are not above a little gay bashing. Nor are liberals. Take the oft-repeated canard about FBI director J. Edgar Hoover prancing around a New York hotel suite in a frilly dress, high heels, and a wig. The story, as homophobic as any coming from conservatives, is relished by the left—even by those who know better. *New York Times* columnist Frank Rich, for example, admitted that "[t]here is no solid proof" of the "delicious" rumors about Hoover, but he could not help adding: "But we can dream, can't we?" Of course we can, and we do, because sexual slander works. As the proprietor of piles of dirt about his enemies' sex lives, and as the century's most sanctimonious morals enforcer—no mean feat, given the competition—Hoover knew this as well as anyone. One need not be accused of something as serious as rape to be brought down; succumbing too readily to the call of the libido is often enough.

• • •

As many of the legal screws on sex loosened over the past century, and as what historian Eric Hobsbawm called the "unlimited autonomy of individual desire" took hold after the Second World War, long-standing fears about the menace of sex reemerged in new, strident forms. More than ever, sex became an issue in power politics, and the sexual habits of individuals became a collective concern. In direct response to growing sexual freedoms, more sex law emerged—much of it no less punishing and irrational than in centuries past. This book aims to trace that process.

In *Sex and Punishment: Four Thousand Years of Judging Desire*, I followed the movement of sex law from the beginnings of Western civilization until the 1895 imprisonment of Oscar Wilde for "gross indecency." If I ventured any further ahead in time in that volume, I feared the noise of the present age would drown out the voices of our ancestors. How could it not? The sexual urge still churns with what Plato called the "most raging frenzy," and sexual morality is ceaselessly debated in every corner of society. The sex rules of Renaissance Venice and Victorian England are fascinating, but those governing the lives of the living demand their own book.

This book's chapters each address different sets of laws, but they all speak to the exercise of power by the strong over the bodies of the weak, based on a roiling mix of sexual mores. They include prostitutes locked up and abused after being "rescued" by clueless religious groups; Nazi-era Jews killed for "defiling" the "master race" with German lovers, and African Americans lynched for sex with white people; homosexuals put through lobotomy "cures" in mental hospitals and poor black girls forcibly sterilized for being "promiscuous"; young children marked as dangerous sex offenders for experimenting with playmates; and sexting teenagers jailed as child pornographers. Being a sex criminal often turns on the bad luck of being caught in the wrong place or decade, belonging to the wrong class or race, or doing something on the wrong side of a passing morality panic.

Modern sex law is a Gordian knot to be examined as a whole and untangled thread by thread. Nevertheless, one recurring theme—the impact of science, technology, and mass communications—is woven too tightly into the subject to be confined to any single chapter. Developments in these areas have upended the ways sex is experienced, discussed, and judged. Breakthroughs in contraception, particularly the birth control pill, fueled the postwar sexual revolution more than any other factor, while new treatments have saved billions of people from the ravages of many sexually transmitted infections. Science has also introduced a host of methods for conception without sex, which have, in turn, called into question our most basic notions about families, children, and social identity. No less influential on sex law have been the social sciences, in particular psychology, which continue to shape our beliefs about what sexual behaviors are transgressive and what kinds of people with "unsavory" desires pose dangers to others.

In this context, the law has been playing a perennial game of catch-up, trying to reconcile long-standing moral strictures with an onslaught of challenges from the men and women in white coats. With its gloss of objective truth, science is often an unassailable basis for determining not only which types of sexual conduct should be condemned outright and which treated as pathologies, but also the types of punishments and treatments that should be imposed. The problem is that justice is impossible unless it is consistent, and in the sciences, the proven truths of one year can well become the next year's falsehoods. The Bible is a poor basis for distinguishing good sex from bad, but at least it doesn't change. When an Alabama court, in a 1966 homosexuality case, invoked "the savage horror practiced by the dwellers of ancient Sodom," the court tapped into clear and fixed fears. By contrast, science discards any notion the instant a better one comes along. While that is essential for the advancement of knowledge, it can be anathema to equality under law. Doctors and researchers make terrible moralizers. Judges do too, but too often they have been made worse by looking to science for guidance.

Once the law signs on to a prevailing theory—say, that homosexuals are mentally ill and should be "treated" with "icepick" lobotomies or castrated; that venereal infections originate from poor, dark-skinned people; or that one may be based on a diagnosis that he or she *may* commit sex crimes—a lot of people will be harmed before the theory is discarded. (The first two of these scenarios have fallen by the wayside, but the third still undergirds the law in many places.)

The same is true with rape. For much of the past century, the law embraced prevalent psychological theories that women claiming rape were probably lying, that nonvirgins had probably consented, that no often really meant yes, and that, deep down inside, many women wanted to be ravaged. While the law is thankfully jettisoning these theories, experts have come forward to pathologize other types of behavior for the first time. Prepubescent children who touch their siblings inappropriately are now being branded as sex criminals, while parents can risk child-abuse charges for bathing their children with their bare hands instead of a soapy cloth. One group of mental-health professionals even called for "intervention" when parents and their kids sleep together. Such arrangements, we are told, risk "emotional incest syndrome" and "oedipal castration anxiety."

The effort to root out the sexually dangerous (particularly in the home) is salutary, but must be leavened with common sense, which crusading mental-health professionals and social workers can have in short supply—especially when they are paid by the state for their opinions and treatments. For example, since the late 1940s a vast medical-prison complex has been built around the idea that sex offenders (a classification that once included homosexuals) are hardwired to reoffend. To enable terrified communities to protect themselves, and to prevent sex offenders from going near schools and playgrounds, there are now more than 750,000 people on public sex-offender registries. They are severely restricted as to where they can live and go, whom they can associate with, and what jobs they can take. Many will remain listed for their entire lives. For those whom prison psychiatrists deem still dangerous after serving their prison sentences, indeterminate "civil confinements" in well-staffed state mental hospitals can await them. However, statistical evidence and recent advances in neuroscience maintain that psychiatrists are no better than coin flippers at predicting which sex offenders will reoffend. In fact, there is a well-founded argument that released sex offenders are *less* likely to commit crimes than other criminals, even violent ones, and that sex registries have not made communities safer from sex crime. Does that mean it is time to erase the registries, let registrants back into communities, and discharge the professionals whose livelihoods depend on the continued terror of sex offenders? Not likely.

Psychiatric professionals also plumb the psyches of victims to find long-buried mental records of sexual abuse. As the number of child sexual-abuse cases grew in the 1980s and 1990s, it became clear that many older cases would not be heard because the victims had no clear memory or no recollection at all of what had happened. Driven by lawyers and victims' groups ready to wage war against wealthy organizations such as the Catholic Church, a push began to validate "repressed memory" as admissible evidence in legal cases. As this effort gained traction, many statutes of limitation were modified and waves of lawsuits were filed. Unquestionably, it has helped to bring sexual abusers to justice, giving long-overdue satisfaction to their victims. But as useful as repressed-memory evidence has been against pedophiles, its reliability remains the subject of intense disagreement. Some people who claim to have been falsely accused of sexual abuse have even organized the False Memory Syndrome Foundation (FMSF). (Interestingly, FMSF's website lists a series of multimillion-dollar lawsuits against mental-health providers for irresponsibly leading patients to believe that they had been sexually abused.) The trauma for sexual-abuse victims, particularly those abused as children, is painfully real, but the movement to provide a remedy for every wrong, even those decades old, should not ride roughshod over basic notions of fairness.

•   •   •

Anyone in the past century who believed that members of the Catholic clergy were somehow immune to sexual desire, or that many were homosexual, should—as the cliché goes—have had his or her head examined. Since well before the 1905 publication of Sigmund Freud's *Three Essays on the Theory of Sexuality*, the sexual urge has been universalized, naturalized, mapped, and documented. Whatever the subtleties or intricacies of Freud's thinking, the message filtered through that the sexual instinct permeates human life from the cradle to the grave, and that its repression is harmful to the individual and, perhaps, even to civilization itself. Freud was far from the first to note the insistent call of the gonads (Saint Augustine wrote in the fourth century that genital "insubordination" was humankind's punishment for original sin), but Freud rescued it from wickedness.

The profound influence of this idea, and those of Freud's contemporaries such as Havelock Ellis, cannot be overstated. No longer was sexual compulsion the sole province of whoremongers, godless libertines, and dark-skinned exotics. It was in everyone, all the time. "Why," asked Ellis, "should people be afraid of rousing passions which, after all, are the great driving force of human life?" While Freud affirmed that civilization is "founded on the suppression of instincts," he criticized enforced abstinence and monogamy. "I have not gained the impression," he wrote, "that sexual abstinence helps to shape energetic, self-reliant men of action, nor original thinkers, bold pioneers and reformers; far more often it produces 'good' weaklings who later become lost in the crowd." For a growing segment of the population—especially those whose faith in moral orthodoxies was rattled by the First World War—these messages were easy to swallow and pleasurable to realize. As the century wore on, few disagreed that a life without sex was a life not well lived. By 1930, one of the US's most eminent jurists, Augustus Hand, would raise few eyebrows by declaring what was already obvious: "The sex impulses are present in every one."

One result of recognizing the pervasiveness of the libido was the birth control movement, most closely identified in the US with Margaret Sanger and in Britain with Marie Stopes. For these women and their confederates, birth control meant much more than the right to say no to their husbands' sexual demands. It also embraced the right to *enjoy* sex without the constant risk—and, for poor and working women, the health burdens—of conception. As recalled in 1936 by the New York bohemian and free-love practitioner Mabel Dodge Luhan, Sanger was "openly an ardent propagandist for the joys of the flesh. . . . [As Sanger] unfolded the mysteries and mightiness of physical love it seemed to us that we had never known it before as a sacred and at the same time a scientific reality." The fight for birth control rights was a battle for female sexual satisfaction as an end in itself. By framing these tectonic demands as "scientific reality," they were invested with objective truth and historical inevitability.

Greenwich Village eccentrics such as Luhan readily integrated these ideas into their personal lives—she even named her dog Climax—but others took the message of sexual freedom much further. The Freud protégé Wilhelm Reich (to whom Freud referred his first patient, an impotence sufferer) made the evangelizing of sexual pleasure his life's work. Possessed of a restless, brilliant, and, in the end, sometimes unhinged intellect, Reich coined the term "sexual revolution" in his 1938 book of the same name and also elevated the consistent achievement of "total orgasms" to an individual and societal imperative. One's wellbeing, Reich believed, depended on the ability to dissolve into orgasmic ecstasy. "There is only one thing wrong with neurotic patients," he wrote in *The Function of the Orgasm* (1927), "*the lack of full and repeated sexual satisfaction.*" The nurturing of true sexual pleasure, he maintained, was also a cure for broader social ills—including the fascism that would drive him from Europe. "The formation of the authoritarian structure," he wrote in *The Mass Psychology of Fascism*, "takes place through the anchoring of sexual inhibition and sexual anxiety."

Reich and Freud inevitably parted ways. Freud believed that giving sexuality free rein was anathema to civilization; Reich thought otherwise. After the break with his intellectual "father," Reich came to the US in 1939 with undiminished zeal for health through orgasmic potency. Soon after his arrival, he invented the orgone energy accumulator, a metal-lined, wooden box about twice the size of a casket that functioned as a hothouse for the libidinous "orgone" energy Reich believed coursed through the atmosphere. When subjects stepped inside (naked, according to Reich's instructions), he believed they would be cured of all that ailed them, from sexual problems to varicose veins. The orgone box became chic, drawing the likes of Norman Mailer, J. D. Salinger, and the young Sean Connery as passionate adherents. William Burroughs claimed he had a spontaneous orgasm in his orgone box, while Woody Allen used an "orgasmatron" as a prop in his film *Sleeper.* In 1964, years after orgone boxes had been banned as fraudulent medical devices, *Time* magazine declared that Reich "may have been a prophet" for the sexual revolution then in full swing, "for now it sometimes seems that all America is one big Orgone Box."

Reich was jailed and his books burned after he defied a court order to stop selling orgone boxes, but his linking of sex and freedom deeply affected sexual attitudes, first on the young and then more broadly. His well-thumbed works were obligatory trophies on the shelves of student radicals in the 1960s and 1970s. In 1968, young revolutionaries in Europe and the US scrawled Reichian slogans on walls; in Berlin, copies of Reich's *The Mass Psychology of Fascism* were hurled at police, while at the University of Frankfurt, student activists were advised: "Read Reich and Act Accordingly!" Without Reich, the famous 1968 revolutionary slogan "When I think of revolution I want to make love" would have been unthinkable. According to *Time*, thanks to Reich's ideas "the belief spread that repression, not license, was the great evil, and that sexual matters belonged in the realm of science, not morals."

If sexual matters belonged "in the realm of science," where does the pseudoscience of eugenics fit in? For early birth control advocates, just about everywhere. Intertwined with the drive to free women from the burdens of multiple pregnancies was the mission to allow the "fit" to reproduce while preventing births among humanity's perceived lesser elements. "Birth control must lead ultimately to a cleaner race," wrote Sanger, whose passion for eugenics remains a point of discomfort for many who admire her. "The most urgent problem today is how to limit and discourage the over-fertility of the mentally and physically defective," she added in another of many pro-eugenics tracts. Sanger didn't maintain the genetic superiority of whites over other races—poverty, lack of intelligence, and physical disability were her main categories of the "unfit"— but the foulest racism permeated the birth control movement. Sanger's British counterpart, Marie Stopes, held similar eugenicist views and even marketed a line of birth control products under the brand name Pro Race.

Eugenics, in its various forms, was anything but a fringe movement in the first half of the century. It was mainstream stuff, embraced by people as respectable as Winston Churchill and Oliver Wendell Holmes. It was only a small step for the law to embrace the "treatment" of sex criminals (among other "defectives") with sterilization. By the 1930s, thousands of homosexuals, prostitutes, and other "moral perverts" had been sterilized in the US, both to deactivate them reproductively and to cleanse the collective gene pool. Denmark, of all places, was the first country to pass a sterilization law, and for forty years after its 1929 passage about one thousand sex offenders there would come under the knife. The Third Reich demonstrated the excesses of eugenics, while the darker roots of the contraceptive movement have largely been purged from the literature of Planned Parenthood.

Ironically, it was a horrible scientific failure that helped to galvanize the US movement to legalize abortion. In 1962, Sherri Chessen Finkbine (known as Miss Sherri to the Phoenix toddlers who watched *Romper Room*, the TV show she hosted) took the drug thalidomide during her fifth pregnancy for morning sickness. When she learned that thalidomide carried a high risk of birth defects, she arranged for a discreet abortion at a local hospital. However, a wave of publicity about her case—and the threat of prosecution—caused the hospital to change its mind and turn her away, sparking lawsuits and a broad firestorm of controversy. Miss Sherri reluctantly found herself on the cover of *Life* magazine.

After being turned down for an abortion in Japan, Finkbine had the procedure done in Sweden, where she learned that the fetus had neither arms nor legs. The case's high profile, and the broad popular sympathy for Finkbine it inspired, blew open the abortion debate. Controversy has raged for fifty years since. As US abortion foes stage a new attack on pro-choice policies by marshaling new theories in neuroscience—for example, that fetuses at an early stage have consciousness and feel pain in the womb, even before viability—it's useful to recall how the discussion began.

In Britain, the abortion issue was jump-started in 1938, after a fourteen-year-old girl was gang-raped and made pregnant. A doctor refused to terminate the pregnancy, reasoning that because the assailants were upper class, she "might be carrying the future prime minister of England." The girl turned to the president of the Royal Society of Medicine's OB-GYN section, Aleck Bourne, who took up her cause and invited prosecution by performing an illegal abortion. He was indeed prosecuted, and he claimed, in his defense, that he had performed the procedure to save the girl from "mental collapse." While Bourne was acquitted, it would not be until 1967 that abortion on demand in Britain was allowed.

In the Netherlands, matters progressed more quickly. In the 1950s, many Dutch women still had to obtain written permission from priests before doctors would explain the details of the rhythm method (a natural form of birth control based on timing ovulation) to them. By 1961, however, birth control pills were widely available, although popular ambivalence about the subject remained, as it would about abortion. In light of the dangers of "back alley" terminations, the Dutch government tacitly allowed the procedure to be conducted at certain clinics. In time, public support increased for broader legalization, which was finally adopted in 1984.

The Soviet Union was the first European country to legalize abortion, a step it took in 1920 as the Bolsheviks reversed czarist-era laws governing sex and reproduction. (Homosexuality was also decriminalized.) The abortion law was reversed in 1936 as the Stalin regime took a sharp sex-negative turn; restrictions were eased again in 1955 under Khrushchev. Poland followed suit in 1956, as the government there began to finance abortions on demand. By the early 1990s, about one million abortions per year were performed in Poland—equal to the number of live births. However, that changed in 1990, when the country shifted from official communist atheism to a much more Catholic-friendly system. Harsh abortion restrictions were passed, and subsidies on birth control pills were eliminated. As a result, Polish women went to German border towns to have the procedure done. In 2010, *Der Spiegel* reported on a woman coming to the German town of Prenzlau for an abortion accompanied by her boyfriend—a Catholic priest—who said that Poland's abortion laws didn't "reflect real life in Poland anymore." The woman's doctor was also assisting a pregnant seventeen-year-old Polish girl. "All the girls in my class have sex," she said. "Afterwards they go to confession."

Five years after the Polish girl made that statement, teen sex has been transformed everywhere by advanced communication technology. While porn sites get more traffic than Netflix, Amazon, and Twitter combined, that heavy visual flow of flesh is augmented by a flood of private exchanges of sexual images, videos, and text messages, particularly among youth. For many kids, "sexting" is a temporary substitute for sex—what one Virginia girl called "a way of being sexual without being sexual." Sexting also may prime teens' hormonal pumps for the real thing. Some research shows that young people who sext are more likely to engage in unprotected sex or sex with multiple partners.

In any event, current law is unsuited to the way the technology is being used. To choose a recent example, after a seventeen-year-old Virginia boy's fifteen-year-old girlfriend sent him pictures of herself, to which he responded with a video, the boy was charged with possessing and transmitting child pornography—which could land him in jail for years, and on a public sex-offender list for life. Prosecutors also sought permission to photograph the boy's erect penis (after giving him an erection-producing injection) to compare with images on his cell phone. Using a law designed to protect children from sexual exploitation, the prosecutors thus attempted to create child pornography.

The nebulous zone between victim and perpetrator that minors often occupy becomes more untenable when teens voluntarily display themselves on webcams for *paying* viewers. This was the case with self-described "cam-whore" Justin Berry, who, starting at age thirteen, built a tidy business undressing, showering, masturbating, and having sex online for hungry fans. Over the course of his five-year venture, he attracted about fifteen hundred paying customers and generated hundreds of thousands of dollars in revenue. If Berry can be considered "exploited," did he exploit himself? What about the company that hosted his websites? In 2007, the web-hosting company's owner, Kenneth Gourlay, was convicted for "child sexually abusive activity" and distribution of "child sexually abusive material." (Berry was given immunity from prosecution in exchange for testifying against Gourlay and others.) Trial testimony revealed that after Berry started his online sex business, he asked for Gourlay's help to bring it "to the next level." The two worked together to set up new websites, establish a "members only" section, and maximize profitability.

Gourlay asked the court to instruct the jury that Berry was an accomplice in the pornography charges. The court's refusal to do so was upheld on appeal, the higher court reasoning that it would be "paradoxical" to label Berry an accomplice when the law was supposed to protect him, and when a child (anyone under eighteen) "could not legally consent to the child sexually abusive activity." Paradoxes notwithstanding, Berry clearly knew what he was doing. Refusing to label him as an accomplice in his own business activity is to ignore reality, which for courts is a dangerous thing to do.

In the context of ventures such as Berry's, the subjects of sexual images are the ones who (at least at first) send them into cyberspace themselves. Other cases, where images are distributed against the subjects' will, are much more disturbing. In 2010, an eighteen-year-old New Jersey college student, Tyler Clementi, leapt to his death from the George Washington Bridge after his roommate secretly used a webcam to stream Clementi's partially clothed encounter with a male companion. The roommate also urged his friends and Twitter followers to watch the streaming of a second such tryst. (This later broadcast never occurred.) In 2012, the hideous rape of an intoxicated teenaged girl in Ohio was recorded, discussed, and bragged about on social media by the students who assaulted her. When the girl awoke, she learned that her peers already knew what had happened to her and had seen a picture of her naked. As horrifying as these cases are, the law has benefited. For just as many of the monsters among us think nothing of recording their misdeeds and boasting about them on social media, by doing so they create a useful trail of incriminating evidence. The perpetrators in these cases left vast numbers of texts, Twitter posts, and other real-time records of what they did and thought, without which their guilt might not have been proven. People who compulsively record their every thought and deed make the work of law enforcement much easier.

• • •

Sex and Punishment covered roughly forty centuries; this volume considers about twelve decades. However, the last century has produced an immense amount of sex law. If it were just a question of volume, however, the story would not hold much interest. Rather, it is the law's effort to keep up with society's transformations, and its attempt to apply moral traditions to a world where they often no longer fit, that makes the current period so absorbing. Biblically inspired rules lose their footing when (to recall Nietzsche) God is dead, when women and minorities are equal (at least in theory) to white men, when sex and procreation are decoupled, and when scientists and doctors come into the picture. Add to that the realities of power politics and potent new demands for laws based on "traditional" sexual morality, and judges can be forgiven for a certain amount of timidity. While the past century has seen large-scale discrediting of old sex laws, no one can agree on what should replace them.

In *On Photography*, Susan Sontag wrote that a photographic image is a "thin slice of space as well as time" defined by the photographer's choice of subject matter and the context in which the picture is presented. Photography thus gives an imperfect "view of social reality consisting of small units of an apparently infinite number." *The Boundaries of Desire* has the same shortcomings: by describing the experiences of certain people, or the rules of some groups at given points in time, the impression may be conveyed that the whole truth is coming through. In fact, the truth is much larger than that. Sex law is central to the lives of all people, all of whom act on it in unique and contradictory ways. Each person, as a spinning atom of moral certainties and doubts, comprises a society as uncomfortable with itself now as it is with its past and future. Merely restating the rules of sexual engagement or describing how they are sometimes applied cannot portray the entire social reality of sex. Until someone figures out how to present the whole of human experience in one bite-size chunk, we shall have to content ourselves with a few compelling snapshots.

CHAPTER 1

FAMILY AND MARRIAGE

"If You Can't Rape Your Wife, Who Can You Rape?"

Questions about sexual power in the home are questions about our interior lives. We all have families in one form or another, and we all have opinions as to what a family is or should be. How can we not? Even with assisted reproductive technologies, we still have mothers and fathers, and everyone's foundational experiences center on the presence or absence of a family, and family dynamics. Our ability to make lasting connections with others is largely governed by our responses to these formative events. To the unending enrichment of psychotherapists and self-help book publishers, we spend much of our adult energies trying to make sense of what happened while we were under our parents' sway. For the student of sex law, matters become interesting when the rules governing sex in the home are set from the outside. The question of who should step in when those rules are broken then arises.

Before going into the modern law of sex and the family, we look back to ancient Rome, to the exalted virgins who were viewed as Rome's wives and sisters, and whose lives illuminate some of the dilemmas women now face. The Vestal Virgins were Rome's top-ranked female priests, selected as girls for their unblemished bodies and perfect pedigrees, and then living in the circular temple of the goddess Vesta in the city's Forum. As long as they eschewed sex, kept Rome's womblike flame alight in the temple, and performed other important duties, they enjoyed more privileges than even emperors' wives. Because their untouched bodies symbolized Rome's unbroken walls, their continued virginity was seen as critical to the city's safety and well-being. When Rome suffered famine or war losses, these troubles were often taken as proof that a Vestal had broken her vow of chastity and that more catastrophes were imminent. Matters could not be set right until the guilty priestess was buried alive.

The Vestals were thus required to live a zero-sum equation: they were either sexless saints or accursed whores. Few females have ever lived under quite this stark a dichotomy, but that is only a matter of degree. Women have long faced the choice of guarding their respectability with sexual restraint or indulging their sexuality and risking ruin. While sexually transgressive females will no longer (at least in the West) be buried alive, or impaled as in ancient Mesopotamia, female sexuality is still incendiary. The Madonna/whore double bind is woven deeply into Western family law. From the beginning, women have been whipsawed between the roles of neutered domestics and sex workers. Assertions of sexual independence by married women routinely resulted in their being socially ostracized, impoverished, and separated from their children. These issues have lost little currency in recent decades. Under long-standing legal traditions, a woman could be either a dutiful wife or sexually independent—not both.

As women have pressed for the right to control their sexuality and reproductive lives, the Western family has also come under examination. No longer is it a given that women are either wife-goddesses to be protected or sluts to be used and jettisoned, and no longer must married or single women pay for their sexual freedom with the loss of their safety. At the same time, as people form living arrangements without intending to have children, or as they use technology to conceive without sex or use the DNA of three people, the push is under way to recognize family structures beyond marriage.

However, we are getting ahead of ourselves. The process toward the normalization of female sexuality has been neither linear nor neat. Nearly every change in law has been decried by opponents as an attack on marriage, family, and the home. In the process, the definitions of these words have been reimagined and sanitized to the point where they mean little. Just as we reflexively call a law "unconstitutional" when we think it is unfair, or brand a country as "undemocratic" because we disapprove of its leaders, nearly every new sexual prerogative for females has been lambasted—often in apocalyptic terms—as undermining the "traditional" family that supposedly forms the bedrock of our way of life. However, amid all the raised voices and mythologizing, no one seems to have given much thought to what marriages, families, and homes were really like before the push for women's sexual and reproductive rights gained legal traction.

The fact that recent changes in sex and family law horrify large segments of the population does not, ipso facto, make the past anything to admire. A century ago, the "family home" was no amber-lit sanctuary where devoted spouses serenely played the roles given to them by a just and loving God. Rather, the law made the home a safe haven for sexual violence and abuse. Even worse, the judges and legislatures who kept this system in place did so using the same "pro-family" rhetoric invoked by today's social conservatives.

Conflicts over the definition and fate of the family have unfolded in a broad array of settings. In 1920, for example, France criminalized all contraception, reasoning that permitting women to choose whether to become mothers threatened civilization itself. In the US, starting in the 1920s and continuing into the 1970s, thousands of poor girls and women were forcibly sterilized for having children out of wedlock. Under the cruel logic driving this policy, they were deemed sexually uncontrollable and "feebleminded," and thus a source of contagion to the human gene pool. For the good of the species, their reproductive capacities were cut short. In Florida in the 1970s, Christian right activists argued that a constitutional guarantee of equal rights for women would "destroy the American family as the very building block of our civilization." (Since Florida was instrumental in blocking the Equal Rights Amendment—a commonsense measure that shows no sign of being revived—we can thank the Sunshine State for keeping civilization intact.) Given these beliefs, it is no surprise that many of the same pro-family advocates greeted the spread of AIDS in the 1980s as a sign of divine displeasure with those leading "anti-family" sex lives.

Heterosexual marriage is no longer the default arrangement for people to have sex and raise children. Rather, it has become one of several options. Vast segments of the reproducing population continue to divorce or rule out marriage altogether, sculpting their unions according to their own tastes or forming families in which sex plays no part at all. In response to these developments, horrified opponents have invested marriage—the one-man, one-woman, no-test-tube kind—with the unique capacity of preventing widespread moral collapse. Whether this will prove to be true is anybody's guess, but under no circumstances ought we to look back fondly on the models of a century ago, when marriage was more akin to state-approved sexual slavery than a society-affirming framework for love and procreation.

Not So Nice Up Close:
Rape and Violence in the Home

Broad sexual attitudes in the early twentieth century differed little from those of the previous two thousand years. The stifling influence of religion in enforcing sex-negative beliefs had abated somewhat, but doctors and scientists were picking up the slack. Sexual sins were becoming symptoms of mental illnesses. Just as medieval religious texts cataloged hundreds of sexual transgressions, the new field of sex research parsed and pathologized vast numbers of sexual acts and desires, from homosexuality and mastur- bation down to passions for striped handkerchiefs and the smell of roses. And while biblical injunctions restricted sex to the marriage bed (and then only to produce offspring), scientific theories now branded much nonre- productive, nonmarital sex as psychopathic. Saint Paul threatened those who pursued sex outside marriage, or for fun, with banishment from the Kingdom of God. Two millennia later, such people could find themselves excluded from earthly society, sterilized, and confined in mental hospitals.

When the purpose of marriage is reproduction, the institution becomes brutal. The personal fulfillment of spouses, especially wives, means little next to the key business at hand. A wife's lack of pleasure in lovemaking, or her ill will toward her husband, raised concerns only to the extent that it affected her ability to conceive. If women sought other sources of intimacy or arousal, the potential penalties were barely less ruinous than those that wives had suffered for centuries. While men were expected to protect their wives from outside dangers and not beat them too severely, long-standing laws still allowed husbands to "rule and chastise" their women. Rather than protecting battered wives, the courts often looked the other way, reasoning that by doing so they were encouraging family harmony and protecting the "sacred" home from government intrusion.

In 1874, in North Carolina, Richard Oliver returned home cranky and hungry after a long night of drinking. His wife prepared him some bacon and coffee, but that only worsened his mood. The meat, it seems, was crawling with insects. Flying into a mad rage, Oliver threw the coffee pot across the kitchen. Then he went outside, fashioned two four-foot switches from a nearby bush, and proceeded to whip his wife "as hard as he could." Had bystanders not stopped him, he would have continued until he "wor[e] her out." For Oliver's efforts, a local court fined him ten dollars—a penalty he thought outrageous. He took the case to the state's supreme court, ar- guing that he had every right to treat his wife as he wished.

Taking sympathy on the wife, the court let the fine stand, but then it doubled back and signaled to the state's other violent husbands that the law was still on their side. "Public policy," the court explained, required courts to protect the "sanctity of the domestic circle" by ignoring all but the most extreme cases of violence where, for example, "permanent injury has been inflicted." Short of that, the court declared, "it is better to shut out the public gaze, and leave the parties to forgive and forget." In other words, unless a wife had been "worn out" by her husband's fists or whip, she had only hope to protect her.

When the *State v. Oliver* case was decided, North Carolina could still claim that it was more protective of married women than ancient Assyria, where a husband could "whip his wife, pluck out her hair, mutilate her ears, or strike her with impunity." However, given that Assyrian law is more than three thousand years old, and that the Assyrians were boorish even by ancient Near Eastern standards, that was not much to boast about. In fact, for much of the nineteenth century, as in ancient societies, American wives were essentially the property of their husbands, with only slightly greater rights than beasts of burden. Under principles reaching back to early English common law, marriage came with a metaphysical oddity called coverture, by which "the very being or legal existence of the woman is suspended" and "consolidated into that of the husband: under whose wing, protection and cover, she performs everything."

The idea of coverture was already coming under criticism by the turn of the twentieth century, at least when money and property were involved. Wives had steadily gained the rights to own and sell their own property, appear in court as individuals, and even sue their husbands for stealing or ruining their stuff. However, this small recognition of a married woman's "natural rights" was the easy part: a wife may have gained control over her deceased mother's silver, but her genitals would remain her husband's chattel for a long time to come.

Traditionally, when a woman said "I do" at the altar, the law heard her say "you can" to her husband for a lifetime of his sexual demands. The rule was put well by England's chief justice, Matthew Hale, in the seventeenth century:

> But the husband cannot be guilty of a rape committed by himself upon his lawful wife, for by their [marriage] the wife hath given up herself in this kind unto the husband which she cannot retract.

According to Lord Hale and three centuries of subsequent British and American jurists, a woman's marriage vows included the promise of limitless access to her body, regardless of her own desires. Brides never actually stated such a promise, of course—most must have thought they could say no at least once in a while—but the law rarely lets reality stand in the way of a good oppressive doctrine. In fact, should a wife later forget her legal status as a sex toy with a pulse, the law permitted her husband to use physical force to remind her.

This rule is referred to in US and British law as the Marital Rape Exemption, though I prefer to call it what it was, a "Rape-Your-Wife Privilege." It proved to be one of the sturdiest doctrines in the history of sex law, outlasting bars against abortion, birth control, and interracial marriage. Until recently, it was enshrined in the laws of every state in the US. The law wasn't even criticized much until the last quarter of the twentieth century, when it was getting worse: rather than cut the Rape-Your-Wife Privilege back or eliminate it, some states were expanding it to insulate men who forced themselves on their live-in girlfriends.

In Britain, the Rape-Your-Wife Privilege first showed a crack in 1949, when a court held that a husband could not force himself on his wife if a court order separating them was already in place. However, a few years later, a British court sided with a husband who raped his wife a year after she had left him and petitioned for divorce. Incredibly, the court found that the wife had still consented to sex with her husband even though he had thrown her to the ground three times before raping her. The Rape-Your-Wife Privilege would not be definitively abolished in Britain until 1991.

It would take relentless pressure from second-wave feminists and anti–domestic violence activists to eliminate the Rape-Your-Wife Privilege in the US. In the 1970s, as one commentator put it, it was still the law that "a husband forcing sex on his wife was merely making use of his own property," but this was changing. In a groundbreaking 1984 decision, New York's highest court exposed the rule for the horror that it was. The case involved Mario Liberta, an abuser whom a court had ordered to stay away from his wife, Denise. Some months later, Liberta lured Denise to his motel room, where he attacked her and, as their two-year-old son watched, forced her to have oral sex and intercourse. Liberta never denied what he did to Denise that night. Rather, he argued that because they were technically married, the law should stay out of their "private" sex lives. In effect, he asked the court to do what courts had always done—protect the "sanctity of the domestic circle." That this circle was now a tawdry motel room and the marriage a shambles were irrelevant details. Liberta and Denise were still husband and wife, and that made violent sex his prerogative.

Three decades later, Liberta's argument sounds like a dispatch from a barbaric netherworld, but it was taken seriously. In fact, he won in the lower court. After years of subsequent legal wrangling, the state's high court declared, finally, that the Rape-Your-Wife Privilege was indefensible on any level. Rape was rape, the court held, and it was nonsense to treat rape committed by a husband differently from that perpetrated by a stranger: "A married woman has the same right to control her own body as does an unmarried woman." As for the idea that the "privacy" of the home should protect a married couple from state intrusion, the court opined that marital privacy "protects consensual acts, not violent sexual assaults."

So much for New York, but the Rape-Your-Wife Privilege had many passionate defenders elsewhere. It was not until 1993, when Oklahoma and North Carolina were dragged kicking and screaming into the civilized world, that marital rape became a crime in every state. The arguments in favor of keeping the law in place still astonish. In 1980, for example, Florida representative Tom Bush argued that governments had "absolutely no business . . . invading the sanctity and intimacy" of a marriage, even when the "invasion" revealed that the husband was raping his wife. The following year, the Colorado Supreme Court *upheld* the rule on the ground that putting a rapist husband in jail was an "obstacle" to the husband and wife eventually reconciling. However, of all the defenders of the Rape-Your-Wife Privilege, California state senator Bob Wilson was perhaps the most forthcoming when, in 1979, he asked a group of women lobbyists: "If you can't rape your wife, who can you rape?"

While spousal rape is now prohibited, it is underprosecuted in the US, and a number of remaining loopholes make it a less severe crime than rape committed by a stranger. Many courts and lawmakers could not shake their indulgence toward sexually violent husbands. In 1985, for example, not long after Pennsylvania eliminated the Rape-Your-Wife Privilege, its highest court complained that "a legal monster" had been set loose, as juries had now been invited "into the privacy of the marital bedroom for the purpose of supervising the manner in which marital relationships are consummated." In other words, how can anyone determine whether sex between a husband and wife was old-fashioned consummation or violent

assault? Someone might have reminded the court that such determinations are *exactly* what courts and juries are supposed to do and that difficulty figuring out whether sex is consensual is no excuse to give up the
effort.

* * *

A century ago, the "sanctity of the domestic circle" was also invoked to protect parents—especially fathers—who abused their children. Parents might
find themselves in hot water if they inflicted serious injuries, but short of
that it was their prerogative to smack their children around—or fondle
them—with little interference from police or the courts. Parents were encouraged to be "strict" with their kids, both to keep discipline in the home
and to rid children of the vices they were believed to have been born with.
Parental discipline, even if savage, was rarely punished. In North Carolina,
for example, the state's highest court refused in 1886 to allow the prosecution of a father who choked his "habitually disobedient" daughter until her
tongue came out of her mouth, whipped her thirty times with a switch, and
dislocated her thumb. The reason? The "best interest in society" would be
ill served by jailing the father, who was only trying to correct his daughter's
bad behavior—especially as a trial would "lift the curtain from the scenes of
home life," where parental control must reign supreme.

The "authority" of parents to sexually abuse their children was marginally less broad than the authority to beat them. In Washington, in 1905,
one E. W. Roller raped his fifteen-year-old daughter Lulu. Thankfully, he
was apprehended and sent to jail, but Lulu also sued her father in civil
court for damages. She won $2,000, but the state's supreme court reversed
that award. Allowing a child to sue her father, declared the court, even for
the "heinous" crime of rape, could be detrimental to the harmony of the
"domestic relations of the home and family fireside." The court allowed
that Roller's rape of his daughter might have *already* blown ill wind into
the cozy confines of their home, but that was secondary to protecting all
parents from the nuisance of being sued by their kids. Where, the court
asked, should the line be drawn? If Lulu were allowed to go to court
against her father, what would stop other kids from suing their parents for
acts less severe than rape?

The recognition of the right of children to not be abused by their parents was slow in coming. It was a long climb from the horrors of the
Roller household to the current recognition that violence and sex have

no place in the parent–child relationship. At the beginning of the twentieth century, however, when parents were presumptively immune from most consequences of mistreating their children, such enlightenment was a long way off.

Adultery and Women-cum-Men

Well into the twentieth century, husbands had the right to sue their wives' lovers for "enticement," "alienation of affections," or "criminal conversation." They all meant the same thing: by having sex with another man's wife, the lover robbed the husband of the wife's exclusive sexual "services" and "defiled" the marital bed. That the wife might have desired the liaison or even initiated it meant nothing. As one British commentator put it in 1937, regardless of the wife's actual desires, the law made her no more capable than a horse of consenting to an adulterous adventure. Neither did it matter when the husband was unable to meet his wife's sexual needs: impotent husbands had the same exclusive right to their wives' bodies as men with functional equipment.

There was no pretense that the adultery laws were reciprocal. In practical terms, women were told to expect their husbands to stray, and to put up with it. The unnamed wife of Frank W. Duffies learned as much in 1890 when a Wisconsin court schooled her on the basics of marital relations. Mrs. Duffies brought a lawsuit claiming that Frank had been enticed away from her. In throwing her case out, the court described the "natural and unchangeable conditions" of matrimony, with which it refused to tamper. Wives were "more domestic" than husbands, the court instructed, and stayed "constantly at home." There, their "purer and better" natures and the "genial influences of home life" primed them to give their husbands the full range of their "comforts and advantages." By contrast, husbands manned the "outside world," where they worked to "protect" their families from privation. Out in the field, husbands met with "temptations, enticements, and allurements" that naturally led them to stray from their wives. Mrs. Duffies should have expected this. Besides, the judge added, if she was allowed to sue for the loss of her husband's affections, wives everywhere would do the same, and all hell would break loose.

The *Duffies* case's portrayal of wives as housebound ciphers and husbands as vigorous masters of the outside world was not just the sentimental musing of a heartland jurist: it was taken as scientific fact. This was an era when women on both sides of the Atlantic agitated in force not only to participate in marriage as equals but also for the rights to suffrage and equal educational opportunities. To put it mildly, their demands were not widely embraced. In fact, they were seen as contrary to nature.

While the *Duffies* court invoked misty stereotypes to justify the shabby treatment of married women, scientists were called on elsewhere to explain why women's full participation in society was not only morally wrong but biologically dangerous. The scientific community did not disappoint. There was no shortage of research "proving" that females were configured solely for the delicate business of reproduction, which demanded that they live in quiet domestic isolation. By wrapping the illusion of objective fact around the rankest sexism, scientists affirmed women's subservience in marriage and society at large. To permit women to engage in worldly intellectual, physical, or political pursuits risked ruining them as child bearers, or even killing them.

In the US, Dr. Edward H. Clarke's enormously influential *Sex in Education; or, A Fair Chance for the Girls*, first published in 1873, framed the issue as follows: "The problem of the women's sphere . . . is not to be solved by applying to it abstract principles of right and wrong. Its solution must be obtained from physiology." Clarke explained why permitting girls to study in a "boy's way" caused "grievous maladies" called leucorrhea, amenorrhoea, dysmenorrhoea, chronic and acute ovaritis, prolapsus uteri, hysteria, neuralgia, and the like. As an example, he pointed to the sad case of "Miss G," who graduated at the top of her class at a coeducational college, well ahead of her male classmates—an act of presumption she paid for with an early death. According to Clarke, her demise was:

> Not so much the result of over-work as of un-physiological work. She was unable to make a good brain that could stand the wear and tear of life, and a good reproductive system that should serve the race, at the same time that she was continuously spending her force in intellectual labor. Nature asked for a periodical remission, and did not get it. . . . Believing that woman can do what man can . . . she strove with noble but ignorant bravery to compass man's intellectual attainment in a man's way, and died in the effort.

In Britain, the stakes of gender equality were put in similar terms. Suffragettes had long been derided as masculine, sexually repellent, and even apelike—slanders that were increasingly pinned to physiological causes.

For example, in 1913, as the women's suffrage movement was reaching its most combustible stage, a prominent Cambridge zoologist named Walter Heape argued that women who engage in "male activities" not only risked sterility but also the loss of their functions as women. A woman's entire being revolved around her reproductive capacity, he argued, so activities that diverted from such functions "perverted" the flow of "energy" away from the reproductive organs and led to the development of "secondary Male characteristics." Intellectual development, physical exercise, political participation—all were "antagonistic to the interests of the woman who is concerned with the production of children." Unless women avoided such pursuits, Heape argued, they risked becoming "waste products" and "their real value to us as a nation" would be lost.

Heape's findings fell into a research tradition reaching back to the early responses against universal education for girls. Men were seen as naturally disposed to physical and intellectual activity, but female health was thought to depend entirely on the "condition of the womb," which was compromised by outside pressures. "The man possesses the penis, but the vagina possesses the woman," said the controversial Austrian philosopher Otto Weininger in 1903. To keep the vagina in shape to do what it was meant to do, women needed to be protected from themselves and kept at home, where the strains of the external world were kept safely away.

These theories went into overdrive when it was discovered that human fetuses had both male and female characteristics. Every female carried a latent male within her, and vice versa. Add to this a large measure of hidebound sexism and a much-discussed 1905 report about a female duck that had transformed into a male; then infuse the mixture with widespread disgust as a response to British suffragettes, and the result was a spate of theories arguing that women must not be given equal rights, lest they evolve in the wrong direction. Suffragettes had long been ridiculed as "unsexed," man-hating spinsters. Now, Heape and his contemporaries lent scientific prestige to the idea that more was wrong with these women than loud voices and questionable grooming: they were sexual reversals in progress.

During the same period that Heape's findings were released, world exhibitions in London, Frankfurt, and St. Louis mounted crowd-pleasing attractions featuring "wild women" and "Amazons" from Africa, Asia, and the Balkans who had assumed male "warrior" identities. Displayed in dioramas depicting their barbarous "natural" habitats, these men-women fascinated middle-class audiences, both for their transgression of gender roles and their avoidance of sexual relations with men. Most importantly, the exhibitions affirmed a value system that equated women who rejected marriage, childbearing, and subservience with circus freaks and wild animals. Such creatures were regarded as not entirely human, or at least not on the same evolutionary level as dutiful European or American householders. They were cautionary examples of just how wrong matters could go when women rejected their roles as wives and mothers.

• • •

By the early 1980s, the broad adoption of no-fault divorce meant that spouses no longer had to accuse each other of bad behavior such as adultery to end their marriages. Anti-adultery laws remained on the books—in 2014, it was still a crime in twenty-one states—but few people were aware, or cared, that it was still illegal to cheat on their spouses. Nevertheless, these vestigial laws allowed law enforcement to handpick sexual miscreants to be punished for the sins of the permissive age. In 1983, Judith Stowell, a married Massachusetts woman who moonlighted as a streetwalker, was convicted along with her married client of adultery for having sex in a van. The client paid his fine and fled the picture, but Stowell decided to fight. She contended that the adultery law, which dated back to 1785, was obsolete and invaded her privacy. Not so, said the court. Even though adultery prosecutions were "practically nonexistent," the state still had a "deep interest" in punishing behavior that "threaten[s] the institution" of marriage and in seeing that "the rules governing marriage are not subverted."

The court never explained how Stowell's few minutes in the van threatened marriage itself, or how an arbitrary prosecution against her would halt adultery elsewhere. With questions of sexual morals, courts rarely use logic to back up their rulings because reason has so little to do with the analysis. The state's power to charge people for adultery, no matter how rarely or arbitrarily applied, prevailed over Stowell's prerogative to govern her own sex life. Faithful marriage as an ideal was more important than the way people were actually living.

By 2010, only seven states still had "alienation of affections" laws on the books. That same year, a North Carolina woman sued her husband's mistress for stealing his affections. The jury decided that the mistress should pay her $9 million for breaking up her marriage. "You don't go after married men and break up families," the wife said, savoring her victory. But these cases are rarities, and it is only in the military that adultery law still has real teeth. Former brigadier general Jeffrey Sinclair learned this in 2014 when he pleaded guilty to (among other charges) having an affair with a subordinate, for which he was demoted two grades, reprimanded, and fined $20,000. He could have received twenty years in jail and been dismissed from the army. The unmarried Kelly Flinn, America's first female B-52 bomber pilot and for a time the face of air force recruiting efforts, was also discharged in 1997 for having an affair with a married subordinate and disregarding an order from her superior to end it.

Righting the Power Balance in the Family

The near-absolute power of husbands over their families diminished considerably in the second half of the twentieth century. Several factors combined to transform the home from an Assyrian-style discipline chamber to one where violence and sexual abuse are forbidden. First, despite the derision heaped upon suffragettes, women received the right to vote in the US in 1920 and in Britain in 1929. These measures heralded what scholar Christina Simmons called the "irreversibility of some kind of equality for women," and lent electoral muscle to activists' efforts to undo laws enforcing female sexual subservience. (The fact that women's enfranchisement did not, after all, cause widespread female-to-male sex reversals, infertility, or lesbianism didn't hurt, either.)

No less important was women's large-scale colonization of the workplace, sparked first by the exodus of men to the battlefronts of the Great War and increasing steadily after the conflict ended. For obvious reasons, women from the lower classes had always worked in greater numbers than their moneyed counterparts, and there were proportionally just as many single working mothers in the US in 1900 as there were in 1960. But the steady acquisition of economic independence by large numbers of women throughout the twentieth century profoundly affected the balance of power in the home.

In the 1920s, the percentage of working married women rose 56 percent; by 1930, approximately 25 percent of professional women and 32 percent of female clerical workers were married. Despite gross pay disparities, growing numbers of women were gaining the wherewithal to leave bad marriages or survive when their husbands abandoned them.

These women also had the money to evaluate suitors on the basis of sexual attractiveness and general compatibility rather than as meal tickets. The rising numbers of working married women caused much unease, especially when legions of married men became unemployed during the Great Depression. In fact, for several years during the 1930s, employers large and small refused to hire married women. Nearly every state and the federal government enacted laws restricting the ability of married women to work; entire cities witnessed crusades to bar them from the workplace. Despite these setbacks, the march toward female economic independence proceeded, with the result that marriage evolved into an institution women could choose, and decide to remain in, on their own terms.

Finally, birth control had incalculable effects on the power dynamic between spouses. Under a nineteenth-century law championed by the puritanical dry-goods salesman Anthony Comstock, it was a crime to traffic in contraceptives. Birth control information, even in medical textbooks, was also attacked as aggressively as hard-core pornography. Hundreds of doctors, advocates, educators, and others were prosecuted for selling contraceptives or even discussing the subject in public. Yet despite the risks, women from all social classes learned where to obtain contraceptives, and how to use them. To birth control advocates such as Margaret Sanger, contraception was *the* critical preventative against poverty. In middle- and working-class families, it was a tool for women to keep their jobs.

Reliable contraception influenced women to reconsider their sex lives from the bottom up. Erotic arousal came to be seen as an end in itself, driven by such ungodly oddities as hormones and resulting from the body's innate and tireless drive for sexual release. This was not news to men, who had long been at liberty to spill their seed wherever they wished. But for women, the acceptance of the sex drive was a world-changing revelation. Even mainstream women's journals joined in. *Good Housekeeping* magazine, for example, ran a long article in 1915 introducing its propriety-obsessed female readers to the libido. Drawing on Freud's early theories on sexuality, the magazine announced that the libido surged within everyone like a "self-propelling torpedo," demanding "every kind of sensory gratification" while silently determining the direction people take in life.

The importance of such articles cannot be overstated. For a society in convulsive change on all fronts, progressive publications such as *Good Housekeeping* set broad standards of decent feminine behavior. Its "Good Housekeeping Seal of Approval" was also the last word on which products should grace the homes of the new middle class. At this point in time, sex itself was becoming a product, and with dozens of column inches devoted to Freud's theories on the sex drive, the female urge for "sensory gratification" had secured its own unimpeachable seal of approval. Add to that Ellis's widely read *Studies in the Psychology of Sex*, which declared that sex was the "chief and central function of life . . . ever wonderful, ever lovely," and sex began to assume a new aspect in the popular imagination.

Birth control allowed working women to ride the "torpedo" while still meeting the demands of their families and employers. For poor women without access to health care, the stakes were much higher. Repeated pregnancies often spelled physical or economic catastrophe, something some urban judges recognized early on. In her memoir, the anarchist (and birth control activist) Emma Goldman told of a New York mother charged for theft after her sickly husband could no longer support their large family. The judge, noting that contraceptives were easier to obtain in Europe than in the US, remarked, "I believe we are living in an age of ignorance, which at some future time will be looked upon aghast as we now look back on the dark ages. We have before us the case of a family increasing in numbers, with a tubercular husband, the woman with a child at her breast and with other small children at her skirts, in poverty and want." Goldman also recalled a Portland judge's remarks after she was arrested in 1915 for speaking publicly about contraception. Setting aside her conviction, the judge observed that "the trouble with our people today is that there is too much prudery. . . . We are all shocked by many things publicly stated that we know privately to ourselves, but we haven't got the nerve to admit it."

These local judges were refreshingly frank, but their opinions had no broad-based effect. It took twenty more years for change to come in a meaningful way. By the mid-1930s, with the introduction of cheap latex condoms, contraceptives were sold widely—if not often in the legal clear. The Comstock Law was already being ridiculed as outdated, but lawmakers lacked the courage to go on record as proponents of "free love." Only a high-ranking, unelected court could cut through the Comstock Law's repressive underbrush and permit contraceptives to reach the legitimate market. That court was the United States Court of Appeals for the Second Circuit, in New York City, when it was called to decide the fate of a little plain-wrapped box that had been seized on arrival from Japan.

The package, which had been ordered in 1936 by Margaret Sanger, contained 120 "rubber pessaries to prevent conception." The pessaries were actually conical rubber diaphragms crafted by a Japanese doctor to stem the growth of his own enormous family. Conical diaphragms were a commercial bust, but that was not the issue. What mattered to the judges was their capacity to prevent the spread of some venereal infections. Although the Comstock Law had no "disease prevention" exception to its blanket ban on contraceptives, the court read one into the law anyway, holding that birth control devices could be prescribed by doctors for the "purpose of saving life or promoting the well-being of their patients." When, by contrast, contraceptives were sold for "immoral purposes"—that is, for recreational sex—the court left the rules barring such sales in place.

The *One Package* decision blew open the birth control industry. The court's attempt to make doctors the gatekeepers of contraceptive sales was widely ignored as torrents of cheap condoms flooded the marketplace. Not long after the decision came down, no fewer than fifteen manufacturers were selling a half million condoms per day at an average price of eight cents each. In 1937, the American Medical Association reversed its position against birth control and by 1942 there were more than eight hundred birth control clinics in the US. At the same time, *Ladies' Home Journal* reported that nearly four-fifths of American women approved of the use of contraception. The era of readily available birth control had arrived, and nothing was going to turn it back. By the middle of the century, it was a given that women could pursue sex for pleasure, protected by contraceptives.

Diaper Changes and Sexual Abuse

The men who once so completely ruled their homes would be hard-pressed to find their bearings today. Regardless of old laws still crowding the books, a husband would be laughed out of court if he complained that his wife had cut off her sexual "services" to him, or that another man had lured her intimate affections away. The profusion of laws punishing domestic violence and childhood sexual abuse has also drastically narrowed the range of permissible intrafamily behavior. No longer do men have legal license to abuse the weaker members of their families. At least in theory, the full power of the state is ready to throw them out of the house—or into jail. Far from ignoring a husband or father who commits abuse, many courts are now *required* to drop everything when such a problem arises, and to deal with it immediately.

No one disputes the wisdom of punishing rampaging parents, especially when they transgress sexually; but it is fair to ask whether we have, in places, gone too far. One might say yes, given the relentless efforts of social workers, courts, and grandstanding legislators to unearth and punish sex offences where none existed before. For example, since 2009 Mississippi has defined parental child abuse not only as parents having sex with their children but also as parents' "toleration . . . of the child's sexual involvement with any other person." How, for example, "toleration" of a child's sexual adventures with his or her peers constitutes abuse, and what kind of intolerance the law requires, is difficult to grasp. Must parents install recording devices in the home, listen in on phone calls for dirty talk, or read their teenagers' text messages for sexual content? The legislature declined to elaborate, with the result that the reach of this awful law will be decided according to the whims of police and local judges.

Much closer to home for parents is the trend of marking quotidian parenting behaviors, including kissing a baby on the belly, appearing nude in front of children, and hugging and kissing as sexually abusive. As cultural studies scholar James Kincaid explains it: "We have expanded the category of sexual abuse to include issues that would have been regarded three decades ago as nuisances or nothing." This development, which has been driven largely by the psychological and social work establishments, can provide cover for harmful court intrusion into the parent–child relationship and, conversely, confuses efforts to root out truly abusive parents.

In 1995, UCLA scholar Paul Okami observed the movement among researchers and social workers to define new forms of "subtle sexual abuse" or "emotional incest syndrome" perpetrated by parents on their young children. Noting the self-interest of professionals in "identifying" new "populations of victims," Okami warned that what had previously been considered "lifestyle" choices "may now be characterized by some mental health professionals as psychosexual disorders." He pointed to a 1987 survey of several hundred Virginia mental-health, law-enforcement, and social-service professionals, as well as lawyers and judges, in which three-fourths of the respondents agreed that state "intervention" was necessary when mothers frequently appear nude in front of their five-year-old sons. Eighty percent of the respondents believed intervention was necessary to stop fathers from sleeping in the same bed as their young daughters, and half saw trouble when fathers entered bathrooms while their daughters were being bathed. Forgetting, perhaps, that in much of the world children sleep in the same rooms (if not beds) as their parents, other researchers have opined that such sleeping arrangements may leave children feeling "powerless" and "endangered," or stricken with "oedipal desire and castration anxiety."

Since that time, in what has been called "definitional creep," child-molestation laws have been expansively interpreted to ensnare some parents whose worst transgressions seem to have been their ignorance of changes in social norms. Even more confounding, as Camille Gear Rich recently pointed out, these "unarticulated" standards can apply differently to male and female caregivers. What a mother does with her children may be blessed by authorities as loving, attentive parenting, while the same behavior by a father may be a felony. The examples of this trend are manifold: a Utah father's rubbing of baby oil on his five-year-old son's body after a bath was used as proof that he had sexually abused the child on a different occasion. A California woman's fiancé was charged with child molestation when he gave her four-year-old daughter a bath, in which he washed the girl's genitals but used his bare hand instead of a soapy cloth. The girl said his finger went in her vagina. As Rich points out about this case, the mother would never have faced child sexual-abuse allegations if she did the same thing, especially as "there is no established social standard that requires a child always to be washed with a washcloth." Other fathers were charged after they helped their children use the toilet, kissed their children during play or diaper changes, or tucked them into bed.

At some point, displays of parental affection are excessive, and no doubt adults, including parents, mask sexual abuse behind mundane caregiving activities. However, the noble goal of halting child abuse does not justify reckless prosecutions; nor should we embrace every diagnostic fad coming out of the psychiatric and social work professions. This is especially the case in that child-abuse prosecutions can leave families in ruins. If parents are in fact molesting their children, then aggressive action by the state is necessary. But if they are not, then the children will certainly be left worse off. Reliance on prosecutors—who are often elected to office—to decide whom to go after is not sufficient. No one in law enforcement wants to be accused of being "soft" on child abuse. Only time will tell whether the drift toward charging parents who appear nude in front of their toddlers or fathers who rub noses with their babies will become the norm, or whether common sense will prevail. In any event, when set against the law's earlier reluctance to interfere with any aspect of the parent–child relationship, this trend shows how yesterday's normal behavior can become today's pathology and tomorrow's crime.

*   *   *

Even absent sexual abuse by parents of their children, the law now meddles with the parent–child relationship with a leaden hand. In New Orleans, for example, a drunken football fan, Brian Downing, was videotaped on Bourbon Street rubbing his genitals on a passed-out fan of the local team. The video circulated on the Internet, outraging local football fans, and Downing was charged with felony sexual battery. Just before his 2012 trial, he agreed to plead guilty to the lesser charge of obscenity, for which he was given a two-year jail sentence. He took the plea deal because a sexual battery conviction would have put him on the sex-offender registry, which in turn would have severely limited his interactions with his young son and other children. "Is it worth the risk of never seeing a Little League game? Or never being able to drop your child off at school?" said Downing's attorney to the press. "[Downing] decided no." Regardless of whether Downing's disgusting stunt descended to the level of sexual battery, the risk of being labeled a sex offender was enough to make two years in a Louisiana prison look good by comparison.

*   *   *

Under the web of restrictions now governing family relationships, the authority of parents in the home is contingent upon their falling in line with quickly evolving, and often controversial, social norms. Christian right activists tapped into a growing feeling of discomfort over parents' waning prerogatives when they invoked the language of the civil rights movement in the fight against the tolerance of homosexuals. If parents no longer had hegemony over their homes, they at least wanted the power to decide who should form families in the first place and who can associate with their kids.

In 1977, Anita Bryant and her group, Save Our Children, led a widely publicized campaign to repeal a Miami ordinance protecting homosexuals from job discrimination. In addition to mining a deep vein of homophobia, their message was direct: the "civil rights of parents" were diminishing, and a law allowing homosexuals to emerge from their closets and, worse, teach their children in schools was the last straw. Bryant argued that the new law would lead to legalized gay marriages and invite gay teachers to "recruit" vulnerable students to their ranks. "Enough, enough, enough!" she cried to her jubilant supporters after the ordinance was repealed. Something was felt to have been lost, and only by reasserting the "rights" of parents over their children, and the primacy of heterosexual marriage, could a sense of order be regained.

Marriage as a Ticket into Society

Despite the large numbers of people opting out of marriage, the law has continually stressed marriage as the only acceptable setting for sexual re-lationships and the only framework for one's full participation in society. Time and again, women—particularly impoverished single mothers—have been forced to pay a heavy toll for having children, or even having sex, outside of formal marriage. Those who pursued such relationships have been branded, variously, as politically disloyal, feebleminded, wel-fare cheats, and sexually deviant. For some, the cost has been loss of a job or state support. Thousands of others were sterilized.

During the red-baiting decades following the Second World War, Soviet communism and sexual transgression were presented as different aspects of the same evil. Americans were constantly reminded of the USSR's purported opposition to marriage and family life. Soviet women were said to register at bureaus of "free love" and give up their offspring for collective child care. Moreover, not only were homosexuals thought to flourish in the Soviet Union, wily Soviet agents were believed to be blackmailing high-placed American homosexuals and other "perverts" for state secrets. A much-publicized 1950 report issued by a blue-ribbon Senate committee stated that Soviet agents were working hard to find and exploit sexual "weaknesses" in American government workers. This statement was folded into American national-security manuals and used to justify decades of exclusion of homosexuals from government.

Out of this paranoid stew came what has been called the Lavender Scare, a highly public effort to purge not only "commies" but also "queers" and "powder puffs" from the government, which is discussed in detail in chapter 2. However, in another example of mission creep, the purge widened to target all "morally degenerate" people with "temperamental unsuitability" for government service, including some unmarried, sexually active heterosexuals. Such people were seen as vulnerable to Soviet influence and, no less importantly, a source of moral rot weakening the US from within. According to Senator Joseph McCarthy: "Once the people of a Nation become complacent about moral degeneracy in its leadership, then that nation has not long to live."

During this period, one's job prospects in government depended on following a narrow sexual and matrimonial path. FBI agents routinely grilled government employees on their views about marriage because, as one agent noted, opposition to marriage was one of the "tenets of the Communist Party." If the civil servants gave wrong answers or pursued sex lives outside marriage, then pink slips could follow. In one case, a State Department language specialist was fired for "immorality" because she had given birth to a child out of wedlock, even though she later married the child's father. Another government employee was dismissed for "moral turpitude" for marrying a woman before his divorce from his previous wife was finalized, while still another unmarried "government girl" was given a lie-detector test during which she was peppered with questions such as: "Have you had sexual relations with a man . . . with a woman? . . . . When did you last have intercourse?"

We don't know how that woman answered the questions, but Marcelle Henry's responses to a similar grilling did her no good at all. During a lengthy interrogation in 1953, the unmarried, French-born State Department employee was told to provide details about her recent sexual encounters with men, and when she bought contraceptives. She made the mistake of telling the truth and admitting that she had had sexual relations with "a number of men." This enraged investigators, who reminded Henry that American moral standards were not the same as they were in France and that sex outside of marriage in the US was illegal. She was fired for showing a "disregard for the generally accepted standards of conventional behavior."

Henry later noted that she was not accused of being a lesbian but rather of "loving the opposite sex too much," and she wondered how homosexuality and heterosexuality could both be dangerous to national security. In fact, the issue was less one of Henry's ardor than her refusal to confine her sex life to prescribed channels. By pursuing "deviant sex," she had allied herself with an immoral alien subculture that depleted the US's ability to fight its enemies. Tabloid journalists Jack Lait and Lee Mortimer summarized the zeitgeist well: "Communism actively promotes and supports sex deviation to sap the strength of a new generation and make the birth of another one problematical." By railroading Henry out of her job, the government had stanched a moral drain.

• • •

The stories of Soviet sexual subversion were complete falsehoods. Not only were no Soviet-serving "perverts" found, the characterization of Soviet society as licentious was untrue. Rather than encouraging free love, open marriage, and homosexual adventure, the USSR enforced sexual standards that were more restrictive than anything American moral crusaders could dream up. In fact, the Soviet Union had its own domestic propaganda campaign that posited a morally corrupt capitalist West against its own more restrained society. Throughout this period, the USSR and the US engaged in an extended contest of virtuous one-upmanship, by which each side elevated its own moral self-regard at the expense of the other.

During the same period when Marcelle Henry was driven out of the State Department, it was illegal to show kissing in most Soviet films; information on sex, reproduction, and birth control was suppressed; homosexuality and sexual "degeneracy" were crimes that brought lengthy terms in the Gulag; and divorce was difficult to obtain. Observed Russian historian Igor S. Kon: "All sexual activity, even marital sexual activity, was considered indecent and unmentionable, a subject only for the degenerate underground." This official prudishness lasted to the Soviet Union's final years. In 1980, an official Soviet journal warned that extramarital sex caused neurotic disorders and sexual dysfunction, while another article advised that intercourse should last no longer than two minutes—men who delayed ejaculation to please their partners risked impotence and psychosis. Even the wearing of shorts in some places was banned until the 1980s. In Siberia, women wearing pants could expect what Kon called official "sexual harassment and aggression."

The Soviet Union did not start out this way. During the heady early years of the Russian Revolution, the traditional family was one of the aspects of bourgeois society that the new regime sought to toss into the dustbin of history. Vladimir Lenin aimed to release women from the "slavery" of "wifery" and "stinking" kitchens and put them into the workforce as equals, while children were to be raised collectively under state supervision. "The [capitalist] family deprives the worker of revolutionary consciousness, said Alexandra Kollontai, the first Soviet people's commissar for social welfare. Leon Trotsky agreed: "Until there is equality in the family, there will be none in social production." Kollontai was radical even for her time, advocating for sidewalk sex booths for the convenience of the masses and arguing that in the new workers' paradise, sex should be "as easily obtained as a glass of water." The booths never happened and water was always more plentiful than sex. But in 1920, Soviet women enjoyed the most progressive marriage and procreation laws in the world. Women were given rights equal to men in all social and private areas. Their involvement in productive labor was supposed to bring them independence from men, as were paid holidays during pregnancy and state-funded child-care nurseries. Abortion was no longer illegal, and neither was homosexuality.

But lasting sexual freedom in the Soviet Union was doomed by the reality of remaking a country in ruins, the discomfort many Soviet leaders felt toward sexual license, and the prudishness that inevitably characterizes totalitarian regimes. Lenin understood the need to "quench" sexual "thirst," but he also questioned whether a normal person would drink from a glass made "dirty from the lips of dozens of people." For him, sex for sex's sake diverted from the revolutionary struggle: "Lack of restraint in sexual life is bourgeois; it is a sign of decadence. The proletariat . . . has no need of intoxication for stupefaction or excitement." Lenin's hesitations about unrestrained sexuality were later hardened by others into the doctrine of subordinating sex and marriage entirely to "class" interests. "All those elements of sexual life that harm the establishment of a healthy revolutionary new generation," warned one influential political tract, "must be mercilessly swept away." In practical terms, that meant sexual repression in all aspects of society and a strict policy enforcing monogamous marriage.

Joseph Stalin's assumption of control over the Soviet Union added new layers of intolerance to this policy. The terrors he unleashed in the 1930s involved, among much deadlier things, what Simon Sebag Montefiore called "the triumph of prissy Bolshevik morality over the sexual freedom of the twenties." The libertine Kollontai was packed off to Sweden, but others fared very badly indeed. Some of Stalin's closest confederates lost their lives after being accused of sexual deviance. To be sure, when Stalin bumped off a political enemy the cause was always political, but accusations of sexual indiscretions were used to heap disgrace on the accused. For those outside of power positions, any action that smacked of bourgeois decadence—whether dancing the fox-trot, indulgence in pornography, or organizing sex education—was subject to punishment. By 1933, homosexuality was recriminalized and the "strong family" was marked as indispensable to Soviet life. Fifty years later, in a televised debate, a Leningrad woman would state, without a trace of irony: "We have no sex here."

• • •

The policy of promoting "traditional" marriage in the US went much further than removing the likes of Marcelle Henry from the State Department. Marriage has been, and remains, the only way to claim the full benefits of citizenship. The push for recognition of gay marriage has been an effort to secure for same-sex couples the more than one thousand legal advantages that married people enjoy over those in other types of relationships. Regardless of how marriage equality issues are ultimately resolved, and despite the vast numbers of people for whom marriage is outdated and irrelevant, an unmarried life is still lived just outside mainstream society.

The government has used penalties, rewards, and persuasion to get the pro-marriage message across. Public funds have been lavished on public-relations efforts to promote marriage as both a passage out of poverty and the only acceptable framework for having sex and children. The government has spent nearly $1 billion over the past two decades—money often diverted from job assistance and food aid—to argue these points on billboards and in subways and print advertisements. In 2005 alone, Congress allocated $750 million to religious and other groups to preach the message that marriage cures poverty. Another $100 million was spent, in the context of abstinence-focused sex education, to convince teenagers that (in the words of the pertinent law) "sex outside of marriage is likely to be physically and psychologically harmful" and that "a mutually faithful monogamous relationship in the context of marriage is the expected standard of human [sexual] activity."

These costly marketing efforts have failed. First, the rates of people living together and having children without getting married are higher than ever. As of 2013, 41 percent of US babies were born out of wedlock (a fourfold increase since 1970), mostly to mothers in their twenties and early thirties. More significantly, the percentage of Americans who disapprove of people living together outside of marriage dropped from 86 percent in 1977 to 27 percent in 2007. Far from toeing the pro-marriage line, 40 percent of Americans now describe marriage as obsolete, and single people now make up more than half of the American population. And despite all the pricey sloganeering, low-income mothers know that marriage has no appreciable effect on their checking accounts. As explained by researchers at the London School of Economics and Princeton, the complex matrix of factors contributing to poverty among the unmarried "cannot be altered with a marriage license." Poverty creates single mothers; not the other way around.

*   *   *

Regardless of the facts on the ground, the US has penalized those who reject the marriage message. Well into the 1970s, unmarried couples living together and having sex were technically committing crimes. While the laws against cohabitation were often ignored, especially as millions of unmarried people formed households without asking anyone's permission, the rules were not mothballed, either. Rather, as explained by Elizabeth H. Pleck in *Not Just Roommates: Cohabitation after the Sexual Revolution,* anti-cohabitation rules have been enforced selectively, first against interracial couples and then as a weapon against the postwar sexual revolution. Few of the laws bothered to explain *why* such "lewd and lascivious" relationships should be criminalized; presumably, the harm of unmarried sex was self-evident. However, Illinois law stated that criminalizing cohabitation was necessary to protect "the institution of marriage and normal family relationships from sexual conduct which tends to destroy them."

Action against cohabiting couples took a variety of forms. Several dozen states required that cohabiting parolees and probationers either cease "living in sin" or return to jail. Other locales used citizen surveillance networks that called in police to bust the couples. There were more such busts than one might now think. One survey of about four hundred prosecutors revealed more than three thousand prosecutions between 1968 and 1972. (Had more prosecutors been surveyed, more prosecutions would undoubtedly have been reported.) The town of Sheboygan, Wisconsin, seems to have been the nation's cohabitation arrest capital during the 1960s and 1970s. In 1967 alone, with a population of only forty-eight thousand, Sheboygan logged eighty-two arrests for lewd and lascivious cohabitation, fornication, adultery, and sexual perversion. When Sheboygan was featured in a *Wall Street Journal* story detailing its aggressive morals enforcement, the town fathers were proud. "We have high principled people who find this kind of conduct abhorrent," said police chief Oakley Frank. The prosecutions included the city's recreation director, James Decko, who was charged with a misdemeanor and lost his job for moving in with a woman after he had left his wife. Decko and his girl-friend had been watched by police for two months—a surveillance effort prompted by a police captain's sister, who lived in Decko's apartment building.

Sixty miles down the road from Sheboygan, Milwaukee's police chief used his vice squad to stake out the homes of several unmarried policemen suspected of living with women. The cohabiting cops were all sacked. Even in New York City, Barnard College student Linda LeClair learned in 1968 that living with her boyfriend could be hazardous to her education. She had given an interview to the *New York Times* about unmarried students living together but had asked that her name be withheld because she and her boyfriend were violating school anti-cohabitation rules. Barnard officials quickly deduced that she was the "Susan" in the story. Concerned that the scandal would impede fund-raising, the school threatened LeClair with suspension. Eventually, Barnard's president offered to let her stay, so long as she avoided the school cafeteria, did not participate in school social events, and followed the school's housing rules. She dropped out.

By the 1980s, most states had either repealed or stopped enforcing their anti-cohabitation laws, but not all. North Carolina's last known cohabitation conviction was in 1993, when well over one hundred thousand unmarried couples were living together in the state. Nevertheless, in 2004, Debora Hobbs, a police dispatcher, was told by her boss to either leave her longtime live-in boyfriend, marry him, or find another job. She quit. Had she been left to her own resources, the story would have ended there: no low-level employee had the funds to last in court against the sheriff's department. Fortunately, a group of do-gooder lawyers offered her free representation as she challenged the law making it a crime for an unmarried couple to "lewdly and lasciviously associate, bed, and cohabit together." Five years after Hobbs lost her job, she won her case and the law was finally gone.

Besides having pro bono legal representation, Hobbs was helped by the fact that she had no children at home. Had kids been involved, and had the children's father objected, the result would likely have been different. Consider Jacqueline Jarrett, a divorced Illinois mother who, in 1979, lost custody of her three young daughters after she moved in with her boy-friend. The judge agreed with her ex-husband that the girls were living in a "sinful environment." The following year, she lost again before the Illinois Supreme Court, which stated that even though the anti-cohabitation law had not been enforced for decades, Jarrett had still "debased" public morality and had, by her example, invited her daughters to do the same.

After the US Supreme Court refused to hear her case, a ruined Jarrett told a Chicago reporter: "If getting married would guarantee getting my children back, I would get married."

Jarrett would get her children back without taking that step. In 1983, the Illinois Supreme Court reversed itself—the result of a change in court personnel and, ironically, the double standards applied to male and female divorcees. First, the liberal Seymour Simon replaced one of the justices who had ruled against Jarrett. The court then took on another child-custody case, this time involving John Thompson, whose bullying had driven his former wife to a battered women's shelter. Despite Thompson's bad behavior, the newly constituted court allowed him to keep custody of his young son. Nothing could have put in starker relief the differing sexual standards applied to fathers and mothers. Having let Thompson off the hook, the court showed a measure of intellectual honesty by going back and changing the result for Jarrett.

At the same time, in the muddy trenches of divorce courts everywhere, judges routinely forced divorced women to choose between having sex and keeping their children. In one 1979 case near San Francisco, Anne Wellman, a divorced mother, had her boyfriend stay with her on weekends. Wellman's ex-husband had no problem with this arrangement, but the judge did. Under threat of removing the children from the house, the judge demanded that Wellman explain in detail how often and where she and her boyfriend had sex, and whether she intended to marry him. The court hearing included the following exchange:

JUDGE: You don't think it would be appropriate to confine your relationship to the daytime or to some premises away from your own home if you are going to have extramarital relationships considering the benefit of the children?

WELLMAN: Yes.

JUDGE: So if you are allowed custody of the children, then this would be one of the understandings you will agree to?

WELLMAN: Yes.

JUDGE: No more overnight visitation unless you are married, and if you are going to have some relationship, then it should be on some other premises?

WELLMAN: Uh-huh, I understand what you are saying.

Having muscled Wellman into making what was in effect a chastity pledge, the judge formally ordered her to have "no overnight visitation with a member of the opposite sex, in the presence of the children, until or unless she is married to that individual." Wellman later reconsidered and appealed the judge's order—something few divorced women have the time or money to do.

The appellate court agreed with Wellman and instructed the brow-beating judge not to "base his decision upon his disapproval of the morals . . . of a parent." The court also noted that by 1980, "mores in regard to cohab-itation have changed radically" and that it was unfair to hold Wellman to sexual standards that had been widely abandoned. Yet even as Wellman won a victory, one of the judges sounded a warning to other divorced mothers. Under slightly different circumstances, he said, he would have been "glad" to pass judgment on Wellman's sex life and "insist" that she adhere to "tra-ditional notions of morality." The message: divorced mothers should not forget that unless they maintain "traditional" sex lives, their days of raising their own children could be numbered.

•   •   •

Litigation is a sport for the wealthy. Anne Wellman received a sexual pass in large part because she found a way to fund a protracted lawsuit and feed her children without government help. Had she depended on welfare to care for her family, her loving new relationship would likely have been condemned as a sordid affair. In the US, impoverished single mothers are presump-tively dissolute. In exchange for government assistance, they are subjected to sexual restrictions the moneyed classes would never abide. This is espe-cially the case with African Americans, whose child-care and food assistance have often been cut off as punishment for having active sex lives. Since the 1980s, women such as Wellman have been able to convince courts that "mature, consenting adults" were moving in together in huge numbers and that their "freedom of . . . sexual conduct" should be respected. Not so with single women at the bottom of the economic ladder. Far from respecting their sexual rights, the law has long forced them to choose between having a sex life and keeping their families fed, clothed, and housed.

The issue starts with the enduring belief that African Americans are sexually dangerous. Before the Civil War, slaves were usually forbidden to marry because slave marriages were seen as a threat to their owners' control over them. Masters feared that such unions would diminish their female slaves' obeisance and incite black men to violence. A slave owner's prerogatives included the "right" to rape slave women, which masters did uncounted millions of times. If black women were allowed to marry, it was feared that their husbands would likely respond with violence when masters came to take their due. Despite the prohibitions, slaves often engaged in informal marriage rituals (such as jumping over broomsticks) and formed families, only to see them ripped apart in the slave markets or when black men were used as "breeding stock" to produce more slaves. A black woman could not simultaneously be a legitimate wife to a black man and a sex object to her white owner; nor could a black man be a breeding "buck" for his owner and a loyal husband to his wife.

The prohibition against African American marriages was lifted after the Civil War, but marriage laws were still used to control the black population, this time by forcing them to marry. Postbellum society viewed marriage as a "civilizing" influence for African Americans, whether they wanted it or not. Unless African Americans had children in the context of marriages, they could be jailed for some combination of adultery, fornication, and unlawful cohabitation. More importantly, forced marriage was a way to saddle black men with the burden of caring for millions of newly freed and desperately poor black women and children. Despite the fact that jobs for African Americans were few and the pay terrible, and the fact that black families had been torn to shreds for generations, freed black men were now supposed to find and support their far-flung offspring (often born to multiple mothers) and, in the process, base their family lives on traditional white models.

In the wreckage that was the South during the Reconstruction era, marriage was framed as a cure for the troubles that befell African Americans—misfortunes slavery had created—which now threatened to do further damage to the economy. The issue was cast in moral terms: the poverty and shattered lives of African Americans were caused not by the legacy of slavery, or by laws cementing their indigence in place, but by their own sexual incontinence. If blacks were impoverished, it was because they copulated indiscriminately and produced children they could not look after. If, however, they married and assumed lives of quiet Christian industry, then they and their children would somehow stay off the public rolls. As one Confederate army officer proclaimed to newly freed African American men: "The loose ideas which have prevailed among you on this subject must cease. You will have to support and take care of your families . . . because it [is] no longer the duty of the white masters to do so."

The beliefs that marriage cures poverty and that unmarried mothers of color don't deserve public assistance have driven public policy to the present day. African American poverty has been blamed not only on purported hypersexuality but also on the alleged schemes of "welfare queens" to use endless pregnancies to enrich themselves at public expense. In 2013, for example, on the fiftieth anniversary of Martin Luther King Jr.'s march on Washington, conservative columnist and talk-show perennial George Will claimed that illegitimate children, not a lack of civil rights, causes poverty among African Americans. Will pointed to a 1965 report by Daniel Patrick Moynihan (later a New York senator, but then an assistant secretary of labor) that pinned "inner city" problems on a "tangle of pathology" causing black families to "break down," and by which black women churned out children their irresponsible paramours refused to support. Will also claimed that the key cause of Detroit's bankruptcy was the city's "culture" of single mothers. Given that Detroit's population is 80 percent African American, the race-based message was not ambiguous.

Vicious stereotypes about African American sexuality, particularly that the root cause of black poverty is the all-too-accessible genitalia of black females, have prompted cruelty to generations of poor women. Unlike the white widows of the First World War, who received the first government aid for single mothers and children, unmarried black women were—in the words of Senator Robert Byrd in 1962 —"welfare chiselers" and "breeders," women whose multiple sexual partners were too busy drinking and shirking work to marry them. The message of Byrd and his ilk fit the times. By the 1960s, the majority of single mothers receiving aid for their children were black. In 1961, the city manager of Newburgh, New York (a town that had recently seen an influx of black migration), called for cutting off all aid to women who "breed illegitimate children at taxpayers' expense." That same year, a Gallup poll showed that about half of Americans believed that *all* unwed mothers should be summarily thrown off the welfare rolls.

In 1960, Louisiana cut off financial assistance to children whose mothers gave birth after they had begun to receive aid. The result: 22,501 children (88 percent of whom were black) risked starvation because their mothers were deemed promiscuous. Many of these mothers then had to give their kids up for adoption, lacking the money to care for them. When that policy was criticized for targeting children, twenty states devised another plan to achieve the same end. Under the new "suitable father" rules (alternately called the "man in the house" rules), a welfare mother's sex partners were required to support her children. If the women were too "immoral" and "shiftless" to have sex without getting married, the thinking went, then the government would convert their boyfriends into stepfathers. In either event, the government was off the hook.

The main tools to find "men in the house" were surveillance and surprise raids of the homes of welfare mothers. If men were detected, then support for these women and their children would likely be cut off on account of "moral unfitness." The women could also be charged with welfare fraud or theft, and the men would be ordered to support the children. It mattered not whether the women and men knew each other well, or whether the men could provide support, or even whether the men knew the children. The mothers and the men were presumably having sex, and that was enough to brand the men as substitute fathers. How much sex should call the rules into play was left to the discretion of welfare workers. Some thought once every six months was sufficient; others felt that more sex was required. Regardless of the frequency, the substitute father rules held poor women to far more restrictive sexual standards than those applied to women with money.

The "man in the house" rules framed sex with destitute single mothers as a variant of prostitution. Unlike the millions of unmarried middle- and upper-class women enjoying the 1960s sexual revolution without legal or economic consequence, a poor woman paid a heavy price. A man in her house during a surprise raid meant that her children would suffer in the foreseeable future. For the man, the price was support of a new family, even if he and the woman had never conceived a child and barely knew each other. Alabama's welfare commissioner Reuben K. King summarized the policy in base terms: "If a man wants to play, then let him pay." During that state's purge, some sixteen thousand children, nearly all of them black, were cut off from aid. Nearly three-quarters of a million children were cut off nationally.

It took a lot of effort to net that many people. By 1962, special "investigation units" had been set up in at least seven states and eighteen cities to stake out houses and apartments. In an East Harlem housing project, an investigator climbed a tree at two in the morning to peer into a woman's window. During Oakland's infamous Operation Bedcheck, the official name given to a blast of raids in 1963, welfare personnel paid surprise visits to the homes of 425 welfare mothers, looking for "unauthorized males" in "husbandly attitude[s]." Fraud investigators and social workers arrived in pairs at the women's dwellings on a Sunday at six thirty AM, one guarding back doors to catch fleeing men while the other rapped on front doors demanding admission. Once inside, the investigators rummaged through every room, paying particular attention to beds, closets, bathrooms, and "other places of concealment."

As if pseudo-commando raids seeking evidence of sex were not bad enough, about half of the women targeted in Operation Bedcheck were chosen at random. Authorities had no reason to believe they had live-in boyfriends. Merely being a mother on welfare raised an institutional suspicion that they were promiscuous welfare cheats. Nevertheless, if any of the women refused to open their doors to the fraud teams, they and their children stood to be cut off from aid. If, on the other hand, they admitted the teams into their houses and a man *was* there—or if there were items around such as a razor, cigar butts, or men's shoes—then the same result would apply, along with possible criminal prosecution.

One welfare worker assigned to Operation Bedcheck, Benny Parrish, saw the raids as "Gestapo-like" and was fired for refusing to participate in them. He sued his superiors, and the case eventually made its way up to the California Supreme Court. The court decided that Parrish had been wrongly fired and that Operation Bedcheck was an unconstitutional fiasco: "It is surely not beyond the competence of the [county welfare] department to conduct appropriate investigations without violence to human dignity and within the confines of the Constitution." By 1967, the federal government had banned such raids altogether.

The *Parrish* decision, as welcome as it was, only nibbled at the edges of the policy of forcing unmarried welfare mothers to refrain from sex. Mass raids like Operation Bedcheck were now forbidden, but the "man in the house" rules themselves remained. Women across the country were still required to make what were, in effect (and in some cases, literal), chastity pledges in exchange for their children's benefits. Even the *Parrish* ruling noted that it was the randomness of Operation Bedcheck's searches, not the "man in the house" rules themselves, that made the operation illegal. The broad challenge to these rules would come out of Alabama, where welfare-receiving single mothers were the worst.

In 1966, an Alabama welfare caseworker told Sylvester Smith, a widowed African American mother of four who worked at a "Negro café," that a "little birdie" told her that Smith had a gentleman coming to her house on weekends. The worker told Smith to end the relationship if she wanted her children to continue to get aid. Smith refused. "If God intended me to be a nun, I'd be a nun," she said. Smith was soon notified that her twenty-nine-dollar monthly welfare subsidy, which comprised 25 percent of her income, had ended—sparking, in turn, one of the mothers of all civil rights cases.

The multiple racial conflicts then unfolding in Selma, where Smith lived, had brought an influx of civil rights attorneys down from the North. However, most of these lawyers, including the ones Smith consulted, were themselves targets of police harassment, which made it difficult for them to take on individual cases. Smith was then referred to the scruffy New York attorney Martin Garbus, who was already a giant of the civil rights bar and was looking for a test case to challenge the substitute-father rules. Smith's situation had the right ingredients for such a case, he decided, because Alabama's rules were more draconian than most and because they were almost exclusively enforced against black women. Indeed, Alabama didn't just cut off families when a mother was found to have an ongoing sexual relationship; it revoked aid when a mother was *thought* to have a relationship with a man, regardless of whether he could support her children or even knew them. To keep her aid, it was the woman's burden to show that each man she saw had no sexual interest in her. Even if Smith had promised her welfare worker that she would end her relationship, it would not have put her in the clear. The rules required her to obtain affidavits from two law-enforcement officials, ministers, neighbors, or even grocers to prove, somehow, that she had no sex life.

Despite fierce opposition, Garbus's challenge to the Alabama substitute-father rules was a complete success. He was assisted by the cluelessness of state officials, who couldn't hide their contempt for their poorest residents. The state's welfare commissioner, Reuben King, for example, testified that sex had nothing to do with the rules but that any mother whose aid was stopped could always choose "to give up her pleasure or act like a woman is supposed to act" and get the support back. Alabama also argued in court briefs that the rules targeted only the "unworthy poor" and that without the rules the state would be "overrun" with "illegitimates." Garbus also had the good luck of drawing a sympathetic trial judge, Frank J. Johnson Jr., who was in the midst of a feud with Governor George Wallace. (Wallace had called Johnson an "integrating, scalawagging, carpet bagging, bold-faced liar.") The final word on the Smith dispute, however—which would ensure its broader effects—would come from the US Supreme Court, which took up the case in 1968.

The evening before the high court was scheduled to hear oral arguments in the case, Garbus met with Mary Lee Stapp, the lawyer for the state of Alabama. Their conversation, as Garbus later recalled, revealed much about the real purpose of the substitute-father rules. Stapp explained that the rules were not anti-black so much as they were anti-fornication. "Good Alabama citizens don't think there should be sex outside of its 'proper' domicile—the wedded couple. You know [African Americans] aren't like us."

Stapp was smart enough to leave this argument out of her written Supreme Court briefs, but the justices got the picture anyway. They were outraged that the rules distinguished between the "worthy" and the "unworthy" poor and also that such distinctions were based on a policy of "discouraging illicit sexual behavior." Wrote Chief Justice Earl Warren: "It is simply inconceivable . . . that Alabama is free to discourage immorality and illegitimacy by the device of absolute disqualification of needy children." By a unanimous vote, the court threw most of the country's substitute-father rules out the window. Within six months, about 750,000 children of single mothers were back on the rolls.

The *Smith* decision, and a few others like it, were victories for single, welfare-dependent women, but the image of the promiscuous African American "welfare queen" only deepened in the ensuing years. Immediate reaction to the *Smith* decision was mixed, with the *New York Times* praising it for "expos[ing] some of the worst vices of the welfare system" while conservatives complained that the decision makes "sin pay" and "adultery profitable." One Michigan legislator declared the decision "incomprehensible," adding: "We can no longer regard the family as a legal unit." Four years after the decision, the Senate Finance Committee held hearings in which Stanford University scholar Roger Freeman testified that *Smith* invited deadbeat dads to "swap" welfare mothers in complex schemes to bilk the government out of money. Lawmakers from both sides of the aisle decried the decision as being hostile to families and, in the words of President Richard Nixon, applying "economic pressure [for families] to split apart."

During his 1976 presidential campaign, Ronald Reagan returned time and again to the false story of a Chicago woman who had eighty names, thirty addresses, twelve Social Security cards, lots of kids, and four nonexistent deceased husbands, and who, Reagan said, was collecting $150,000 per year in welfare. The story was widely disproved, but the facts did nothing to dispel the stereotypes it advanced. By the 1990s, the idea had coalesced that providing aid to the families of unmarried women encouraged immorality. Vilifying sexually active single women on welfare became a key strategy on the Republican and, to a lesser extent, Democratic Party agendas.

In 1996, President Bill Clinton signed the Personal Responsibility and Work Opportunity Reconciliation Act (PRWORA), which turned the heat up even further. The law was based in part on Congress's "findings" that marriage is an "essential institution of a successful society," but Florida congressman John Mica put it more candidly when he argued that providing support to poor women (whom he compared, strangely, to alligators) would only spur them to have more indiscriminate sex, produce more children, and scheme for more government handouts. Under PRWORA and the raft of harsh state laws it spawned, unless a poor woman produced children with a lawful husband, her kids ate less. Assistance to the children of single mothers was slashed, and morality tests were reinstated for even the reduced amounts. Unannounced home visits by welfare officials looking for live-in boyfriends resumed, and while the presence of men did not automatically trigger cutoffs, the men's incomes were usually imputed to the mother—resulting in smaller checks or no checks at all. In San Diego County, where 14,600 such home visits took place in 2002 alone, women were prosecuted for fraud even when their boyfriends refused to share their earnings.

Not to be outdone, the administration of President George W. Bush championed a Healthy Family Initiative that lavished hundreds of millions of dollars on the active promotion of "healthy, two-parent, married families" as a cure-all for poverty. The initiative was no more successful than its predecessors. As the economic and political journalist Annie Lowrey observed, "Uncle Sam tends to make a poor cupid. The preponderance of the evidence is that Washington instead has, over the years, wasted hundreds of millions of dollars . . . to no real effect on marriage rates or child poverty or anything else."

Sterilization of the Poor and Sexually Unfit

The substitute-father and similar rules punished children for the crime of being born to an unmarried woman—but other measures prevented such children from tasting life at all. For about sixty years, under the banners of marriage promotion and preventing illegitimate babies, more than sixty thousand females were forcibly sterilized in the US. Most of them were poor and nonwhite; some were no more than girls and were not even told beforehand about the procedure. Under the ghastly patchwork of laws that encouraged such deception to happen, women and girls were admitted into clinics for one procedure, such as giving birth, and left with their fertility destroyed.

The sterilization of impoverished females is one of the more shameful aspects of the US's extended romance with the pseudoscience of eugenics, during which the "unfit"—a protean label that included the "feebleminded," moral and sexual "perverts," epileptics, and felons—were judged a threat not only to society but to the human gene pool. While some states had been sterilizing and castrating "undesirables" since the mid-nineteenth century, the practice of disabling the reproductive equipment of single women picked up steam in the late 1920s. Such people were deemed less than worthless, both for their rejection of marital norms and for the seeds of sexual incontinence they were thought to carry in their blood.

The green light for mass sterilization was given by the US Supreme Court in a 1927 case, *Buck v. Bell,* which concerned a young, white, un-married Virginia woman who had given birth. Seventeen-year-old Carrie Buck had the bad luck of being used by local health authorities to test the limits of a new Virginia law called the Eugenical Sterilization Act. Buck's medical records echoed her doctors' opinion that she came from a "shiftless, ignorant, and worthless" class that was breeding out of control. Her mother had been institutionalized for "immorality" and had given her up to a foster family when she was a child. Buck's foster parents, in turn, had her put into the same institution after she gave birth. Both Buck and her mother were said by hospital staff to have low "mental ages" and Buck's six-month-old daughter, after a brief examination by a nurse, was also diagnosed as mentally deficient. In their court papers, hospital officials argued that Buck and her mother's "feeblemindedness" had been passed down to the child, a process that sterilization would halt once and for all.

The Supreme Court, per Justice Oliver Wendell Holmes, accepted these arguments and, "to prevent our being swamped with incompe-tence," ruled:

> It is better for all the world if, instead of waiting to execute degenerate offspring for crime or to let them starve for their imbecility, society

can prevent those who are manifestly unfit from continuing their kind. The principle that sustains compulsory vaccination is broad enough to cover cutting the Fallopian tubes. . . . Three generations of imbeciles are enough.

Chilling stuff, but from that point on, it was law. Rather than "waiting to execute" the likes of Buck's next baby, or caring for such children during their accursed lives, the court found that it was better to prevent their coming into existence at all. Buck was the first person sterilized under the Virginia law, and by 1930, thirty states had followed suit with laws of their own. By this time, eugenics was mainstream science and social theory, taught widely in universities, promoted by a variety of respected professional organizations, and approved by notables including Theodore Roosevelt, Winston Churchill, and John Maynard Keynes. The most notorious proponent of eugenics, Adolf Hitler, had not yet become a household name, but he had already written admiringly of American eugenics practices in *Mein Kampf.*

Had Justice Holmes and his brethren bothered to look carefully at Buck's situation, and had her awful lawyer offered up evidence on the subject, the court would have learned that her pregnancy had resulted from her being raped by a member of her foster family. She was institutionalized to protect the family from scandal. The court would have also known that Buck was *not* born out of wedlock as hospital authorities had said, so there was no basis for accusing her mother of promiscuity or for inferring that some kind of "slut gene" had been passed down to Carrie. Finally, had the court not been so enamored of eugenics, it might have asked how a nurse's cursory examination could have determined that Buck's child was feebleminded, or how feeblemindedness could traverse generations.

After *Buck v. Bell,* a woman who engaged in nonmarital sex could be pronounced "sexually delinquent" and unfit to reproduce. The decision unleashed a surgical blitzkrieg against women on the margins of society who, by choice or compulsion, had sex while unmarried. A catalog of the horrors unleashed by the eugenic sterilization laws would fill many thick volumes. By the time the procedures finally stopped in the 1980s, Virginia had sterilized more than seven thousand people; North Carolina more than eight thousand; and California almost twenty thousand. In fact, some states *expanded* their eugenics programs after the grim details of Third Reich medical practices were known. Said Mississippi legislator

David Glass in 1958, advocating for the sterilization of *all* unwed mothers, "The Negro woman . . . because of child welfare assistance, [is] making it a business, in some cases, of giving birth to illegitimate children." Under Glass's proposed scheme, such women could avoid sterilization by getting married.

•   •   •

Half of the purportedly feebleminded women sterilized in North Carolina were poor single mothers. Most of them were African Americans suspected of using babies to scam the government for welfare benefits. As in most other states with eugenics laws on the books, North Carolina's scheme gave medical authorities wide latitude to determine what constituted feeblemindedness. Their conclusions were rarely questioned by the state's Eugenics Board, especially when the target female, or her parents, were seen to have sexually misbehaved. Here was the considered medical thinking: promiscuity was not only a sign of mental deficiency; it also made the patient's condition worse. Mental defectives were addicted to orgasms, and every sexual climax they pursued exacerbated their idiocy and criminality. Since sex was the main occupation of the feebleminded, and sexual addiction was passed down through the generations, a diagnosis of sexual uncontrollability was a sure strategy for convincing the Eugenics Board that a patient was feebleminded and sterilization the only solution.

Given the stereotypes that African American females were both hypersexual and had built up profitable baby-making rackets, they bore the brunt of North Carolina's sterilization efforts. So did their children, especially when they showed signs—such as girls sending flirtatious notes to classmates—that they had inherited their parents' sex addiction. State authorities saw it as urgent to get to these girls early, before they started to produce offspring and before they infected humanity by enticing "normal-minded" people to conjoin with them.

These loose standards were ignored even when girls were victims of sexual assault. In such cases, North Carolina officials still pinned them with the dreaded label of promiscuity. Take Elaine Riddick, a poor thirteen-year-old African American girl who was raped and impregnated by an older man in 1967. Hospital social workers diagnosed her as promiscuous and feebleminded and threatened to put her in an orphanage unless her illiterate grandmother consented to her sterilization. The grandmother signed the consent form (with an X), and the social workers went to the state Eugenics Board for clearance to perform the operation. The board was presented with the following summary of the girl's life:

Delores Elaine Riddick - (N) - Perquimans County

Social information: Age 13. Single. Pregnant. Psychological

April 5, 1967. MA 9-6: IQ 75

This thirteen-year-old girl expects her first child in March 1968. . . . She has never done any work and gets along so poorly with others that her school experience was poor. Because of Elaine's inability to control herself, and her promiscuity—there are community reports of her "running around" and out late at night unchaperoned, the physician has advised sterilization. . . . *This will at least prevent additional children from being born to this child who cannot care for herself, and can never function in any way as a parent.*

Diagnosis: Feebleminded.

The board, which approved about 90 percent of such petitions in fifteen minutes or less, granted this one without dissent. When Riddick went to the hospital to deliver her son, no one told her that she was about to be sterilized as well. She did not learn what had happened until years later, when she and her husband tried to conceive a child. Still bitter over her treatment, she later told news reporters that she had been "raped twice . . . once by the perpetrator and once by the state of North Carolina." In another interview, she said: "They took away my right to be a woman. . . . I was a little bitty kid and they cut me open like a hog."

Several years later, after the collapse of her marriage, Riddick sued the members of the Eugenics Board, but the case went down in flames. To make matters worse, one of the board members, Jacob Koomen, testified that he thought they were doing right by Riddick and the other women who were sterilized: "We were doing a favor; indeed, we were often asked—not often—we were sometimes asked to sterilize those who had not yet menstruated."

Another black North Carolina woman, eighteen-year-old Nial Cox, was bullied into consenting to tubal ligation in 1965, soon after she had been impregnated by a white man and had given birth to a girl. As with Elaine Riddick, Cox's pregnancy coincided with North Carolina's effort to sterilize unwed African American mothers at the earliest possible ages.

Cox and her daughter were not on welfare but her mother and siblings were, which meant that threats from the local welfare department still had particular force. "[The social worker] would always tell me, 'Your family is going to starve because of what you did,'" Cox later recalled. "'If you don't do this, we going to take this check away from [your family].'"

Not long after Cox's daughter was born, Cox was forced to choose between consenting to sterilization and watching her family go hungry. "What am I supposed to do? Why should my family—my sisters and brothers—starve for something I did?" Cox signed her consent. From that point, it was a quick process for the Eugenics Board to approve the procedure. The petition to the board stated that Cox was argumentative and lazy and "would not assume the responsibility of supporting all the children she would bring into this world. . . . Our agency is thoroughly convinced that the only way to keep a family of this type from reproducing itself is to rely on sterilization."

Cox was sterilized three months after her child was born. She eventually went to New York City, where she found work as a nurse's aide. In 1973, she filed a class-action lawsuit against the Eugenics Board and others involved in the sterilization program, claiming that she and others like her had been robbed of a series of constitutional rights. She lost, as Riddick had, but the publicity generated by the suit helped to hasten the disbanding of the Eugenics Board. The last sterilization in North Carolina took place that same year, just as fourteen other states were considering new bills to force women on welfare to undergo sterilization. As the sponsor of one of the bills declared: "People who live like animals should be treated as such."

The year 1973 also saw a series of well-publicized eugenics cases burst out of South Carolina. An obstetrician in the genteel town of Aiken, Clovis H. Pierce, was the only doctor who would deliver the poor's babies, but he refused to assist women on welfare with more than two children unless they also agreed to have their Fallopian tubes tied. Hospital records indicated that more than half of his thirty-four deliveries the previous year included sterilizations. Pierce defended the practice as a way to reduce welfare expenditures. Soon the national news media swarmed Aiken and published stories about the injustice of forced sterilization.

At about the same time, a federal judge in South Carolina expressed outrage that two black girls aged twelve and fourteen had been sterilized without even their parents' knowledge. The judge started issuing orders against the use of government funds to sterilize disadvantaged females. By 1978, new regulations strictly limiting the practice were in place. The last legally compulsory sterilization in the US took place in 1981.

In 2002 the *Winston-Salem Journal* published a lengthy series of articles titled "Against Their Will," which exposed the darkest aspects of North Carolina's eugenic sterilizations and highlighted the program's racist and sexist dimensions. The articles led to a public apology by the state's governor and the appointment of a commission to consider paying reparations to surviving victims. In 2013, the state approved $10 million in compensation, slated for distribution in 2015. North Carolina, where the record in this regard is among the worst anywhere, was the first state to make restitution to the victims—a landmark by any measure. In 2002, the governor of Oregon also apologized for that state's eugenic sterilization program, going as far as declaring an annual Human Rights Day in memory of those the program had victimized.

Despite these apologies, deep popular resentment remains against poor women who have the temerity to produce children outside of marriage, and there is also support for the use of government power to stem the growth of the "surplus poor." It remains an article of faith among social conservatives, such as Charles Murray, that births outside of marriage are "more important than crime, drugs, poverty, illiteracy, welfare or homelessness *because {they} drive everything else.*" Recent economic downturns have only intensified those beliefs. In 2009, an ardently pro-life Louisiana legislator, John LeBruzzo, proposed paying women on welfare $1,000 to have their tubes tied while at the same time proposing tax incentives to educated elites to have more kids, a move revealing what law professor Linda Fentiman called a "closet eugenics feeling in the United States."

Among the ironies generated by these debates, few are as glaring as the fact that abortion-rights activists were among the first to raise an outcry over compelled sterilization. This happened in 1973, when the scope of the sterilization abuse issue was first widely revealed, and just when the *Roe v. Wade* decision legalized most abortions. In the 1977 Hyde Amendment, passed during the same year coerced sterilizations were outlawed, the pro-life lobby pushed through legislation almost completely cutting off public abortion funding for poor women, while Medicaid and most insurance plans still happily pay for almost the entire cost of sterilization.

*   *   *

The family these days is a beautiful mess: beautiful because marriage no longer gives men license to rape their wives; beautiful because the law is starting to embrace arrangements that veer from narrow, oppressive models; beautiful because same-sex couples are adopting, having, and raising children who are no better or worse adjusted than those of heterosexual parents; beautiful because the rate of interracial marriages has more than doubled in the past three decades, and with each union the stigma against interracial children abates; and beautiful because marriage has flourished even as it is being reinvented. More than $70 billion is spent yearly on weddings (more than on pets, coffee, toothpaste, and toilet paper combined), while divorce rates have dropped from their high of two decades ago. And beautiful because now, more than ever, a family can be formed on the basis of a couple's choice, love, and devotion.

The family is a mess because the law simply cannot keep up. The goal of protecting children from abuse now runs against the right to have children at all. In New York, for example, in 2003, two homeless drug addicts had a child who tested positive for crack cocaine. The court removed the baby from the parents and ordered the parents not to procreate until (among other things) they regained custody of the child. Obviously, the sympathy here is for the baby, but one legal case builds on another, and the next one might not be so morally clear-cut. At present, courts are split on whether no-procreate orders violate the right to reproduce, even when it is likely that children will be born into neglect.

Other questions arise when parents have a child in order to mine its body for donor cells. For example, in 2000, two parents created a baby specifically to save their existing child, who suffered from a rare blood disease. The baby's embryo was selected from several because of its compatibility with the sick child, and the use of stem cells from the baby's umbilical cord did no harm to the baby. But what if the parents created a child to harvest one of its kidneys for an ailing sibling? And what if the new child was harmed in the process? At what point does the new child's right to keep his or her body intact trump the parents' loving efforts to save another child? As science advances, the competing rights of parents and children will need to be delicately balanced, and the long-standing rights of parents to make medical decisions on behalf of their children will likely need to be curtailed.

The advent of assisted reproductive techniques has also been a strain on the law. It started with the *Baby M* case, in 1987, when a court ruled that a surrogate mother, not the biological parents, could keep the baby. The contract between the surrogate and the parents violated public policy, the court ruled, and was "illegal, perhaps criminal, and potentially degrading to women." Almost thirty years later, the law governing surrogacy and assisted reproduction is all over the map. In Kansas, a man who answered a lesbian couple's Craigslist request for sperm, and who donated his own to the couple after renouncing his rights as a parent, was ordered in 2014 to pay child support. In 2009, Amy and Scott Kehoe purchased sperm and egg cells through brokers and then hired Laschell Baker to carry the embryo—or embryos, as twins were born. Baker then convinced a court to let her keep the babies. Neither she nor the Kehoes had any genetic link to the twins. In New York, an unmarried couple conceived in 2011 with a sperm donor and in vitro fertilization. However, the mother fell into a depression and killed herself a few months after the child was born. More than a year of litigation later, the baby was given to the mother's sister. The court ruled that the "father" was a biological and legal stranger to the child, despite his desperate desire to continue the family he and the mother had started.

Then there are the babies who are conceived with surprise genetic material. In London, a fertility clinic owner secretly used his own sperm—and not that of other donors, as he had told the mothers—to create up to six hundred babies, while in Utah, a fertility clinic receptionist substituted his sperm for that of donors. The families were more than a little distressed to learn who the father of their children was, but what should the legal effect be? Should the secret donors be compelled to pay for the upbringing of their far-flung offspring? What if they decide to claim custody rights of some of the children? These questions are rarely resolved to anyone's satisfaction.

Finally, what happens if parents die before their children are even conceived? The US Supreme Court ruled in 2012 that children born using a dead father's frozen sperm aren't entitled to his Social Security benefits, while a New York court ruled in 2007 that children created with their dead father's frozen sperm could inherit potentially millions of dollars from the father's father. This decision, and others like it, may well create new and unexpected populations of family members and heirs. Every frozen embryo and every human being born from preserved egg or sperm cells is, after all, someone's genetic child or grandchild.

CHAPTER 2

HOMOSEXUALITY

From Sin to Sickness

In 2013, Ukraine was divided over whether to integrate with the European Union or deepen its ties with Russia. The issues were mainly economic, but gay sex entered the debate. In December, one thousand icon-carrying Orthodox Christians marched in Kiev against European integration, lest Ukraine become infected with homosexuality. "We are against the Euro Sodom," said a marcher. One month earlier, in Syria, Sunni Muslim fighters from the Islamic State (ISIS) jihadist group severed the head of a man believed to belong to an enemy Shi'a group. They held the head up before a crowd, warning that Shi'as "will . . . rape the men before the women. That's what these infidels will do." These two episodes took place outside the boundaries of the West, but before any readers begin to feel smug they should remember that the same anti-gay slanders have also pervaded American and, to a lesser extent, European jurisprudence over the past century.

The belief that homosexuality is a contagious illness is woven through twentieth-century law. In 1955, for example, a Boise, Idaho, judge slapped members of a homosexual "ring" with long jail terms to prevent "mass conscience deterioration" and "social disorder." The judge shared the local media's fear of the "cancerous growth" of gay sex, against which "immediate and systematic cauterization" was required. In 1978, five years *after* the American Psychiatric Association (APA) declared that homosexuality was not an illness, the top US jurist, William Rehnquist, compared the activities of a campus gay-rights group to the spread of measles. And in the 1980s, the AIDS pandemic was widely linked to the "gay lifestyle." The fear of gay contamination of the American body politic was so acute that, from 1952 until 1990, homosexuals were technically barred from entering the US.

The Ukrainian protesters' horror of "Euro Sodom" followed the same range of beliefs, especially as Russia offered a clear alternative. A few months before the Ukrainians' march, a top Russian media executive brought cheers from an audience when he said that Russian rules against "homosexual propaganda" should be augmented with laws that "banned [homosexuals] from donating blood [and] sperm," and added that "[homosexuals'] hearts, in case of an automobile accident, should be buried . . . or burned as unsuitable for the continuation of life."

The ISIS fighters' smear of their enemies as homosexual, and homosexuals as sex criminals, also follows a familiar pattern. For much of the past century, Western law associated homosexuals with rape and violence of all kinds. Measures against "predatory perverts," child molesters, and serial killers often made homosexuals prime targets, regardless of the victims' sex. In 1954, for example, after a little girl in Miami was raped with a tree branch and brutally murdered—a crime for which there were no leads— police immediately descended on the city's gay bars, while newspapers demanded an aggressive "pervert cleanup." Until recently, many people convicted of having consensual gay sex were put on public registries of dangerous sex offenders.

In the first half of the twentieth century, considerable mischief resulted when the law started approaching gay sex as the symptom of an illness rather than as a sin against God. Homosexuality became a pathological identity, and gay men were seen as naturally inclined to commit violent crimes outside the bedroom. This characterization of homosexuality as a dangerous mental illness worsened the visceral disgust gays have long elicited in much of the straight population, which still exists. In a 2004 study, *Hiding from Humanity: Disgust, Shame, and the Law*, philosopher and law professor Martha Nussbaum dissects this reaction, and does so well enough to merit an extended quotation:

> The central locus of disgust in today's United States [is] male loathing of the male homosexual. . . . What inspires disgust is typically the male thought of the male homosexual, imagined as anally penetrable. The idea of semen and feces mixing together inside the body of a male is one of the most disgusting ideas imaginable—to males, for whom

the idea of non-penetrability is a sacred boundary against stickiness, ooze, and death. The presence of a homosexual male in the neighborhood inspires the thought that one might oneself lose one's clean safeness, one might become the receptacle for those animal products. Thus disgust is ultimately disgust at one's own imagined penetrability and ooziness, and this is why the male homosexual is both regarded with disgust and viewed with fear as a predator who might make everyone else disgusting. . . . *The gaze of a homosexual male is seen as contaminating because it says, "You can be penetrated." And this means that you can be made of feces and semen and blood, not clean plastic flesh. (And this means: you will soon be dead.)*

This is why participants in a 2001 University of Virginia study expressed more negative feelings toward gay sex than they did toward incest or even a man masturbating while a dog licked his genitals. It is also why some of the literature supporting a 1992 Colorado referendum against gay rights claimed that gay men ate feces and drank blood. It is also one reason the law has been indulgent toward men who kill homosexuals. And it is why, as we examine the law's approaches to gay sex, we must keep in mind homosexuality's capacity to elicit irrational responses in seemingly reasonable people.

Early Labeling Events

The words "homosexual" and "heterosexual" were invented in 1869 by the Hungarian *littérateur* Kàroly Mària Kertbeny (born Benkert), who wrote that homosexuals were held in "bondage" to a congenital urge for gay sex. While Kertbeny was not a scientist, a growing body of late-nineteenth-century European medical researchers were turning their attention to a wide range of sexual aberrations, including coprophilia (arousal by feces), urophilia (arousal by urine), mysophilia (love of filth), fetishism (for example, for boots, rosebuds, striped handkerchiefs, metal screws), necrophilia, gerontophilia (sex with the aged), sadism, masochism, voyeurism, and exhibitionism. Homosexuals (also called inverts, and urnings) were just one of the many types of "perverts" coming under scrutiny. However, as the new century began, no one could have predicted that attention to homosexuality would surpass all the others, or that the homosexual/heterosexual dichotomy would emerge, as the historian Dagmar Herzog put it, "as the great contrast pair organizing the sexual universe."

At the turn of the twentieth century, straight and gay sex were not always seen as mutually exclusive. Female–female sex took place furtively and well under the radar, while many men had sex with both males and females and did not see themselves as maladjusted for doing so. While "sodomy"—a protean category of crime that included anal sex—was illegal in the US, Germany, Austria, Britain, Sweden, and Denmark, it was technically not forbidden in France, Italy, the Netherlands, Belgium, or Spain. Sodomy was one sexual sin among many and was seen as a product of uncontrolled lust, like whoremongering. The law's hostility was not necessarily focused on men having sex with men but on men seeking sexual release outside marriage. In some quarters, the term "heterosexual" denoted a person who was *too* interested in sex for pleasure alone rather than one attracted to the opposite sex.

Along with the burgeoning population of female prostitutes, there was a prodigious "rough trade" in the cities that saw lower-class young men (workers, soldiers, sailors, bathhouse attendants, and so on) providing sex to other men for money or favors. While some of these "rent boys" presented themselves as effeminate or in drag, many were not exclusively attracted to men; nor were their customers. And while there were substantial numbers of people who desired only gay sex, "homosexuals" were not yet clearly marked out as a subspecies of humanity.

That said, no one regarded gay sex as normal, especially not the researchers in the new field of sexology. Under one popular theory, the urge for gay sex came from an "inverted" sexual instinct, a defect in the nervous system resulting from evolutionary reversal. In essence, inverts had not evolved properly and thus were condemned to a life of misdirected sexual energy. Inversion, for example, was blamed for the perceived lesbianism and mannish features of British suffragettes. Another theory pegged a predisposition to sexual perversion on a mix of factors: a bad brew of weak chromosomes, poverty, and even inclement weather could spark the urge for gay sex, profanation of corpses, or rape. American researchers added a thick dollop of racism to the mix, associating homosexuality with the supposedly primitive sexual excesses of the "Southern Negro" and even with prehistoric "troglodytes."

The most influential of the early sex researchers was the German Richard von Krafft-Ebing, whose encyclopedic *Psychopathia Sexualis* (first published in 1866 and later expanded) stands as the enduring sexological document of the era. Covering hundreds of case histories and dozens of perversions (including masochism, a term he coined), it also focused on homosexuality, a "perversion" he blamed on a hereditary degeneration of the nervous system. For Krafft-Ebing and many of his contemporaries, homosexuals should not have been imprisoned as criminals but medically treated as their condition demanded. Homosexual men had no choice but to show "feminine timidity, frivolity, obstinacy and weakness of character," as well as paranoia, bouts of insanity, and pathological emotional states. Lesbians were driven to wear their hair short, dress like men, and go in for sports and male pastimes. In the same way, medical researchers sought to identify the "congenital" criminal, the inborn prostitute, and the "hysterical" woman.

Krafft-Ebing's calls to eliminate German criminal penalties for sodomy were ignored, but the characterization of homosexuality as a deviant personality type stuck. This "pathologizing discourse" bred self-hatred among homosexuals. "Law and its penalties made homosexuals into outsiders," wrote historian Jeffrey Weeks, while "religious residues gave them a high sense of guilt, and medicine and science gave them a deep sense of inferiority and inadequacy." One of Krafft-Ebing's correspondents wrote, "I am very unhappy with my condition and have often considered suicide." The Irish nationalist Roger Casement recorded the dimensions of his pickups' sexual organs in his diary, but he also felt that he had been inflicted with a "terrible disease." As Weeks observed, "countless" homosexuals saw their orientation "as a disability, a sickness, a personal disaster. The self-consciousness of male homosexuals was deeply fractured by the prevailing norms."

No less fracturing and defining were a series of high-profile trials, most notably that of Oscar Wilde. The essentials of Wilde's collapse are well-known: the brilliant man of letters lived in London comfort with his wife and children, but he also made little effort to conceal his taste for rent boys or his romance with the dissolute young aristocrat Lord Alfred Douglas ("Bosie"). Nor did Wilde veil his idealization of handsome young men, as his great novel *The Picture of Dorian Gray* (1890) attested fulsomely. The book was reviled by critics for its "immoral" content, but Wilde, by outward appearances, could not have cared less. By 1895, his plays were hits in London and New York; his journeys "to the depths in search of new sensations" had drawn no adverse consequences; and he was the most interesting person in any room he entered. He was untouchable—at least to those who mattered to him.

Or so he believed. First came visits from blackmailing rent boys. He paid, and then he paid some more. Then, more ominously, Bosie's father arrived. The ninth Marquess of Queensberry, a truculent little man consumed with anger over Wilde's involvement with his son, threatened to "thrash" Wilde if the relationship continued. Wilde's response: "I don't know what the Queensberry rules are [Queensberry had penned a set of boxing rules], but the Oscar Wilde rule is to shoot on sight." Further insults were later hurled, after which Wilde stupidly sued Queensberry for libel in 1895. At the close of several highly publicized trials, Wilde was sentenced to two years of hard labor for "gross indecency." The response of the London *Evening News* was representative: "England has tolerated the man Wilde and *others of his kind* too long. . . . We venture to hope that the conviction of Wilde for these abominable vices, which were the natural outcome of his *diseased intellectual condition*, will be a salutary warning."

The pivotal issue was not whether Wilde had committed particular acts of gross indecency but whether he *was* homosexual, and on this point he had not covered his tracks. In a searching cross-examination, Queensberry's lawyer demanded that Wilde explain *Dorian Gray*'s homoerotic passages, as well as the love letters exchanged by Wilde and Bosie and Wilde's distaste for "ugly" young men. By the time it was all over, Wilde's marriage, children, and position had been buried in the quicksand of sexual inversion. He was no longer an eccentric genius; he was now equal parts evil and insane. Thanks in part to Wilde, men who had sex with men were no longer people who *did* bad things; rather, they *were* bad, to the last cells of their corrupted bodies. Homosexuals were, in the later words of an English judge, "stamped with the hallmark of a specialized and extraordinary class as much as if they had carried on their bodies some physical peculiarities." As Michel Foucault observed: "The sodomite had been a temporary aberration; the homosexual was now a species."

The Wilde trials were "major labeling events" for male homosexuals in the English-speaking world. Soon France went through a similar process. In a 1907 trial that drew intense public attention, two men from "excellent families" were charged with corrupting youth by involving boys in "black masses" and "orgiastic bacchanalias" at a swank Paris apartment. In truth, Baron Jacques d'Adelswärd-Fersen and Count Albert Hamelin de Warren were merely oddballs with an immoderate interest in Baudelaire, but their use of underdressed boys in bizarre *tableaux vivants*—in one, the boys posed in togas while incense burned, flutes played, and the defendants read *La Mort des Amants*—called the nature of homosexuality into question.

Sodomy itself had not been a crime in France for more than a century, so the question was not whether sex had taken place. (It seems it had not.)

Rather, the issue was whether the two men had "corrupted" the boys by exposing them to the poisonous fumes of homosexuality. During the trial, a mental disorders specialist reviewed the "defects" in d'Adelswärd-Fersen's bloodline (insanity, epilepsy) and suggested that his degeneracy resulted from "hereditary factors," which the doctor said merited a "certain indulgence." This seems to have been given in the form of short jail sentences and modest fines. However, the price of that indulgence was the linking of homosexuality with inborn defects and immoral behavior.

Germany soon had its own gay labeling event, which reached all the way to Kaiser Wilhelm II and his intimate circle. For years, gossip had circulated about homosexuality in German high society. The steel heir Friedrich Krupp was booted off the island of Capri for his indiscretions with boys; the king of Bavaria fancied his coachman; the king of Württemberg cast longing looks at his mechanic; and, on a private Black Forest estate with Wilhelm himself present, a senior military official died of a heart attack while doing a *pas seul* clad in a ballerina's tutu. In Europe, gay sex came to be known as the German vice. On the walls of Paris pissoirs, "Do you speak German?" became a familiar graffiti message. Yet these matters were considered unsuitable for a broad public discussion, much less a press scandal, until 1908, when the kaiser's political foes decided to lift the lid.

Wilhelm had made many enemies since taking power in 1888—none more influential than the "Iron Chancellor," Otto von Bismarck, who left the government in disgust and started to feed scandalous tidbits to Maximilian Harden, publisher of the weekly *Die Zukunft* (*The Future*). Harden's loathing of the kaiser was tied to his concern about what he saw as Germany's weakening geopolitical position. Like Bismarck, he believed that Wilhelm's advisors (whom he called a "sinister and effeminate camarilla") were guiding the kaiser toward a disastrous conciliation with France and Britain. Breaking the German press's deference toward the ruling class, Harden smeared the Kaiser by impugning the manliness of his closest associates. In articles published in 1906 and 1907, he exposed a thick sexual affair between Wilhelm's dearest friend, the diplomat Prince Philip von Eulenburg, and his "one and only Cuddly Bear," the military commandant of Berlin, Count Kuno von Moltke. While the articles referred to the two men as "Sweetie" and "the Harpist," no one doubted who they really were. Displaying his typical strength of character, the kaiser sacked the two men immediately.

Moltke sued Harden for libel, claiming (falsely) that he was neither homosexual nor Eulenburg's lover. The trial was a circus, with Moltke's shrew of an ex-wife, Lily, testifying that he had refused to make love to her and preferred Eulenburg. When Eulenburg wasn't available, Lily said, Moltke contented himself by sniffing his lover's handkerchiefs. Others among Harden's sixty witnesses revealed Moltke's and Eulenburg's clandestine trysts in forests and Moltke's indulgences with handsome young soldiers at officer-hosted sex parties. Harden also called Dr. Magnus Hirschfeld, a prominent sex researcher (and, ironically, a long-standing activist for gay rights), to give his expert opinion that Moltke was a homosexual. Hirschfeld based his assessment on Lily's remarks and on his observations of Moltke's telltale mannerisms (and face makeup). Within the context of a trial obsessively followed in Germany and throughout Europe, the notion of homosexuality as a medically diagnosed identity was thus further cemented into the public consciousness.

The Eulenburg affair wore on in court for several years, with various parties winning and losing in turns, falling ill, suffering nervous breakdowns, and providing nourishment to a popular press that now fed on the sex lives of public figures. During this time, at least six unrelated military figures committed suicide while being blackmailed for having homosexual affairs. The kaiser, stung by his association with people characterized as perverse weaklings, compensated in part by ramping up an aggressive posture in foreign affairs. Wilhelm became so bellicose that some see the Eulenburg affair as a factor contributing to the outbreak of the First World War in 1914. Harden later said that launching the scandal was the worst political mistake of his life.

Each of these episodes dramatically accelerated the hardening of early twentieth-century attitudes toward homosexuals, who were increasingly perceived as effeminate, dangerous to the young, and helpless before the perverse demands of their illnesses. In the run-up to the Great War, homophobia spiked sharply in Britain, France, and Germany, and the nascent movement to decriminalize sodomy stopped in its tracks. As the century progressed, however, another series of dark traits would be attached to sexual inversion. Not only were inverts supposedly sick, they came to be understood as destructive as well.

Homosexuals at War

The connection between gay sex and treason was made in 1913 when Alfred Redl, an Austrian colonel and top intelligence officer, shot himself after he was exposed both as homosexual and for passing military secrets to Russia. "Passion and levity have destroyed me," he wrote in his suicide note. "I pay with my life for my sins. Pray for me." By "passion and levity," he meant his taste for men, over which the Russian enemy had been blackmailing him for about ten years. In exchange for large sums of money that fueled a sybaritic lifestyle, he gave Russia information that resulted in the deaths of Austrian agents. He is also believed to have passed Austrian attack and mobilization plans to Russia, along with details of Austria's eastern fortifications. The extent to which Redl's treachery contributed to Austria's astounding loss of half a million men during the war's first battles cannot be pinpointed, but there is no doubting his lasting damage to the image of homosexuals. When Austrian agents broke into Redl's Prague apartment, they were shocked to discover pink whips, cosmetics, women's underwear and clothing, photos of Redl and other officers in drag and having sex, and . . . top-secret Austrian battle plans.

The scandal in all its musky detail was soon made public, and it rattled the already feeble Austrian state to the core. Not only was there moral rot at the top of the military, the decay was gay. Until his espionage was revealed, Redl had enjoyed a brilliant military career, sporting a chest full of medals and a personal commendation from Emperor Franz Josef. Now he was just another one of the "inverts" doctors were talking about, and one whose unrelenting compulsions trumped his oath of loyalty to the empire. In the panicked, xenophobic years of the First World War, and as Austria lost vast amounts of men and territory, the Redl scandal would solidly link homosexuality to betrayal, not just of sexual norms but also of all that is dear and worthy in humanity itself. Redl was an arch-traitor, brought down by his unbalanced "passion and levity."

In his fascinating 1937 book *The Sexual History of the World War*, Magnus Hirschfeld asked: "Would Redl have found it necessary to sell himself to Russia if his sexual life, his erotic self-expression, had not . . . been regarded as criminal?" The answer, of course, is no. Redl was targeted for blackmail precisely because his sexual orientation was a crime, and a shameful one at that. "The persecution of homosexuality contributed to digging a grave for [Austria and Germany], for if Redl had not feared to have the secret of his weakness made public, he would not have betrayed his country so grievously." (This logic would be reversed in the coming decades, particularly in the United States, where the oppression of homosexuals was justified by their purported innate disloyalty. In 1950, for example, American lawmakers invoked Redl's memory as proof that homosexuals had weak "moral fiber," "lack of emotional stability," and inborn criminality. Rather than recognize the harm of stigmatizing homosexuals, the Americans concluded that *more* stigma was needed to neutralize the perfidious homosexual menace.)

Hirschfeld also sifted through copious firsthand soldier accounts to explain why, despite all the risks, so many German "urnings" rushed to fight in the war, and fought with such bravery. He noted that because they "lack in family sense," they were inclined toward "unsettled" lives, which "explains why so many of them are to be found among sea-faring men, explorers, and vagabonds of all sorts." Hirschfeld also wrote that "many an urning" ran into the "thickest rain of bombs and the most deadly attacks" hoping "that a bullet might put an end to their life which they regard as being a complete failure." To the extent this last point is correct, it poignantly captures the desperation of men who were made to believe that their sexuality was incompatible with life.

Hirschfeld noted another aspect of life for gay German soldiers: in the occupied sectors of France, "the native population . . . looked with sympathetic understanding" on sexual love among the German occupiers, and often allowed "such friends" to meet in their houses for assignations. The German soldiers' search for privacy was well warranted. Harsh military punishment awaited any erotic affection in the ranks, even kissing. On the British side of the battle lines, there also was also abundant homoeroticism among soldiers. According to Paul Fussell, in his literary study of the British trench experience, *The Great War and Modern Memory*:

> Given [the] association between war and sex, and given the deprivation and loneliness and alienation characteristic of the soldier's experience—given, that is, his need for affection in a largely womanless world—we will not be surprised to find . . . the homoerotic. I use that term to imply a sublimated (i.e., 'chaste') form of temporary homosexuality. Of the active, unsublimated kind there was very little at the front.

Fussell may not have been looking in all the right places. If the poet-soldiers he surveyed confined their "temporary homosexuality" to their thoughts, their less erudite (and more numerous) comrades most likely acted on their thoughts, as did soldiers in all the fighting forces.

• • •

The surge of nationalistic fervor that accompanies the outbreak of war often can be seen as a drive for national cleansing, renewal, and recovered virility. Through shared sacrifice and the use of explosive force against a demonized foe, war promises nations purification and individuals escape from the emptiness of quotidian life. The suffering and horror of previous conflicts never diminish war's seductions. Each new generation of fighters has its own urgent need for combat, and its own pulsing desire for an immersion in blood. "Could it be," asks a character in James Jones's war novel *The Thin Red Line*, "that *all* war is basically sexual? . . . A sort of sexual perversion? Or a complex of perversions?" I take the liberty here of answering the question: yes. I also add Robert Graves's description, in his poem *Recalling War*, of the orgasmic joy young British men felt at the start of the Great War:

> And we, oppressed, thrust out
> Boastful tongue, clenched fist and valiant yard.
> Natural infirmities were out of mode,
> For Death was young again; patron alone
> Of healthy dying, premature fate-spasm.

Fate-spasm, indeed. As Hirschfeld observed: "Everybody who was acquainted with sexual dissatisfaction or misery of any kind greeted the outbreak of war" as an opportunity to "pull off [the] shackles" and "indulge infinite erotic desires."

At the war's end, with the world completely transformed, the return to prewar mores was well-nigh impossible. Too much had happened, too much erotic freedom had been tasted. As with the other armies, the returning American doughboys were innocent no more, and their return caused no shortage of dislocations at home. Many had permanent injuries, others had gone insane, and still others wanted to continue tasting the intimate company of men. One response on the home front was the aggressive enforcement of morals laws, particularly those against homosexuality, of which the US Navy's 1919 persecutions in Newport, Rhode Island, is a case study. The navy deployed handsome young sailors to pick up men in Newport's cruising zones and take them to designated locations for sex, after which the targets were arrested. The sting operation would likely be forgotten by now had it not been approved by Franklin D. Roosevelt (then a young assistant secretary of the navy) or ensnared a respected military chaplain, and had the hunky decoys not been coached to have sex with their targets "to completion." However, these "ifs" did happen, and the purge of the "Ladies of Newport" became a national scandal.

With about twenty thousand sailors pouring into Newport during the war, a gay subculture was inevitable. It took no effort to find liquor, cocaine, and a swirl of parties where cross-dressing sailors (known, for example, as Theda Bara and Salomé) provided sex for a price. Known as pogues and fairies, they played passive sexual roles with "trade," the masculine men for whom sex with fairies was not necessarily deviant. As the writer John Loughery put it: "Trade did the fucking; trade never sucked. Trade wasn't queer." Fairies and trade did little to hide themselves, as was evident in the wide-open pickup scene at the local YMCA and in the loose talk at the naval hospital. Such gossip deeply distressed chief machinist's mate Ervin Arnold. After overhearing chatter about the sex-saturated revelry one too many times, Arnold made it his personal mission to bring the entire party to an end. He pushed shrill reports up the chain of command, and before long Roosevelt himself approved "a most searching and rigid" investigation.

Following on Roosevelt's superb choice of words, what ensued was an entrapment scheme of the most penetrating kind. Arnold's cadre of sailors went to the YMCA and wherever else "perverts" were to be found and did what was necessary to bring "cocksuckers and rectum receivers" to justice. Arnold made sure that his young decoys would not be prosecuted for sodomy, so long as they acted like trade and kept to the active sexual role. They took their responsibilities seriously. "I entered the room with Trubshaw," wrote one in his report, after which "I took off my pants and jumper and got under the covers," whereupon Trubshaw "took my penis in his mouth and sucked it until I had an emission of sperm." Arrests soon began, and some of the terrified men taken into custody implicated others. With more than a dozen men arrested, a preliminary court of inquiry found that there was enough evidence to court-martial most of them. They received prison terms of five to twenty years. A report on the operation recommended that the decoys be commended for their "zeal" in their work. "Surely," wrote historian B. R. Burg, "this was the first time in the history of the US Navy that sailors were officially commended for committing homosexual acts."

There the matter might have ended, but the arrest of the Reverend Sam Neal Kent, a forty-six-year-old chaplain with a sterling reputation, backfired badly. When two operatives testified that Kent had performed homosexual acts on them, it was the first time the public grasped that America's young sailors were being deployed not to defend the country but to have gay sex. When one testified that he was told to let Kent "play with my penis" until "I had an emission," the public's reaction went against the navy and in sympathy for Kent, who was acquitted. Still tone deaf, the navy and Roosevelt took Kent to trial again, and the matter blew up into a major scandal. The cream of Newport society lined up to testify on Kent's behalf; he was acquitted a second time. High-level investigations by both the navy and the US Senate began, focusing on the government's debauching of sailors. A Senate committee concluded that Roosevelt's actions were "reprehensible." The *New York Times* headline:

"LAY NAVY SCANDAL TO F. D. ROOSEVELT . . .
DETAILS ARE UNPRINTABLE."

Roosevelt, of course, survived the scandal. The Ladies of Newport left the news, several men rotted in jail for the crime of having gay sex, and the matter was put to rest. However, some remarks made in the Senate about homosexuality during the scandal are worth remembering. Two senators noted that doctors and scientists now viewed homosexuality as a mental illness and recommended that gays in the military be discharged and given medical care rather than imprisoned. "Perversion is not a crime," said Senator Henry Keyes, "but a disease that should be properly treated in a hospital." This recommendation found no takers, but it still showed the degree to which the medicalization of homosexuality was being absorbed at the highest levels of government.

• • •

Until the Second World War, the American military had no official policy for keeping homosexuals out of its ranks. Gay sex in the armed forces had been a crime since the founding of the republic, but not homosexuality as such. However, that changed just before the start of the war as part of psychiatrist-influenced efforts to exclude "mental defectives." Among the list of "deviations" targeted for exclusion from the army were "homosexual persons" and those with "homosexual proclivities," both said to have "psychopathic personality disorders." Draft-inductee examiners were told to check recruits for signs of homosexuality, such as discomfort with their naked bodies, undue curiosity or embarrassment about masturbation, and sensitive, effeminate, or immature character traits.

By 1942, new directives stated that "persons habitually or occasionally engaged in homosexual practices" were unsuitable sexual perverts and should be excluded, and listed three possible indicators for such types: "feminine body characteristics," "effeminacy in dress or manner," and a "patulous [open or distended] rectum." The next year, another checklist developed by doctors warned that men who marked their "occupational choices" as interior decorators, dancers, or window dressers had difficulty accepting the "male pattern" and should be screened out.

The Second World War also marked the first time that American women were allowed to serve in military capacities other than as nurses. Before then, the military paid no attention to lesbianism. As the historian Allan Bérubé noted: "Not only in the law but in most areas of American life lesbians were ignored as either nonexistent or less significant than gay men." The military saw no advantage in aggressively keeping women out, especially as service for them was voluntary and paid less than jobs at home. Until 1945, most women went into the army without taking any psychiatric exams, much less ones designed to ferret out lesbians; and even then, exclusion efforts were halfhearted. In 1945, Pat Bond went to her Iowa recruitment center to enlist in the Women's Army Corps (WAC). Bond followed the example of her "butch" acquaintances, who enlisted wearing men's pinstripe suits and short haircuts: "the whole bit." Once Bond was in the WAC, she saw that "everybody was going with someone or had a crush on someone. The straight women . . . tended to ignore us, tended to say 'Who cares? It leaves all the men for us.'" Few, if any, women were kept out of the military as lesbian or masculine.

Out of eighteen million Americans examined for service during the Second World War, the military rejected only about four to five thousand as homosexual. For all the instructions to be on the lookout for "patulous" rectums and "effeminate" occupational choices, military screeners were no match for legions of homosexuals already adept at hiding their identities. As the war ground on and the military's need for bodies increased, recruiters focused more on meeting enlistment goals than keeping otherwise qualified people out. Yet even as the rules were circumvented, the overall effect of publicly branding homosexuals as defective was profound. They were further marked as a breed beneath the rest of humanity. This stigma became a painful part of military life.

Getting into the American armed forces was the easy part for gays and lesbians. What recruiters overlooked, officers in the field often did not. The military kept up a constant hunt for homosexuals, and those caught having sex or implicated as queer could expect treatment ranging from cruel to life-threatening—that is, unless bodies were needed to hurl into enemy gunfire, or if they had managed to gain the protection of senior officers. Before being discharged as undesirable, gays endured brutal interrogation by officers and psychiatrists, lockup in "queer stockades" or "queer brigs," and confinement to mental wards. About ten thousand GIs received some combination of these measures, but the terror of exposure and persecution permeated the entire military establishment.

Interrogators wanted detailed confessions and names of other suspects for future roundups, and nothing short of full cooperation was tolerated. Humiliating techniques were used—some GIs were interrogated by panels of smirking officers while standing nude—as were false promises of immunity and threats to tell all to loved ones at home. These tactics worked. "A single rumor that someone was gay," observed Bérubé, "could lead to full-scale purge, filling the stockades with suspected 'queers' who were held for interrogation." There, many found the comfort of kindred spirits as well as guards who treated them hatefully. One group of inmates, at the Treasure Island Naval Station near San Francisco, was told they would be eating out of garbage cans. Others were put to use servicing guards sexually. In one stockade in Noumea, New Caledonia, guards took gay prisoners to the latrine and forced them to perform oral sex. "The guards were all getting done," explained a GI, "and then guarding the people that were blowing them. . . . They could have put the whole goddamn armed forces in the brig!"

From 1941 until 2011, when the Clinton administration's idiotic Don't Ask, Don't Tell policy was finally revoked, about 114,000 men and women were discharged from the US military for homosexuality. Some straight men avoided service by claiming they were homosexual, although this ruse was most frequently used during the Vietnam War. When, for example, the actor Chevy Chase told a military psychiatrist that he "liked" both boys and girls, the doctor asked which he preferred. "Boys," he replied. He was dismissed from consideration due to a "mental defect."

• • •

Male homosexuality was also criminalized in the British military during the Second World War. Officers were told to watch out for "feminine types and confirmed homosexuals," but this exclusion policy was often ignored in practice. There was no screening process for homosexual inductees, and if they were subsequently outed, they were often treated humanely. Of the estimated 250,000 to 500,000 gays and lesbians serving in the armed forces, only about 800 were court-martialed for "indecency." The British brass took a more pragmatic approach than the Americans. If homosexuals were discreet and, most importantly, held up under the strains of battle and gained their comrades' loyalty, they usually avoided military punishments.

As everywhere, the ability to pass as straight was a survival skill that British gays and lesbians had developed in civilian life. "You've got to be as you would say, normal," recalled one serviceman. "It's no good going on about it and saying 'Oh I'm gay . . . take pity on me' because I'd have probably got my papers straight away and been working down in a coalmine or something." If that cover was blown, as happened to Richard Briar when an officer saw him in flagrante behind a bush with his sergeant major, it was not certain that punishment would follow. In fact, the officer turned and walked away. On another occasion, a respected soldier, Crank Dyer, was even provided with a "lad" to "use" while assigned to the Fourteenth Battalion Light Infantry Division. Far from being sent to jail or discharged, Dyer was accommodated.

A key factor contributing to the lenient treatment of homosexuals in the British armed forces was the belief that not all gay sex made one a "confirmed" homosexual. Sexual incidents seen as isolated and driven by war's deprivations didn't count as much. One gay soldier, Dennis Campbell, recalled that he and other gay men had sex with married soldiers because "they simply wanted their rocks off. In many places, there was not a woman about. What do you do? . . . In many cases it was sexual relief rather than actual gayness." How this comported with a military code condemning homosexuality and equating it with bad soldiering is explained by the exigencies of warfare. The rules had little to do with ground conditions. If a gay person's fighting skills increased his companions' chances of survival, his methods for getting his "rocks off" were irrelevant.

. . .

The Nazi hostility toward homosexuals reached back at least to 1934, when Hitler engineered a purge of the Sturmabteilung or SA (the so-called

Brownshirts) and the murder of its leader, the openly gay Ernst Röhm. The Nazis broadened German sodomy laws the next year to punish the seduction of minors as well as mutual masturbation, kissing, and even erotic glances. By the end of the war, approximately one hundred thousand men had been prosecuted for same-sex activities. About half of them were sent to prisons and concentration camps, used in medical experiments, or sacrificed in Wehrmacht suicide missions. The Röhm, Eulenburg, and Redl affairs made the Nazis touchy about appearing queer—a slander their enemies constantly repeated—especially as homosexuality embodied nearly everything the Nazi ideal was not. Hitler thought homosexuality was a "plague" transmitted by perverted men to susceptible youths. To guard the Third Reich's vitality, all cases of homosexual behavior "among our youth" were to be addressed with "barbaric severity." To be gay in Nazi Germany, whether as a civilian or in uniform, was to be in danger.

The elite Schutzstaffel (SS) and its leader, Heinrich Himmler (who would eventually oversee not only the SS but the Gestapo and the concentration camp system as well), enjoyed an increase in power and influence after the Röhm purge. Himmler affirmed the Nazi position on homosexuality in a 1937 speech in which he waxed nostalgic about an old German custom of throwing weighed-down sodomites to drown in muddy bogs. In a 1941 decree issued in Hitler's name, death was prescribed for homosexual offenses among the SS and police, with all such cases to be handled secretly in SS courts. Hitler worried that the very existence of such a rule would reveal that there were homosexuals in elite Nazi circles, so he also demanded that it be kept secret, leaving Himmler to transmit the message to the rank and file in an "appropriate fashion." Himmler ordered that they be told about the decree verbally and commanded not to reveal its details to outsiders. All units were to be kept free of "vermin of a homosexual nature."

There were no exceptions to Hitler's decree, but they emerged anyway. For example, in 1943 an SS medical expert rationalized a policeman's gay encounters and spared the man's life, explaining that the man had "an abnormally large sex organ" that few women could accommodate. The doctor believed the policeman had been led astray by his unusual anatomy and would return to normal upon treatment (whatever that could mean). The same doctor found that a police corporal's swelling of the brain explained his multiple sexual encounters with chickens (bestiality and homosexuality were both forbidden under the same law), so he was not responsible for his actions. In still another case, a gay Waffen [Armed]-SS man was spared death in 1942 because he was "feebleminded." Normally, feeblemindedness was itself grounds for euthanasia under Nazi eugenics law, but the SS man was jailed for five years instead.

Hans G., a young SS sergeant major, had no such excuses. In 1944, the former concentration camp guard and decorated fighter was turned in for directing sexual attention toward his soldiers on the eastern front. One of his men woke up to find G. masturbating him, after which G. climbed onto the startled soldier and started to moan and gasp. Another time, G. thrust his erect member between the thighs of one of his men while he kissed him. In all, five completed and two attempted homosexual acts, any one of which merited swift death, came to the SS court for judgment. Yet the lengthy investigations that ensued, and G.'s appeal, reveal the difficulties of applying even the clearest decrees amid the dense sexual fog of war, especially a war the Germans were losing.

G. did not deny his actions. He did, however, dispute that he was homosexual, explaining to the court that "normal" sex was unavailable on the frontline. He also claimed to have been unaware of the 1941 decree, or even that the things he did were homosexual acts. This was plausible, at least in theory, given that some of the homosexuals he saw at the prison camps would have worn badges bearing the letter A, denoting "ass fucker" (*arschficker*). As G. had not fucked an ass, and as he had sex with women when he could, he considered himself straight. He also pointed to the fact that several years earlier he had turned someone in for making homosexual advances.

The judges were unmoved by G.'s defense and sentenced him to death. However, within a week, an SS general made a strong plea for clemency. The general said G. was an exemplary soldier and his sexual misconduct was a "psychic or erotic aberration . . . formed by the conditions of war." More investigations followed, this time by the authorities in Berlin's Reich Central Office for Combating Homosexuality. In early 1945, when Berlin was in ruins and Germany's defeat all but certain, investigators still occupied themselves with inquiries about why G. had left a Catholic school twelve years earlier, and about his early relations with females. They also brought G. in for further interrogation at the central office in the bombed-out center of the city, asking how often he had sex with women when he was a guard at Dachau, and whether or not he enjoyed it. The file stops here. We don't know G.'s fate, but we see that while homosexuality was one of the Third Reich's cardinal sins, especially in vanguard units like the SS, difficulties of definition remained. The law barred any kind of homoerotic act without exception, but G. was still able to offer excuses and justifications. Even in Nazi Germany—among the most homophobic environments in history—homosexual sex did not necessarily make one a homosexual.

Lesbianism on Trial: *The Well of Loneliness*

Radclyffe Hall's best-selling 1928 novel, *The Well of Loneliness*, meant a lot of things to a lot of people, but for some women the book was survival itself. The melodramatic story of a female English "invert" who discovers her sexuality had incalculable effects on women coming to grips with their attraction to females. One woman who read it in Polish reportedly survived the Nazi concentration camps by clinging to the hope that one day she might know a woman's kiss. From a book with little kissing and no explicit sex, in which the protagonist declares herself a "freak" and an "awful mistake," and calls her life "pure hell," this camp survivor had precious little to go on. But *The Well*'s deeply sympathetic view of female–female love made it the signature lesbian novel of the interwar period. Other books dealt with lesbianism, but none with *The Well*'s literary ambition and popular success. The book's power to "corrupt" women, and the nature of lesbianism itself, was at the center of bruising censorship battles in both England and the US.

Hall was the child of a cruel mother and a caddish father who was in bed with the maid when she was born. Her grandfather's death left her with enough money to avoid having to work or marry for financial security. Taking the first name John, wearing mannish clothing, and smoking green cigars, she embarked on a series of affairs with women and, eventually, a writing career. Some of her affairs were brief and disastrous, others lengthy and fulfilling, but none came close to social acceptance in mainstream English society. During the 1920s, Hall and her lover, Uma Troubridge, mingled with the likes of Noël Coward, Colette, and W. Somerset Maugham, but few people breathed the rarified air of such sophisticated company. Outside tightly circumscribed circles, lesbianism was not discussed, and only the smuttiest books even acknowledged that it existed. Hall took it upon herself to "smash the conspiracy of silence." In 1927, at age forty-seven, she took a room in a posh Paris hotel and wrote *The Well*.

The book's protagonist, a female named Stephen, is raised in an idyllic country setting. The "narrow hipped, wide shouldered" girl is proficient at hunting and fishing, disdains frilly things, and longs to be male. At seven, she develops a crush on the family maid and is crushed in turn when she sees the maid kissing a man. In adolescence, she is revolted when a friend named Martin proposes marriage. Surprised by the intensity of her feelings, she asks her father whether there is something "strange" about her. Her father had already been consulting the work of Krafft-Ebing (probably *Psychopathia Sexualis*), and he dies before explaining what he learned, but she later consults the same book and realizes that she is an "invert." With both relief and vexation, she declares: "There are so many of us—thousands of miserable, unwanted people, who have no right to love, no right to compassion, because they're maimed, hideously maimed and ugly—God's cruel; he let us get flawed in the making." Stephen's love affairs with females all come to naught. At one point, she uses an elaborate lie to save a lover from the desperate life of the inverted. The lover ends up in the arms of Martin, crushing her further. The book closes with Stephen's plea to God and society to accept the invert: "Give us also the right to our existence!"

The Well drew a mixed response upon its release in England. The *Daily Telegraph* thought it "finely conceived and finely written," while the *Sunday Express* called it "poison" and demanded that it be suppressed. Within a few months the book was seized and a court obscenity trial began. As lesbian sex was not technically illegal, the question was whether writing about it could be. To the prosecution, the very topic of sexual love between women was obscene and should be discussed only in medical textbooks. The publisher's attorneys had lined up a cadre of eminent people, including D. H. Lawrence and Virginia Woolf, to explain the merits of the book, but the judge would not hear from them. The book was declared obscene and all remaining copies were ordered to be sent to the "King's furnace." On appeal, the judges found *The Well* "disgusting" without reading it. The book remained banned in the UK for decades.

Given the events in London, Hall's American publisher, A. A. Knopf, bowed out even before the official English verdict was handed down. Four other US publishers turned the book down as well. But respectability isn't for everybody, and Covici-Friede, a start-up publishing house with no compunction about releasing a "dirty" book—especially one with such advance buzz—bought the rights and sold the book for twice the normal retail price. Within a month of the American release, it sold more than twenty thousand copies; within a year, one hundred thousand copies. At the same time, no one doubted that the book would end up in court, and for that Covici-Friede turned to Morris Ernst, the attorney who would later represent Random House in clearing *Ulysses* of obscenity charges. The adversary was the New York Society for the Suppression of Vice (NYSSV), a long-standing antisex juggernaut that had recently launched a successful attack on a lesbian-themed play, *The Captive*. Buoyed by this victory and *The Well*'s demise in England, the NYSSV's leader, John Sumner, sharpened his teeth for an attack on a book he called "literary refuse."

To prepare for the legal contest, Ernst read everything about lesbianism he could get his hands on, from Mary Mills Patrick's *Sappho and the Island of Lesbos* to *Psychopathia Sexualis*. Ernst also consulted Havelock Ellis's *Sexual Inversion*, which argued that inverted women had "masculine" characteristics, including deep voices, a tendency to crimes of passion, a taste for cigars, and an aversion to needlework. However, Ernst's reading showed up only obliquely in his legal briefs. As his private notes reflect, he avoided the word "lesbian" in court. "This is a story of a woman not fully developed; thwarted in life," he wrote, adding: "If the word 'homosexual' is used, we should get a doctor to define it."

When the trial began in 1929, Sumner used the same strategy that had succeeded in England: he read the most troublesome passages to the court, turned up his nose, and let the text speak for itself. Ernst, on the other hand, had much to say. First, he argued that a much more explicit book on a similar theme, *Mademoiselle de Maupin*, had been cleared by the courts in 1922, so there was precedent for allowing Hall's much tamer book. Unlike *Maupin*, he argued, *The Well* had "not one dirty word, not a single indecent scene, not a single suggestive episode. On the contrary, it is written with extraordinary restraint and delicacy." Ernst described Stephen's relationships as "pitiable" and wrote that the "outstanding feature of her life is . . . that she is thwarted in the development of her emotional life. . . . In short, her life is one of poignant tragedy."

To scholar Leslie Taylor, Ernst's decision to "evacuate lesbian desire" from the book was "tactically sound" in court but "philosophically at odds with the author's intent." By characterizing Stephen's emotional life as "thwarted," and her relationships as pathetic, he also framed Hall's lesbianism as a toxic condition—something to be treated and pitied. At the same time, for Ernst to argue that lesbianism should be accepted on its own terms would have required a departure from even the most progressive medical/scientific thinking of the time, none of which framed lesbian love or sex as normal. However crafty Ernst's methods may seem, they worked. In April 1929 the court cleared *The Well* of all obscenity charges.

Almost immediately, Covici-Friede released a two-volume edition of the book for the astronomical sum of twenty-five dollars. Printed on hand-made paper, it featured Ernst's summary of the trial, the court's opinion, and Hall's autograph.

Psychopaths and Cross-Dressers

In 1915, a California court agreed that expert medical help was needed to explain how the sexual abuse of a child could arouse a homosexual's "lust or passions or sexual desires." "The normal man," wrote the court, could not divine "the neurotic or orgiastic effect of such indecent acts." In the coming decades, medical experts would repeatedly explain the desires of gay people, and what they said often involved violence and perversion. Building on the medical diagnosis of homosexuality as a mental illness, the very word "homosexual" came to be synonymous with child molester, sex criminal, pervert, and sexual psychopath. Along the way, homosexuals were seen not only to "corrupt" the young by "recruiting" them to their ranks but also to be driven to attack them. Mainstream news sources typically referred to them as "vile," "wicked," "criminal," and "depraved." In 1947, *Newsweek* reported as fact that gays "committed the most dastardly crimes" and "should be placed in an institution." Homosexuals became go-to suspects for all manner of violent crimes, particularly against children. Between 1947 and 1955, twenty-one states and the District of Columbia had laws targeting homosexuals as sexual psychopaths.

To give police maximum latitude to lock up homosexuals, states also started to punish fellatio and other unspecified "lascivious acts." Most of the time, the new rules were responses to homosexual scandals, such as the one in Long Beach, California, in 1914, when undercover cops brought thirty-six men into various compromising positions (short of anal sex) and then arrested them. The public outrage over these homosexual "devils" was exceeded only by the frustration that no law made what they did a serious crime. The next year, fellatio was added to the law as a felony. In response to a man's horrible murder of a little girl in 1949—a crime with no homosexual elements—California further amped up its laws to make repeated oral copulation and sodomy convictions grounds for life imprisonment. (Notably, these laws also covered sex acts commonly practiced by heterosexuals.) Sodomy laws were also amended nationwide to criminalize the "enticing" of children to masturbate, taking "improper" or "indecent" liberties with minors, contributing to a minor's delinquency, committing "lewd and lascivious" acts on children, and catch-all crimes such as "lewd vagrancy." All were aggressively enforced against gay people.

There was never evidence that homosexuals were prone to sexual violence any more than heterosexuals, but facts rarely impede a compelling myth. As observed by law professor William Eskridge, "Demonized as sexual psychopaths, sex perverts, and child molesters, homosexuals became the new enemy of the people." Far from preventing violent sexual crime, the expanded sex laws were effective only in making the lives of thousands of homosexuals miserable. Many of those caught having consensual sex in public restrooms or parks, for example, ended up on public registries of sex offenders, thus putting them on the same level as child rapists. Homosexuals could also be locked up in state mental hospitals based only on a conviction for, or sometimes just a charge of, consensual sodomy. There they could be subjected to a range of harsh treatments such as castration, shock therapy, and lobotomies. While it is nearly impossible now to grasp how consensual sex between two adults could elicit such harsh responses, the fact is that the characterization of homosexuality as a mental disorder, and the conflation of homosexuality with violent crime, was embraced at all levels of society. With a 1960 *Newsweek* headline asking whether we should "punish or pity" gays and lesbians, and with *Time* magazine in 1966 describing homosexuality as a "pathetic little second-rate substitute for reality," the law was well in line with popular attitudes.

The methods used to ensnare gay people were aggressive, to say the least. Few people complained to police or came forward with evidence, so vice officers went "to the crime" and relied on their own observations. This often meant using decoys or hanging around bars, beaches, restrooms, and parking lots looking for gay (usually oral) sex. Vice cops perched above public toilets, lurked in parks, peeked through holes in walls, and followed gay-seeming men around the streets. In 1963, two vice cops followed Eldridge Rhodes, an African American man suspected of propositioning sailors, as he walked into a hotel with Thomas Earl, a white man. The men took a room and the cops waited outside the door. Before long, they heard "kissing-type" noises and bed squeaks. Peeking through a crack in the door, and also through a glass transom, the cops saw Rhodes and Earl committing a felony: oral sex. They forced their way into the room and made arrests. Both Rhodes and Earl were convicted, certified as sexual psychopaths, and sent to a state mental hospital for indeterminate sentences.

When this kind of shoe-leather detective work was too difficult, police staged mass "jump" raids on bars, clubs, and bathhouses. While these raids rarely netted sodomy convictions—few men were caught having or soliciting sex—patrons could always be charged with more fluid infractions such as disorderly conduct. By the 1950s, mass raids were frequent. In 1955, for example, a raid on the Pepper Hill Club in Baltimore netted 162 arrests for disorderly conduct; a 1960 raid on the Tay-Bush Café in San Francisco resulted in 103 arrests (89 men and 14 women) for same-sex dancing and disorderly conduct.

Most famously, in 1969, at the Stonewall Inn in New York City's Greenwich Village, police claimed to be enforcing the liquor laws when they invaded, swinging billy clubs and spitting insults. The riots known as the Stonewall Uprising ensued, and over the next several nights police and queers clashed in the streets. In 2003, at the Power Plant club in Detroit, several dozen police officers, guns drawn, stormed the premises and told patrons to "hit the floor." More than three hundred people were arrested for "loitering inside a building."

The vast majority of the anti-gay arrests were made against men, although lesbians faced escalating police harassment starting in the 1950s. The arrests would often be for violating long-standing sumptuary laws against cross-dressing. In Chicago, for example, it was a crime "to appear in a public place in a state of nudity, or in a dress not belonging to his or her sex." In Toledo, Ohio, it was a crime for a "perverted person" to appear in clothing intended for the opposite sex. Other laws required people to wear at least three articles of gender-appropriate clothing. Some of the more oblique rules included a New York law prohibiting people from assembling while "disguised" and a California law making it a crime to "masquerade" in another person's attire for unlawful purposes. Butch lesbians took the brunt of sumptuary law enforcement. They were arrested if they were unable to prove, on the spot, that they were wearing the required articles of female clothing, or if they appeared to police to be "disguising" their true sex.

. . .

Even without cross-dressing laws, women who were seen as insufficiently feminine found their rights curtailed, sometimes severely. In 1960, as Sara Quiroz tried to cross from Mexico to the US, an immigration officer sized up the permanent US resident and household maid as a lesbian. Investigators grilled her on her sex life, getting her to "confess" that she had had sexual encounters with two women, and also that she "enjoyed" sex "more with women than with men." An immigration court later found that "her relations with several women . . . demonstrated a pattern of behavior which was antisocial [and] irresponsible [and that] she has manifested a disorder of the personality." Because Quiroz was marked as a lesbian, she was perforce a psychopath, which in turn required that she be deported. (While psychopaths and those with "abnormal sexual instincts" had been separately barred from entering the US for decades, a 1952 Senate report connected the two types, stating that the law excluding psychopaths "is sufficiently broad to provide for the exclusion of homosexuals and sex perverts.")

Quiroz later recanted her "confession" and denied that she was a lesbian, pointing to her nine-year-old child as proof. The government's response: a heterosexual affair a decade earlier, which ended when the man deserted her, meant nothing. If anything, she might have turned to lesbianism because her heterosexual fling had ended badly. Two weeks before she was to be sent to Mexico, she played her last card by getting married. Her lawyers argued that the marriage proved she was "normal" and "no longer a psychopathic personality." Again, no one believed her. Despite legal appeals reaching up to the Fifth Circuit Court of Appeals, she was deported.

Had the Quiroz case stopped at low-level immigration hearings, we could dismiss her treatment as the handiwork of vile bureaucrats operating in an intolerant age. But the Quiroz deportation went too far up the ladder of power to be disregarded. It was reviewed and approved by a tribunal second in stature only to the US Supreme Court. More importantly, the law was clear: as psychopaths per se, homosexuals were unwelcome. The methods used to determine Quiroz's lesbianism were ludicrous, but bad laws always produce absurdities. Only in 1990 would American immigration law change to stop the automatic exclusion of homosexuals.

Michel Foucault famously wrote that sexuality functions as a "dense transfer point for relations of power." Nowhere is that observation more apt than at an international frontier, where a quick once-over by a man with a badge could deprive a trouser-wearing woman of her home.

Killing Homosexuals

The more gay people were identified as pathological sex criminals, the more the law turned a sympathetic eye on people who killed them. According to some psychological researchers, a sexual advance by a homosexual, even if nonviolent, can so distress a straight man (all the cases involve men) that he might lose control and respond with homicidal violence. Given that he was not in his "right mind," and his loss of self-control was triggered by the sexual advance, he did not have the requisite mental state for the killing to be called murder. While there has never been an official "homosexual panic" murder defense in courts—it has popped up, technically, as temporary insanity, diminished capacity, provocation, heat of passion, or self-defense—it has nevertheless been a path away from the gallows for some people who killed homosexuals. It also carved out a channel for juries to express their darkest anti-gay hatreds.

The idea of homosexual panic was first cooked up in 1920 by the psychiatrist Edward Kempf, who coined the phrase for his patients who self-identified as straight but were actually repressed homosexuals, which caused them anxiety "due to the pressure of uncontrollable perverse sexual cravings." The mental clash between homoerotic urges and the horror of being gay could, Kempf theorized, also cause the patient to be "swept . . . into a hell of hallucinated temptations and demons of destruction." At their most distressed, patients reacted with dangerous aggression toward others. Later psychiatrists built on Kempf's thinking by, among other things, emphasizing that temporary insanity takes hold when the subject is in situations where his homosexuality can no longer be avoided and his straight self-image collapses. In 1952, "homosexual panic" was included in the first edition of the Bible-like *Diagnostic and Statistical Manual of Mental Disorders*.

In criminal courtrooms, however, men who killed in response to gay advances never had to lean too heavily on the niceties of psychiatric theory; nor were they always required to proclaim that they were self-loathing repressed homosexuals. Rather, they tapped into widespread visceral disgust for homosexuality. We see this by looking at the readiness of juries to excuse the killers of gays even before homosexual panic was formally defined as a mental disorder, and the continued vitality of the defense after homosexuality was declassified as a mental disease in 1973.

When Nathan "Babe" Leopold and Richard "Dickie" Loeb were put on trial in 1924 for murdering a fourteen-year-old boy, their sexuality was used against them. One of their own expert witnesses highlighted their strained sexual relationship, and the prosecutor referred to them as "perverts" who indulged in "vile and unnatural practices." Their attorney, the famed Clarence Darrow, saved them from the executioner, but Loeb still met an unnatural end. In 1936 a fellow inmate, James Day, slashed his throat with a straight razor in the prison shower. Facing a murder charge, and despite the absence of any evidence of struggle with Loeb, Day claimed that he was defending himself against Loeb's sexual advances. The jury acquitted him in less than an hour. While this was not technically a homosexual panic–related defense, it shows the early indulgence of courts and jurors toward men who kill in response to homosexual advances. Loeb was already widely reviled, but it was his purported homosexuality that brought Day an acquittal.

Homosexual panic–related defenses came into use in the courts in the 1960s, although they were never more than a hit-and-miss prospect. For example, in 1972, John Parisie was given a ride in a car by a man who unexpectedly turned down a secluded road and demanded sex. Parisie killed him. At his trial, Parisie claimed that he "blew up, went crazy" in response to the sexual advance and could barely remember what happened. A psychologist testified that Parisie was a "highly latent" homosexual with strong feelings of inferiority, and a psychiatrist testified as to the contours of homosexual panic. The jury rejected the defense and convicted Parisie of murder. Three years later, while two male neighbors sat together watching television, one of them initiated sex. The other man said he "kind of went blank" in response. "I remember breaking loose from him and starting to stab him," he said, adding that "queers and freaks upset me a lot." His lawyers had psychiatrists explain to the jury that the client's "violent emotional reaction to a homosexual situation" stemmed from his need to "conceal his homosexual tendencies at any cost." This time, the jury was persuaded, and the killer evaded a murder conviction.

In 1995 a heterosexual man, Jonathan Schmitz, went on the *Jenny Jones* tabloid television talk show, expecting to meet a female "secret admirer." Instead, Scott Amedure came onstage and titillated the audience with descriptions of his frothy sexual fantasies involving Schmitz. All was taken in good humor in front of the cameras, but three days later Amedure sent Schmitz a note inviting him to his house. Seeing the note as a sexual come-on, Schmitz went out and bought a shotgun, after which he went to Amedure's house and shot him twice in the chest. At Schmitz's trial for first-degree murder, he claimed that he had experienced homosexual panic due to his embarrassment about his appearance on the *Jenny Jones* show and the note. The jury agreed that he had "diminished capacity" when he pulled the trigger and convicted him of second-degree murder instead.

Other killers of gay men sought lenient treatment by arguing that gay sexual advances threw them into a heat of passion. In 1978, for example,

David Mills met Billy Brinkley in a bar, where Mills agreed to service Brinkley sexually for twenty dollars. The two drove in Brinkley's car to a secluded spot, where Brinkley reached for Mills's genitals. Mills demanded the money, but when Brinkley said he had none, Mills pushed him out of the car, chased him, kicked him in the head and chest, and then threw him against rocks. Mills then took Brinkley's jewelry and fled in Brinkley's car. Despite ample evidence of murder, the jury agreed that Brinkley's initiation of sex had spurred Mills into the heat of passion, and it convicted him of only manslaughter.

In 1991 another young man, Timothy Schick, killed and robbed a man with whom he had agreed to have sex. The victim had picked up Schick in his car late at night. Schick asked where he could get a blow job, and the victim volunteered. The two walked out to a field, where the victim dropped his pants and attempted to grab Schick's genitals. Schick beat, kicked, and stomped the victim to death, took his money, and fled. At his murder trial, his lawyer argued for a verdict of manslaughter in light of the "sudden heat" Schick experienced on the field. The jury obliged and Schick got away with murder—literally.

How anyone could have believed that Mills or Schick were provoked in these circumstances can only be explained by powerful anti-gay hatred. Both had agreed to sex (one for money), neither was ever in physical danger, and both had the presence of mind to rob their victims after they killed them. Despite all this, only one fact mattered: the victim's initiation of gay sex. Would the results have been the same if the victims had been straight men and the killers females? No one can say for sure, but it is likely that had women done the killing and robbing in these circumstances, murder convictions would have followed.

The best-known example of the homosexual panic defense came in 1998, after Matthew Shepard, an openly gay Wyoming college student, was beaten to death and tied to a fence. Two young men were charged with murder. One of them pled guilty to avoid the death penalty. The other, Aaron McKinney, took his chances in court. At the opening of the trial, McKinney's lawyer told the jury that Shepard had grabbed McKinney's crotch and licked his ear shortly before the killing, while they were riding in McKinney's truck. That upset McKinney, the attorney explained, because when McKinney was a boy, a bully had forced him to suck his penis and have sex with other boys. McKinney had also been traumatized sometime earlier when he wandered into a gay and lesbian church and saw men kissing. These experiences, and McKinney's prodigious use of alcohol and methamphetamines before the killing, combined to cause his "past" to "bubbl[e] up in him" and to make him "leave his body" and lose control.

The judge first attempted to shut this line of argument down, saying that a provocation defense based on "homosexual rage" did not exist in Wyoming, but then he inexplicably permitted McKinney's lawyers to call two other male witnesses to testify that Shepard had been sexually aggressive with them. The judge also allowed McKinney's lawyer to argue that Shepard's sexual advance had triggered the beating. Whatever was going through the judge's mind, the homosexual rage defense didn't work. McKinney was found guilty of murder and sentenced to life imprisonment. In a later prison interview, McKinney admitted to ABC News that he had made up the story about Shepard making a pass at him. The murder was simply a robbery gone wrong, committed by two despicable men.

More recent is the so-called trans-panic defense, which is typically deployed when a man has sex with another man he believes is female, subsequently learns of his mistake, and then kills the partner. The killer then claims in court that the victim's deception provoked him into a heat of passion, and that he should, therefore, not be held liable for murder. While this defense has met with mixed results, it has been embraced by some courts and juries. For example, in 2003, seventeen-year-old Gwen (born Eddie) Araujo was beaten to death by several young men after they discovered that Araujo had male genitalia. (Two of her assailants, José Merél and Michael Magidson, had been Araujo's sex partners.) The men were charged with first-degree murder. Merél's and Magidson's lawyers argued that they had been provoked by the discovery that they had had sex with a man. During the first trial, the jury could not agree on whether Merél and Magidson had committed first- or second-degree murder; in the second trial, they were found guilty of second-degree murder.

• • •

While defenses related to homosexual panic have always been a long shot, they are still raised. The fact that courts allow them at all normalizes gay hatred and privileges violence in response to homosexual advances. The responses "stop," "I'm not interested," or simply walking away are somehow deemed insufficient when a straight male is faced with the seismic indignity of another male's sexual advance. A woman who kills in response to an unwelcome kiss, grope, or sexual proposition would never have such a defense available. On the contrary, as the scholar Cynthia Lee has written, "Women in this society are supposed to accept a certain amount of unwanted male attention. . . . [T]hey are not supposed to use violence to dissuade or thwart men who suggest [sex]. . . . The woman who is the target of male attention is supposed to be flattered."

When women are subjected to aggressive sexual propositioning by male strangers outside the workplace, they are on their own unless the harassment is repeated or extreme, and even then their chances in court are iffy. In one 1976 case, a woman who was surprised in her college dormitory lounge at three thirty AM by a man who repeatedly demanded sex, saying he "never ate pussy before," was able to prove a case of harassment. However, one of the dissenting judges dismissed the man's behavior as "petty nastiness," writing that "such incidents are too frequent for a justice system to handle them effectively," and also that allowing the woman's harassment claim to go forward ran the risk of criminalizing "generally accepted behavior."

Women have more protections in the workplace, but not always. Take, for example, the California woman in the late 1990s whose coworker placed his hand on her stomach and then, after she pushed him away, forced his hand underneath her sweater and bra and fondled her breast. She removed his hand and told him he had "crossed the line," but he stopped only when another coworker arrived. She filed suit for sexual harassment, but her case was thrown out of court. The appellate judges reasoned that a "single, rather unsavory episode" was not "severe" or "pervasive" enough to create a hostile work environment: "If a single incident can ever suffice to support a hostile work environment claim, the incident must be extremely severe. . . . [She] was harassed on a single occasion for a matter of minutes in a way that did not impair her ability to do her job in the long-term." If what this woman was subjected to could not even support a civil sexual harassment claim in the year 2000, imagine her fate had she killed the aggressive coworker.

The law comes down much harder when queer males are accused of sexually harassing straight men in the workplace, even when the harassment is comparatively mild. In 1996, for example, a male supervisor in Louisiana told his male employee, "I see you got a girl. You know I'm jealous," and later came up to the employee from behind and rubbed his rear end. The employee fell into a depression, lost sixty pounds, and began to drink heavily. The court gave his sexual harassment case the green light. Another case at about the same time, in Colorado, was allowed to proceed.

In this case, a male employee's supervisor "rubbed his . . . hands up and down his thighs with his pelvis thrust forward in a fornicating gesture," and later suggested that the employee use semen to lubricate workplace machinery. In light of the homosexual panic–related murder defenses, the supervisor was lucky the employee filed a lawsuit rather than come after him with a gun.

The message of these cases is consistent: male sexual advances on men, even when nonviolent, are intolerable, while male advances on women are simply a part of life. Unlike their female counterparts, men who kill sexually aggressive men can often find a way at least to argue that violence was reasonable under the circumstances; and men who are sexually harassed by men at work have a solid chance of walking away from court much the wealthier. The law should resolve this double standard by getting rid of homosexual panic–related defenses once and for all, and requiring men to develop the same thick skin expected of women.

Gay Europe after the Second World War

To say that Europe was raped by the war is not an exaggeration. In the conflict's last weeks alone, Soviet troops raped up to two million German women and tens of thousands more Hungarian and Austrian women. In the final Red Army assault on Berlin, about one hundred thousand females were raped, often repeatedly, while Polish women, concentration camp survivors, and those who had been in hiding were ravaged everywhere by Soviet forces. While rapes by other nations' armies were less frequent, that would have been cold comfort to the many thousands of females on whom Allied troops forced themselves. Aside from these horrors, 5.5 million Germans, 5.8 million Poles, and tens of millions of other Europeans lost their lives. In the chaos of the war's aftermath and the unhinged sexual behavior that attended six long years of fighting, the urge for a return to sexual normalcy (however imaginary) was powerful. For the men whom the war had given de facto license to have gay sex, conditions would change rapidly.

The postwar years were hard ones for homosexuals. In France, Vichy-era rules criminalizing same-sex encounters between males, over and under twenty-one were retained, and it was not until 1975 that the gay journal *Arcadie* could be sold openly. From 1960 to 1980, France also had a law declaring that homosexuality was a "social scourge," even if it was not technically illegal between adults. In the Netherlands during the decades after the war, prewar restrictions on gay sex between adults and minors were applied, and castration and imprisonment were common, as were registration and police surveillance of gay men. Homosexuals lived in constant fear of blackmailers. In Germany and Austria, men who had been persecuted during the war for homosexuality were denied reparations, and many found themselves imprisoned again for new infractions under anti-gay laws that the Allied occupiers refused to repeal.

The British law against "gross indecency" also remained in place, leaving gay men as sitting ducks for blackmailers and the police. Most notable was the prosecution of Lord Montagu of Beaulieu, who, along with two acquaintances, was convicted in 1954 for "conspiracy to incite male persons to commit serious offenses with male persons." The prosecution arose out of a country weekend involving the three men and, alleged the prosecution, one boy from a group of boy scouts who had been camping on the Montagu estate. The case went nowhere, but in a new trial the three men were sentenced to jail for up to eighteen months. For Home Secretary David Maxwell Fyfe, the case at first seemed like political cakewalk. As many as one thousand men were locked up each year for homosexual offenses, and including the young Montagu in Fyfe's drive to "rid England of this plague" must have been too tempting to pass up. However, the case backfired badly. Public opinion ran squarely in Montagu's favor and, most critically, sparked movements to reform the law. In 1957, a government committee recommended that gay sex among adult men be legalized, and a decade later that recommendation became law. (Prosecutions for gay sex among minors, however, would soon triple.)

The brave souls elsewhere who challenged the status quo were rebuffed by conservative postwar regimes, but eventually the screws loosened. Same-sex sexual activity was legalized in West Germany in 1969, in Austria and Finland in 1971, and in Norway in 1972. While some members of the Eastern Bloc such as Czechoslovakia, East Germany, and Hungary decriminalized gay sex in the 1960s, nearly all prohibitions fell in the years following the collapse of communism. The European Court of Human Rights, which initially avoided the gay-rights issue, finally ruled in favor of gay plaintiffs in 1981. As of 2014, gay sex is legal in every jurisdiction in Europe. Of all places, Turkey has not forbidden homosexual sex since 1858.

On the gay marriage front, there is a wide division between East and West. In 2001, the Netherlands became the first country in the world to recognize same-sex marriages, followed over the next thirteen years by Belgium, Spain, Norway, Sweden, Iceland, Denmark, France, and the United Kingdom. Most countries have opted to legalize only civil partnerships, as has the Republic of Ireland, which will hold a referendum on gay marriage in 2015. In Russia and most of Eastern Europe, gay marriage is banned. A 2013 Pew Research poll found that three out of four people in Russia believe that society should "reject" homosexuals. That same year, Russia also forbade foreign same-sex couples from adopting Russian children.

"Once a Homo, Always a Homo"—
Gay Sex as a Risk to American National Security

Soon after Lyndon Johnson's 1964 election victory, one of his aides asked a subordinate to explain the federal government's policy of barring homosexual employees. In particular, the aide asked whether people with past same-sex liaisons could be "rehabilitated" by getting married. The rules allowed for rehabilitation, but Johnson's aide wanted to know if that ever happened. The response, by personnel officer John W. Steele, was telling. Not only was homosexuality treated "much more severe[ly]" than other forms of "immoral conduct," Steele wrote, but few believed that a homosexual could ever go straight. "Some feel that 'once a homo, always a homo,'" he wrote, adding: "Our tendency to 'lean over backwards' to rule against a homosexual is simply a manifestation of the revulsion which homosexuality inspires in the normal person. What it boils down to is that most look upon homosexuality as something uniquely nasty, not just as a form of immorality."

Steele's memo is refreshing in its candor, but it contained no secrets. For decades, the government had aggressively purged homosexuals from its ranks, based on their "unsuitability" and the risk they were said to pose to national security. What it really "boiled down to," however, was the belief that homosexuals were equal parts revolting and scary. In the cruel alchemy of Cold War politics, homosexuals were also cast as treasonous communists, and the oppression of gays and lesbians became an act of patriotism. "Commies" and "queers" were not only indistinguishable threats, they were said to be working together to upend American life. The "purge of the perverts" in the federal government, which lasted roughly from 1947 until 1975, resulted in the firing of an estimated five thousand or more suspected gay federal employees. Many more thousands, having endured brutal treatment by government security personnel, re-signed to avoid further disgrace.

The federal government emerged from the war much larger and with a more direct influence on the lives of ordinary Americans than ever before. So long as it hounded gays and lesbians from its ranks—or, indeed, anyone who had ever had gay sex—then homosexuals would remain a breed apart from normal life. The groundwork for the persecutions was laid by FBI director J. Edgar Hoover, who grasped the destructive force of homosexual slander earlier than anyone. While Hoover had been stockpiling exten-sive dossiers on prominent gay people since at least 1937, he also used FBI muscle to stanch the incessant murmurings about his own sexual inclinations. Starting in 1943, Hoover had FBI agents strike out against anyone who so much as gossiped about his suspected homosexuality. As the postwar government came to target gays as national-security threats, it was a small step for the FBI to set up a broad-based "sex deviates" pro-gram and, in short order, become a national clearinghouse for information about homosexuals, their organizations, and their political activities.

Inclusion in an FBI sex-deviate file could bring misery not only to high-profile political figures such as Adlai Stevenson but also to people with no possible impact on national security. In 1942, for example, a young man was expelled from the University of Illinois for making a pass at a male student. The FBI found out about this and tailed him from office job to office job for years afterward, informing his employers and coworkers that he was gay. As late as the 1960s, FBI agents would show up at his house to press him for the names of other homosexuals.

One of Hoover's early dossiers concerned Sumner Welles, the blue-blooded undersecretary of state in the Franklin D. Roosevelt administration. With his chauffeured Rolls Royce, smug manner, and lifelong connections to the Roosevelt family, the man known as FDR's "global strategist" gath-ered enemies as easily as he did accolades. FDR knew about Welles's taste for men, but until then gay men in high places had been able to manage double lives. There was no reason to think Welles would be any different. However, when Welles was caught in 1940 propositioning a black railroad porter—an incident possibly leaked by Hoover—FDR could not contain the damage. Hoover's file on Welles was 160 pages thick and ensured that more trouble was likely even if the railroad-porter situation was kept quiet.

The president stood by Welles for two years, but after one of FDR's opponents threatened to go public with a Senate probe, he had no choice but to demand that Welles resign. The details of Welles's resignation were kept out of the newspapers, but they were still the talk of Washington insiders. More importantly, the State Department would soon be stuck with a reputation as a haven for "Russian-loving pansies."

After the war, congressional Republicans used rumors that the Democratic Truman administration (particularly the State Department) was "honeycombed with homosexuals" to maximum political advantage. In 1947, the Senate admonished Secretary of State George Marshall for allowing the State Department to harbor communists and "admitted homosexuals." The response was a new series of "security principles" to weed out disloyal and unsuitable personnel. Communists and their fellow travelers were targeted, as were "sexual perverts" whose "basic weakness of character and lack of judgment" inclined them to subversion. This became the model for subsequent homosexual purges and a basis for later government-wide security programs. Over the next three years, the government investigated about two hundred employees for sexual perversion. Most of them were fired or resigned. During the same period, about seventeen hundred job applications were denied because the applicants "had a record of homosexuality or other sex perversion." The gay purges were starting, but they had not yet become the stuff of water-cooler or kitchen-table conversations. That would change with two dizzying revelations.

In 1950, one week after Senator Joseph McCarthy muscled into the public consciousness with a fiery speech about communists in the State Department, John Peurifoy, the department's new security head, caused another sensation when he revealed that ninety-one homosexuals had been fired in the past three years. Coming on the heels of McCarthy's speech, the impact of Peurifoy's revelation could not have been greater. McCarthy and his Republican colleagues had landed on the perfect issues with which to hammer the Truman administration. "Commies and queers" were framed as two parts of the same threat. In fact, only one-quarter of McCarthy's constituent mail during this period expressed fear about "red" infiltration; the rest complained of sexual depravity in government.

The fear of pervasive homosexuality was heightened by the 1948 release of Dr. Alfred Kinsey's best-selling *Sexual Behavior in the Human Male*, which reported that more than one-third of the men surveyed had had homosexual experiences, and 4 percent were exclusively gay. Extrapolating from these percentages, agitators warned that at least five hundred thousand civil servants and 192 members of Congress could be considered homosexual security risks. In the coming years, what historian David Johnson calls the Lavender Scare would proceed alongside the Red Scare.

Pressure mounted for a high-level probe into homosexuals in government, which took the form of a Senate subcommittee inquiry led by conservative North Carolina Democrat Clyde Hoey. A spats-wearing relic of the Old South, Hoey started the investigation convinced that homosexuality was sinful but clueless about what gay people did in bed. When, for example, he was told about lesbians in government, he asked an aide, "Can you please tell me, what can two women possibly do?" Yet Hoey and his colleagues learned enough to form politically expedient opinions. The material gathered by his subcommittee was a mix of selective history and anti-gay invective unburdened by analysis. Despite great effort, Hoey found no evidence that any gay or lesbian US government employees had ever been blackmailed for sensitive information. Instead, the subcommittee dredged up the pre–First World War case of Alfred Redl, the gay Austrian turncoat, which became the sole example on which it would conclude, in its much-discussed report, that "the pervert is easy prey to the blackmailer." The report also stated that homosexuals' "lack of emotional stability" and weak "moral fiber" made them "susceptible to the blandishments of the foreign espionage agent." In light of this, the subcommittee concluded that "Persons who indulge in such degraded activity . . . constitute security risks in positions of public trust."

The Hoey report was covered heavily in the press and lent prestige and credibility to the idea that gay people were, by their very nature, security risks. The report also found that homosexuals were a "corrosive influence" on "normal" employees, particularly young ones, because they "frequently attempt to entice" them into perverted practices. "One homosexual," the report warned, "can pollute an entire Government office." The subcommittee castigated the government for taking a "head-in-the-sand" approach toward homosexuals in its ranks and failing to get rid of them. It noted, for example, the "deplorable" fact that 457 of the "perverts" recently arrested in Washington, D.C., anti-gay sweeps were federal employees who should have been promptly fired. "To pussyfoot or to take half measures," the report warned, "will allow some known perverts to remain in Government."

With the Hoey investigation and report, the government moved closer to an all-encompassing anti-gay policy. The army had already, in 1949, directed all enlisted personnel to report any "overt acts of homosexuality," and over the next decade the expulsion of lesbians serving in the army outpaced that of gay men. In 1952, homosexuals, as "persons afflicted with psychopathic personality," were barred from entering the US. The most important anti-gay measure came in 1953, when newly elected President Dwight D.

Eisenhower signed Executive Order 10450, which added "sexual perversion" as grounds for the dismissal of *any* federal employee. Following Eisenhower's 1952 campaign promise to "clean house," the purge of gay federal employees was in full swing and would last for two decades.

In 1953, a State Department clerical worker read about the homosexual "house cleaning" and decided to help. Her first target was her boss, "Miss McCoy," with whom her relations were strained. In a note to security officers, she accused McCoy of having "lesbian characteristics," including "peculiar lips" and regular communication with a woman with a "mannish voice." When the worker met with investigators, she also reported her "funny feeling" about a male coworker with a "feminine complexion" and a "girlish walk," and added that another female employee had a deep voice and an unfeminine face. The investigators took extensive notes, and McCoy and the other two employees were investigated. As 80 percent of such investigations that year ended in confessions, it is likely that this roundup netted some dismissals. Five years later, another government employee, Madeleine Tress, was accused of being a lesbian and going to lesbian gathering places. During an interrogation, investigators named some of Tress's lesbian acquaintances and demanded that she confirm spending time with them. Then the interrogation turned really nasty. "How do you like having sex with women?" one investigator asked. "You've never had it good until you've had it from a man." After Tress resigned, she learned that a coworker had reported her "mannishness," "bohemian lifestyle," and calls from single women.

McCoy's and Tress's experiences were typical of what happened to thousands of federal employees. Under constant pressure to "name names," and not knowing when an anonymous accusation would bring trouble, suspicion among gays and lesbians was kept at a feverish level. "You didn't know who your friends were," Tress recalled. Conditions in Washington, D.C., were particularly bad on account of ongoing police "pervert elimination" campaigns, in which homosexuals were hunted down in Lafayette Park, bars, and other gathering places. Given the high number of government workers in the nation's capital, the arrests produced a bumper crop of firings. In 1956, for example, a federal employee was fired for perversion after seventeen years of service. The charge was based on an arrest—not even a conviction—for loitering in Lafayette Park.

The Lavender Scare also struck in high places. When, in 1953, the son of Lester Hunt, an anti-McCarthy Democratic senator from Wyoming, was arrested in Lafayette Park for soliciting sex from an undercover cop,

Hunt's enemies went to work. He received a threat from Styles Bridges, a pro-McCarthy senator, that unless he declined to run for reelection, the world would know about his son. After some initial resistance, Hunt buckled under the pressure. He withdrew from the race, brought a rifle into his Senate office, and killed himself.

Yet gay smears also boomeranged on McCarthy through his chief aide, the barely closeted Roy Cohn, and another of his aides, the sexually ambiguous G. David Schine. While McCarthy was mostly spared direct accusations about his own sex life, Cohn and Schine were not, and accusations against them helped bring about the senator's downfall. In 1953, Cohn and Schine had gone to Europe on a "fact-finding tour"; their conduct there earned them the sobriquet "The Two London Lovers." For a "man's man" such as McCarthy, the affair was unseemly but manageable. But when he angrily stood by Cohn despite the latter's efforts to secure special treatment for the recently conscripted Schine—which occurred as McCarthy started to focus on subversion in the army—the army went on the attack.

The resulting Army-McCarthy Hearings, broadcast on television in 1954, painted a seamy (and perhaps inaccurate) picture of Cohn trying to pull strings for his handsome lover and of McCarthy entangled in a web of unnatural relations, even if not gay himself. "Does the assistant [Cohn] have some hold on the Senator?" asked Senator Ralph Flanders. The question was never answered, but asking it made the point. When, in the hearings' most dramatic moment, Joseph Welch demanded of McCarthy, "Have you no decency, sir?" Welch was referring to McCarthy's attack on one of Welch's associates. However, by that point the concept of decency, at least when applied to McCarthy and his team, could also have carried a sexual connotation. As the historian Andrea Friedman put it, McCarthy had become "a man who betrayed the nation for his own degenerate desires."

The courts occasionally stepped in to limit anti-gay persecution, but in the 1950s, the victories were few. Only with the help of groups such as the Mattachine Society of Washington (MSW), founded in 1961 by a fired government astronomer, Frank Kameny, did momentum start to build against the Lavender Scare. Kameny had unsuccessfully challenged his dismissal in court as an example of discrimination. Had he won, he likely would have returned to astronomy, but his loss—and the fact that, as a homosexual, his science career was over—pushed him toward a life of militant activism. Against constant harassment from the FBI and police, the

MSW pressed its case for an end to anti-gay discrimination in the courts, in legislatures, and on White House picket lines. Teaming up with the ACLU, it scored a key victory for Clifford Norton, a gay NASA employee who had also been fired for immorality. In 1969, after years of litigation, a federal appeals court held that immorality was not, in itself, grounds for dismissal. Such a judgment, the court said, "connotes a violation of divine, Olympian, or otherwise universal standards of rectitude," which government personnel officers had "neither the expertise nor the requisite anointment to make." Unless there was a rational connection between an employee's off-duty conduct and his or her dismissal, the dismissal could not stand. Six years later, the government finally deleted the words "immoral conduct" from its list of disqualifications for employment, and a key locus of stigma against homosexuals was removed.

The *Norton* decision came down the same week as the Stonewall Uprising exploded in New York City. While Stonewall is rightly remembered as the watershed event that gave rise to the gay-rights movement, it was not the first. Groups such as the MSW had already developed much of the rhetoric and many of the tactical methods that the LGBT movement would later use, and *Norton* marked a key early advance in the long march toward the lifting of legal penalties against gay sex.

The 1970s

By the 1970s, sodomy laws were enforced only sporadically, but they were still invoked to support anti-gay discrimination on other fronts. As dozens of new organizations fought for gay rights, the message slowly and unevenly began to sink in that gay sex should not automatically lead to jail, discrimination, or harassment. A 1975 *Time* magazine cover story on "the gay drive for acceptance"—the first to feature a photograph of a publicly gay man or lesbian—noted the repeal of several anti-sodomy laws since Stonewall and that the federal government and some large companies now hired "openly avowed gays." However, the tone of the piece was still one of alarm. The article rounded back repeatedly to worries that "homosexuality will spread, especially among the young, if the social sanctions are removed." The demand by gays for "full acceptance" makes many Americans "apprehensive," the article continued. "It is one thing to remove legal discrimination against homosexuals. It is another to mandate approval." The article's layout also telegraphed ambivalence. Next to a passage about advances in gay rights was a photo of a bewigged and bearded drag queen, while the section on "how much approval" gays should be given was placed next to a picture of a gay man signaling his sexual "dominance" with a strategically placed key chain. As for gay sexual culture, it was "fast and loose." The APA's 1973 vote to declassify homosexuality as a mental disorder, an immense gain by any measure, was buried in the article's twenty-sixth paragraph and then diminished as an "awkward compromise by a confused and defensive profession."

For middle-of-the-road *Time,* the link of gay sex to illness was too entrenched to give up easily. On the law-enforcement side of the debate, there was no effort to be judicious. Explaining his refusal to talk to gay leaders about police harassment, Los Angeles police chief Ed Davis said in 1972: "It's one thing to be a leper. It's another thing to be spreading the disease." In 1978, as noted above, Chief Justice Rehnquist likened the presence of a gay-rights organization on a college campus to a group infected with measles. And in a bizarre twist of logic, a gay man in 1985 was given the death penalty after the prosecutor convinced the jury that sending him to prison "isn't a very bad punishment for a homosexual." In other words, being raped in prison suits gay men. They like it.

More than anything, the entry of religious fundamentalists into secular politics directed the debate about homosexuality. Alarmed by school desegregation, the Equal Rights Amendment, and the 1973 *Roe v. Wade* abortion decision, and vexed over the widespread shift away from Judeo-Christian "family values" (a phrase coined at this time), Protestant, Catholic, and Jewish fundamentalists fought hard against the "homosexual agenda." Given the momentum to relax anti-gay laws—by 1977, there were at least three dozen new local laws against anti-gay discrimination, and sodomy bans were falling—the law was the central arena for the religious right to wage its cultural battle. Florida's hard divide between a permissive urban minority (mostly in Miami) and a deeply conservative majority made the Sunshine State a natural setting for the religious right to make a stand. No one could have predicted, however, that a former beauty queen and orange-juice pitchwoman would be the one to carry a message of anti-homosexual hatred.

Anita Bryant's vitriolic 1977 Save Our Children crusade against a Miami law barring anti-gay job discrimination caught much of the US by surprise, but it was not the first time Florida had struck out against homosexuals. From 1956 to 1964, the "Johns Committee" of the state's legislature had directed a witch hunt against gays, particularly those in public education. Teachers, professors, and students were yanked out of class by uniformed police, brought to interrogation rooms, and badgered into naming names. Pressure was then put on administrators to fire or expel them. Dozens of people were dismissed, and hundreds more dropped out of school or resigned after being interrogated. They included the University of Florida's president and dean of students. Explaining its focus on schools, the committee's final report, known as the Purple Report for its purple cover and prodigious use of gay pornography and sexual imagery, had this to say:

> The homosexual . . . prefers to reach out for the child at the time of normal sexual awakening. . . . The homosexual's goal and part of his satisfaction is to "bring over" the young person, to hook him for homosexuality. . . . Whether it be with youth or older individuals, homosexuality is unique among the sexual assaults considered by our laws in that the person affected by the practicing homosexual is first a victim, then an accomplice, and finally himself a perpetrator of homosexual acts.

Bryant adopted this rhetoric of homosexual contagion wholesale. As the Johns Committee had done, she focused her efforts on the supposed menace of gay and lesbian teachers. Rather than using police and subpoenas, Bryant used her celebrity and headed a well-organized propaganda campaign to secure the repeal of the new law. Only by keeping schools free of gay teachers—"human garbage," in her words—and preventing their "lifestyle" from spreading to the young could the "homosexual agenda" be stopped. According to one Save Our Children ad: "The recruitment of our children is absolutely necessary for the survival and growth of homosexuality. Since homosexuals cannot reproduce, they must recruit, must freshen their ranks." Adding to this frightening picture, another Save Our Children ad warned that homosexuals use "outright seduction and molestation, a growing pattern that will predictably intensify if society approves laws granting legitimacy to the sexually perverted." Calling not only for a vote in favor of anti-gay discrimination but also for "God's judgment" against "these vile beastly creatures," the crusade also sparked the appearance of "KILL A QUEER FOR CHRIST" bumper stickers and a wave of anti-gay violence.

With the help of the rising Baptist preacher Jerry Falwell ("Gay folks would just as soon kill you than look at you") and the support of Miami's Catholic archbishop, local newspapers, conservative rabbis, and Florida

Governor Reuben Askew ("I would not want a known homosexual teaching my children"), the antidiscrimination law was repealed by a two-to-one margin. Bryant then went on tour, preaching for the repeal of other antidiscrimination laws, and was successful in several regions. Oklahoma passed a law in 1978 allowing schools to purge both gay teachers and those who "advocated" or "encouraged" homosexuality in a way that may "come to the attention" of schoolchildren. However, that law was eventually struck down by the courts, and a similar 1978 initiative in California was defeated at the ballot box. Soon Bryant faded back into well-deserved obscurity, but the religious right had tasted victory on an issue dear to its heart. With the formation of Falwell's Moral Majority at the end of the 1970s, more battles were coming.

• • •

In 1979, almost 90 percent of Americans lived in states that had, in whole or in part, decriminalized sodomy. The push for equal rights for gays, mostly centered in urban areas with vocal gay populations, was gaining steam. However, two developments would change not only the playing field but also the rules of the game and the players themselves.

First, in 1980, the religious right found a key ally in newly elected President Ronald Reagan. With the help of the Moral Majority and other religious groups, Reagan had won the presidency by a landslide. From that point forward, the revitalized Republican Party would be doing the bidding of the religious right on sexual issues and would adopt "family values" as the defining message of its social agenda. Second, in 1982, a medical condition with a rising death toll was termed acquired immune deficiency syndrome (AIDS). AIDS had no cure and was transmitted through blood and semen—a common exchange in anal sex. Just nine years after homosexuality had been taken off the APA list of mental disorders, the "gay plague" remedicalized gay sex—with a vengeance.

The AIDS outbreak recharged the paradigm of homosexuality as a diseased state and fit within a long tradition of victim-blaming. Homosexuals were said to become sick and die because of their "depraved lifestyle." Before the outbreak, the news media had regularly reported that gays and lesbians were sexually voracious. *Time* magazine, for example, reported as fact that "the most obvious aspect of the male gay culture is its promiscuity." Once the AIDS outbreak began, the media reflexively pinned it on the "promiscuous gay lifestyle," pointing to its spread in "hotbeds of homosexual promiscuity." Ever the opportunist, Falwell amplified this theme. "A man reaps what he sows," he said. "If he sows seed in the field of his lower nature, he will reap from it a harvest of corruption."

The link between AIDS and homosexual depravity was also made early on by some medical researchers. Because many of the first cases involved gay men, epidemiologists presumed that its transmission was confined to gay sex. "You get heterosexual doctors examining gays and they jump on the first possible hypothesis, that it must be due to the sexual behavior of gays," admitted James Curran, the leading AIDS researcher at the Centers for Disease Control (CDC). However, perhaps more was going on than mere prejudice. The CDC, which was the key source for AIDS-related information at the time, inexplicably waited until mid-1982 to report that one-fifth of the earliest cases involved heterosexual intravenous drug users, and it waited another three years to officially take note of infected homosexual IV drug users. Reports of infections among straight hemophiliacs and drug transfusion recipients were also delayed. This dearth of information at such a critical time helped to frame AIDS as a "gay disease."

By the mid-1980s, the link between AIDS and "immoral" homosexual sex was forged in steel. The New Right saw the outbreak as a vehicle to stir up hysteria against gays and sexual liberalism generally. "The gay chicken created by sexual liberation has come to roost in everybody's back yard, thus endangering everyone," Falwell warned. "His disease-ridden root must be destroyed." The Southern Baptist Convention concluded that God had created AIDS to show his disapproval of homosexuality. In 1983, the reactionary columnist (and soon the Reagan White House's communications director) Patrick Buchanan wrote, "The poor homosexuals—they have declared war upon Nature and now Nature is exacting an awful retribution." As for the Reagan administration, it couldn't be bothered to care. It was not until 1985, when AIDS cases already exceeded fifteen thousand, that the White House started to pay attention to the issue. It was not until 1986—five years into the epidemic—that Reagan would pronounce the word "AIDS" in public. The White House's message was unambiguous: AIDS was the lot of sexual perverts whose claim to life was already tenuous. To the extent anything was to be done, the objective, according to Health and Human Services chief Margaret Heckler, was to stop its spread "before it affects the heterosexual population."

Even the goal of protecting straight people collided with the Reagan administration's pro-family agenda. The administration refused to encourage condom use, as doing so would be seen to condone immorality and dilute the core messages of premarital chastity and spousal fidelity. Notably, Reagan's surgeon general, C. Everett Koop, took a different approach. In a 1986 report, he called for both condom use and "frank" and "open" AIDS education for young children. Instead of avoiding the subject of gay sex, Koop spoke to it directly and without gratuitous condemnation, observing: "We can no longer afford to sidestep frank, open discussions about sexual practices—homosexual and heterosexual."

This was too much for the White House's social conservatives, who saw Koop's position as "homosexual propaganda" and the surgeon general himself as a traitor. In the end, Koop lost this ideological battle, and in 1987 Reagan signed on to a policy condemning "irresponsible sexual behavior," validating sex only within marriage and allowing sex education that contained no useful information other than encouragement to avoid premarital sex. Not long afterward, Reagan signed a law forbidding the CDC from doing anything to "condone homosexual activities."

The consequences of ignorance as policy are grave. Fire officials refused to resuscitate suspected homosexuals. Utah passed a law in 1987 barring AIDS patients from marrying. In Texas, an HIV-positive man was convicted of attempted murder for spitting on a prison guard. It was punishable in some cases for HIV-positive people to have sex at all, even if they did not know of their condition. Merely by leading a homosexual "lifestyle," one court held, a man should have known that he had been exposed to the AIDS virus and that his sexual partner would be as well. Parents pulled their kids from schools because HIV-positive children were allowed to attend. Most famously, thirteen-year-old Ryan White, a hemophiliac who had contracted AIDS through a blood transfusion, was expelled from his Indiana school. According to his mother, "People said that he had to be gay. . . . We heard God's punishment a lot. That somehow, some way he had done something he shouldn't have done or he wouldn't have gotten AIDS." After a punishing legal contest, he was finally readmitted to school but was forced to use separate bathrooms and eat with plastic forks and knives; he was also barred from physical education classes. Someone fired a bullet through his family's window.

In 1990, not long after White died, President George H. W. Bush signed a substantial aid package for the care of AIDS patients called the Ryan White CARE Act. However, the law gave money only to states that first criminalized the intentional transmission of HIV. The states obliged, some punishing *any* sex between HIV-positive and HIV-negative people, even with a condom. One such law was passed in Iowa, where Nick Rhoades, an HIV-positive man, had met Adam Plendl online and had sex with him once using a condom. At that time Rhoades's viral load was almost undetectable, which made the risk of transmission nil. When Plendl learned that Rhoades was HIV positive, he went to the hospital for treatment. As would be expected, Plendl had not been infected with HIV, but Rhoades nevertheless went to prison—on a *twenty-five-year* sentence. Fortunately, Iowa has recently decriminalized the theoretical transmission of HIV. Rhoades's conviction was finally tossed out in 2014, and the Ryan White Act no longer requires states to have criminal HIV transmission laws. However, about twenty-five states still criminalize sex that has a low-to-negligible risk of HIV transmission.

Meanwhile, as the risk of HIV transmission through heterosexual sex sank into the public consciousness, the market responded. In 1986, a spate of news stories on the dangers of AIDS to heterosexuals was heavenly manna for the condom industry. Sales exploded, and the stock price of Carter-Wallace, manufacturer of Trojan condoms, leapt by 55 percent in 1986 alone. The long-standing refusal of media and advertising channels to carry condom ads also started to evaporate. By the end of 1986, magazines such as *Modern Bride*, *Vogue*, and *Family Circle* were running condom ads. By the following year, nearly all print magazine bans had fallen away, including those of *Time*, *Newsweek*, and *US News and World Report*. The next citadel to fall was television broadcasting. In 1987, a Harris poll showed strong popular support for TV condom ads, but it was not until 1991 that Fox Television became the first of several networks to accept them. The first prime-time condom ads ran on the WB network in 2005. Over time, protections against job discrimination have been extended to people afflicted with HIV, as have access to health care and disability rights. In 2009, President Barack Obama finally lifted a twenty-two-year ban on the admission of HIV-positive people to the US.

While these and other changes in the law are welcome, the lack of comprehensive public education about HIV/AIDS has been devastating. The percentage of people in the US who believed that HIV could be transmitted by, for example, swimming in a pool or sharing a drinking glass with an HIV-positive person (between 10 and 20 percent) did not change from 1987 to 2009. Half of the adults surveyed in 2009 by the Henry J. Kaiser Foundation said they would be uncomfortable having their food prepared by someone who was HIV positive. With HIV/AIDS still closely associated with gay sex, homosexuals remain stigmatized as an engine of worldwide infection. That sense of disgrace often dissuades those who are infected from seeking care.

The Opening

Since 2003, when the US Supreme Court threw out anti-sodomy laws, the legal landscape for people who engage in gay sex has transformed. Not only may homosexuals now serve in the military, an army color guard led a gay pride parade, a general attended a same-sex commitment ceremony at an army base, and gays and lesbians performed in drag at an air force show, presenting themselves as "Chocolate Sunrise," "Artemis Faux," and "Manny Nuff." In 2014, thirty-five years after being booted from the army for being gay, Lisa Weiszmiller—one of the more than one hundred thousand service members discharged for their sexual orientation since the Second World War—won her fight to have her discharge upgraded to "honorable." By January 1, 2015, some thirty-six states, the District of Columbia, and about seventeen other jurisdictions around the world permitted same-sex marriages. Even the pope now says that homosexuals should not be marginalized: "If a person is gay and seeks God and has good will," said Pope Francis in 2013, "who am I to judge him?"

What the hell has been going on? Quite a bit. The process started in 1969, with the Stonewall Uprising and the *Norton* court ruling. It continued through the 1972 Democratic National Convention, when openly gay speakers shocked TV viewers with demands for full civil rights, and went on to presidential candidate Jimmy Carter's (ultimately broken) 1976 promise to end anti-gay discrimination. It exploded in the 1980s with outrage at the government's grotesque response to the AIDS epidemic, which pulled many gays and lesbians out of the closet and helped to galvanize the "gay vote" as something for politicians to reckon with. It gained new urgency in 1996, with President Bill Clinton's craven endorsement of the Defense of Marriage Act. On issues of gay rights, the past two decades have been a convulsive seesaw of hard-won gains and bitter losses.

As the new century began, it was clear that any lasting expansion of gay civil rights turned on the decriminalization (if not the normalizing) of gay sex itself. Unless the law stopped treating what gays did in bed as a "crime against nature," the pariah status of homosexuals would remain intact. Even if sodomy laws were rarely enforced, their very existence validated not only the disgust widely felt about gay sex but also a range of other stigmatizing and disabling laws. By 2002-2003, 58 percent of Americans still believed that same-sex relatio..s were "always" or "almost always" wrong. This was a dramatic improvement from 1987, when 82 percent of Americans held such beliefs, but still far from a consensus.

The question of whether gay sex could still be outlawed fell to the Supreme Court, and before it answered no in *Lawrence v. Texas* (2003), it answered yes in *Bowers v. Hardwick* (1986). The deciding vote in *Bowers* came from Justice Lewis F. Powell, a skilled jurist but also, like Senator Hoey a half century earlier, a man in the dark about homosexuality. During deliberations, the seventy-eight-year-old justice claimed never to have met a homosexual. (This oft-repeated anecdote may not be entirely accurate. During the same period, Powell reportedly asked one of his law clerks, who was gay, about the mechanics of gay sex.) Nevertheless, he believed that homosexuals—whom he said were addicted to sodomy as other people were hooked on drugs—could never form loving homes the way straight people did. The very idea seemed to repel him.

Beyond Powell's ignorance, there were other thorny issues in *Bowers*: many anti-sodomy laws were gender neutral, meaning they barred many forms of straight sex such as fellatio and cunnilingus. If the court upheld rules against sodomy, would that mean it also condemned common forms of sex among heterosexuals? If, on the other hand, homosexuals were given the right to have sex, would that start the process of normalizing gay relationships all the way to marriage? Finally, few people were actually charged with sodomy. Was there really a reason to overturn long-standing precedent to get rid of laws that were so rarely enforced?

For gay-rights attorneys, the answer to this last question was a strident yes. Sodomy prosecutions were few but they still happened, and the proscriptions against anal and oral sex were the bedrock foundation for widespread anti-gay harassment and discrimination at every level of society. Moreover, as lesbians became more visible as a group, gay mothers in divorce cases were finding that their rights to child custody and even to visitation of their children were denied on morality grounds. Emphasizing the reach of sodomy laws into the lives of all people, rather than just homosexuals, the gay-rights legal establishment mounted an effort in *Bowers* to challenge the constitutionality of anti-sodomy laws. Thanks to Powell's deciding vote, it lost.

On the most basic level, the case was about fellatio. One evening in 1982, Michael Hardwick was having mutual oral sex with another man in his Atlanta bedroom when he looked up and saw a policeman standing by the bed. Hardwick had had other run-ins with the same cop in the recent past, and the circumstances of the arrest were dubious—but as the case unfolded, that was not the point. Hardwick had been caught giving and receiving blow jobs, and Georgia law prescribed up to twenty years in jail for "any sexual act involving the sex organs of one person and the mouth or anus of another." Hardwick challenged the law, along with a married couple who claimed that their sexual rights had also been infringed.

When the case reached the Supreme Court six years later, four justices agreed with Hardwick's legal team that the key legal issue was personal privacy, namely, whether the law should meddle with "intimate sexual conduct in the privacy of the home"—*everyone's* homes, not just those of gay people. To the five justices, including Powell, who sided with them for the majority, gay sex was the key question: "The issue presented is whether the Federal Constitution confers a fundamental right upon homosexuals to engage in sodomy," wrote Justice Byron White. "This we are quite unwilling to do." Georgia's lawyers encouraged this narrow, gay-only view, denouncing gay sex in their brief as "purely an unnatural means of satisfying an unnatural lust." In a concurring opinion, Chief Justice Warren Burger added that "millennia of moral teaching," including the Judeo-Christian tradition, ancient Roman law, and England's common law—all of which punished gay sex with death—backed up Georgia's power to jail homosexuals for sodomy. In a stinging dissent, Justice Harry Blackmun scolded his brethren for their "almost obsessive focus on homosexual activity" and their refusal to recognize the law's clash with the constitutional right to privacy. If privacy meant anything, he wrote, "it means that, before Georgia can prosecute its citizens for making choices about the most intimate aspects of their lives, it must do more than assert that the choice they have made is an 'abominable crime not fit to be named among Christians.'"

The *Bowers* decision was heavily criticized for its result, its reasoning, and its selective and inaccurate description of legal history, but from 1986 forward, it was the law. Oral or anal sex between straight people would continue to be overlooked, but when two women or two men had the same kind of sex, serious criminal penalties could still follow. Under *Bowers*, gay sex would remain dangerously abnormal under the law. It remained open season on barring homosexuals from the military, civil-service and law-enforcement work, professional licenses, housing, adoptions, and, of course, the more than one thousand benefits flowing from marriage.

When Falwell congratulated the court for its "clear statement that per-verted moral behavior is not accepted practice in this country," he knew that the issue was not only gay sex. It was whether or not homosexuals themselves could be granted the full benefits of citizenship. Sex was the linchpin.

It would take seventeen years, substantial changes in Supreme Court personnel, and another gay arrest in a private home for *Bowers* to be re-versed. In 1998, Houston police were called to John Lawrence's apartment by Robert Eubanks, who was drunk and livid that his boyfriend—African American Tyron Garner—had been flirting that evening with Lawrence. Eubanks told police that a black man was "going crazy" inside the apart-ment and that he was "armed with a gun." With guns at the ready, the police arrived and found Lawrence and Garner having sex in the bath-room. Arrests for violating Texas's Homosexual Conduct Law followed and another epic legal battle commenced.

When the case came to the Supreme Court, Lawrence's and Garner's attorneys had arranged for a wide array of organizations such as the APA, the Cato Institute, and the American Bar Association, as well as church groups, professors, historians, and others, to file friend-of-the-court briefs, also called amicus briefs. Each brief buttressed the main arguments that the time had passed for laws criminalizing gay sex, that such laws sup-ported other anti-gay laws and practices, and that *Bowers* should be re-versed. The amicus briefs defending Texas's sodomy law, by contrast, made Anita Bryant seem liberal. The American Center for Law and Justice claimed that homosexuals were insisting on a "misuse" of sexual organs," while other briefs claimed that Texas's law was a bulwark against pedo-philia, incest, bestiality, and necrophilia—all of which were supposedly encouraged by the dreaded "homosexual agenda."

In the end, none of this mattered. Six justices (four of whom were not on the court when *Bowers* was decided) were intent on striking down sodomy laws. They also were ready to hold that the laws "demean[ed] the existence" and wrongly "control[led] the destiny" of homosexuals. The question, wrote Justice Anthony Kennedy for the majority, was not just the right of homosexuals to engage in sodomy, any more than the purpose of marriage is to facilitate straight sex. Rather, the pivotal issue was the level of state power to enter into people's private lives. Absent a legitimate state interest justifying such intrusions—which moral disap-proval, even by a majority of citizens, is not—sodomy laws violate the Constitution. Despite the fact that Lawrence had been caught in a brief sexual hookup, Kennedy made clear that "intimate" same-sex relationships, whether fleeting or long-term, deserve the same protections as those between heterosexuals.

Going further, the court corrected Burger's simplistic history of sodomy law, noting that it was only recently that laws targeted homosexuals specifically and that many states and the European Court of Human Rights had already condemned anti-sodomy laws. Even if the laws carried light penalties, they still extended "an invitation to subject homosexual persons to discrimination both in the public and in the private spheres." For these and other reasons, *Bowers* was overturned, the Texas law was thrown out, and all other anti-sodomy laws were tossed as well. According to the court's majority, the right of homosexuals "to liberty under the Due Process Clause gives them the full right to engage in their conduct without intervention of the government."

● ● ●

Gay-rights activists wept while Kennedy read the historic *Lawrence* opinion aloud in open court, but Justice Antonin Scalia's dissent, also read aloud, was a reminder of what they had been up against. The dissent sounded like a polished-up version of the religious right's amicus briefs. "Today's opinion," Scalia read, "is the product of a Court . . . that has largely signed on to the so-called homosexual agenda, [which aims at] eliminating the moral opprobrium that has traditionally attached to homosexual conduct." Continuing, he observed: "Many Americans do not want ['open' homosexuals] as partners in their business, as scoutmasters for their children, as teachers in their children's schools, or as boarders in their homes. They view this as protecting themselves and their families from a lifestyle that they believe to be immoral and destructive." With the court "tak[ing] sides in the culture war," Scalia complained, these Americans could no longer protect themselves. But worst of all to Scalia were the slippery-slope effects of the majority's decision. Once sodomy laws were outlawed, "laws against bigamy, same-sex marriage, adult incest, prostitution, masturbation, adultery, fornication, bestiality, and obscenity" would inevitably be called into question.

Most horrifying to Scalia and the religious right was the prospect of legalized gay marriage. If moral judgments no longer supported rules against gay sex, Scalia wrote, "what justification could there possibly be for denying the benefits of marriage to homosexual couples[?]" None, as matters turned out. What Scalia did not predict was that his dissent in *Lawrence,* and his equally bilious dissent in *United States v. Windsor,* which threw out the Defense of Marriage Act's ban on federal recognition of same-sex marriages, would be cited in many of the later court rulings striking down state bans on gay marriages. In one representative passage, penned by a district judge in Ohio in 2013:

> And now it is just as Justice Scalia predicted—the lower courts are applying the Supreme Court's decision, as they must, and the question is presented whether a state can do what the federal government cannot—i.e., discriminate against same-sex couples . . . simply because the majority of the voters don't like homosexuality (or at least didn't in 2004). Under the Constitution of the United States, the answer is no.

By predicting doom, Scalia hastened it for the anti-gay contingent. By July 2014, a panel of appellate judges, in striking down a Virginia gay-marriage ban, would not only cite Scalia's dissent in *Lawrence,* it would also close its ruling with the following observation:

> The choice of whether and whom to marry is an intensely personal decision that alters the course of an individual's life. Denying same-sex couples this choice prohibits them from participating fully in our society.

My, how far we have come. Until the twenty-first century, the entire point of the law concerning homosexuals was to stop them from "participating fully in our society." By October 2014, a majority of Americans lived in states where gay marriage was legal, and with the Supreme Court refusing that month even to address court rulings overturning bans on same-sex marriages, the way is clearer than ever for gay people, finally, to participate in society as married couples.

· · ·

The importance of the gay-marriage rulings cannot be overstated, but the full integration of gays and lesbians into society still has a ways to go. As of October 2014, for example, there were five states where it was legal for same-sex couples to marry and where it was also legal for employers to fire someone for being gay. The inconsistent patchwork of laws governing discrimination on the basis of sexual orientation and sexual identity will keep access to housing, employment, and government benefits a touch-and-go proposition for millions of people. Given the deep divisions in Congress at present, it is unlikely that any federal laws will be passed in the near future to create national standards for treating married same-sex couples equally.

Perhaps most concerning is the continued distaste felt by a large number of Americans toward gay sex itself. A 2014 study by the Public Religion Research Institute found that 51 percent of those surveyed believed that gay sex was morally wrong, while 43 percent said it was not. Compare this to the 53 percent of Americans who support legalizing gay marriage and the 41 percent against it. Moreover, while about 70 percent of millennials (aged eighteen to thirty-three) now support same-sex marriage, only 56 percent of those surveyed think that gay sex is morally acceptable. Young Americans are thus more tolerant of gay marriage, but only slightly less disapproving of gay sex than the general population. In both groups, there is a substantial minority of those who are tolerant of gay marriage while still believing that gay sex is morally unacceptable. Obviously, the high tolerance of millennials toward gay marriage is a good thing, but their continued attitudes toward gay sex means that they may still try to mold their gay children in their own straight image.

Ever since homosexuality was framed as a mental illness, people have been trying to cure it. In 1894, Krafft-Ebing wrote that posthypnotic suggestion may "remove the impulse to masturbation and homosexual feelings, and . . . encourage heterosexual emotions with a sense of virility." At about the same time, Graeme Hammond, a neurologist, suggested extensive bicycle riding as a cure. Since then, the methods used to alter the sexual orientation of homosexuals have often been gruesome: electroshock treatment, castration, clitoridectomy, aversion therapy, hormone treatment, lobotomy, and so on—all performed legally, and often by doctors on government payrolls. The pioneering British computer scientist Alan Turing was given a choice after being arrested for gross indecency in 1952: jail or chemical castration with female hormones. He chose the latter, and killed himself not long afterward, thereby depriving science of one of its most brilliant minds.

At California's Atascadero State Hospital, thousands of homosexuals were given "ice pick" lobotomies and experimental drugs. When the singer Lou Reed was a gay-leaning Brooklyn teenager, his parents had him put through twenty-four high-voltage electroshock treatments. In 1962, the British psychologist I. Oswald injected a man with nausea-inducing drugs while playing audiotapes of men having sex and surrounding the man with beakers of urine. The goal was to "overdose" the man with homosexuality and vile sensations so that he would turn to women for sexual relief.

While reputable medical organizations now condemn sexual-orientation-change efforts, and an American court held that the Russian use of electroshock treatments to "cure" lesbians constitutes persecution, that has not stopped the "gay cure" trade, especially where youths are concerned. As of February 2015, only California and New Jersey had barred sexual-orientation-change efforts for minors, while other states are considering such measures. Internationally, only in Ecuador and Brazil have there been any substantial (if tentative) efforts to limit such therapies. In 2013 a leading US gay-cure group, Exodus International, gave up its cause after decades of promoting sexual-orientation change through prayer and psychotherapy. Its leader, Alan Chambers, even conceded that such treatments did not work and caused extensive trauma. Since then other groups have stepped in. These include the religiously oriented Alliance for Therapeutic Choice and Scientific Integrity, Restored Hope Network, and Friends of Ex-Gays and Gays. Not only do these groups contend that homosexuality can be cured, they argue that restrictive rules such as California's discriminate against their own religious and speech rights.

So far these arguments have not found any takers in the courts, but given the Supreme Court's recent decision to let privately held companies refuse, on religious grounds, to give employees insurance coverage for birth control, there may be an opportunity to use religious freedom to halt further bans of gay cures. However this issue resolves itself, one thing is for sure: the controversies over gay sex will not end any time soon.

CHAPTER 3

DANGEROUS TO MINORS

Sex and Children

In Scotland, among other places, it was commonly believed in the early twentieth century that a man could cure himself of sexually transmitted infections by "having connection" with a virgin female. This "abominable superstition" resulted in the rape and infection of quite a few girls and caused deep public concern. A Child Outrage Committee was formed in Edinburgh. It recommended harsh criminal penalties for offenders who infected girls. Police personnel called for them to be whipped, castrated, or even exposed to X-rays. After 1910, men who infected girls through "lewd, indecent, and libidinous practices" were tried in the high courts, where their crimes would be treated with the severity they deserved. The message was clear: virgin girls were off-limits.

Yet for all the hue and cry, the courts and their medical advisors were doubtful about recognizing this form of abuse. If the victims came from the lower classes, courts were inclined to hold that their infections came from "worms or uncleanly habits." In 1913, after one Jessie B. was raped by her father in their Glasgow tenement, her vaginal discharges were attributed not to her father's assault but to the "general uncleanliness of the house," her "lack of personal cleanliness," and her "fingering of the parts." Even when sexually transmitted infections were found to result from "criminal interference," the girls were punished. Their "innocence" gone forever, they were viewed less as victims than as sources of danger—they were now said to have "undesirable" sexual "habits" that "they all too readily teach to others," and which could lead to prostitution. For the sin of being raped, many girls were put in locked wards, asylums, and children's homes, both to isolate them and to halt the spread of moral contagion.

This paradox has been repeated, in various forms, up to the present day. With few exceptions, no crime causes as much outrage as the sexual abuse of children, and for good reason. If civilized society means anything, it means the weak are protected, and the mission of guarding children from sexual abuse has become a defining element of modern law. Yet with every protective measure, the distrust of kids lingers. The Puritan idea that children are born in sin and inclined toward wickedness has not fully dissipated, nor has the loathsome sexual desire some adults feel toward the young. Modern sex law has too often blamed children for tempting adults into sex just as it has affirmed that sex is perilous to minors. This contradiction has become even more glaring as the law has expanded the definition of childhood to include adolescence.

At the turn of the last century, the age of consent for sex coincided roughly with the onset of puberty, which meant that in most places it was perfectly legal for a fifty-year-old man to have sex with a thirteen-year-old girl. That age limit was raised as lawmakers agreed that children were incapable of reasonably making such decisions. Regardless of what they subjectively desired, sex with them became statutory rape. However, placing the bodies of children and adolescents off-limits did not dispel the age-old distrust of wicked youth, and the law's protections proved to be far less than absolute. As statutory rape laws were applied, adults were charged for having sex only with young people of "chaste character," which left many kids exposed to mistreatment. Even as police hunted for child predators, underage victims were routinely punished for enticing their attackers. In the late 1980s, when public outcries against child sexual abuse grew the loudest, the trend of charging even prepubescent kids with sex crimes began, and children began to appear on public registries of dangerous sex offenders. And now, as child pornography surges through cyberspace, teens who sext each other are treated as traders in kiddie porn. The legal line between victim and victimizer, unclear to begin with, has now all but vanished.

When we think of sex crimes involving children we generally think of the perverted adult relative or neighbor, the freak lurking at a playground, or, lately, the priest, scout leader, or teacher crossing lines with kids under his care. Those criminals will be covered in detail, but we will also address others caught in the crossfire. Harmless people, including young kids playing "doctor" and teens doing what teens have always done, are now being labeled, often for life, as registered sex offenders. Faced with the specter of sex crimes against children, a terrified populace will support any kind of response so long as it is "tough," even if innocents are harmed in the process. It remains to be seen whether we will decide that ruining the lives of young and nondangerous people is unacceptable collateral damage in the battle against child abuse, or whether hotter heads will continue to prevail.

Sex and youth will always be a volatile, emotionally fraught combination. It is perhaps asking too much of the legal system to resolve the quandaries raised by youthful sexual desire, or to figure out who poses a real risk to children, but it is the only system we have and it needs improvement.

One or the Other: Determining a Child's Sex

Before addressing the issue of sex with children, we start with the sex *of* children—specifically, who may decide a child's sex, and why. Most of the time, biology makes the decision. Babies with unambiguous sexual characteristics are recorded as male or female in their birth records and their lives proceed. Some will assume different gender identities in later years, but that is their choice to make—assuming local law and custom cooperate. However, for the 1 to 4 percent of the population born with atypical reproductive equipment—what the medical community calls "disorders of sex development"—matters become complicated. The law rarely has patience for ambiguity, and when "hermaphrodites" or, in current parlance, "intersex people" come into the picture, the legal system has been outright hostile. With very few exceptions, people are required to adhere to one sex or the other. There is no third category. The results of this binary approach are harsh for intersex children, whose bodies are often surgically mutilated ("normalized") to shove them into a single sex classification.

In most cases, parents authorize these procedures to guard their intersex children from what they fear will be a traumatic life astride the hard cultural line separating male and female, and also to relieve their own distress. In 1997, Stanford University's chief of pediatric urology, Linda Shortliffe, explained that she operated on intersex children because "we consider it sort of an emergency because it is upsetting to parents."

Pointing to expectations raised by prenatal ultrasound and chromosome-typing techniques, one of Shortcliffe's colleagues, Ray Hintz, observed, "It can be difficult to get the family to accept the child as what they are. They can't just go home and throw away those blue curtains and bedspread and get pink." This dynamic is changing with an accumulation of research showing that "normalizing" medical procedures can cause more damage to intersex children than they resolve, and that rejects the view of intersexuality as an urgent medical problem—not one, in any event, that the children should not eventually address themselves. Led by recent changes in Colombian law, a patient-centered model of dealing with intersexuality is starting, ever so slowly, to gain acceptance.

Starting in the late nineteenth century and continuing for roughly five decades, scientists and doctors held to what bioethicist Alice Dreger calls the "gonadal definition" of sex, by which a newborn's "true" sex is determined by doing a visual once-over of the gonadal tissue and then declaring it either ovarian or testicular. This has preserved a strict separation of male and female and imposed one immutable sexual identity on everyone, regardless of other aspects of one's sexual anatomy or one's later gender self-identification. By denying any middle ground, clarity in the social order was maintained. Those with testicular tissue but also with other ambiguous anatomical characteristics were labeled male pseudohermaphrodites—the "pseudo" meaning that they were still "true" males.

This strict either/or perspective was shoved aside in the mid-twentieth century by the doctrine that one's sex is not necessarily determined by looking at gonads but also by psychosocial factors. This theory, developed mainly by John Money, a professor of pediatrics and psychology at Johns Hopkins University from 1952 until his death in 2006, held that people are born gendered tabula rasa, and that their sexual identities develop in response to a matrix of external stimuli. Money nevertheless maintained that being male or female still required "convincing-looking genitalia," and deviations from this norm can cause mental trauma and "unsuccessful" gender identity. As maleness is widely considered to depend on a normal-sized penis, inferior but "repairable" members (2.5 or more centimeters when stretched) of "XY" infants have been fixed and enlarged. XY babies whose penises haven't measured up have been castrated and reconstructed to resemble females. On the other hand, newborn girls, believed to require petite "nonerectile" clitorises, have been subjected to surgeries to trim them—even at the price of diminishing sensitivity.

These decisions are usually made by the child's parents soon after birth, often under pressure from doctors and in a state of acute angst. The children, of course, have no idea what is going on and are not always told about the tinkering that took place when they were infants. In fact, telling the truth in this regard is arguably unethical. In 1995, a medical student was given a cash prize in medical ethics by the Canadian Medical Association for an article advocating that patients with androgen insensitivity syndrome (AIS) be deceived about the facts of their condition. The crafty student argued that "physicians who withhold information from AIS patients are not actually lying; they are only deceiving" because they are selectively holding back information. As Dreger observed in 2000, "in intersex cases the doctor still typically plays the role of an almost superhuman benefactor who knows best and who, in his noble efforts to save an otherwise doomed patient, need not tell the patient or parents all he knows."

During the second half of the twentieth century, Money cut exactly such a superhuman figure. To the parents of young Bruce Reimer, he was messianic. A Harvard-trained psychologist and cofounder of the Gender Identity Clinic at Johns Hopkins, Money was the medical profession's unquestioned authority on gender identity in 1966, when Reimer's parents saw him on Canadian television. Money and his team had already achieved renown for their work with intersex people, and their theory that intersex children could be molded—through surgery, hormonal treatments, and psychological conditioning—into either sex, so long as the process began within a few weeks of birth but not later than two and a half years. To Money, all babies, intersex or not, were sexually neutral. It was just a matter of deciding which direction to take and then never looking back.

When the Reimers saw the handsome, charismatic Money tout his successes on television, they had good reason to pay close attention. One of their nine-month-old twin sons, Bruce, had recently suffered a botched circumcision that had destroyed his penis. The parents were desperate to find a way forward for Bruce, and Money seemed to have all the answers. "Something told me that I should get in touch with this Dr. Money," recalled Bruce's mother. She and her husband did, and before long Bruce came under Money's care. This young, uneducated working-class couple from Winnipeg didn't know it, but they had given the publicity-loving Money a perfect opportunity to exhibit the universality of his gender-identity theories. With identical, nonintersex twins, Money could demonstrate once and for all that everyone could be subject to gender assignment. Bruce would be made into a girl while his twin brother, Brian (whose circumcision had gone well), would be the experiment's "control" and remain a boy.

Money was eager to get started, and within a few months Bruce was brought to the Johns Hopkins medical complex in Baltimore. There, his testicles were removed, and his remaining scrotal and other tissues were reconfigured to resemble rudimentary female genitalia. That was only the beginning: the child, now named Brenda, was not only to be raised as a girl, she would also undergo years of unremitting and often bizarre conditioning to solidify her female identity. Moreover, neither Brenda nor Brian was to be told the truth about Brenda's sex reassignment until much later. If the Reimers stuck to the program and did nothing to "weaken the child's identification as a girl and a woman," then, Money told them, there was "no reason that it shouldn't work." Everything Money required spelled deliverance for the Reimers and their unfortunate child. "I looked up to him like a god," said the twins' mother. "I accepted whatever he said."

Money always had a lot to say, and in the coming years what he said, and demanded, was increasingly difficult for Brenda to live with. First, Brenda was never comfortable in the guise of a female. As a child, she tore off her dresses and ignored the girly toys her parents showered on her. She preferred to urinate while standing up. "I recognized [Brenda] as my sister," Brian later recalled, "but she never, ever acted the part. . . . When I say there was nothing feminine about [Brenda,] I mean there was nothing feminine. She walked like a guy. She talked about guy things, didn't give a crap about cleaning house, getting married, wearing makeup. . . . We both wanted to play with guys, build forts and have snowball fights and play army." None of this went unnoticed at school, where Brenda was mercilessly ridiculed and shunned by the other children. "Even the [kindergarten] teacher didn't accept her," recalled the mother. "The teachers knew there was something different." As she went through various schools, she was called "cavewoman" and "gorilla."

The twins also made periodic visits to Money's office at Johns Hopkins, which became ghoulish in the extreme. Money believed that children must be made to understand the differences between males and females, and how reproduction is accomplished, as early as possible. To reinforce gender and identity roles, he showed the twins explicit photographs of adults having sexual intercourse—what he called "the things that moms and dads do." He also had the twins inspect each other's genitals. Starting at age six, he had them simulate intercourse, with Brenda playing the female role and Brian the male, while Money took pictures. Money made Brenda take a position on all fours while Brian pressed his genitals against her from behind. He also had Brenda lie on her back with her legs spread while Brian simulated mounting her. To Money, these sessions were merely the "sex rehearsal play" most kids engaged in, which he said was a vital step toward forming a healthy—if heterocentric—gender identity. To Brenda and her brother, they were torture.

From about second grade, Brenda was convinced that she was not a girl, no matter what anyone did or said or what she looked like. Yet Brenda's mother, who fervently wanted the treatment to succeed and wished to please Money, sent Money letters reporting what a good "girl" Brenda was turning out to be. In 1972, relying on these letters and ignoring Brenda's manifest boyishness and resistance to "treatment," Money announced the success of his experiment with six-year-old Brenda and her brother. The case was a sensation, in no small part because the notion of a malleable "gender identity" (a term Money coined) perfectly fit the progressive zeitgeist. In January 1973, Money was lionized in *Time* magazine: "This dramatic case," the article reported, "provides strong support for a major contention of women's liberationists: that conventional patterns of masculine and feminine behavior can be altered." The experiment's purported success found its way into textbooks on subjects ranging from sociology to pediatric urology to endocrinology. For the next several decades, Money's influence was, in the words of Brown University's Anne Fausto-Sterling, "almost monolithic. . . . It solidified the practice of doing surgery on young infants who had unusual genitalia so that it became the only acceptable practice." Hundreds of such surgeries were performed each year.

Brenda continued to deteriorate as Money collected honors. As she headed into puberty, she didn't take her estrogen pills consistently. She also dressed like a boy and refused to submit to additional genital surgeries. Finally, in 1980, her despairing father told her the truth, and "all of a sudden everything clicked," she later recalled. "For the first time things made sense and I understood who and what I was." One month before the twins' sixteenth birthday, Brenda underwent another sex change—this time to return, to the extent possible, to being a male. Now calling himself David, he also started a course of hormonal treatments and had a mastectomy. While he was relieved to assume his true identity at last, he was physically, reproductively, and psychologically ravaged. David eventually married and adopted his wife's children, but the travails of a life spent as a guinea pig in a reckless medical experiment were too much to bear. His marriage failed and in 2004, at the age of thirty-eight, David ended his bitter life with a shotgun.

The failure of David's sexual reassignment was not publicly revealed until 1997, after two of Money's rivals in the medical community located David and told him that his case had been the precedent for thousands of ill-advised sex reassignments. "There are people who are going through what you're going through every day," one of the doctors told David, "and we're trying to stop that." David's suffering brought a wave of outraged publicity. Articles appeared about his case, he told his story on Oprah Winfrey's television show, and sex "normalizing" surgery finally started to come under serious scrutiny. For his part, Money said little, but he did respond that the Reimer exposé was the result of right-wing media bias and "the antifeminist movement," adding that his detractors "say masculinity and femininity are built into the genes so women should get back to the mattress and the kitchen."

At least until 2006, the birth of an intersex infant was still considered a medical and social crisis requiring immediate surgical intervention. That year, the American Academy of Pediatrics (AAP) issued a new policy statement urging caution before intersex children are put under the knife—noting particularly the risks to girls of having their clitorises cut for "cosmetic" reasons, and highlighting the potential for intersex children to lead fulfilling lives without such radical interventions. Yet no law in the United States bars such surgeries, and parents are still within their rights to have doctors surgically alter the sex of their intersex children.

Colombia has led the way in setting limits on the power of doctors and parents to surgically alter the genitalia of their intersex children. In a historic set of decisions, the Constitutional Court of Colombia required, in 1999, that children's "best interests" be put ahead of parental anxieties over the consequences of sexual ambiguity. For the first time anywhere, intersex people were found to constitute a minority entitled to protection against discrimination. Surgery, the court held, may be a violation of a child's autonomy and bodily integrity. The court allowed parents to consent to surgery only after they have been given accurate information about the risks and alternative treatment paradigms that rule out early surgery. Additionally, parents' consent must be given more than once and over an extended period of time to ensure that they understand the ramifications of their decision. Colombian parents also cannot grant consent to surgery on children more than five years old. By that time, a child has achieved "autonomy," and the child's gender identity has already come into being—factors that diminish surgery's urgency and potential benefits.

Other countries have followed Colombia's lead, but none have gone as far. In 2013, Germany became the first European country to permit parents of babies without "clear gender-determining physical characteristics" to mark birth certificates with an X, signifying neither male nor female. The idea is not to recognize a third sex but to let the child decide later which direction to take. Other legislation around the world shores up the rights of transsexuals and people whose gender identity varies from the sex listed on their official birth documents. Argentine law now permits individuals to change their names and sexual identities on official documents without the approval of a doctor or judge, and also requires insurance plans to pay for hormone therapy and gender-reassignment surgery. Australia recognizes a neutral third gender based on self-identification, as do Nepal and New Zealand. The United States does not. While other countries make strides toward recognizing the right of people to determine their own gender identities, the debate in the US has focused on marginal issues such as which bathrooms gender-nonconforming children may use in school. (For its part, Facebook permits its users to identify themselves from a menu of dozens of gender identities, including "two-spirit," "cisgender," "pangender," intersex, "neutrois," "androgyne," "agender," and "gender fluid.") As intersexuality becomes less an object of horror and more a question of discrimination and equal treatment, then the law should eventually accept that intersex children should not be surgically modified according to the anxieties and potentially outdated values of their parents.

•   •   •

Even leaving aside the simulated sex among child siblings, the Reimer case is shocking, but no less startling is the fact that we are alarmed at all. To the question "How can we have allowed a child to be put through this?" we must add the queries: "Why do many of us now find such treatment to be cruel when until so recently it was seen as merciful?" and, "How do moral certainties about sex change so quickly?" Our horrified response to the treatment of David Reimer reflects just one of many abrupt shifts in popular views about youth and sex. Every period has its dominant set of beliefs in this regard, which are invariably framed as moral, natural, and right. That is, until a new set of precepts replaces them and yesterday's kindnesses are remembered as abuses. This is particularly true over the past century, when the law hitched its moral and ethical wagons to the protean beast of science. But scientific and medical thinking changes too quickly to guide sex law, especially when children are involved. The law stood silent as Reimer was surgically mutilated and then pushed into a female gender identity because Money himself answered the question of whether doing so was right or wrong.

At least as late as the year 2000, the AAP channeled Money's theories by urging early surgical intervention for intersex infants, lest they experience psychological trauma throughout their lives and are unable to form successful gender identities. Six years later the AAP took an opposite approach, stating that "available data" supports "male rearing" (that is, no surgical castration) of boys born with "micro" genitalia and warning of the psychological trauma caused by gender-reassignment surgery. The abrupt discarding of Money's theories is all to the good for science, where a truth prevails only until a better one emerges, but it is of little comfort to those who have already been made to suffer. Hopefully the US and other countries will follow Colombia's example and pass laws recognizing that intersex infants have rights against such interventions. But until that happens the casualties will continue to mount.

Money was not a mad doctor experimenting on children in some secluded dungeon. On the contrary, he stood at the apex of the medical establishment and seemed to be genuinely dedicated to finding innovative methods to help his patients. In her 1998 book *Lessons from the Intersexed*, Suzanne Kessler writes that Money's views about sexual flexibility at birth enjoyed "a consensus that is rarely encountered in science." We should also recall that Money's was the only available treatment regime that promised solutions to parents. As Johns Hopkins surgeon William Reiner said: "It allowed me [to tell parents of boys with atypical genitals that] we have a surgical solution, because we have a psychological solution. . . . We can construct the child as a female and your child will grow up and be a successful, happy girl or woman."

Money's ideas also "dovetailed with a lot of ideas that were being produced," said Fausto-Sterling, particularly those coming out of the women's movement, for which Money provided scientific proof that differences between the sexes resulted from societal prejudices, not inborn human characteristics. At the same time, his belief that "convincing" genitals were essential to healthy gender identity affirmed the belief that intersex people are mistakes of nature and cannot develop normally. By claiming that people belong in one of only two acceptable sex slots, and that surgery is required for those who traverse such categories, Money validated both gender malleability and sexual intolerance.

Had intersex people enjoyed even a small measure of acceptance when Bruce Reimer was born, his parents might not have put him under the knife. Had Money not been guarded behind a high wall of prestige, he might have been more reticent about showing the twins pornography or forcing them to simulate sex with each other. Money might also have been removed from his post at Johns Hopkins for his positions on sex *with* children. He told *Time* magazine in 1980, "A childhood sexual experience, such as being the partner of a relative or an older person, need not necessarily affect the child adversely." In his book of the same year, *Love and Love Sickness*, he suggested, somewhat ironically, that parents, priests, and teachers be charged with criminal child abuse for not permitting children to engage in sexual rehearsal play. These notions were all elements of what Money saw as a progressive, reason-based approach toward sexual development. When he voiced this last idea, it did little more than raise some eyebrows. A few decades later, he sounds like a disturbed child molester. So does towering sex researcher Alfred Kinsey, who wrote, in *Sexual Behavior in the Human Female* (1953), that there is no reason except society's adverse "cultural conditioning" why a child "would be disturbed at having its genitalia touched, or disturbed at seeing the genitalia of others, or disturbed at even more specific genital contacts."

Kinsey echoed Wilhelm Reich, who had advocated sexual contact among youths and wrote in *The Sexual Revolution* (1930)—the bible of the sexual counterculture—that the only plausible reason for parents not to have sex in front of their kids is that it might interfere with the parents' pleasure. In this context, Money's display of pornography to the Reimer twins and his requirement that they simulate intercourse look less like criminal perversions than applications of the advanced thinking of the time.

Few people now would agree with the above sentiments of Money, Reich, or Kinsey, and fewer still would invite these men to babysit their children. Any encouragement by adults of sexual activity among or with children, and any display of pornography to children, now smacks of child abuse. Will our beliefs change again with the rise of another movement or charismatic theorist? As we work through these questions in the coming pages, the challenge will be to recognize that our attitudes, no matter how fervently we may hold onto them at any given time, are always subject to change.

Bright Lines and Teen Temptresses—
Age-of-Consent Laws

The push to widen the sexual barriers around the bodies of children began late in the nineteenth century. The basic idea of age-of-consent laws is simple: sex with people below a specific age is statutory rape, full stop. Yet each time that age is raised, new populations of innocents are penalized while more harmful actors avoid sanction. After more than a century of tinkering with the laws, it has become plain that formulaic age limits on sex do not work—in large part because no one can agree on who is really being harmed, and why. A sex law may look clear as day on paper, but the distinction between perpetrator and victim often blurs in application. Do age-of-consent laws protect kids from themselves or from others? What if the "child" is seventeen, sexually experienced, and invited the encounter? Should sex between two fourteen-year-olds be treated the same as sex between a fourteen-year-old and a person who is ten, twenty, or fifty years old? Why does the law bless sex between married youths but call it rape if the same people happen to be unmarried? These issues and others make the rules inconsistent and, all too often, capricious.

In the 1880s, only the very youngest girls were considered incapable of consenting to sex. The usual age of consent in England and the US was ten or twelve, although Delaware put the age at seven. Girls over these ages who had sex did so as adults. If they consented, even with men many times their age, then no rape of any kind resulted under the law. Given that consent could be inferred when females did not fight back to the death, or even if they were not virgins, most sexual encounters were taken as consensual. In practice, then, young girls were outside the law's concern. In England, a shifting coalition of religious and early feminist reformers, including the evangelical Josephine Butler, contended that these lax standards condemned "a large section of female society" to lives of "administering to the irregularities of the excusable men." For years, their demands for a raise in the age of consent were ignored. Members of Parliament saw Butler and the other reformers as noisy nuisances and had no intention of legislating against their own sexual prerogatives. They had raised the age to thirteen in 1875, and the consensus among lawmakers was that that was high enough.

That changed in 1885, when the muckraking London newspaperman W. T. Stead caused riots with a series in the *Pall Mall Gazette* about "Lily," a young waif sold by her venal mother to a white slave trader, who then took his pleasures with her and sold her off to the "fleshpots" of Paris. In column after column of feverish prose, Stead thundered that Lily was just one of "many thousands" of poor girls "served up as dainty morsels to the passions of the rich" and then "killed and done away with," a scourge that only a higher legal age of consent could stop. It was later revealed that the entire story was a hoax. There was no white slave trade on the scale Stead represented, and it was Stead who had played the role of Lily's white slaver. He had indeed terrorized the poor girl, but rather than selling her off in France, he'd had her held secretly by the Salvation Army. Before any of this came out, however, a petition bearing 393,000 signatures and demanding a raised age of consent (among other things) was brought to the House of Commons—in a Salvation Army carriage pulled by white horses and accompanied by a clanging brass band. A rattled Parliament passed several new laws protecting girls from exploitation, including one lifting the age of consent to sixteen.

Ironically, Stead was the first casualty of the new laws; he was jailed for three months after his fraud and kidnapping were revealed. Yet despite Stead's disgrace in Britain, his "Maiden Tribute of Modern Babylon" articles were game changers. If the story hadn't exactly been true, it had a large measure of what Stephen Colbert would call "truthiness": it *felt* like it was true, even without pesky facts to back it up. Stead became a worldwide hero to moral reformers—particularly in the US, where religious reformers such as the Women's Christian Temperance Union (WCTU), suffragists, early feminists, and workers' unions took up the cause of protecting girls from predatory men. Within a few decades, it was illegal in every state for anyone to acquire "carnal knowledge of a female child" who was less than sixteen or eighteen years old. By the strokes of a few pens, countless millions of sexual encounters—many consensual, others not, and all in line with cultural norms that had prevailed for thousands of years—were criminalized.

To justify the new laws, American advocates pointed to the influx of young females to cities to work in factories, mills, and sweatshops. Living in unsupervised housing, their virtue (that is, virginity) was under constant threat by men of means. Without the threat of prison against such men, generations of (white) girls stood to be ruined and left without options for marriage and respectable lives. A young woman's virtue, said Colorado reformer Clyde Holly, was more valuable than "life itself," and a man who trampled on it for a passing thrill was worse than a murderer.

However, legislators still had doubts about the girls they were being asked to protect—suspicions that found their way into the laws. As the laws were written, only underage girls with no sexual past could be statutorily raped. If, however, they had already sampled the erotic fruits of urban life, then men were free to prey on them to their libidos' content. What started as an effort to protect young women thus became, in effect, yet another tool for examining, judging, and controlling female sexuality. The "chaste character" exception, which put every statutory rape victim through a rigorous moral gauntlet, would not be completely purged from US statutory rape laws until 1998.

Lawmakers and courts were also concerned that a higher age of consent would invite scheming young females to blackmail helpless men for payoffs or, worse, marriage proposals. Far from viewing teenage girls as passive victims, many saw "designing females" looking to profit from their forbidden sexuality. One Iowa legislator warned that raising the age of consent would permit females to "inveigle unsuspecting and susceptible [young men] into situations in which yielding to an almost irresistible temptation will place them within the power of the female." The medical profession agreed. One medical journal, *Medical Age*, warned that a higher age of consent would invite the "licentious, designing *demi mondaine*" to entice an "innocent, ignorant schoolboy to her *bagnio*" and, after compromising him, take him to court for all he was worth. The "chaste character" requirement, as well as rules excusing men from statutory rape liability if they mistakenly believed girls to be of age, was meant to protect against these hazards.

As matters unfolded, the moral reformers, dubious lawmakers, and doctors were all wrong. The ranks of poor and working-class girls crowding the cities did not, for the most part, fit the blushing, virginal stereotype pushed by the WCTU and its confederates. Nor were they hell-bent on extorting money from the wealthy. Separated from the restraints of family, they pursued sex happily, most often with people from their own age groups and backgrounds. To the extent they were victimized sexually, the culprits usually came from their own families, or their families' neighbors or friends. Many of the girls whose statutory rape cases ended up in court had run away from abusive or oppressive home settings. Moreover, far from being victimized by deceitful females, many accused men learned that their real adversaries were the girls' parents, who used the laws to retrieve runaway daughters or disrupt their consensual relationships. Indeed, in many of these cases up to the present day, the girls refuse to testify against their lovers.

Once sex-restrictive laws are adopted, they are rarely repealed, and if they don't work as planned, then they are deployed for other purposes. Rather than guard feminine virtue against male aggression, the laws were used in a series of efforts to police young women's voluntary sexual habits—including patrols of amusement centers, hotel raids, and so on—and placements of suspect girls in juvenile detention centers and reformatories. To the girls, the idea that they were being protected from predatory men would have sounded like a bitter joke. The men were usually given mild or no penalties when courts even suspected that girls had been sexually active.

In 1915, police in Oakland, California, arrested thirteen-year-old Louise Blake and her boyfriend, nineteen-year-old George Fields. Blake admitted that they had been having sex, which was apparently enough for the court to conclude that she was a temptress and Fields was the real victim. "The circumstances of this case are such as would test the moral backbone of persons far better equipped to resist than [Fields] had been," said a court officer. The judge agreed and let Fields off with no jail time. Blake was put into a juvenile detention home while she awaited trial. If she was treated like other girls in her position, she would have been subjected to compulsory examinations to determine whether or not she was a virgin. If doctors discovered that her hymen had been ruptured or that her vaginal opening was "relaxed," she would have been interrogated about details of her sex life and for the names of the men and boys she had been with. The names would then have been given to police and new arrests made.

The law was supposed to make sex with an underage girl a crime regardless of her consent, but courts still demanded to know whether she had wanted sex with the accused man. In one 1910 case, the judge himself badgered a young girl with questions such as: "Whatever you did, you did of your own free will?" and, "What did you go in the house for?" and, "Did you know what you were going to get when you were undressing yourself?" Given that the law was supposed to take the girl's "freewill" out of the equation, these questions were irrelevant—but who was going to say so to the judge? Even when girls were taken with force, the same suspicions remained. In 1914, a fourteen-year-old girl was violently raped by a janitor in a cannery after following him into a secluded office. The man admitted his guilt and no one disputed that the girl had been a virgin. Nevertheless, he was set free. "She was an inexperienced girl," said a court officer, "but her willingness to accompany [the janitor] into the office alone placed him under special temptation."

As the century progressed, the law continued to focus on controlling, rather than guarding, young female sexuality. In California, girls were arrested and detained for transgressions such as being "in danger of growing up to lead an idle, dissolute or immoral life." They could also be charged with "sex delinquency," another term for having sex outside of marriage. Sex delinquency or other morals charges would often follow arrests for nonsexual offenses, such as truancy, running away from home, and shoplifting, after which the girls would be physically examined and grilled about their sex lives. Nearly half the girls so charged were placed in reformatories or juvenile detention centers, or made to work as maids in private homes, before their cases were even decided. According to historian Mary Odem, the female officials who sent teenage girls to do domestic work "thought that placement in a middle-class home would provide [the] girls with maternal supervision and household training supposedly lacking in their own homes." The girls disliked the work, but it was better than institutional life, where girls were hosed with frigid water, given bread-and-water diets, and put in solitary confinement. All for having sex.

The active enforcement of statutory rape laws continued into the late twentieth century. On one hand, the laws helped to facilitate prosecution against hideous characters such as John Geoghan, a Boston Catholic priest whose abuse of at least 130 children from the 1960s to the 1990s stands as one of the most egregious cases in the church's ongoing sex scandals. The laws, which by the year 2000 were all gender-neutral, were also critical to the prosecution of Mary Kay LeTourneau, a Washington State teacher whose passionate romance with a twelve-year-old student resulted in a seven-year prison sentence, despite entreaties by the boy and his mother that she not be jailed. (LeTourneau and her young lover produced two children before the boy's fifteenth birthday and married after her release from jail.)

At the same time, the statutory rape laws continue to generate injustices. Take Kevin Gillson, who at eighteen years old was prosecuted in Wisconsin in 1997 for having sex with and impregnating Stephanie, his fifteen-year-old fiancée. While he was spared jail time, he was still required to register as a sex offender and was barred from any contact with her. At Gillson's trial, Stephanie submitted this statement into the court record: "Thanks to the court system, I have lost the love of my life and the father of my unborn baby." Among the cruel ironies in the case is the fact that Kevin and Stephanie had decided to marry after they learned that she was pregnant. Kevin had also taken a full-time job to obtain health insurance for Stephanie and the baby. In slightly different circumstances,

Kevin would be praised for forming a family along traditional lines and meeting his obligations as a father. Yet he and Stephanie had succumbed to their passions before their wedding day, for which their family was put to ruin before it started.

During the later decades of the twentieth century, age-span provisions (also known as Romeo and Juliet exceptions) were also widely adopted. These rules reduce penalties for sex among similarly aged minors on the theory that there is less potential for abuse, and that young people should not be charged with felonies for following their "natural" urges. These rules mark a salutary change in the law, but they still don't always work as designed. For example, Nushawn Williams, twenty, an HIV-positive crack dealer in upstate New York, bedded many girls and young women—hundreds, by his own reckoning—and infected at least sixteen of them with HIV by the time he was arrested in 1997. Under New York's Romeo and Juliet exception, Williams could be prosecuted for statutory rape only for having sex with someone under the age of fourteen, which meant that the vast majority of his sexual conquests—most of whom were homeless runaways who remained loyal to him—carried no penalty. (Had he been twenty-one years old, the exception would not have applied.) He was convicted of one count of statutory rape and one count of reckless endangerment with, respectively, only the girls willing to testify against him.

Another sexual encounter that slipped through the cracks of a Romeo and Juliet exception concerned Genarlow Wilson, a seventeen-year-old student who, in 2003, had the misfortune of being videotaped while a fifteen-year-old girl performed fellatio on him at a party. As the sex was consensual, a Georgia jury absolved Wilson of forcible rape, but he was still convicted of "aggravated sexual assault on a minor." Because Wilson and the girl were close in age, the Romeo and Juliet exception would have reduced the penalties, but the law applied only to sexual intercourse, not oral sex. Wilson was sentenced to a mandatory minimum of ten years in prison and lifetime sex-offender status. Prosecutors had offered Wilson a plea bargain that would have carried a short prison sentence, but he still would have been marked as a sex offender, which would have barred him from contact with his younger sister.

The case drew widespread attention on account of the harshness of the sentence and what many saw as racist undertones in the prosecution: Wilson and the girl on the tape were both black. In 2006, Georgia reduced some of its penalties for oral sex among minors, but legislators refused to make the new law retroactive to benefit Wilson. Ugly litigation ensued, and after twice turning away Wilson's appeals, the state's supreme court finally released him, declaring that it was "cruel and unusual" to hold him after the law was changed.

Wilson's prosecution came on the heels of a big legislative push to beef up statutory rape laws, especially with regard to the poor population. In 1996, President Bill Clinton signed a wide-ranging welfare-reform measure—the Personal Responsibility and Work Opportunity Reconciliation Act—that urged states to "aggressively enforce statutory rape laws" and also directed the Justice Department to study the "link between statutory rape and teen pregnancy." After the law was passed, no fewer than ten states increased their statutory rape penalties. Starting in 2013, Mississippi went further by requiring doctors to harvest the umbilical cord blood of young birthing mothers where the father is over twenty-one or paternity is in question. Somehow, this gathering of evidence against male sex partners is supposed to reduce teen pregnancy. The law's focus is misplaced, however. In Mississippi's public schools, no methods of pregnancy prevention other than abstinence are taught.

If being black or poor leaves one susceptible to statutory rape charges, being gay is of no help either. In 2013 a love affair between eighteen-year-old Kaitlyn Hunt and a fifteen-year-old female classmate was discovered by the younger girl's parents, who pressed charges for two counts of "lewd and lascivious battery on a child age twelve to sixteen," crimes that can result in a prison sentence of thirty years. Florida prosecutors offered Hunt a plea deal that included two years of house arrest and registration as a sex offender, but she refused. As adverse publicity about the case, including charges of anti-gay bias, continued to build prosecutors offered her a more lenient deal. However, that offer was withdrawn and Hunt was jailed after it was discovered that she and her girlfriend had exchanged thousands of text messages as well as explicit videos and photos, despite the judge's order that they have no contact with each other. For good measure, Hunt was also charged with the crime of "transmission of material harmful to a minor by electronic equipment" —that is, sexting. She finally pled guilty to lesser charges and served several more months in jail. To the parents of the young girlfriend, Hunt did more than break the law: "She definitely took our daughter's innocence away," said her father. To the ACLU, Hunt's ordeal was part of a broad trend of "criminalizing teenagers," something "all too common, whether they are male or female, gay or straight." To Hunt, her girlfriend was a joy: "She could cheer you up in five minutes."

In Spain the age of consent is thirteen. In Germany, Italy, and Hungary, it is fourteen. In France, Sweden, and the Czech Republic, it is fifteen, and in the United Kingdom it is sixteen. In 1990, the Netherlands adopted a flexible system acknowledging the sexuality of adolescents between twelve and sixteen, but that also includes multiple safeguards against exploitation and abuse. Each of these countries has more liberal age-of-consent laws than most of those found in the US, which raises the question of whether those societies are less protective of their young. The answer is no. Strict rules prescribing harsh penalties for sex among ever-larger groups of people have only swelled jail populations and sex-offender registries. Denying and punishing the sexuality of teens has not then reduced adolescent sex; instead, it has made it more dangerous.

Targeting Young Children

In 1989, when Josh Gravens was twelve years old, he touched his eight-year-old sister's genitals. "It was experimentation," Gravens later said of the encounter, "and sadly my sister was a victim of that experimentation." Josh, however, paid a greater price. The same day Josh touched his sister, she told their mother, who then contacted a Christian counseling center near their Texas home for advice. That call sparked a chain reaction that no one, least of all Josh's family, anticipated or wanted, and that still continues. The counseling center immediately called the police to report the sexual assault of a child. Officers arrived at the Gravens home the next day and arrested Josh. He spent three and a half years in prison for aggravated child assault (sexual assaults of people under fourteen are all "aggravated" in Texas). There, because of his youth and the low regard in which prisoners hold sex criminals, his safety was always in jeopardy. Upon his release on parole in 2003, Gravens was placed on the state's public sex-offender registry—a searchable website accessible to anyone—until at least 2021. Additionally, his parents were ordered to lock him in his bedroom at night and put locks on his windows. If he needed to use the bathroom, he had to pound on his door until someone let him out.

Gravens attended high school after his release. He did well and was accepted by his peers, until a list of local sex offenders went out to neighbors. Overnight, everyone—classmates, friends, teachers—stopped speaking to him. That was painful, but it was even worse later, at Texas Tech University, when his picture appeared in a news story about sex offenders and he started to receive death threats. An anonymous note, telling him to leave school or be killed, appeared under his door. Men threw beer bottles at him from a passing truck, yelling: "Get out of our school, you child molester! I wish I could kill you!" He dropped out, but his subsequent life brought no relief.

Because of his status as a sex offender, jobs were short-lived when they were available at all. He was fired from his first job, at a construction company, after vigilante coworkers threatened to throw him off a tower. Landlord after landlord refused to rent apartments to him and his new family. He also racked up two additional felonies for failing to notify authorities promptly enough when he changed locations. (In one instance, he notified police after he moved rather than before.) Taking his kids to school, attending parent–teacher conferences, spending time in the park, the library, or any other place where children gathered were out of the question. As a registered sex offender, he was considered a danger, even to his own kids.

After a lengthy and sympathetic article about him appeared in 2012 in the *Texas Observer*, Gravens was able to persuade the court to take him off the sex-offender registry—something that is almost never done in Texas. He was also awarded a fellowship in 2013 to educate the Texas government and legal establishments about the harms of placing children on sex-offender registries. The aggravated sexual assault charge and the other two felonies remain on his criminal record.

Until Gravens had the rare good fortune of having his ordeals detailed in a respected publication, his case was fairly typical. According to a 2009 Justice Department analysis, more than one-third of those people "known to police" for committing sex offenses against minors are juveniles themselves. Half of them are between fifteen and seventeen years old, which at least puts them on the road to adult responsibility, but about one in eight are younger than twelve. Of the 17,835 sexual assault incidents reported in Texas in 2012, about 1,800 of the accused perpetrators were fourteen years old or younger. Baffling as it is, young kids—the very people society seeks so urgently to protect due to their vulnerability and their inability to make responsible decisions about sex—make up a substantial portion of those condemned as child predators.

How did this barbarity happen? Why have we criminalized and stigmatized young children for sex offenses, often for life? When did youthful sexual play and experimentation, something toddlers and children have always engaged in, become pathologized to the point of being equated with adult sex crimes? The answer to the last question is the late 1980s, when it was wrongly believed that youngsters with aggressive sexual tendencies were likely to become sexual predators as adults and when a vocal group of child-sexual-abuse researchers, therapists, and experts—whom the influential sociologist Howard S. Becker would call "moral crusaders" or "moral entrepreneurs"—started to push to broaden the definition of child sexual abusers to include children themselves.

It was an auspicious period for such an effort, as child abduction and sexual abuse were crowding the headlines and the world seemed to be under siege by deviant forces bent on the ruination of the young. This was the time when hundreds of adults (many of whom had been trusted operators of day-care centers and preschools) were put on trial for mangling and raping children in "satanic" sexual rituals, when the word "pedophile" entered the common lexicon, and when the US Congress heard testimony (by an "expert" in a major satanic sexual-abuse trial) about a worldwide network of pornographers, pedophiles, and day-care center operators who abducted children and used them in pornographic movies. It was when missing kids first appeared on milk cartons, when parents stopped letting their children walk to school or play outside, and when a senator sparked a burst of "public awareness that sexual abuse happens everywhere" by announcing that she had been molested as a child. The late 1980s was also when government money started to pour in for studies and measures against child sexual abuse, and when new child-protection bureaucracies sprang up everywhere.

Driven by the new institutional apparatus and the fast drumbeat of panic-inducing publicity about an "epidemic" in child sexual abuse, reports of such crimes jumped from about 6,000 in 1976 to about 350,000 in 1988. A Chicago television station circulated a pamphlet called *To Save a Child* that wrongly stated: "Nearly 2,000,000 children . . . disappear from their homes each year. Many end up raped, forced into prostitution and pornography." In Congress, it was announced, again incorrectly, that "4,000 to 8,000 missing children each year are found dead and probably a majority have experienced some type of sexual exploitation." Toy stores and fast-food restaurants distributed abduction-prevention materials. The Sharper Image catalog cashed in by selling anxious parents a special transmitter, called the Guardian Angel, to track children when they were absent—even from the house. New child-protection laws were passed at a fast clip, academic conferences were arranged, college courses were offered, and police task forces were deployed. What sociologist Joel Best called a "child abuse

establishment" came into being, with medical and psychological professionals, law enforcement, and protective agencies all enjoying increased
resources and broad spheres of influence. In turn, this new establishment
"became a base from which further claims-making could be staged," which
would, of course, further redound to its collective benefit.

In this heated environment, the traditional definition of child abuse—
adult neglect of, sexual contact with, or violence against children—came
to be seen as too narrow to catch all the horrors going on, and the language
of abuse loosened. In the space of a few years, the term was applied to virtually anything potentially harmful to children, including secondhand
smoke, tobacco use by pregnant women, violent and sexual rock lyrics,
circumcision, illicit drugs, inadequate social services, fervent religious education, and even the teaching of children to abide by traditional gender
roles. Parents who appeared nude in front of their children or slept with
them, and fathers who washed their young daughters' genitals in the bath,
came to be seen in some quarters as possible perpetrators of "emotional
sexual abuse," "emotional incest," "covert sexual abuse," and "seductive
sexual abuse," all of which, some experts opined, required state "intervention." Child abusers were suddenly everywhere, and soon no one—not
even children—would be free from suspicion.

During this period, some of those involved in promoting and profiting from the child-abuse panic raised the call to include children in the
pool of potential child sexual abusers. For example, in a 1988 paper titled
"Child Sexual Abuse: Very Young Perpetrators," published in the journal
Child Abuse and Neglect, Hendrika Cantwell, MD, expressed outrage that
kids under ten who engage in sexual play with each other were not being
"reported" or "investigated," and that "courts usually provide no assistance since society regards sexual play between children as innocent."
While Cantwell allowed that "it is not clear to what extent sexual play
among children is normal," she wrote that "evidence is mounting" that
"child perpetrators may be a large reservoir for future adult perpetrators."
Thus, families who don't allow authorities to interview suspect children
"may well be protecting [the family's] 'secrets,' allowing the child to grow
undisturbed into a perpetrator . . . and leaving a trail of victims who
are themselves at risk to imitatively perpetuate the abusive behavior."
In short, according to Cantwell, we don't know if what kids are doing is
normal, but it seems like it is not, so the law should step in.

Cantwell's article came at the same time as an influential series of articles by Toni Cavanaugh Johnson, a respected child-sexual-abuse therapist

and entrepreneur and a close associate of Kee MacFarlane, one of the most vocal "experts" promoting the satanic-ritual-abuse panic. In these articles, Johnson coined the terms "children who molest" and "child sexual abuser," and argued forcefully against the "denial and minimization of the seriousness of yet another population of [sex] offenders . . . children 13 years old and younger." Sounding the alarm that such children may engage in "even more serious perpetration behavior as they mature," Johnson warned that "the behavior of these child perpetrators must not be ignored any longer." Among other horrors, her articles referenced a seven-year-old girl who "molested" her twelve-year-old adopted brother, a case of "pathological" "sodomy" committed by a six-year-old against an eleven-year-old, and the "rape" of a ten-year-old girl by two six-year-old boys.

In a 1989 article discussing female "offenders" aged four to twelve who had "demonstrated developmentally inappropriate sexual behavior," Johnson complained,

> None of the girls . . . were filed on by the police, and therefore none were prosecuted. None of these girls ever spoke to a probation officer, and none of them were placed on probation. Child abuse reports were not filed. Not one of these children was mandated to treatment.
>
> While filing, criminal prosecution and involvement in the criminal justice and probation system may not be considered necessary for some of these child perpetrators, it should at least be considered. Not only does this type of intervention demonstrate to the girls the seriousness of their sexually abusive behavior, but it also makes their parents take heed of the behavior.

While Johnson had admitted earlier that standards "do not presently exist for what is normal sexual behavior of children," she nevertheless called the girls "perpetrators" of "serious offenses" who may be on a trajectory toward further offending as adults.

Perhaps sensing the trouble inherent in using these damning terms so loosely, Johnson cooked up her own checklists and standards of child sex pathology, which she still uses and sells, in various forms, in her own therapy and child-sexuality consulting business and which are widely employed when evaluating children. The problem is that these standards (which she later admitted were "never subjected to empirical verification") only muddy the picture further. Among the behaviors of kindergarteners through fourth-graders she describes as requiring "professional help" are "endless questions about sex after curiosity satisfied" and "telling 'dirty' jokes or making sexual sounds, even after exclusion from school and fun activities." Children under five are recommended for professional help when they, for example, "refuse to leave people alone in the bathroom" or use "dirty words" after "strong scoldings."

In criticizing this willy-nilly pathologizing of child "sexual" behavior, scholar Paul Okami noted in 1992 that under Johnson's standards, "virtually any" child sexual behaviors are subject to being labeled as abusive. Okami also pointed to the self-interest of "crusaders" like Cantwell, Mac-Farlane, and Johnson in pushing for expanded definitions of sexual abuse, as they stood to benefit from the "copious funds" flowing for research, prevention, and treatment. When, for example, Johnson demanded that "child perpetrators must not be ignored any longer," she was in effect arguing for a larger pool of clients and increased funding for the Support Program for Abuse Reactive Kids (SPARK), which she and MacFarlane had recently established and which was already receiving government support. The program, "one of the first . . . to treat sexual behavior problems among pre-adolescent children," has since received public grants to develop model treatment programs. In 2010, SPARK's umbrella organization used public money to launch a program that works with courts and other public authorities to, among other things, "help youth control their sexual impulses."

Cantwell, Johnson, and MacFarlane were in the vanguard of the movement to pathologize young children for sex abuse, but there were many other advocates. The Justice Department noted that there was a "surge of interest" in the subject starting in the 1980s, including hundreds of studies, a fortyfold jump in the number of juvenile sex-offender treatment programs from 1982 to 1992, and a broad "dissemination of information" about child sex offenders. Woven through all of this was the conviction that child perpetrators will continue to offend into adulthood. By the mid-1990s, despite the fact that there was no concrete definition of just what constitutes juvenile sexual misconduct, the idea that young kids could be branded as sex abusers had gone mainstream. In 1994, in the Princeton journal *The Future of Children*, scholar Judith Becker surveyed the available research and noted the presence of *five-year-old* children in a database of sex offenders.

The results of this movement were predictable: close behind the pathologizing of child sexual behavior came demands for aggressive responses by the law, which were amplified by community pressure to "get tough" on juvenile crime as a whole. The law responded with increasingly punitive measures. Not only are children like Josh Gravens now being arrested and imprisoned, they are registered as sex offenders. By 2009, thirty-six states had laws requiring sex-offender registration for juveniles, with only a few exempting children younger than twelve. Even worse, Congress, in the 2006 Adam Walsh Child Protection and Safety Act, required sex-offender registration of all people fourteen and older who, like Gravens, commit "aggravated sexual assaults." Some juveniles must continue to register with law enforcement every few months for their entire lives.

Gravens's sex-offender status was lifted, but that small measure of mercy is the exception that proves the rule. The lamentable fact is that children are being treated as sex criminals for doing what kids have always done:

- In 1996, a neurologically impaired twelve-year-old who groped his younger stepbrother in the bath was required to register as a sex offender.

- In 1999, police busted a child "sex ring" in Pennsylvania, in which kids as young as seven "taught each other to have sex." Six of them were convicted of charges including rape and indecent assault at a girl's sleepover party and outdoors. These criminal dens were so impregnable that detectives used an "elaborate investigation" to infiltrate them.

- In 2001, an eleven-year-old Minnesota boy was required to register as a "predatory sex offender" for life after he had sex with an eight-year-old girl; that same year, a twelve-year-old Illinois boy was put on the sex-offender registry for life for having sexual contact with other boys.

- In 1993, after spending two years in a California jail for proposing sex with his sister when he was fourteen, a boy escaped and tried to return to his father. He was chased by SWAT teams as police loudspeakers warned local residents that a dangerous sex offender was on the loose.

- In Texas, a twelve-year-old boy who mooned some five- and six-year-old children was placed on the state's sex-offender registry.

- In 1996, an eleven-year-old boy who "admitted" to penetrating his cousin was placed on the New Jersey sex-offender registry for life, despite a therapist's opinion that he had a learning disability and did not understand the terms "sex," "rape," or "penetration" when he made the admission.

- In 2000, in New Jersey, a twelve-year-old boy inserted a "douche" in his six-year-old half brother's anus. When asked why he did it, he replied: "I don't know." He subsequently pled guilty to aggravated sexual assault and was sent to a juvenile placement center. After incarceration, he was required to register as a sex offender for life.

- Dominic G. was charged in 2006 with molesting his sister when he was fourteen and she was twelve. When Dominic turned twenty-one, he was released from jail and placed on the sex-offender registry, after which his sister admitted that she had lied under pressure from police. "He never touched me," she said. "[The police] kept telling me that I was going to jail if I didn't tell the story right." Not long afterward, Dominic slashed his wrists. His frantic grandmother, knowing that he could not go to the hospital without permission, called his parole officer, who threatened to have him arrested unless he went to the parole office first to sign papers. They complied, and Dominic spent two weeks in the hospital.

The stories go on endlessly and show no sign of letting up. At least six countries besides the US have sex-offender registries, but none allow such a wide inclusion of kids. The heavy weight of criminal liability not only drops kids into the inferno of the justice system, it also disrupts efforts toward therapy and rehabilitation. If, for example, a child offender is in therapy, anything he or she divulges about other sexual activity may result in more charges and further penalties. Moreover, if a therapist keeps the child's confessions confidential, then he or she may be exposed to legal action for not reporting sex crimes.

Matters have clearly gotten out of hand. Even if a child's sexual behavior may signal future antisocial conduct, the policies of punishment and shame have, as observed by social worker and sex-offender specialist Christopher Lobanov-Rostovsky, only "increased the youth's risk of stigmatization, peer rejection and isolation from families and home communities," which in turn "aggravate rather than mitigate subsequent risk." Moreover, in the short time since Johnson et al. complained that "children who molest" were slipping through the law's cracks, sound research has refuted the utility of treating kids as sex criminals. It is now widely agreed that children who experiment with sex are not a "reservoir" of future "adult perpetrators." The truth is that they have a very low risk of reoffending, so placing them on sex-offender registries does not protect communities. In 2013, Human Rights Watch issued a thorough and blistering report detailing the problems of registering youths as sex offenders and recommending that the practice be stopped. The report should be mandatory reading for any lawmaker calling for "get tough" measures against juvenile sex crimes.

● ● ●

What now? Johnson, for one, has stepped back from her earlier positions. In an article she coauthored called "Children Twelve and Younger with Sexual Behavior Problems: What We Know in 2005 That We Didn't Know in 1985," she argues that "children should not be judged by adult standards regarding their sexual behaviors." She also maintains that using the words "victim" and "perpetrator" to describe children is misleading and might have unfair legal consequences, especially given that abnormal sexual behavior in young kids is not necessarily abusive. Most significantly, Johnson now expresses deep concern about young children being marked as sex offenders: "Since there is no empirical evidence . . . that children who molest . . . will continue to sexually offend . . . it is cruel and unusual punishment to condemn them to a lifetime stigma as a sex offender." Johnson reaffirmed this position in 2013, wisely adding: "Most adults would not want to be labeled for life for their childhood sexual behaviors, no matter how serious."

This is a much different Toni Johnson than the activist who complained that "child perpetrators" had not been sent to the police. While Johnson should be commended, the fact is that her earlier positions—and those of others who called for harsh treatment of sexually misbehaving children—are now woven into the law and cannot be undone readily. In surveys, up to 92 percent of judges have expressed concern about placing juveniles on sex-offender lists, but the law gives them little room for discretion or mercy. In the current political climate, it would take a brave group of lawmakers to risk accusations of being "soft on child molesters" by advocating change to the law, but stranger things have happened. After all, just a few decades ago, we started to treat seven- and eight-year-olds as sex criminals.

Kids as Prey: Sexual Psychopaths and Pedophiles

Peter Lorre's bug-eyed facial expressions, Mitteleuropean accent, and fey mannerisms were the butt of jokes throughout his cinematic career. The diminutive actor is now remembered chiefly as a small-time crook and comic foil in classics such as *Casablanca* and *The Maltese Falcon*, but Lorre's first starring film role, in Fritz Lang's *M* (1931), scared the daylights out of audiences. As Hans Beckert, a tortured Berlin loner who lures little girls with candy and balloons and then kills them for a few moments' sexual gratification, Lorre was an avatar of a Depression-era public menace that, judging by the spike in newspaper coverage and resulting hysteria, was thought to be waiting in every shadow for a chance to abduct, molest, and kill children: the sexual psychopath.

After killing eight girls, Beckert is captured by a band of thieves, who set up a kangaroo court to put him on trial and punish him. Hysterical, Beckert begs them for understanding:

> I can't help myself! I have no control over this, this evil thing inside of me, the fire, the voices, the torment! It's there all the time, driving me out to wander the streets . . . I can't escape, I have to obey it!

The "judges" are unimpressed with this argument, but Beckert's psychological condition lived on as the target of a spate of new laws that remained in force long after *M* left the movie houses. The laws, mostly written by the psychiatric community, defined the sexual psychopath as one who was not necessarily insane but whose "utter lack of power to control his sexual impulses" made him likely to attack "the objects of his uncontrolled and uncontrollable desires." At the end of *M*, after Beckert has been tried by a legitimate court, the grieving mother of one of his victims laments that nothing can bring back the dead children. She then closes the film with this admonition to the audience: "One has to keep closer watch over the children. . . . All of you!" The sexual-psychopath laws were meant to keep sexual psychopaths off the streets and in jails and mental hospitals—forever, if necessary.

As with the other bogeymen in twentieth-century sex-crime panics—including the white-slavery panic, the alarm over "predatory" homosexuals, the satanic-ritual-abuse panic of the 1980s, and the recent sex-trafficking scares—the sexual psychopath was thought to target children. In just a few years, spurred by fears of a sex-crime "wave" relentlessly promoted by the *New York Times* and other newspapers, Peter Lorre's lone pervert had become an omnipresent source of terror in American cities. In 1937, FBI director J. Edgar Hoover claimed that "the sex fiend, the most loathsome of all the vast army of crime, has become a sinister threat to the safety of American childhood and womanhood." In a later article called "How Safe Is Your Daughter?"—which was printed with the image of a giant male hand about to snatch three adorable little girls—Hoover declared that "the most rapidly increasing type of crime is that perpetuated by the degenerate sex offender," and added: "Should wild beasts break out of circus cages, a whole city would be mobilized instantly. But depraved human beings, more savage than beasts, are permitted to rove America almost at will."

Hoover could take credit as the single-most influential person driving the sex-crime hysteria, but he was simply wrong on the facts. The sexual-psychopath panics of the 1930s and later decades were not driven by a rise in severe sex crimes. Arrests for sexual offenses always shoot up during sex panics, but they are usually for minor, consensual, or less violent transgressions. However, as observed by sociologist Edward Sutherland, "Fear is seldom or never related to statistical trends in sex crimes." All it takes is a few sufficiently gruesome and well-publicized attacks, and a sex-crime "wave" is born. In New York in 1937, there were sensational sexual attacks on, and murders of, four girls, a shock repeated the same year in California, where lynch mobs formed in response to the murder of three girls. In 1949, during a frenzied week in which police searched for Fred Stroble, the killer of a six-year-old girl found on a Los Angeles rubbish heap, dozens of molestation reports rolled in to law-enforcement officials, while the *Saturday Evening Post* reported—with no substantiation—that "at least tens of thousands" of "sex killers" were "loose in the country today."

In each of these (and other similar) episodes, citizens demanded measures to stop the carnage and lock up offenders, and politicians gladly obliged. Resolutions were adopted, blue-ribbon panels put to work, experts consulted, and studies made. Inevitably, broad "tough" laws were passed, money allocated, and police mobilized. During the 1930s panic, five states passed sexual-psychopath laws; in the second wave, between 1947 and 1955, twenty-one more states and the District of Columbia joined in with laws of their own; and by the 1960s, thirty states had such laws.

A common feature of the sexual-psychopath laws is their targeting of a personality type rather than a species of crime. Regardless of whether the targets were charged with exhibitionism, sodomy, or child rape, the laws allowed them to be confined indefinitely in state mental hospitals or psychiatric wards until a psychiatrist declared them no longer a menace. Some states didn't require a conviction before committing someone, while others went further and allowed people to be locked up without even being charged. All it took was a psychiatric evaluation.

The omnipresence of psychiatrists was no accident. As they often had a hand in writing the laws, the problems and solutions were framed in psychiatric terms. Psychiatrists also stood to benefit from both the diagnosis and treatment of psychopaths and the research money allocated to study sexual pathology. Observed Sutherland in 1950: "The psychiatrists, more than any others, have been the interest group [behind] the laws." Illinois's sexual-psychopath law, for example, was drafted by a committee of psychiatrists and neurologists. In 1934, Ohio psychiatrists were unable to secure funding for the separate treatment of psychopathic criminals. A few years later, following a rash of newspaper articles on rampaging sex offenders, the laws were changed to allow the indefinite commitment of presumed psychopaths to state mental hospitals.

The sexual psychopath thus became what anthropologist Roger Lancaster calls the "shared province" of law enforcement and psychiatry, which solidified psychiatrists' authority within the criminal-justice system and augmented their considerable popular mystique. Noting that Chicago had added one thousand cops to its police force after the 1946 abduction and death of a little girl, the *Saturday Evening Post* opined that the money had been ill spent: "Fifty psychiatrists, backed by sensible laws, could do more to halt crime waves in a city like Chicago than 5,000 extra policemen could."

Immediately following the Stroble drama, California governor Earl Warren summoned a panel of psychiatrists for advice. They suggested that every sex offender be examined by a psychiatrist, psychologist, or criminologist for "classification for correction or treatment," and that the state immediately start funding the research and training of psychological and other personnel. Research money began flowing almost immediately, as did funds for a civil commitment program created by the new sexual-psychopath laws. The laws also sparked a boom in construction of specialized mental institutions, including California's $10 million Atascadero facility. There, patient-offenders became human guinea pigs for trendy new treatments such as insulin, electroconvulsive therapy, sterilization, and—in a surprising number of cases—frontal lobotomies.

By the 1960s, what had begun as an effort to use psychiatry to neutralize child molesters had become a hodgepodge of rules more effective at locking away oddballs and unpopular minorities than protecting kids. In fact, most of the cases under the laws had nothing to do with children. Some examples:

- New Jersey's law in 1950 allowed indefinite commitment to a mental hospital for possession of obscene literature or "indecent" communications with females.

- In 1952, a young District of Columbia man was placed in a mental hospital for fifteen years for his "tendency to indecently expose himself in public." Had he not been declared a sexual psychopath, he would have spent, at most, ninety days in jail. After his release in 1967, a judge again put him in the hospital for indecent exposure, even though the examining psychiatrists thought it wasn't necessary to do so.

- Soon after New Jersey's law was passed, a homosexual man was committed to a mental hospital after he passed a bad check.

- A New Jersey black man was committed for following (but not touching or even approaching) a white woman.

- In 1943, a Minnesota father of six was hospitalized as a sexual psychopath after he committed unspecified "sexual excesses . . . upon his wife." He challenged the commitment in court, claiming he was not dangerous, but he lost. A medical expert had determined that his "craving for sexual intercourse and self-abuse by masturbation" was, if unsatisfied, "like steam under pressure." As his wife was no longer available to help him let off steam, the expert believed he might molest other women, even though he had never done so before. The record stops there, but it is likely that he stayed in the hospital until he was able to convince doctors that he no longer "craved" sexual release.

With results like these, the laws became increasingly difficult to defend. By the 1960s, they were criticized by both the legal and medical communities. The core of the problem, as critics saw it, was the impossibility of arriving at a consistent definition of "sexual psychopath" and applying it fairly. In his influential 1962 book *Sex and the Law*, Judge Morris Ploscowe wrote that the laws "fail miserably" at separating dangerous offenders from minor ones, mainly because psychopathic personalities are "elusive even to psychiatrists." The Group for the Advancement of Psychiatry further cautioned that "psychiatric knowledge and terminology are in a state of flux." Once a term like "sexual psychopath" is burned into the law, it "attains a fixity unresponsive to newer scientific knowledge." In other words, psychiatric thinking constantly changes, and it is a mistake to write laws based on a moment's snapshot of research. In 1977 the group went even further, stating that the laws "have failed." By this time, the higher courts were ready to join in. In truth, opined a prominent appellate judge in 1969, the whole system had become "what is essentially a warehousing operation for social misfits." The following year Michigan, which had been the first state to adopt a sexual-psychopath law, also became the first to abolish the legal category of "criminal sexual psychopath." The laws fell into disuse, and before long only about a dozen states even kept them on the books.

• • •

The demise of the sexual psychopath in the 1960s and 1970s, and the events that followed, call to mind Jean-Paul Sartre's remark about Jews: if they did not exist, their enemies would have to invent them. As an object of visceral, irrational fear, the sexual psychopath had become outmoded—but the need for such a monster remained. To fill the vacuum a new menace had to be invented. During this period's tumult of changing mores and sexual habits, the same pattern of isolated crimes and grotesque overreaction would repeat itself. A new series of scares would spark even more draconian measures against what was feared to be a vaster army of child predators. The old sexual-psychopath laws were written against isolated drifters and freaks. The law's new targets included the trusted next-door neighbor, teacher, doctor, coach, clergyman, relative, and even, as we have seen, kids themselves. Essentially, anyone who had contact with children came under suspicion as a potential pedophile and child abuser. Yet before this kind of threat could be embraced, the ground had to be softened with a public education effort and a new vocabulary.

Prior to the late 1970s, there was little available to read about child sexual abuse, but in the ensuing years an avalanche of material crowded the shelves of bookstores and university libraries. Examples include, *The Sexual Assault of Children and Adolescents* (1978), *Sexually Victimized Children* (1979), *Betrayal of Innocence* (1979), *The Best-Kept Secret* (1982), *Child Sexual Abuse* (1984), and *Father-Daughter Incest* (1981). All of them, by varying degrees, added to the profile of the omnipresent army of child molesters walking undetected in our midst. To meet a threat of this breadth, and to understand it, an augmented institutional apparatus was required. Organizations dedicated to protecting children started to spring up. They included, in 1976, the International Society for the Prevention of Child Abuse and Neglect. In 1984, the newly created National Center for Missing and Exploited Children (NCMEC) started working with government agencies to, among other things, "eliminate child sexual exploitation and prevent child victimization," and in the process became a dominant force in disseminating extreme claims about child endangerment.

That same year, the Justice Department sponsored a national symposium on child molestation. As awareness rose that child sexual abuse took place on all social strata, new mandatory reporting laws swelled abuse statistics, and amid the noise of news stories about pedophile rings, child pornography, and kiddie "snuff" films, the conviction grew that all children were at risk all the time. Then, just as in the 1930s, a rash of murders kicked the late-century child-sexual-abuse panics into high gear.

The NCMEC was formed in response to several horrifying abduction/ murders, including those committed by John Wayne Gacy, who was arrested in 1978 and charged with the rape and murder of thirty-three boys and young men; the 1979 disappearance of six-year-old Etan Patz from a New York City street; and the 1981 abduction from a Florida shopping mall of six-year-old Adam Walsh, whose decapitated head (but not his body) was later found. Each of these (and other) murders triggered seismic waves of fear, but it was their sexual elements that drove public discourse, even when there was no evidence of sexual molestation. For example, no one was ever arrested for Walsh's murder; nor was there evidence of sexual assault. Nevertheless, Walsh's father (later to become the host of the television program *America's Most Wanted*) spread the rumor that his son had been abudcted by a pedophile—a story that, through incessant repetition, came to be accepted as fact. In 2006, Adam Walsh's name was given to a major piece of federal legislation intended, among other things, to "protect children from sexual exploitation and violent crime [and] to prevent child abuse and child pornography."

Fact is invariably followed or replaced by fancy in sex-crime scares—the more bizarre, the better. The fear caused by these murders was brought to a boil by thousands of charges against day-care center and preschool operators for the "satanic ritual abuse" of small children. To say the charges were outlandish is to say way too little. They included the rape of children with knives; animal mutilations; forced participation in pornographic films; forced consumption of blood, urine, and feces; children thrown in water with sharks; and baby sacrifices—all in service of Satan and taking place at the facilities, in secret tunnels and chambers, on boats, and in hot-air balloons. How any of these charges ever gained credibility is stupefying, but they did. Fanned by unrelenting news coverage, the cases quickly metastasized into a full-blown international panic.

In 1988, Margaret Kelly Michaels was convicted of urinating in the mouths of three- to five-year-olds and sexually abusing them with kitchenware and peanut butter at the Wee Care Day Nursery in Maplewood, New Jersey. None of the kids showed any signs of injury, but they were cajoled and coerced into saying they had been molested. Six years later, Michaels's conviction was overturned and she was released from prison. At the Little Rascals Day Care Center in North Carolina, five workers were accused in 1989 of molesting and murdering babies, in addition to rape, fellatio, and sodomy of children. On evidence provided by kids whose memories had been "refreshed" through months of "therapy," one of the defendants, Bob Kelley, was given twelve life sentences. That conviction was also later overturned. A panic in Martensville, Saskatchewan, began when a woman who ran a day-care center and babysitting service came under suspicion. Eventually, more than one hundred accusations were made against twelve people, including five police officers, concerning a satanic cult called the Brotherhood of the Ram, which supposedly sexually abused children at something called the Devil Church. The day-care center owner's son was found guilty, but authorities later concluded that the original investigation was motivated by emotional hysteria. In 2014, day-care center operators Frances and Dan Keller were freed after more than two decades in prison. Based on coerced stories from children, unqualified expert testimony, and weak physical evidence, they were accused of running a business at which babies, dogs, and cats were torn apart in front of children; children were transported to Mexico to be sexually abused by soldiers there; blood was put in children's Kool-Aid; and children were forced to carry the bones of bodies exhumed at a cemetery.

The mother of all the satanic-ritual-abuse cases arose out of the McMartin Preschool in the Los Angeles suburb of Manhattan Beach, where an accusation by a mentally unbalanced mother of a two-year-old set off a panic that resulted in one of the longest and most expensive trials in US history. In 1983, Judy Johnson (later diagnosed as a paranoid schizophrenic) claimed that Ray Buckey, son of the school's administrator, Peggy McMartin Buckey, had sodomized her son. Those accusations soon grew into claims that Ray Buckey had sodomized the boy while his head was in a toilet, among other things. Buckey was arrested, parents were notified about possible sex crimes at the school, and accusations started to mount. Before long, the police handed much of their mushrooming investigation over to Kee MacFarlane, who interviewed about 400 kids and concluded that more than 350 of them had been abused.

MacFarlane's methods of interviewing the kids were, to put it lightly, aggressive. In response to one eight-year-old boy who told her that he had not seen anyone playing a "naked movie star" game at the school, she said: "What good are you? You must be dumb." The boy then changed his mind. MacFarlane became a central expert witness in the case and a celebrity in her own right. In September 1984, she appeared before Congress as an expert in the treatment of sexually abused children. There she stunned the audience by announcing her suspicion that a wide network of child predators used day-care centers as covers for child pornography operations. She also said that the McMartin Preschool "serves as a ruse for a larger unthinkable network of crimes against children," which "may have greater financial, legal, and community resources at its disposal than those attempting to expose it."

By the time the Buckeys were indicted on 354 counts involving about as many alleged victims, it was common belief that their school was a modern vampire castle replete with dungeons, tunnels, and kids living out scenes from Hieronymus Bosch paintings. No physical evidence was ever found—no blood, bruises, or cuts; no semen; no pornography involving the kids; no sacrificed animals or babies. However, that stopped nothing. The trial got under way in 1987, the same year in which television host Geraldo Rivera claimed, in a special broadcast, that more than a million satanists were plying their trade in the US *right at that very moment.*

MacFarlane and several confused kids were star witnesses. Two years of convulsive trial proceedings later, Peggy McMartin Buckey was acquitted—but the jury was deadlocked on thirteen charges against Ray Buckey. Still, about 90 percent of respondents to a poll believed the accusations, and prosecutors, responding to pressure from parents, took him to trial again. In 1990, the jury deadlocked a second time. By that time Ray

Buckey had spent five years in jail, and prosecutors had spent $15 million of public money. By 1989, MacFarlane's Children's International Institute had received $11 million in government grants and her associate, Toni Cavanaugh Johnson, was starting up a campaign to recognize young children as a new population of child molesters.

With each sensational trial, article, book, and television program about abused children, calls grew louder for the law to do something—*any-thing*—to stop pedophiles. However, there was one problem: the pedophile was easy to fear but impossible to define. While killers like Gacy fit the traditional mold of the lone, sex-crazed child murderer, experts emphasized that pedophiles were often ordinary men and women, even members of a victim's family or inner circle. (For his part, Malcolm Gladwell recently wrote: "The pedophile is often imagined as the disheveled old man offering candy to preschoolers. But the truth is that most of the time we have no clue who we are dealing with.") While such warnings increased the general level of terror and suspicion, they gave no useful guidance to parents or the legal system. Without a working profile of a pedophile (or "child sexual abuser," "child abuser," "sex offender," "child molester," "child rapist," or "victimizer"—all terms used interchangeably with "pedophile"), parents didn't know who to avoid, police didn't know who to chase, and lawmakers couldn't write workable rules. Again, the law turned to the professionals for guidance, and again it got nothing but confusion in return.

Along with the innumerable publications on pedophilia came as many explanations of who pedophiles are and what they do. Depending on whom one listened to and when, a pedophile could be: an adult who masturbates—even once—while thinking about a child; one who has watched child pornography; one who has had sex with anyone under the age of eighteen or sixteen; one who has had contact with a minor who then feels sexually abused; one who desires sex with people under the age of eighteen, even if it never takes place; one who makes verbal propositions to a minor; one who "watches" children but does not touch them; a minor who has sex; and so on. There is even something called corporate paedophilia, which the Australia Institute calls the marketing of products using children in sexually suggestive ways.

With each twist on the definition, new questions arise. For example, if, as has been true in Virginia since 2008, adults who "French kiss" kids under thirteen are so dangerous that they are put on the sex-offender registry, are non-Virginians who do the same also dangerous? What about those who French-kissed kids before 2008? And if the law is repealed, will they no longer be dangerous? There are no consistent answers. In fact, after all the efforts of professionals over the past few decades, there is no universal definition of child sexual abuse.

The issue is more than just theoretical. Absent a clear idea of who child molesters are and what constitutes child sexual abuse, it is impossible to predict whether someone will abuse kids in the future. Even if, for example, one has completed a jail sentence for raping or tongue-kissing a minor, we still don't know whether it makes sense to warn communities that the offender lives nearby, to bar the offender from the company of children, or to keep the offender under lock and key. Will the child rapist rape again? Will the tongue-kisser repeat the crime or do something worse? According to two Canadian experts, Andrew John Rawson Harris and R. Karl Hanson, sex-crime "risk assessments" over the past two decades have been so problematic, and have changed so often, that the task of developing better ones has been "like rebuilding a ship at sea, continually replacing one plank at a time when we sprang a leak."

Between 2003 and 2008, an average of 176 risk assessment–related papers were published each year. As none of these assessments has become standardized, hundreds of thousands of convicted sex offenders around the world have been evaluated according to inconsistent and often conflicting standards. In a 2013 article titled "The Science of Sex Abuse," the journalist Rachel Aviv noted that the current methods used to predict someone's potential for reoffending work "about as well as the S.A.T. forecasts freshman grades. Neither correlation is particularly strong." Nevertheless, we accept them, even if they "confer a stamp of scientific precision on a judgment that psychologists have proved ill-equipped to make." In fact, as a prominent psychiatrist told Aviv, there is *no* research showing that abnormal sexual desires are any harder to control than normal ones. "Psychiatry," said the psychiatrist, "is being co-opted by the criminal justice system to solve a problem that is moral, not medical."

Sex-Offender Registries

For a society binging on a supersized diet of fear, no measure against an enemy is severe enough—but we are getting close. In addition to long prison terms, we now have a matrix of sex-offender registry laws mandating that offenders be publicly exposed, closely tracked, and ostracized.

The rules are always adopted under the banner of protecting children from pedophiles, but in application they veer far from that goal. With courts deferring to grandstanding legislators, the sex-offender registry system now encompasses not only genuine sex criminals but also people who pose no danger to anyone. With agonizing names like Adam, Jacob, Megan, Amber, Jessica, Carlie, and Samantha—all child victims of horrible crimes—the registries have now ensnared more than three-quarters of a million people in the US, too few of whom meet anyone's idea of dangerous.

Sex-offender registries were created in the late 1930s as a resource for police to keep track of the "usual suspects" in sex crimes. In 1937, New York mayor Fiorello La Guardia ordered police to make a list of "all known de-generates," including those convicted of sex crimes in the previous twenty years. Chicago did the same, as did Los Angeles, where in 1938 police started to catalog sex offenders' photographs, fingerprints, psychiatric eval-uations, and descriptions of their criminal "methods." California was first to set up a statewide registry, in 1947, requiring anyone convicted of one of eleven crimes (mostly concerned with young victims) to register with police. Over the next twenty years, California's modest example was followed by Alabama, Arizona, Illinois, and Nevada. None of the lists were public.

There matters stood until the 1990s, when a spate of new laws changed everything. In 1994, Congress passed a law named after a Minnesota boy, Jacob Wetterling, who had been abducted by an armed, masked man while he was riding his bicycle. The Wetterling Act established a na-tional database of sex offenders and encouraged states to create their own registries. By the end of the decade, every state had done so. In 1996, in response to the abduction, rape, and murder of seven-year-old Megan Kanka by a neighbor with a record for sex crimes, Congress required that communities be notified of the presence of "potentially dangerous sex of-fenders." Under Megan's Law and its subsequent amendments, commu-nity notification systems proliferated rapidly everywhere. By 2006, all states had registries accessible to the public, in whole or in part, on the Internet. That same year saw the passage of the Adam Walsh Act, which mandates registration for indecent exposure, kidnapping, false imprison-ment of a child, public urination, rape, incest, indecency with a child by touching, and possession of child pornography.

These are just a few of the new laws. States and cities have joined in with their own crowd-pleasers. In 2006, for example, California voters over-whelmingly passed Jessica's Law, which was named after a nine-year-old girl who had been raped and murdered by a sex offender. This law requires that felony sex offenders (whether dangerous or not) be tracked by GPS monitors for their entire lives. They also may not live within two thousand feet of a school or a park, which makes most populated areas off-limits. These restrictions have been widely duplicated, and cities have added more rules such as barring offenders from living near bus stops. Many cities are also building "pocket parks": tiny spots of green to mark additional radii in which sex offenders cannot live. In Los Angeles, for example, a park of less than one thousand square feet was built for this purpose, and more are in the works. The park is too small to use, but relieved residents love it. "I think it's great," said Patti O'Connell, who lives near the park. "It's scary that there's sex offenders all around with all these little kids here."

If the laws were tailored to keep people like the killers of Jessica, Adam, Megan, and Jacob away from children, then O'Connell's comment would be well-founded. But the laws go much further than that, and in any event, recidivism rates for sex offenders of all types, violent or not, are extremely low. No less important than the laws' ineffectiveness at stopping future crime is the affirmative harm they cause. The lives of hundreds of thousands of people (and, often, their families) are damaged, if not ruined, to address sex-crime scares they had no part in creating. In the process, the painful memories of the children commemorated by the laws are trivialized more than they are honored.

Keeping in mind the horrific sexual crimes against Jessica, Megan, and the others, one should ask whether any such threats are implicated in the following scenarios:

- In 1986, in Massachusetts, Juan Matamorous urinated near a parked car while celebrating the birth of his daughter. He was charged and convicted of "lewd and lascivious behavior." Twenty-one years later, this mishap came back to haunt him in Florida when he and his family were forced to leave their home because his neighborhood was off-limits to sex offenders.

- In Miami, where sex offenders cannot live within twenty-five hundred feet of a school, day-care center, or park, as many as 140 homeless sex offenders were forced to live under a bridge in 2009. There was nowhere else for them to go. However, at least they were out of jail. In New York City, sex-offender-residency restrictions now include homeless shelters. As a result, dozens of offenders who have served their sentences are being held in prison, because there is nowhere else to put them.

• In South Carolina, Dean Weisart was required to register as a sex offender because he had been caught, more than two decades earlier, skinny-dipping with his girlfriend in a hotel pool.

• As of 2010, anyone who robs a minor in Georgia is automatically put on the state's registry of sex offenders. The state's supreme court was unconcerned that sex has nothing to do with robbery, as requiring robbers to register still meets the goal of "protecting children from those who harm them." The ruling added: "The fact that [a robber's] offense did not involve sexual activity is of no consequence."

• In Illinois, in 2002, a man who kidnapped his granddaughter for ransom but who committed no sexual offense against her was required to register as a sex offender because there was the "possibility" that the child would have been sexually molested. Thus one can be marked for life as a sex offender because of the *opportunity* to commit a sex crime, even though it never happened.

With variations depending on where they live, people of sex-offender registries have all been banished from their communities. Many are also forced to disclose their Internet passwords, usernames, and telephone numbers to police. They are required to submit to searches of their personal computers and monitoring of their Internet usage, and their employment and housing opportunities are limited. Some laws bar them from opening their doors to kids on Halloween.

Again, if the sex-offender rules prevented sex crimes they might be defensible—but they do not. After an exhaustive 2011 study at the University of Chicago, researcher Amanda Agan concluded:

I find little evidence to support the effectiveness of sex offender registries, either in practice or in potential. Rates of sex offense do not decline after the introduction of a registry or public access to a registry via the Internet, nor do sex offenders appear to recidivate less when released into states with registries. . . . There is little information one can infer from knowing that a sex offender lives on one's block.

Other studies have shown similar results. One in New Jersey in 2008 found that sexual-offense rates, on a downward trend since 1985, declined fastest before 1994 (the year registration laws were passed) and slowest after 1995 (the year registration laws were implemented). In another major study, in 2011, researchers found that the registries may actually *increase* sex-offender recidivism because the burdens they put on sex offenders' lives "offset the benefits to offenders of forgoing criminal activity."

So why are we doing this? Why does the law still run a "race to the harshest" treatment of sex offenders when so little of value is being accomplished? The first answer is ignorance. When, for example, Patti O'Connell said that a pocket park made her neighborhood safe from sex offenders, she apparently believed the term applied only to those who prey on small children. Her last personal involvement with the issue was likely in 2006, in the wake of saturation news coverage about the rape and murder of Jessica Lunsford, when voters passed Jessica's Law. Jessica had been attacked by a convicted sex offender, so voters concluded that the law would keep such killers away from kids. Only deep in the thickets of the law's fine print was it revealed that people convicted of public urination, streaking, sexting, and consensual teen sex were also included. Those who voted for Jessica's Law also could not have known that its residency restrictions would lead to one-third of the state's paroled sex offenders being homeless, making them even more difficult to track and raising a host of new public-safety risks.

"There's not a shred of research that supports residence restrictions," said Tom Tobin, who as vice chairman of California's Sex Offender Management Board knows what he is talking about. Addressing the fallout from Jessica's Law, Tobin added: "We do things that are not so wise, because we want to do something"—which brings us to the next reason for harsh sex-offender laws. If a threat is scary enough, society has consistently proven itself capable of doing unwise things so long as something is *done*—and done aggressively. That the threat to children from registered sex offenders is miniscule, and that the rules don't prevent sex crime, simply doesn't matter. In voicing support for Jessica's Law, California's governor Arnold Schwarzenegger, cannily, didn't say what the law would do. Rather, he stoked fear. In one radio broadcast, he asked: "What kind of a society do we create here when we cannot even let the children go out on the playground, and you always have to worry about them getting abducted and sexually molested and all those things?" So long as our inquiries stop at rhetorical questions and we don't also look at what exactly we are doing to address our worries, bad laws will continue to pile up.

Molesters in Plain Sight

More than 90 percent of child sexual abuse occurs not at the hands of strangers skulking around parks or schools, but at the hands of people walking into children's lives through the front door: family, family friends, close acquaintances. Therefore, the key justification for sex-offender registries—to announce the presence of offenders to communities—doesn't apply to most child molesters. We see this in stark relief when we look at the recent scandals involving the clergy, sports coaches, teachers, Boy Scout leaders, and others who have access to minors in close settings. Like most large enterprises, the Catholic Church, schools and universities, and others value their own survival and prestige more than they are willing to condemn wrongdoing by their individual members, even when sexual molestation is concerned.

The Catholic sex-abuse cases—involving, by the church's own count, more than six thousand clerics "not implausibly" or "credibly" accused by more than seventeen thousand victims in the US alone—will smolder in the courts and in the hearts of victims at least for our lifetimes. Litigation has been going on for some time, with over $3 billion in settlements paid out, but the church's defensive imperative remains. Despite Pope Francis's gestures in 2014 highlighting his "zero tolerance" for sex abuse by priests, the church will never make itself fully accountable for the malignant liberties taken by its members on minors in their care. Nor will the church likely purge itself of the high-level enablers who protect them—not when the Holy See still withholds data on priest abuse, imposes what the UN's Committee on the Rights of the Child calls a "code of silence" on clergy members, bars its members from reporting child abusers to the law, and "moves child abusers around the world in a shell game designed to cover up the crimes."

The full scope and implications of the Catholic Church child sexual-abuse scandals go beyond the brief of this book, but it should be noted that most sexually abusive priests in the US have avoided the sex-offender laws. Most of the accusations against them have not been formally proven, and many of the offenders have never been publicly identified. The very few convicted of child sex abuse have been put on sex-offender registries, but others—whose cases haven't gone to court but who have been removed from the ministry—have vanished, their fates often a mystery to their victims, their parishioners, and even their attorneys. If this is because the church was complicit in shielding them from justice, then the church should be condemned. As observed by the UN Committee on the Rights of the Child: "The practice of offenders' mobility has allowed many priests to remain in contact with children and to continue to abuse them." However, every case is different and, as disturbing as the accusations typically are, the presumption of innocence still applies to priests. If the accused priests have walked free because the charges against them simply didn't stick or were too old, then the fact is that they still are innocent under law.

The Catholic Church's unique position on the world stage has given it a lot of latitude in its self-preservation efforts, but other organizations have followed its playbook in putting their own interests ahead of the safety of the individuals they serve. Penn State University allegedly covered up the serial violations of its assistant football coach Jerry Sandusky for more than a decade before they were revealed, and before the school agreed to pay $60 million to about two dozen of Sandusky's victims. Given that Penn State's annual budget exceeds $4 billion, and that its insurance will likely cover the settlement and legal fees, the settlements are a sweet deal for the school.

Starting in about 1920, the Boy Scouts of America (BSA) kept thousands of top-secret "perversion files" detailing the sexual abuses of its adult volunteers. The BSA said that the files were used to keep "bad apples" out of the organization, but lawyers for abused former scouts, including one who obtained an $18.5 million verdict in 2010, said the files should have been made public decades ago. (In that case, the former scout had been molested by a volunteer who was kept on after he admitted to abusing seventeen boys.) The perversion files contain multiple molestation accusations against scout leaders—for example, the commission of "indecent liberties with a child" and "second degree sodomy," and showing kids pornography—none of which were reported to police. In fact, the files were kept in such a way as to prevent their being subpoenaed in court cases. Some of the perversion files were released only after years of attempts by the BSA in court to keep them under seal.

While Judaism, like Islam, has no "church" per se, some powerful, insular Orthodox Jewish sects have gone to great lengths to guard their members from legal exposure for child abuse. This is particularly true in the Orthodox communities in New York, where sexual abuse has long been suspected of running rampant but community intimidation keeps potential accusers silent. A 2012 trial was the first to crack the system. The case concerned the Satmar sect of Williamsburg, Brooklyn. A twelve-year-old girl had been sent to Nechemya Weberman, a respected "spiritual counselor," after she had failed to dress according to Satmar modesty standards. Rather than instruct her on restraint, however, Weberman molested her at least fifty-nine times over three years, acts that included forcing her to reenact some of his favorite scenes from pornographic movies. The abuse was bad enough for the girl, but the idea of reporting it seemed worse at the time: "Satmar would have kicked me out, and if Satmar kicks you out, nobody accepts you," she said. "No one in Williamsburg would accept me."

Her fears were well-founded: when the charges first came out, and throughout the subsequent criminal trial, she and her family were ostracized by the Satmar community. Charges were also brought against several Satmar men for trying to use bribery and threats to interfere with the prosecution. After Weberman was convicted, a rabbi who supported the girl had bleach thrown in his face by a pro-Weberman supporter. Nevertheless, on account of the girl's uncommon courage, Weberman will now spend the rest of his days in jail, and hopefully more such cases will come to light. "The veil of secrecy has been lifted," said Charles Hynes, the Brooklyn district attorney who won the case. "The wall that has existed in parts of these communities has now been broken through." Perhaps, but even one victory in such a secretive community is a welcome breakthrough.

Children and Pornography

In 2012, UK police paid a visit to the house of Timothy Ford, a registered sex offender in Northamptonshire, where they found computer and related equipment containing child pornography. The discovery prompted police to contact the UK's Child Exploitation and Online Protection Centre, which in turn led to a global investigation called Operation Endeavor, involving UK, Australian, and US authorities, as well as the International Justice Mission, an NGO. Within two years, forty-six people in twelve countries were arrested in connection with a network in which customers paid to see live streaming of Filipino children (some as young as six years old) being forced to have sex. Evidently, their impoverished parents received $100 to $200 in exchange for serving up their children for the online pleasure of men in France, the US, Hong Kong, Norway, Switzerland, and other wealthy locales. Ford was sentenced to more than eight years in prison, which put a halt to his plans to move to the Philippines and set up his own Internet café.

Operation Endeavor was exemplary police work. Rather than running Ford out of his house with residency restrictions (which do not exist in the UK), British authorities focused on addressing real risks and securing law-enforcement cooperation across three continents, not only to stop Ford from committing further crimes but to get to the source of the problem. No one believes that the problem of child exploitation can be solved in one or even one hundred such operations, particularly in impoverished locations such as the Philippines, but that does not mean anyone should give up, especially where customers pay to see children abused in real time.

The mission of halting the use of children in pornography is not controversial, or at least it shouldn't be so long as law enforcement uses its powers reasonably. But reason is never in large supply when children and pornography come together, and efforts to stop "kiddie porn" often go off the rails. The specter of the child pornographer took form in the 1970s. In advance of the Democratic National Convention in New York in 1976, some raids on Times Square sex shops turned up a few already-illegal examples of kiddie porn. From that discovery (and a few others) came a panic, replete with crusaders passing around bogus statistics and stirring up calls for tough new laws. In 1977, child psychiatrist Judianne Densen-Gerber told Congress that about 1.2 million children were victims of child sexual exploitation, including in snuff films in which they were killed for the sexual arousal of viewers. Nothing she said was correct, but the figure was repeated so often that it was soon accepted as true. That same year saw the passage of the Protection of Children Against Sexual Exploitation Act, which added new prohibitions against the production and distribution of obscene materials involving kids under sixteen. The law was later amended, among other things, to change the age definition of "child" to a person under eighteen and to allow prosecutions involving even nonobscene materials.

With these and other laws in place, the stage was set for coordinated efforts to bring down the kiddie-porn industry. However, despite claims that the business was an enormous machine generating huge profits—one newspaper said it used about 2.4 million youngsters to generate $46 billion in revenue—the truth was that, by 1978, the trade had already been beaten down to nothing. Two years later, after searching under every rock for child porn, the FBI came up empty-handed. With little to do in this regard, law enforcement went in alternate directions. First, it circulated child porn itself in sting operations to nab people with a predisposition toward pedophilia. This was done so aggressively that by the end of the 1980s, cops were far and away the largest, if not the exclusive, distributors of kiddie porn.

Law-enforcement officials also used the new child pornography laws to crack down on mainstream publications. One of the first casualties was *Show Me!*, a sex-education book for kids, originally published in 1974 by a Lutheran Church–sponsored education group in Germany. What the book "showed" was educational text written by a Swiss psychiatrist, accompanied by high-quality photos of kids and adolescents engaged in sexual play. Carrying the subtitle *A Picture Book of Sex for Children and Their Parents,* the coffee-table book came to the US in 1975 and soon sold more than one hundred thousand copies. It received generally favorable reviews as well as several awards. However, law enforcement was not pleased, and as new laws allowed authorities to go after materials that were not technically obscene, the publisher had to pull the book from circulation after no fewer than four prosecutions. It is still almost impossible to get.

Following that auspicious beginning came the seizure of the film *The Tin Drum* (an adaptation of the novel by Nobel Prize–winning author Günter Grass) from a video rental store, as well as a number of prosecutions stemming from parents' photographs of their nude children. In that predigital era, clerks in Fotomats and other photo-developing services would leaf through batches of prints and report customers to police if they considered the images to be pornographic. One father was dragged from his house in handcuffs after being reported for pictures he had taken of his six-year-old son. His children were also taken away to be examined for sexual abuse. No evidence of abuse was found and the man was not tried for any crime, but he was barred from his home for two months. In 1990, the San Francisco art photographer Jock Sturges had all his equipment, negatives, and business records confiscated and was the subject of a worldwide investigation for his nonerotic nude photos of adolescents, mostly shot at naturist colonies and nude beaches in Europe. FBI agents even demanded client lists from art galleries representing Sturges. The ordeal lasted nearly two years and resulted in no indictments, but the message from law enforcement was made: shoot photographs of nudes under eighteen and your life will become hell.

Sturges was arrested just before the Internet would breathe new life into the child-pornography business. Those involved in the trade are classified under a new taxonomy of perversion, including "browsers," "trawlers," "groomers," "secure" and "nonsecure" collectors, "physical abusers," "distributors," and "producers." All of them are subject to serious criminal penalties. While online exchanges and streaming Web channels open new opportunities for law enforcement, they also are nearly impossible to control because much of the material originates in countries where the laws are either lax or unenforced. Nevertheless, as Operation Endeavor and other prosecutions attest, the trade in child pornography is now widespread, and courts are taking a tough line. In the past fifteen years, sentences in the US for child-porn offenses have increased more than fivefold, averaging about ten years, which is about the same as the average punishment for a physical sex crime.

Once people are locked up, the issue arises as to what to do with them once they have served their sentences. If their crimes were confined to looking at child pornography but they have never touched any children, is it just to keep them locked up on the fear that they would someday act on their fantasies? The story of "John" illustrates some of these issues. In 1998, John met two young female undercover law-enforcement agents in a park for what he thought would be a sexual encounter. John had "met" one of them online. She had identified herself as Indy-Girl, and he told her that he was a "real-life pedophile" who had already had sex with underage girls. He later said that was false—he was just trying to "impress" Indy-Girl—but in fact he had already downloaded thousands of images from child-porn newsgroups.

After four years in prison, John was released, but he was later caught with kiddie porn again and sent back to jail for two more years. As his new release date approached, prison psychologists diagnosed him as a pedophile in the "high range of risk" for committing a new sex crime. He was classified as a "sexually dangerous person" and held until a new trial could determine whether he should be put in a mental ward indefinitely. That happened four years later, when an expert testified that John would likely grow unsatisfied with pictures of kids and would "seek out children for sexual activity." The judge agreed, and John was committed to an indefinite "therapeutic confinement" in a mental hospital. There he remains.

The issue here is not whether John feels compelled to consume child pornography—he is an admitted addict—or whether he is a loathsome character. He is. The question is whether he will molest children if he returns to the streets. We have seen that the business of making risk assessments for sex offenders is sketchy at best, but it is even more so when we try to predict whether a child-porn addict will commit the worse crime of physically molesting a child. In this case, the judge relied on a study showing that child-porn aficionados are likely to molest. The study is a "statistical outlier" because its results conflict with similar studies, but it confirms a gut-level suspicion about people like John, so it has been given more credit in courts than it deserves. Even more troubling is the fact that the American Psychological Association has already come out against indefinite commitments, calling them a "serious assault on the integrity of psychiatry." In 2007, about forty-five hundred sex offenders were civilly committed nationwide after serving their jail sentences; just over 10 percent had been released.

Unlike the other child-sex panics of the past century, which had little or no basis in fact, the global online exchange of child pornography is a real danger and a worthy target of extensive law-enforcement efforts. That said, our disgust for those who fantasize about sex with children should not lead us to keep them incarcerated if they are not dangerous to others. "Doing something" about kiddie porn is right and necessary; doing *anything* is not.

CHAPTER 4

VAMPIRES AT NOON

Obscenity and Its Uses

Obscenity should be a dead issue by now. Smartphones make, display, and distribute homemade pornography, ten-year-olds effortlessly outwit the most daunting Internet filters, and television is crowded with sex. Well before the advent of the Internet, society's sensitivities to the subject seemed to have dulled. *Playboy's* once game-changing "girl next door" photo spreads had become quaint and given way to ultra-graphic fare. Gratuitous hard-core passages in popular books, such as the fine one on pages 23 and 24 of *The Godfather*, had become go-to sales boosters; and video-rental stores did better business with the likes of *Caught from Behind, Part II* than mainstream movies. Once the world went online and the perverse became pervasive, the battle against smut appeared finally to be lost. At least forty million Americans now spend quality time with Internet pornography (average viewing time: twenty to forty minutes), and while estimates differ as to how much worldwide Internet traffic is X-rated, no one disagrees that it is a mind-numbing amount. With this kind of market penetration, it looks like efforts to ban, or at least severely restrict, access to sexual material have flopped and should be abandoned altogether.

Rather than concede defeat, however, pornography's opponents have redoubled their efforts. Just as porn viewing was reaching saturation levels, crusaders from the left and right joined to assail porn as a detonator of violent crime and to mark those who are aroused by it as rapists in training. Feminist activist Andrea Dworkin warned legislators in 1986:

"Pornography is used in rape—to plan it, to execute it, to choreograph it, to engender the excitement to commit the act." After describing the grisly rape and murder fantasies of porn enthusiasts, scholar Catharine MacKinnon concluded: "Sooner or later . . . the consumers want to live out the pornography further in three dimensions. Sooner or later, in one way or another, they do." Smut is even said to motivate war crimes. According to British journalist Linda Grant, the rapes of about fifty thousand Bosnian women in the 1990s were influenced by the recent influx of pornography into the region. The Serbian "rape camps became porn studios without cameras, where sexual fantasy was freed from the prison of the imagination." As for judges who hesitate to send distributors of porn to jail, they are, according to MacKinnon, interested in "keep[ing] the world a pornographic place so they can continue to get hard from everyday life." When the stakes are put in these terms, the fight shows no signs of abating.

Over the past century, immense efforts have been made to halt public displays, descriptions, and even discussions of sex. In addition to war crimes and sexual violence, pornography has been blamed for mental illness, political subversion, child exploitation, juvenile delinquency, scattered perversions, impotence, and excessive masturbation, among other things. However, the sheer numbers of harms pegged to smut tend to cancel themselves out. *Nothing* can be so perilous in so many ways, especially when—let's face it—so many otherwise harmless people get off on it. Every anti-porn initiative evokes the same question: What are we really afraid of? Are the medical and birth control publications suppressed as obscene a century ago as harmful as *Mad* magazine or Arthur Miller's *Death of a Salesman,* both of which were banned in 1959? Is the film *Black Bun Busters*, listed as obscene by a high-level government commission in 1986, as dangerous as the racy photos of left-wing activist Angela Davis that the FBI kept in its sprawling "Obscene" file? Are female "ejaculation" videos, recently banned in the UK on online pay sites, any worse than the ubiquitous videos featuring men ejaculating? What really differentiates ordinary pornography, which is legal in most cases, from the "obscene" stuff that can still bring jail sentences? In millions of pages of legal decisions and commentary, there are no answers to these questions that make even the smallest bit of sense.

In the end, the legality of sexually stimulating materials depends on the setting in which they are presented. Anti-obscenity activists, for example, have long staged peep shows to appreciative audiences with no consequence. In 1873, in support of a sweeping anti-indecency bill, the US vice president's office was transformed into a "chamber of horrors," where attendees tut-tutted their way through a series of "lowbrow publications" and "other abominations." In 1968, a well-attended X-rated film festival for legislators was held in the US Capitol, supposedly to stir moral outrage at the "filth" on display. And a few years before the Andy Warhol film *Lonesome Cowboys* (1968) was the subject of an FBI obscenity investigation, an anti-gay Florida legislative report plastered gratuitous displays of "confiscated" gay pornography on its cover and inside pages. Apparently, the report's call for the severe repression of homosexuality made the materials legally palatable.

Is it acceptable, then, to savor sexual materials so long as one clucks disapprovingly while being titillated? The answer would seem to be yes, although no one admits it. The truth about obscenity laws is that they are based entirely on emotion. As the eminent judge Richard A. Posner observed about his colleagues' unusual preoccupation with a law prescribing which garments strippers may remove onstage: "Nudity and the erotic are emotional topics even to middle-aged and elderly judges." The case to which Posner was referring, *Barnes v. Glen Theatre*, shows how flummoxed jurists can become when faced with bare breasts and pubic hair. After Posner's Chicago-based court fixated on the subject for some time (not using three judges, as is typical, but the entire court), the US Supreme Court took the case on, holding that nude dancing is "expressive conduct" protected by the First Amendment but adding, nonsensically, that pasties and G-strings were necessary to protect "order and morality."

With obscenity, context is everything, and context is always in flux. A dance, painting, or downloaded file can be permissible and criminal simultaneously, depending on who is watching, where the watching occurs, and why the viewer is aroused—judges included. In 1933, when considering the alleged obscenity of James Joyce's *Ulysses*, New York judge John M. Woolsey applied what has since been called the "erection test." Seeking to discover whether the book would cause readers to have "sexually impure and lustful thoughts," Woolsey consulted his own genitals and those of two trusted male friends. If their penises reacted with interest while reading *Ulysses*, then government authorities could continue to ban and burn the book; if Woolsey's and his mates' members stayed in repose, publication could go forward. Fortunately for subsequent generations of literature students and professors, *Ulysses* had no visible effect on the three readers, although Woolsey wrote that it sometimes made him nauseous.

The book was released after more than a decade of suppression. Had Woolsey's erection test produced a different result, then what is arguably the English language's twentieth-century masterpiece would have remained criminal contraband. As scholar Mary Lydon observed about the *Ulysses* case, "*throwing* up is a legitimate reader response; *getting* it up is taboo."

As we hack through a century of high-minded legal cant about obscenity, Woolsey's and Posner's candor is a rarity. Advocates or jurists rarely say what they really believe on the subject, because the truth remains shameful. When professional courtroom experts such as Judith Lynne Hanna argue that an "exotic dance" in a strip club has "serious artistic value" comparable to the choreography of George Balanchine, or when cities impose a four-foot distance between strippers and patrons to prevent the supposed spread of sexually transmitted infections, they are all being disingenuous. The point of going to a strip club, and the aim of most other sexually oriented diversions, is to bring about the very "lustful thoughts" Woolsey looked for when he read *Ulysses*. Woolsey was simply candid enough to admit it.

The erection test never caught on as formal legal policy, although it is as logical a standard as any. In the hundreds of laws and court decisions tinkering with the question of which sexual representations can be outlawed, the rule, roughly, is this: If, applying community standards, (1) a work excites an average person's "prurient," "morbid," or "shameful" interest in sex (rather than his or her "good, old-fashioned, healthy" sexual appetites); (2) the work is patently offensive; and (3) it accomplishes nothing other than causing one to become sexually aroused, then it can be outlawed as obscene. Exactly *why* catalysts of unadulterated sexual excitement (without any other merits) should be outlawed has never been adequately explained, and neither is there useful guidance on how to distinguish morbid sexual appetites from "old-fashioned" and "healthy" ones. Judges and juries just improvise.

Since at least the 1920s, commercial enterprises have used ever-more-base sexual messages to hawk products, which, historian Estelle Freedman observed, has kept the public "in a state of constant sexual excitement." I can recall, during the 1980s, seeing a large Los Angeles billboard showing a bikini-clad woman with an orgasmic facial expression straddling an oversized electronic paging device. The ad's unsubtle message: "Buy from us, and this woman will mount you like she is doing to this pager." Is that appeal "old-fashioned healthy" or morbid? For the pager company, it seemed healthy indeed: the billboard towered over a busy intersection for a long time. For the bikini model, it was exploitative in the extreme, although she was presumably paid for her pose. And of the billboard's millions of viewers, at least a few fools might have taken the advertisement's message literally—a scary thought. During the same period, a commission headed by US attorney general Edwin Meese badgered twenty-three convenience store chains to stop selling soft-core magazines such as *Playboy* and *Penthouse*. At least one of the targets, Southland Corporation (owner of the 7-Eleven chain), succumbed to the pressure and stopped selling the magazines for a time. Both the billboard and the magazines used sexual arousal to pull money from the wallets of excitable customers: the billboard sold pagers, while the magazines advertised products. Which sexual appeal was morbid and which was healthy?

Distinguishing Pornography from Prostitution

In earlier times, a prostitute was defined as a woman with multiple sexual partners, regardless of whether she was paid. Money is a now a part of the definition, but that has brought little clarity to the matter, especially when others pay to watch. Consider the pornographic performer, for whom sex is no less a living than it is for a streetwalker. Both engage in sex for money, yet the streetwalker's business is criminal while the porn actor's job is perfectly legal in many places. As matters stand, whether a paid sexual encounter amounts to prostitution or legitimate acting depends chiefly on one fact: whether a camera in the room is set to "record." Don't kick yourself if you miss the reasoning here—there is none. The law often ties itself into illogical knots, especially with regard to the adult-film industry.

In 1987, porn producer and director Harold Freeman hired several people through a Los Angeles "modeling" agency to have anal, oral, and vaginal sex in a piece of cinema verité titled *Caught from Behind, Part II*. As part of a local crackdown on commercial sex, Freeman was convicted of pimping in connection with the film. The guilty verdict was an easy call for the jury; he had arranged for the troupe of "models" to have paid sex. However, the California Supreme Court held that no laws had been broken, and that the film was protected under the First Amendment, because Freeman did not pay for his own or the actors' "gratification." Rather, he paid them to *simulate* pleasure before the camera. If no camera had been rolling, or if the actors had actually enjoyed the sex, then each time they were "caught from behind" on film they would have been engaging in prostitution. How the court measured the gratification levels of Freeman or the actors, it did not specify.

The rationale behind the *Freeman* decision, which blessed California's hard-core-movie industry, is somewhere between bad and laughable. Both the prostitute and the adult-film actor have sex for money, during which they both act like they are enjoying it. (Their financial success depends, in large part, on their ability to simulate sexual arousal.) It is illegal for people to pay one another for sex, but after *Freeman*, if the people paying and being paid are not "gratified" and a camera is rolling, then an act of rank prostitution enjoys the same lofty free-speech protections as those given to a documentary film about politics or climate change.

Although *Freeman* was decided well before video cameras became ubiquitous, the rule now applies to homemade porn as well. Eleven years after *Freeman*, a restless former court bailiff in New Hampshire offered a couple money to have sex while he watched. He was caught and convicted of arranging prostitution. On a later occasion, he again hired a couple to have sex while he remained a voyeur, but this time he also videotaped the encounter. Again he was caught, but the state supreme court let him off. It held that no law had been broken because the sex was arranged for the "legitimate" purpose of making a videotape, as opposed to "sexual arousal or gratification." Thus, the bailiff was in the same hallowed company as the producer of *Caught from Behind, Part II*.

Given the thin, irregular line between prostitution and free speech, even an experienced pornographic actress can become confused. In 2012, the chairman of the Miramax film studio, Richard Nanula, bridged his fantasy life with reality by arranging a sexual encounter with the porn actress Sarah Shevon at a Malibu, California, estate. Nanula had already tried, through an intermediary, to induce Shevon to take $1,500 in exchange for a single act of fellatio, but she saw that as prostitution and refused. Undaunted, he tried again, this time setting up a fake video shoot at the Malibu house, where he assumed the false persona of a porn actor named Mr. Rich. Believing that she would be working with a fellow actor, Shevon took the deal. Dressed as a schoolgirl, she performed fellatio on him while a camera rolled, took $300 in cash, and went home. When Shevon later saw pictures on a website of another porn actress, Samantha Saint, having sex with the same man—this time correctly identified as Nanula—she realized that she had been duped.

While both Shevon and Saint were angry that "Mr. Rich" had misrepresented himself, they both rightly believed that the presence of video cameras protected them against criminal prostitution charges. (Saint took an additional precaution by posting her scene with Nanula on an adult website.) As for Nanula, he got what he wanted. For a sum far smaller than the $10,000 he was said to pay prostitutes, he received the intimate attentions of two seasoned sex workers. However, he should have known that the presence of cameras during his sessions with Shevon and Saint made his public exposure a certainty. Shortly after the video stills from the Saint shoot made their way onto the Internet, he stepped down from his post at Miramax.

Taking *Freeman* one step further, paying people to have sex in front of a webcam while a customer watches from another location may or may not be illegal, depending in part on who is performing and who is turned on by the encounter; but if the customer pays a third-party provider, who then hires the couple to copulate in front of the webcam, and if the actors make sure not to enjoy themselves, then the ignoble affair could be classified as free expression. It is fine legal distinctions like this that make the law ridiculous in the eyes of many. So long as there is widespread agreement that prostitution should be illegal, there is no rational reason to allow it on a mass scale in the form of pornography production. Using logic more contorted than the sexual positions in *Caught from Behind, Part II*, the courts have allowed the pornography industry to flourish while making low-end sex workers, such as streetwalkers and their pimps, into criminals. It should be noted that the state of Utah—where prostitution laws are fiercely enforced—boasts the greatest per capita number of Internet pornography subscriptions in the US.

Obscenity and Theatrical Performance

Battles over sex and performance raged long before the excitable New Hampshire cop and Messrs. Freeman and Nanula arrived on the scene. A century ago, the controversy centered on sexually charged live performances, where the distinction between acceptable highbrow art and illegal gutter obscenity was never clear. Depending on its location, its audience, and the mood of the judge involved in the case, the same performance could elicit a judicial yawn, provoke raids—or, in some instances, both.

In Europe, during the years preceding the First World War, performances evoking the mysteries of the "Orient" or ancient Greece were much in vogue, particularly when they involved erotic dances by unclothed women. For innovators such as Isadora Duncan, who modeled dances on Greek statues and vase figures, it was natural to "fall into Greek positions" as she "danc[ed] naked upon the earth." For the many lesser talents who followed in Duncan's wake, acclaim came in the form of stylized evocations of "exotic" worlds ancient and modern, where sexuality was thought to be less restricted and passions readily indulged. The American performer Maud Allan, for example, was promoted as "a delicious embodiment of lust"; the Dutch dancer/prostitute/spy Mata Hari was billed as the incarnation of the "Kama Sutra and the Oriental arts of love."

Whether or not such performances would be shut down by police usually depended on the social class of the audience and the brand of sexuality evoked by the dancers. The minor French danseuse Adorée Villany, for example, had been doing underclad characterizations of mythic princesses and Greek muses for years in European capitals before coming to Munich in 1911. Her first two shows there were well received by audiences and at least a few critics, but the police arrested her for indecency during her third. Villany had unwittingly sparked a frothy morals debate between the old-line Bavarian Catholic hierarchy, who were horrified at her "shameless prostitution" onstage, and the city's arty liberal types, for whom her arrest was an embarrassment before the "educated world."

The core of the controversy was Villany's body. Had it been presented to be leered at, as her detractors asserted, or was it dirty-minded even to suggest that such an artistic presentation would excite lust? To Munich's arts community, the government had no business dictating the merits or legality of Villany's performance, while the morals crowd countered that decency must be at the top of the public agenda. Otherwise, they argued, the state was open to moral decay and the "dictatorship of Eros." The police took the unusual step of contacting Villany's audience members to ask for volunteers to testify that her performances were offensive. When no one came forward, the indecency charge was dropped. Nevertheless, she was forced to leave Bavaria. Meanwhile, European newspapers had a jolly time ridiculing German prudishness and, as one Paris critic joked, the envy of Bavaria's stocky "Gretchens" toward Villany's "lovely figure."

Given the Parisian press's smug response to the Villany affair in Germany, and the city's preeminence in matters of artistic taste, Villany believed that her 1913 performances in the French capital would be free from legal trouble. She was incorrect. Villany was again charged with indecency, and again a brouhaha ensued. The controversy had been treated with utmost seriousness in Munich, but in Paris it became the butt of mockery. Her brief trial was treated as a sideshow; even the judge and prosecutor couldn't resist a few vulgar cracks. Nevertheless, she was convicted and fined. Chastened, she continued her shows at the Folies Bergère clad in flesh-colored fabric. In commenting on the Villany affair, the *Pariser Zeitung* observed that the city was happy to tolerate immorality so long as it as it didn't pretend to be art. That was true as far as it went. Villany aside, artistic sex displays were mostly ignored by the law unless the sex veered toward the homosexual, in which case the city became narrow-minded indeed.

In 1907, at the famed Moulin Rouge nightclub, the writer (and Villany defender) Colette and her female lover, the Marquise de Morny, performed a pantomime called *Rêve d'Egypte* (*Egyptian Dream*). In it, a male archaeologist discovers a female mummy, which seductively unwraps itself and kisses the startled explorer. The first performance sparked an instant uproar. Under pressure from de Morny's family, the police threatened to close the show if the two women performed together again. The marquise buckled at these demands, but the show was shut down anyway. In 1908, after a more explicit sexual performance between two scantily clad women called *Rêverie d'éther* (*Ether Intoxication*), a court jailed the manager of the Moulin Rouge for three months. The performers were fined for exposing their "bare flesh" and acting in a way the judge said "appealed to the grossest, most excessive and dangerous lubricity" and "nervous passions."

In 1907, the city of Chicago enacted the first law in the US to censor sexual content in films, which has been followed to the present day by a shifting series of governmental and film-industry rules. Goaded by the Catholic Legion of Decency, Hollywood toughened its own censorship rules (known as the Hays Code) in 1934 by banning, among other things, portrayals of adultery, lustful embraces, undressing, and dances that evoke "indecent passions." One of the many casualties of the Hays Code was a love scene between Tarzan and Jane in *Tarzan and His Mate* (1934), which was edited out, as were all references to lovemaking between the Humphrey Bogart and Ingrid Bergman characters in *Casablanca*. The Hays Code was finally abandoned in favor of the now-familiar rating system in 1966, but individual films, even those with top cultural credentials, still occasionally faced legal trouble. For example, in 1972, after a two-year legal battle, the US Supreme Court overturned a Georgia ban on the Mike Nichols film *Carnal Knowledge,* and also the conviction of a movie theater owner for showing the film.

Sex Displays and the First World War

In matters of public sex displays, as in all other aspects of society, the First World War changed everything. As Europe blew itself to shreds, its sex habits degenerated into a hybrid of cruel abandon and bitter intolerance. On the battlefronts and in the cities, the war unleashed what the German doctor and sex researcher Magnus Hirschfeld called a "madness of corporeal surrender" and "war nymphomania." Everywhere, Hirschfeld observed, "the pleasure of the moment was what decided the action of the individual, for the present moment was the only certain one." Married women leapt into adulterous "whirlpools of pleasure" as they succumbed to the "hellish and brutalizing onslaught of sexuality," while in the trenches of the Western Front, sexual release became a savage diversion. When prostitutes were unavailable, soldiers masturbated compulsively— during bombardments, while listening to comrades tell dirty stories, and to the abundant pornography they carried in their packs. They had sex with each other, with the overheated nurses who cared for them, and with the horses, donkeys, and swine that accompanied their regiments. The details didn't matter: the release was the thing.

Wartime propaganda often read like pornography. To bring their populations to maximum states of hatred against their enemies, each side luridly accused the others of rape, bestiality, homosexuality, the consumption of excrement, and necrophilia. In truth, sex crimes were committed by every army on every front, but in this, the first mass-media war, it was seen as imperative to drive home the message that the enemy was a horde of sexual psychopaths. This was particularly true in Britain, where immense war losses sparked frenzied xenophobia and fears that foreign-influenced moral rot was weakening the empire from within.

One would have thought that about one million British casualties would cause the performance of an Oscar Wilde play by an underclad dancer to pass unnoticed, but quite the opposite occurred. The legal spectacle set off by the play became a media-friendly vehicle for right-wing extremists to rail against homosexual contagion on the home front. When Maud Allan agreed in 1917 to perform Wilde's *Salome* in London, she was already a famous dancer of the "exotic" variety. Ten years earlier, she had performed *The Vision of Salome* in a London run spanning 250 shows. Reviews had praised her "animal-like and carnal" interpretation of the biblical story as "a reincarnation of the most graceful and rhythmic forms of classic Greece," and as a "writhing" enactment of the "voluptuousness of Eastern femininity." Her earlier performances had been popular with the liberal upper classes and had brought Allan the friendship of Prime Minister Herbert Asquith and his wife, Margot. With friends at the apex of the social scale, this slender "embodiment of lust" had enjoyed some of the highest acclaim that prewar Britain had to offer.

However, three years into the miserable war, the social and cultural landscapes were poisoned. Britain was exhausted, its edge dulled and its military now seemingly unequal to the task of protecting the empire. When the fighting had begun in 1914, many hoped that a quick and decisive victory against the "Hun" would cleanse British society of the fey decadence that had seemed to set in at the turn of the century, of which the "cult" of Oscar Wilde was the most visible example. Yet war's "purifying fire" had only weakened the empire and incinerated its precious sons. In 1917, Britain had little to show for its suffering other than casualties on an unimagined scale. The fighting was nowhere near its end and there was genuine fear that Britain would be defeated.

Proto-fascist politicians such as Noel Pemberton Billing exploited this sense of dread. The newly elected backbencher found a large and receptive audience for his charges that the homosexual-laden German government was working with well-placed British perverts—by blackmail and otherwise—to subvert the war effort. In January 1918, Billing's newspaper *The Imperialist* (soon renamed *The Vigilante*) reported that the enemy kept a one-thousand-page "black book" listing the names of forty-seven thousand Britons with "sexual peculiarities" of the kind practiced in "Sodom and Lesbia," and reaching to the highest levels of government, business, and the media. Each of them, the paper charged, had been drafted into Germany's service.

The article caused a stir, but not enough to draw out the libel suits Billing hoped would provide a larger platform for his tirades. That opportunity came a few weeks later in the form of an announcement for the new production of *Salome* in which Allan was to play the biblical temptress. The play's revival was a satin-wrapped publicity gift for Billing, an almost too-easy pretext for him to redouble his charges of German-influenced immorality and treason. Among his allies was Lord Alfred Douglas, Wilde's former lover and the object of the disgraced playwright's "love that dare not speak its name." In the years since Wilde's 1895 imprisonment for "gross indecency," followed by Wilde's flight from England and death in Paris, the cantankerous Douglas had repackaged himself as a Catholic family man, an anti-Semite, and a shrill homophobe. Nursing a limitless hatred of anyone who dared to evoke his gay past, he spent considerable time in court and at his writing desk attacking Wilde's biographers and former associates. In the months to come, Douglas worked with Billing to slander Allan and Wilde, whom Douglas would later testify was "the greatest force for evil that has appeared in Europe during the last 350 years."

Six days after the advert for *Salome* appeared, Billing's newspaper ran a front-page article headlined "The Cult of the Clitoris," which charged that the audience for the new production would include many of the forty-seven thousand German-loving perverts he had warned of earlier. The term "clitoris" was used, mistakenly, to denote lesbian activity, but whatever a clitoral cult may have consisted of, Allan resented being associated with it. She reacted just as Billing had hoped, with a suit for criminal libel. On one level, the case was a political brawl. Billing's enemies, who included Prime Minister David Lloyd George, could not have cared less about Wilde or Allan. They saw the affair as an opportunity to end Billing's career by pegging him as an immoral crackpot. A woman was hired to lure Billing into a male brothel, where he would be caught and then disgraced. However, rather than entrap Billing, she jumped into bed with him, after which she joined his cause and turned against her employers. At Billing's urging, and before a packed courtroom, she falsely testified that she had seen the infamous black book and that it contained the names of Lord and Lady Asquith, as well as the judge on the case, Charles John Darling. The trial went downhill from there.

The Billing–Allan case was also a reckoning with the legacy of Oscar Wilde and the anti-homosexual hatred that still pervaded British society. Not only did Douglas testify against Wilde and homosexuals generally, he also charged that *Salome* was intended to be "an exhibition of perverted sexual passion." For his part, Billing said that his reference to the "Cult of the Clitoris" was nothing next to the "cult of sodomy" that Wilde had "founded" in England, which still perverted youth through plays such as *Salome* and which, somehow, assisted the enemy. The black book was never produced—it never existed. Neither was any German blackmail of British homosexuals ever proven; nor was the political disloyalty of *Salome*'s patrons remotely established. In the end, none of that mattered. Billing had gotten his message across and he had won. After the jury's verdict of Billing's innocence was announced, the entire gallery erupted in cheers—a similar reaction to that which greeted Wilde's disgrace in court in 1895. Rather than suffer for its leader's hubris, Billing's Society of Vigilantes saw a swift rise in membership. His fight "for a cleaner England" pressed on with renewed vigor. Allan resumed her career, but her popularity waned. She died in a California convalescent home in 1956. Homosexual sex between men would remain a criminal offense in Britain until 1967.

Bumping and Grinding

The end of the war in 1918 cleared the way for a surge of live shows about sex on both sides of the Atlantic. The 1925–1926 New York theater season included some brilliant productions by the likes of Eugene O'Neill and Noël Coward, but the real crowd-pleaser was *Sex*, written by and starring the savvy actress and promoter Mae West. The critics hated the show, but that only helped its success. So did ads advising that patrons "who cannot stand excitement" should seek medical help before "visiting" West. Manhattan physicians must have been busy, because 325,000 people paid West "visits" in the theater before the city's acting mayor, Joseph V. ("Holy Joe") McKee, had the show raided. West managed the controversy masterfully, refusing to shut down *Sex* in exchange for dropped charges and publicly endorsing the grand jury's assessment that the show was "obscene, indecent, immoral and impure." After happily losing the case, she made a publicity stunt out of her limousine ride to jail, and she later boasted that she wore silk underwear during her eight nights in captivity.

If New York law enforcement became an unwitting dupe for Mae West's canny promotion of herself and *Sex*, the joke did not last long. In the 1930s, the brief flowering of burlesque—a lighthearted combination of tame striptease, bawdy humor, and Vaudeville shtick—would be snuffed out by morals agitators, a compliant city government, and the rising belief that the sight of partially clad women onstage caused men to become mentally unhinged. The demonization of burlesque, and especially the tie between sexual entertainment and sex crime, would foreshadow anti-obscenity efforts in the decades to come.

The Great Depression and competition from Hollywood movies took a steep toll on legitimate theater in Times Square, causing the closure of stages and a drop in rents that permitted burlesque operators to move in from outlying neighborhoods. The first burlesque theater opened there in 1931, and within a few years there were fourteen such establishments within a few blocks of each other. With them came a clientele of working-class and unemployed men, few of whom were accompanied by women. Local merchants and business leaders were not enthused. Sexual innuendo had long been a recurring element of legitimate theater, but as long as the plays drew people with money to spend, there was not much that morals agitators could do about it (*Sex* notwithstanding). However, that changed when the theatergoing toffs vanished and the subway started disgorging packs of near-destitute men into the area. By aligning with neighboring property owners and attacking the moral character of the burlesque audience (rather than the shows themselves), censorship advocates made gains that would have been unimaginable just a few years earlier.

The issue often arose in the context of theater license renewal proceedings, during which burlesque patrons were repeatedly denigrated as "lewd and dissolute" and, as the argument soon developed, so crazed by what they saw onstage that they were driven to rape women passing through the neighborhood. The movement against burlesque found a powerful ally in Fiorello LaGuardia, who had been elected mayor in 1934 on a promise to "be the mayor of a clean American city and protect its morals." His close alliance with Catholic anti-obscenity activists was both a shrewd political move and an expression of genuine beliefs. During his tenure, groups such as the Knights of Columbus and the National Legion of Decency usually got what they wanted, and they wanted smut stamped out.

Matters heated up in 1937, when the rape and murder of several New York girls drew sensational media attention and sparked a national sex-crime panic. No evidence linked the crimes to Times Square burlesque. Nevertheless, closing burlesque theaters would communicate that something was being done about the sex-crime "wave" that the newspapers incessantly claimed was taking place. LaGuardia and his allies got to work. As theater licenses came up for renewal, opponents refined their arguments, claiming that the sexual stimulation dispensed at burlesque houses bred sexual violence. As observed by historian Andrea Friedman: "No longer did they argue that burlesque attracted sexual perverts; now they declared that it created them." While LaGuardia launched a much-ballyhooed "investigation" into the matter, on the other side of this debate there was . . . no one. In this frenzied climate, admitting that one went to the shows, or arguing that burlesque was a harmless diversion, would have been tantamount to admitting that one was a sex criminal.

With no reasoned debate, and with no evidence that any sex criminals had ever attended or been inspired by burlesque shows, the down-on-his-luck burlesque patron of the early 1930s had been transformed in the popular imagination into a criminal of the worst order. By 1942, the bump-and-grind and ribald humor of burlesque was largely finished, and no theaters featuring it were left in Times Square. In the wake of this purge was the lasting belief that obscenity in all its forms caused men to become sex criminals, a canard used by both the left and the right until the present day.

After the Second World War, the law continued its attempts to distinguish erudite art—in which nudity and eroticism were usually tolerated—from low-end fare, which would remain in the legal cold. Nudity itself has long been the stuff of "serious" performance art, from the exotic evocations of Maud Allan and Isadora Duncan to the work of George Balanchine, whose 1936 ballet *Slaughter on Tenth Avenue* was inspired in part by the strip shows at Paris's Crazy Horse Saloon. When Martha Graham integrated intercourse-like pelvic thrusts into her dances, no one doubted the value of what she was doing, and when the Washington Shakespeare Company performed a fully nude version of *Macbeth* in 2007, it drew critical reactions of "eerie, intelligent, and visually arresting"—but not "dirty" or "obscene."

The line becomes fuzzier when satire and pop culture come into the picture. Take *Oh Calcutta!*, the title of which was drawn from the French exclamation "Oh, quel cul tu as!" ("Oh, what an ass you have!"). The revue lampooned modern sex culture with nude sequences, sexy skits, striptease numbers, and sophomoric humor. (Example: "Q: 'What do you think about fucking onstage?' A: 'Oh, I can dig it, but what do you do on your day off?'") The show's creator, Kenneth Tynan, brought in the likes of Samuel Beckett, John Lennon, Sam Shepard, and Edna O'Brien to write sketches, so its artistic bona fides were intact. After its successful 1969 Off-Broadway debut, it became a perennial (if increasingly dated) tourist draw on Broadway and in London's West End.

London and New York swallowed *Oh Calcutta!* without so much as a hiccup, but that tolerance did not extend to the US's squeamish interior. In 1970, a filmed version of the play was scheduled for broadcast on closed-circuit television in twenty-six cities, including Cincinnati, Ohio—the home of Charles Keating, a lawyer who convinced a court to bar the broadcast. Normally, US courts recoil at restricting any but the most dangerous forms of speech (for example, instructions on building a hydrogen bomb) before they take place, such measures being "prior restraints" and anathema to freedom of expression. In fact, five years before Keating went to court against *Oh Calcutta!*, the Supreme Court unanimously held that state censorship boards had no authority to ban films. However, in 1970, the prospect of naked people telling dirty jokes was still enough for the Ohio court to stop the broadcast. The following year, a showing of a videotape of the play brought a federal indictment in Corpus Christi, Texas. Given the culture wars going on at the time in the US, these panicked responses were expected, if unfortunate. The musical *Hair* (which had one brief nude scene) caused similar reactions. What was surprising, however, was the uproar *Oh Calcutta!* caused when it came to Chattanooga, Tennessee, in 1991, long after sex-themed entertainment had penetrated every corner of the country.

The one Chattanooga theater suitable for staging a large production was publicly owned. The city's fathers refused permission to use the venue, declaring the play too sexual for delicate local sensibilities. The play's producers ran to court, arguing that the profusion of far racier material on cable TV, in video stores, and in local movie theaters put the play at the low end of the sexual scale, and well within the bounds of the law. Two decades after the play's opening, they argued, it no longer made sense to exclude it from Chattanooga's cultural mix. In response, the city agreed that times had changed, but in its view sexual decency standards had *tightened* since the free-for-all 1960s, and *Oh Calcutta!*'s "promotion of promiscuity," which "caused" AIDS, was reason enough to ban the show. The judge didn't know what to think, so he recruited a group of citizens, called an "advisory jury," to watch a video of the play and report back to him. They confirmed that the play was offensive but not obscene. The judge reluctantly agreed, opining that the play's advocacy of free sex "was more appropriate in the late 1960s" than in 1991. Nevertheless, he let the play go on. (It didn't do very well.)

Right about the time that *Oh Calcutta!* went on trial in Chattanooga, the strip club industry was experiencing a worldwide surge, although in that pornography-soaked period, it is difficult to say why. Perhaps men flocked to strip clubs because they wanted the illusion of personal connection with a living person (particularly during "private dances"), even when the better part of their reason told them the illusion was false. It seems that strip clubs filled a niche for men too lonely to continue masturbating to videos, too frightened to pick up streetwalkers, and too frugal to pay for higher-end prostitutes. Whatever the reasons, the business boomed. As of 2012, there were about four thousand such establishments in the US. Two strip club companies are publicly traded in US financial markets and listed on the NASDAQ: VCG Holding Corp. (VCGH) and

RCI Holdings (formerly Rick's Cabaret International, Inc. [RICK]). In the UK, the number of strip clubs rose 1,150 percent from 1997 to 2010. In 2008 alone, a lap-dancing club opened in Britain almost every week. Most strip clubs are zoned in underpopulated and industrial neighborhoods, where their mix of loud rock music and silicone-inflated arousal are dispensed without incident. However, because they are licensed by municipalities, grandstanding officials have been able to implement zoning rules so restrictive that they can make it impossible for such businesses to operate profitably. Are rules mandating distances between dancers and patrons really necessary to prevent disease transmissions or drug transactions, as proponents claim? Obviously not, and neither are rules mandating ultra-bright lighting, but the local judges who uphold such rules don't care. If local sentiment runs against the clubs, chances are they will be driven out of town.

Local governments sometimes launch direct attacks against strip clubs and their employees. In 1999, for example, a grim little Maryland club called Showcase was stormed by a thirty-person riot squad in combat gear. The ten dancers and twenty customers who had the bad luck to be there were forced to lie spread-eagled on the floor lest police officers make good on their threats to "use physical force and fuck you up." The dancers were told to sign papers stating that they were forced by the club owners to dance nude, which they refused to do. The owners and dancers were then charged with multiple counts of criminal "conspiracy to violate public indecency laws." What followed was a multiyear legal, legislative, and political battle, pitting the club owners against a well-funded anti-nudity lobby allied with local politicians. The goal, according to Maryland politician Arthur Dorman, was to use all available means to make life miserable for Showcase and similar clubs "until they get the hell out of here." While the litigation ground on, new adult entertainment ordinances (some barring "simulated nudity") were passed and struck down. More raids were conducted, and more lawsuits were filed.

There is no reason to believe that strip clubs will ever come completely into the legal clear, just as there is no way to come up with a consistent distinction between high art, low debauchery, political statement, and humor. (While arresting Lenny Bruce after a performance in San Francisco, a policeman asked, "Why do you feel that you have to use the word 'cocksucker' to entertain people?" Bruce's reply: "Well, there are a lot of cocksuckers around, aren't there? What's wrong with talking about them?") Public nudity was barred in New York, but not when women appeared topless to protest an anti-nudity law or exposed their breasts in other "noncommercial" ways; that is, until police gave up and decided not to enforce the law against breast exposures at all. Nude sunbathing is allowed in many places, but not when the sunbather "lewdly" presents his or her body. Nude dancing can be protected as artistic expression, but often not in strip clubs, no matter how sublime the strippers' movements may be to their beholders. In Arizona, one commits sexual indecency by having intimate contact with an animal's anus or genitals while someone else is present—*if* the animal lover is "reckless" about whether or not the witness would be offended or alarmed. Simple, right?

Obscenity in the Global Village

Since 1957, the question of whether something can be labeled obscene and therefore be banned has, in large part, turned on whether it fits the "standards" of a particular locality. As explained later by the Supreme Court, the good citizens of (presumably prudish) Maine or Georgia should not have to "accept public depiction of conduct found tolerable in Las Vegas or New York City." The Internet has erased any rational basis for this standard, as anything can be viewed or downloaded from anywhere by anyone. Yet the local community standard persists. In fact, it has become a tool for law enforcement to accomplish the *opposite* of what the court sought to achieve: rather than protect the heartland's fragile sensibilities, the local standards of the rural US are now being foisted upon the entire country, if not the world.

All that a crusading law-enforcement agency needs to do to start an obscenity case against a faraway target is download the offending material. Once that is done, the material has technically been brought into the locality and can be judged by the locality's standards. If the case goes well for prosecutors, the distant pornographer can be hauled before local courts and then punished just as if he had staged a sexual exhibition at the courthouse. This is not just a quirk in the law exploited by backwoods extremists; it became an integral tool in anti-obscenity enforcement. In 2008, the George W. Bush administration created an Obscenity Prosecution Task Force dedicated "exclusively to the protection of America's children and families through the enforcement of our Nation's obscenity laws." During Bush's years in office, some 361 defendants were charged with obscenity violations (more than twice as many as under President

Bill Clinton), and many of them were charged according to the standards of the most conservative regions.

One of the task force's victories came in Tampa, Florida, where officials downloaded some trailers and ordered some DVDs depicting sadomasochism from an adult website. The site's operator, Paul Little (aka Max Hardcore), a small-time operator who lived in California, was dragged to Tampa, where the site's wares were judged by that locality's tight standards. Little was put in jail for almost four years. On appeal, his lawyers argued that it was wrong to use Tampa as the benchmark for sexually explicit material on the Internet and that a national standard should be adopted. The court brushed that argument away.

In 2005, a Florida adult-website operator found himself in extremely hot water for retransmitting images from the Second Gulf War that were embarrassing to the US military. Sheriff's deputies in Polk County, Florida, stormed the home office of Chris Wilson, the proprietor of nowthatsfuckedup.com, a website featuring a politically explosive mix of sex and military violence. Users not only swapped explicit pictures of their wives and girlfriends as well as other sexual imagery, they also uploaded hundreds of gory pictures of dead and injured Iraqis and other war casualties—images the government was keen to suppress. Wilson was arrested and hit with three hundred counts of obscenity and faced the real possibility of spending the rest of his life in prison. It was one of the stiffest obscenity charges in the history of the Internet.

Wilson had not intended that his one-man operation should enter the minefield of military public relations. In fact, he only wanted to resolve some of his users' credit-card problems. After launching the site, he received emails from American soldiers in Iraq who couldn't get beyond its paywall because of bank verification issues. Wilson offered to let any soldier use the site for free if he sent photographic proof that he was in fact serving in Iraq. The first images that came in showed soldiers with their weapons and in their barracks. Then came photos showing, for example, a severed Iraqi head in a bowl of blood, dismembered limbs, and a child with bloody pulp where his face once was. That caused considerable discomfort in high places, where another Abu Ghraib–type scandal was the last thing anyone wanted. The army launched an investigation, but unlike the children of Iraq, Wilson was outside the military's reach. It had no jurisdiction over him, and its investigators couldn't pinpoint which soldiers had uploaded the bloody images. According to a *Rolling Stone* source, a call was then made to Florida's governor, Jeb Bush, and Wilson was arrested the next day.

The local sheriff who went after Wilson, Grady Judd, was the right man for the job. A longtime anti-pornography obsessive, Judd had already been instrumental in shutting down more than one hundred adult businesses—mostly through raids, impossibly aggressive charges, and then comparatively lenient plea bargains. Judd went after Wilson with such ferocity that it took herculean efforts by his attorneys just to keep the website operator out of jail—and this was before he was convicted of anything. Had Wilson been given a fair trial before an impartial jury, he would never have been convicted. The sex images were run-of-the-mill and the First Amendment protected the pictures of Iraqi casualties. Yet Wilson still had good reason to fear that he would emerge from the case in a prison uniform. With everything to lose, he took a plea deal and shut down the site. Through a baseless prosecution brought solely to suppress evidence from a dirty war, and with the help of a maniacal local law-enforcement regime, the army got what it wanted.

Perhaps inspired by this kind of success, prosecutors decided to go after bigger fish. In the pornography world, that included John Stagliano, known as Buttman. As a director and the head of Evil Angel Pictures, based in Los Angeles, Buttman graced his customers' collections with such gems as *An American Buttman in London* and *Nudes a Poppin 7*. In 2007, an FBI agent paid $57.48 for Evil Angel's bondage-, enema-, and urination-themed titles *Jay Sin's Milk Nymphos* and *Storm Squirters 2: Target Practice*. The agent also used his computer to watch the trailer for *Fetish Fanatic 5*. That was enough: Stagliano was soon charged with federal obscenity violations and faced thirty-two years in jail and $7 million in fines. Rather than hear the case in a hinterland venue like Florida, prosecutors charged Buttman in Washington, D.C., where the case would bring more publicity. Shockingly, Buttman won. The judge, who seemed to be pulling for the government at the start of the case, threw the charges out on technicalities. Not long afterward, the Obama administration quietly shut the task force down.

The Buttman prosecution would have likely achieved a different result had it been brought in a more accommodating forum. However, even in conservative regions, the Internet creates a barometer of tastes and habits that can belie what residents admit in public. In 2008, a savvy Florida lawyer, Lawrence Walters, used Google search data to show that local residents were *not* the abstemious prudes they claimed themselves to be. In fact, they were more likely to search for terms like "sex" and "orgy" than "apple pie." "Time and again you'll have jurors . . . who will condemn material that they routinely consume in private," said Walters, who added that the charges against his client—a Pensacola porn-website operator— were dropped as soon as this issue was raised.

Child and Revenge Pornographers

Every parent who has asked his or her kids to explain the hidden proper- ties of a smartphone knows that the lives of today's youth are intertwined with the digital world. It should therefore come as no surprise that young people's sex lives are also integrated with their computers and phones. The law, however, seems to be confused as to how to set limits on sexual communications among kids and teens, with the result that some young people are being labeled as criminals for harmless activities while others get away with truly reprehensible behavior.

Take the advent of sexting—the use of cell phones and other devices to exchange sexually explicit images and messages. Precise figures don't exist, but studies (and much anecdotal evidence) suggest that a vast number of teens have sent or, more often, received "sexually suggestive" messages. While it is baffling to many of us, sexting is emerging as a common element of the drama of adolescent sexual awakening. Adults can generally sext without penalty, but when teens do so—even by sending explicit "selfies" to their boyfriends or girlfriends—they often violate child-pornography laws unwittingly and expose themselves to draconian penalties. In many states, for example, the age of consent for sex is sixteen, but if sixteen-year-olds send nude pictures of themselves they become child pornographers and could be forced to register, sometimes for life, as sex offenders. Minors can thus be punished for recording their own legal sexual activity. For teens, this simply does not compute.

Two Florida teens, aged sixteen and seventeen, took pictures of them- selves having sex with each other and passed them back and forth via email. In 2007, the photos came to the attention of law-enforcement au- thorities. The girl was charged with the felony of promoting a sexual per- formance by a child—that is, herself. The boy was convicted of possessing child pornography. In upholding the convictions, the court offered the following wisdom:

A number of teenagers want to let their friends know of their sexual prowess. Pictures are excellent evidence of an individual's exploits. A reasonably prudent person would believe that if you put this type of material in a teenager's hands that, at some point either for profit or bragging rights, the material will be disseminated to other members of the public.

Apparently, the court reasoned that it was better to convict the amorous teens for felonies now than take the chance that they may be embarrassed later.

A year later, several female high school students in Pennsylvania used their phones to photograph each other in bath towels or underwear. The local district attorney, George Skumanick, launched a criminal investigation into possible violations of child-pornography laws and threatened to charge the girls with felonies unless they enrolled in a counseling program to learn, among other things, about "what it means to be a girl in today's society." Skumanick told the girls' parents that criminal charges would be filed if they did not agree. Fortunately, the parents resisted the pressure and convinced a court to bar Skumanick from filing charges. However, the case went on for years, undoubtedly to the lasting detriment of the girls and their families.

Not all law-enforcement efforts are ill-willed, but the ubiquity of teen sexting, combined with the profound legal penalties attached to it, and the fact that sexts can end up in the possession of limitless numbers of kids, still puts police into a bind. In one recent Virginia case, a mother's report about compromising pictures of her daughter that were circulating online started an investigation that revealed that many other girls' photos were being traded among her high school classmates. Some of the photos showed girls partially disrobed; others showed them masturbating or having sex with multiple boys. Soon, the police had confiscated hundreds of kids' phones, and new leads arose with each student they interviewed. "We got to draw the line somewhere," said Donald Lowe, a local deputy sheriff, "or we're going to end up talking to every teenager in the damned county!" As his investigation progressed, Lowe's characterization of the girls he saw on Instagram went from "victims" to "I guess I'll call them victims" to "they just fell into this category where they victimized themselves. . . . We don't want to label them as child molesters."

The law has been erratically easing the penalties associated with the sexting phenomenon, but millions of kids technically remain felonious sex offenders. As of November 2014, about twenty states had made adjustments to the law, but that leaves the majority of kids who take sexy selfies, or who send pictures of their peers, or who retransmit the images, in the same status as producers of child pornography. In the Virginia case above, each one of the confiscated smartphones could lead to multiple felony prosecutions.

It is not always easy to separate a merely ill-advised sext between consenting viewers from the malicious dissemination of such images, or to balance the rage of victims (and their families) with the mercy that should be afforded to minors. This is especially true given a spate of recent cases in which photos of girls who were victims of sexual assaults were circulated. In San Jose, California, in 2013, Audrie Pott, fifteen, hanged herself after several teenaged boys sexually assaulted her and then circulated pictures of the attack. A few days earlier, a Canadian high school girl named Rehtaeh Parsons died after attempting to commit suicide in a similar set of circumstances. Canadian police initially did little about the case, but after a public uproar they agreed to reopen the matter. By September 2014, the boy who photographed Parsons—who was drunk and vomiting out of a window while a friend penetrated her from behind—pleaded guilty to making child pornography. What punishment, if any, should be meted out to those who retransmitted the images of Pott and Parson after receiving them? How can we know which of these people re-sent the images maliciously, or should ill will even matter? This is uncharted territory.

Then there are the revenge-porn cases, each of which is an independent argument for the doctrine of original sin. Consider the Maryland man who, in 2010, put eighty-eight compromising images of his ex-girlfriend, Annmarie Chiarini, for bid on eBay and sent links to the sale page to her family and friends, as well as her colleagues at the college where she worked as a professor of English. About a year after the auction, the ex-boyfriend created a website, featuring the tagline "HOT FOR TEACHER? WELL, COME AND GET IT!," on which the photos were posted—with Chiarini's full name and address. The police refused to do anything about it other than ridicule her. There is also the woman who runs a site where women post compromising photos of their husbands' mistresses, and the fraternity brothers who amused themselves by posting photos of unconscious nude women or women in sexual positions. "I banged her lol," bragged a frat boy about one of the women. Then there is the worst of the worst, Kevin Bollaert, who ran a profitable site charging men to post intimate photographs (and identifying information) of their ex-wives and ex-girlfriends (about ten thousand photos in all), and who then created a parallel operation in which he charged the women to take the photographs down. Short of this extreme are the day-to-day blackmailers, vengeful ex-partners, and bottom crawlers whose possession of compromising images of others gives them the power to torment. According to one 2013 study, one in ten people in the US have faced threats by their ex-partners or spouses to post embarrassing images of them online.

In 2014, the UK passed a law allowing up to two years in jail for distributing "private sexual images of someone without their consent and with the intention of causing them distress." Israel also classifies revenge porn as a sex crime, as do about fifteen American states, although the rush by legislators to "do something" about the problem may cause other issues down the road. Arizona's law, for example, is so broad that it seems to criminalize most photography involving naked bodies, even those images that are clearly newsworthy; other laws are also quite broad and are likely, as with Arizona's, to be tied up in court for quite some time. Even with no specific revenge-porn law, a Texas jury awarded a woman $500,000 after her ex-boyfriend posted a recording he made of one of their sexy Skype chats, among other things. And no revenge-porn law was needed for a grand jury to indict Hunter Moore for allegedly paying hackers to source images for his site. Increasingly, couples who sign prenuptial agreements also agree not to post nude or embarrassing photos of each other. But advocates say that too much revenge porn is slipping through the cracks, and without laws specifically targeting the practice, any woman (again, the victims are almost always women) who has been the subject of a compromising photograph or videotape is a sitting duck.

. . .

It seems clear that one who is harmed economically by revenge porn—such as by losing a job—should be able to sue his or her tormentor in court for damages, but there are others whose losses can't be readily quantified. What about children used in kiddie porn, such as a little girl, called Amy in court papers, whose uncle raped her and then circulated photos of her on the Internet? The images became among the most widely viewed child pornography in the world. "Every day of my life I live in fear that someone will see my pictures and recognize me," she later wrote, "and that I will be humiliated all over again. It hurts me to know that someone is looking at them—at me—when I was just a little girl being abused for the camera. I did not choose to be there, but now I am there forever in pictures that people are using to do sick things. . . . It's like I am being abused over and over and over again."

What is that suffering worth in court? A lot, as it should be, but trouble arises when victims such as Amy try to collect not only from the demons who took and first circulated the images but also the downstream creeps who leer at them afterward. Amy's uncle was sentenced to twelve years in prison for his crimes and was ordered to pay her $6,325, but that amount does not begin to compensate her for her losses. Steady employment has been difficult for her; she also has a need for long-term therapy, legal bills, and other losses. All told, she has suffered about $3.4 million in damages. Under the 1994 Violence Against Women Act, she should have the right to get the "full amount" of her losses from anyone producing, distributing, or possessing the images. Amy has gone after about 180 people who were charged with possessing the images and has collected dozens of awards in amounts from less than $10 to more than $1 million. But when a court ordered Doyle R. Paroline, who was found guilty of possessing hundreds of child-porn images, including two of Amy's, to pay Amy's whole claim, the US Supreme Court reversed the order. In a confused 2014 decision, the court held that holding one person responsible for Amy's entire losses was unacceptable; the link between her millions of dollars in damages and Paroline's individual misconduct was too attenuated. The court sent the case back to the lower courts to figure out how much of Amy's total losses should be attributed to Paroline. How this can be accomplished, given the thousands of people who have contributed to Amy's predicament, is impossible to say.

In response to the decision, Amy said she was "surprised and confused" and didn't understand "where this leaves [her] and other victims . . . [and] how restitution will ever be paid to kids and other victims of this endless crime." She was right to be disappointed, and while Paroline is as unsympathetic as anyone can be, the court's reasoning was not entirely off base. At least the court's majority held that she was entitled to something, even if it could not say how much. Three of the dissenting justices (Roberts, Scalia, and Thomas) thought the law allowed her to get nothing.

The issue of compensating victims of pornography first emerged in the 1980s, when Andrea Dworkin and Catharine MacKinnon wrote up a model law giving violent crime victims the right to sue pornographers (as well as porn sellers and distributors) and claim that pornography somehow caused their assailants to attack them. The law was adopted in Indianapolis in 1984 and, thankfully, was struck down by the courts.

A few years earlier, a grieving mother sued *Penthouse* magazine, claiming that her fourteen-year-old son, who died while engaging in "autoerotic asphyxiation," tried the hazardous masturbation technique after reading about it in the magazine. She won big before a sympathetic jury, but the verdict was reversed on appeal. The magazine article, no matter how ridiculous or sleazy, was protected by the First Amendment because it did not directly incite the boy to harm himself.

Striking down laws like Indianapolis's and throwing out the verdict against *Penthouse* are easy calls, because people should be required to pay only for harms they really cause. Much harder is the Supreme Court's decision against victims such as Amy. The stolen innocence and continued agony of child-pornography victims must be compensated and should be done so without forcing them to chase down everyone who is gratified by the illegal images. In my opinion, Amy should be allowed to collect her full damages from Paroline. If he then wishes to find and sue other guilty parties and sort out who is more or less responsible for Amy's losses, then that should be his burden.

To Forbid and Foment

The underlying issues in obscenity law often concern *who* may consume pornography as opposed to whether it should be available at all. Much of the legal Sturm und Drang about porn over the past five centuries has been, at bottom, an effort by one audience group to bar another from accessing titillating materials. In one form or another, pornography has always been around, but inefficient technology limited its distribution. As the elements of mass culture took shape, the game changed, and for the first time sexually explicit materials were condemned as harmful—at least for the lower classes.

When the elites of Renaissance Europe rediscovered ancient Greek and Roman art, philosophy, and literature, many developed a special interest in antiquity's many explicit depictions of sex. However, while plenty of aristocrats were (in Paula Findlen's phrase) "masturbating to the classics," sexual material was sparsely circulated. Any one item of pornography was certain to remain just that: a singular object for private consumption. That exclusivity ended when modern printing and reproduction techniques came into use in the late fifteenth century. A mass market for pornography materialized almost overnight. Had such materials remained in manuscript form and circulated only among the elites, obscenity restrictions would likely never have been imposed. Yet the advent of a large consumer audience for pornography sparked a rush by secular and religious authorities to control it. What had been harmless fun among friends became dirty and dangerous.

Early editions of printed porn were, like their manuscript predecessors, literate and geared to snobby tastes. The growing mass market demanded earthier fare. As a prostitute urges in the *Dialoghi* (*Dialogues*) of Pietro Aretino, sixteenth-century Italy's most infamous pornographic work: "Speak plainly and say 'fuck,' 'prick,' 'cunt,' and 'ass' if you want anyone except the scholars at the University of Rome to understand you." The new crop of budding printer-pornographers took this as sound marketing advice and set about supplying Europe with cheap, blunt, and explicit works. Aretino, who in 1537 published lusty sonnets accompanying sixteen hard-core images lifted from the Vatican's own collection, was the Renaissance world's premier pornographer. The book came to be known as *Aretino's Postures* and was reproduced everywhere, an accomplishment that placed his work at the bull's-eye of the church's first major censorship initiative. The *Postures* soon joined the select company of the works of Martin Luther, Johannes Kepler, and Niccolò Machiavelli, among others, in the Vatican's inaugural Index librorum prohibitorum (List of Forbidden Books). The index was primarily intended to suppress heretical religious and scientific works, but it also banned books concerning "things lascivious or obscene."

The church went prudish, right down to covering up the exposed genitals of the figures in Michelangelo's Sistine Chapel fresco *The Last Judgment* with painted wisps of fabric and fig leaves. However, an immense pornographic consumer culture was already in place, and nothing could eliminate it. If printing Aretino's works in Italy was dicey, less regulated printers elsewhere were only too happy to do the job. Pornography was as easily accessible as liquor was in the US during Prohibition. By the end of the sixteenth century, cheaply printed erotic images were sold in Venice's Piazza San Marco along with sexy depictions of famous courtesans.

In many ways, the situation in the United States at the turn of the twentieth century was similar. A federal law from 1873 banned the transportation of anything having to do with sex or reproduction. The country's main morals enforcer (and the namesake of the anti-pornography law), the maniacal Anthony Comstock, bagged convictions left and right and confiscated vast amounts of naughty playing cards, medical and other books dealing with reproduction, pills, powders, and "rubber goods." During his forty-year career as an anti-smut crusader, Comstock claimed to have confiscated sixteen tons of "vampire literature," organized more than four thousand arrests, and convicted enough people to fill sixty train coaches. In the words of one proud prosecutor, the US had become "one great society for the suppression of vice."

This was only partially true. Many of Comstock's targets were outliers, far from the centers of wealth and power and helpless before the relentless legal juggernaut he commanded. In 1902, for example, he secured a five-year prison sentence against Ida Craddock, a stenographer and "divine science" authority who wrote *Advice to a Bridegroom*, a pamphlet that advised young men on attaining "sweet and wholesome" satisfaction with their brides. This conviction came after Comstock had forced Craddock to serve a prison sentence for selling another oddity called *The Wedding Night*. Rather than return to jail, Craddock killed herself, just as fourteen other Comstock targets would do.

Morals advocates such as Comstock maintained that the mere suggestion of sex was dangerous. Sexual materials sparked the urge to masturbate, which was still considered to be harmful to health and a source of weakness in societies. Even Sigmund Freud and his followers had difficulty letting go of the belief that solitary sex *had* to be harmful in some way, even if it was not as lethal as previously imagined. Primarily, however, it was the flights of fantasy during the act of self-gratification that caused the most persistent fears. Such thoughts were believed to lead to antisocial behavior, lassitude, and even homosexuality. Sexual fantasies were tools of the devil, and Satan's most vulnerable victims were children. As Comstock thundered in his manifesto *Traps for the Young*:

> Satan is more interested in the child than many parents are. Parents do not stop to think or look for their children in these matters while the arch-enemy is thinking, watching, and plotting continually to effect their ruin. Thoughtless parents, heedless guardians, negligent teachers, you are each of you just the kind that old Satan delights to see placed over the child. He sets his base traps right in your very presence, captures and ruins your children, and you are all criminally responsible.

Comstock was in a position to know this firsthand. He had masturbated so furiously in his youth that he feared he might be driven to suicide. His own experiences seem to have influenced his work. In his book

Frauds Exposed, he wrote that sex "fastens itself upon the imagination . . . defiling the mind, corrupting the thoughts, leading to secret practices of most foul and revolting character, until the victim tires of life and existence is scarcely endurable." He warned: "Every new generation of youth is sent into the world as sheep in the midst of wolves. Traps are laid for them in every direction. . . . Once in the trap, the victim will love it and press greedily forward."

That the prohibitive sweep of the Comstock Act included books such as Craddock's, which were addressed to married couples, was lost in the rush to suppress everything remotely sex-related. Nor was it relevant to morals enforcers that the medical works and birth control information they attacked were focused on health rather than the erotic. Most troubling, those who pushed against obscenity ignored the fact that the usual ages of consent for sexual relations were ten or twelve years old, or that the rape of children was rarely taken seriously by courts. Youngsters could thus be taken sexually, often by force, without penalty, but if a word or image conceivably incited children to have sexual desires, then the purveyors of such "vampire" materials stood to be branded as criminals.

The clarion call of "saving" children from sexual fantasies would animate obscenity law throughout the century. While the Comstock Act was a dead letter by the 1980s, its ghost lingered. In 1994, for example, US surgeon general Jocelyn Elders was forced from office for stating, following a speech at the United Nations about HIV/AIDS, that masturbation should be discussed in schools as an alternative to risky sexual activity. That comment sparked a conservative outcry in Congress, in which Elders and her boss Bill Clinton were accused, among other things, of preaching "free sex" and ruining the country's "moral fiber." (Never one for taking a principled stand on questions of sex, Clinton fired Elders.) In 2012, Wisconsin governor Scott Walker did his part to repair the country's moral fiber by signing a bill permitting schools to refuse mention of something as inflammatory as puberty in sex-education classes.

None of this is to say that morals enforcers don't allow themselves the opportunity to savor the same materials that "ruin" children. As part of Comstock's 1873 campaign for his anti-obscenity law, he brought to Washington a collection of smutty stuff that students had purportedly been ordering in the mail. Setting up shop in Vice President Schuyler Colfax's office, he staged a pornography exhibition for lawmakers that he called a "chamber of horrors." There he displayed "lowbrow publications and their advertisements, gadgets purportedly designed to stimulate sexual potency, and 'fancy books' and . . . other abominations." As legislators toured and retoured the show, the bill's official sponsor, Representative Clinton Merriam of New York, argued that "low brutality" threatened to "destroy the future of the Republic by making merchandize of the morals of our youth." The *New York Times* joined in, expressing its disgust at the sexual materials "sent by post to the girls and boys in our schools" and lionizing Comstock for having already seized tons of "the most loathsome printed matter ever sent into the world to do the devil's work." Fully sated, the lawmakers approved Comstock's bill.

Stiff pornography laws are a godsend for law enforcement. Government funding flows, the problem never goes away, and police get to spend considerable time examining the materials they confiscate. Nowhere was this more the case than at the FBI, when, starting in the 1920s, the agency thrust itself into anti-obscenity enforcement and set up a giant file of sex-related material that eventually swelled to more than one hundred thousand separate sub-files. Most of it was not used in criminal investigations. Rather, it was obtained because the FBI's pornography-obsessed director, J. Edgar Hoover, wanted the bureau to cast the widest possible net. For a long time, the FBI was the largest repository of smut in the US. Aside from the incriminating material the bureau kept to intimidate political enemies, the files contained an impressive catalog of African American "race music," the garbled pop hit "Louie Louie" (which claimed substantial bureau resources before agents gave up trying to decipher the song's lyrics), comic books, pulp novels, playing cards, "novelties," and mountains of films and photographs. The files grew after Hoover's death in 1972. In 1980–1981 alone, as X-rated videocassettes became widely available, agents submitted more than thirteen thousand items.

Access to these files was coveted within the FBI. Hoover ordered the material secured to prevent "undue curiosity," but the temptation for bureau personnel to peek was too much to endure. Former assistant director William Sullivan wrote in 1979 that "within hours a file with compromising photographs would be opened and closed [by agents] so many times that the tape would lose all of its adhesiveness." Hoover guarded his own access to the files jealously and reacted with fury when he was not alerted to new caches of spicy material. In 1970, for example, agents broke into the apartment of left-wing activist Angela Davis and found photographs of her having sex with her boyfriend. Given the FBI's intense interest in Davis, one would have thought Hoover likely to commend the agents involved; but they had made a big mistake by not sending the director the photos immediately. After he learned about them, he demanded to see them at once and poisoned a responsible agent's personnel file with a brutal letter of censure.

The FBI did more than compile a giant porn collection. In 1968, for example, two agents were dispatched to a San Francisco film festival to watch a midnight screening of Andy Warhol's film *Lonesome Cowboys*. The comic value of crew-cut G-men scowling in a California art house cinema, scribbling notes while a transvestite sheriff cavorted onscreen, was omitted from their report, but the following observations were included: "All of the males in the cast displayed homosexual tendencies and conducted themselves toward one another in an effeminate manner," "The position of the male and female [actors] suggested an act of cunnilingus," "A cowboy fondl[ed] the nipples of another cowboy," and so on. The obscenity case against Warhol and *Lonesome Cowboys* went nowhere, but the agents, at least, had been treated to a bureau-paid trip to San Francisco and an eyeful of the Wild West, 1960s style. By the end of the decade, as loosening obscenity standards gave the green light to what the bureau called "nude art-type movie films" such as Warhol's, the FBI's stores of such materials were cleared out to make room for more explicit stuff.

Another axis of anti-porn activity was Citizens for Decent Literature (CDL), a group that used a heady mixture of lawsuits, lobbying, and pornography displays to—in the CDL's words—"arouse" the public and "stimulate community action." Headed by Charles Keating, the Cincinnati lawyer who went to court against *Oh Calcutta!*, the CDL racked up an impressive array of victories, including lawsuits resulting in a ban (in some locations) of Russ Meyer's breast-shaking 1968 classic *Vixen!*, as well as bans of *Mad* and *Playboy* magazines. The CDL also played a leading role in undermining President Lyndon Johnson's Commission on Obscenity and Pornography, which had concluded that pornography was, in many instances, not harmful.

Keating himself was a mixed bag. At his office, he was known to leer at the blonde, buxom women he hired, whom he frequently pressured to have breast-enlargement surgery. He is now best remembered as one of the worst crooks in the fraud-soaked Savings and Loan Crisis of the 1980s and 1990s, for which he was convicted in a number of courts. However, in the 1960s he was known as a passionate anti-pornography activist— who used sex to deliver his message. In 1962, as the CDL cheered on obscenity charges against Henry Miller's *Tropic of Cancer*, it distributed a pamphlet featuring the book's "nineteen dirtiest passages." The next year, the CDL released *Perversion for Profit*, a film that mixed fabricated facts (for example, most porn ends up in the hands of kids; porn causes communist sympathies and homosexuality) with images from gay, straight, and fetish skin magazines. The ostensible object of the film was to educate the public about the pornography industry and its risk to children, but the effect was also stimulating, to say the least.

In 1965, at a CDL conference at New York's Waldorf Astoria hotel, a display behind an "adults only" door featured nudism, S&M, bestiality, and other outré subjects. At other CDL functions, where largely religious audiences were shown hard-core materials, Keating explained that the displays were mounted "to inform you of what is available on your newsstands, and what, very possibly, your children are reading." In 1968—in a replay of Comstock's "chamber of horrors"—the CDL and Senator Strom Thurmond staged an X-rated film festival in the US Capitol, ostensibly to derail the appointment of Abe Fortas as chief justice of the Supreme Court. The films (a CDL production called *Target Smut* and some stag shorts) were shown as examples of the "floodtide" of "filth" that Fortas's liberal obscenity decisions had purportedly unleashed, and were seen by "an untold number of senators," who all feigned outrage. The event contributed to dooming the Fortas nomination.

The CDL's use of pornography to provoke censorious government action was hypocritical to the core, but not unique. Anti-porn activists often exploit, and seem to relish, what they condemn. Even the strident and influential 1993 book *Only Words* by feminist law professor Catharine MacKinnon begins on a perversely smutty note:

> Imagine that . . . you grow up with your father holding you down and covering your mouth so another man can make a horrible searing pain between your legs. When you are older, your husband ties you to the bed and drips hot wax on your nipples and brings in other men to watch and makes you smile through it. Your doctor will not give you drugs he has addicted you to unless you suck his penis.

MacKinnon wrote in a footnote that the scenarios in this quote—which is only a short excerpt of a lengthy, feverishly sadistic pastiche—were taken from true sources, but that does not explain why she gives off such a strong whiff of the aficionado, like so many who claim outrage at pornography.

Hoover and Keating maintained the pretense of public service to the end, but not Australia's David Haines. In 1994, after fourteen years as one of that country's chief censors, Haines jumped ship and started making his own X-rated films. His 1996 magnum opus, *Buffy Down Under*, was a huge success, in no small part because Haines knew just how far a sex film could go and still avoid government intrusion. Haines also gave himself a (clothed) role in *Revenge Aussie Style*, which also did well. But the fortunes of his films were less important than the veneer of respectability he gave to the nascent Australian pornography industry. "I've got no problem wanting to arouse people," the self-described "conservative Englishman" said in 1999, adding, "I've never had a problem with explicit movies." Haines gave the lie to decades of government-sponsored sanctimony and showed how similar the opposing sides of censorship issues can be.

If there was an award for prurience wrapped in sanctimony, it would go to Independent Counsel Kenneth Starr's probe into President Bill Clinton's sexual hijinks with White House intern Monica Lewinsky, which culminated in a graphically detailed report and impeachment proceedings in late 1998. Starr had spent years looking into Clinton's personal financial dealings, with little to show for his efforts, when news of Clinton's relationship with Lewinsky surfaced. In short order, what novelist Philip Roth called "an enormous piety binge," during which the "president's penis was on everyone's mind," was unleashed.

The findings of Starr's investigation are phrased in the report in somber bureaucratic style. The document purports to trace a pattern of grievous presidential misconduct, but its real purpose was to dish out all the crummy details of Lewinsky's and Clinton's sexual encounters. Every ejaculation, every stain, every grope, fondle, and phone-sex encounter between them is detailed and footnoted. Examples: "I wanted him to touch my genitals with his genitals"; "The President inserted a cigar into Ms. Lewinsky's vagina, then put the cigar in his mouth and said: 'It tastes good.' After they were finished, Ms. Lewinsky left the Oval Office and walked through the Rose Garden"; "Ms. Lewinsky performed oral sex on him, again until he ejaculated." It goes on in a similar vein, interminably.

The *Starr Report* was calculated to justify Clinton's impeachment, and it worked. The process dragged on well into 1999. Clinton eventually beat the impeachment and served out his second term, but not without lasting damage to the presidency. It is risky to speculate what would have happened had the president's semen not become a general topic of conversation, but it is certain that without the report or the impeachment proceedings, the Democratic candidate for president in 2000—Clinton's former vice president, Al Gore—would have been in a much stronger position to win the election.

No one was arrested for downloading or reading the *Starr Report*. On the contrary, Clinton's congressional enemies pressed for its immediate release on the Internet, and it is safe to assume that most every reader searched for the "hot" parts first, just as boys once did with *Playboy*. However, the *Starr Report* stands on its own as a cultural/pornographic artifact—its perversity heightened by the faux-horrified tone its author struck throughout its 154 double-columned pages. Starr wrote that it was "regrettable" that he forced people to testify about "sensitive personal matters," and gave lip service to the "private family life" we are all "entitled" to enjoy. But those concerns, he averred in the same high-minded legalese, were nothing next his own grave duty to guard the presidency as an "inspiring symbol of all that is highest in American purpose and ideals." Five years after Starr finished smearing Clinton, he signed on as dean of the law school at Pepperdine University, a Christian institution where sex among unmarried students is banned. Perhaps Starr could reconcile his record of prurience with his avowed Christianity, but in truth he is no less a scoundrel than Comstock, Keating, or the other Bible-thumping porn hounds who preceded him.

The *Starr Report* was guilt-free sex reading for the ruling class, but that does not hold for other legal pornography. While the consumption of most X-rated material is now permitted, at least for adults, the stigma attached to enjoying it remains intact, and exposure of one's viewing habits can lead to career-killing sanctions. Being exposed as an avid pornography consumer means disqualification for high public office, as do other even mildly transgressive sexual thoughts and deeds. As one reporter for *GQ* magazine discovered in 2012, when he underwent a simulated vetting process for vice presidential candidates:

> Less than an hour after I meet the vetter for the first time, he asks me if I've always been faithful to my wife. Next he wants to know if I've ever been accused of sexual harassment. And then whether I've ever paid for sex. Before long he's asking me about any past history I might have with sadomasochism. Internet-porn memberships? Sexting?

That was before the interrogation turned to homemade sex tapes, about which the reporter was asked many more questions. In effect, unless candidates have married their college or high school sweethearts and remained faithful in both body and mind, they should forget about running for high-profile public office. Former New York congressman Anthony Weiner learned this in 2011, when the world discovered that he had sent pictures of his crotch (with an impressive erection) and exchanged explicit messages over social media with several women who were not his wife. None of these communications violated the law, but that was not the point. Weiner had no choice but to resign from Congress. Two years later, when he reemerged to run for mayor of New York City, his early lead in the polls signaled that the city might forgive his former trespasses. However, the revelation that his cybersex escapades had continued, this time under the moniker Carlos Danger, tanked his candidacy. He will not be holding public office in the foreseeable future.

Anthony Weiner's pornography production with himself as the subject put him farther down the road of sexual transgression than even blasé New Yorkers could stomach. By contrast, the ascent of Clarence Thomas to the US Supreme Court was almost derailed by his taste for commercially produced pornography, a habit everyone agreed was inconsistent with a position as a premier interpreter of the law. In 1991, after Thomas was nominated to the court, his former employee Anita Hill claimed that he had (among other foul things) told her of his interest in X-rated films. Thomas denied everything, but other acquaintances of his privately confirmed his regular rentals of porn videotapes (including those featurng a rotund actress known as Bad Mama Jama), his comprehensive *Playboy* magazine collection, and his trips to adult movie theaters during his law school days at Yale. One law school friend, Henry Terry, remembered Thomas enthusiastically describing such films in detail. "It was a thing with him," said Terry. "Everyone knew it. That's just what he did."

However unabashed Thomas might have been in law school, by the time he reached groping distance of the Supreme Court, his personal "brand" had changed. He was now presented to the Senate and to the country as a devoutly Christian champion of traditional values, and "porn lover" did not fit that profile. As the issue heated up, Thomas's key supporter in the Senate, John C. Danforth, extracted a commitment from Joe Biden, the Democratic chairman of the Senate Judiciary Committee, that Thomas would not be asked about his interest in pornography during his confirmation hearing. If that happened, Danforth threatened, Republicans would throw their own pile of sexual dirt on Hill, which might include accusations linking

Hill with lesbianism, placing her own pubic hairs onto her students' school papers, and a delusional disorder called erotomania.

Thomas angrily denied Hill's accusations, calling them (and her sexual-harassment allegations) a "high-tech lynching" and a racist ploy to hold down an "uppity" black man. Backed by a formidable legal and public-relations team supplied by the White House and his supporters in Congress, he was confirmed in a close vote. However, wary of any other damaging information emerging, the White House advanced his swearing-in ceremony by nine days, to October 23, 1991. That turned out to be a prescient call. On that day, *Washington Post* reporters confirmed Thomas's considerable record of porn-video rentals—but it was too late. He was on the court for life, and the true extent of Thomas's fantasy relationships with the likes of Bad Mama Jama no longer mattered.

Had the whole truth emerged, it would have ended the Thomas nomination. High-placed judges may view porn in order to rule on its lawfulness—that is part of the job description—but compulsively seeking it out for their own masturbatory pleasure is too much. Yet Thomas's personal interest in pornography is irrelevant to his ability to discharge the duties of a Supreme Court justice. Just as it was wrong to demand that Clinton account for his sex life under oath and then to impeach him for not telling the truth, it would have been a grave error to demand that Thomas testify about his embarrassing but entirely legal masturbation habits.

Smut at Work and Behind Bars

As the law stood in 1991, it was anyone's guess whether Thomas's on-the-job braggadocio about his porn-viewing habits would support a legal claim for sexual harassment. However, had Thomas gone one step further and shown Bad Mama Jama videos to Hill at work, and had Hill then brought a complaint to an impartial court and not a pack of Senate hyenas, she would likely have prevailed. The display of pornography in the workplace is a classic ground for a "hostile environment" sexual-harassment claim. In this context, the legality of the pornography under free-speech laws is less important than maintaining a harassment-free workplace. The right to view Bad Mama Jama's oeuvre may be constitutional, but anyone who believes it to be appropriate viewing at the office can expect a rude shock in court. In this way, sexual harassment law can allow an end run around the broad protections of the First Amendment.

Even the most ardent pornography advocates would admit that hard-core films and images are often offensive. For many, pornography's turn-on value is increased to the degree that it disgusts others. Yet what about nonpornographic material? Would Hill had have cause to complain if her boss had showed her a nude image by an acknowledged master? Should a priceless painting from the Louvre's collection be considered in the same manner as an image taken from *Caught from Behind, Part II*? Quite possibly, depending on the fragility of the employee and the cravenness of the employer. Soon after the Hill–Thomas imbroglio, for example, a professor at Penn State University was assigned to teach in a classroom decorated with a reproduction of Francisco Goya's *Naked Maja*, a painting depicting a nude woman lying on her back, legs closed, arms up, and with a rather inviting expression in her eyes. The original painting (along with its companion, *Clothed Maja*) is in the collection of Madrid's Prado Museum and has long been a source of both Spanish pride and American consternation. In 1930, after Spain issued postage stamps emblazoned with *Naked Maja*, the US barred and returned all mail bearing the stamps. However, by 1992 times had changed considerably, and by no stretch of the law could Goya's masterpiece be tagged as obscene.

Or so it would have seemed. Not only was the professor, Nancy Stumhofer, irritated by the image, she later wrote:

> I felt as though I were standing there naked, exposed and vulnerable. . . . After my initial embarrassment passed, I became angry because I knew none of my male colleagues would ever find themselves in a similar situation, nor would the students in my class.

Stumhofer complained that she could not do her job in the company of *Naked Maja*. School officials offered her another classroom, but she refused. They also offered to remove the print while Stumhofer was in the classroom, but she refused that solution as well because "every female student in every class scheduled in that room would have to be subjected" to the "chilled classroom climate" the image imposed. The painting constituted sexual harassment, "whether it was a *Playboy* centerfold or a Goya," the professor said. "It's a nude picture of a woman which encourages males to make remarks about body parts." The print was removed before a lawsuit could be filed. Whether or not Stumhofer was being touchy to a fault was evidently less important to the university than the financial risk and adverse publicity a sexual harassment lawsuit would have brought.

If a world-class painting is susceptible to employee complaints, then images with sketchier artistic provenance are even more vulnerable. In 1993, the University of Nebraska ordered a graduate student to remove a snapshot from his desk. The picture, of the student's wife in a bathing suit, purportedly also created a hostile workplace environment for female staff, faculty, and students. In another incident a few years later, an assistant school superintendent in Murfreesboro, Tennessee, named Laurie Crowder crossed the rotunda of the town's city hall and was shocked to confront *Gwen*, a twelve-by-sixteen-inch painting of a mostly nude woman by artist Maxine Henderson. The painting, along with Henderson's other paintings of churches, landscapes, and still lifes, had been installed in the rotunda at the invitation of the city's art commission. The next day, Crowder filed a sexual harassment complaint charging that *Gwen* was "pornographic," and "very offensive to and degrading to [her] as a woman," and that it was unlawful for the city to "thrust" the painting "in [her] face" as she went into a meeting with her superiors, most of whom were men. The painting was removed, which prompted Henderson to file her own lawsuit—this time for the infringement of her First Amendment rights as an artist. Henderson won the key parts of that case, but the painting never went back on the rotunda wall.

The removals of *Gwen*, *Naked Maja*, and the snapshot of the student's wife were intended to guard against substantial jury awards arising from "hostile" workplace environments. With few exceptions, this "hostility" refers to the sexual aggression of men toward women, something believed to be simmering in the male psyche that even mild images can trigger into bad behavior. However speculative the connection between a painting and male aggression, the practical reality is that the door to the marketplace of sexual ideas closes in face of sexual-harassment law. About a year after the Hill–Thomas hearings, an expert in a closely watched sexual-harassment case opined that even "sexist advertising" had the effect of "priming" men to act in a sexist manner toward female employees and job applicants. The court warmed to this theory: "Sexual stereotyping," the court said, "is relevant to the question [of] whether women were sexually harassed."

Standards in Prison and Mental Hospitals

Given the supposition that even anodyne images can cause men to become beasts, it would follow that incarcerated sex offenders should be separated from pornography. Yet in California's Coalinga State Hospital, a locked treatment facility for sex offenders, including rapists and pedophiles, pornography can be plentiful. At least during 2008–2010, if an offender was in therapy, he could be shown images of adults having sex, children in bathing suits, and so on, while a plethysmograph—a device wrapped around his penis to measure erection-inducing blood surges—signaled the man's arousal response. If, however, the offender wanted diversion without therapy, he was allowed to watch pornographic videos during which, presumably, the blood flowed plentifully. Given that these offenders have little hope of leaving Coalinga (very few are ever discharged), hospital administrators evidently saw little public risk in letting patients live out their condemned lives in porn-induced sexual fantasy.

While California's convicted sex offenders pass the time with pornography, no one can seem to agree on whether other prisoners should be allowed any sex materials at all. In 2006, a California man in prison for murder was penalized for having an article from *Men's Health* magazine on the subject of female orgasms. A court upheld the penalty: "Although *Men's Health* magazine is not what one would normally characterize as an obscene publication, and may contain useful and socially acceptable articles properly suited for the adult eye in mainstream America, its content may not be suitable for prison inmates." In other words, even a magazine for sale in health clubs can be banned in prisons if it has some sort of sexual content.

However, in 2013, another California court allowed a prisoner in a maximum-security prison to cuddle up with *The Silver Crown,* a novel of the "werewolf erotica" genre. The book concerns a female werewolf hunter who falls in love with one of her prey, leading, the court said, to "a great number of graphic sexual encounters," including "detailed descriptions of intercourse, sodomy, oral-genital contact, oral-anal contact, voyeurism, exhibitionism, and *ménage à trois.* Semen is mentioned." (The court added that "no bestiality is portrayed [unless werewolves count].") Despite *The Silver Crown's* howling hard-core content, the court was troubled that prison authorities had not measured its "serious literary value" before confiscating it. Had they done so, said the court, they would have found that the book's plot and character development were "more than a mere sham" and that, taken as a whole, it was not legally obscene. Refusing to give prisons carte blanche to arbitrarily confiscate any sexual materials, the court required prison authorities to perform a sophisticated constitutional analysis—even with a book describing oral–anal sex between a woman and a werewolf.

That the same state's penal system can ban *Men's Health* magazine while allowing *The Silver Crown* exemplifies the jumble of prison porn standards throughout the US. Connecticut recently banned all "pictorial depictions of sexual activity or nudity" from its jails, a measure it said protected female prison staff from hostile sexual work environments. Several prisoners contended that access to porn was their constitutional right—something the California court ruling in the werewolf-erotica case seemed to accept—but that argument fell on deaf ears. In Connecticut, as in many other regions, prisoners' rights are of little concern to anyone but the prisoners themselves. In any event, the fortunate reader of *The Silver Crown* would have been well advised not to celebrate his legal victory too vigorously, even under the sheets: he was still subject to a prison rule barring "intentionally sustained masturbation without exposure."

• • •

In 1968, the noted First Amendment lawyer Charles Rembar wrote a thick book called *The End of Obscenity*, which traced the steady liberalization of obscenity law in the US and predicted that Western society's "distorted, impoverished, masturbatory" obsession with sexual materials will "diminish as the restraints on expression recede." As society sheds the last vestiges of Comstockery, he predicted, no one will care about sexual words or images anymore. "Pornography, which is in the groin of the beholder, will lose its force." Referring to the lifting of bans on books such as Henry Miller's *Tropic of Cancer*, Rembar observed that it was only the "grownups" who were aroused by these works. "The younger generation is much less excited by the new freedom in literature—in both senses: it is less alarmed and it is less titillated."

How wrong Rembar was. Almost fifty years later, the world is more soaked in sexual representations than he could have imagined. Indeed, many now are so inured to smut that ever more precise and bizarre iterations are required for arousal to take place. More importantly, we have lost none of our ambivalence on the subject; the regions with the most restrictive obscenity laws are those with the highest per capita consumption of pornography. Writing about the prevalence of sex and violence in the media, former New York governor Mario Cuomo observed: "We are . . . caught in this uncomfortable contradiction: the desire for what disgusts us, the disgust for what we desire."

As sexual depictions become more commonplace—perhaps because they are everywhere—many of us are increasingly convinced that they must be harmful. Recently, British Internet providers made "family-friendly filters," which block sexual websites, the default for customers. Prime Minister David Cameron promoted the initiative to prevent what he called the corrosion of childhood, notwithstanding that a study produced by his own government concluded that a "causal relationship" between pornography and risky sexual behavior among young people "could not be established." True, nearly all teenagers who engage in sexually risky behavior have tasted Internet pornography, but so have teens who don't take such risks. But the truth matters here less than perceptions. So long as sex remains (in the words of Justice William Brennan) "a great and mysterious motive force in human life" and a "subject of absorbing interest to mankind," its depictions—both beautiful and hideous—will cause vexation. The law just follows.

CHAPTER 5

THE LIMITS OF CONSENT

Rape and Sexual Harassment

We start with four short anecdotes:

- In 1961, a sixty-year-old West Virginia man was acquitted of raping a nine-year-old girl because the girl had already had intercourse with a teenaged boy.

- Fourteen years later, an English man encouraged three of his drunken friends to have sex with his wife while he watched, telling them not to stop if she resisted them. (She was "kinky," the husband said, and was aroused by force.) Britain's highest court ruled that the friends should walk free if they honestly believed the woman had wanted sex, even if her struggle during the ordeal made that belief unreasonable.

- In 2013, an Israeli judge, considering the gang rape of a thirteen-year-old girl, opined: "There are some girls who enjoy being raped."

- A rape counselor at a major American university said in 2008 that she would never advise a female student to avoid risky situations such as getting drunk and climbing into bed with a boy because that "sends the message [that rape] is the victim's fault."

Other than causing bile to churn in the stomach, these stories each highlight issues driving the ongoing debates over rape. While the attackers mentioned above would presumably all agree that rape is a terrible crime, none saw themselves as rapists. In the first example, the girl's previous sexual encounter trumped everything else—even the law's protection of those considered too young to make decisions about sex. The rules have since changed to bar evidence of a victim's sexual past, but the "chastity" issue still hovers over rape cases, even those involving children. In 2014, for example, a Texas judge declined to jail a man for having sex with a fourteen-year-old girl because she was sexually experienced, and thus "wasn't the victim she claimed to be."

The men who gang-raped their friend's wife, in the second example above, had a way out of jail (at least in theory) if they believed they had carte blanche to take her sexually. British law soon changed to require men to pay closer attention to their sex partners' feelings, but a subsequent case involving another man who "gave" his wife to a pal brought the same result. The woman sobbed throughout the ordeal, and the husband's friend walked free. These examples are, admittedly, extreme, but consent remains the key issue in every adult rape case. The basic rule is that sex between adults is not rape if both sides consent, but deciding whether there was consent is one of the most confounding tasks the law demands of juries. The onus remains on the victim (who is nearly always a woman) to communicate her lack of consent with ringing (and provable) clarity, or she will likely be found to have "wanted it."

In the third example, the Israeli judge's Paleolithic remarks about female rape fantasies cost him his job, but he is less of an outlier than he might seem. The idea that women crave rape and project their fantasies onto men has long been woven into the law. More than a few women have been found to have either desired forced sex or dreamt up the episodes entirely. This leads us to the campus counselor, in the fourth example, who won't give female students rape-avoidance advice. In an effort to halt the practice of blaming victims, the counselor puts her convictions over common sense. It is true that victims don't cause their own rapes—on dates, at parties, or anywhere else—but that should not forestall caution and good thinking.

In recent decades, the recognition that rape involves more than a stereotypical violent stranger leaping out of the dark, and in fact occurs most often among people who know each other, has brought broad changes to the law. Rape has come to be seen as one part of a web of women-subordinating power dynamics. "All sexist behavior [is] an extension of the paradigmatic act of rape," as the feminist writer Ellen Willis said. Sexual harassment, girly magazines, sexist advertising, rape—they are all viewed as elements of the same oppression. Because sexual harassment law is an outgrowth of efforts to fix the entire legal matrix concerning sexual force, we consider both rape and sexual harassment in the same chapter.

The Hateful Tradition

Until the mid-twentieth century, rape law was essentially as it had been for many hundreds of years: severe penalties awaited those convicted of the crime, but the path to convictions was mined with obstacles. Early English law required the victim to raise an immediate "hue and cry" and display her bloody garments to the nearest group of respectable people. Then she had to make reports to various public authorities and describe the assault precisely the same way each time. Any variance in the reports or other missteps destroyed the case and exposed her to imprisonment for making false charges. This was no mere threat. Approximately half the females who accused men of rape ended up in jail themselves. In 1320, a ten-year-old London girl was dragged off the street and raped. No one doubted that her attacker had "ravished her maidenhead," but he was acquitted because one of her accounts said that she was attacked on a Sunday, and another said it occurred on a Tuesday. The man then sued her and her father for filing a false case. Even when the reporting was consistent, there was also a requirement that rape be brought to "completion." In 1287, a seven-year-old English girl was sexually attacked so violently that blood flowed from several parts of her body, yet her tiny size prevented her rapist from ejaculating inside of her. Finding the attack a "worthless act," the court threw the case out.

By the late seventeenth century, rank misogyny was hardwired into the common law. The rules punishing rape were viewed less as a means of protecting women than as a way for vindictive females to ruin men with false accusations. Lord Matthew Hale, chief justice of England, articulated this perspective in his hugely influential *Historia Placitorum Coronae* (*History of the Pleas of the Crown*), published in 1736. Hale warned that rape was "an accusation easily to be made and hard to be proved, and harder to be defended by the party accused," and urged judges to protect men against "malicious and false" women. These exact words would be repeated innumerable times in the coming centuries throughout the Anglo-American legal system.

Lord Hale was a Puritan prig of the most austere order, but his views on sex and women were typical. When he wrote that husbands could use violence to force their wives into sexual submission, he was simply re-stating a long-standing legal principle: a wife was her husband's prop-erty, and any resistance to his sexual demands was no more acceptable than the stubbornness of a disobedient horse. Hale also presided over one of England's last and most venomous witchcraft trials, in which two widows went to their deaths for casting spells on children, causing lice "of extraordinary bigness" to colonize their bodies, and making large nails erupt from their mouths. There was good evidence casting doubt on the charges—starting with the fact that no hardware ever emerged from anyone's mouth—but Hale still piously signed the death warrants. Had a more thoughtful, merciful, or courageous judge been presiding, the women could have survived, but Hale was no such man, and his hostility toward women resonated for centuries.

Hale's positions on rape were invoked by courts in the US, Britain, and Australia well into the twentieth century. Judges routinely cau-tioned juries that rape was a crime "easily charged and not easily dis-proved," and also that the woman's testimony should be taken with "caution." This skepticism, unique in criminal law, existed at all levels of the justice system. In the 1970s, for example, a rape suspect arrested in the US had a 60 percent chance of being charged and only a 35 per-cent chance of being convicted. In absolute terms, a man reasonably suspected of rape stood a seven-in-ten chance of walking free. During rape trials, the woman's entire sex life would come under close scrutiny, as would any "enticements" she may have made, whether her resistance had been genuine, how promptly she complained to police, and whether, deep down, she really wanted the sex. Even when these questions were answered against the accused rapist, the suspicion remained that the woman might be lying or fantasizing. Her account often had to be cor-roborated by other witnesses—an impossible task when no one else was around. In brief, a rape trial had two objectives: first, to decide whether the suspect had committed the crime; and second, whether the victim's life and psyche made her a deserving victim.

This legal dynamic was given authoritative heft by American John Wigmore, a major legal authority who cloaked Hale's misogyny with the credibility of medical and social science. Wigmore's eleven-thousand-page treatise on evidence, first published in 1904 and updated constantly since, has had an immense effect on the law's approach to rape. Like Hale, Wigmore fervently warned against "the evil of putting an innocent man's liberty at the mercy of an unscrupulous and revengeful mistress." When he wrote that women fantasized about rape, he explicitly relied on Sigmund Freud and other psychological authorities, thus giving them the force of law. And when he wrote that rape trials should proceed only after the woman's "social history and mental makeup have been examined . . . by a qualified physician," he put victims on the defensive while validating the modern belief that psychiatry can decode the mind.

Wigmore's distrust of women surpassed even Hale's. At times he sounded like a Renaissance-era witch hunter—albeit one who backed up his noxious theories with portentous-looking research papers rather than religious texts. In its 1970 edition, Wigmore's treatise noted the prevalence of "female types of excessive or perverted sexuality," a notion he supported with a quote from a 1930 paper by one Dr. Otto Mönkemöller about females of "intensely erotic propensity," which cautioned:

> One must not be deceived by a madonna-like countenance that [a] girl can readily assume; nor by the convincing upturn of her eyes. . . . To be sure, the coarse sensuousness of her demeanor, coupled with a pert and forward manner, usually leaves no doubt about her type of thought. Even in her early years can be seen in countenance and demeanor the symptoms of the hussy-type.

Wigmore was not alone in his views. Academics, courts, and social scientists of all stripes added their own glosses to this dark portrayal of women. An influential *Yale Law Journal* article from 1952, for example, generalized about females' "malicious or psychopathic accusations" in rape cases and "explained" how a no from a woman to a sexually aggressive man could really mean yes, even when he used physical force:

> When [the accuser's] behavior looks like resistance although her attitude is one of consent, injustice may be done the man by the woman's subsequent accusation. Many women, for example, require as a part of preliminary "love play" aggressive overtures by the man. Often their erotic pleasure may be enhanced by, or even depend upon, an accompanying physical struggle. The "love bite" is a common, if mild, sign of the aggressive component in the sex act. And the tangible signs of struggle may survive to support a subsequent accusation by the woman.

The author then picks up pseudo-Freudian steam to a climax of male innocence:

A woman's need for sexual satisfaction may lead to the unconscious desire for forceful penetration, the coercion serving neatly to avoid the guilt feelings which might arise after willing participation. But the desire thus generated for the "attack" is likely to clash with the civilized "superego" which vehemently rejects such unrestrained sexuality. . . . To illustrate: a woman whose sexual desire and superego are in conflict may alternate rapidly between "approach" and "rejection" responses to the man, first scratching and pushing him, at the next moment soliciting his caress. In other women, the anxiety resulting from this conflict of needs . . . may cause her to flee from the situation of discomfort, either physically by running away, or symbolically by retreating to such infantile behavior as crying. . . . But the conclusion of rape in this situation may be inconsistent with the meaning of the consent standard and unjust to the man. . . . *Fairness to the male suggests a conclusion of not guilty, despite signs of aggression.*

In other words, a woman's crying, scratching, or running away should not matter if she unconsciously wanted "forceful penetration." In such situations, she still consented to the sex, so no rape occurred. In 1966, the *Stanford Law Review* weighed in with an article specifically addressing women's "masochistic tendencies" and the "no-means-yes" trope:

Although a woman may desire sexual intercourse, it is customary for her to say, "no, no, no" (although meaning "yes, yes, yes") and to expect the male to be the aggressor. . . . It is always difficult in rape cases to determine whether the female really meant "no." . . . The problem of determining what the female "really meant" is compounded when, in fact, the female had no clearly determined attitude—that is, her attitude was one of ambivalence. . . . Furthermore a woman may note a man's brutal nature and be attracted to him rather than repulsed. Masochistic tendencies seem to lead many women to seek men who will ill-treat them sexually.

In 1971, Menachem Amir, a prominent Israeli sociologist and criminologist, coined the term "victim-precipitated" for rapes taking place after a woman leads a man to believe he has the go-ahead for sex but then gives contrary signals, or when she puts herself in situations "charged with sexuality." Amir echoed Morris Ploscowe, a New York judge and widely read authority on sex law, who warned prosecutors to be "continually on guard" against a rape charge brought by "the spurned female that has as its under-lying basis a desire for revenge, or a blackmail or shakedown scheme."

Notions like these are now confined to extreme right-wing politicians bent on career ruin, but that has only recently become the case. For most of the twentieth century, the works of Ploscowe, Amir, Wigmore, and others were the mainstream. They formed a solid intellectual foundation for approaching rape accusers as crazy, malicious, or promiscuous, and also for assuming that accused men were victims of regretful females trying to salvage their reputations. This chorus of doubt included the voice of none other than Alfred C. Kinsey, the author of two of the century's sem-inal works on sex, *Sexual Behavior in the Human Male* (1948) and *Sexual Behavior in the Human Female* (1953), and an influential voice on the lib-eralization of sex laws. According to one of his colleagues, Kinsey took a rather insouciant view of rape, often declaring that the "difference be-tween a 'good time' and a 'rape' may hinge on whether the girl's parents were awake when she finally arrived home."

Victims on Trial

Lord Hale's observation that "in a rape case, it is the victim, and not the defendant, who is on trial" remained true for most of the twentieth cen-tury. At every stage of the process, the cards were stacked high against the victim. Never, for example, has the law required mugging victims to explain why they walked on a dangerous street, or why they "tempted" thieves by flashing their iPhones or jewelry. But demands for such ex-planations by rape victims were par for the course. Victims of nonsexual assault have not been required to fight back, but a rape victim who did not struggle (and thus increase her risk of injury) was often considered to have consented. In other violent crime cases, the victim's testimony alone is sufficient to sustain a conviction—but not in rape trials, where vic-tims were often compelled to back up their accounts with other evidence. Being raped was simply not enough to arouse the law's concern. One also had to be a "worthy" victim.

With few exceptions, the first step in any rape case is a report to the police, who must be convinced that something is likely amiss before taking action. However, police were trained to treat rape complaints with extreme suspicion. A 1970s edition of the popular police manual *Patrol Procedures,* for example, stated as fact that "forcible rape is one of the most falsely reported crimes" and that rape accusations often stem from a woman's regrets after going "out on the town" and being unfaithful to her husband. In her landmark 1975 book *Against Our Will: Men, Women, and Rape*, Susan Brownmiller gave several accounts of police indifference to rape. How typical they were is impossible to say—Brownmiller argued, with characteristic vigor, that they were common and "shared by the rest of the male culture"—but the examples she cites are chilling. In one account, a woman arrives at a police station, declaring: "I want to report a rape." The policeman's reply: "Aw, who'd want to rape you?" When Brownmiller herself visited a New York City police precinct in 1972 and, examining relevant records, noted that just 5 percent of rape complaints had resulted in arrests, the police captain told her not to worry because the women were merely "prostitutes who didn't get their money."

Indeed, the notion that a prostitute could ever be raped was usually unthinkable. Prostitutes stood at the far end of what Michelle J. Anderson, dean of the law school at CUNY, calls the "chastity requirement," by which rape convictions become less likely as the victim's sexual history lengthens. At the other end of the chastity requirement were virgins. In between these two extremes stood the vast majority of women whose prior sexual experience made them less worthy of the law's protection. Here is the official statement of the law given to California juries in 1970 about nonvirgins who claimed they had been raped:

> A woman of unchaste character can be the victim of a forcible rape but
> it may be inferred that a woman who has previously consented to sexual
> intercourse would be more likely to consent again.

Knowing this, it is not surprising that in 1989–1990 the police in Oakland, California, would quickly decide that about half the rape complaints that came in—involving prostitutes and/or drug abusers—were unfounded, or that the Philadelphia police would, in 1966, ignore most complaints by women who said they had been raped in cars by people they knew.

Cases that survived the police's winnowing process were then evaluated by prosecutors, who would, logically, bring them to trial only if they believed a jury would convict. In a fascinating study conducted in 1989–1990, Lisa Frohman found that prosecutors rejected cases when the victims were viewed as somehow sexually dishonorable. One such prosecutor rejected a case involving a "real skinny and gangly" woman who had been raped and severely beaten by at least six "gang-bangers." The woman was possibly a "strawberry" (crack-addicted prostitute) who was likely to have been "hooking or looking for a rock"; but the prosecutor was still sure that "somewhere along the line [the sex was] not consensual." Nevertheless, the prosecutor decided that a jury would not believe a rape allegation coming from such a woman. In another of Frohman's examples, a woman was raped and "really messed up" by two men after she went to a bad neighborhood late at night. There was "no doubt . . . that she was raped," the prosecutor said, but he rejected the case because the victim could have been accused of trading sex for drugs, in which case the jury would see the attack as her fault. Finally, Frohman told of a young woman who claimed that she was raped in a car. Because the attack occurred at a location where prostitutes brought clients, the case was dropped. Rather than focusing on what happened in that car, the prosecutors thought the victim would be seen as lying to avoid a prostitution arrest.

Other studies, conducted in the 1970s and 1980s, showed that previous relationships between victims and accused rapists also caused prosecutors to drop cases. If a victim had had voluntary sex even once with a defendant, few believed she wouldn't do it again. Experienced prosecutors did not always believe these scenarios. Rather, they channeled the prejudices of juries. In none of these cases did drug abuse, prostitution, or previous relationships constitute a legitimate rape defense, but there is a big difference between legal technicalities and what really happens in court. If the women were susceptible to being branded as the "hussy type," then bringing a case to trial was useless.

For the few rape cases surviving the gauntlet of police indifference and prosecutorial reluctance, further barriers awaited in the courtroom. The victim was typically forced to defend her resistance to the attack and to explain her past relationship with the defendant, her promptness in reporting the rape, and also her sexual conduct with other men. Until very recently, a rape defendant's attorney had wide latitude to grill a victim about all these factors, especially her sex life. Actual examples of questions posed by defense lawyers include the following:

"Isn't it true that you have acted lewdly with other men in the late hours at bars when you were in a drunken state?"

"Isn't it true that you have been known to kiss men at public parties?"

"Isn't it true that you have had sexual intercourse many times before with a number of different men?"

Even if answered with a firm no, the questions suggest to juries that the victim is so "loose" that she probably leapt at the chance to have sex with the defendant. These inquiries were not perceived as cheap shots. Rather, a thorough airing of a victim's sex life was taken as critical to a fair trial. As one court held in 1955: "Justice and the defendant's constitutional right to a fair trial require that his counsel be permitted to cross-examine [the victim] thoroughly as to any prior act of lewdness with the accused and with other men." If the victim was humiliated in the process, such were the wages of her sexual sins. In fact, it was the positive *duty* of defense lawyers to dig into victims' sex lives. Anything was fair game, including the victim's use of birth control, her frequenting of bars, and her employment history. In a San Francisco rape case in the early 1970s, the victim, after answering repeated questions about her former employment as a cocktail waitress, her affair with a married man, and other sexual incidents, asked if *she* was the one on trial. The defense lawyer apologized and then pressed on, suggesting that her children engaged in perverted erotic games. The defendant was acquitted.

Faced with a victim with no sexual past, defense lawyers used other tactics. In 1975, a hotshot young Yale Law School graduate named Hillary Rodham (now Clinton), when defending one of two Arkansas men accused of raping a twelve-year-old girl, filed an affidavit in court saying that she had been "informed" that the girl was "emotionally unstable with a tendency to seek out older men and engage in fantasizing." Clinton also wrote that a child psychologist had told her that children in early adolescence "tend to exaggerate or romanticize sexual experiences," especially when they come from "disorganized families, such as the [victim]." The victim, now in her fifties, says there was no basis for these accusations— but they worked. The men were given very light sentences. For her part, Clinton (through a spokesperson) said that she "had an ethical and legal obligation to defend [her client] to the fullest extent of the law. To act otherwise would have constituted a breach of her professional responsibilities." Given the times, she was correct on that point.

Juries were often a harder sell than judges. Arguably, the most formidable barrier to conviction was their visceral hostility toward female victims. A widely published 1966 study found that juries were "lenient" with accused rapists whenever there were suggestions that the victims somehow contributed to the attacks. In forty-two rape cases during the mid-1950s, a guilty verdict was returned just three times. The judges would have convicted the defendants seven times more often. In one of the cases, described by the judge as a "savage rape," the woman's jaw had been fractured in three places. The jury voted for acquittal because it emerged that she might have had sex on previous occasions. In another of the study's cases, three men kidnapped a young woman from the street late at night and took her to an apartment, where they all raped her. The jury acquitted the attackers in clear response to the fact that the victim had two illegitimate children. The judge called the verdict a "travesty of justice."

Finally, if a rape case made it through all these stages and the defendant was convicted, he had another potential ticket out of jail: the appellate court, which can reverse a conviction if it finds that a defendant has not been given every legal chance to defend himself. Typical is a case from North Dakota, where two couples went drinking and driving in the countryside one night in 1953. The outing degenerated into a sordid, violent scene, during which one of the men raped one of the women. A jury convicted the attacker of rape, but the verdict was reversed on appeal because the trial judge had not let the jury learn about a sexual affair between the victim and another man three years earlier. "To exclude the tendered proof of her . . . having sexual lust and unlawfully indulging it—is simply to remove actual and real fairness from the trial and to reach judgment from mere appearances," the appellate court ruled. In other words, unless the defendant is permitted to smear the victim, a fair trial is impossible.

Familiarity Breeds Consent

It was quite difficult to make a rape charge stick when the victim and attacker had a prior sexual relationship, or even knew each other. Hence the acute (and well-founded) concern about "date rape" and "acquaintance rape" in the present day. The closer the relationship, the more violence required to obtain a conviction, and the lower the conviction rates overall. This helps to explain the troubling result in *State v. Alston*, a 1984 North Carolina case in which the victim had been involved with the defendant for six months before the attack. The court described their sex during this period as consensual, but that was quite a stretch: he beat her periodically and she often agreed to sex "just to accommodate him" and while "remain[ing] entirely passive." After he hit her one time too many, she went to live with her mother. About a month later, he showed up at the school she attended, grabbed her by the arm, threatened to "fix" her face to show he was "not playing," and told her he "deserved" sex from her. He then took her to his friend's house, where she told him the relationship was over and she didn't want to have sex. Nevertheless, he undressed her, pushed her legs apart, and had his way with her. She cried while he did so and called the police that same day.

The jury was convinced she had been raped, but a higher court was not. The court accepted that the defendant's conduct was scary, but still held that she had not been "in any way intimidated" into having sex. While it is impossible to read the judges' minds, it seems clear that had there been no prior relationship between the victim and the defendant, the court would have agreed that the sex was rape. Yet as so many rape victims discover, existing relationships between victims and aggressors—even those plagued by violent episodes—often give the men broad leeway to extract sexual submission by force. A woman's having sex freely with a man one day reduces her protection against rape the next.

A blurred line between seduction and rape has also marked encounters between people who barely knew each other. In many of these cases, a woman's subjective feelings of terror were not enough—she had to fight back, even if that made the situation worse. A female bartender in Wyoming learned this in 1973 when, shortly before closing time at the bar where she worked, a patron with whom she had been chatting asked her for a ride home. She refused. When she later got into her car, he emerged from nowhere, sat himself in the passenger seat, and repeated his request. Again she said no, but he wouldn't leave the car, so she drove off with him. During the journey, he asked her to stop at a gas station and took the keys with him while he used the lavatory. When he returned, he told her he intended to rape her. Sometime later, he told her to turn into a side road. As she tried to persuade him to leave her alone, he placed his fist against her face and said: "I'm going to do it. You can have it one way or the other." As she undressed, a male friend of hers drove by, but she did not send a distress signal. Her attacker had sex with her two or three times, during which she begged him to let her go. He didn't do so until he was through.

The trial judge found the man guilty of rape, stating that a woman need not "subject herself to a beating, knifing, or anything of that nature. As long as she is convinced something of a more serious nature will happen, she is then given by law the right to submit." Not so, ruled a higher court, which sent the case back for another trial. The trial judge had been too lenient on the woman, the higher court held, because her *subjective* fear of harm meant little. Rather, her fear "must be based on something of substance . . . of death or severe bodily harm." Whether or not what took place on that Wyoming road was substantial enough, the appellate court did not say—but it was skeptical, especially as the victim's hair had not been put in disarray; nor had her clothes been torn or her body bruised, and the defendant had not hit her. The court also pointed out that *she* had removed her own panties and failed to signal her distress to anyone. In all, the court found the situation "sketchy" and "far from overwhelming."

This ruling, and the many others like it, are brutal in the extreme, but they typify the "rape culture" that still colors attitudes toward sexual violence—what Andrew Taslitz defined in 2005 as "a culture that implicitly sanctions frequent male indifference to a woman's desires and a significant degree of male violence in sexual encounters." The requirement that rape victims put up "utmost resistance" has been dropped. But the fact remains that blood, bruises, and torn panties are still taken as the best proof that a rape really took place. More distressingly, while rape victims no longer must fit strict character requirements, the underlying attitudes have lingered. In the Wyoming case, the victim was a divorced mother who worked in a bar. The court noted that she "had experience in such work." The subtext: she is a floozy barmaid; rough encounters with patrons come with the job.

Fortunately, many of the more pernicious sexist assumptions in rape law have come under close scrutiny in recent decades, and substantial progress has been made. However, before looking at these advances, there is also the question of race, which has influenced the treatment of sexual violence as much as sexism.

The Race Factor

During the first half of the twentieth century, rapists were most often imagined as black men, and rape victims as white females. The many reasons for this go beyond the scope of this book, but W. E. B. Du Bois, in 1919, offered a trenchant summary: "The charge of rape against colored Americans was invented by the white South after Reconstruction to excuse mob violence [lynching]" and was "the recognized method of re-enslaving blacks." Cast as congenital rapists incapable of suppressing their violent sexual instincts, black men were not only marked as a danger to the flower of white society but also easier to characterize as too savage to vote, hold public office, or have the other rights and privileges of full citizenship.

These beliefs extended well beyond the borders of the Old South. For instance, in 1872, a Rochester, New York, crowd tried to drag a black man out of jail and lynch him for allegedly raping a white child. The man would have been hacked to pieces had the local militia not stepped in. The *Atlanta Constitution* seized on the affair to remind the North of the benefits of mob justice ("a swift penalty on the brutal assassin of priceless innocence") and the inborn violence of African Americans. If the Negro were given political and social rights, the newspaper warned, "the hereditary slave and semi-brute . . . will not forget his barbarian instincts at once. . . . There is a heap of nature in this." Northern newspapers affirmed that rape was a "Negro crime" and that the lynching of accused black perpetrators was "richly deserved." In the last century's early years, lynching in response to rape accusations was rarely prosecuted. When it was, an "unwritten law" allowed white people who killed blacks suspected of ravaging their kin to avoid murder charges. The same was true for victims. In 1892, the *New York Times* reported that an Arkansas woman was "accorded the privilege" of lighting the "funeral pyre" of the black man she had accused of sexual assault—a man others suspected had been her consensual sexual partner.

Given this legacy, it is not surprising that black men have been convicted of rape at a much higher rate, and punished more severely, than whites—especially when white women were the victims. Statistics are legion, but one should give the picture. Between 1930 and 1977 (when capital punishment for rape was outlawed), 455 men were executed for rape; 405 of them were black. Nearly all the victims were white. In 1931, nine black Alabama youths, soon known as the Scottsboro Boys, would be railroaded to conviction—based on sketchy evidence and coerced confessions—for gang-raping two white women with whom they had been riding a rail car. Eight of them were sentenced to death. (The ninth boy, a thirteen-year-old, escaped a death sentence by one juror vote and spent six years in jail.) However, the speed of the convictions and the fact that the boys were extremely young sparked widespread protest. The Scottsboro Boys case would not follow the pattern of other quick-and-dirty rape convictions of black males. A series of appeals, retrials, and myriad other twists and turns kept the case going for decades, and while none of the boys would avoid imprisonment, the case moved the needle of justice toward more fairness for African Americans accused of rape.

The Scottsboro Boys trials focused national attention on the injustices routinely meted out to black men in sexual-assault cases. Twice the US Supreme Court reversed the Alabama courts: once because the boys had been given awful lawyers, and again because there were no African Americans on the jury rolls. As the trials and retrials wore on, the boys were given prison terms instead of death sentences. In 1937, after the defendant had spent years in a prison so decrepit that it was declared "unfit for white prisoners," the charges against four of them were dropped. Over the ensuing decade, four of the others were paroled. (Another defendant, Haywood Patterson, escaped from prison in 1948 after his fourth conviction, following which he was convicted for killing a man in a barroom fight.)

Moreover, the fact that the women involved were not models of white virginity—they both had sex with black men before riding a rail car with the Scottsboro Boys—helped to start the process of normalizing black–white sexual relations. One of the judges told jurors to presume that no white woman would ever *want* to bed a black man, but the facts told a different story. Most importantly, after the Scottsboro cases, death was no longer the knee-jerk sentence for African American men accused of raping white women, and sex between black men and white women was not reflexively labeled as rape. Black men were by no means treated the same as whites in such cases, but the dynamics were starting to change.

In 1989, the last surviving Scottsboro Boy, Clarence Norris, died in New York City at the age of seventy-six. Three months later, another racially suffused rape case exploded in New York, summoning the worst demons of Scottsboro. A white, twenty-eight-year-old investment banker, identified later as Trisha Meili, was beaten viciously and raped while jogging in Central Park. The attack was horrifying: her left eye socket was crushed, her skull was broken through to the brain, and she had lost 80 percent of her blood by the time she was found, gagged and unconscious. That Meili survived was miraculous; no less of a gift from above was her inability to remember the attack. Within two days, five Harlem teenage boys, four of them black and one Hispanic, were arrested. They had been in the park that night on a "wilding" spree and causing considerable trouble. In an instant they were publicly condemned, not only for what they supposedly did to Meili but for every jolt of fear felt by white people passing dark-skinned youths on sidewalks. The *New York Post*'s Pete Hamill, in a column called "A Savage Disease," had this to say about the indicted boys:

> They were coming downtown from a world of crack, welfare, guns, knives, indifference and ignorance. They were coming from a land with no fathers. . . . They were coming from the anarchic province of the poor. And driven by a collective fury, brimming with the rippling

energies of youth, their minds teeming with the violent images of the streets and the movies, they had only one goal: to smash, hurt, rob, stomp, rape.

The fallout from the attacks, and the demand that the five youths pay for them, was, in the words of journalist Jim Dwyer, "like a centrifuge. Everyone was pinned into a position—the press, the police, the prosecution—and no one could press the stop button." In the frenzy of racial hatred that brooked neither reason nor contrary opinions, Donald Trump ran full-page ads in four newspapers demanding that "these muggers and murderers" be "forced to suffer and . . . executed." The city's mayor, Ed Koch, was quoted as calling the boys "monsters" and complaining that juvenile criminal laws were too lenient. Within two weeks of the attack, five New York newspapers published 406 stories about the case, totaling 3,415 column inches of print coverage, much of it calling for blood. Fifty-seven years after the start of the Scottsboro case, it seemed that whites were still convinced that dark-skinned males were sexual monsters and that "good" white women were their chief targets.

The imperative for both the police and the courts was to serve up rape convictions. The boys were charged with assault, robbery, and attempted murder, but public bloodlust would be sated only with sex-based verdicts. "If we don't get a rape conviction," said one of the detectives, "we lost the case." When asked whether a conviction for attempted murder—technically a higher count—would not be considered a victory, the detective replied no, it had to be a rape conviction. Within a very short time after their arrests, the boys were intimidated and tricked into confessing to the attack. Not long afterward they retracted their confessions, claiming they had been coerced, but by then the train had left the station and nothing was going to stop it: not the absence of blood matches, not the fact that the semen in Meili's cervix could not have come from any of the boys, not evidence pointing to another attacker, and not the troubling inconsistencies in the boys' confessions. They were convicted.

The real attacker, Matias Reyes, had raped and beaten a woman in the same part of Central Park just two days before Meili was attacked. He had been identified by police but had not been caught, and while the boys were being pushed toward prison, he continued to rape women in Meili's Upper East Side neighborhood, killing one. The boys' attorneys were never told about this. While in prison for another crime in 2002, Reyes found religion and confessed to the attack on Meili. After serving prison sentences ranging from seven to thirteen years, the boys—now men—were released. They subsequently sued the city, police, and prosecutors, and after more than a decade of hard-fought litigation, the case was settled for about $40 million in 2014.

The mishandling of the Central Park Jogger case has been well aired, particularly in a 2012 documentary and in the course of the civil lawsuits. However, the case has broader implications. The instant labeling of the boys as maniacs, with "one goal . . . to rape," matches the most despicable portrayals of sexually predatory black males dating back 125 years. In 1901, in a conference addressing the "Negro question," North Carolina academic George T. Winston bemoaned the "unbridled and unrestrained . . . black brute . . . lurking in the dark, a monstrous beast, crazed with lust. . . . A whole community is now frenzied with horror," particularly the "women and children of the white race." Had Winston's sentiments been published in 1989 or 1990 about the boys in Central Park, they would have had plentiful company. Even the thoughtful African American journalist Bob Herbert attacked the boys, dismissing them as "teen-age mutants."

The crimes against Meili were hideous, even by 1980s New York standards, but race was a key reason the case generated such vengeful reactions. (Perhaps race was also the reason so little attention was paid to the black woman in New York who was raped and thrown down an elevator shaft the same week Meili was attacked.) The fact is that Winston's stereotype of the "black brute . . . crazed with lust" had not abated. In many ways it had become so widely accepted that police and prosecutors could frame the five boys and get away with it for more than ten years.

While some at the time noted the parallels between the Central Park and Scottsboro cases, there were few such voices and they went largely unheard. Despite the many similarities, however, there remains one central difference: even when African Americans were denied anything approaching full citizenship, and when about ten lynchings per year were still being carried out, the Scottsboro Boys enjoyed a fair amount of public support and the backing of organizations such as the Communist Party and the National Association for the Advancement of Colored People. In May 1933, some four thousand people, black and white, marched in Washington, D.C., to demand justice for the Scottsboro Boys and to present the White House with a 145,000-signature petition. By contrast, the five Harlem youths had little public support at the time outside of their families, some black publications, and a few church organizations.

The New Normal

Since the 1970s, the debates over rape law have focused on what kinds of sexual behavior are "normal" or, even more amorphously, "natural." What are the norms for seduction and sex between strangers, acquaintances, lovers, and former lovers, and how should they be signaled? When and how should those norms be adjusted? Is rape a natural result of a man's not having his "normal" sexual desires satisfied, as a prosecutor argued in 1983 about a man who raped two thirteen-year-old girls? Or is sexual intercourse itself rape, as Andrea Dworkin famously posited? ("The thrusting is persistent invasion. She is opened up, split down the center. She is occupied.") Can rape ever be considered natural, and if so, what effect should that have on the law?

In Stanley Kubrick's 1971 film *A Clockwork Orange*, a band of young thugs in jumpsuits and codpieces roams near-future London in search of violent amusement. They gain admittance to a posh house, where they rape a seductively dressed woman and force her husband to watch. The scene, along with other bits of sexually infused "lashings of the old ultra-violence," caused an intense furor. Despite the film's ample artistic merits, it was withdrawn from British distribution. It also sparked revealing commentary. A *Newsweek* reviewer wrote that the film was "a statement of what it is to be truly human. [Alex, the gang's leader,] appeals to something dark and primordial in all of us." Added Kubrick: "Alex symbolizes man in his natural state, the way he would be if society did not impose its 'civilizing' processes upon him. . . . It is in this glimpse of the true nature of man that the power of the story derives."

From a certain feminist perspective, Alex and his "droogs" embody state-sanctioned masculinity. In this view, Catharine MacKinnon's suggestions that rapists do "little different than nondeviant men do regularly" takes on a new resonance. "Instead of asking what is the violation of rape," she writes in a brilliant 1983 essay, "what if we ask, what is the nonviolation of intercourse? To tell what is wrong with rape, explain what is right about sex." Taking the intercourse-as-rape point one step further, MacKinnon argues that "the law sees and treats women as men see and treat women," and the state uses the law to "institutionaliz[e] male power." The reason why "the wrong of rape has proven so difficult to articulate," she continues, is because rape and intercourse have been defined as two different events, "when for women it is difficult to distinguish

them." Under conditions of male dominance and institutionalized violence against women, "to be rap*able*... defines what a woman *is*."

Mackinnon's arguments are as compelling as they are challenging. Her
extensive writing and advocacy, as well as those of other feminists such
as Susan Brownmiller and groups such as the National Organization for
Women, have sparked a robust international debate calling into question
received wisdom about sexual violence. While the movement's broadest
goals have met with mixed results, the inequities of rape law have stayed
on the international agenda and significant changes have been achieved.
The first and perhaps the most significant one was the eradication of the
Rape-Your-Wife Privilege (see Chapter 1). Gone also is the gender-spe-
cific definition of rape limiting it to a crime committed by men against
women. The requirements that victims be of "chaste character," that they
put up "utmost resistance," and that they provide corroborative evidence
of their violations are also, for the most part, wiped from the law books.
As awareness spread that rape is more often than not committed by people
the victim knows, acquaintance rape has also been recognized. As usual,
MacKinnon framed this issue in colorful terms, asking, "In whose interest
is it to believe that it is not so bad to be raped by someone who has fucked
you before as by someone who has not?" Regardless of the specific answer
to that question, the message is sinking in: rapists are not, by definition,
ultra-violent strangers.

In 2012, the FBI also announced a "long overdue" redefinition of rape
in its *Uniform Crime Reports*. The definition eliminates the requirement of
physical force by the rapist and the need for a victim to fight back. From
1927, rape had been defined as "the carnal knowledge of a female, forcibly
and against her will." The revised definition includes "penetration, no
matter how slight, of the vagina or anus with any body part or object, or
oral penetration by a sex organ of another person, without the consent of
the victim." Significantly, the new gender-neutral definition also includes
homosexual victims as well as instances when a victim is incapacitated
(including on account of drugs or alcohol).

Equally overdue have been efforts to give all women the same protections from sexual violence as blushing virgins, and to encourage victims
to come forward. To this end, jurisdictions throughout the US passed
laws in the 1970s and 1980s barring the exposure of victims' sex lives
in rape trials. The laws, known as rape shields, reflected the growing
realization—so obvious now that it seems foolish even to say it—that

women who have sex voluntarily with one man do not necessarily consent to sex with another. It is debatable whether such laws came about because "both sexes had become increasingly feminist," as the cognitive scientist Steven Pinker contends, but the influence of feminists cannot be overestimated.

Most influential was women's refusal to be condemned for having active sex lives. Many rape victims who came of age in the birth control–friendly, permissive climate of the 1960s and early 1970s found this unpalatable and were no longer afraid to say so. As was commonly said, the personal had become political, and the safety and privacy of rape victims had become a political matter. When President Jimmy Carter signed the federal rape-shield law in 1978, he emphasized that it would "end the public degradation of rape victims" and "prevent a defendant from making the victim's private life the issue in the trial." Merely stating these points as positives reflected a huge shift in public attitudes toward sexually active women.

The rape-shield laws were not universally supported, even on the left. The American Civil Liberties Union, for example, which had long defended African American men accused of rape, had a lively internal debate over the issue. ACLU board member Jeanette Hopkins argued that white women used rape allegations to gain power over black men and secure white men's approval. Because "a disproportionately large percentage of the defendants in rape prosecutions are black men," she added, the ACLU should stand against rape-shield laws. Another ACLU board member, Lawrence Herman, went further, claiming that a woman's decision to have sex with a maintenance man, a casual acquaintance, or a group of strangers was key to determining whether she would later consent to sex in a similar setting. In other words, evidence that she had done it once is evidence that she would do it again. Herman's arguments were criticized by feminists within the ACLU, but the group nevertheless registered its opposition to the laws.

The ACLU lost the debate over rape-shield laws. They were passed, in various forms, in nearly every state and on the federal level. Yet Hopkins's and Herman's sentiments managed to live on. The laws are so riddled with exceptions, and smart defense lawyers have been so adept at circumventing them, that they are more accurately viewed as sieves than as shields. And when a victim's sexual past surfaces at trial, it can make a jury more inclined to give a rapist a pass. In a 1982 study, mock jurors looked at rape cases that were identical except for one variable: in one scenario, the victim's sexual past was not mentioned; in the next, she had limited sexual experience; and in the third, she was labeled as promiscuous. The subjects rated the rape as most serious when the victim's past was not mentioned, less serious when she had limited experience, and least serious when she was promiscuous. In a 1983 study, mock jurors were also given identical rape scenarios with one variable: the victim was either a virgin or sexually experienced. Four-fifths of the jurors voted for conviction when the victim was a virgin, while just three-fifths wanted to convict the attacker of the sexually experienced victim.

Many appellate judges also cannot seem to shake the belief that the sex life of a rape victiim—even a child—is fair game. In 2006, for example, a thirteen-year-old Missouri girl was ravaged by a man named James Baker after he had been eyeing her at a swimming pool. Atypically, she reported the crime and Baker received a lengthy prison term for statutory rape. The conviction was later reversed on appeal because Baker's lawyers had not been allowed to show that the girl already was carrying a sexually transmitted infection. The higher court found that this evidence—useful only to show that she was not a virgin—was not barred by the rape-shield law and should have come out at trial. In 1994, an army sergeant was convicted of having sex with a nine-year-old girl. His conviction was also thrown out because the girl's sexual interactions with another girl had not come out at trial. The court said that this information could have shown that she "had knowledge beyond her tender years." And a 1988 New Hampshire rape conviction was reversed because the jury had not learned of the victim's "openly sexually provocative behavior toward a group of men" in a tavern before the rape took place. According to Judge David Souter (who was later appointed to the US Supreme Court), the woman's barroom cavorting could be a sign of her "likely attitude at the time of the sexual activity in question." The state's rape-shield law was thus rendered as powerless as the victim.

Talented defense lawyers can also comply with rape-shield laws and still get their messages across. Take, for example, the trial of the Kennedy family scion William Kennedy Smith, who was charged with raping Patricia Bowman after meeting her at a Palm Beach nightclub in 1991. They danced at the club until about three AM, after which they went to the Kennedy estate and strolled on the beach. Sex occurred. She called it rape; he said it was consensual. He won. In truth, Bowman didn't have much of a chance—not with Kennedy's attorney, Roy Black, putting her through this kind of questioning on the witness stand:

BLACK: And you had a difficult time with your daughter's father?

BOWMAN: I had a difficult time losing my daughter's twin.

BLACK: And one of the worst parts of it is that you didn't get support from the man involved, did you?

Despite a strict rape-shield law, Black still elicited a sluttish impression of Bowman: she had a child outside of marriage; she was the type of woman who jumps into bed with a deadbeat; she was familiar with casual sex. Why would anyone think she would not do the same after a long evening of flirting with a member of the Kennedy family?

When basketball star Kobe Bryant was accused in 2003 of raping a young woman in a Colorado hotel room, another "he said, she said" contest arose, again involving sex after flirtation and again turning on whether the woman consented. She told police she had gone to Bryant's room, where they kissed, after which he pushed her over a chair and forced himself on her. Bryant said she willingly had sex with him, which his representatives argued was no surprise. With the assistance of the Bryant defense team's copious leaks to the press, the public learned much about the accuser, including her name, her appearance, and her email and home addresses. (She began receiving death threats.) It was also revealed that her panties had traces of another man's semen when she had her rape exam, raising the possibility that she had had sex with others near to the time she was with Bryant. The judge ruled that the rape-shield law did not bar evidence about her sexual activity in the three-day period before her rape exam. Soon after that ruling, she indicated that she no longer wished to testify and the case fell apart.

Just before Bryant's accuser pulled out of the case, the legal journalist Dahlia Lithwick offered excellent observations about rape-shield laws:

> [They have] led to two unappealing alternatives: Either the defendant's legal presumption of innocence is flipped on its head, since rape shield laws unambiguously deny him access to potentially exculpatory evidence, or—as a practical matter—the woman's sexual history goes on trial regardless, permitting humiliating public scrutiny often likened to a second rape. . . . Enacted with the best of intentions, rape shield laws don't work, particularly in high-profile cases. These laws either don't protect victims, or undermine defendants' rights to a fair trial.

Often they do both. Add the press to the mix and you have a perfect storm—with either accuser or accused twice victimized.

It is often said that hard cases make bad law. With rape, every case is hard and the law is never good enough. When people are on trial for such a serious felony, the law must do its level best to ensure that they are not convicted wrongly. When the victim and accused rapist are acquainted (if only briefly) and the case turns on the woman's consent, the familiar swearing contest arises, and proving lack of consent becomes a grueling task. After the Bryant rape case was dismissed, Bryant stated: "Although I truly believe this encounter between us was consensual, I recognize now that she did not and does not view this incident the same way I did." If she said no (as she claimed), shouldn't that be sufficient, even if he honestly (but contemptibly) understands no to mean yes or "keep on trying"? These questions, in various forms, are raised daily in the criminal courts— and there are no satisfactory answers.

Rape-shield laws are supposed to protect women from having their sex lives held up as generalized expressions of sexual consent. However, the law's commitment to this end has not been absolute, and, for most practical purposes, slut-shaming is alive and well (if inconsistently applied) in the courts. While rape-shield laws led to the increased reporting of rapes, especially by acquaintances, they have not resulted in higher conviction rates. Whether they have reduced the actual amount of rape going on we cannot know, but we can hope.

Institutional Rape— on Campus, in the Military, and in Prison

In Chapter 1, we looked at the conflict between the supposed "sanctity of the home" and the need to protect women from their husbands' sexual predations. Here, we look at rape in three other insular environments. Obviously, universities, military organizations, and prisons are not entirely closed, but society has decided that their unique missions require different legal frameworks—particularly with regard to rape—than elsewhere. People in the military or in prison have fewer rights in this regard than those on the outside, while university students, curiously, have both more and fewer.

As the definition of rape came to include date and acquaintance rape, studies emerged showing that rape was far more prevalent on college campuses than previously imagined. In 1987, *Ms.* magazine published the shocking results of a study reporting that about one-fourth of all college females would be raped or the victims of attempted rape by the end of their undergraduate years—and that 90 percent of victims knew their attackers. (The term "date rape" entered common parlance due to this study.) The rapists weren't always creeps hiding behind the school library; they were guys in class and dudes manning beer kegs at parties. Interestingly, three-quarters of the women in this study did not think they had been raped. Many of them continued having sex with the same men. But when they replied to loosely worded questionnaires about their sexual experiences, which the people conducting the study classified as rape afterward, much higher numbers resulted. Applying the conclusions of this study to the fourteen thousand female students at UC Berkeley in 1990, for example, some two thousand of them would have suffered three thousand rapes and attempted rapes that year alone. In fact, just two rapes were reported to police, and a few dozen students sought help from the campus rape counseling service.

According to the widely cited 2007 Campus Sexual Assault Study funded by the National Institute of Justice, an astonishing 19 percent of all the female students surveyed reported experiencing attempted or completed sexual assault since entering college. The study summarized the online responses of students at only two universities, and it included "forced kissing," "fondling," and "rubbing up against you in a sexual way, even if is over your clothes," in its definition of sexual battery, but the one-in-five figure for campus rape has nevertheless stuck. President Barack Obama has cited it repeatedly, as have endless numbers of legislators, pundits, editorial writers, and activists. But even acknowledging the weaknesses in that or other rape studies, the undeniable fact is that a lot of forced sex is going on. Also undeniable is the fact that nearly all of the perpetrators go free and also that few rapes are even reported. Over the past few years, the existence—some still say the myth—of a sexual-assault crisis on college campuses has stayed on the front pages as schools both famous and obscure scramble to guard their reputations while attempting to meet new government standards to address the problem.

The questions fall under two main headings: what constitutes rape in the college setting, and who should deal with it when it takes place? On both fronts, a growing panic mentality—both by victims who feel left in the cold and institutions worried more about their standing in the community than their students' safety—has precluded clear thinking and has often trivialized a complex problem. As for what constitutes rape, college students are increasingly living in a separate reality, where sex is judged by much tighter standards than those applied to others. In California and on a growing number of campuses, rape is said to result unless "affirmative," "specific," and "unambiguous" consent is given throughout a sexual encounter. As Yale law professor Jed Rubenfeld pointed out:

> Under this definition, a person who voluntarily gets undressed, gets into bed and has sex with someone, without clearly communicating either yes or no, can later say—correctly—that he or she was raped. . . . [The rule] encourages people to think of themselves as sexual assault victims when there was no assault. People can and frequently do have fully voluntary sex without communicating unambiguously; under the new consent standards, that can be deemed rape if one party later feels aggrieved.

Proponents say that the new rules merely simplify what have long been vexingly complex questions regarding consent, but others, such as journalist Heather MacDonald, deride these "legalistic caveats" as both unworkable and "laughably out of touch with reality."

Other schools now say that a student's agreement to sex while under the influence of alcohol or drugs is not consent, so anyone—male or female—who has sex while drunk but not completely incapacitated may now have been raped. That would seem to include quite a few college sexual encounters. For a time, Duke University's rules added to the ambiguity by stating that sexual misconduct could arise when there are "real or perceived power differentials" between those involved—whatever that could mean. None of these rules coincide with rape law as it exists outside the ivory tower. If binge drinking is a trigger of sexual misbehavior, then universities should revisit their tacit toleration of alcohol and drugs on and off campus. Most universities issue warnings about mixing intoxicants with sex, but they are ignored. The cringe-worthy spectacle of students drinking or drugging themselves into oblivion is taken as a given—a rite of passage into adulthood that should pass without significant consequence.

Moreover, it is not only females who get drunk or high and have sex; their male partners are presumably no less intoxicated. According to a group of twenty-eight Harvard Law School professors, Harvard's new rules for situations in which both students are "impaired or incapacitated" are "starkly one-sided as between complainants and respondents and entirely inadequate to address the complex issues in these unfortunate situations." I expect that as more males are accused of rape in circumstances where alcohol and/or drugs are present, they will claim that they were intoxicated and pushed into sex, particularly by the women bringing rape charges against them. If both parties were presumptively raped because they were heavily intoxicated, and no one else was there to witness the encounter, what is a college disciplinary board to do? Nothing, most likely. The contraction of the consent standard in the new campus rules may, in the end, clear a path out of liability for bad actors.

More troublesome is the expanding use of university-staffed kangaroo courts to make rape determinations and mete out punishments. If we have learned anything over the centuries about rape law, it is that determining whether one consented to sex is a devilishly hard thing to do. Since 2011, the federal government has mandated that universities transform themselves into criminal tribunals and undertake fact-finding missions of the most subtle kind. Repeatedly, we read of botched investigations, cynical cover-ups and other administration stratagems to protect institutions' reputations, mismanaged secret hearings, and, inevitably, lawsuits by aggrieved students on both sides of the disputes who claim they were not given a fair shake. Returning to Harvard, the twenty-eight law professors complain that the school's procedures "lack the most basic elements of fairness and due process [and] are overwhelmingly stacked against the accused [students]." Criticisms include the failure to ensure that accused students, particularly those without a war chest, are adequately represented.

Rape is a serious felony and should be treated as such. When adults are guilty of rape, significant punishments should result, but only after they are given a fair chance of acquittal before an impartial judge or jury. The university hearing process turns this paradigm on its head. In the first place, even if they were really interested in addressing the problem, universities can't really punish anyone for rape. Their worst sanction, expulsion, is nothing compared to the crime and, most importantly, does not stop a rapist from raping again. In the upside-down world of university justice, stealing a keg of beer brings a harsher penalty than drinking the beer and then violently forcing sex on a classmate. When rape cases come to university hearing boards, the likelihood of a bad result is built into the system. The government now requires that rape be found if student accusers show by a "preponderance of the evidence"—a mere 51 percent likelihood—that the rape took place, even in cases emerging from the miasmas of drunken parties, mixed signals, and imprudence by all involved. In criminal courts, the standard of proof is the much-harder-to-meet "beyond a reasonable doubt." The person charged in court with stealing beer has far more legal protections than a student accused of rape.

At the center of the controversy are victims who, for reasons we see elsewhere in this chapter, hesitate to go to the police once they have been assaulted. Rather than undergo the indignities of callous police conduct, unused rape kits, prosecutions refused, (rare) trials, and (even more rare) convictions of their attackers, the majority choose the college disciplinary process, hoping it to be more understanding, discreet, and efficient. Yet they often walk away feeling ignored, mishandled, and betrayed, and fewer than one-third of those found by colleges to have committed sexual assault were expelled, much less criminally punished. By January 2015, ninety-five schools were under investigation for their sexual-assault investigations possibly violating students' civil rights.

There is also the significant question of why college students should have greater protections than their counterparts off campus, especially as women who don't go to college are significantly more likely to be raped. A recent American University study, based on government statistics from 1995 to 2011, found that female college students (ages eighteen to twenty-four) were about one-third less likely than women who were not in college to be sexually assaulted or raped. Going further, women with college degrees are four times less likely to suffer sexual violence than those without high school diplomas. While rapes on campuses are no less devastating than those outside school gates, neither should the safety of the privileged be a greater concern than that of others.

Adjudicating rape is always a hard business, and as alienating and infuriating as the court system is, at least it has the teeth to bring wrongdoers to justice and the rules and the procedures necessary to minimize mistakes. It is easy to adopt expansive definitions of rape, but contending with the high numbers of rape victims created by the new campus rules is much more difficult. Matters such as plagiarism and cheating on exams are suitable for informal adjudication on campus, but not something as grave as rape, at least not without the close involvement of law enforcement.

. . .

Planes that operate off aircraft carriers have hooks on their tails, called tailhooks, which grab ropes on the giant ships' runways as they land. Tailhook also is the name of a private association of active-duty and retired US Navy and Marine pilots. For several years the word "tailhook" become shorthand for a frenzy of sexual assaults on women during the association's 1991 Las Vegas convention, which was attended by five thousand people, including nearly one thousand officers, active-duty admirals, and generals, as well as the secretary of the navy, H. Lawrence Garrett III. At hotel "hospitality suites" hosted by flight squadrons, there were numerous strippers as well as "butt biting," "ball walking" (men strolling around with their genitals exposed), and, most infamous, a hallway "gauntlet," which involved a double line of male aviators by whom female service members were groped as they struggled to get through.

More than eighty women claimed they were mistreated in the gauntlet. One of them was navy lieutenant Paula Coughlin, a helicopter pilot and admiral's aide, who claimed that she was pulled into the gauntlet and treated savagely. "Help me!" she implored a pilot, who, she said, then molested her too. "It was the most frightened I've ever been in my life." She said she "squatted down to break [her main attacker's] hold and bit him and somebody reached between my knees and tried to grab my panties." In the coming months, the Tailhook scandal—with its investigations, charges of cover-ups, and countercharges of mistreatment of America's "top gun" war heroes—resulted in the referral of 119 navy and 21 marine corps officers for possible discipline. Fifty-one people were found to have lied during the investigations. However, none of the cases resulted in courts-martial. (Coughlin's charges against one man were dropped for lack of evidence.) Ultimately, however, the careers of fourteen admirals and about three hundred aviators were ruined or damaged by Tailhook. Garrett himself also resigned. Additionally, the promotions of about forty-five hundred officers were put on hold pending inquiries about their association with the notorious convention.

The Tailhook scandal unfolded just as the US was celebrating its victory in the 1991 Gulf War and also as polarizing sexual-harassment charges against US Supreme Court nominee Clarence Thomas were being played out on the national stage. The hijinks of boozed-up young men wearing "Women Are Property" T-shirts now looked unsavory. While many saw the entire process as a whitewash—Frank Rich of the *New York Times* sneered, "The [Tailhook] scandal has been swept under the Navy's rug: 140 marauding Navy and Marine pilots; 83 assaulted women;

0 Courts-Martial"—many others felt differently. In a scathing commentary, for example, law professor Kingsley R. Browne wrote that the scandal caused more damage to the navy than the 1941 Pearl Harbor attack. Navy personnel were sacrificed, he said, to please a rabid public with a lingering "witch-hunt mentality," and under a politically correct double standard for females in uniform that harmed the entire military. Now that women were being integrated into the armed forces, Browne wrote, "a decision must be made . . . can women take care of themselves, or can't they?"

To show how the military had become excessively politically correct after Tailhook, Browne pointed to Lieutenant General Claudia Kennedy, who in 2000 accused Major General Larry G. Smith of touching her in a sexual manner and trying to kiss her, a charge that derailed Smith's appointment to a higher position. Quoting a *Washington Times* columnist, Browne asked, "Our women warriors, who insist they should be permitted to lead men in battle, cannot handle so much as a touch on the upper arm?" and, "Heck, why not close down the Army and replace it with a sewing circle?" Browne added, "The core lesson that the military and its civilian overseers need to take to heart is this: extraordinary attempts to 'help' women ultimately harm their position within the military."

Browne's commentary came in 2007, five years before the jaw-dropping scale of rape in the US armed forces was revealed. To choose just a few relevant figures, the Pentagon estimates that there were twenty-six thousand cases of rape and other sexual assaults in 2012, a leap from nineteen thousand in 2011. For the few brave souls who reported their attacks, about 60 percent of them said they were subject to retaliation afterward. The controversy over sexual assault in the military became a major embarrassment to the US government and shows no signs of slowing down. So far, the efforts to address the problem have not been impressive—not when Senator Saxby Chambliss attributes it to hormones; or when the army's top sex-crimes prosecutor, Lieutenant Colonel Jay Morse, received only a reprimand after molesting a female officer at a sexual-assault-prevention conference; or when military commanders still make key decisions over the prosecution of sexual-assault cases; or when more than half of the estimated cases of rape and sexual assault are committed against men. Reports of sexual abuses will continue to come fast and furious for at least the next several years, or until the system of military justice is fixed to give sexual-assault victims safe and reliable channels to make their claims heard.

• • •

There is no more closed society than a prison and, at least in the American penal system, rape is often the coin of the realm. Sexual violence between prisoners is often tolerated and promoted by prison authorities, both to control prison populations and, in some instances, as an opportunistic crime by guards. To be raped in prison is to become a "punk," the lowest form of prison human life and a cheap piece of property to be traded, sodomized, and sold like a slave. Guards have been known to place troublesome prisoners with known rapists either as a disciplinary measure or as a reward to the rapist and his confederates for helping to maintain order. As a Louisiana prison guard described:

> There are prison administrators who use inmate gangs to help manage the prison. . . . Is inmate "X" writing letters to the editor of the local newspaper and filing lawsuits? Or perhaps he threw urine or feces on an employee? "Well, Joe, you and Willie and Hank work him over, but be sure you don't break any bones and send him to the hospital. If you do a good job, I'll see that you get the blondest boy in the next shipment."

A heart-rending 1999 exposé in *Salon* described the fate of Eddie Dillard, a California prisoner who, after he kicked a guard, was put in the cell of a prisoner known as the Booty Bandit, who raped, beat, and tortured Dillard for several days. From that point forward, Dillard was a punk, open to be abused by the rest of the population. For his services, the Booty Bandit was given new shoes and extra food.

In 1994, the US Supreme Court ruled that prison officials must protect prisoners from rape and that "deliberate indifference" to rape is cruel and unusual punishment. Cruel, indeed, but still far from unusual. Twenty years later, rape levels in prison are still stubbornly high, and despite legislation requiring prisons to improve their detection and prevention of rape, little has been accomplished. In fact, as of May 2014, seven Republican governors had refused to comply with new national standards designed to improve the situation.

One reason for the lack of movement to protect prisoners from sexual assault is that about half of the perpetrators are staff members. (About one-fifth of youth victims of staff sexual misconduct experience physical force or threat of force, while more than one-third were offered protection or given drugs or alcohol in exchange for sex.) Even taking out false accusations against disliked guards, this still leaves a lot of staff-initiated sexual assault. "An inmate is just as threatened by staff as . . . by other in-mates—this wasn't the prevalent though: iust a few years ago," said Jaime Fellner, who served on the Natior.! Rape Elimination Commission. A growing number of rape lawsuits have been filed of late by prisoners, but without substantiation by other witnesses these cases are the longest of long shots. And regardless of what happens in court, the last word almost always lies with prison authorities. In 2012, a female prisoner in Utah who had won a $1.4 million court judgment after being raped by a guard was found dead in her cell.

My Daddy the Rapist

In about half the US states, rapists have the same broad array of parental rights—including rights to custody, visitation, and input on a child's up-bringing—that other fathers have. When a child is conceived through rape and carried to term, this leaves the rape victim/mother tethered to the very person she wishes least to see, much less consult about the welfare of the child. As one woman expressed:

> I was raped in [North Carolina] and the rapist won "joint" custody. Torment does not come close to describe what I live. . . . [The courts] have not only tied and bound me to a rapist, but also the innocent child that was conceived by VIOLENCE! [The rapist's] violence has earned him even more control over my life.

Another rape survivor wrote: "I was raped . . . and the rapist has been taking me to court for five years for the right to see his son. . . . I am being tormented to death. I just want to die." In 2009, the child of a Pennsyl-vania rape victim was placed with foster parents at the age of three. At that time, the child had not been potty-trained and did not speak. After two years in the foster home, the child improved and the foster parents sought to adopt him. Enter the father/rapist, who by that time was in trouble with the law on other counts and was living in someone's base-ment. Still, he managed to block the adoption and gain custody of the child. The child regressed and was soon back in diapers. Just as alarming is the use a rapist can make of his parenting rights to avoid the full con-sequences of his crime. In 2004, for example, a rape victim who became pregnant tried to put the child up for adoption, but she first had to get permission from the father—who was in jail awaiting trial for the rape. He told her he would sign the adoption papers on condition that she not testify against him. "What do I do?" the woman asked. "Protect society or protect [the child]?"

The problem is more widespread than one would think. About twenty-five thousand rape-related pregnancies occur each year in the US, and about one-third of rape victims who became pregnant carry their pregnancies to term. While about half of the states give rape victims superior parental rights, the laws have flaws. Some require that the father be formally convicted before his parental rights are curtailed. As most rapes (*if* they are reported, prosecuted, and tried) do not result in convictions, and appeals can eat up years, chaos still reigns in the lives of the mother and child. Before she knows the outcome of the prosecution, she must decide whether to place the child up for adoption or raise it herself—all with the father's participation. Even if the father is convicted, a judge can still decide to allow him to be involved in the child's upbringing.

Some laws go too far in the other direction by terminating a father's parental rights even if he did nothing worse than have consensual sex with a barely underage female—which could apply to cases where he and the girl were prepared to start a family. In such situations, the child could well benefit from the presence and involvement of the father. Other laws, which allow a father's parental rights to be cut off *absent* a criminal conviction, raise the potential for fathers to be punished even when they have been acquitted in court or when prosecutors perceive a case as too weak to bring to trial.

The elephant in the room in this debate is the pervasive belief that women could not possibly love the human results of rape and should not rest until their wombs are purged. Women who decide, for religious or other reasons, to keep children conceived through rape clash with motherhood models embraced by both abortion advocates and opponents. In the years before 1973, when *Roe v. Wade* legalized most abortions, pregnancy terminations in cases of rape were widely permitted. Rapists were still popularly understood as violent strangers, and the children of rape victims were seen as wickedness incarnate. In the 1960s, pro-choice advocates pointed to abortion-seeking rape victims to refute the argument that women who had abortions selfishly chose their own pleasures over motherhood. Having been impregnated by violence, abortion-rights supporters argued, such women had no choice but to terminate the pregnancies.

The rape exception continues to be widely accepted, even by much of the anti-abortion movement. In 1977, in the first major victory against *Roe*, the law changed to bar the use of government funds to pay for abortions *except* for health reasons and for those pregnancies resulting from rape and incest. The rape and incest exceptions were removed in 1981 but restored in 1993, on the assumption that poor rape victims (in the words of Washington senator Patty Murray) would otherwise be "forced" to obtain "back-alley" abortions. Two years later, when Congress revisited the question, Representative Nancy L. Johnson framed the issue like this:

> Think. Rape is someone grabbing you, assaulting you, overwhelming you with fear for your life and then violating you in the most deeply personal and destructive way. Please, leave to the victim the decision as to whether to carry or not to carry any possible product of such violent, vicious and terrible act as that of rape.

For female rape victims, then, abortion was required for emotional healing and, as another congressperson put it, was a medical "necessity." At this point, questioning the necessity of abortion in rape cases is political suicide, as Indiana Senate candidate Richard Mourdock learned in 2012, when he said rape victims should be denied abortions because rape-conceived children are a "gift from God." (Missouri Senate candidate Todd Aikin also suffered opprobrium when he said the rape exception is unnecessary because pregnancies don't result from "legitimate rape.") While these comments were cheered by a slice of the extreme right wing, nearly everyone else—including Republican leaders—ran for cover. Mourdock and Aikin lost their races and their remarks were blamed in part for the party's broad losses in that year's election. A few months later, the anti-abortion Republican New Mexico legislator Cathrynn Brown introduced a bill to punish abortions following rape on the theory that the fetus constitutes evidence needed to prosecute the crime. The bill elicited an outcry from both the left and the right and died.

So long as rape narratives rely on the stereotype of a violent stranger-rapist, children conceived by rape will be seen as vile creatures that no rational woman would want to keep. The issue is not whether a woman should be permitted to abort; that should be her choice in any event. The relevant, and far more difficult, question is the extent to which a rape victim should have primary parental rights. Should the man be deprived of *all* rights concerning the child? Is a rapist father worse than no father at all? If he is barred from personal contact with the child, should he still provide the child financial support? If he has been acquitted of rape under the stringent criminal standards, should there be a more lenient standard for cutting off his parental rights? More than anything, what is best for the child? These questions, urgent as they are, are not conducive to legislative solutions, much less to rushed decisions by overworked family law judges. But until a better system is created, the statehouse and courtroom are where such questions will be resolved.

• • •

The definitions of rape, and the rules for proving it, are in perpetual flux. Is rape drastically underreported, as advocates and government statistics suggest, or does it only seem so because a broader range of behavior is now included in the definition? The lawyer and law professor Alan Dershowitz (who normally has no trouble taking sides) asserts that rape is "*both* the most overreported and underreported serious crime in America," adding that false allegations of rape should be criminalized. Was Steven Pinker correct when he wrote, in 2011, that "feminists won the battle against rape" so conclusively that incidents of the crime have declined 80 percent in recent decades, or is he just another man who refuses to see the truth of rape for what it is?

Going beyond the statistics, perhaps Catharine MacKinnon was correct when she wrote that the real culprit is institutionalized male dominance over women, in which "sexuality is a sphere of male power" and "forced sex [is] paradigmatic." In its grotesque extreme, MacKinnon's statement evokes Josef Stalin, for whom rape was the prerogative of the strong. When told in 1945 that some people were angry about Soviet troops raping German women by the millions, he mused: "What is so awful about [a soldier] having fun with a woman after such horrors?" On a broader level, MacKinnon's link between sex and male power has been integrated into the law. It is no accident that it was MacKinnon who popularized the term "sexual harassment" in 1979, when she and others were also arguing for expanding the reach of rape laws. The core issue was not just forced sex but the wider abuse of gendered power relationships. Thus the "imposition of sexual requirements" on women in the workplace was no less ripe for correction, and a new field of law was born.

Sexual Harassment in the Workplace

On the first page of her groundbreaking 1979 book *Sexual Harassment of Working Women*, Catharine MacKinnon placed rape and sexual harassment on the same continuum of male power abuse: "American society legitimizes male sexual dominance of women and employers' control of workers." MacKinnon didn't argue for sexual harassment at work to be criminalized. Rather, she and other advocates sought to frame it as a form of discrimination under existing civil rights law, which in fact occurred the year after her book was published. In the thirty-five years since, sexual harassment law has developed and mutated at a rapid pace. In some instances—such as a six-year-old boy's suspension from school for "sexually harassing" a student with a kiss—the term is applied to behavior having nothing to do with sex, harassment, or a workplace. In other situations, the concept is applied so narrowly that a state governor's (and future president's) alleged demand that a female employee "kiss" his exposed penis was found to be trivial. In many respects, the rules regarding sexual harassment have followed a similar track as rape law, adopting nearly all the "she wanted it," "I thought she wanted it," "don't believe her, she's crazy," and "she's a bad girl" defenses that have made rape such a vexing crime to address.

Before we start on the short, chaotic path of sexual-harassment law, we visit the Iowa dental office of James H. Knight, DDS. In 2010, Knight fired his dental assistant, Melissa Nelson, because he was sexually attracted to her. The two had worked together without incident for ten years, and Nelson considered Knight to be a father figure. However, six months before she was sent packing, Knight started to discuss sex with her—often. He complained that her tight shirts were distracting and added that if she also wore snug pants, he would "get it coming and going." He texted her to say that if she saw his pants bulging, she would know her clothes were too revealing. Another time, he asked her in a text about her orgasms. (She didn't reply.) Still another time, he told her that her infrequent sex life was a waste, like "having a Lamborghini in the garage and never driving it." Whatever his skills at repairing teeth, Knight is clearly a boor, a dinosaur, and the sort of slimeball with power that working women know all too well.

Knight's wife discovered the texts and told him to fire Nelson. Knight later acknowledged that Nelson was a fine worker and had done nothing wrong, but he was concerned that he would try to have an affair with her one day. Knight's behavior hadn't particularly offended Nelson, but she nevertheless claimed that she would not have been fired had she been male. She sued Knight for sex discrimination, and lost. The case ended up before the Iowa Supreme Court, which noted that while Knight's "inappropriate" actions "are of a type often seen in sexual harassment cases," it was still perfectly legal for him to fire Nelson. "Even if the reasons for the termination are unjust," the all-male panel declared, Knight's treatment of Nelson "does not bring about [a sexually abusive] atmosphere." Rather than focus on Nelson's loss of her (and her children's) livelihood despite her exemplary workplace behavior, the court penalized her for Knight's adulterous intentions. In Iowa, as elsewhere, being female and coming to work can be a firing offense.

Even if Nelson had expressed outrage at Knight's smarmy behavior when it was occurring, she would still likely have lost in court, because she stayed on the job. Women who continue or, worse, excel at their work despite pats on the rear end, groping of breasts, or even forced intercourse have found that their ability to withstand indignities is a liability in court. As the lawyer and commentator Susan Estrich observed: "Those who suffer in silence often find their silence is used against them . . . often because of the presumption that the harassment couldn't have been so bad . . . if the woman did not complain." For her part, Nelson was put in a *quadruple* bind. She did not encourage Knight but was nevertheless fired because she triggered his desires and his wife's jealousy; she continued to work despite Knight's come-ons, but by preserving her means of support, she undermined her rights. Sexual harassment is evidently something a full-blooded man cannot help but commit when he is attracted to an employee. If his urges threaten his marriage, the law (at least in this instance) lets him solve the problem by eliminating the object of his attraction. Rather than protect Nelson from Knight's rogue sexuality, as the sexual-harassment laws are supposed to do, the opposite occurred. Once Knight's juices began to flow, she was in trouble.

• • •

The bar against job discrimination "because of sex" was a last-minute add-on to Title VII of the Civil Rights Act of 1964, which also outlaws discrimination on the basis of color, religion, and national origin. In fact, the addition of sex as a protected category was a caustic joke by Virginia congressman Howard Smith, who used it to highlight what he saw as the absurdity of the entire law. He hoped it would contribute to the law's defeat in Congress. In a speech, Smith read from a crackpot constituent's letter complaining that there were fewer women than men in the US. The amendment, Smith implied sarcastically, would address his constituent's concerns by allowing the government to correct the gender imbalance and help legions of "spinsters" find "nice" husbands. Smith's stunt backfired. The law passed with the prohibition against discrimination based on sex.

Sexual-discrimination complaints started to pile up soon after Title VII was voted in, but because the law gave no guidance on just what was meant to be prohibited, judges applied their own views of appropriate sex relations. In 1975, for example, two female clerical workers at Bausch and Lomb sued the company after their boss made repeated "verbal and physical sexual advances" toward them and other female employees. The case was thrown out. To the court, the boss had done nothing worse than "satisfying a personal urge," something men with authority had always done. Two years later, a female government employee was fired for refusing her boss's sexual entreaties even after he promised her a promotion in exchange. This time, the employee was allowed to sue, but the court was still troubled that her complaint merely described "social patterns that to some extent are normal and expectable."

Many judges of this era had a difficult time imagining a world where bosses no longer pawed female employees, promised rewards for sex, or made life difficult for those who did not cooperate. Courts also worried about giving employees the right to sue the employing company—where the money is—when a boss misbehaved. Even the most liberal courts were concerned about how far the new doctrine would reach, and whether sexual harassment law was the right vehicle for broad-based social engineering. Opined the federal court in San Francisco:

> It is conceivable . . . that flirtations of the smallest order would give rise to liability. The attraction of males to females and females to males is a natural sex phenomenon and it is probable that this attraction plays at least a subtle part in most personnel decisions. Such being the case, it would seem wise for the Courts to refrain from delving into these matters.

By 1980, however, the link of sexual discrimination to unwelcome workplace sexual behavior had been forged. Federal guidelines coming out that year defined sexual discrimination as "unwelcome sexual advances, request for sexual favors, and other verbal or physical conduct of a sexual nature." In 1986, the growing sexual-harassment litigation industry received a solid boost when the US Supreme Court announced that an employee not need to be harmed economically to be sexually harassed; nor were employees always required to be put in the position of trading sex for jobs or benefits. Merely working in a hostile or abusive environment was enough to sustain a lawsuit.

The Supreme Court chose a rather extreme case to make that ruling. A low-level bank employee, Mechelle Vinson, had sex with her boss, Sidney Taylor, soon after he hired her. Vinson said she had been afraid of losing her job if she refused, and Taylor's demands never let up. They had sex on more than fifty occasions, several of which she claimed were accomplished by Taylor's use of physical force. Taylor also fondled her in front of other employees, followed her into the bathroom, and exposed himself to her in the office. Taylor denied everything, but the lower court didn't bother to determine whose story was true. Even if Vinson was believed, the judge said, the sexual relationship was still "voluntary" and had "nothing to do" with her bank employment. (She was, in fact, promoted three times while the affair was taking place.) Vinson's case wandered through the courts for years, eventually reaching the Supreme Court—with the addition of Catharine MacKinnon to Vinson's legal team. The high court ruled that if Vinson's allegations were true, she had indeed been sexually harassed. "Without question," the court held, "when a supervisor sexually harasses a subordinate because of the subordinate's sex, that supervisor 'discriminate[s]' on the basis of sex."

The court's ruling was unanimous, but it was not a total victory for Vinson or other women in her position. The justices remained suspicious that Vinson had enticed Taylor and thus brought her problems upon herself. As the main question was whether Taylor's sexual behavior was "unwelcome," the justices said that evidence that Vinson had spoken or dressed provocatively, or had smutty "fantasies" (a subject much discussed in the lower court), would clarify whether she had welcomed Taylor's conduct. By confirming that a woman can be the cause of her own sexual harassment, the court gave its seal of approval to the same character-based attacks that had long been leveled at rape victims. Boiled down, the question in sexual harassment cases became: "Was she asking for it?" If her skirts are too short or, as dental assistant Nelson discovered, she causes a bulge in her boss's pants, the answer will likely be yes. Just as women were held responsible for their own rapes by their dress, demeanor, fantasies, or past sex lives, it was open season on making the same charges against women claiming sexual harassment.

Even with its limitations, the *Vinson* decision sparked an increase in the number of sexual-harassment cases, but it still went unnoticed outside limited circles. For the term "sexual harassment" to enter common parlance, it would take another five years and a mud-wrestling match in the US Senate over Clarence Thomas's allegedly freaky behavior toward a subordinate. The hearings—which political and social science professor Nancy Fraser called a "national teach-in" on sexual harassment—concerned Thomas's nomination to the Supreme Court. The story told by Thomas's former employee Anita Hill was bizarre in its details: Thomas allegedly demanded to know whose pubic hair was on his Coke can; he described pornographic movies featuring animals, rape, group sex, and people with giant genitals; he talked about the impressive dimensions of his own penis; and he remarked that Hill was wearing a "provocative slip." As unique as these charges were, the underlying gestalt between Hill and Thomas struck a familiar chord with many women, particularly the predicament of having one's livelihood turn not only on doing a good job but also on surviving a superior's sexual torment.

The accused harasser was a young Republican favorite about to enter the highest reaches of power, which guaranteed wall-to-wall news coverage, as did the fact that both players were African Americans, which gave commentators material for endless chatter on race relations. Moreover, even Democratic senators were ambivalent about Hill's claims. Senator Howard Metzenbaum of Ohio said: "If that's sexual harassment, then half the senators . . . could be accused." This ambivalence allowed Thomas's more resolute supporters the latitude to use all available means to smear Hill. The fact that the drama played out in the Senate, rather than in a courtroom, meant that there was only a slim pretense of fairness, and there was no credible decision as to who was telling the truth. The Senate's vote, as with Thomas's original nomination, was purely political.

According to Hill, soon after she came to work for Thomas at the Department of Education in 1981, he began asking her out on dates—which she refused. In response, she asserted, he brought up all the above-mentioned subjects to punish her by making her uncomfortable. The more disquiet she showed, she said, the more it "urged him on, as though my reaction of feeling ill at ease and vulnerable was what he wanted." Hill said she found Thomas's patter degrading and disgusting, and told Thomas that she didn't want to discuss "these kinds of things." At the same time,

Thomas's future in Republican administrations was glowing bright. If Hill played ball and remained loyal to Thomas, she stood to benefit from his promotions—not bad for a woman whose previous employer rated her as "uneven" and only "generally adequate." So Hill said she kept her mouth shut and made no formal complaints about Thomas's conduct. "I was really upset," she later explained when asked why she did not complain. "I felt my job could be taken away or at least threatened."

This was still the case in 1982, when, after just nine months at the Department of Education, Thomas was tapped to head the Equal Employment Opportunities Commission (EEOC), the agency tasked with enforcing sexual-harassment laws. Hill followed him there, where she said his harassment became worse. Now, however, Thomas was in a more untouchable position. Hill knew that no one would believe that the top official in charge of preventing sexual harassment would conduct himself like that. She continued to endure, developing stomach problems that were likely stress-related and wondering what to do with herself. Her situation was not unusual. From the early 1980s until the start of the next decade, fewer than 5 percent of women who believed they had been sexually harassed filed official complaints. Susan Estrich put Hill's quandary in context:

> Hill never complained . . . because she was afraid to burn her bridges. She was a vulnerable young woman at the beginning of her career. She moved from one post to another with Thomas because she hoped for the best, thought it might stop, and needed her job. . . . You maintain a cordial relationship because the man may be called as a reference, because you don't want to be known as a troublemaker.

In 1983, after receiving an opportunity to leave government work and teach law school, Hill returned to her native Oklahoma to take up a post at Oral Roberts University. She later recalled that, on her last day at the EEOC, Thomas told her: "If you were ever to tell anyone what went on between us, you could ruin my career."

When Hill's story came out publicly a decade later, after Thomas had been nominated for the high court, the backlash against her was both unfamiliar and predictable. Women who claimed sexual harassment were often accused of lying—but never by a bank of seething US senators. Such women had also been threatened, but Hill faced menacing words on the Senate floor. Alan Simpson of Wyoming said that Hill "will be sucked right into the maw, the very thing she wanted to avoid most. She will be injured and destroyed and belittled and hounded and harassed—real harassment—different from the sexual kind." That threat was kept. Within a very short time, Hill would be branded as a lesbian, an "erotomaniac," a schizophrenic, a fantasist, a vengeful spurned woman, a perjurer, and a fool, all on television before an astounded country and with no real chance to respond. No woman before her, much less an African American, had seen her accusations met with a claim that the accused harasser was suffering a "high-tech lynching." Yet despite the unique circumstances, Thomas's defense followed a familiar playbook. Women who charge powerful men with sexual harassment are routinely maligned. If they hadn't raised a complaint immediately, or if others had not witnessed it, they are accused of making everything up. To the extent their charges are believed, they are imputed to have either enticed or enjoyed the sexual advances. Thomas was confirmed in 1991.

One key gain for sexual harassment claimants was lost in the ugly noise of the Thomas–Hill hearings: even during their most outlandish moments, no one seriously thought that if Hill's allegations were true, Thomas would be confirmed for the high court. If Hill had been believed, then even Thomas's defenders would have agreed that he lacked the necessary "temperament" for the Supreme Court and would be unfit to hold any other high position. Rather than argue that Thomas's talk about pornography, pubic hair, and so on, was the "normal and expectable" banter that a woman should expect, the goal of Thomas and his defenders was to show that nothing Hill charged ever took place. On October 12, 1991, as he spoke to Thomas, Utah senator Orrin Hatch made no secret of the stakes:

> And I have to tell you this has come down to this, one woman's allegations that are 10 years old against your lifetime of service over that same 10-year period. I have known you almost 11 years. And the person that the good professor [Hill] described is not the person I have known. We are going to talk a little bit more about . . . how one person's uncorroborated allegations could destroy a career.

Even Simpson, who later admitted to being "pissed [off] to the core" at Hill and treating her "monstrous[ly]," and who didn't personally think her allegations were that serious, did not say, "So what?" publicly. Rather, he attacked Hill as untruthful, saying she suffered from a "delusional disorder." Somewhere along the way, the kind of loutish behavior described by Hill went from being written off as a common expression of a "personal urge" to being illegal and wrong.

Immediately after the hearings, polls showed that only about one-quarter of registered voters believed Hill was telling the truth, while about double that amount believed Thomas. Nevertheless, the hearings raised awareness about sexual harassment immeasurably, and, aided by changes in the law allowing a broad range of money damages in such cases, the number of cases filed soon went through the roof. Between 1980 and 1985, only sixteen sexual-harassment charges were filed with the EEOC. In the years after the hearings, forty-six hundred sexual-harassment complaints poured in annually.

Meanwhile, another more important sexual-harassment case was brewing in Arkansas. It would spark a chain reaction leading to the impeachment of a sitting president. If the Hill–Thomas imbroglio was a "teach-in" on sexual harassment, then Paula Jones's suit against Bill Clinton was an advanced seminar on the use of such claims as a weapon of political destruction. In 1991, Thomas could deflect questions about his sex life by invoking the "sanctity of my bedroom," refusing to discuss the "most intimate parts of my privacy," and claiming that such inquiries were "ruining the country." A few years later, any pretense of such privacy protections had vaporized. Clinton was forced to testify about his sexual encounters not only with Jones but also with other women. Not long after that, his plentiful ejaculations were being discussed everywhere, and his semen deposit on a White House intern's dress would be mentioned no fewer than twenty times in a report by Independent Counsel Kenneth Starr. "If it can happen to me it can happen to anybody," Thomas had warned. "Our institutions are being controlled by people who will stop at nothing." Clinton learned that all too well. Barely more than a decade after sexual harassment came into its own as a legal claim, it was clear that *no one*, not even a popular US president, could avoid its reach.

While Jones lost her lawsuit in the end, her personal victory or defeat in court was never the real point. From December 1993, when the Jones story broke, to the Monica Lewinsky drama, and then on to Starr's investigation and Clinton's impeachment in 1998, the entire case was a hit job—one of many tactical strikes in the ideological guerrilla war waged against Clinton by his enemies. Since Clinton's "zipper problem" was already known to anyone who was paying attention, and because sexual-harassment lawsuits gave litigants the right to inquire extensively into an accused harasser's sex life, Jones's case was a useful vehicle for taking Clinton down. As later confessed by David Brock, the self-titled "right-wing hit man" who first exposed Clinton's alleged request for sex from Jones: "Sex is [Clinton's] 'Achilles' heel,' after all." It just took the right case—and Clinton's prevarications about his relationship with Lewinsky—to bring it all out.

Brock had gained national notice in 1993 with his best-selling book *The Real Anita Hill*, a fierce attack on the "myth of Anita Hill" and the liberal groups that supported her. Eight months later, Brock launched what he called "the print equivalent of poison-gas canisters on the Clinton White House" with a lengthy story, sourced mainly though Arkansas state troopers, detailing Clinton's seamy extramarital sex life with "dozens of women" while he was governor of Arkansas. In what Brock later called an oversight, the story mentioned a young state employee, Paula, by her first name. The article reported that Clinton had spotted her at a conference at Little Rock's Excelsior Hotel and told troopers to bring her to an upstairs suite he had taken for assignations. After one hour there with Clinton, the story continued, Paula told a waiting trooper that "she was available to be Clinton's regular girlfriend, if he so desired."

The Paula, of course, was Paula Corbin (later Jones), who stepped forward a couple of months later with a different story. As described in her lawsuit, Clinton had indeed had a state trooper take her to his hotel suite, but that is where the stories diverged. According to Jones, after a few minutes of conversation Clinton started to flatter, kiss, and fondle her. "I'm not that kind of girl," she said, but the governor would not be deterred. Clinton allegedly went to the sofa where she was sitting, dropped his pants as he sat down next to her, brandished his erect penis, and told her to "kiss it." She refused and soon left the room, but only after Clinton gave her a "stern look" and told her: "You are smart. Let's keep this between ourselves."

The saturation coverage given to every development in the *Jones v. Clinton* lawsuit precludes the need to recount it here. Clinton ultimately won the legal case, but his lies under oath about his sexual relationship with Lewinsky, and his decision to keep lying about it afterward, gave his political enemies more than enough material to ensure that he would end his presidency in disgrace. Jones emerged from the process divorced, impoverished, and discarded by those who had championed her cause. Two years after the case ended, she posed nude for *Penthouse* magazine, which led conservative firebrand Ann Coulter to lament: "Paula was my Rosa Parks. . . . She used to be my hero in a David-and-Goliath conflict. She used to have dignity and nobility and tremendous courage. Now she's just the trailer-park trash they said she was." The truth was that Jones, having served her purpose, was expected to disappear quietly.

Political sex scandals have always been with us and will never go away. The Thomas–Hill and Clinton–Jones cases, however, have gone a long way toward equalizing the power dynamic in such cases. Not only is sexual misbehavior a potential political embarrassment, it can also be a legal liability and a pretext for wide-ranging and embarrassing investigations. If there are patsies available with stories to tell, and who don't mind weathering savage counterattacks, a sexual-harassment case is an effective forum for fighting political battles. As for the private lives of public figures, that is a thing of the past.

* * *

The hoopla over Clinton, Jones, and Lewinsky obscured another key event: in 1998, the Supreme Court vastly increased the potential number of sexual-harassment claimants by recognizing that men can be sexually harassed and that harassment can occur between people of the same sex. The decision dealt with an offshore oil-rig worker whose male coworkers shoved a bar of soap into his anus and threatened to rape him. He quit his job, claiming that otherwise he would have been "raped or forced to have sex." The lower courts ruled against him, holding that men cannot sexually harass other men, but the Supreme Court took the opposite position. For a court that still blessed anti-sodomy laws, the inclusion of same-sex harassment as a violation of law was a no-brainer. If sexual harassment is to be forbidden, "it must extend to sexual harassment of any kind," the court ruled.

While same-sex harassment is illegal, gay and transgendered people are still far from equal under the law, especially when harassment comes in their direction. Sexual orientation is not an explicitly protected category under Title VII, and when gay people sue for sexual harassment, courts often employ tortured reasoning to bar their claims. Consider the gay Coca-Cola employee who claimed that coworkers assaulted him, called him a "sissy," and was told: "Everybody knows you're as gay as a three-dollar bill," "Everybody knows you're a faggot," and "Everybody knows you take it up the ass." The court, in 2000, threw his case out, saying his coworkers were merely harassing him because of his sexual orientation, not because of sex itself. If the coworkers had propositioned him for sex or treated him in a way that was "sexually charged," then the court would have shown more interest; but anti-gay taunting was not the concern of civil rights laws.

Coca-Cola has cleaned up its act since that decision by instituting broad policies protecting employees from discrimination based on sexual orientation, as have many other companies large and small. In 2000, about half the Fortune 500 companies had such policies in place. By 2015, that number had jumped to 89 percent for sexual orientation and 66 percent for gender identity. Additionally, a patchwork of states and localities have instituted their own policies against LGBT job discrimination. Yet in twenty-nine states, employers can still fire people—or refuse to hire them in the first place—because they are gay. In thirty-two states, employers can, similarly, refuse to hire someone on the basis of gender identity.

As the reach of sexual-harassment law broadens, the number of human-resources consultants, lawyers, and other hangers-on who guide businesses on avoiding liability has also grown. An employer can often mitigate liability for sexual harassment if it has systems in place to police harassment and shows that it has done what it can to deal with problems as they arise. Several states now *require* large employers to provide sexual-harassment training to supervisors, which is seen as essential to avoid big punitive-damages awards. This requirement, plus a stream of big and well-publicized jury verdicts, has moved businesses to become almost maniacal in their policing of all sex in the workplace—an effort with which the consulting industry is only too happy to help.

The pitch from sexual-harassment consulting services—and there are hundreds of them—is always the same: hire us now or your business could be at risk. One such service, HRM Consulting, warns that "sexual harassment within the workplace is an area of critical exposure for business owners and corporations alike," and that "failure to provide [sexual-harassment] training can result in expensive legal consequences." This is not just a hard-sell pitch. In 1994, Rena Weeks, a secretary at the world's largest law firm by revenue, Baker & McKenzie, had the misfortune of being assigned to Martin Greenstein, a powerful partner and serial groper of women. In what initially looked like a quixotic effort, Weeks sued Greenstein and the firm for sexual harassment—and she won, big. After learning about Greenstein's long history of harassment, which the firm had tolerated, the jury awarded her a total of $7.1 million. In addressing the jury, Greenstein's lawyer said the problem stemmed from recent "uncertainty" about "what is O.K. and what is not O.K. in the workplace." After the *Weeks* verdict, employers were far less ready to test those questions in court.

The specter of women such as Weeks obtaining multimillion-dollar jury awards led to the wide adoption of zero-tolerance policies, which demand more employee restraint than the law requires. In workplaces everywhere, these policies prohibit not only illegal behavior but also consensual flirting, dating, sexual jokes, and innuendo. In 2004, for example, the California Department of Justice announced that under its zero-tolerance policy, "corrective action" would be taken against employees who violate the policy, "even if the violations are not so serious as to be unlawful." Two years later, a Web publication called the *HR Daily Advisor* went even further, counseling HR managers to make zero-tolerance policies so broad so that they put employees on guard against their own thoughts: "Employees should feel uneasy about even thinking of their co-workers in sexual terms." And with each twist in the law come new rounds of seminars, training sessions, and lawyered-up amendments to company policies and employee manuals.

It is impossible to say how much sexual harassment these policies have prevented; proving a negative proves nothing. However, we do know that their excessive breadth has sometimes caused injustice. In one 1994 incident, a Chicago Theological Seminary professor, while teaching a course on sin, told his class the same illustrative story he had been using for decades: a man falls off a roof, lands on a woman, and accidentally has intercourse with her. The professor told students that the Talmud absolves the man of sin, as his penetration of the startled woman was unintentional. A female student filed a complaint, and before long the professor was formally reprimanded. Notices saying that he had "engaged in conduct of a sexual nature" that had the effect of "creating an intimidating, hostile, or offensive environment" were put on all students' lockers. His anecdote did not remotely trigger any law, but all his lectures were recorded from that point on to ensure that he kept his remarks nonsexual.

Also in 1994, several female bank tellers had a laugh over some cutouts of male nudes from *Playgirl* magazine, which caused a male teller to complain. The women were suspended without pay and ordered to apologize to him. The following year, a low-level "leadman" in an envelope factory was suspended for not taking action against employees who looked at a *Penthouse* magazine featuring the figure skater Tonya Harding sans costume. The men had viewed the pictures unobtrusively and did not discuss them with others. However, someone told a female coworker, who then complained to management, who in turn conducted an investigation and suspended the leadman. The leadman sued the employer in arbitration, but the arbitrator was not interested in whether anyone at the factory had actually been sexually harassed. The company's policy prohibited anything with "sexual content"; the magazine had sexual content, and therefore the leadman should have been disciplined. With rulings such as this one, it is no wonder that so many companies are uncompromising in maintaining what Vicki Schultz calls a "sanitized workplace," even if workers are steamrolled in the process.

As most every adult reader of this book knows from experience or observation, the workplace remains a hothouse of sexual energy. Liaisons and romances occur regardless of the rules. According to a 2013 survey by the Society for Human Resources Management, approximately one in four employees have been or are involved in workplace romances. As such relationships (particularly between management and subordinates) are recipes for disaster in court, the question is what to do when they occur. Among the solutions, perhaps the most bizarre is the "love contract," which is supposed to protect a company when such a relationship collapses. One such contract, written by a lawyer for a manager to send to his love interest, reads as follows:

Dear _____ :

I very much value our relationship and I certainly view it as voluntary, consensual and welcome. And I have always felt that you felt the same. However, I know that sometimes an individual may feel compelled to engage in or continue a relationship against their will out of concern that it may affect their job or working relationships.

It is very important to me that our relationship be on an equal footing and that you be fully comfortable that our relationship is at all times voluntary and welcome. I want to assure you that under no circumstances will I allow our relationship or, should it happen, the end of our relationship, to impact on your job or our working relationship.

The letter encloses (presumably along with an expensive gift) the company's sexual-harassment policy and also designates a place for the recipient to countersign, just below the following text:

I have read this letter and the accompanying sexual harassment policy and I understand and agree with what is stated in both this letter and the sexual harassment policy. My relationship with _____ has been (and is) voluntary, consensual and welcome. I also understand that I am free to end this relationship at any time and, in doing so, it will not adversely impact my job.

One can only imagine the responses letters like this elicit, but it is safe to say they are likely not to be affectionate.

Is everyone's skin getting too thin? With college students demanding "trigger warnings" ahead of reading or viewing assigned materials in schools, with animal keepers suing for sexual harassment after a gorilla allegedly demanded (through sign language) that they expose their breasts, and when a six-year-old boy is suspended from school for sexually harassing a classmate by kissing her on the hand, it would seem so. But these examples are the reductio ad absurdum of a positive movement, and the expansion of protections against sexual predation in the workplace is too long in coming. For every ludicrous example of excessive victimhood, there are others in which one has been asked to trade his or her dignity for a livelihood. If the price is a sanitized workplace, then that is the price we must pay.

CHAPTER 6

HARMFUL VICTIMS

Prostitution and Sex Trafficking

To grasp prostitution's place in modern law, we return again to ancient Rome, this time to the pious sixth-century Byzantine emperor Justinian and his wife, the reformed "actress" (that is, prostitute) Theodora. Justinian felt an irritated sympathy for the half-starved harlots filling Constantinople's streets. Disgusted by their licentiousness, he nevertheless tried to redeem them. For centuries, the Romans had tolerated and taxed the skin trade—but that changed when Rome adopted Christianity as its state religion. Justinian's predecessor, Constantine, also considered prostitution a filthy institution, but rather than arrest prostitutes, he confined them to certain districts. Justinian, however, believed that more was needed than zoning rules. He prohibited prostitution altogether in the capital, fined brothel owners, and had pimps flogged and expelled.

He didn't stop there. At Theodora's insistence, he had more than five hundred marketplace strumpets rounded up and locked away in a convent called the Metanoia ("Repentance") high on the bluffs above the Sea of Marmara. There, the bewildered women were forced to give up sex and adopt the grim routines of nuns. Many of these "reformed" prostitutes perceived their new lives as hellish and, despairing of ever escaping the convent, hurled themselves off the cliffs into the rocky waters below. Trading their bodies for money had been no picnic, but forced service to God was—apparently—much worse.

That is one version of the story. Another has Constantinople's prostitutes grateful for their rescue at the loving hands of Justinian and Theodora, and joyful at the chance to pursue pious lives. We'll never know which account is accurate. Each advances an opposing perspective about the wisdom of outlawing prostitution and "saving" prostitutes—just as there is still no consensus on whether to ban prostitution or whether efforts to rescue prostitutes do more harm than good. Under the banner of saving women from "the life," lavishly funded "anti-trafficking" task forces smash into massage parlors and similar establishments, manhandle the women inside, and then sometimes jail them even before finding out whether they have been trafficked. In poor countries, swashbuckling agents of the "rescue industry" mount media-friendly brothel raids to "save" prostitutes, only to park them in refugee camps and locked shelters, deport them to unsafe countries, or consign them to oppressive and low-paid service or manufacturing jobs. To many of these women, rescue is like imprisonment. Moreover, in places such as Sweden, where selling sex is technically legal but clients are criminals, sex workers complain that anti-trafficking reforms have driven the trade further underground, putting their lives in greater danger as a result.

Fifteen hundred years after Justinian decided that Constantinople's whores preferred to be nuns, bitter disputes as to whether anyone could freely choose to sell sex remain. For the radical feminist Andrea Dworkin, prostitution was equivalent to gang rape and could never be accepted as a free choice. Even if that were true, is it still right to "save" prostitutes if doing so might result in more hardship? Do women who return to prostitution suffer from what some activists call "false consciousness"— the inability to recognize their own oppression? Are they, as journalist Nicholas Kristof wrote about a Cambodian woman who returned to prostitution, so "shattered and stigmatized" that the only place where they feel they belong is the brothel? Or are they, like billions of people across the world with no choice but to do dangerous work, chosing the best of a series of bad options? Is poverty the root cause of prostitution, or is it the moral failings of prostitutes and customers? Finally, if prostitutes are victims, why use the criminal-justice and penal systems to protect them? Wouldn't legalizing prostitution, or at least providing prostitutes with increased services and protections, be more effective?

There is no consensus on any of these issues, and the result has been a global mess of competing and incompatible laws and law-enforcement approaches, from the United Nations down to small-town police precincts. Yet despite all the noise, arrests, and global dragnets, the situation for sex workers rarely seems to improve.

Under emerging legal norms, immigrants locked in airless third-world brothels, independent "escorts" advertising on the Internet, and

$15,000-a-night courtesans have all been recast as victims of sex trafficking, while customers are likened to rapists. Increasingly draconian criminal laws have often made the words "prostitute," "sex slave," and "trafficking victim" interchangeable. While these last two labels fit too many people caught in the sex trade, one unintended effect of recent policies has been to leave vulnerable sex workers more prone to danger. Moreover, while enforcement efforts against the sex trade grow, the trafficking of domestic workers, sweatshop and farm laborers, and hair and nail salon workers (among many others) grows worse. Why the asymmetrical emphasis on sex work? In short, sex sells and sex motivates. The plight of imprisoned maids or restaurant workers is not as compelling to activists, or as conducive to splashy media exposés, as that of sex workers. The feminists, evangelical rescue operators, NGOs, and law-enforcement agencies fighting prostitution might not agree on much, but they coalesce around the fervent conviction that all commercial sex must be stopped at all costs. Other trafficked and exploited labor—the kind that makes daily life in the West easier and less expensive—is simply par for the course.

One can presume that Justinian and Theodora were quite pleased with themselves for rescuing Constantinople's streetwalkers, while their slaves fed them, emptied their chamber pots, and prepared their baths. By the same token, when actress Mira Sorvino—on a rescue mission to Cambodia with a CNN documentary crew filming everything—screamed, "It's not OK to sell children!" at a group of suspected traffickers, she must also have felt self-satisfaction. And when actress Demi Moore, whose journey to Nepal was also covered by CNN in a documentary called *Nepal's Stolen Children*, brought a rescued sex worker back to her family, she was clearly pleased with her efforts. Sorvino and Moore were well intentioned, and the CNN specials directed attention to an important issue. Yet the documentaries' producers and the actresses themselves gave no airtime to the misery of the people who, for example, clean Cambodian and Nepalese hotel rooms, or the suffering of the millions other trafficked laborers in the West whose unspeakable living and working conditions escape star treatment.

What Is a Prostitute?

The word "prostitute" comes from the Latin *prostare,* to "stand out," and from the beginning until the present day, prostitutes have been marked apart. Historically, the definition was based on a woman's moral shortcomings rather than her means of earning money. If she was considered freely available for the pleasure of men, she was a whore. The question was: How many men? Some authorities said five within a certain time frame sufficed; others as few as two or as many as twenty thousand. Whatever the variations, there was no distinction between a woman whose virtue was for sale and one who was merely promiscuous. Both had the same rock-bottom legal and social positions. Money is now part of the definition of prostitution (at least in the West), but prostitutes are still viewed as unworthy of the same basic rights as others—and also as objects of intense sexual interest, whether admittedly or not. Whether they are seen as victims or vulturine whores, they remain the embodiment of everything the respectable classes are not.

As attitudes toward sex have evolved, so has the place of prostitutes (both female and male) in the popular imagination. They have been perceived as the embodiment of disease, the face of foreign immorality, the casualties of a licentious age, or even feminist heroes. However, these perceptions are neither static nor uniform, and when sex and morality are involved, the law almost always moves at a different pace than popular attitudes. In some settings—such as the hazy intersection of prostitution and marriage—the courts have had to step in to legitimize relationships that laws on the books still condemned.

This happened in Malibu, California, where tough-guy actor Lee Marvin lived with the actress Michelle Triola from 1964 until 1970. The couple moved in together soon after meeting on the set of the aptly named film *Ship of Fools*. While they never married, the wealthier Marvin supported Triola, and she changed her last name to Marvin. However, after he abruptly married a former sweetheart in Las Vegas, he had her evicted from his Malibu house. As a settlement, he agreed to give her $833 per month for five years—but he stopped making payments after a year and a half. Triola ran to court for more money, but before that question would even be considered, she needed to convince a series of judges that she had not been for sale.

The case became an eight-year delight for tabloids and gossip columns worldwide, in part due to the showboating of Triola's attorney, the celebrity divorce lawyer Marvin Mitchelson, who was always ready to show off his Rolls Royce automobiles, pricey suits, and office hot tub. But Mitchelson's quirks paled next to those of his client and her opponent. Before the case ended in 1981, the world learned of Triola's abortions and miscarriage, Lee Marvin's occasional impotence, their mutual drug abuse, and other sordid details of the lives two rather mediocre people with too much money to spend. Triola eventually won the case (at least in principle), but only after the courts tackled the threshold question of whether a live-in girlfriend was more akin to a wife or a prostitute.

In its landmark opinion in *Marvin v. Marvin*, the California Supreme Court recognized that "during the past 15 years, there has been a substantial increase in the number of couples living together without marrying," arrangements that had achieved "social acceptance." However, the court noted, without marriage licenses the law still viewed such couples as living in sinful "meretricious" relationships—that is, arrangements in which sex was traded for money. Any financial understandings between the two halves of such couples were treated the same as those negotiated through open car windows between streetwalkers and customers. The court decided that the law needed updating:

> To equate the non-marital relationships of today with [prostitution] is to
> do violence to an accepted and wholly different practice. . . . The mores
> of the society have indeed changed so radically in regard to cohabitation
> that we cannot impose a standard based on alleged moral considerations
> that have apparently been so widely abandoned by so many.

If, the court reasoned, Lee Marvin had given Triola a good reason to expect lifetime financial support, then the law should not stand in the way. Where there was no written contract that detailed such an arrangement, then the courts needed to look at the "conduct of the parties" during the relationship to deduce what they had in mind.

This was a watershed moment in the history of marriage and prostitution. Triola was transformed overnight from a gold-digging prostitute into something closer to a wife. However, her troubles were just beginning. Traditional wives were entitled to alimony, regardless of what their husbands wanted. Triola had to prove that Marvin had agreed to support her after they broke up. In the end, this was more than she or her loudmouth lawyer could do. After an eleven-week trial with sixty witnesses, the court awarded her nothing. (Triola's case wasn't helped by a young man who testified that he had sex with her in Micronesia for ninety straight days while Marvin was making a movie nearby.) Triola won on the law, lost on the facts, and became forever associated with the new concept of "palimony," something for which she never qualified.

The *Marvin* decision was soon applied to gay couples, for whom marriage was unavailable. One of the first such cases came in 1982 and involved the flamboyant entertainer Liberace and Scott Thorson, his former travel secretary, chauffeur, animal trainer, and lover. Thorson claimed that Liberace had promised him $70,000 per year for life, plus $30,000 per year for pet care and the use of one of the pianist's homes in Palm Springs and one in Beverly Hills. Thorson also said that, at Liberace's request, he had forgone his own career as a dancer and had plastic surgery "to more closely conform his facial features to those of Liberace." Liberace denied that he ever made such promises. The two eventually settled out of court, with Liberace promising Thorson $75,000 in cash, two dogs, and three cars, but Thorson later went back to court and tried again, this time settling for $95,000 and no dogs or cars. In 1981, tennis champion Billie Jean King was also sued for palimony by her former secretary and lover, Marilyn Barnett. The case outed King as a lesbian and caused the cancellation of all of her lucrative endorsement deals but brought no fortune to Barnett. The court threw the case out.

•　•　•

In most Western societies, live-in lovers will not be classified as prostitutes when their relationships are seen as affectionate and supportive—in essence, more marriage-like than straight sex-for-money trades. Yet even without quasi-marital trappings, a few types of commercial sexual exchanges have been blessed by the law. In pornography production, for example, paid sexual performers—prostitutes by any logical yardstick—can ply their trade so long as their sexual encounters are recorded on tape and no one involved is "gratified." That potentially millions of people will gratify themselves while watching the recording and that the performers endure humiliation while *looking* gratified (a key skill of prostitutes) are aspects of porn production that the law overlooks. If a camera is running while a person is being paid to be smacked, penetrated, or ejaculated upon in a hotel room, then that is perfectly legal. If the camera is off, then the room is a crime scene.

Another example of permissible commercial sex twists logic even further. From 1972 until 2014, vice cops in Hawaii were allowed to have paid sex with prostitutes "in the course and scope" of their duties, which purportedly gave police the "flexibility" they needed for thorough investigations. The law was not the first of its kind. In the eighteenth century, Parisian police patronized brothels to "learn" what was going on within. Following the Second World War, police measures against prostitutes and homosexuals regularly involved sexual contact—some of it forced—before arrests were made. Present-day sex-worker advocates report endemic police abuse, either in the form of violent rape or demands for sex in exchange for lenient treatment. But only in the Aloha State did the law explicitly allow police to enjoy prostitutes. No one paid much attention to this until Hawaii's legislature took up a new anti-prostitution bill that omitted the rule, and Honolulu police pushed to have it put back in. The resulting publicity embarrassed the force and soon it gave up the effort. The four-decade prerogative of Hawaiian police to have paid sex with prostitutes and then haul them to jail came to an end.

• • •

A more serious and legally ambiguous exception to prostitution law concerns sex surrogates, a term encompassing therapists who provide paid sexual contact to clients who, because of psychological or physical handicaps, have acute difficulties in achieving sexual fulfillment. Such patients include Mark O'Brien, a poet disabled by polio, who wished to experience some sort of sexual contact before dying (as depicted in the 2012 film *The Sessions*). Sex surrogates can provide a path—sometimes the only one—out of a crippling, lonely existence. The sex-surrogacy profession is regulated by a number of trade groups, and sex surrogates can rarely be hired unless recommended and supervised by a licensed psychotherapist, but for opponents that is all a distraction from the fact that sex is being exchanged for money. Said one criminal-defense lawyer in New York City: "It doesn't matter if the client is disabled, it doesn't matter if he is suffering from some kind of emotional distress—that just makes it kind of sad. They have agreed to pay money for a sexual experience, and everyone understands that's the transaction. In my view, that's prostitution."

The French National Ethics Committee agrees. In 2013, it issued a report criticizing the practice as the "unethical use of the human body for commercial purposes." In France, prostitution is technically legal, but soliciting and pimping are not. Therefore, while a sex surrogate may be paid for sex, marketing oneself as one or referring patients to one is a crime. French government officials, among them Marie-Arlette Carlotti, a minister responsible for issues involving people with disabilities, approved the report. She called the practice "a form of prostitution." That decision has not stopped people in France from seeking sex surrogates, however.

Laetitia Rebord is a French woman in her thirties who is almost completely paralyzed and confined to a wheelchair. After unsuccessfully looking for sexual relationships through friends, websites, and male escorts, she told the *New York Times* in 2013 that she intended to find a sex surrogate in Switzerland or Germany, where the practice is legal. "A disabled person is seen as a child," Rebord said. "So inevitably, child[ren] and sex don't go together." Other disabled people in France seek surrogates closer to home. A female Dutch surrogate trained in Switzerland and working underground in France explained: "During the session, I can be a friend, the lover, whoever they want. If someone is in the wheelchair, I start in the wheelchair. I start playing the game of getting undressed in the wheelchair." To the untrained or unsympathetic ear, and to the French government, such statements evoke role-playing, which clients of prostitutes sometimes seek. The fact that prostitutes are now signing up for training as sex surrogates (along with nurses and physiotherapists) is not likely to help the profession there find legitimacy before the law.

If US sex surrogates are supervised by licensed therapists and follow professional ethical guidelines (condoms required, emotional attachment discouraged, etc.), the encounters will usually not bring legal trouble—although there is no guarantee. As crackdowns on prostitution become more aggressive, local law-enforcement agencies are free to decide that a client's disabilities or psychological needs do not trump prostitution laws. There are advocates for a clear exemption from prosecution under prostitution laws for sex surrogates, but so far their voices have not been heard.

Whatever the fate of this therapeutic niche, its very existence highlights an important step in the evolution of Western sexual beliefs: that fulfilling sex is an essential component of a well-lived life, regardless of whether one is married or attempting to produce children. "Sex helps the disabled reincarnate themselves and recover their human aspect," said Marcel Nuss, a disabled French sex-surrogacy advocate. Cornell law professor Sherry F. Colb agrees: "Disabled people certainly . . . have a right to sexuality that is of no lesser weight than the rest of the population." While that may seem obvious now, the fact that sexual satisfaction is equated with one's "human aspect" reflects a substantial, if not universal, shift in sexual norms. In places such as France, the law requires Nuss and Rebord to seek their pleasures abroad or illegally: "The sexuality of the disabled cannot be considered a right," said Anne-Marie Dickelé, a member of the National Ethics Committee. Time will tell whether Dickelé's view will prevail. It should not.

* * *

While prostitution is legal in Australia, New Zealand, Switzerland, Canada, Germany, the Netherlands, and other places, it is still a crime in the majority of Western jurisdictions—although degrees of enforcement vary widely. Prostitutes laboring at the bottom of the profession, particularly those who still sell themselves on street corners and in doorways, have dim hopes of ever seeing their work legitimized by the psychotherapeutic community or the law. The men, women, children, and transgendered people who work the streets have always suffered more legal and social oppression than their counterparts servicing a wealthier clientele. In Louisiana, for example, some of them have been labeled as dangerous sex offenders on a par with child rapists, and their services have been classified as sex crimes of a high order.

An 1805 Louisiana anti-homosexual law condemned oral and anal sex as "crimes against nature." In a 1982 amendment targeting gay prostitutes, the law also criminalized offering oral and anal sex for money. Given that such sex acts are also part of the menu of services offered by straight prostitutes, the amended statute gave law enforcement a choice with regard to virtually every prostitute hauled in: to charge him or her with the mild crime of garden-variety prostitution, or to ratchet up the legal stakes with a much more severe crime-against-nature charge.

In 1991, this second option became even more harsh, as anyone convicted of a "crime against nature"—even for the first time—was put on the state's registry of sex offenders, which effectively barred the person from social services, employment, housing, and even, in some instances, homeless shelters and drug-treatment centers. Those on the registry had their driver's licenses and identification cards marked to announce in bright orange letters that they were sex offenders. They were also forced to disclose their sex-offender status to neighbors, landlords, employers, and schools. Whereas most crimes requiring sex-offender registration involve children or the use of force or violence, a charge of "crimes against nature" did not even require sex to take place; merely offering it could bring a conviction.

Inevitably, most of those convicted under the law were poor people of color, including homeless gay and transgendered people navigating a precarious existence by selling sex on the streets. In New Orleans, as of 2012, about 40 percent of all registered sex offenders had been convicted of "crimes against nature"; 75 percent of them were women, and

79 percent were African American. In the early 2000s, a homeless young man was sent to jail for four years on a crime-against-nature charge for uttering the words "fifty dollars" to an undercover cop. Upon his release, he was designated a sex offender—therefore, as noted, homeless shelters would not take him, much less social-service providers or potential employers. Had he been charged with ordinary prostitution, he would have served little or no jail time and been spared the penalties of sex-offender registration.

In 2011, Louisiana finally ended the travesty of branding street prostitutes as criminals against nature, but it took years of subsequent, hard-fought litigation to force the state to lift sex-offender status for the nearly seven hundred people who had already been convicted. However, even after this important step was taken, police were still charging homosexuals with "crimes against nature," even when no prostitution was involved. In 2013, male undercover police officers in Baton Rouge were soliciting men for sex in parks and then arresting them for "crimes against nature"—despite the fact that laws against adult consensual gay sex had already been declared unconstitutional by the US Supreme Court. After protests about these arrests from the gay and civil rights communities brought Baton Rouge police a rash of negative publicity, the police department pledged to "learn from this, make changes, and move forward."

Prostitution and Purity
in the Early Twentieth Century

In the early twentieth century, prostitution was seen as an amalgam of nearly everything that was wrong with the world. In the US, the issue was first a moral one and, secondarily, one concerning public health. In a 1908 opinion of the US Supreme Court, prostitutes (as well as, incidentally, women who had unpaid "indiscriminate intercourse with men") were said to embody all that a decent, sex-only-in-marriage society should not be:

> [Prostitutes] are in hostility to the idea of the family as consisting in and springing from the union for life of one man and one woman in the holy estate of matrimony; the sure foundation of all that is stable and noble in our civilization; the best guaranty of that reverent morality which is the source of all beneficent progress in social and political improvement.

Social-purity crusaders at the time regarded prostitutes as one of several suspect populations infecting society, both morally and physically, with their licentious ways. (Others included poor immigrants and African Americans.) Some moral reformers advocated for education, rehabilitation, and increased social-health measures to check vice and the spread of disease. Others adopted platforms promoting a return to a pastoral, idealized past, supposedly free from the dreaded influences of industry and modernity. It was the latter group that posed the greatest risk to the well-being of sex workers.

During the "white slavery" panic of the late nineteenth and early twentieth century, foreigners and Jews were falsely accused of abducting innocent white country girls for exploitation in the cities. Within eight years of the passage of the Mann Act in 1910, almost twenty-two hundred people would be convicted for transporting women across state lines for "immoral purposes." Other laws passed that same year facilitated the deportation of not only foreign-born prostitutes and procurers but also those who were employed "where prostitutes gather." Brothels in urban red-light districts had long been tacitly accepted but were now being shut down everywhere, putting more low- and working-class prostitutes on the streets and at the mercy of often-violent pimps. Yet that was not enough for many reformers, who soon trained their sights on the unwashed masses themselves.

These anti-prostitution movements were backed by highly publicized vice surveys and studies overseen by blue-ribbon panels in dozens of cities. People with clipboards and pencils roamed the seediest neighborhoods to observe and quantify immorality in all its manifestations. Predictably, they were not pleased with what they encountered. The researchers saw sex being sold in saloons, dance halls, parks, cafés, "immoral hotels," chop suey restaurants, and railroad stations; on streets; and everywhere else the lower classes were found. (The vices of the moneyed classes were, of course, indulged in more discreet locations, and thus evaded the investigators' gaze.) One 1912 study found that New York City had more than eighteen hundred "vice resorts," along with an estimated fifteen thousand prostitutes. The results of these studies further fueled the closure of red-light districts and the end of the de facto toleration of commercialized vice that had prevailed in the later nineteenth century.

Not all studies of vice and prostitution were setups for police raids. Prostitutes were also examined as members of a new criminal class first being identified by the psychiatric community: the sexual psychopath. While the contours of sexual psychopathology would change much throughout the century, American psychiatrists in the 1920s and 1930s often applied the term "sexual psychopath" to prostitutes and women viewed as hypersexual. Providing intellectual heft to this growing branch of psychiatry was the work being done in the US's first specialized treatment institution for psychopathic criminals—nearly every bed of which was occupied by a prostitute. The hospital, called the Bedford Hills Reformatory for Women, was bankrolled in 1916 by oilman John D. Rockefeller, who was no stranger to the issue: he was already devoting his philanthropic largesse to the study and elimination of prostitution through his Bureau for Social Hygiene.

Much of the research concluded that prostitutes were feebleminded and otherwise defective, which, in turn, resulted in calls for their exclusion from the greater gene pool. In Chapter 1, we saw how eugenics laws were used to surgically sterilize poor females of color, especially those who had children outside of marriage. Their "promiscuity" was interpreted as a sign of congenital sexual delinquency and idiocy, which justified sterilizing them lest they conjoin with "normal" people. Women who were paid for sex were put into the same category. In Georgia, for example, a 1919 "mental hygiene" survey sought to confirm "the highly important relationship which feeblemindedness bears to the whole question of prostitution and venereal disease." Not surprisingly, the study found that most infected prostitutes had "serious mental abnormalities" that rendered them unfit to reproduce, even if their infections were cured.

Prostitutes thus became prime targets for segregation and sterilization in jurisdictions where eugenics practices were accepted. In fact, prostitution was the only specific job category targeted in most eugenics laws. Margaret Sanger, the founder of what would become Planned Parenthood and a giant in the field of birth control advocacy, called for the exclusion of immigrant prostitutes and the segregation of sex workers to "farms and open spaces for as long as necessary for the strengthening and development of [their] moral conduct." In Sweden, some sixty thousand women were sterilized without their consent between 1930 and 1970 on grounds such as having an "unhealthy sexual appetite."

Prostitution and War

Prostitution is a component of any sustained armed conflict, and not just for the people directly involved in paid sexual exchanges. To understand its lasting effects on wartime populations, we can look to the ongoing controversy over Japan's Second World War–era enslavement of up to two hundred thousand mostly Korean "comfort women" to sexually service its soldiers. In 1993, in what became known as the Kono Statement, Japan apologized and set up a fund to provide some compensation to surviving comfort women, but this long-delayed acknowledgement of accountability was too little for many Koreans and too much for some Japanese. In 2007, Prime Minister Shinzo Abe's cabinet declared that there was no documentary evidence of coercion of comfort women and that the Kono Statement was not binding government policy. In February 2014, as a sop to Abe's far-right supporters (who resent what they see as unfair condemnations of Japan's wartime behavior), his chief cabinet secretary said that the Kono Statement would be revisited. That announcement infuriated South Koreans, who had been demanding much more in the way of apology and compensation, and who have missed few opportunities to raise the issue.

Korean rage has been expressed symbolically—through gestures such as the placement of statues of comfort women in front of Japanese embassies—and on the geopolitical stage. Only after Abe, at the US's urging, promised in 2014 not to tamper with the Kono Statement ("We must be humble in front of history," he said) would South Korean president Park Geun-hye agree to meet with Abe at a nuclear summit in the Netherlands. While this issue continues to play out on the world stage, and while the oppression of the comfort women was unique both in its scale and its systematic enslavement of women, the fact is that most women who are used for sex by soldiers during wartime become prostitutes from acute economic need or are coerced at the point of a bayonet. The conditions in which they do so range from poor to deeply miserable. None comes out unscathed.

During the First World War, prostitutes were considered by commanders on all sides as the source of a one-way flow of sexually transmitted infections (STIs) into the bodies of soldiers. The US military shared this concern, although its initial responses were rather naive. Soon after America entered the war in 1917, soldiers were told to practice abstinence overseas and thus don the "invisible armor" they needed to avoid infection. Soldiers were also told that "sex organs do not have to be exercised or indulged in, in order to develop them or preserve virility," and were urged to "forget them, don't think about them, or dwell upon them. Live a good vigorous life and they will take care of themselves." A pamphlet distributed to troops, "Keeping Fit to Fight," stated: "Women who solicit soldiers for immoral purposes are usually disease spreaders and friends of the enemy." These entreaties, as well others intended to keep soldiers from prostitutes, were as futile as would reasonably have been expected. As STI rates among soldiers increased, and as crowds of women made themselves available for hire near army bases and battlefronts, condoms were eventually distributed to soldiers, treatment centers set up, and brothels and saloons placed off-limits in overseas ports. At home, no fewer than fifteen thousand prostitutes near army bases were arrested en masse and forcibly detained for periods averaging ten weeks. No troops were arrested for patronizing prostitutes.

For European participants in the Great War, prostitution was further associated with intrigues. As the fighting on the Western Front settled into an entrenched stalemate on French and Belgian territory, German army commanders were concerned that local prostitutes would do their "patriotic duty" by deliberately infecting their soldiers with STIs, as they were said to have to done to German soldiers during the 1870–1871 Franco-Prussian War. Whether or not that happened, prostitutes on all sides were deployed as spies. The Belgians, for example, informed their "light cavalry" that they would not be prosecuted for bedding the enemy if the encounters produced good information for use against the Germans. "The tricks of prostitution remained relatively the same everywhere," observed Magnus Hirschfeld: "to chat, to boast, then, if necessary, to drug the victim and run through his pockets."

For many prostitutes, between-the-sheets espionage was a minor variation on the sexual confidence games they had long practiced. "The best women spies were nearly always *grandes cucottes*, *mondaines* and *demi-mondaines* who had gone through the mill," wrote Hirschfeld. Among the best of them, "the journey between the first coquettish glance and the removal of the last garment was so long that many a man gave away his secrets long before" lovemaking commenced. The women did their work in grand Swiss, Polish, British, and Russian hotels, on boats and trains, and anywhere else that men with useful information gathered. This excerpt from a letter from one such spy gives the flavor of the work:

> Yesterday I had a rendezvous with a deck officer. The poor devil is passionately in love with me and is even desirous of marrying me. . . . He invited me to visit him aboard the vessel which invitation I gladly accepted and I succeeded in following him into the map room. There two eyes did the rest.

Another prostitute-spy prevailed on her love-struck German paramour to bring her a gift of the newest German gas mask, which she sent along to Allied commanders. "At that time, it was a great puzzle why suddenly the masks became useless, and why thousands of German soldiers were destroyed despite the fact that they were wearing gas masks," wrote Hirschfeld.

The best known of the seductress-spies was Mata Hari, née Maragarethe Zelle, a renowned courtesan, performer, and "mistress of the Kama Sutra" whose wartime loyalties and liaisons were so convoluted that even she must have been confused. While the details of her intrigues still remain obscure, she had agreed (according to statements she supposedly made) to act as a French spy in German-occupied Belgium. Naturally, she did not bother to inform French intelligence that she had been engaged previously to spy on behalf of the Germans. Zelle was executed in Paris as a German spy in 1917. Despite her renown and the legions of powerful men who had occupied her bed and declared their love, she died alone. No one claimed her body, which was left "to anatomy for the advancement of which her much loved limbs were cut up into little fragments."

Mati Hari and her ilk notwithstanding, nearly all of the hard labor of wartime sex commerce carried no glamor whatsoever. Encounters were quick, often savage, and frequently undercompensated. The ample numbers of field brothels serving troops were housed in abandoned and partially ruined buildings, barracks, or even empty wagons. Brothels for officers were often fairly comfortable—for the officers if not the women—but those for soldiers everywhere presented a similar grim spectacle. The British poet Robert Graves, in his autobiography *Goodbye to All That*, describes the brothel at Béthune, northern France, where 150 men were usually found lined up outside the door, waiting to spend a few moments with one of the three women inside. The reader can do the math, but suffice it to say that it was exhausting work: "Each woman served nearly a battalion of men every week for as long as she lasted," Graves added. The women usually endured only a few weeks before they were unable to continue.

What drove the women to work in these brothels? Poverty and hunger. Most wartime prostitutes did what they did because, in a world blown inside out, there was no other way of obtaining the means to eat or relieve the misery of those who depended on them. When Graves describes being greeted in Le Havre by a tangle of ragged kids tugging at the his coat and begging him to have "very good jig-a-jig" with their sisters "very cheap," there is no doubting the reason such scenes took place, or the uncounted other such encounters behind the battlefronts. The lines of men at the brothels mirrored the queues in which their distant wives and daughters waited for food. The difference was that the food often ran out before the waiting women could all be served, while the brothels had an inexhaustible supply of desperate females ready, if not willing, to be used.

In Serbia under occupation by the Austro-Hungarian Empire, food was particularly scarce and most of the native men were away fighting. There were plentiful brothels, but some Serbian women also formed "relationships" with well-placed members of the occupying forces. This "soft" prostitution brought these women moral castigation by their neighbors and punishment once the war ended. Serbian women were traditionally seen as guardians of national honor, and females who deviated from virtue were reviled as much as paid prostitutes. By allowing the enemy into their bodies, they opened the sacred recesses of the Serbian soul to occupation—a violation no less grievous than the presence of foreign guns. Most of these women were doing what was necessary to survive, but that mattered less to their detractors than the stain they put on Serbian national identity. There was no "I had no choice" defense to sexual treason.

When the war finally came to a close in 1918, it was time to settle scores and, through retribution against women who had consorted with the former occupiers, claw back a measure of Serbian honor. "Immoral" women, many of whom the war had left widowed and without male protection, often had whatever property they had managed to keep taken away. This was especially the case with housing, of which the war had left a severe shortage. In one instance a landlord went to the police to evict Jelena, a female tenant he accused of leading a "licentious life with Austrian soldiers during the enemy occupation." Her neighbors chimed in, telling the court that "Jelena is an immoral woman" who had been "living in sin" with the enemy. The landlord claimed that he had been unable to do anything about Jelena's behavior during the war because "the [enemy] authorities tolerated this lifestyle, which they deemed to be necessary for their troops." But now that the Austrians were gone, he wanted her out. Jelena's failure to pay rent was treated almost as an aside; the economic rationale for her eviction was subordinate to the sexual-moral reason. Jelena had traduced Serbia by living off her sexual relationship with Austrians and now, for the sake of the country as well as the landlord, she would be called to account. Her story was repeated time and again.

Comfort Markets in the Second World War

As in all theaters of armed conflict, sex was a form of currency during the Second World War—particularly in Nazi Germany and the lands it occupied. While prostitutes (and other "deviants") were initially sent to concentration camps in the tens of thousands for "conspicuously . . . inciting immoral acts," the regime later changed its tune and treated prostitution as a necessary outlet for male sexual urges. Access to brothels came to be understood as a deterrent to homosexuality in young men, and also as a reward for work well done. While the "sanitation of the street scene" (the removal of streetwalkers, pimps, and so on) was seen as critical to the family-friendly image the Nazis wished to project, the state-managed brothel system emerged as a tool to augment male vitality, flare off excess sexual energies, and increase male productivity in the cities and on the battlefields. Prostitutes were always condemned as "asocial" (as were people who engaged in interracial sex and those who cultivated a "strongly erotic impression"), and "oversexed" women were still subject to sterilization, but they were also warily deployed for the good of a vital Thousand-Year Reich.

The subject of prostitution during the Third Reich is extensive. Here we shall look at a small subset of the system—specifically, the ten or so concentration-camp brothels set up for the pleasure of favored male prisoners. These were established by SS chief Heinrich Himmler in 1942, after he visited the Mauthausen-Gusen camp and its nearby rock quarries, where slave laborers extracted granite for use in Hitler's grandiose construction projects. Himmler did not accept the received wisdom that slaves work to about half the productivity of free workers. To his mind, it was only a question of using carrots and sticks to get more out of them. As he considered a series of rewards, he affirmed that denying sex to hardworking prisoners was "out of touch with the world and life." To provide incentives to prison laborers to meet production targets, he ordered that a small number of male prison laborers be given the sexual company of select female prisoners—some formerly prostitutes, others not.

Himmler's sex-incentive plan conformed to Nazi racial beliefs. Only "Aryans," which included Germans, Dutch, Belgians, and Scandinavians, were permitted to patronize and work at the camp brothels. Jews and Soviet POWs were excluded. The prostitutes were culled from acceptable populations such as Germans, Dutch, and some Poles; there is no evidence that any of them were Jews. (Polish women were also recruited for sexual service to Ukrainian SS guards, as Ukrainians were considered unfit to have sex with Germans.) Sometimes "volunteers" were sought from among the women working the most difficult details; they were falsely promised release after six months in exchange for service in the brothels. Other women would be selected by guards and pressed into service. Still other female prisoners sought the work, as camp prostitutes had a slightly better chance of survival. "The main thing was that at least we had escaped the hell of Bergen-Belsen and Ravensbrück," said one camp prostitute. "The main thing was to survive at all."

Magdalena Walter, a German, was selected for prostitution service in the Ravensbrück camp and transported to Buchenwald. There she was told she would receive better food, and would not be harmed so long as she cooperated. She was relieved that she was not put into a brothel for the pleasure of SS officers and was, at least at first, glad to escape the beatings that came with work on a road construction crew. She was given a white plaid skirt, panties, and a bra to wear. After a full day of work, what she described as the "terrible two hours" in the evening began, when the male prisoners had finished their work and were brought in:

> Now, every night we had to let the men get on top of us, for two hours. That meant they could come into the brothel barrack, had to go to the medical room, to get an injection, could go to the [numbered room,] could do their thing, into the room, on top, down, out back to the medical room, where they again got an injection. . . . And then right away there came the next one. Non-stop. And they didn't have more than a quarter of an hour.

Only the prisoners at the top of the camps' complex hierarchy—that is, the ones who already had more food and performed less physical labor than the majority of inmates—were permitted this vile luxury. Most of the men were too starved, ill, or exhausted to even consider sex. (Some prisoners masturbated from time to time, noted historian Robert Sommer, not to satisfy any sexual desire but "to see whether they were still alive.") However, an elevated position among the prisoner population still did not bring these men any appreciable measures of humane treatment by the SS guards. Some were forced to visit the brothels against their will, either as vicious jokes or for more sinister reasons. For example, the Buchenwald brothel's first patron was a prisoner-collaborator. By giving him the "honor" of crossing the brothel's threshold first, the guards telegraphed his turncoat status to the camp—which likely exposed him to a violent end at the hands of the inmates. In another instance, an exhausted group of prisoner-workers, coming off a grueling shift making missiles, were directed to the camp brothel:

> The men were stupefied. . . . The poor fellows were drunk with fatigue and only wanted to sleep after twelve hours of work. The first line was put one in front of each door and commanded to drop their trousers. The doors were still closed. . . . The second order was given: 'Enter!' They went in, trousers lowered. . . . Delarouche found himself face to face with a woman who was waiting. He was worried and blushing with confusion.

The humiliation didn't stop there. The doors to the little sex chambers had peepholes for the guards to look through, which they often did, providing crude commentary on what they saw. Guards also enforced only "normal," missionary-position sex, and ensured that it was brought to a close within the quarter-hour allotment. If men stayed after ringing of the fifteen-minute bell, guards rushed into the rooms and beat them. Yet despite the risks, some of the men and women tried to form relationships beyond those permitted. A few men tried to smuggle gifts to the women; others simply wanted to feel a kindred human presence. To prevent close relationships from forming, the SS made the women change rooms constantly, so the men never knew whom they would be visiting. For any prisoners trying to visit the women at night in their barracks, the prescribed punishment was death.

Incredibly, after the war ended and the surviving forced laborers began to agitate for compensation, the women who had worked in the camp brothels found that they were unable to claim damages because of the supposed "voluntary" nature of their labor. Others never came forward because of the shame and stigma of sex work, even though the circumstances had been extraordinary. Most remained silent about it for the rest of their lives.

There were other insidious sexual exchanges taking place in the German camps at the direct instigation of privileged prisoners and at the expense of lower-ranked females or boys. Food rations for much of the prison population were insufficient to sustain life, so obtaining food from other sources became a matter of survival. Those resources were often controlled by higher-ranked prisoners. If one had a little food or other essential items to trade, sex was not difficult to obtain. "Since time began," boasted one privileged inmate, "there has never been such an easy market for female flesh!"

One such exchange, between the Jewish prisoner Gisella Perl and a better-situated Polish inmate in the Auschwitz-Birkenau complex, this time for a needed piece of string, captures the desperation and opportunistic cruelty that must have been repeated time and again:

> I stopped beside him. . . . He looked me over from head to foot, carefully, then grabbed me by the shoulder and hissed in my ear: "I don't want your bread. . . . I want you . . . you. . . . Hurry up . . . hurry up . . ." he said hoarsely. His hand, filthy with the human filth he was working in, reached out for my womanhood, rudely, insistently.

Many of the surviving women were too ashamed to later admit what they had done, especially given postwar suspicions that survivors must have either collaborated or prostituted themselves. Yet such accusations wrongly presume that those who traded sex to survive exercised freewill in doing so. "I was only a shadow without identity, alive only by the power of suffering," wrote Perl. Shadows do not make reasoned decisions.

Outside the prison camps, the rules for sex with occupiers were no less blurry—that is, until the fighting ended and sex with the enemy was punished as treasonous collaboration. Fraternization with enemy forces had taken place on a huge scale, particularly in the Western European sectors where occupying German troops were stationary and had little to do. There were brothels nearly everywhere for German troops, but the populations of certain occupied countries such as Denmark and Norway were believed to have a similar racial makeup to that of Germans, so the Nazi authorities allowed romantic relationships as well. In Norway, about one in five women under the age of thirty had romantic/sexual relationships with Germans during the war; in Demark, the ratio was about one in ten. Nearly fifteen thousand babies were born in both countries from these relationships. The number of love children born in France was much greater: about two hundred thousand.

We are talking here about a lot of sex between peoples at war. No doubt a large number of these relationships involved genuine affection, although there were also mercenary aspects. For women in occupied regions, sex with the enemy could bring food, coal, favors, intimacy (both real and imagined), and tit-for-tat reprisals against philandering mates. The one constant was that in all locations, in all languages, and in the opinions

of sniping neighbors in every town, women who consorted with the occupiers were considered whores. They represented frailty over strength,
depravity over rectitude, and moral chaos.

The rage caused by these sexual encounters was exploited by opposing
armies. American, British, German, and Soviet planes dropped millions
of leaflets reminding soldiers that their wives and sweethearts were having
sex with the enemy and loving every second of it. Almost as infuriating was
the fraternization of women with Allied soldiers, which combating armies
also exploited. German-produced leaflets directed at the French depicted
French women in the arms of British soldiers or, in leaflets dropped across
the English Channel, English women in ecstatic embraces with Americans.
The Japanese army left leaflets on the battlefields of New Guinea, where its
soldiers were fighting Australia, showing Americans taking their pleasure
with Australian women. One showed a grinning American officer with a
partially disrobed Australian woman in his arms, telling her not to worry
about her husband: "He'll be on the next casualty list."

Historian Dagmar Herzog sums up the long-term effects of wartime
female infidelity:

> The long-standing assumptions about vast differences between wives
> and prostitutes had collapsed. Wives had come to be understood as
> sexual beings who actively sought pleasure for themselves. There was
> no longer any difference between good girls and bad girls. And—no
> minor matter—from now on men would have to compete to be the
> objects of female desire.

Returning, war-weary soldiers were in no mood to accept the free sexual
agency of their wives or sweethearts, especially when that entailed "hor-
izontal" collaboration. When the fighting stopped, retributions against
such women were sometimes hateful. Relatively few women were tortured
or killed—usually they had their heads shaved, although some were tarred
or marked with swastikas in paint or lipstick. The message was that the
women had crossed sexual bounds treasonously and that anyone thinking
about ever doing the same would be well advised to think again.

• • •

Japan's network of enslaved "comfort women" grew out of the privately
organized, prewar sex-trafficking system that accompanied the country's

expanding commercial and colonial interests in the Pacific. When Japan's imperialist military adventures gained steam in the 1930s, the system fell under the control of the Imperial Japanese Army, which oversaw the sexual enslavement of thousands of women from conquered territories. Armed with condoms that the army branded as "Assault No. 1," Japan's fighting forces penetrated not only enemy territory but the enemy herself—and in so doing, deepened the humiliation of the defeated populations in Korea, Manchuria, the Philippines, and the Dutch East Indies (Indonesia).

In the early part of the twentieth century, Japanese prostitutes were shipped to Singapore, Perth, and various Russian ports (among other places), where they serviced clients of all nationalities and collected much-needed foreign currency to send home. Many of the women had been deceived by labor brokers, who induced them to leave Japan using false promises of legitimate, well-paid overseas work. Once under the brothel owners' control abroad, the women were saddled with inflated debts that took years to repay (if they ever could be) and that kept them in indefinite bondage.

With the intensification of Japan's colonization of Korea and its invasion of China in 1938, the military transported subjugated local women to "comfort stations" near Japanese army bases and forward combat positions. It is impossible to know how many women were sexually enslaved before the war's end, but the best estimates range from eighty thousand to one hundred thousand. Most of them were Korean, but many also came from Taiwan, China, the Philippines, Indonesia, and Malaysia. One comfort station, set up in Borneo in 1942 with four abducted Indonesian women, was the handiwork of a young paymaster in the Imperial Navy named Yasuhiro Nakasone, who would be prime minister of Japan from 1982 to 1987.

The conditions in which the comfort women lived and worked were almost indescribably hideous, and became worse as Japan's military reversals mounted and its soldiers became increasingly desperate. As described by one Korean woman, Mun P'ilgi, who had been transported to a comfort station in China:

> There were many times when I was almost killed. If I refused to do what one [Japanese soldier] asked, he would come back drunk and threaten me with his sword. Others simply arrived drunk, and had intercourse with their swords stuck in the tatami. . . . This sort of behavior was more of a threat to make me accede to their desires and give them satisfaction.

Mun P'ilgi also described being beaten and branded with a red-hot iron for refusing the humiliating demands of another soldier. In the Philippines, approximately ten young females were kept by each company-size army unit. During the day they would do the cooking and washing for the company, and in the evenings they would be required to submit sexually to five to ten soldiers each. Many of the women became addicted to drugs; others killed themselves by ingesting the chemicals they were given to clean their genitals. Some were killed in enemy attacks and some committed double suicide with their depressed "customers." There are tens of thousands of such stories, all of which testify to the sexual pathology that accompanies warfare. When the war ended, most of the comfort women were abandoned by the retreating Japanese army. In 1945, Mun P'ilgi was left behind in Manchuria, where she faced the imminent danger of rape by invading Soviet armies.

The comfort-women system did not end with Japan's surrender in August 1945. Rather, it was reestablished in Japan itself, this time using native women to serve the war's victors. Japanese authorities had anticipated a wave of rape by occupying troops—a concern that had some foundation, given that American soldiers had gang-raped Okinawan women during the extensive combat there. To create a sexual "breakwater" or "kamikaze" unit to draw the Americans' "wild feelings" away from respectable Japanese women, government authorities (in league with businessmen and shady labor brokers) rushed a network of brothels into operation. There the bodies of disfavored Japanese women—many coerced or deceived into service—were sacrificed "for the sake of the nation and for the safety of the Japanese people." By the time US troops arrived on Japanese shores, these brothels awaited them.

Within one day of the first landing of American troops, five hundred to six hundred GIs could be found waiting in line at a brothel called Komachien, or "The Babe Garden." Each of the women there endured the rough affections of fifteen to sixty clients per day. In Hiroshima, where the nuclear bombing had caused chaos and widespread starvation, prostitutes were lured into service with food and other basic provisions. In addition, teenage girls whose families had been killed by Allied bombs were coerced into becoming comfort women, as were women responding to deceptive notices offering decent pay for legitimate jobs. The Americans were aware of the Japanese military's comfort-women system prior to the invasion of Japan, but it was low on their initial list of concerns. Nor were the Allies too troubled about the wretched circumstances of Japanese women selling sex to US troops. A memorandum dated December 6, 1945, from a well-placed officer in the occupation's General Headquarters, confirmed that "in urban districts, the practice of enslaving girls [for sex], while much less prevalent than in the past, still exists."

Moreover, as historian Yuki Tanaka points out: "The physical hardship that the Japanese comfort women faced was strikingly similar to that endured by Asian comfort women during the war. The only difference was that these Japanese comfort women were paid properly, in most cases, whereas the former had received hardly any payment." American troops were also known to rob comfort women at gunpoint, and some military police were not averse to demanding "free service." In September 1945, three Australian former prisoners of war dragged some comfort women back to their hotel and gang-raped them along with seven additional soldiers.

The sexual free-for-all in and around the Japanese comfort stations continued until March 1946, when General Douglas MacArthur, concerned about the spread of STIs and adverse publicity at home, placed the brothels off-limits to American troops. Just as suddenly as the comfort stations had opened in 1945, about 150,000 Japanese women were now out of work and more destitute than ever—although many continued to sell sex to the occupiers through other channels. In a 1949 survey of five hundred Japanese prostitutes servicing American GIs, about 25 percent of the women said they became prostitutes in order to subsist. Another 22.8 percent said they became comfort women in despair after being raped by Allied troops. However, even this survey is probably skewed in that it did not tabulate the deaths of comfort women that had already taken place. In one case, nineteen-year-old Takita Natsue—who worked at the Babe Garden—jumped in front of a train a few days after the brothel opened in 1945. Was her brief life less worthy of living than the women Japan sought to protect at her expense? Of course not. The bare outline of Natsue's last days is enough to affirm that in wartime, no one side holds the moral high ground.

• • •

Back in the US, the official policy, instituted in 1941, was that prostitution near military bases was a federal crime. The government also set up a Social Protection Division (SPD) to act as a watchdog over women's morals. The SPD and other government agencies exerted considerable

pressure on local governments to stamp out prostitution everywhere soldiers were based and quartered, but their efforts were not always welcome.
In San Bernardino, California, for example, businessmen argued that
without red-light districts, soldiers from a nearby military base would
prey on local females. Other groups, echoing Japanese logic, argued for
a "buffer of whores" to protect respectable women. Many regions, such
as Hawaii, operated without hindrance. Honolulu's sprawling vice district served about 250,000 soldiers and sailors per month. The average of
three dollars paid by troops for three minutes of a prostitute's attention
was seen as socially beneficial. It was better for men to go to regulated
brothels than to turn, as one newspaper stated, to "our young girls and
women—whether by rape, seduction, or the encouraging of their natural
tendencies." For the duration of the war, regulated prostitution was the
rule in Hawaii.

While the libidinous "tendencies" of soldiers were taken as a fact of
nature, women's sexuality was viewed quite differently. Here we encounter the hybrid wartime female identity known, variously, as the Kha-
ki-Wacky, the Victory Girl, the Grass Grabber, the Good-Time Charlotte,
and, most expressively, the Patriotute. This last moniker, a blend of "pa-
triot" and "prostitute," was coined by a US Public Health Service official for women who too enthusiastically answered the government's call
to support the war effort. It aptly encapsulates the ambivalent messages
women received about sex with men in uniform.

Women were not only recruited to work in munitions factories and the
like. They were also called upon—by the United Service Organization
(USO) and other organizations—to build morale by providing wholesome
companionship to the troops at activities such as dances. That this war
service would take a quick sexual turn should have come as no surprise.
Advertisements encouraged women to go "all the way" for the war effort
by wearing enticing perfume, donning provocative clothing, and generally making themselves alluring to soldiers. One article in the magazine
Coronet, headlined "Johnny Get Your Fun," focused on female entertainers
and observed: "The gal with the G-string, the taxi-dancer, and the chorine
in the nightclub with the black net stockings up to her mezzanine; in
their own way they're all doing war jobs."

The nightclubs' patrons would, undoubtedly, have agreed with the
Coronet writer's opinion, but the government did not. The campaign
against traditional prostitutes broadened to include sexually indiscriminate females, the girls who "live and give lightly." According to the SPD,

such a type was "not criminally motivated." Rather, she was likely to be a "casual, fun-seeking girl, wanting male companionship, a young experimenter; someone lonely, easing her conscience for defying social and moral codes by quixotic references to patriotism." At the same time, she was likened to a prostitute: "The old-time prostitute . . . is sinking into second place," wrote one "expert." "The new type is the young girl in her late teens and early twenties, the young woman in every field of life who is determined to have one fling or better." In a very short time, the sweet USO girl-next-door had morphed into a bed-hopping hussy, a source of disease, and the focus of repressive government attention.

Soon, all women became potential prostitutes. "The non-commercial girl . . . is supplanting the prostitute as the main source of venereal infection," announced the US surgeon general in 1944. They were supposedly everywhere, in "boom towns, trailer towns, cities and villages," and "they were driving our national standards of morality down." Prostitution, warned the authorities, now "may be practiced in many different ways, few of which are outwardly apparent." GIs were warned against "booby traps"—attractive women who would poison them with STIs. "You are badly mistaken if you think you can tell whether or not a girl has Venereal Disease by her looks or her clothes or by listening to her story," advised one military handout to troops going on leave.

Given the expansive definition of prostitution, a broad cross-section of American females found themselves under suspicion. One married waitress, who attracted attention for eating lunch alone in a train station, was arrested for vagrancy and jailed for seven days. Notwithstanding the negative results on a test for STIs and her protestations that she had sex only with her husband, she was sent to an isolation hospital. Over the course of the war, prostitution arrests rose about 20 percent. Arrests for related offenses such as vagrancy, disorderly conduct, frequenting bars too much, and other crimes against "common decency" also rose steeply, mostly among young females. From 1940–1942, there were nearly thirty thousand arrests of girls for juvenile delinquency.

The idea that "good girls" did war duty by chastely comforting lonely servicemen while "Patriotutes" engaged in heavy petting and more shows the reality-challenged double bind that American women faced during wartime. The truth is that young people are usually hungry for sex and take advantage of most opportunities to have it. Moreover, far from being encouraged to stop at holding a soldier's hand, many girls were not-so-subtly made to believe that having intercourse with a serviceman before he was shipped out—perhaps never to come back—was a patriotic duty. Yet by showing sexual interest in the men lionized by the wartime propaganda machine, women compromised their own respectability and risked time in jail. Servicemen were never charged with morals offenses for having paid sex with prostitutes or informal encounters with Khaki-Wackies. Women, on the other hand, were subject to arrest even "on suspicion of" various morals offenses.

* * *

The Third Reich's unconditional surrender in 1945 resulted in the occupation of Germany by the US, France, Britain, and the Soviet Union. Berlin, the ruined capital, was divided into four sectors; each was administered by one of these Allied powers and subject to its own set of rules. This unique situation, along with the city's position as a focal point of the Cold War, generated a host of international political issues. But for Berliners trying to survive the early postwar years, geopolitics was of secondary importance. First on their list was finding food and shelter, and many young men and women earned the money to do so by selling sex.

The situation for Berlin's female population was particularly dire. First, there were the mass rapes committed by the invading Soviet troops. Second was the persistent belief that venereal disease originated with female prostitutes, which meant that young women and girls suspected of prostitution were routinely forced to undergo crude, invasive examinations. For example, in November 1945, four fifteen- and sixteen-year-old girls were rounded up in the street and, for no reason other than their failure to carry sufficient identification, forced to strip in front of American military police and undergo invasive gynecological exams. One of the girls, a virgin, begged to be spared the exam, but her pleas were ignored. After a night in jail she was returned to her outraged parents. In response to their complaints, the police merely noted: "It is impossible to differentiate between good and bad girls," as even those from good homes have "discovered their bodies as a means by which to lead an easy life."

The many boys and young men who sheltered in the rubble of Berlin's destroyed buildings and lived by picking up men at the city's infamous train stations (*Bahnhöfe*) were treated differently. Whereas girls were rounded up merely for congregating in public, the *"Bahnhof* boys" generally had to be caught having sex with their clients to be arrested. Even then, they were treated—at least at first—more like war victims than as a source of trouble. Rather than going to jail or being subjected to rough medical exams, they were sent to youth centers and provided increased social services. Girls were viewed as public health risks; boys were to be reclaimed as productive citizens.

Further complicating the situation were the occupying authorities' differing approaches as to what constituted illegal male–male sex. The infamous Paragraph 175 of the German Criminal Code (originally adopted in Prussia in 1871), which criminalized homosexual sex among adult men as well as purchased sex with youths, was still in place, but it was enforced differently in each of the city's four sectors. Authorities in the Soviet-occupied zone—and the emerging German Democratic Republic (GDR)—required physical proof of an "intercourse-like act" before a criminal charge could stick, while the American, British, and French authorities were content with the Nazi-era interpretation that even "shameless" behavior such as kissing and mutual masturbation violated the law. Consider Otto N., a forty-nine-year-old office worker who, in 1951, picked up a young man at a pissoir near the Friedrichstrasse *Bahnhof* in Berlin's Soviet sector. The two masturbated each other and then journeyed to West Berlin, where they were arrested—apparently at the urging of Otto's wife. At the subsequent trial, Otto reminded the court that mutual masturbation was legal in the Soviet sector, where he had picked up the young man. He was correct—but in the western sectors such an act was still forbidden, and Otto received a six-month prison sentence. (The fate of his marriage is not known.)

The Friedrichstrasse *Bahnhof* was also the scene of a pickup in 1948 by a married man, Gerhard Z., and a young hustler named Karl-Heinz S. While being followed by police, the two men repaired to a destroyed apartment complex known for hosting sexual assignations. The cops mishandled the case by startling the men before they had begun to have sex in earnest. Although the policemen admitted they had likely arrived too soon, Gerhard still insisted on going to the police station to ensure that the matter was handled with discretion—so that his wife would not learn of the extent of his sexual interests. It is likely that he was not penalized, as the "intention" of having sex with a man was not a crime in the eastern sector. Karl-Heinz, however, was probably detained, because merely offering himself for the "purpose of abuse" was grounds for intervention.

In yet another encounter beginning at the same *Bahnhof*, an off-duty police officer and a fourteen-year-old male prostitute spent a long, drunken evening together before something soured between them. The boy called for the police, claiming that the officer had fellated him without permission. The cop, who vehemently insisted upon his heterosexuality by referring more than once to his pregnant fiancée, was not charged because there was no physical evidence to support the boy's accusation. (The police had returned to the scene of the altercation looking for traces of semen, but rain had made their investigation futile.) The boy was sent to a youth home for no less than two years of "reeducation."

It's no surprise that the policeman in the last example was let off—he was in law enforcement, after all. Yet "johns" were given mild treatment for other reasons, such as the deleterious effects of their wartime experiences. When a middle-aged laborer was accused of having repeated sexual contact with a neighbor boy, he argued that he had developed health problems during his captivity by the Soviet army that made sex with women impossible. He was treated with leniency by the court, likely also on the belief that returning soldiers with major injuries were prone to homosexuality. As the war crept further into the past, this "medicalization" of homosexual behavior continued to work to the advantage of men who had solicited male prostitutes, while the mercenary motives of the young prostitutes earned them less sympathy. In the eastern sector, male hustlers came to be viewed as lacking the socialist "values" required to contribute to the new communist state. Invoking Nazi-era laws, judges sentenced young offenders to indeterminate sentences in grim youth facilities and workhouses to learn how to become productive, heterosexual citizens. In both East and West Germany, male hustlers came to be characterized as predators, while their better-heeled customers were seen as prey.

By the time Germany unified in 1989, East and West had developed profoundly different systems of sexual regulation. East German authorities equated the capitalist West with gender inequality, exploitation of women in the workplace, and especially retrograde and commodifying attitudes toward sex. Contrary to West Germany's lenient prostitution rules, East Germany (the GDR) criminalized prostitution in 1968. At about the same time, however, restrictions on travel from the West were loosened, and soon bans on holding Western currency were eased. This development created new opportunities for bed-based spying. Ironically, just when GDR officials trumpeted their suppression of prostitution, the communist state went into the business. Prostitution came under the control of the Ministry for State Security—the notorious Stasi—which strong-armed prostitutes into spying on Western visitors. In return for information gained in bed, the Stasi let them continue to service foreigners and spend the hard currency they earned on luxury goods. From the early 1970s onward, prostitute-agents were fixtures in the bars and lobbies of East German tourist hotels.

Sex Trafficking and the Hazards of Compassion

In the run-up to the 2014 Super Bowl game in East Rutherford, New Jersey, more than fifty law-enforcement agencies teamed up with the FBI to strike against what has repeatedly been called "the largest human trafficking event on the planet." The state's governor, along with other stern-faced dignitaries, announced that large resources were in place against the expected influx of sex traffickers and prostitutes. The same scene has been taking place for years in advance of the World Cup, the Olympics, and other major sports events, where authorities routinely warn that up to one hundred thousand "forced prostitutes" (including children) are being brought in to work the events. Invariably, authorities then assure the populace that the situation is under control, that extra law-enforcement muscle and technology are in place, and that offenders will be found and jailed. No less consistently, press releases boasting of mass arrests (or, in current parlance, "rescues") of sex slaves and their traffickers begin to fly after the games.

There is one problem with these narratives: they are shams. The predictions of human trafficking are untrue and the waves of arrests usually do more harm than good. As noted by Kate Mogulescu, supervising attorney at the Trafficking Victims Advocacy Project, despite all the raids and incarcerations that accompany these events, "the actual number of traffickers investigated or prosecuted usually hovers around zero." This was the case with the 2010 World Cup in South Africa, the 2010 Olympics in Vancouver, Canada, and the 2004 Olympics in Athens, Greece, where the sports-event sex-trafficking myth first arose. During the 2014 Super Bowl festivities, many alleged prostitutes (including some minors) were arrested, but no traffickers were brought in. What was hyped as a high-tech operation against sex slavery and child exploitation was, like its predecessors, only a traditional but expensive vice roundup.

The false link between sex slavery and major sports events has long been reported, but law-enforcement agencies receive too much money and publicity from the pretense to let it go. "I don't know if the increased number [of enslaved prostitutes] is a legend or not," said Anthony Favale, vice unit coordinator of the New York Police Department, before the 2014 Super Bowl, "but I am exploiting the opportunity." Media outlets know of the fallacy but carry the story anyway. In a frank self-assessment, the *Dallas Morning News* expressed the following thoughts after the 2011 Super Bowl in Arlington, Texas:

> The routine is the same in every Super Bowl city. The media beats the drum of impending invasion, warning that anywhere from 15,000 to 100,000 hookers will soon arrive. Politicians lather on their special sauce of manufactured outrage. Cops and prosecutors vow stings and beefed up manpower. . . . Of course, we in the media are equally culpable. We dutifully relay the fraud . . . rarely bothering to check if it's remotely plausible. And by this time, there's no going back. The fraud must be upheld. Charities have raised money to help the innocents. Politicians have brayed and task forces have been appointed. Editors and news directors have ordered five-part series. . . . After all, children in distress sell.

That the media and governments exploit bogus sex and morals panics is not news, but these events fall into a larger and more disturbing pattern of anti-sex-trafficking initiatives worldwide. Aside from being a colossal waste of resources, the sports-event raids highlight the conflation of prostitution with human trafficking that characterizes modern vice enforcement, and the use of the wrong tools to address the problem.

Prostitution is one thing; human trafficking and slavery are something else altogether, and the overlap of the two is not always clear. Has a Bulgarian woman been trafficked when she takes herself to London to escape poverty and then sells herself because it is the only way there to earn money? Does she become enslaved when her debts to a brothel owner require her to continue servicing men? Is her bondage exacerbated by zero-tolerance vice and immigration laws that guarantee her arrest if she reaches out to police? What of Hanna Morris, who ran an escort agency and who, in 2009, called police when two men threw petrol around her flat in Surrey, England, and threatened to set it on fire? After helping police with the investigation, she was convicted under a new brothel-keeping law and fined more than £65,000. (The attackers were not charged.) Cases such as this one lead to what Chrissy Browne, of Central London Action on Street Health, calls the silencing and further endangerment of vulnerable sex workers. The trend of equating all prostitution to sex trafficking and then punishing it as such overlooks complex and important issues regarding globalization, the exploitation of labor, and sexual morals generally, and does little good for those who most need help.

No one questions the law's obligation to free those who are enslaved, whether in sex work or not. But passing overaggressive enforcement laws, staging bogus "rescue" operations, and ignoring the distinctions between voluntary and involuntary sex work have often caused more harm than good. More than other aspects of modern sex law, the modern anti-sex-trafficking movement represents the integration of extreme right-wing social beliefs into criminal law-enforcement policy—something accomplished with the assistance of zealous feminists on the left. For both constituencies, the subtleties are secondary to the core conviction that all sex work is morally wrong and the criminal justice system should stamp it out. By characterizing it all as slavery and dressing up vice raids as rescue operations, old-fashioned morals crusaders have garnered previously unimaginable public support and secured sharp changes in the law.

The first casualty in the war against sex trafficking has been the truth about whom the law should protect and whom it should punish. Too often, no distinction is made between sex workers held against their will and those working independently, or the many shades of sex work in between. This precludes a coherent strategy for helping the truly enslaved, and invites misguided enforcement efforts. Anti-trafficking initiatives worldwide, particularly US-financed efforts in the developing world, often rely heavily on crime-fighting methods such as raids and mass arrests. This approach is dangerously ill-conceived. If the goal is to rescue sex-trafficking victims, then rounding them up, holding them indefinitely, and exposing them to the risk of deportation back to dire situations is a poor way to accomplish it.

Knowing what happens when "rescuers" get involved, would anyone locked into sex work, especially someone with less-than-perfect immigration status, ever risk reaching out to the law for help? Probably not, especially in areas where police corruption is rampant. "[I have] never seen an issue where there is less interest in hearing from those who are most affected by it," said Phil Marshall, a UN official involved in fighting trafficking in Southeast Asia's Mekong Delta region, in 2003. Yet the raids continued. That same year, a US-funded religious NGO, International Justice Mission, acted in "partnership" with Thai police to stage a late-night raid of a brothel in Chiang Mai (with news crews recording everything). Twenty-eight Burmese women were arrested, immediately separated from each other, and then put into isolation. Their belongings and cell phones were confiscated. Some escaped their "rescue" quickly, but others were locked up for weeks and were subjected to relentless interrogations by members of another US-funded anti-trafficking NGO. The women who told interrogators that they wanted to remain in Thailand were held until they agreed to "recant." Eventually, about half the women escaped, after which they were surprised to learn that their ordeal had been trumpeted as something for their own welfare. They thought they were to be either held in prison indefinitely or, if they failed to "cooperate," to be deported back to Burma, the place they had left because it was so dangerous.

Who really benefits from this supposed fight against sex trafficking? Certainly law enforcement, funding for which surged after sex trafficking became an international priority at the turn of the millennium. Certainly, also the myriad private organizations, religious and secular NGOs, consultants, conference organizers, media outlets, rescue operators, academics, and others making careers in the rescue industry—all of whom, to greater or lesser degrees, feed from the public trough. No doubt there are numbers of women, men, and children who have been kept against their will and forced to sell themselves, and for whom rescue efforts were a godsend, but this positive has been, at least thus far, marred by an ill-conceived enforcement regime.

The women in Chiang Mai, for example, claimed that in Burma, before going to the Thai brothel, they were told about the true nature of the work they would be doing in Thailand and the pay arrangements, and that they had been free to leave once they got there. Like millions of migrant workers in dozens of industries, they had crossed a border for the work, but doing so did not automatically mean they had been deprived of their liberty—that is, until the police, NGO workers, and news crews showed up that night.

Underlying the global effort against trafficking are the unshakable beliefs that *all* prostitution is by definition coerced, that genuine consent to an exchange of sex for money is impossible, and that purchasers of sex are all potential slavers and rapists. These simplistic perspectives form the common ground between the evangelical Christians and feminist activists whose joint efforts have helped to shape sex-trafficking policy. They also help to explain why anti-trafficking raiders often don't fuss over the individual circumstances of the women involved. Whether they are New York escorts profiting from Super Bowl fans, Burmese women in a Chiang Mai brothel, or Eastern European migrants in London, they are all "enslaved."

The idea that all prostitution is bondage has also given rise to a new front in the fight against sex trafficking: the aggressive targeting of customers. While going after the "demand side" of the prostitution equation may have some initial appeal—without demand, there would be no supply, as advocates repeatedly state—in practice it has driven the sex industry further underground and made sex workers less safe. Is the London "kerb crawler," or the man responding to a Backpage.com advertisement, or, for that matter, former New York governor Eliot Spitzer (who used an expensive New York escort service) on the same moral plane as a smuggler of human beings? Is a German sex tourist in Cambodia, where prostitution is technically illegal, as guilty as he would be visiting a prostitute at home, where the trade is permitted? When all prostitution is reduced to a simple moral equation, the answer to these questions is yes.

Sex trafficking is like terrorism: everyone agrees that it is a terrible thing and its perpetrators are criminals of the worst kind. However, as we have seen since both issues rose to the top of the international debate, a fearful populace asks too few questions about the methods used to stamp out a menace. As with the "war" on terror, good intentions do not always lead to good results. The temptations to mischaracterize and oversimplify the issues, to abridge the rights of the innocent, and to grab the enforcement money that inevitably pours in from above are too great for the unscrupulous to resist.

• • •

The roots of the modern anti-sex-trafficking movement reach back to the apocryphal "white slavery" panics of the late nineteenth and early twentieth century, when disfavored segments of the population were accused of abducting and transporting innocent white women for sexual exploitation. Underlying this movement was the fervent belief that all prostitution—not just sex trafficking—was a profound moral wrong, and what began as a push to stop the transport of women for "immoral purposes" took shape as a broad social-purity crusade to abolish prostitution altogether. While it succeeded in closing dozens of red-light districts on both sides of the Atlantic and thousands of brothels, as well as the passage of much-abused laws such as the Mann Act, it failed to eradicate, or even significantly stem, commercial sex.

In the late 1990s, a similar effort was mounted, this time in the context of labor trafficking and human exploitation in the global manufacturing, agricultural, and service economies. The worldwide volume of *non*sex trafficking is at least three times that of the sex sector, but sex and prostitution have been the focus of advocates and law enforcement. Workers on farms and in restaurants, hotels, private homes, and factories are trafficked and exploited in immense numbers, but the issues are often numbingly complex and, in the end, too few consumers want to sacrifice to improve workers' lives by paying more for food, domestic service, or beauty treatments.

Between 2000 and 2005, the number of US sex-trafficking prosecutions rose nearly 900 percent, while prosecutions in the nonsex sectors about doubled. Since then, the volume of sex-trafficking cases investigated and filed, as well as the number of convictions obtained, has outpaced the prosecutions in the nonsex sectors, sometimes by large margins. And when nonsex-sector traffickers are brought to trial, they can hope for more lenient treatment. For example, from 2000 to 2008, an Indonesian man living in Virginia kept twenty Indonesian women in his basement and farmed them out as domestic workers to wealthy households. The man had promised the women higher pay and less work, but once he had them in his control he charged them high rent for his basement, plus transportation and other "taxes." Some of the women slept three to a bed. He kept them in check by holding their passports, threatening both to deport them and to kill their families at home. He also sexually assaulted two of the women. For this, a Virginia judge fined him $2,000 and imposed no jail time. Had the Indonesian women been kept for sex work, the case would have carried a simpler narrative—one that the public could embrace without condemning itself—and the case would likely have resulted in a lengthy jail sentence. The "brothel captive" is simply a more compelling object of pity than the imprisoned maid or the exploited migrant farm worker.

Whatever their beliefs about labor trafficking generally, the evangelicals, conservatives, and feminists who have pushed for harsh anti-sex-trafficking laws, whom we can call neo-abolitionists, have more in common than a hatred of prostitution. By invoking the horrors of sex slavery, they found an easily digestible platform to strike out against late-twentieth-century sexual permissiveness. For evangelicals and conservatives, the widespread acceptance of casual sex, omnipresent pornography, sexual content in mass media, and high divorce rates are all a perilous departure from traditional norms. For feminist neo-abolitionists, consumer-driven sexuality drives violence against women. Renowned anti-trafficking activist Donna Hughes, for example, attributed sex trafficking not only to prostitution but also to a sexist society that fuels men's desire for sexual services, including "media depictions of prostitution and other commercial sex acts, such as stripping and lap dancing, that romanticize or glamorize these activities." Others blamed "TV commercials . . . billboards . . . marketing . . . [and the] sexuality that keeps on increasing . . . where there is no more protection over our physical bodies." Add to that the advent of high-volume sex tourism to Latin America, Eastern Europe, and Southeast Asia, and the cheap air travel that facilitates the sale of women from the developing world in Europe and North America, and the time was ripe for an attack on commercial sex generally.

The neo-abolitionist coalition had combined to fight pornography in the 1980s, with mixed results, but this time it made up for past mistakes. Rather than arguing that *images* of sex spurred oppression of women, it now maintained that purchasing sex was *itself* an act of violence. Prostitutes were ipso facto sex slaves. As explained by feminist activist Sheila Jeffreys, prostitution damages all women—if one woman is considered a prostitute, all women can be treated as such as a consequence. The new anti-trafficking coalition, galvanized by this simple message, was impressively broad-based. As one activist gushed to scholar Elisabeth Bernstein:

> A whole consortium from the farthest left to the farthest right was in favor of making all prostitution trafficking . . . a coalition that included Salvation Army and the lesbian-feminist Equality Now, and CATW [Coalition Against Trafficking in Women] up in New York and Michael Horowitz who's very conservative. . . . That's new politics. I had never before seen a group like that.

In addition, established feminist groups such as the National Organization for Women and the Feminist Majority, along with Christian groups such as the International Justice Mission, Focus on the Family, the Family Research Council, and Concerned Women for America all joined the fight.

With the backing of faith-based constituencies, the neo-abolitionist cause drew support from the international community and, significantly, the deeply conservative administration of George W. Bush. In 2000, after protracted negotiations in the United Nations and under pressure from the Bush administration, the UN adopted the Protocol Against Trafficking in Persons, which defines all prostitutes who cross borders as trafficking victims, regardless of whether they travel voluntarily. Congress then picked

up the issue and, in a series of legislative acts, took the neo-abolitionist approach over the goal line. The Trafficking Victims Protection Act (TVPA)
was passed in 2000 and broadened in 2003, 2005, and 2008. It not only
equates trafficking with prostitution, it also set up a well-funded enforcement apparatus to *eradicate* prostitution both domestically and abroad,
punish countries and NGOs that do not toe the neo-abolitionist line, and
lavish money on faith-based rescue operations.

The breadth of the TVPA is matched only by the hyperbole used to
secure its passage. The bill was introduced by the socially conservative
congressman Christopher Smith (R-NJ), who announced that "50,000
innocent women and young children are forced, coerced, or fraudulently
thrust into the international sex trade industry with no way out" each
year. This assertion was echoed by the National Organization for Women,
which noted that "sex trafficking, referred to by many of us as *the* modern
form of slavery, is thought to victimize 50,000 women and girls every
year in the US." This is an alarming number, and a false one. In truth,
that figure was an estimate of *all* female trafficked labor into the US,
including maids, sweatshop workers, and agricultural laborers. The estimated number of sex workers was later downgraded to eighteen thousand
to twenty thousand, but by then the shock had had its effect, and the law
had passed. Abused migrants and workers in the nonsex sectors have no
friends in Congress, except when their numbers can be used to inflate
estimates of sex slaves.

Even when focusing exclusively on sex work, it is impossible to come
up with reliable trafficking figures because there is no consensus on how to
classify prostitutes as slaves. *New York Times* columnist and anti-sex-trafficking activist Nicholas Kristof observed: "Some commentators look at
prostitutes and see only sex slaves; others see only entrepreneurs. But in
reality there are some in each category and many other women who inhabit a gray zone between freedom and slavery." People use the numbers
that suit the ends they wish to achieve, and, according to law professor
Janie Chuang, "Unsubstantiated figures often [are] recycled and accepted
as true, as if sheer repetition guarantees veracity."

In a 2003 speech at the UN, President Bush said that each year "hundreds of thousands" of girls "fall victim to the sex trade," adding that
"governments that tolerate this trade are tolerating a form of slavery."
Was Bush referring to abducted Burmese girls, women in Amsterdam's
brothel windows, or the millions worldwide (including in the US) for
whom prostitution was the only economic option? He didn't say, but his

administration's all-of-the-above position had already been made clear. In 2002, Bush issued a national security directive stating explicitly that US policy "is based on an abolitionist approach . . . [which] opposes prostitution and any related activities . . . as contributing to the phenomenon of trafficking in persons." The neo-abolitionist community hailed this document as "crucial in fighting trafficking," especially in its refusal to "legitimize prostitution as a form of work for women." In 2004, the Bush administration issued a "fact sheet" that stated: "Where prostitution has been legalized or tolerated, there is an increase in the demand for sex slaves." The Bush and Obama administrations enforced the TVPA aggressively. In 2005, after the act created a new crime, domestic sex trafficking— until then, the term had meant transporting people across international borders—the government started handing out large sums of money to local police departments to crack down on street prostitution. Rarely had local vice been the target of big-ticket federal law-enforcement efforts, but the new policy drew little opposition because the target was recast as sex trafficking and the victims as sex slaves. With the stroke of a pen and the cutting of a check, run-of-the-mill vice patrols—usually low on law enforcement's status heap—were elevated into operations against "organized, sophisticated, criminal syndicates."

Under the rules, pimps can be charged with sex trafficking and given ninety-nine-year prison sentences, as opposed to the typical sentences of several months. For some bad actors—such as pimps who use runaway girls, control their every move, and force them to service men across the country—harsh sentences are appropriate. The prostitutes themselves, however, are a much more delicate matter, and when they are apprehended in anti-trafficking operations, they can find themselves subject to beatings, arrests, and deportations. In one 2009 New York case, "Jin" had been sentenced to six months in jail before her status as a trafficked person was even identified. Here is how she described her contact with her rescuers:

> There were so many policemen; the whole house was filled with maybe 15 officers. . . . I didn't know anything. I saw the auntie run so I ran too and as I was running a police officer struck me in the back of the head with the back of a gun and I fell to the floor and I passed out. . . . I had no idea they were police when they all broke in. . . . I woke up because someone was picking me up. It was a female officer and she opened up my skirt and revealed my undergarments in front of everyone to see if I was hiding anything on me. I was scared, I didn't even know what

they wanted to do. At that point I would do whatever they said I was so frightened.

Events such as this exemplify what Elizabeth Bernstein calls an "unprecedented police crackdown on people of color who are involved in the street-based sexual economy." The situation reached such a critical point that, in 2014, the UN Human Rights Committee urged American police to stop prosecuting trafficking victims for crimes they were forced to commit. The UNHRC was concerned that cops show little interest in identifying and helping trafficking victims, and it urged the US to "take all appropriate measures to prevent the criminalization of victims of sex trafficking, including child victims, to the extent that they have been compelled to engage in unlawful activities."

As with the global war on terrorism, international efforts against sex trafficking are largely directed by the US, which uses its superpower and superdonor status to muscle other countries into allowing American citizens to raid brothels, and into adopting measures that conform to US priorities. In this way, the TVPA has also become a tool of American foreign policy. The act forms the basis for funding foreign rescue missions, punishing other countries for not meeting US trafficking standards, and, until recently, under a companion law, withholding funds to combat HIV/AIDS unless the recipient organizations condemn all prostitution.

The foreign rescue missions have been a bonanza for American NGOs and have provided the news media with ample material to scare and titillate audiences. The International Justice Mission (IJM) is one of the most prominent faith-based rescue players, receiving more than $6 million in US government funds by the end of 2012. (That year, its president, Gary Haugen, was paid about $250,000 in base compensation.) IJM specializes in conducting media-friendly raids. In "partnership" with often-corrupt local law-enforcement officials, IJM personnel go undercover as potential prostitution clients to "investigate" brothels and then—often with police guns drawn and sirens blaring—burst in and deliver the inmates to "safety." This law-and-order approach makes for exciting television but does little to alleviate anyone's suffering.

As in the Chiang Mai raid described above, many IJM and other rescues have failed badly. Surprisingly high numbers of involuntarily "rescued" women escape their rescuers and return to the brothels because American-style deliverance is seen as worse than prostitution. Remaining in the brothels may be preferable to deportation (for some, the choice amounts to being "raped for free" in their home country or actually being paid for commercial sex work) or confinement in dangerous shelters for months or even years. In a series of raids in the notorious Cambodian village of Svay Pak outside Phnom Penh, dramatically covered by *Dateline NBC* in its popular episode "Children for Sale," thirty-seven women and girls were snared; within a short time, many of them had returned to the brothel. Some of those caught in the rescue operation, such as a noodle seller suffering from high blood pressure, were not even sex workers. IJM staff members were told of her condition, but she was not released or provided with medical care, and she died in custody. (Her body was returned to her family with teeth missing; prison guards had pulled out the ones containing gold fillings.)

After the raid, the number of child prostitutes in Svay Pak went up: the families of the rescued girls sent their siblings back to pay the girls' debts to the brothel owners. The siblings were joined later by the rescued girls themselves, who had escaped their shelters. The IJM and police kept up their efforts for months afterward, but that seems to have only dispersed the problem. The women and girls of Svay Pak who hadn't returned to Vietnam (where most of them had come from originally) had been relocated to Phnom Penh and Siem Reap, where they presumably returned to sex work. When Nicholas Kristof came to Svay Pak some years later, he found prostitution reduced in scale but still available. Rather than having virgins at the ready, a brothel keeper told Kristof, one could be available in a day or two.

Do women who flee their rescues suffer from "false consciousness," a condition by which they cannot recognize their own enslavement? Kristof himself answered the question in his book *Half the Sky*: "Many prostitutes are neither acting freely nor enslaved, but living in a world etched in ambiguities somewhere between these two extremes." So long as the brute law-enforcement practices encouraged and funded by the US ignore these questions, and the fact that sex work, even when done by teenagers, is often the sole means of support for sex workers and their families, little will be accomplished in providing effective help to prostitutes to escape poverty or avoid violence.

The link between showbiz and the sex-trafficking rescue industry reached both its apogee and its nadir with Somaly Mam, a telegenic and charismatic Cambodian activist who attracted the vocal support of, among other luminaries, Oprah Winfrey, Hillary Clinton, Nicholas Kristof, Queen Sofia of Spain, Susan Sarandon, and Facebook COO Sheryl Sandberg. Both Sarandon and Sandberg were on Mam's foundation's advisory board.) When Mam was named a *Time* magazine "hero" and one of the world's 100 most influential people in 2009, Angelina Jolie wrote her profile. She also received numerous awards from the US government, foundations, and news organizations worldwide. Why the star power? Her story was powerful. According to an account she gave at the White House, she was sold into sex slavery in Cambodia at age nine or ten and spent a decade as a captive in a Phnom Penh brothel, after which she escaped to France in 1993. In 1996 she returned to Cambodia, where she started an anti-trafficking NGO, gaining worldwide attention with her own heroic story and presenting the heartbreaking stories of other young women.

One of Mam's early advisors, Pierre Fallavier, recalled that donors started to send "their people," as well as news crews, to meet her and the women she served: "I used to tell Somaly to send them away, that all they wanted were exotic stories of violence and sex with pictures of a beautiful hero saving children so they could sell their papers. But they came with the funders." By 2012, Somaly Mam's foundation had taken in nearly $13 million in grants and contributions and was operating in several Southeast Asian countries. However, in 2014, the foundation closed its doors after it was revealed that Mam and others connected to it had fabricated key facts about their experiences as victims of the sex trade. The lesson here is not that sex trafficking in Southeast Asia does not occur—it surely does, and Mam's foundation assisted people who badly needed it. Rather, the foundation's demise is a cautionary tale of the hazards that befall Western governments and organizations when they incentivize private groups to distort the truth about prostitution. "She used the system, and she was used by the system," said Mam's ex-husband. "I've worked with a lot of organizations, and you confronted the same issue when you wanted money. If you have no story, you don't have money."

.   .   .

Besides funding rescue efforts, the US uses an annual ranking system to pressure countries to counter prostitution. Tier 3 countries are deemed to have the worst trafficking records; Tier 2 indicates borderline cases; and Tier 1 countries are ranked highest. The cost of a Tier 3 ranking is the possible loss of US aid and American opposition to loans through the International Monetary Fund and the World Bank. While a 2004 State Department fact sheet amplified the government's "strong position against legalized prostitution" and noted that "where prostitution has been legalized or tolerated, there is an increase in the demand for sex slaves . . . many likely victims of human trafficking," the rankings do not always bear that out. For example, Germany, New Zealand, the Netherlands, and Australia are consistently ranked as Tier 1, notwithstanding that prostitution is legal and widespread in those countries. A Tier 3 status, on the other hand, often seems to be a punishment for hostility to the US. Perennials on that list are North Korea, Cuba, Iran, and Russia. Venezuela was also given a Tier 3 ranking in 2004 after its stridently anti-American leader, Hugo Chávez, survived a referendum. Citing Venezuela's record on trafficking, the US then pulled support for loans Venezuela had requested from international banks.

The efforts of Thailand, a center of sex tourism, to placate the US have caused human-rights problems of their own. According to a coalition of sex-worker-rights groups there called EMPOWER, Thai women have been brutalized by police, detained at borders, held for extensive periods, and deported, all "in an attempt to please the US government and satisfy the American anti trafficking agenda." Added EMPOWER's director, Chantawipa Apisuk: "We have now reached a point in history where there are more women in the Thai sex industry being abused by anti-trafficking practices than there are women exploited by traffickers." The Thai government's efforts have nevertheless not satisfied the US government, which in 2014 dropped Thailand to Tier 3. Whether that will change in the years to come is anyone's guess, but the question will likely be resolved on political or economic grounds rather than on the well-being of Thai and migrant sex workers.

The last and perhaps most ludicrous element of the neo-abolitionists' attempts to stamp out prostitution is the targeting of customers. According to the Coalition Against Trafficking in Women (CATW), "The male demand . . . is the most immediate cause of the expansion of the sex industry. . . . It is indisputable that a prostitution market without male consumers would go broke." Based on this logic, and an exaggerated faith in police and jails to solve social problems, CATW and other neo-abolitionist groups have successfully advocated for sharply increased penalties against johns. "End Demand" policies have been adopted in various forms in Sweden, Iceland, Norway, the United Kingdom, and hundreds of American states and cities, among other places. Aside from increased jail time and fines, the policies include publishing the names of johns on billboards, on the Internet and television, and in newspapers and letters to families, employers, and friends. Additionally, johns' cars and other property have been seized; they have been forced to enroll in "john schools" (paid courses about the moral, legal, and health dangers of prostitution); and they have been caught on surveillance cameras that broadcast prostitution transactions on YouTube in real time.

In the US, these efforts have had the full support of the federal government, which, in 2005, authorized a $50 million grant to local law-enforcement and social-service agencies "to develop and execute programs targeted at reducing male demand and to investigate and prosecute buyers of commercial sex acts." A subsequent State Department fact sheet added this endorsement of End Demand ideals:

> If there were no demand for commercial sex, trafficking in persons for commercial sexual exploitation would not exist in the form it does today. This reality underscores the need for continued strong efforts to reduce demand for sex trafficking by enacting policies and promoting cultural attitudes that reject the idea of paying for sex.

The facile logic and questionable efficacy of End Demand policies are enough to fill a lurid chapter of their own, but for our purposes here we can make a few observations:

Advocates of End Demand policies contend that all men who buy sex are of a type: they have violent tendencies, are unconcerned about the circumstances of prostitutes' lives, are avid consumers of pornography and inclined toward rape, and derive their pleasure, at least in part, from dominating women. However, for every study backing these conclusions, there are others refuting them. The truth is that men of all ages, economic positions, and races buy sex. Any effort to shove them into one psychopathological profile is futile, as are predictions of their response to End Demand laws. Moreover, the idea that johns "drive" sexual exploitation cannot hold up even to cursory analysis. For that to be accepted as true, we would also need to accept that purchasers of blue jeans, precious metals, Apple products, or industrially grown vegetables are also culpable for "driving" the forced-labor chains that bring these products to market.

For neo-abolitionists, the most alarming aspect of prostitution should be, as concluded by Bridget Anderson and Julia O'Connell Davidson, that "the vast majority of those who buy sex . . . are ordinary people." Assuming this is the case, and given the reality that many prostitutes are not trafficked in any rational sense of the word, it is simply wrong to upend the lives of so many people in a foolhardy effort to eradicate an entire industry.

If the law's goal is the safety of prostitutes, then End Demand policies have fallen short. We can see this by looking at places where the selling of sex is technically legal but the buying of it is not. The first country to implement such a law was Sweden, which in 1999 passed the Sex Purchase Act, making it a crime to buy sex but decriminalizing its sale. The Swedish model's focus on punishing johns, assisting prostitutes as victims, and framing prostitution as a form of male violence has made it the darling of the world's neo-abolitionist community and a model for other legislative initiatives. Despite its stated objective of protecting and destigmatizing sex workers, however, the results have been mixed at best.

In a thorough study of the impact of the Swedish law, presented in The Hague at the 2011 workshop Decriminalizing Prostitution and Beyond: Practical Experiences and Challenges, feminist historian Susanne Dodillet and social commentator Petra Östergren concluded that the law "*cannot* be said to have decreased prostitution, trafficking for sexual purposes, or had a deterrent effect on clients to the extent claimed" by the law's supporters. They also concluded that the law caused "serious adverse effects . . . [on] the health and well-being of sex workers." Street prostitution in Sweden dipped soon after the law was passed, but then it returned, while the volume of "indoor" sex work (by which appointments are made by telephone or on the Internet) seems to have increased. Moreover, while prosecutions for buying sex have increased since 1999, actual demand has not changed. Most importantly, with increased risk to customers, "sex workers experience higher levels of vulnerability in their contact with clients. . . . Sex workers might not be able to demand safer sex practices [and] they take greater risks and accept lower prices." Additionally, "[sexual] services have to be carried out in even more hidden, and therefore unprotected areas." As one informant stated: "[Swedish prostitutes] are exposed to violence and sexually transmitted diseases. If the client demands unprotected sex, many of the prostitutes cannot afford to say no. Harassment by the police has increased . . . and [prostitutes] use pimps for protection."

Finally, the Swedish law's motives were not completely benevolent. It appears that Swedish authorities were also alarmed about immigrants coming west from the collapsed Soviet Bloc. The new law was a rather crafty way to make Sweden a less attractive destination for foreign immigrants.

Bernstein also notes that the reduction of street-based sex commerce in high-priced tourist cities such as Stockholm and Göteborg has "conveniently served to displace streetwalkers from the very downtown areas that government and real estate officials are interested in developing."

End Demand policies such as exposing accused johns on billboards, via the media, or through letters to family, friends, and employers seem to be motivated more by malice than anything else, especially given that the exposed men have usually been only arrested and not convicted. The practice is also subject to abuse. In Kennebunk, Maine, where a Zumba instructor-cum-prostitute serviced at least 150 men, including, presumably, some prominent figures, a judge's decision to release part of the woman's client list resulted in considerable confusion. The judge ordered that the names be released without identifying information such as addresses. One man, who shared a name with one of the suspects, was then wrongly connected with the affair. "I'm almost to tears and I'm 65 years old," he said. "This is how bad it hurts me." Some cities that are strongly committed to combating demand, such as San Francisco, do not publish the names of johns because of the impact it may have on spouses and other friends and family members.

•   •   •

In 2013, the Canadian Supreme Court unanimously struck down that country's anti-prostitution laws, ruling that they were overbroad and endangered the "health, safety, and lives of prostitutes." In response to the decision, Canada's legislature drafted new laws on the Swedish End Demand model, targeting mainly pimps and johns and ushering in all of the problems that come with criminalizing half of the players in paid sexual encounters. Meanwhile, in New York City, where more than one hundred thousand people suffer from HIV/AIDS, the safety of street-level prostitutes has been under attack. Police regularly confiscate condoms from them and, when arrests are made, use the confiscated condoms in court against them. Thus the very people most at risk for STIs are being forced into making a terrible choice: protect their health with condoms or avoid trouble with the law. Hopefully, the judges in the city's new "prostitution courts" will put a halt to this practice.

In Zurich, where prostitution is legal, authorities took a brilliant step in 2013 by outlawing streetwalking and installing drive-in "sex boxes" where prostitutes and johns can park and do their business, and where counseling, sanitation facilities, and police are close at hand. Should the john become troublesome, the prostitute can press an accessible alarm button and use an emergency exit. The goal is safety—not criminality or shame—for the sex worker: "Most women won't be doing this forever, and we do want them to be healthy [for the future]," said Ursula Kocher, a Swiss social worker.

This frank approach—also followed in the Netherlands and Germany—is perhaps too much to hope for in any but a few limited locales. Instead, the Swedish model seems to be taking hold. In 2013, the French National Assembly passed such a law—pushed by a coalition of feminists and "survivors"—on the ground that prostitution is always exploitative of women. Whatever one believes in this regard, criminalizing everything but the sale of sex does not protect sex workers; nor can it end the demand for prostitutes. Whenever sex between strangers is sold, danger to the seller will arise. The reduction of this danger should be the law's only goal.

CHAPTER 7

MONGRELS AND MYTHS

Sex across the Color Lines

Marie Antoinette Monks's fingernails and heels gave her away, as did the "negroid contour" of her calves, the "pallor" at the back of her neck, and a telltale wave in her hair. These characteristics (among others) convinced courtroom "experts" that Marie Antoinette, the light-skinned second wife of the deceased, white Allan Monks, was not the white French countess she claimed to be. Rather, her body—and her conduct in court—indicated that she was one-eighth "Negro." Because even partial black ancestry made one nonwhite, and interracial marriages were strictly forbidden, Marie Antoinette's nine-year marriage to Allan was declared a legal nullity. Furthermore, by telling Allan that she was of "pure" French (that is, white) descent, she had tricked him into marrying her—it was inconceivable, after all, that a white man would knowingly marry the "descendant of a Negro." The judge ruled that Allan's will, which left Marie Antoinette his property, was also void, and that his former wife—the white Ida Lee—should receive his property instead.

Like her namesake one and a half centuries earlier, Marie Antoinette was branded as a sexual predator, a vampire who used her wiles to lure a hapless white man into her bed. "[Monks] was dominated by the will of [Marie Antoinette]," another court later found. Only by exposing her "hybrid" racial ancestry, and nullifying both the marriage and her inheritance, could matters be set right. In the mid-twentieth-century US, the "vamp" role was routinely ascribed to women of color, particularly African Americans, who were thought to be hypersexual and to seduce unsuspecting white men of means. Add to that the prevailing belief that *any* mixture between whites and other races degraded the white race and the fate of Marie Antoinette starts to look inevitable. The fact that Ida Lee used these racial theories to grab her ex-husband's property was immaterial. A white man's love for a woman even one-eighth black could not receive the law's blessing.

Marie Antoinette's downfall took place in 1939, in a San Diego courtroom. Technically, the case concerned the law of Arizona, where she and Allan had married, but it could have played out in any of the thirty states that outlawed interracial marriage—miscegenation—at the time. These laws were part of a larger matrix of rules governing sexual relationships not only between blacks and whites, but also among a dizzying array of other real or imagined racial groups. Many states barred people of different races from marrying or living together while engaging in "lewd and lascivious fornication," while others criminalized interracial sex altogether. In Arizona, people of mixed ancestry were even barred from marrying each other.

The rules reached back to the southern slave-based economy. When black women were property to be taken at will—and taken they were, by the millions—their children inherited their slave status. Rape was not only the birthright of propertied white men, it also spawned valuable human capital. However, matters became more complicated in the early twentieth century, a few decades after slaves were formally emancipated and much of the black population was moving north. Preventing them from becoming equals required a new set of slanders and pretexts, particularly sexual ones. Black women were recast as temptresses, while black men were seen as rapacious sexual monsters aching to ruin white womanhood. As the century progressed and immigrants arrived from around the world, these same theories were applied to Asians, Africans, mestizos, and others, all of whom were barred in one degree or another from sexual relationships with whites.

That Marie Antoinette Monks's fate could hinge on "expert" opinions on the "Negro characteristics" of her neck, fingernails, and legs was par for the course. A host of theories, under the broad heading of eugenics, held that race was a biological rather than social construction and demanded the ban of sex between races. Interracial sex was not only deviant, the theory went, it put the entire white population at risk. Even "one drop" of "inferior" blood in the collective white "germ-plasm" threatened the degradation and extinction of the race, and with it Western civilization.

In this way, the lowliest white dirt farmer assumed a social status superior to the black sharecropper laboring in the next field or the black school-teacher down the road. Traditional race hatreds took on a respectable scientific veneer. When Calvin Coolidge wrote that "biological laws tell us that certain divergent people will not mix or blend," he was more politic than Harry Truman, who asked, "Would you want your daughter to marry a Negro?" but no less racist than Dwight D. Eisenhower, who sympathized with white parents' fears about their "sweet little" girls going to school with "big overgrown Negroes." These US presidents all made the same point: sex between whites and people from other races was wrong and should not be allowed.

Foucault's critical observation about sexuality being a "dense transfer point for relations of power" applies well to interracial sex—especially in the US, where sex and marriage laws were used to implement crushing racial repressions. South Africa, of course, also used laws against interracial sex and marriage, passed in 1949–1950 and repealed in 1985, as key elements of Apartheid. In Europe, where eugenics theories were first developed (and where they reached their apotheosis in Germany during the Third Reich), the rules concerning interracial sex developed along a different trajectory. Laws calling for the sterilization of "imbeciles" and social outcasts were widely adopted, but clear legal rules forbidding sex and marriage between races were confined to fascist regimes. However, that does not imply widespread comfort with the subject, as periodic flare-ups in France, Italy, the UK, and Germany into the present day demonstrate.

Colonial Discomforts and Nazi Purges

More than a little sex took place between the rulers and the ruled in France's African and Asian colonies. Generally, as long as it was confined to violations of native women on foreign soil and did not upset the social order, the state paid no attention. Sex with natives was a perquisite of colonial service. However, that changed with the start of the First World War in 1914, when French authorities realized that the country's stock of young men was insufficient to sustain a total war against Germany. France brought in approximately five hundred thousand *troupes indigènes* as well as hundreds of thousands more workers—from colonies in Africa and Indochina—to labor, fight, and die on its behalf. To the intense dismay of the French, the foreign troops also trained their libidinous eyes on French females. To the troops' delight, many of the women retuned their looks with keen interest. The readiness of French women to have sex with the *troupes indigènes* undermined the strict racist hierarchy that reinforced French power over its colonies. French officials tried to prevent such wartime unions. At a minimum, they hoped to stop the word from spreading in the colonies that French women—so unattainable in, say, Saigon—were available, ready, and willing in Paris. Both efforts were spectacular failures.

As colonial troops and workers ranged over the countryside and crowded city streets, they found sexual companionship not only in brothels but also in the beds of respectable bourgeois women, as well as nurses and peasants. For many, sex with French women was a kind of payback for lifetimes of humiliation by colonial authorities. As one Madagascan wrote in a letter, white women in the colonies "regard us rather like lepers," while one of his countrymen wrote that in Madagascar "we fear them, [but] here they come to us and solicit us." An Indochinese solider, after noting how difficult it was to approach French women back home, observed that all it took now was two francs "to have fun with them."

Colonial soldiers not only bragged about their sexual conquests, they sent pictures home as proof. By 1918, authorities had intercepted almost one hundred thousand photos and postcards featuring, among other images, nude French women, mixed-race children, and Franco–Indochinese couples. Would the *troupes indigènes* still bow to the stiff rod of French power when they returned home after the war? How could the colonial color line be maintained when their subjects now saw French women as easy sexual marks? French authorities worried about the long-term effects of the "loathsome copulations" taking place on French soil, especially the resultant mixed-race babies, who were thought to degrade French bloodlines.

The activities of French nurses were of particular concern, as many provided extended care to wounded foreign troops—which sometimes included enthusiastic sexual attentions. Yet, try as the authorities might, this "hysterical folly" was impossible to stop even when male nurses were assigned to hospitals treating foreign fighters. Other efforts to halt interracial relationships were no less futile, as when authorities jailed an Indochinese man for fifteen days for "daring to fall in love with a French girl." Two weeks in jail mostly likely increased the man's resolve.

With more than half a million colonial subjects in France, any efforts to build a sex firewall around them were not going to work. To the authorities' credit, they did not expend too much effort trying to do so. They had much bigger fish to fry in a massive, unending military conflict. However, the discomfort remained even after the war ended. In 1921, three years after the fighting stopped, a French official in Tunisia noted that "the impropriety of too many [French] women have succeeded in destroying the respect [Tunisian soldiers] had for us." We can't pinpoint how much this demystification of French womanhood really weakened French colonial rule, but we do know that, for many of the sexually sated *troupes indigènes*, white superiority no longer existed.

* * *

The 1935 Italian invasion of Ethiopia was propagandized as the epitome of the fascist ideal of pitiless, dominant masculinity. It was also a sexual-exploitation fantasy fulfilled. Ethiopian women, long depicted as bare-breasted, licentious beauties waiting for white men to come and take them, were a key enticement for conquest. Reports were promising. One young man was said to have "bought" a twelve-year-old Muslim girl from her father for a good price. The Italian later sold her to an officer to add to his harem. Cohabitation arrangements between whites and indigenous women were also common, adding to sexual opportunities unimaginable on Italian soil. The children of these unions were given the possibility of obtaining Italian nationality.

Italy's leader, Benito Mussolini, was against the idea of Italians getting too close with natives. After the victory in Ethiopia, he ordered that no Italian civilian or military official was to remain there for more than six months without a wife. From that point on, the *meticciato*, or mixed-race child, was held as a freak of nature and a degradation of the virile fascist identity. Soon, laws were passed barring interracial marriages at home and in the colonies, including marriages with Jews. By 1940, Italian fathers were forbidden from recognizing their *metticci*.

However, men will be men, and sex with indigenous African women was tolerated as long as there was no affection involved. If, however, the relations assumed a "conjugal nature," then love-struck Italians faced up to five years in prison. Evidence of an Italian's sexual loyalty to a native woman was taken as proof of his "guilt," as were gifts, visits to the woman when she was sick, and expressions of jealousy over her involvements with others. In a few short years, the Ethiopian "Black Venus" was transformed from an object of exotic desire into poisonous bait. In a colonial court case in which an Italian man was charged with excessive affection for an African woman, the judges declared that he would have been innocent if he had "used the woman only as a prostitute . . . and then dismiss[ed] her after satisfying his sexual needs." In another case, in 1939, an Italian man confessed his deep love for an indigenous woman and his desire to marry and start a family with her. The judges were horrified. In their view, "The soul of the Italian man is itself disturbed; he is entirely devoted to the young Black woman." The judges gave him one and a half years in prison to realign his priorities.

* * *

In German East Africa, there were important limitations to the colonists' de facto sexual license. Most critical was the fact that Germans, like all colonists, were vastly outnumbered by their native subjects, which caused them no end of anxiety. The Germans had firepower available for use against the Africans, but it was more practical to keep them in line with the implicit threat of violence and with strict behavioral rules to mark each group's relative status. The German colonists were intent on maintaining a high level of African subservience, lest their authority lose its omnipotent mystique. Domestic servants, for example, were forbidden from looking their masters in the eye, as that would have "revealed the Europeans as fallible men and women rather than as untouchable authoritative figures." German men, however, often fixed their gaze on their servants and used them sexually whenever they wished. According to historian Heike I. Schmidt, "To some male colonizers, it made little difference which body they appropriated—woman, man, child—so long as it was at their convenience." At the same time, members of the tiny, backbiting German community (mostly centered in Dar es Salaam) watched each other closely and, when it suited their purposes, cast aspersions on each other for sexual misconduct.

This dynamic played out in a series of lawsuits between the governor of German East Africa, Albrecht von Rechenberg, and a local newspaper editor, Willy von Roy, on the eve of the First World War. After Roy published an article insinuating that Rechenberg and his ruling circle were homosexuals—a high crime under German law—Rechenberg sued him for libel in a colonial court. Rechenberg won the case, but Roy kept digging for evidence. Using native spies and paid informants, he learned that Rechenberg was indeed forcing one of his male servants to submit to regular anal sex. Again, Rechenberg sued Roy, this time not only for defamation but also for "enticing" natives to make scandalous accusations against

Germans. These charges really attracted the court's attention because they involved bringing natives into the filthy little disputes of Europeans. The judges were furious at Roy's use of natives to "undermine the standing of the white population" and railed against "any communication to blacks about actual lapses on the part of whites." Rechenberg's forcing himself on a servant violated German law, but that paled next to Roy's exposure of German foibles to Africans. To contain the damage, the judge kept the entire proceedings secret. Roy was expelled.

* * *

By the mid-1930s, when the Nazis took power in Germany, the subject of interracial sex had assumed a much more destructive aspect. No longer was the law merely concerned about the impression such encounters made on colonial populations. Rather, the focus turned to the "defilement" of the German race through sex with "inferior" groups. In this context, the Third Reich was playing catch-up with the US, which already had an extensive system in place punishing interracial sexual relations. In 1933, Germany's Law for the Protection of German Blood and Honor, commonly called the Nuremberg Laws, drew on the American example and added its own anti-Semitic gloss by (among other things) punishing sex between Germans and Jews with lengthy prison sentences. The Nuremberg Laws spawned a wave of "race-defilement" trials, many more investigations and denunciations, and the definitive union of sex law, eugenics, and state-sponsored voyeurism.

The first result of the Nuremberg Laws was the overnight illegality of long-standing sexual relationships throughout the Reich. As arrests began taking place almost immediately, some couples protected themselves by breaking up; others continued their relationships in secret. Convictions depended on whether forbidden sexual encounters took place after the laws' passage, so quite a few couples claimed that they hadn't touched each other since then. These claims were rarely believed. For Jews convicted under the laws, the consequences were usually fatal. Jail conditions were extremely harsh, and sentences often ended with relocation to a concentration camp. In the Sachsenhausen camp, Jewish "race defilers" were suffocated in broom closets and hosed with freezing water. Even if they somehow survived prison and were released, their incarceration often precluded any chance they may have had to emigrate, which in turn left them open to other anti-Semitic measures.

Most of the race-defilement cases arose from denunciations by hateful neighbors and family members. One man denounced his brother-in-law to the Gestapo in 1937, after hiring a detective to spy on him. In another case, a neighbor told investigators that she was certain that a forbidden sexual relationship had taken place, as she heard the "rhythmic squeaks" of bedsprings coming from the apartment next door "until the door was opened fifteen minutes later." Another denouncer sent an anonymous post-card to the Gestapo complaining of the German "bitches" and "whores" who had sex with Jews including that "little so-and-so, Miss Lange." Notably, the Nuremberg Laws made only men liable for race defilement, so Miss Lange would probably have escaped imprisonment, if not a solid public shaming. The same would not be true for her paramours.

While there were many race defilement cases, obtaining convictions was not always easy. As in the US, it was often difficult to determine whether one belonged to an "inferior" race. As only "full" Jews (those who had at least three grandparents who "adhered" to Judaism) fell under the law's prohibitions, the inquiry often turned to the religious observance of long-deceased ancestors. How anyone's adherence to religious rituals could affect his or her physical racial composition, or that of the person's descendants, was not explained, but that logical gap did not stop the inquiries; nor did it keep adjudications of Jewishness from turning on flimsy testimony from neighbors and acquaintances.

Despite the difficulties of determining who was a Jew, there was no doubt about Jewish sexual morality. Jewish women were branded as promiscuous vipers who often concealed their identity from the Aryan men they seduced. The court described one woman in terms that could have been applied to Marie Antoinette Monks. She was a "sexually predatory, morally depraved" Jewess who held two Aryan men "in her thrall." Another Jewish woman was said to show "exceptional tenacity" in the seduction of Aryan men. For their part, Jewish men were seen as hideous sexual monsters, intent on injecting disease and depravity into the pure Aryan bloodline.

Investigators and courts were intensely interested in the mechanics of forbidden sex. Interrogations of accused sexual miscreants were unending, covering their precise sexual activities, whether any "perversions" or "gratification" occurred, and so on. Even sex that did not occur was examined minutely. On one occasion, an Aryan woman who had confessed to fully clothed embraces with a Jewish man endured relentless questioning on whether their sexual organs had "touched" through their garments, and whether the man might have climaxed as a result. Another case file recorded that an accused Jew had "tried two or three times to engage in oral sex with her. . . . Whether on this occasion Miss Geyer took the defendant's member in her hand and stroked it could not be determined."

The searching interrogations required by German law sometimes backfired by eliciting too much information. In 1938, the Jewish Leo Wallach was caught making visits to a "massage institute," where he paid a woman to parade in front of him nude and dressed in lingerie. The case—and, in effect, Wallach's life—hinged on whether or not this constituted sex. Wallach's lawyer argued that no sex had taken place, as the two had had no "contact," and that his client had refrained from masturbating in the company of the woman. True, his hand had been in his right pocket during the first visit, but the lawyer argued that Wallach "carries himself to the left," so there was no likelihood of stealth self-abuse. The "masseuse" testified that she had not seen signs of Wallach being aroused, and the court allowed that "she must be considered something of an expert in such matters." Over the strident objections of the prosecutor, Wallach was acquitted on account of insufficient evidence.

The "Negro Question" in the United States

In April 1901, Colonel Hilary A. Herbert, former secretary of the United States Navy, addressed a conference of luminaries at the American Academy of Political and Social Science in Philadelphia who had gathered to examine "America's race problems." The symposium covered Cuba and the Philippines, which had recently been acquired, but the "Negro Question" was uppermost on the conferees' minds. Herbert opened the proceedings with a rant against the granting of voting rights to African Americans three decades earlier. He said that suffrage had "wronged the Negro" because it "tempted" him away from the "field of labor into the field of politics, where . . . he could understand nothing that was taught him except the color line." Even worse, voting rights for blacks created a "bitterness" between the races "that had never existed between the ex-slave and his former master."

Expanding on the Negro Question was George T. Winston, a North Carolina academic a former president of the University of Texas. Winston recalled his contented childhood in the warm company of his father's slaves, listening to their stories and witnessing their steady transformation from "savage to a civilized man." Even the babies who emerged from "social intercourse" between masters and slave women were a net positive in Winston's estimation, as such children were "quicker, brighter, and more easily refined than the Negro."

However, Winston's idyll had been lost. No longer could the "Southern [white] woman with her helpless children" sleep securely while black men guarded her doors, men so loyal they would "freely" give their lives in her defense. Now, "when a knock is heard at the door, she shudders with nameless horror. The black brute is lurking in the dark, a monstrous beast, crazed with lust. His ferocity is almost demoniacal. A whole community is now frenzied with horror." Every day, black men committed "crimes that are too hideous to describe" against the "helpless women and children of the white race," Winston reported—"crimes that were unknown in slavery." The "new generations of Negroes," born in the thirty-five years since the end of the Civil War, were a wild race of degenerate sex criminals, making the "condition of things too horrible to last."

This is crazy stuff, but not atypical of its time. Well into the twentieth century, grotesque sexual slanders against African Americans were front and center whenever the Negro Question was discussed, and sexual restrictions were a key part of the legal toolkit used to control African Americans and deny them basic human rights. Both northern and southern whites believed that the emancipation of slaves had unleashed a latent sexual criminality in black males that posed a clear and present danger to white women.

In the South and border states, the most shameful response to this fear came at the hand of "Judge Lynch." Between 1889 and 1940, at least thirty-eight hundred African Americans were tortured, mutilated, and murdered in carefully staged public spectacles. Many of them were men accused of sexual transgressions against white women. While none of the lynchings were strictly legal, they often had support at both the top and bottom of white society. South Carolina senator Ben Tillman claimed that "civilized men" were well justified in their desire to "kill kill kill" the "creature in human form who has deflowered a white woman." Another senator from that state, Cole Blease, put it even more directly: "Whenever the Constitution comes between me and the virtue of white women of the South, I say to hell with the Constitution!"

Critical to the wave of lynchings was the belief that black men were not only destroying the sexual jewels of the South but also using their preternaturally large genitals to do so. As crowds gathered to picnic and watch black men lose their lives in agony, the spectators were especially interested in the castration and genital maiming that were so often part of the show. Many took pieces of the victims' penises home as souvenirs. The swirl of lurid accusations, the endlessly retold stories of "pure" white women raped by sexually unstoppable blacks, and the frenzied stares of lynch mobs all combined to create what Jacqueline Dowd Hall called "a kind of acceptable folk pornography in the Bible Belt."

The truth of the accusations against lynching victims was beside the point. Aside from the cathartic release that came from watching black men suffer, the underlying aim of lynchings was to terrorize all African Americans, particularly males. "We will hang two, three, or four of the Negroes nearest to the crime until the crime is no longer done or even feared in all this southern land we inhabit and love," wrote Atlanta editor John Templeton Graves. The true crime, according to Graves and his ilk, was being a black male and thus part of a dangerous group against whom established protections were inadequate. "No law of God or man can hold back the vengeance of our white men," added Graves.

Sexual slander against African Americans was plentiful above the Mason-Dixon Line, too. In 1899, during the depths of the lynching craze, no less a mainstream voice in American jurisprudence than the *Yale Law Journal* argued that sexual assaults by black men were a "daily terror" to southern women and brought "uneasiness" to their "Northern sisters." Without questioning the racism that motivated lynching, or the typical absence of proof against its victims, the article concluded that lynching was "caused" by sex crimes perpetrated by these "ruffians." In total disregard for such quaint niceties as due process of law and fair trials, the article's author asked: "Is it too much to say that if the courts are not ready to [act against black men] the people will?" The solution, the anonymous author concluded, was court-ordered castration, a technique that was also useful to stop "imbeciles," "paupers," and the "feebleminded" from producing children. Only castration could simultaneously prevent sexual assault and end the family lines of people who were "misusing the earth" by existing. Domestic animals had long been castrated to "make them safe to keep about us," the author observed, so why not use the same remedy against black men who attack the "weaker sex"?

•   •   •

Lynching did not occur in isolation. It was part of a web of formal and informal measures against the imagined hypersexuality of blacks and immigrant populations from Eastern and Southern Europe, Asia, and Latin America. While no persecutions approached the savagery of "Judge Lynch," the difference was one of degree rather than kind. Blacks were marked as morally depraved, but so were Italians, Jews, Hispanics, Filipinos, Chinese, and others providing disposable human-labor capital. Governing these groups meant containing their sexuality, especially where sex and marriage with the white population were concerned. As historian Catherine Cocks observed: "Racial fears and sexual ideologies were intimate bedfellows at the turn of the century."

During the same decade that George T. Winston railed against "monstrous" black "beasts" raping southern belles, Eastern European Jews took the rap for a (fictitious) wave of "white slavery" said to claim the honor of innocent girls throughout the heartland. In truth, female Jewish refugees were being traded in an international network of prostitutes, particularly for the South American market; but the preferred narrative was that Jews were the cause of the problem rather than its victims. In 1909, the influential muckraking publication *McClure's* published an exposé accusing immigrant Jewish "scum" (among other groups) of "cruising" the American countryside looking for innocent girls and then plucking them up for deposit into a "closely organized machine" of sin from which there was no escape. The two articles described girls smoking opium, drinking, and shrieking from their makeshift urban prisons: "My God, if only I could get out of here!"

Soon, President William Howard Taft began giving speeches about the "urgent necessity" for new laws against the white-slave trade. In the literature that amplified the general alarm, white slavers were repeatedly characterized as foreign, particularly as "Jew traders," "typical Jew pimps," and other "outcast filth" who fed on corruption and immorality in the cities. A federal report added that diseased alien females had infected "innocent wives and children" by having sex with respectable men, and thus had "done more to ruin homes than any other single cause." The main legislative result of the white-slavery panic was the Mann Act of 1910, a measure its sponsors said was necessary to halt a trade "more horrible than any black-slave traffic ever was." The law created a new form of criminal: one who "knowingly transport[s] in interstate commerce . . . any woman or girl for the purpose of prostitution or debauchery, or for any other *immoral purpose*, or with the intent . . . to induce, entice, or compel" any female to do something immoral."(Italics added.)

The law could not have had a broader reach. The phrase "immoral purpose" covered much more than white-slave traffic and it was quickly put to wide use. The prizefighter Jack Johnson, for example, had sparked deep white resentment after becoming the first black heavyweight boxing champion in 1908. That victory led to a search for a "Great White Hope" who could end the charade of black strength and defeat him. Two years later, in a bout called the Battle of the Century, Johnson beat Jim Jeffries, a white former champion who had been coaxed out of retirement. Deadly riots ensued.

If Johnson refused to be brought to heel in the boxing ring, then it would have to happen in a courtroom. Just as Johnson flaunted his wealth—a dangerous presumption for black men—he also made no secret of his attraction to white women. In 1912, he was able to beat an abduction rap brought by the mother of one of his white girlfriends, but the following year he was put on trial again, this time under the Mann Act, for transporting a white prostitute from Pittsburgh to Chicago for "immoral purposes." The all-white jury had no trouble convicting him, even though his involvement with the woman occurred before the Mann Act was passed. As crowds shouted for a lynching, and after the Chicago district attorney called for a tough sentence "to set an example to Johnson's race," the boxer fled the country. He returned in 1920 to serve a yearlong prison term. Over the following decades, many people, including Chuck Berry, Charlie Chaplin, and Charles Manson, would find themselves facing Mann Act charges.

The Mann Act was one of a series of efforts at the time to address the ills, real and imagined, brought by industrialization, the influx of destitute foreigners, and the spike in commercial sex in the cities. Some of the measures, such as laws limiting child labor, brought workers a needed measure of relief from exploitation. Too many others, however, were directed against the underclasses, particularly against what was thought to be their excessive sexuality. The movement to stem the rising rates of sexually transmitted infections provides a good example. Medical research was identifying the organisms making up syphilis and gonorrhea, and the rudiments of effective diagnostic exams were falling into place. However, for all the advances in the laboratory, the medical community held fast to the conviction that the spread of these infections was caused by the immorality of African Americans and poor immigrants. "The tide [of venereal disease] has been rising owing to the inpouring of a large foreign population with lower ideals," said one leading American gynecologist in 1910. African Americans in particular were seen as a "syphilis soaked" race, and red-light districts (populated mainly by blacks and immigrants) were considered venereal "swamps" that sent "countless currents flowing daily from the houses of the poorest into those of the richest." Not only were minorities threatening white women, they were injecting sexually transmitted infections into the white bloodstream.

Ignoring that the majority of prostitutes were native-born Americans, or that their patrons were mostly white, urban health officials and citizen "vice commissions" launched attacks on brothels and closed more than one hundred during the First World War. In what medical historian Alan Brandt called "the most concerted attack on civil liberties in the name of public health in American history," officials orchestrated mass detentions and quarantines of anyone "reasonably suspected" of harboring a sexually transmitted infection. For prostitutes, especially those of foreign lineage, the result was devastating. Whatever protections they had in brothels vanished: they were forced to take to the streets and endure the often violent exploitation of pimps. Meanwhile, the rate of infection kept rising. Certain health officials advocated treatments rather than moral castigation, but such measures were expensive and were never adopted widely enough to have much of an impact. Besides, vice raids were more newsworthy.

By the mid-1940s, penicillin had become generally available for the treatment of syphilis. Suddenly, treatments no longer required weeks of painful (and marginally effective) injections. By 1948, gonorrhea could also be cured with a single injection. In some cities such as Baltimore, infection rates declined steeply. Could anything be wrong with that? According to some hidebound purity advocates, yes. In 1948, the prominent Johns Hopkins bacteriologist and syphilis researcher Thomas B. Turner gave a talk to the American Social Hygiene Association called "Penicillin: Help or Hindrance?" Rather than rejoicing in the new drug's effectiveness against syphilis, Turner was dubious. Penicillin did nothing, he said, to raise the community's "moral, spiritual and economic health," and with the advent of the drug he feared that people would no longer associate sex with infection. To Turner, the real causes of sexually transmitted infections were sin and promiscuity, and they were far from cured.

●　●　●

The association of syphilis with African Americans took a ghastly turn with the infamous Tuskegee, Alabama, experiment, in which hundreds of black sharecroppers were told they were being treated for "bad blood" while in fact they were being studied as they slowly died from untreated syphilis. The study lasted from 1932 until 1972. Not once were the sharecroppers treated for the disease; nor were they even told they were infected. Even after penicillin became widely available, the men were denied simple treatments that would likely have saved many of their lives, as well as those of their families. Such trivialities as medical ethics or even common mercy were anathema to the "science" behind the Tuskegee study. The goal of the experiment—which, incidentally, was not kept secret from anyone but the subjects themselves—was to observe what advanced syphilis does to the bodies of black men and then "bring them to autopsy." "The success of the experiment turned on what happened to [the men] while they were dying," observed historian James H. Jones.

The magnitude of the race crime perpetrated by the government doctors, nurses, and bureaucrats involved in the Tuskegee study exceeds the scope of this book, but some points bear noting. First, the experiment was fueled by the same notions of black inferiority that drove racist sex laws. African Americans were seen as less human than whites, and while their sexually transmitted infections were objects of scientific curiosity, their own suffering simply didn't matter. They were treated as lab rats. That the men's infections were transferred to their wives was also of no concern. Even in the late 1960s, after ethical objections were raised, the study's directors resolved to withhold treatment and continue until the last subject died. Among the many bitter ironies in this case, the experiment turned out to be worthless as a scientific exercise—in part because several of the sharecroppers received some treatment for syphilis from other sources. As one health official concluded: "Nothing learned will prevent, find or cure a single case of infectious syphilis."

With the exception of the Nazis' experiments on human beings, it is hard to top the Tuskegee study as an example of cold-blooded medical research. But then there's Guatemala. From 1946 to 1948, US government researchers intentionally infected hundreds of Guatemalans—including institutionalized mental patients—with syphilis and gonorrhea, without their knowledge (but with the Guatemalan government's cooperation). This was accomplished through the use of infected prostitutes and direct injections. The researchers were trying to determine whether penicillin could prevent as well as cure sexually transmitted diseases. While many of the subjects were later treated, it is unclear whether these treatments worked or the patients were given proper medical care. The study was kept hidden until 2010, when it was exposed by a women's studies professor researching the Tuskegee experiment. She also learned that the Guatemala experiment was managed by John C. Cutler, who was later one of the researchers in the Tuskegee study.

Cutler went to his grave in 2003 defending the Tuskegee study, and had he been confronted about his research in Guatemala he might well have done the same. American political officials have done quite a bit of apologizing, however. As soon as news of the Guatemala study broke in 2010, Secretary of State Hillary Clinton and Health and Human Services Secretary Kathleen Sebelius expressed outrage at the "clearly unethical" and "abhorrent" work done there. In the wake of the exposure of the Tuskegee study, a class-action lawsuit was filed. It resulted in the government's agreement to pay about $10 million to the Tuskegee survivors and their heirs. In 1997, sixty-five years after the sharecroppers were first told they were being treated for "bad blood," President Clinton said: "The American people are sorry—for the loss, for the years of hurt. You did nothing wrong, but you were grievously wronged. I apologize and I am sorry that this apology has been so long in coming. . . . No ground is gained and, indeed, much is lost if we lose our moral bearings in the name of progress."

The Limits of Love—Miscegenation

The Tuskegee study would not have been conducted had there not been rules in place preventing the sharecroppers' infections from spreading to the white population. Like more than two dozen other states, Alabama maintained an arsenal of laws criminalizing sex and marriage between whites and people of color. It was, for example, a felony for a white person to marry or "live in adultery of fornication" with anyone who had at least one black *great*-grandparent. While definitions of white, Negro, mulatto, and such exotic mixtures as octoroons (one-eighth black), marabous (five-eighths black), and sangmelees (one sixty-fourth black) varied from region to region, the purpose behind all miscegenation laws was to preserve white privilege and reconstitute a white racial "purity" that—assuming it ever existed—was already long gone.

The rules expressed a sense of race hemophilia, by which interracial sex caused an unhealable and disfiguring wound on the body of the white race, and fed the fear that white civilization was in irreversible decline. Wrote premier American eugenicist Madison Grant in his immensely popular *The Passing of the Great Race*:

> It must be borne in mind that the specializations which characterize the higher races are of relatively recent development, are highly unstable and when mixed with generalized or primitive characters tend to disappear. Whether we like to admit it or not, the result of the mixture of two races, in the long run, gives us a race reverting to the more ancient, generalized, and lower type. The cross between a white man and an Indian is an Indian; the cross between a white man and a Negro is a Negro; the cross between a white man and a Hindu is a Hindu; and the cross between any of three European races and a Jew is a Jew.

The truth, of course, was that sex between the races—and among the offspring of interracial unions—had been taking place since the beginning of history and had occurred untold millions of times since Europeans first arrived in the Western Hemisphere. However, that reality only caused white supremacists to redouble their efforts with ever-more-stringent rules mandating that "pure" whites reproduce only with each other. Adolf Hitler, an enthusiastic student of eugenics who referred to *The Passing of the Great Race* as his personal "Bible," argued that nonwhites were a "poison which has invaded the racial body," an infection which needed to be "eliminated so long as there still remains a fundamental stock of pure racial elements." Both Hitler and mainstream American white supremacists believed that time was short in safeguarding the "fundamental stock" of white blood. Hitler applied his racial beliefs in a well-known fashion against Jews, Slavs, and Romanis. For its part, the US turned, among other measures, to restrictions on sex and marriage, using rules that would outlast Hitler's by decades.

The Return of Pocahontas in Virginia

Virginia's state slogan promotes it as a place for "lovers," but that was not always the case. In 1924, when it passed its Racial Integrity Act to "suppress the shameful intermixture of races"—the law required couples to prove they were of the same race before they could marry—it was clear that only one kind of love was acceptable. Like those in other states,

Virginia's miscegenation rules had antecedents reaching back centuries, but the 1924 law was the most restrictive yet. From that point forward, anyone carrying even a trace of nonwhite blood was not permitted to marry a white person, and those who lied to state authorities about their race faced a year in prison.

The law's main booster was John Powell, a pianist and the founder of the Anglo-Saxon Clubs of America, a group devoted to "racial integrity," the "intelligent selection and exclusion of immigrants," and the "fundamental and final solution of our racial problems in general, most especially of the Negro problem." Powell enlisted the most eminent eugenicists of the day to help him goad legislators into passing the law. Madison Grant gave his "unqualified endorsement," adding, "It would be a frightful calamity . . . to civilization itself . . . if the struggle for the supremacy of the white race were in any way diminished." This view was echoed by Lothrop Stoddard, author of *The Rising Tide of Color against White Supremacy*, who warned that the fight against intermarriage was a "matter of national and racial life and death" and that "no efforts should be spared to guard against the greatest of all perils—the peril of miscegenation." Powell also had the backing of Dr. Walter Plecker, head of the state's Bureau of Vital Statistics, the agency that would enforce the law. Plecker later praised the law as "the most perfect expression of the white ideal, and the most important eugenical effort . . . in 4,000 years." The bill passed with only a few dissenters.

Powell's triumph was not complete, however. To his endless chagrin, the bill had been amended to allow whites to marry people with traces of American Indian ancestry. Powell had evidently forgotten that Virginia's "first families" nurtured the idea that they had descended from the marriage of Jamestown settler John Rolfe and Pocahontas, the original Indian princess. Unless the law sanctified this lineage, no fewer than sixteen Virginia legislators (and many more Virginians of rank) would have lost their cherished whiteness overnight, with the added indignity that their marriages would likely have been declared criminal and their children classified as bastards. The pedigree of, for example, the Jefferson, Lee, Randolph, and Marshall families would have forever been sullied, their members dropped to the same social level as their black maids. Thus was born what became known as the Pocahontas Exception.

The idea of an entire social class tracing its lineage to the loins of an abducted Indian teenager is preposterous, as is the notion that she had happily submitted to the embraces of one of her captors. The myth of willing Native American girls throwing themselves at European settlers, however, was long-established. Soon after the Jamestown settlers first arrived in Virginia in 1607, stories circulated in England that said a white man, on his arrival, could look forward to a "brace of young Beautiful Virgins" being "chosen" to "wait upon him that night for his particular refreshment." While some native females were likely served up to colonizers in the name of peace, the predominant truth was that native women, and later female slaves, were raped by the millions—a legacy no amount of mythologizing could sanitize.

In his 1952 novel of race and identity, *Invisible Man*, Ralph Ellison examines the myth of racial purity and suggests that even in the whitest of genealogies, a little color can be found. The book's black protagonist takes a job at the Liberty Paints factory, on which was erected a large electric sign:

"KEEP AMERICA PURE WITH LIBERTY PAINTS."

Liberty's signature paint product, "the purest white that can be found," was called Optic White. The protagonist soon learns the secret alchemy behind Optic White's brilliance: in each bucket, ten drops of a mysterious "glistening black" liquid are stirred in. Those black drops mixed into Optic White represent the seed, the soul, and the suffering of people of color, without which the ideal of white purity, and privilege, could not be attained.

Literary irony was absent in Virginia's eugenics movement, however. While the state's first families understandably (if contemptibly) preserved their own prerogatives, the Pocahontas Exception revealed the futility of restricting marriage and sex along racial lines. In truth, there are no such lines, and the exceptions immediately swallow the rules. If "science" required that "no efforts be spared" to prevent race mixing, and if a white person was defined as one with "no ascertainable trace" of nonwhite ancestry, then no exceptions could be brooked. Certainly, this is what Powell believed when he warned that because of the Pocahontas Exception, "civilization and our race will be swallowed up in the quagmire of mongrelization." (No doubt Powell would have also been disappointed to learn that the Third Reich would exempt people of Japanese ancestry from its racial purity laws, and that some useful German Jews would be named "honorary Aryans.")

Just a few months after the passage of Virginia's Racial Integrity Act, Powell's warnings materialized in the person of Atha Sorrells, whose application for a license to marry a white man was denied by a county clerk. Because Sorrells's records indicated that her ancestors had included a "free colored person," the clerk reasoned that her marriage would violate the law. However, Sorrells argued that her ancestor was in fact a Creek Indian and that the "colored" designation had been made before the Racial Integrity Act was passed. In the subsequent court proceedings, Plecker himself stepped in to produce mountains of records that he said showed that Sorrells was at least partially black. Sorrells countered with a family genealogy backing her story. In the end, Sorrells won—not because the judge had any affection for people of color but because he recognized that it was impossible for anyone to prove the "negative"—that they do not carry "mixed blood":

> In twenty-five generations one has thirty-two millions of grandfathers, not to speak of grandmothers, assuming there is no intermarriage. Half the men who fought at [the Battle of] Hastings [in 1066] were my grandfathers. . . . Certainly in some instances there was an alien strain. . . . I cannot prove that there was not. [T]here is no inhibition against the intermarriage of those who are unable to prove absence of a trace of blood of stock prohibited . . . and since nobody can prove this, we find ourselves where we were in the beginning. Alice [in Wonderland] herself never got herself into a deeper tangle.

Powell and Plecker were apoplectic over the *Sorrells* court decision. They lobbied for the law to be amended to plug the "breach in the dyke," but there was nothing they could do. However, that did not stop Plecker from enforcing the law aggressively in the coming years, or from sounding the alarm against interracial sex. He investigated racially "suspect" Virginians with an eye toward annulling or preventing their marriages. He also pressured an orphanage to remove a child of "questionable" background. In 1943, when there were no delusions about Nazi intentions toward Jews, he boasted that his bureau's "information and pedigree charts" on the racial origins of Virginians were so meticulously prepared "that Hitler's own genealogical study of the Jews is not more complete."

No one can accuse Plecker or other Virginia officials of slacking in their efforts to channel white sexual energies away from people of color. In 1928, for example, Mary Hall, a "white woman," and her new husband, Mott Hamilton Wood, who was one-sixteenth black and had lived his entire life as a white man, were sentenced to two years in jail. Although the couple had considerable local support, the state's governor denied Hall's request for a pardon, maintaining: "The necessity of racial integrity is so important . . . that I find myself unable to act favorably on this application." Plecker also instituted a system of notation on existing birth certificates of people he suspected of having misrepresented their race, in order to justify later refusals of birth certificates to their children.

Plecker could not fully plug the dike because racial purity was a zero-sum game. Either the white race was white, or it was not. There was no consolation prize for putting in a good effort. There was also no chance that any society could ever undo the results of millennia of interracial unions; nor would any law ever stop them from occurring. On the simplest level, the law could be avoided by taking a short drive to another jurisdiction, as Mildred (black) and Richard (white) Loving did in 1958, when they went from their home in Central Point, Virginia, to Washington, D.C., to marry. True, they were banished from Virginia, but the marriage continued and the couple had three children. (It would take years of bruising litigation and a landmark Supreme Court decision in 1967 before the Lovings could finally return to Virginia as a married couple.)

Just as racial definitions shifted in Virginia, there was no general agreement as to who belonged to what race. Oklahoma law, for example, classified as "white" everyone who was not black, including, for example, people of Asian descent. However, in several other states, Asians were forbidden from marrying whites. Moreover, not all states used Virginia's "one-drop" definition. One could be legally black in Georgia, and thus forbidden from marrying whites, while also being considered white across the state line in Florida. South Dakota prohibited marriage with Koreans, while Arizona included Hindus in its anti-miscegenation statute. The laws of Delaware, Kentucky, Louisiana, West Virginia, and Wyoming—all of which barred miscegenation—had no definition of "Negro" at all. As if these laws were not discordant enough, there was also the patchwork of ad hoc methods individual courts used to determine people's racial makeup—including their "reputation" and physical features—which doomed the project of using marriage laws to achieve white "purity" before it began.

Yet facts rarely impede an ideological theory, and the project of demonizing interracial sexual relations proceeded apace throughout the US. Even the representation of such relationships was forbidden in many places, most notably in the movies. The Motion Picture Production Code of 1934, known as the Hays Code, was stringent in prohibiting depictions of "sex relationships between the white and black races." The restriction lasted until 1967, when Sidney Poitier, playing a middle-class doctor, briefly kissed a white woman in the film *Guess Who's Coming to Dinner?* Notably, the kiss was shown through the rearview mirror of a taxicab—to the discomfort of the cab driver. The cabbie's reaction mirrored the long-standing attitude of much of the public, even in areas where interracial marriage was not banned: the cabbie was uncomfortable with what he saw, but he still looked. While movie producers had agreed to avoid interracial sex, the news media picked up the slack by covering the issue as it unfolded in the courts. Sex between the races fascinated and titillated even as it elicited displays of moral indignation.

One of the most dramatic examples of this paradox took place in New York in 1925, when Leonard Kip Rhinelander went to court to annul his six-week marriage to Alice Jones. He claimed that she had deceived him into believing that she was white. The trial, held in suburban New Rochelle, was breathlessly covered on a minute-by-minute basis by the national news media, in no small part because Rhinelander came from one of New York's oldest and wealthiest blue-blood families. However, Rhinelander was a dullard. The real object of fascination was Jones, a pretty taxi driver's daughter whose quiet dignity in court never fit the persona Rhinelander's lawyers tried to pin on her—that of the sexually voracious, scheming vamp. During this period Jones became, in the words of one journalist, "the most talked about, read about, and maligned Negro woman in American history."

The case fed on familiar storylines: a scion of old wealth driven more by his libido than loyalty to his name; a working-class woman looking to elevate herself through seduction and marriage; the son's family attempting to save him from his mistakes; and a sensational trial dispensing a stream of interracial sexual tidbits. Yet more was involved here than a ne'er-do-well rich boy falling into bed with a low-born woman. In Jones, the public saw the ambiguities of female blackness in the Jazz Age. Her ancestors had not been southern slaves; rather, her parents hailed from England. Her mother was white, and her father was a descendant of the colonial West Indians. The government clerk who issued the couple their marriage license had marked her as white—a designation she accepted, just as she embraced both her parents and her sister's marriage to an African American man.

Jones's premarital trysts with Rhinelander were anything but predatory. Rather, for reasons few understood in the end, she loved him and was loyal to him, and she dearly wanted to be his wife. As matters unfolded, it was her sexual availability before marriage that won the case for her, as the lovers' three-day embrace in a Manhattan hotel room proved that nothing had ever been hidden from Rhinelander. However, before her victory in court, Jones would get dragged through the filthiest mud by both Rhinelander's and her own legal teams.

Although he never showed up in court, Rhinelander's overbearing father was a key player in the drama. He had long tried to squelch the romance, and when he had learned of the marriage he bullied his son into leaving Jones. The father then tried, unsuccessfully, to pay Jones to agree to an annulment, after which he supplied Rhinelander with a pricey attorney to undo the marriage in court. It must have seemed obvious to the father that a Rhinelander would never knowingly marry a woman who wasn't white, and also that Jones must have used seductive artifice to reel in his son. Certainly, that was the story advanced by the Rhinelanders' lawyer when he argued to the jury that Rhinelander had been helpless before a gold digger with a light complexion and a dark racial past.

In a surprise move, Jones's lawyer conceded that Jones did, in fact, have "colored blood," but he also argued that no fraud had taken place because her racial makeup was known. The young Rhinelander had spent many evenings with her family, had raised glasses of wine with her black brother-in-law, and had, sneered Jones's lawyer, "cared not a button."

It was the lovers' sex life during their courtship that drew the rapt attention of both the jury and the public. Much of the trial was consumed with the prodigious correspondence between Jones and Rhinelander, which described the details of their couplings in frank terms. More than four hundred letters were read to the jury, eliciting the collective impression that the couple had loved each other passionately and with a mutual interest in sexual experimentation. Jones silently wept as the missives were read. Far from coming off as a schemer preying on a rich dupe, she was shown in the letters to have succumbed to Rhinelander's endearments. His attempts to deny this in court made him appear more cad than gentleman.

The turning point in the trial occurred when Jones's lawyer had her disrobe and display herself to the jury. Even in the arid bureaucratese of the trial record, the misery of the scene is plain. Here, the record picks up as Jones, her mother, and the lawyers leave the courtroom for the adjoining jury room, where the exhibition took place:

> [Jones and her mother] then withdrew in to the lavatory adjoining the jury room and, after a short time, again entered the jury room. [Jones], who was weeping, had on her underwear and a long coat. At [her lawyer's] direction, she let down the coat, so that the upper portion of her

body, as far down as the breast, was exposed. She then again, at [her lawyer's] direction, covered the upper part of her body and showed to the jury her bare legs, up as far as the knees.

Following this exhibition, they returned to the packed courtroom, Jones crying bitterly and near a state of collapse. Taking advantage of the moment's drama, her lawyer demanded that Rhinelander confirm that her body complexion (apparently darker than her face) was the same shade as it had been during those days of sexual abandon in the hotel room. Rhinelander admitted that it was. The rest of the trial had twists and turns, but Rhinelander no longer had a chance. He had gone into the marriage with his eyes wide open. The jury ruled for Jones.

To save his client from being adjudged a deceitful temptress, Jones's lawyer had treated her like a piece of ass. By having her strip and submit to the stares of a roomful of white men, he transformed her into a sex object with no claim to personal dignity. The public thrilled to the spectacle, and newspaper sales jumped with each imagined rendering of the events in the jury room. Yet while Jones's ordeal was both extreme and newsworthy, it was not so very different from the bodily inspections other African Americans suffered as courts determined whether "colored blood" flowed in their veins.

While there was no rule against intermarriage in New York, the entire trial operated on the assumption that some amount of African ancestry still made one black. In most race trials, the defendants tried to prove themselves white. Jones's attorney won by proving that she was black, but in so doing he subjected her to the same disrespectful treatment other African American women suffered. Had Jones and Rhinelander not married, or had Rhinelander not come from a prominent family, little notice of their relationship would have been taken. But once they went public by marrying, the accumulated weight of American racism proved too much to bear. In the 1920s, passing for white was not good enough. Whether one was in the North or in the South, one's racial past could always come back and haunt.

Sex, Segregation, and the School Play
in Little Rock, Arkansas

One of the main civil rights battlefields in the 1950s and 1960s was the schoolyard, where fights over desegregation were charged with sexual issues—especially the fear that school integration would put whites and blacks in sexual proximity. Even the presence of a few African American youths in schools with thousands of white students was thought to be dangerous, not only to the safety of white students but also to the white race.

At Central High School, in Little Rock, Arkansas, the court-ordered enrollment of nine black students in 1957 caused a full-scale panic among white parents and students. On the first day of school, after Arkansas governor Orval Faubus was ordered to remove a phalanx of armed state troopers that had been blocking black children from entering the building, a mob of hysterical parents outside the building saw their world go to pieces. "My daughter's in there with those niggers. Oh my God, oh God," wailed one mother, while a female student—apparently convinced that she was about to be raped—jumped out the window of a second-floor classroom and ran to her mother. Other students did the same.

The fear of sexual mixing at Central High went beyond rape to the prospect of white girls offering themselves for the pleasure of black boys. As one segregationist parents' group publicly asked: "Would the Negro boys be permitted to solicit white girls for dances?" Also: "When [a school play] script calls for the enactment of tender love scenes, will these parts be assigned to Negro boys and white girls?" How, the parents further demanded, would integration work at the most sexually unhinged of all high school rituals—the senior prom? Reaching even deeper into the parents' fears, the White Citizens' Council of Arkansas circulated a flyer depicting a preschool-aged white girl dancing with a black boy and then black men embracing provocatively attired white women. The caption asked: "Is this YOUR little girl's future?" The idea that a white girl would choose a black male for sex, thus opening her womb to racial contamination, was in many ways more mortifying for parents than their worries over rape, but in either case the girl's ruin would be total. After conjoining with black men, warned one flyer, white females were "nevermore . . . one with [their] white race again."

Notably, there was no rhetoric in Little Rock against potential sex between white boys and black girls. In keeping with long-standing traditions, and given that the offspring would be considered black, such a thing fell into the "boys will be boys" category. That is not to say, however, that black females were viewed as harmless prey. Like all African Americans, they were thought to be primary carriers of sexually transmitted infections and thus posed yet another risk to the white population. The threat was not only through sex. A segregationist flyer stated that "uncontested medical opinion [held that] girls under 14 years of age are highly susceptible to [venereal] disease if exposed to the germ through seats, towels, books, gym clothes, etc." Because of such beliefs, there were mass refusals by white girls to take gym showers so long as black girls were present.

The chaos caused by the desegregation of Little Rock's schools resulted in school closures for nearly a year. To break the deadlock, Faubus proposed opening and desegregating some schools as long as they were segregated by sex. As awful as it was to segregationists, school integration had become the law of the land; sooner or later, it would be implemented in Little Rock. *Sexual* integration, however, was simply too much to accept.

On the Margins

Faubus and the angry Little Rock parents saw matters in black-and-white terms. There was no outcry about people of, say, Chinese, Filipino, or Hispanic ancestries, because those minorities did not live in Arkansas in substantial numbers. In regions where such populations were found, laws limiting their sexual relations with whites, other minorities, and sometimes even with each other inevitably arose. In the West in particular, the rules governing interracial sex and marriage became quite elaborate as lawmakers responded to the influx of poor populations from Latin America and the Pacific Rim. Early laws targeted Chinese laborers. Later, as Japanese immigrants arrived, the laws covered them either specifically or as part of the catchall group "Mongolian." As other groups arrived, the laws were changed to include them as well. Along with each of these measures came the usual lies concerning each race's sexual excesses, disease-carrying proclivities, and moral threats to the white population.

Restricting sex with these minorities was no more manageable than it had been with African Americans. Additionally, American foreign policy, military adventures, treaties, and the like sometimes demanded that sex with once-forbidden groups suddenly be permitted. How, for example, could Japanese women continue to be marked off when, following the Second World War, boatloads of American GIs were coming home married to them? They couldn't, so the law was amended, and Madame Butterfly morphed into a virtuous suburban housewife. The net effect of governing sex according to short-term political expedience was to put sex laws on even thinner logical and moral ice than they were in the South, thus hastening their ultimate removal.

Laws against marriage with people of color were most often deployed to keep property in the hands of whites. In a typical case in 1921, in Oregon, Ophelia Paquet asked the court for permission to take control of the property that had belonged to her recently deceased longtime husband, Fred. Out of the mists came Fred's brother, who claimed that the marriage was a nullity because Ophelia was Native American. Unlike Virginia with its Pocahontas Exception, there was no indulgence in Oregon toward Native Americans—especially those born into the nearly extinct Clatsop tribe, as Ophelia had been.

The court held that Ophelia's thirty-year marriage to Fred carried no more legal weight than a thirty-minute date with a prostitute. The judge could have ruled in her favor had he wished to do so: it seems that Fred had followed local Clatsop custom and paid Ophelia's mother fifty dollars for her daughter's hand in marriage. Oregon law held that Indian marriages were valid, even when they involved "peculiar habits and customs." Yet the court circumvented this rule with the meaningless observation that the couple had not physically been on an Indian reservation when they married, so Indian custom had no effect. Had the court been more forthcoming, it would have declared that there was no way it would let a white man's property go to a Native American when a white relative was claiming it. Ophelia had acted the part of the "good and faithful wife," but in the end that meant nothing.

Matters were more complicated with Filipinos, who first immigrated after the US acquired the Philippines in 1898 but who began arriving in large numbers during the Great Depression. Nearly all of them were male laborers between sixteen and thirty years old. Most of them wanted female company, and—to the vexation of white men—many white women were ready to provide it. Before the influx of Filipino men, the Philippines had been thought to be populated by headhunters, dog eaters, and, according to colonial "experts," people resembling "little brown monkeys." However, the men crowding the taxi-dance halls, buying fast cars, and dressing in flashy suits rattled the stereotype. Their attractiveness to white women was attributed to their supposed primitive sensuality and readiness to lavish money on dates—money that unemployed white workers did not have. In 1936, commenting on sexual relationships between Filipinos and white girls, one judge wrote in the *San Francisco Chronicle*: "Girls of tender age are being ruined and led astray by the strange influence these men seem to have on women of a certain type." Pointing to Filipino spending habits, the judge didn't mince words: "When decent white youths can't find a job for love or money, it's enough to make a man's blood boil, and mine is boiling this minute!"

Fortunately for Salvador Roldan, this was not the judge who ruled on his request to marry a white woman. In 1931, a Los Angeles clerk had refused Roldan a marriage license on the ground that Filipinos fell within the law barring "Mongolians" from marrying whites. The judge disagreed, holding that Roldan was in fact an "an Illocano, born . . . of Filipino progenitors in whose blood was co-mingled a strain of Spanish." He was not, therefore, a Mongolian. Los Angeles officials appealed, but Roldan won again. This time, the court declared that Filipinos were "Malay," while Mongolians were limited to "the yellow peoples of China." As Malays were not Mongolian, the court told Roldan that he was free to marry any white woman who would have him.

To put it mildly, the *Roldan* court decision did not meet with universal approval. Anti-Filipino riots had already broken out in several California locations, and popular resentment against men like Roldan for "taking" both white women and jobs was too strong for the state's timorous legislature to ignore. Within weeks a new law outlawing marriage between Malays and white people was passed. It invalidated Roldan's marriage as well as all existing white–Filipino marriages across the state. However, having so few of their countrywomen available, Filipino men evaded the new law by taking their brides out of state to marry. They also freely married Japanese, Chinese, and Mexican women. In fact, most mixed couples in Los Angeles during the 1930s and 1940s were Filipino–Mexican. Given that people of Mexican ancestry were categorized as white, these romances were forbidden as much as those with snow-white daughters of privilege, but no one seemed to mind. The anti-Filipino race rioters made no claim to be protecting the sexual honor of Mexican women.

•   •   •

Prior to the Second World War, the worst racist xenophobia against any Asian population was directed against the Chinese, and with it the most hateful sexual restrictions. Through aggressive immigration restrictions and barriers to intermarriage, Chinese laborers were effectively denied wives of *any* race. As with other foreigners providing cheap physical labor, sexual slanders against Chinese people piled up to justify a policy that prevented them from forming families. By the turn of the twentieth century, it was commonly believed that Chinese men were latent rapists.

For their part, Chinese women were pegged not only as disposed toward prostitution but also as carriers of incurable sexually transmitted infections—to which they were supposedly immune but which were lethal to whites. In 1875, Congress passed the Page Law, which barred immigration by Chinese women who came for "lewd and immoral purposes." The law theoretically allowed genuine Chinese wives to immigrate while keeping out sex workers, but it was applied so aggressively that nearly all Chinese women were barred from entering the country. Out of 39,579 Chinese people who immigrated in 1882, for example, only 136 were women. If you were Chinese and female, you were presumed a tramp and had no place in American society.

In California, where a large number of Asian immigrants lived, the hatred of the Chinese was translated into a state policy of segregation and sexual restriction. As delegates met to draft the state's 1879 constitution, the chairman of the Committee on the Chinese left no doubt as to his position on intermarriage:

> Were the Chinese to amalgamate at all with our people, it would be the lowest, most vile and degraded of our race, and the result of that amalgamation would be a hybrid of the most despicable, a mongrel of the most detestable that has ever afflicted the earth.

From 1881 onward, California prohibited marriages between whites and "Mongolians." A new federal law upped the stakes by stripping American women of their citizenship if they married Chinese or other Asian men. Federal law also barred American-born Asian women from marrying foreign-born Asian men. Together, these laws left Chinese men with virtually no options for marrying. "Permitted neither to procreate nor intermarry," observed Megumi Dick Osumi, "the Chinese immigrant was told, in effect, to re-emigrate [or] die out—white America would not be touched by his presence." As Chinese men turned to prostitutes for temporary relief, the accusations of perversity only increased.

The first real measure of respite for Chinese people in the US came not from a courtroom or legislature but from the serendipity of plate tectonics. The 1906 San Francisco earthquake and fire did more than anything to facilitate the initial wave of Chinese women immigrating to the US. After the destruction of roomfuls of official records, Chinese men began claiming that they were native-born citizens, which allowed them to bring their Chinese wives over to join them. Between 1907 and

1924, this ruse resulted in about ten thousand Chinese women entering the country, as opposed to about forty-five hundred such women in all the years before 1900. It would take decades for anything approaching an appropriate gender balance to be reached among Chinese in the US.

Clamping sexual and immigration restrictions on the Chinese might have made Americans feel safe from the "Yellow Peril," but a huge demand for cheap labor still existed. Filling the gap were Japanese laborers, who were initially brought to Hawaiian plantations and then migrated to the mainland. By 1900 there were about thirty thousand Japanese people in California, and the number was growing. However, thanks to pressure from the Japanese government on American lawmakers, Japanese immigrants soon brought brides and family members with them. In 1900, there were almost five Japanese men for every Japanese woman. By 1920, the ratio had dropped to 1.6 to 1.

Japanese laborers were thus able to form families and avoid the perennial bachelorhood that so bedeviled their Chinese counterparts. Nevertheless, through force of habit or the tendency of the ignorant to smear all Asians with the same poisonous brush, the Japanese endured considerable sexual typecasting. Japanese females were widely viewed as no better than prostitutes; Japanese men were accused of harboring lascivious designs on American schoolgirls, and their families were seen as a weakening agent of American "stock." One California legislator warned of the danger of white girls "sitting side by side with matured Japs, with their base minds, their lascivious thoughts, multiplied by their race and strengthened by their mode of life." California's 1905 anti-miscegenation law announced that all Asian immigrants were a threat to the "self-preservation of the [white] race."

The war between Japan and the US between 1941 and 1945 impacted every aspect of the lives of Japanese Americans. The imprisonment of more than one hundred thousand of them in concentration camps is well-known, as is the visceral hatred leveled at all people of Japanese ancestry. No accusation of immorality or cruelty directed against the Japanese was taken as too outrageous or far-fetched. Not only was the Empire of Japan a military enemy, the Japanese were seen as America's racial foe. Few disagreed that they were subhuman.

Given such boundless hostility toward the Japanese, one would have expected them to be the last group to receive an exemption from American sexual restrictions. However, something always happens in war zones: people trained to hate each other fall in love, and American troops and

Japanese women did so in substantial numbers in US-occupied Japanese territories. Pressure from soldiers and sailors demanding the right to bring their new loves home resulted in laws allowing Japanese "war brides" to enter the US. About 80 percent of the forty-five thousand Japanese who immigrated to the US during the 1950s did so as brides of US servicemen. In a matter of a few years, Japanese females were no longer infectious harlots; they were dutiful Truman- and Eisenhower-era wives.

• • •

The war fought a century earlier between Mexico and the US had laid the groundwork for the first major crack in the interracial marriage laws. At the end of that conflict, in 1848, the Treaty of Guadalupe Hidalgo added immense stretches of land to the US and made Mexican nationals in those territories eligible for US citizenship. As only "white" people were allowed to naturalize at the time, the treaty made Mexicans white by default—and Mexicans were never singled out by any state's anti-miscegenation laws. That they would ever share the same legal status as whites would have come as a bitter surprise to many Mexicans in coming decades, given the persecution they had suffered since Mexican soil became American. The fact that the Mexican population had long comprised a mélange of people of European, Indian, African, mestizo, and other ancestries displeased racial separatists at the time. Nevertheless, the treaty was an extraordinarily good deal for the US, and in exchange for territories now forming part of California, New Mexico, Arizona, Nevada, Utah, Wyoming, and Colorado, a little racial ambiguity was not too high a price to pay.

History was not on the minds of Sylvester Davis and Andrea Pérez when, in 1947, the lovers went to the Los Angeles County clerk to get a marriage license. Davis was African American and had recently returned from military service abroad; Pérez was the dark-skinned daughter of Mexican immigrants. They had fallen in love a few years earlier while working at a wartime munitions factory. While Mexican–black marriages were rare in Los Angeles, the couple was determined to spend the rest of their lives together. The clerk had other ideas, though, and the license was rejected on the grounds that marriages between African Americans and whites were forbidden under California law. The law categorized Pérez, a Mexican American, as white. Baffled and angry (Pérez considered herself "Mexican," not white), the couple decided to fight.

Had Davis and Pérez gone to Mexico or traveled to an accommodating state, they could have married without a problem. Indeed, had they gone to the outlying parts of California where clerks ignored the law and allowed marriages between Mexicans and nonwhites (particularly Punjabis), a marriage license would have been forthcoming. But Davis and Pérez were not like that. Devout Catholics, they were intent on marrying in their local church on the same terms as other Californians. To do so, they would first have to challenge California's anti-miscegenation statute—which would not be easy, given that the rules were becoming more restrictive over time rather than less so. They retained a noted civil rights lawyer, Dan Marshall (for whose family Andrea had babysat when he was a teenager), and filed suit directly in the state's highest court. Marshall first framed the issue as one of religious freedom, arguing that the law denied his clients the right to participate in the Catholic sacrament of marriage. He hoped to enlist the support of the Catholic Church or even the National Association for the Advancement of Colored People, but no religious or civil rights group would sign on. The church worried, oddly, that the case would stir up communist rebellion, while African American groups were focused on other issues such as housing. Most importantly, none of these groups thought that a challenge to intermarriage laws could win. Spurned by the civil rights community, Marshall worked the case alone.

The state argued the familiar eugenic claptrap: "mental incompetents" would result from "mongrelizing" the races, etc. However, these theories, which had long been accepted by the legal community as fact, now encountered sharp resistance in court. A remarkable exchange took place between the attorney defending the law, Charles Stanley, and Justice Roger Traynor:

TRAYNOR: What is a Negro?

STANLEY: We have not the benefit of any judicial interpretation. The statute states that a white cannot marry a Negro, which can be construed to mean a full-blooded Negro, since the statute also says mulatto, Mongolian, or Malay.

TRAYNOR: What is a mulatto? One-sixteenth blood?

STANLEY: Certainly certain states have seen fit to state what a mulatto is.

TRAYNOR: If there is 1/8 blood, can they marry? If you can marry with 1/8, why not with 1/16, 1/32, 1/64? And then don't you get into the ridiculous position where a Negro cannot marry anybody? If he is white, he cannot marry black, or if he is black, he cannot marry white.

STANLEY: I agree that it would be better for the Legislature to lay down an exact amount of blood, but I do not think that the statute should be declared unconstitutional as indefinite on this ground.

TRAYNOR: That is something anthropologists have not been able to furnish, although they say generally that there is no such thing as race. . . . *The crucial question is how can a county clerk determine who are Negroes and who are whites?*

That was it. In a bureaucratic age, a bureaucratic analysis did the trick. Dispensing with the question of whether Davis and Pérez were white, black, or anything else, or whether this was a question of religion, Traynor seized on the impossibility of anyone—especially the functionaries who hand out marriage licenses—making such determinations at all. The court ordered no "expert" inquiry about the significance of the moons on Pérez's fingernails, as happened with Marie Antoinette Monks; neither was Andrea forced to disrobe in front of a jury, as happened with Alice Jones. Rather, by throwing out California's miscegenation statute, Traynor declared that the entire exercise of regulating marriage according to race was futile, immoral, and unconstitutional. The law was "too vague and uncertain" to keep, especially when the "fundamental right" of marriage was involved. This was especially the case, Traynor wrote, given the "stead[ily] increas[ing] number of people of mixed ancestry." In short, in a world in which races have already been mixing for a long time and show no signs of stopping, the entire endeavor of using racial classification to govern who can legally marry whom was a fool's errand.

Traynor did not have the support of all his colleagues on the California Supreme Court, three of whom continued to warn against the perils of race mixing and the "retrogression" and "eventual extinction" of the white race that intermarriage would bring. The dissenting justices even cited the opinions of a South African politician who had recently given a speech in San Francisco warning that the "free mixing of all the races" would "only lower the general level." Those arguments lost the day, however, at least in California, and from 1948 onward that state no longer barred interracial marriage. Davis and Pérez were free at last to seal their union in their neighborhood church. (However, one problem remained: Pérez's father was dead-set against his daughter marrying a black man, regardless of what any court ruled. Until the couple had their first baby, he would not enter their house.)

Pérez v. Sharp, as the case was known, was a giant step forward in the development of sex law, but twenty-nine states still had anti-miscegenation laws on their books. Over the next several decades, thirteen states would repeal their laws against interracial sex and marriage, just as others would enforce theirs more vigorously. In those regions, interracial couples often avoided marriage, choosing instead to live together in informal arrangements. However, as some of them found out, no sexual relationship between people of different races was immune from judgment.

Shacking Up in Florida

Dora Goodnick was not happy when, in 1961, she spied a "colored man" through the window of one of her tenants, Connie Hoffman. Hoffman told Goodnick (falsely) that the man was her husband, but that hardly assuaged the landlord. Hoffman was white and interracial marriages were taboo in Florida. Other tenants were already complaining about the goings-on in Hoffman's apartment. Nevertheless, money talks with a convincing voice, and there was little demand at the time for Goodnick's tatty Miami Beach "efficiency" units. Rather than evict Hoffman and lose rent, Goodnick reluctantly let her stay—until she saw something that shocked her into action. As she just happened to be peering, again, into the Hoffman apartment, she saw the same black man walking nude out of the shower and then using the toilet. The sight of his body (and likely his genitals) was too much for Goodnick, and so began a legal wrangle ending three years later at the US Supreme Court.

Soon after her second eyeful, Goodnick and two police officers were pounding on Hoffman's front door. Hoffman was not at home, but the "colored man," Dewey McLaughlin, was in—and refused the policemen entry. Having already been deported back to his native Honduras twice before, McLaughlin panicked and tried to flee out the back door. He was immediately apprehended, hustled back into the apartment, and then interrogated in the pointed manner with which black men were all too familiar. Telling him to answer honestly or he would have "trouble," the officers demanded to know whether he was having sex with Connie Hoffman. McLaughlin answered yes, but said it had only happened once. The lie was obvious: the apartment had a double bed and two of McLaughlin's shirts were hanging there. The cops stuffed him into an unmarked police car and arrested Hoffman later that day.

Within a week, Hoffman and McLaughlin were charged with the crime of "Negro Man and White Woman, not Being Married to Each Other, Habitually Living in and Occupying in the Nighttime, the Same Room." Seven other states as well as Houston, Texas, had similar prohibitions. Striking directly at sex rather than marriage, these laws took the state as far as it could go into the lives of interracial lovers. Florida's law dated to the slave era, when it was used to encourage white slave owners not to flaunt their black mistresses in public. In the twentieth century, the law and those like it became part of the white-supremacist arsenal against any mixing of the races.

The US Supreme Court had blessed these rules back in 1883, in *Pace v. Alabama*, when a black man and a white woman were jailed for two years for occasionally meeting for sex. Had they both been white (or black), the punishment would have been much lighter, but because interracial sex carried the same risk of racial "amalgamation" that came with mixed marriages, the court held that more severe punishments were justified. The law's aim was to prevent contact between the genitals of whites and those of other races, and whether that happened in the marital bed, a hotel room, or out in a field was immaterial.

After their arrests, Hoffman and McLaughlin had more pressing concerns than the fine points of Supreme Court precedent. Hoffman's child had been taken away from her, and they both faced a year in jail and a big fine. At trial, McLaughlin tried to show that he was Latino rather than black—but that defense failed against Florida's ad hoc racial classification system. Apparently, only light-skinned Hondurans were considered Latino, while their darker countrymen—including McLaughlin—were classified as Negroes. The judge also swatted away their attorney's arguments against the constitutionality of interracial sex laws. The jury took twenty minutes to convict them, and they were sentenced to monthlong jail sentences and fines. Relying on *Pace v. Alabama*, Florida's highest court upheld the convictions. The segregationist judge who wrote the decision also rejected any "supposed social and political advances" that would argue for a change in the law.

However, everything changed once the case left the South and reached the US Supreme Court. The court took the opportunity to toss *Pace v. Alabama* onto the dung heap of racist history and declared that it was no longer good law. Florida's argument that its interracial-fornication rule upheld "basic concepts of sexual decency" was also rejected unanimously, as were the shibboleths about biracial offspring. Most importantly, the court held that making racial classifications related to sex was "arbitrary," "invidious," and a violation of the Constitution's guarantee of equal protection before the law. Significantly, however, the court stopped short of throwing out the rules barring interracial marriage, so any marriage plans McLaughlin and Hoffman may have had were still off the table. This, and the larger question of whether the government could ever stop people of different races from having sex, would have to wait for another day. As matters unfolded, that day was only three years off, when the conviction of Mr. and Mrs. Loving for marrying across the color line came up for review.

The Road to Loving

The *Pérez* and *McLaughlin* decisions scored solid hits against laws interfering with sex between people of different races, but they did not put the issue to rest. The impact of *Pérez* stopped at California's borders. *McLaughlin* got rid of the noxious *Pace v. Alabama* but still allowed states to meddle with interracial marriages. For example, when it was revealed in 1963 that one of the University of Georgia's first black students, Charlayne Hunter, had married a white classmate and was living in New York City, Georgia state officials (including the school's president) publicly declared the marriage "shocking," "disgraceful," and a violation of Georgia law. They announced that the couple would be arrested and prosecuted if they ever tried to return. Two years later, Frances Aline Jones, who was African American, and Jesse Marquez, of Mexican descent, were refused a marriage license in Oklahoma on grounds of race. The couple tried to convince the courts that the times had moved on from such restrictions, but the Oklahoma Supreme Court disagreed. Until they received direct instructions to the contrary from the nation's highest court, the judges said, interracial marriages would remain illegal in Oklahoma.

The edifice would finally fall in a case out of Virginia, where the rules against intermarriage were grounded on the most primitive white-supremacist beliefs. There, in 1958, Mildred Jeter and Richard Loving received a surprise nighttime visit from the local sheriff and two of his deputies. The cops stormed into their bedroom, shined flashlights into the couple's bleary eyes, and demanded that Richard explain, "Who is this woman you are sleeping with?" Mildred answered: "I'm his wife," and pointed to a marriage certificate on the wall that the couple had obtained a few weeks earlier in the District of Columbia. The sheriff's response was: "That's no good here." The reason? Richard was white; Mildred was not.

The two were hauled off to jail. Not only did Virginia's law bar interracial couples from marrying, it also forbade them from marrying out of state and then returning. At their trial, the judge sentenced them to a year in jail. However, he ruled that they could avoid prison if they left the state and did not return as a married couple. For four years, the Lovings put up with this exile, living in Washington, D.C., and visiting their families in Virginia separately. Yet banishment never sat well with them, and in 1963 Mildred wrote a letter to Attorney General Robert F. Kennedy, asking if he could help them return to Virginia to live near their loved ones. Normally, citizen appeals to high-ranking government officials have as much chance of genuine personal attention as letters to Santa Claus, but this one was read and acted upon. After centuries of restrictions on interracial sex and marriage, it was time for the laws to be junked once and for all.

Kennedy referred the case to the American Civil Liberties Union, which had already become active in the fight against anti-miscegenation laws. Years of tortured litigation began. The Lovings' case bounced back and forth among a number of different courts. Along the way, the judge who had originally sentenced the Lovings—Leon M. Bazile—not only refused to change his decision banishing them, he dug in his heels, adding this pearl of religious anthropology to the law of intermarriage:

> Almighty God created the races white, black, yellow, malay and red, and he placed them on separate continents. And but for the interference with this arrangement there would be no such marriages. The fact that he separated the races shows that he did not intend for the races to mix.

Had Judge Bazile spent much time in Caroline County, Virginia, where the Lovings grew up and wished to return, he would have seen evidence that God's plan had long been disregarded. Not only was Mildred's family a mix of African American, Native American, and white ancestry—as one of Mildred's cousins put it, "Richard isn't the first white person in our family"—the county had also gained a reputation for having a high number of light-skinned black inhabitants who could be taken for white. Richard and Mildred had met there and fallen in love as kids. When Mildred became pregnant at eighteen (Richard was twenty-four), they decided to get married. Their families did not object to the union, but someone else in the neighborhood did: it was an anonymous tip to the sheriff that had led to their arrest and prosecution.

In 1967, the case moved to the US Supreme Court. By that time, the Civil Rights Act of 1964 and the Voting Rights Act of 1965 had been passed (among other major civil rights advances), and the court was ready to fix the problem of racial equality in the bedroom. The Lovings' attorneys threw every rationale they could think of at the court: miscegenation laws were the last "relics of slavery"; they violated the Constitution's due process and equal protection clauses; eugenics theories were discredited; marriage was a fundamental right; miscegenation laws violated religious freedom; and so on. Virginia countered with evidence about the dangers of race mixing. Realizing, however, how little currency eugenics-based arguments held outside the South, Virginia's lawyers also advanced what they hoped was a more contemporary argument. They told the justices that families formed by interracial couples suffer undue "pressures and problems," not least because such parents "have a rebellious attitude toward society, self-hatred, neurotic tendencies, immaturity, and other detrimental psychological features." Since the state had a strong interest in "maximizing the number of successful marriages," and interracial unions produce children with "almost insuperable difficulties," it was right for Virginia to prevent such families forming.

Not one of Virginia's arguments passed muster. A unanimous court, in a decision handed down on June 12, 1967, demolished Virginia's miscegenation law and those of the fifteen other states that still criminalized interracial marriage. For the Lovings, the most important sentence of the written opinion was the last: "These convictions must be reversed." No longer did they have to choose between jail and living in their hometown. No longer were their three children illegitimate. No longer could the state determine one's right to love, make love to, or make children with anyone else on the basis of race. *Loving v. Virginia* marked a sea change in the application of race to sex law, to the effect that race-based restrictions on sex and marriage no longer had the support of the Constitution.

The defenders of Virginia's miscegenation laws were correct on one point, however: interracial couples and their families were widely reviled. That a number of recalcitrant states and judges had to be nudged to permit interracial marriages was to be expected, even after *Loving*. In 1970, President Richard Nixon's administration sued the state of Alabama and one of its judges to force them to allow a black army sergeant to marry a white woman.

Alabama didn't formally repeal its anti-miscegenation law until 2000, and even then 40 percent of the state's voters wanted to keep the law. In 2009, a Louisiana justice of the peace refused to marry a black man and a white woman. "There is a problem with both groups accepting a child from such a marriage," he said. "I think those children suffer, and I won't help put them through it." In 2011, Republican Party primary voters in Mississippi were asked: "Do you think interracial marriage should be legal or illegal?" The responses: "legal," 40 percent; "illegal," 46 percent; "not sure," 14 percent.

Regardless of what the law said, in much of the popular imagination, sex between people of different races remained transgressive, if not pathological. For example, in 1966—just before the Supreme Court ruled in the *Loving* case—the liberal, peer-reviewed *Journal of Sex Research* published a curious piece of psychobabble called "Interracial Sexuality as an Expression of Neurotic Conflict." The article, written by psychiatrist Thomas L. Brayboy, notes the historical hostility toward interracial sex but then cites that legacy to conclude that such relationships must involve some form of psychopathology or "acting out" of "neurotic complexes." Brayboy details several cases of interracial relationships, each deeply fraught with violence and mental illness. In one case, a "pretty" but "insecure" white woman "consorts" with "socially inferior" black men to spite her racist father, eventually driving her father to suicide. Another case involved a black civil rights activist seeking to avenge his childhood suffering by abusing white women, including his wife, who desired him excessively and accepted his abuse as atonement for the oppression of African Americans. Brayboy concludes: "The so-called 'Negro Problem' is a multi-faceted and extremely complicated social and psychological dilemma." What he was actually implying was that until the golden age of racial tolerance arrived, there would be something pathological about interracial sex.

None of the people Brayboy described had had children, but if they had, there is little doubt he would have thought such "heterogeneous mixing" unsuitable for child rearing. He would not have been alone in this opinion. Interracial unions were immune from prosecution after *Loving*, but courts still found ways to punish them—especially when they involved divorced white mothers who had sex with black men. Such women were seen as irresponsible parents who put their own sexual quirks ahead of their children's welfare. In 1978, the supreme court of Louisiana found that a white mother who had had a brief affair with a black man had shown a "lack of love and consideration for her children." Even if it was no longer possible to criminalize interracial sex, the court still opined that it ran against "established moral principles," and any mother who engaged in it was "morally unfit or otherwise unsuitable" to raise white children. This mother's children were taken from her.

In 1981, an Iowa court held that a divorced white woman went against her children's "best interest" and made their future lives "more difficult" when she formed a relationship with a black man. The court sent the kids to the ex-husband. A few years later, the US Supreme Court stepped in to say that fear of racial prejudice should not govern custody disputes, but it is impossible to say how many judges still force women to choose between having sex outside their race and keeping their children.

As of 2010, one in seven new US marriages was interracial or inter-ethnic—more than double the rate in 1980 and six times the rate in 1960—while more than 60 percent of Americans now say that it "would be fine" with them if a family member married outside his or her racial or ethnic group. In 2011, one in ten people in England and Wales was living with or married to someone outside his or her racial or ethnic group—a 35 percent jump from 2001 and one that reflects a broad change in attitudes toward interracial relationships. In 1986, half of the British public was against marriage across ethnic lines. The number now stands at just 15 percent.

This is all to the very good, but we have seen that as social attitudes change, dead-enders cling to their prejudices all the harder—and not just the uneducated. In 2013, for example, in Greenwich Village, a man recently employed at Goldman Sachs pointed to a mixed-race couple at a restaurant and hissed: "You n——s are why I lost my job!" Presumably, using the N-word is forbidden in the hushed confines of Wall Street investment banks, and few in such places would admit to using it. But let some strain, such as the loss of a job, come into the picture and the racist monsters return in force.

Not surprisingly, interracial sex is still a detonator. Would Anthony Walker—a young black man axed in the head by two racist thugs in Merseyside, UK, in 2005—still be alive if his killers had not seen him with his white girlfriend? No one can say for sure, but given the history of violence against black men for having sex with white women, it's a reasonable assumption. The UK never had the kind of anti-miscegenation laws that plagued the US, but even without a tradition of state-sanctioned intolerance, the very availability of a white woman to a black man remains potentially incendiary. In the US, fortunately, the law no longer provides cover for such hateful attitudes, and while life is no picnic for interracial couples, it is no crime either.

CONCLUSION

Nothing derails a conversation like telling a group of people that one is writing a book about sex law. It's happened to me more times than I can count. Once I say what I am up to, there comes a pause, followed by smirks and then embarrassed facial expressions, as if I had revealed that I or, worse, they had done something unspeakably perverse. Philandering politicians and broad issues like gay marriage are suitable for party chit-chat, but the lines marking legal from illicit sex in our own lives are too close to home. Most of us have crossed those lines, or at least want to, but we don't want our transgressive deeds or appetites to become known. If the conversation continues, people are unsure how to talk about this book without implying that it may pertain to them. Soon, I rescue the room from its discomfort by changing the subject.

I don't blame people for their responses. To be caught on the wrong side of desire's frontiers is not only to experience intense shame but also possibly to be removed from one's family and livelihood. While many of the people discussed in these pages committed acts of harmful depravity, too many others were wrongly condemned. The young children branded as sex offenders; the sexting teens charged as child pornographers; the homosexuals jailed for how they looked, thought, and made love; and the African Americans mutilated for "poisoning" the white race through sex—all were punished, as the saying goes, for being themselves. Never before the past century had sexual self-actualization been put at such a premium; nor had it been so hazardous. The rising "autonomy of

individual desire" has been accompanied by what Wendell Berry identi-
fies as a tyrannical "politics of sexuality." Sexual behavior has been freed
from many social and familial restraints, but into the vacuum has rushed
a confused and often inhumane tangle of laws. And while families can discipline only their own members, sex laws often condemn entire categories
of humanity—an abstract form of judgment that Berry calls the "lowest
form of hatred." Pre-twentieth-century sex law focused mainly on what
people *did*. The laws of the past dozen or so decades have moved, for better
or worse, into what we think and who we *are*.

Given the tension between individual desire and collective retribution,
it is no wonder this book causes unease. Sexual release is a flame to which
everyone is drawn, but shifting laws make the fire more volatile than
ever. Keeping one's bearings in this environment is a challenge. To give a
few examples, while volumes of pornography are legally available on the
Internet, mistakenly downloading an image of a mature-looking seventeen-year-old can land one in jail, on a sex-offender list, and, potentially,
on the hook for the minor's damages resulting from his or her exploitation. The 570 men across the US who made online appointments with
prostitutes during the 2015 Super Bowl weekend, and who were then arrested in a much-publicized sex-trafficking "sting operation," were surely
surprised that the operation's leaders made "no distinction" between johns
and sex traffickers. And while gay and lesbian US government employees
have been protected against job discrimination since 2011, Kansas's
LGBT state employees recently saw their employment-discrimination
protections revoked.

Meanwhile, many of those branded as society's worst sexual monsters—the defendants in the satanic-ritual-abuse cases of the 1980s and
1990s—now look like victims of a legal system run amok. Not only
have nearly all of their convictions been reversed, an appellate court
recently characterized the "highly questionable" cases as the result of a
vast "moral panic." The entire episode now appears as unhinged as the
witch hunts of the sixteenth and seventeenth centuries. But it happened,
and nearly everyone went along with it. I lived and practiced law in Los
Angeles while the most notorious of those cases—the one involving the
McMartin Preschool—unfolded there. I cannot recall one time during
that period that I or any of my learned friends or colleagues seriously
questioned the bizarre allegations in that case. Rather, we accepted the
constant media reports that psychotic sex rings had infiltrated day-care
centers and preschools.

In November 2014, as the panic about rape on college campuses was reaching a feverish level, there emerged a defining scandal about the University of Virginia's (UVA) alleged mishandling of a horrific gang rape at one of its fraternity houses. A few days after *Rolling Stone* published a nine-thousand-word article about the case, UVA suspended all of its fraternities, while one of the school's law students published an op-ed in *Slate* calling for "rogue fraternities" to be treated by the law as "criminal street gangs." But the case unraveled before formal charges were even filed, and before long police announced that they had no evidence to support the rape allegations. Even before this, the *New York Times* called the scope of the campus rape problem into question, particularly the oft-repeated statistic that one in five female college students is sexually assaulted before she graduates, and people questioned why college personnel were being required to adjudicate rape cases rather than forming partnerships with law enforcement and the courts.

* * *

There is something about sexual crime that makes it more alarming, more urgent, and more demanding of quick and rough solutions than other crimes. In the face of imagined sexual psychopaths, predatory homosexuals, satanic child abusers, and rogue rapists (among others), we have consistently shown ourselves ready to jettison both logic and legal norms. In our rush to punish sexual malefactors, niceties such as evidence, proof, and the presumption of innocence seem like outdated hindrances, even to the courts. In the case of one falsely accused child molester at a New York preschool, the judge announced—before she heard any evidence—that "there was never any doubt in my mind" that the defendant was guilty. If he did not plead guilty, the judge threatened to sentence him to consecutive terms on each of the hundreds of charges he faced. Facing the likelihood of several lifetimes of prison, he pleaded guilty. After serving thirteen years, the only adult witness against him recanted, as did five of the children who had initially said (after being badgered by investigators) that they had been abused.

The law is often rightly derided for its sluggishness. It adjusts too slowly to changing social norms and clings too tightly to noxious rules. The resilience of anti-miscegenation laws and the Rape-Your-Wife Privilege are two examples of this. But caution is necessary, even if it rubs the majority the wrong way, and especially when legions of wrongdoers seem to pop up out of nowhere. Before we establish new categories of sexual wrongs, mark new populations of sex miscreants, and further radicalize the politics of sexuality, we need to stop and take a long breath.

Just as the sexual urge demands satisfaction, so does the drive to condemn others for sexual wrongdoing. After centuries of being blamed for everything from insanity to death, masturbation is now considered a harmless pastime. However, the "autoerotic pleasure of despising other[s]" still kills.

ACKNOWLEDGEMENTS

This book was completed with a lot of help: from the many scholars on whose work I relied, from the direct assistance I received from others, and from the first-rate publishing team that gave me a platform to do my work.

No work of scholarship is unique in itself. Everything builds on the work of others. I turned to a body of historians, scholars, and journalists without whose achievements this book would be inconceivable. Chief among them are Michelle Anderson, Elizabeth Bernstein, Allan Bérubé, Lisa Carstens, Douglas Charles, Janie Chuang, John Colapinto, Alice Dreger, Andrea Dworkin, William Eskridge, Susan Estrich, David Finklehor, Estelle Friedman, Julie Greenberg, Karen Gustafson, Marjorie Heins, Dagmar Herzog, Philip Hoare, David Johnson, Roger Lancaster, Judith Levine, Catherine MacKinnon, Mary Odem, Paul Okami, Peggy Pascoe, Elizabeth Pleck, William Prosser, Kavita Ramakrishnan, Heike Schmidt, Vicki Schultz, Na'ama Shik, Gretchen Soderlund, Robert Sommer, Yuki Tanaka, and Jeffrey Weeks. These are just a few of the giants on whose shoulders I stand.

Building on my efforts was the research assistance I received from Marine Galvez, an impressive young woman who will certainly be making waves in the years to come, as well as the insights of Lawrence G. Walters, a First Amendment and obscenity lawyer of the first rank, and Diana Adams, a New York attorney at the forefront of issues regarding sexuality and marriage. Along the way, I received critical input on drafts from Adam Kaufman and Tony DeToro. Most important in this regard was the editing and guidance I received from Mitchell Albert, whose advice on structure, style, tone, and focus were indispensable. Thanks again, Mitch.

On the business end were my terrific agent, Andrew Stuart, and my tireless publicist, Elizabeth Shreve. At Counterpoint, this project was expertly shepherded by Jack Shoemaker, Rolph Blythe, Kelly Winton, Megan Fishman, and Sharon Wu, among others. Making sure the text was right was copy editor extraordinaire Ryan Quinn and Claire Berkowitz, who made the first effort at untangling her dad's often mangled bibliography and end notes.

And every day was made possible by Lawrence, Claire, and Gillian, my children, and Jennifer, the love of my life.

BIBLIOGRAPHY

"2009 Survey of Americans on HIV/AIDS: Summary of Findings on the Domestic Epidemic." Kaiser Family Foundation, April 2009.

"About FMSF—Introduction." False Memory Syndrome Foundation, November 26, 2013.

Adams, Jane Meredith. "$7.1 Million Award for Sexual Harassment." *Chicago Tribune*, September 2, 1994.

Agan, Amanda Y. "Sex Offender Registries: Fear without Function?" *Journal of Law and Economics* 54, no. 1 (February 2011).

Agency for International Development v. Alliance for Open Society International, Inc., 570 U.S. (2013).

"Alabama Man Pleads Guilty to Obscenity for Sexually Taunting LSU Fan in Video after BCS Game." *Washington Post*, October 2, 2012.

Alexander, David. "Pentagon Report Shows Big Jump in Sex Crimes in Military." Reuters, May 7, 2013.

Altman, Dennis. *Global Sex*. Chicago: University of Chicago Press, 2001.

America's Race Problems: Addresses at the Annual Meeting of the American Academy of Political and Social Science, Philadelphia, April Twelfth and Thirteenth. New York: McClure, Phillips and Co., 1901.

Amir, Menachem. *Patterns in Forcible Rape*. Chicago: University of Chicago Press, 1971.

Anderson, Bridget, and Julia O'Connell. "Is Trafficking in Human Beings Demand Driven? A Multi-Country Pilot Study." International Organization for Migration, 2003.

Anderson, Michelle J. "Chastity Requirement to Sexuality License: Sexual Consent and a New Rape Shield Law." *George Washington Law Review* 70, no. 1 (2002): 51–162.

Angier, Natalie. "The Changing American Family." *New York Times*, November 25, 2013.

"Anita Bryant vs. the Homosexuals." *Newsweek*, June 6, 1977.

"Anti-Porn Crusader Dworkin Dies." BBC News, April 13, 2005.

"AP: Adults Who French Kiss Minors Must Register as Sex Offenders." NBC News, March 8, 2008.

Apuzzo, Matt. "Uncovered Papers Show Past Government Efforts to Drive Gays from Jobs." *New York Times*, May 20, 2014.

Archambault, Sergeant Joanne, and Kimberly A. Lonsway. "Clearance Methods for Sexual Assault Cases." End Violence Against Women International, July 2007.

Astor, Maggie. "In Another Era, a Barnard Student Makes National Headlines after Moving in with Boyfriend." *Columbia Daily Spectator*, April 27, 2008.

"Attorney General Eric Holder Announces Revisions to the Uniform Crime Report's Definition of Rape." US Department of Justice: Office of Public Affairs, January 6, 2012.

Attorney General's Annual Report to Congress and Assessment of U.S. Government Activities to Combat Trafficking in Persons: Fiscal Year 2010. US Department of Justice: Office of Legal Policy, 2011.

"Attorney General's Commission on Pornography: Final Report ('The Meese Report')," 1986, http://www.porn-report.com/.

"Audrie Pott Suicide: Three Teens Arrested for Alleged Sexual Assault of Calif. Girl Who Committed Suicide." CBS News, April 12, 2013.

Aviv, Rachel. "The Science of Sex Abuse." *New Yorker*, January 14, 2013.

Ball, Aimee Lee. "Who Are You on Facebook Now?" *New York Times*, April 4, 2014.

Banda, P. Solomon, and Nicholas Riccardi. "Coy Mathis Case: Colorado Civil Rights Division Rules in Favor of Transgender 6-Year-Old in Bathroom Dispute." *Huffington Post*, June 24, 2013.

Bankoff, Caroline. "White Guy Punched Out after Yelling Racist Crap." *New York Magazine*, July 13, 2013.

Barnes, Robert. "Supreme Court Declines to Review Same-Sex Marriage Cases, Allowing Unions in 5 States." *Washington Post*, October 6, 2014.

Bassett, Laura. "New Mexico Bill Would Criminalize Abortions after Rape as 'Tampering with Evidence.'" *Huffington Post*, January 24, 2013.

Bazell, Robert. "U.S. Apologizes for STD Experiments in Guatemala." NBC News, October 1, 2010.

Bazelon, Emily. "Another Sexting Tragedy." *Slate*, April 12, 2013.

Becker, Howard S. *Outsiders: Studies in the Sociology of Deviance.* New York: Free Press, 1963.

Becker, Judith V. "Offenders: Characteristics and Treatment." *Future of Children* 4, no. 2 (1994).

Beevor, Antony. "An Ugly Carnival." *Guardian*, June 4, 2009.

Begos, Kevin. "Lifting the Curtain on a Shameful Era." *Winston-Salem Journal*, March 18, 2013.

Belkin, Aaron. "A Sting He Didn't Deserve." *Washington Post*, September 1, 2007.

Bell, Ellyn. "First Offender Prostitution Program (FOPP)." Sage Project, October 2013.

Bennett, Lisa. "The Perpetuation of Prejudice in Reporting on Gays and Lesbians: Time and Newsweek: The First Fifty Years." Joan Shorenstein Center on the Press, Politics and Public Policy, September 1998.

Bennett-Smith, Meredith. "Louisiana Police Sting Targets, Arrest Gay Men for Sex Using Unconstitutional Anti-Sodomy Law." *Huffington Post*, July 29, 2013, sec. Huffpost Gay Voices.

Berger, Stephanie M. "No End in Sight: Why the 'End Demand' Movement Is the Wrong Focus for Efforts to Eliminate Human Trafficking." *Harvard Journal of Law and Gender* 35 (2012): 524–70.

Berger, Vivian. "Man's Trial, Woman's Tribulation: Rape Cases in the Courtroom." *Columbia Law Review* 77, no. 1 (January 1977): 1–103.

Berkowitz, Eric. "Desperate Hours: Legal Aid Attorney Protima Pandey Works against the Clock to Protect Battered Women." *California Lawyer*, August 2012.

———. *Sex and Punishment: Four Thousand Years of Judging Desire*. Berkeley, CA: Counterpoint Press, 2012.

Bernstein, Elizabeth. "Carceral Politics as Gender Justice? The 'Traffic in Women' and Neoliberal Circuits of Crime, Sex, and Rights." *Theory and Society* 41, no. 3 (2012): 233–59.

———. "The Sexual Politics of the 'New Abolitionism.'" *Differences: A Journal of Feminist Cultural Studies* 18, no. 3 (2007): 128–51.

———. "Temporarily Yours: Intimacy, Authenticity, and the Commerce of Sex (2007)." In *The History of Sexuality in Europe: A Sourcebook and Reader*. London: Routledge, 2011.

Bernstein, Elizabeth, and Laurie Schaffner, eds. *Regulating Sex: The Politics of Intimacy and Identity*. New York: Routledge, 2004.

Bérubé, Allan. *Coming Out under Fire: The History of Gay Men and Women in World War Two*. New York: Free Press, 1990.

Best, Joel. *Threatened Children: Rhetoric and Concern about Child-Victims*. Chicago: University of Chicago Press, 1990.

Bhumiprabhas, Subhatra. "Sex 'Trade,' Not 'Traffic.'" *Nation*, March 6, 2012.

Bien-Aime, Taina. "France Takes First Steps towards Abolition of Prostitution." *World Post*, April 15, 2014.

"Big Data, for Better or Worse: 90% of World's Data Generated over Last Two Years." *Science Daily*, May 22, 2013.

Bingham, John. "Love across the Divide: Interracial Relationships Growing in Britain." *Telegraph*, July 3, 2014.

Birmingham, Kevin. *The Most Dangerous Book: The Battle for James Joyce's Ulysses*. New York: Penguin Press, 2014.

Bitar, Kara N. "Parental Rights of Rapists." *Duke Journal of Gender Law and Policy* 19 (2012): 275, 276.

Black, Edwin. *War against the Weak: Eugenics and America's Campaign to Create a Master Race.* New York: Four Walls Eight Windows, 2003.

Blackstone, William. *Commentaries on the Laws of England.* Edited by George Sharswood. Philadelphia: J. B. Lippincott, 1890.

Blake, John. "Return of the 'Welfare Queen.'" CNN, January 23, 2012.

Bogdanich, Walt. "Reporting Rape, and Wishing She Hadn't." *New York Times,* July 12, 2014.

"A Bold Plan to Aid Sex-Trafficking Victims." *New York Times,* September 25, 2013.

Boorstein, Michelle, and William Wan. "After Child Abuse Accusations, Catholic Priests Often Simply Vanish." *Washington Post,* December 4, 2010.

Boyle, Louise. "Meet the Mom Who Runs a Revenge Porn Website Filled with Explicit Pictures of 'Home Wrecking Mistresses' (but NOT the Cheating Husbands)." *Daily Mail Online,* December 13, 2013.

"Boy Scouts Ordered to Pay Oregon Man Kerry Lewis $18.5M in Sex Abuse Case." *Daily News,* April 24, 2010.

Brady, Bob. "8 Elements Your Sexual Harassment Policy Must Have . . . and Why Just Having a Strong Policy Isn't Enough." *HR Daily Advisor,* June 18, 2006.

Brandt, Allan M. "AIDS: From Social History to Social Policy." In *AIDS: The Burdens of History,* edited by Elizabeth Fee and Daniel M. Fox. Berkeley: University of California Press, 1988.

Brayboy, Thomas L. "Interracial Sexuality as an Expression of Neurotic Conflict." *Journal of Sex Research* 2, no. 3 (1966): 179–84.

Bremner, Robert H., ed. *Children and Youth in America: A Documentary History.* Vol. II, 1866–1932, Parts 1–6. American Public Health Association, 1971.

Brier, Jennifer. *Infectious Ideas: U.S. Political Responses to the AIDS Crisis.* Chapel Hill: University of North Carolina Press, 2009.

Brisbane, Arthur S. "Confusing Sex and Rape." *New York Times,* November 19, 2011.

Brock, David. "Confessions of a Right-Wing Hit Man." *Esquire,* July 1997.

———. "The Fire This Time." *Esquire,* April 1998.

———. "Living with the Clintons." *American Spectator,* December 1993.

———. *The Real Anita Hill: The Untold Story.* New York: Free Press, 1993.

Browne, Kingsley R. "Military Sex Scandals from Tailhook to the Present: The Cure Can Be Worse Than the Disease." *Duke Journal of Gender Law and Policy* 14 (2007).

Brownmiller, Susan. *Against Our Will: Men, Women, and Rape.* New York: Fawcett Columbine, 1975.

Brozan, Nadine. "Witness Says She Fears 'Child Predator' Network." *New York Times,* September 18, 1984.

Bruce, Lenny. "The People of the State of California vs. Lenny Bruce (from How to Talk Dirty and Influence People, 1965)." In *Sexual Revolution,* edited by Jeffery Escoffier. New York: Thunder's Mouth Press, 2003.

Bruce, Steve. "Young Man Enters Guilty Plea in High-Profile Nova Scotia Child Porn Case." *Chronicle Herald,* September 22, 2014.

Brundage, James. *Law, Sex, and Christian Society in Medieval Europe.* Chicago: University of Chicago Press, 1990.

Bryden, David P. "Rape in the Criminal Justice System." *Journal of Criminal Law and Criminology* 87, no. 4 (1997): 1194–1384.

Brynie, Faith. "Brain Sense." *Psychology Today,* December 13, 2013.

Buchanan, Patrick. "Florida's Vote: Hopeful Symptom." *Reno Evening Gazette,* June 15, 1977.

———. "Nature's Retribution." *New York Post,* February 24, 1983.

Bullough, V., and B. Bullough. *Women and Prostitution: A Social History.* Amherst, NY: Prometheus Books, 1987.

Bullough, Vern L. "Masturbation: A Historical Overview." *Journal of Psychology and Human Sexuality* 14, no. 2/3 (2002): 17–33.

———. *Sexual Variance in Society and History.* Chicago: University of Chicago Press, 1976.

Burg, B. R. *Gay Warriors: A Documentary History from the Ancient World to the Present.* New York: New York University Press, 2001.

Burke, Matthew M. "Senate Bill Would Provide Clean Service Records for Discharged Gay, Lesbian Troops." *Stars and Stripes,* February 12, 2014.

Burleigh, Nina. "Super Bowl Prostitution Crackdown: Inside the NYPD's New Strategy." *Time,* January 31, 2014.

Burnham, John C. "The Progressive Era Revolution in American Attitudes toward Sex." *Journal of American History* 59, no. 4 (March 1973): 885–908.

Burns, Marshall. "Origin of the Sex Offender Registries." SOL Research, August 26, 2009.

Burns, Sarah. *The Central Park Five: The Untold Story behind One of New York City's Most Infamous Crimes.* New York: Vintage Books, 2011.

Byrnes, Sholto. "Mixed Blessings." *Guardian,* January 20, 2009.

Caldwell, Michael F., Mitchell H. Ziemke, and Michael J. Vitacco. "An Examination of the Sex Offender Registration and Notification Act as Applied to Juveniles: Evaluation of the Ability to Predict Sexual Recidivism." *Psychology, Public Policy, and Law* 14, no. 2 (2008): 89–114.

Campbell, D'ann. *Women at War with America: Private Lives in a Patriotic Era.* Cambridge: Cambridge University Press, 1984.

Cantwell, Hendrika B. "Child Sexual Abuse: Very Young Perpetrators." *Child Abuse and Neglect* 12, no. 4 (1988): 579–82.

Capehart, Jonathan. "Gay Marriage Victories Only Go So Far." *Washington Post*, October 13, 2014.

———. "Gays and Lesbians Owe Thanks to President George W. Bush and Justice Scalia." *Washington Post*, October 20, 2014.

Capers, I. Bennett. "Cross Dressing and the Criminal." *Yale Journal of Law and the Humanities* 20, no. 1 (2008).

Caplan, Arthur. "Past Horrific Human Experiments Stir Concerns of Today." NBC News, October 1, 2010.

Carey, Jane. "The Racial Imperatives of Sex: Birth Control and Eugenics in Britain, the United States and Australia in the Interwar Years." *Women's History Review* 21, no. 5 (2012): 733–52.

Carleo-Evangelist, Jordan. "Police Sign of Shame Set for Its First John." *Times Union*, October 3, 2009.

Carpenter, Catherine L., and Amy E. Beverlin. "The Evolution of Unconstitutionality in Sex Offender Registration Laws." *Hastings Law Journal* 63 (May 2012): 1071–1134.

Carpenter, Dale. *Flagrant Conduct: The Story of Lawrence v. Texas.* New York: W.W. Norton and Company, 2012.

Carpenter, Morgan. "Australia Can Lead the Way for Intersex People." *Guardian*, June 17, 2013.

Carstens, Lisa. "Unbecoming Women: Sex Reversal in the Scientific Discourse of Female Deviance in Britain, 1880–1920." *Journal of the History of Sexuality* 20, no. 1 (2011).

Cassell, Paul. "The Crime Victim's Reaction to Today's Supreme Court Decision." *Washington Post*, April 23, 2014.

Chafe, William H. *The Paradox of Change: American Women in the 20th Century.* New York: Oxford University Press, 1991.

Charen, Mona. "The General's Protracted Charge." *Washington Times*, April 10, 2000.

Charles, Douglas M. *The FBI's Obscene File: J. Edgar Hoover and the Bureau's Crusade against Smut.* Lawrence: University Press of Kansas, 2012.

Chen, Christina Pei-Lin. "Provocation's Privileged Desire: The Provocation Doctrine, 'Homosexual Panic,' and the Non-Violent Unwanted Sexual Advance Defense." *Cornell Journal of Law and Public Policy* 10 (2000): 195–235.

Chesler, Ellen. *Woman of Valor: Margaret Sanger and the Birth Control Movement in America.* New York: Simon and Schuster, 1992.

Chiarini, Annmarie. "I Was a Victim of Revenge Porn—I Don't Want Anyone Else to Face It." *Alternet*, November 19, 2013.

"Chronology of the McMartin Preschool Abuse Trials." University of Missouri–Kansas City School of Law, n.d.

Chuang, Janie A. "Achieving Accountability for Migrant Domestic Worker Abuse." *North Carolina Law Review* 88 (2010).

———. "Rescuing Trafficking from Ideological Capture: Prostitution Reform and Anti-Trafficking Law and Policy." *University of Pennsylvania Law Review* 158, no. 6 (2010): 1655–1728.

Clark, Kenneth R. "Sen. Paula Hawkins: Sexual Abuse Happens Everywhere to So Many." *Chicago Tribune*, November 2, 1986.

Clarke, Edward H. *Sex in Education; Or, A Fair Chance for the Girls*. Boston: James R. Osgood and Company, 1873.

Cocca, Carolyn. *Jailbait: The Politics of Statutory Rape Laws in the United States*. Albany: State University of New York Press, 2004.

Cocks, Catherine. "Rethinking Sexuality in the Progressive Era." *Journal of Gilded Age and Progressive Era* 5, no. 2 (April 2006): 93–118.

Colapinto, John. *As Nature Made Him: The Boy Who Was Raised as a Girl*. New York: Harper Perennial, 2000.

———. "The Case of Joan/John." *Rolling Stone*, December 11, 1997.

———. "Gender Gap: What Were the Real Reasons behind David Reimer's Suicide?" *Slate*, June 3, 2004.

Colb, Sherry. "Sexual Surrogacy: Better Than Prostitution?" *Verdict: Legal Analysis and Commentary from Justia*, July 24, 2013, sec. Health Law.

Cole, Jeff. "Young Expectant Father Gets Probation." *Milwaukee Journal Sentinel*, June 25, 1997.

Colin, Chris. "Lou Reed." *Salon*, May 16, 2000.

Collins, Jeffrey, and Michael Biesecker. "Army General Fined, Reprimanded in Sex Case." *Yahoo News*, March 20, 2014.

"Colombia's Highest Court Restricts Surgery on Intersex Children." Intersex Society of North America, n.d.

Commonwealth v. Judith Stowell, 389 171 (Mass. 1983).

Commonwealth v. Mlinarich, 498 A.2d 395, 403 (Supreme Court of Pennsylvania 1985).

Comstock, Anthony. *Traps for the Young*. New York: Funk and Wagnalls, 1883.

"Congressional Authorization." National Center for Missing and Exploited Children, n.d.

Connelly, Mark Thomas. *The Response to Prostitution in the Progressive Era*. Chapel Hill: University of North Carolina Press, 2011.

"Consultations to Professionals." Toni Cavanagh Johnson, PhD, Licensed Clinical Psychologist in Independent Practice in South Pasadena, California, n.d.

Contenta, Sandro. "Pope Francis Names Sex Abuse Victim as Adviser." *Star*, March 31, 2014.

"Convention on the Rights of the Child." United Nations, February 25, 2014.

Coulter, Ann. "Clinton Sure Can Pick 'Em." *Jewish World Review*, October 30, 2000.

"Couple Given Six Months to Pay Back Brothel's Money." *GetSurry*, October 7, 2011.

Courtney, Susan. *Hollywood Fantasies of Miscegenation: Spectacular Narratives of Gender and Race, 1903–1967*. Princeton, NJ: Princeton University Press, 2005.

"Crimes Against Nature by Solicitation (CANS) Litigation." Center for Constitutional Rights, n.d., http://ccrjustice.org/crime-against-nature#files.

Culp-Ressler, Tara. "23 Years Later, Senator Who Interrogated Anita Hill Still Doesn't Understand Sexual Harassment." Think Progress, May 7, 2014.

Cuomo, Mario. *Reason to Believe*. New York: Simon and Schuster, 1995.

Curry, Neil. "Demi Moore Sees Plight of Sex Slaves." CNN, June 23, 2011, sec. The CNN Freedom Project: Ending Modern-Day Slavery.

Dank, Meredith, Bilal Khan, Mitchell P. Downey, Cybele Kotonias, Deborah Mayer, Colleen Owens, Laura Pacifici, and Lilly Yu. "Estimating the Size and Structure of the Underground Commercial Sex Economy in Eight Major US Cities." Urban Institute, March 2014.

Dao, James. "In Debate over Military Sexual Assault, Men Are Overlooked Victims." *New York Times*, June 23, 2013.

"Database of Publicly Accused Priests in the United States." BishopAccountability.org, n.d.

Davidson, Roger. "'This Pernicious Delusion': Law, Medicine, and Child Abuse in Early-Twentieth-Century Scotland." *Journal of the History of Sexuality* 10, no. 1 (2001).

Davies, Lizzy. "UN Committee against Torture Criticises Vatican Handling of Sex Abuse." *Guardian*, May 23, 2014.

Davies, Nick. "10 Days in Sweden: The Full Allegations against Julian Assange." *Guardian*, December 17, 2010.

"Dear Colleague Letter: Sexual Violence." United States Department of Education: Office for Civil Rights, April 4, 2011.

De Grazia, Edward. *Girls Lean Back Everywhere: The Law of Obscenity and the Assault on Genius*. New York: Vintage Books, 1993.

De la Baume, Maia. "Disabled People Say They, Too, Want a Sex Life, and Seek Help in Attaining It." *New York Times*, July 4, 2013.

Delgado, A. J. "Crying Rape." *National Review Online*, May 19, 2014.

D'Emilio, John. *Sexual Politics, Sexual Communities: The Making of a Homosexual Minority in the United States, 1940–1970*. Chicago: University of Chicago Press, 1998.

D'Emilio, John, and Estelle Freedman. *Intimate Matters: A History of Sexuality in America*. Chicago: University of Chicago Press, 1988.

DePrang, Emily. "Josh Gravens, Subject of Observer Feature, Removed from Sex Offender Registry." *Texas Observer*, December 7, 2012.

———. "Life on the List." *Texas Observer*, May 31, 2012.

Dershowitz, Alan M. *The Abuse Excuse: And Other Cop-Outs, Sob Stories, and Evasions of Responsibility*. New York: Back Bay Books, 1995.

Deutsch, Linda. "Billie Jean King Wins 'Palimony' Suit." *Telegraph*, November 20, 1982.

Dewan, Shaila. "Georgia Man Fights Conviction as Molester." *New York Times*, December 19, 2006.

Diaz-Duran, Constantino. "Sterilized for Being Poor?" *Daily Beast*, January 16, 2010.

Diaz, Joseph, Jenner Smith, and Alexa Valiente. "Fla. Teen Jailed for Same-Sex Relationship with Underage Girlfriend Ready to 'Move On.'" ABC News, February 14, 2014.

Dickinson, Edward Ross. "'Must We Dance Naked?': Art, Beauty, and Law in Munich and Paris, 1911–1913." *Journal of the History of Sexuality* 20, no. 1 (2011): 95–131.

Dillard, Carter. "Future Children as Property." *Duke Journal of Gender Law and Policy* 17 (2010).

Ditmore, Melissa, ed. *Encyclopedia of Prostitution and Sex Work*. Westport, CT: Greenwood Press, 2006.

———. *The Use of Raids to Fight Trafficking in Persons*. Sex Workers Project at the Urban Justice Center, 2009.

Dockterman, Eliana. "Hawaii Police Won't Get to Have Sex with Prostitutes Anymore." *Time*, March 26, 2014.

Dodillet, Susanne, and Petra Ostergren. "The Swedish Sex Purchase Act: Claimed Success and Documented Effects." The Hague, 2011.

Dreger, Alice D. "'Ambiguous Sex'—or Ambivalent Medicine? Ethical Issues in the Treatment of Intersexuality." *Hastings Center Report* 28, no. 3 (1998): 24–35.

———. "Ethical Problems in Intersex Treatment." *Medical Humanities Report* 19, no. 1 (1997).

———. *Hermaphrodites and the Medical Invention of Sex*. Cambridge, MA: Harvard University Press, 1998.

Dworkin, Andrea. *Intercourse: The Twentieth Anniversary Edition*. New York: Basic Books, 1987.

Dworkin, Roger B. "The Resistance Standard in Rape Legislation." *Stanford Law Review* 18 (February 1966): 680–89.

Early, Gerald. "Rebel of the Progressive Era." PBS, n.d.

Eaton-Robb, Pat. "Connecticut Prisoners Express Anger over Porn Ban." CBS Connecticut, October 8, 2011.

Edelman, Benjamin. "Red Light States: Why Buy Online Adult Entertainment?" *Journal of Economic Perspectives* 23, no. 1 (Winter 2009): 209–20.

"Editorial: State Must Move Ahead on Compensation Process." *Winston-Salem Journal*, August 23, 2013.

Effron, Lauren. "I Love You, You're Perfect, but Watch What You Facebook: Social Media Prenups." ABC News, June 3, 2014.

Eichenwald, Kurt. "Making a Connection with Justin." *New York Times*, December 19, 2005.

———. "Through His Webcam, a Boy Joins a Sordid Online World." *New York Times*, December 19, 2005.

Eifling, Sam. "Police Lobby to Remain Exempt from Law against Prostitution." *Honolulu Star Advertiser*, March 21, 2014.

Elizey, Don. "JP Refuses to Marry Couple." *Daily Star*, October 15, 2009.

Ellis, Randy. "Gay Soldier's Discharge Upgraded to Honorable." *Military .com News*, June 16, 2014.

Ellison, Ralph. *Invisible Man*. New York: Vintage International, 1947.

Elton, Catherine. "Jail Baiting: Statutory Rape's Dubious Comeback." *New Republic* 217, no. 16 (1997).

Emily, Jennifer. "Judge Says Sexually Assaulted 14-Year-Old 'Wasn't the Victim She Claimed to Be.'" *Dallas News*, May 1, 2014.

"Empower Writes to Thai PM Re 'Anti-Trafficking' Raids." Global Network of SexsWork Projects (NSWP), June 8, 2012.

Epps, Garrett. "The Twilight of Antonin Scalia." *Atlantic*, August 21, 2014.

Erdely, Sabrina Rubin. "A Rape on Campus: A Brutal Assault and Struggle for Justice at UVA." *Rolling Stone*, November 19, 2014.

Ernsdorff, Gary M. "Let Sleeping Memories Lie—Words of Caution about Tolling the Statute of Limitations in Cases of Memory Repression." *Journal of Criminal Law and Criminology* 84, no. 1 (1993): 129–74.

Ernst, Morris L. "Reflections on the Ulysses Trial and Censorship." *James Joyce Quarterly* 3, no. 1 (1965).

Eskridge, William N. Jr., *Dishonorable Passions: Sodomy Laws in America, 1861–2003*. New York: Penguin Books, 2008.

———. "Privacy Jurisprudence and the Apartheid of the Closet, 1946–1961." *Florida State University Law Review* 24, no. 703 (1997): 721.

"Estimating the Numbers." PBS, February 7, 2006, sec. Frontline.

Estrich, Susan. "It's a Case of the Powerless versus the Powerful." In *Debating Sexual Correctness: Pornography, Sexual Harassment, Date Rape and the Politics of Sexual Equality*, edited by Adele M. Stan. New York: Delta, 1995.

———. *Real Rape*. Cambridge, MA: Harvard University Press, 1987.

————. "Sex at Work." *Stanford Law Review* 43 (1991): 813–61.

"Eugenics: Three Generations, No Imbeciles Virginia, Eugenics and Buck v. Bell," sec. "Carrie Buck Revisited and Virginia's Apology for Eugenics." University of Virginia: Historical Collections at the Claude Moore Health Sciences Library, 2007.

Evans, Jennifer. "Bahnhof Boys: Policing Male Prostitution in Post-Nazi Berlin." *Journal of the History of Sexuality* 12, no. 4 (October 2003): 605–36.

Evans, Lynn. "Confusion in the Court: Sexual Harassment Law, Employer Liability, and Statutory Purpose." *Loyola of Los Angeles International and Comparative Law Review* 21 (1999): 521–52.

Executive Order no. 10450, "Security Requirements for Government Employment," National Archives, n.d.

Fackler, Martin. "Japan's Foreign Minister Says Apologies to Wartime Victims Will Be Upheld." *New York Times*, April 8, 2014.

————. "Japan Stands by Apology to Its Wartime Sex Slaves." *New York Times*, March 14, 2014.

————. "U.S. Emerges as Central Stage in Asian Rivalry." *New York Times*, March 22, 2014.

Faison, Seth. "Child-Abuse Conviction of Woman Is Overturned." *New York Times*, March 27, 1993.

Fallet, Mareike, and Simone Kaiser. "Concentration Camp Bordellos: 'The Main Thing Was to Survive at All.'" *Spiegel Online International*, June 25, 2009.

"Famous American Trials: Illinois v. Nathan Leopold and Richard Loeb, 1924: Excerpts from the Psychiatric ('Alienist') Testimony in the Leopold and Loeb Hearing (August 18–August 19, 1924)," n.d.

Fee, Elizabeth. "Sin versus Science: Venereal Disease in Twentieth-Century Baltimore." In *AIDS: The Burdens of History*, edited by Elizabeth Fee and Daniel M. Fox. Berkeley: University of California Press, 1988.

Fejes, Fred. "Murder, Perversion, and Moral Panic: The 1954 Media Campaign against Miami's Homosexuals and the Discourse of Civic Betterment." *Journal of the History of Sexuality* 9, no. 3 (2000): 305–47.

Fidelis, Malgorzata. *Women, Communism, and Industrialization in Postwar Poland*. Cambridge: Cambridge University Press, 2010.

Findlen, Paula. "Humanism, Politics and Pornography in Renaissance Italy." In *The Invention of Pornography: Obscenity and the Origins of Modernity, 1500–1800*, edited by Lynn Hunt, 49–108. New York: Zone Books, 1993.

Finkelhor, David. *A Sourcebook on Child Sexual Abuse*. Thousand Oaks, CA: Sage Publications, 1986.

Finkelhor, David, Richard Ormrod, and Mark Chaffin. "Juveniles Who Commit Sex Offenses against Minors." US Department of Justice: Office of Juvenile Justice and Delinquency Prevention, December 2009.

Fisher, Bonnie S. "Measuring Rape against Women: The Significance of Survey Questions." US Department of Justice, 2004.

Fitch, W. Lawrence, and Richard James Ortega. "Law and the Confinement of Psychopaths." *Behavioral Sciences and the Law* 18, no. 5 (2000): 663–78.

Fitzsimmons, Emma G. "Alan Turing, Enigma Code-Breaker and Computer Pioneer, Wins Royal Pardon." *New York Times*, December 24, 2013.

Fogarty, Richard S. "Race and Sex, Fear and Loathing in France during the Great War." In *Brutality and Desire: War and Sexuality in Europe's Twentieth Century*, edited by Dagmar Herzog. London: Palgrave Macmillan, 2009.

"Forcible and Statutory Rape: An Exploration of the Operation and Objectives of the Consent Standard." *Yale Law Journal* 62, no. 1 (1952): 55.

Ford, Dana. "Representatives Knock Sen. Sax by Chambliss' Comments on Sexual Assault." CNN, June 5, 2013.

Ford, Kishka-Kamari. "'First, Do No Harm'—The Fiction of Legal Parental Consent to Genital-Normalizing Surgery on Intersexed Infants." *Yale Law and Policy Review* 19, no. 2 (2001): 469–88.

Foucault, Michel. *The History of Sexuality, Vol. 1: An Introduction*. Translated by Robert Hurley. New York: Pantheon Books, 1978.

Foulkes, Imogen. "Zurich Introduces 'Drive-in' Sex." BBC News, August 26, 2013.

"France's New Approach to Curbing Prostitution." *New York Times*, December 8, 2013.

Frank, Gillian. "'The Civil Rights of Parents': Race and Conservative Politics in Anita Bryant's Campaign against Gay Rights in 1970s Florida." *Journal of the History of Sexuality* 22, no. 1 (January 2013).

Franke, Katherine M. "The Central Mistake of Sex Discrimination Law: The Disaggregation of Sex from Gender." *University of Pennsylvania Law Review* 144 (1995).

Franks, Angela. *Margaret Sanger's Eugenic Legacy: The Control of Female Fertility*. Jefferson, NC: McFarland and Co., 2005.

Fraser, Nancy. "Sex, Lies, and the Public Sphere: Some Reflections on the Confirmation of Clarence Thomas." *Critical Inquiry* 18, no. 3 (1992): 595–612.

Freedman, Estelle B. "'Crimes Which Startle and Horrify': Gender, Age, and the Racialization of Sexual Violence in White American Newspapers, 1870–1900." *Journal of the History of Sexuality* 20, no. 3 (2011): 465–97.

———. *Redefining Rape*. Cambridge, MA: Harvard University Press, 2013.

Freud, Sigmund. *"Civilized" Sexual Morality and Modern Nervousness (1908)*. Aylesburg, UK: Chrysoma Associates Limited, 2000.

————. "The Economic Problem in Masochism." In *Freud on Women: A Reader*, edited by Elisabeth Young-Bruehl. New York: W. W. Norton and Company, 1990.

————. "'Uncontrolled Desires': The Response to the Sexual Psychopath, 1920–1960." *Journal of American History* 74, no. 1 (June 1987).

Friedersdorf, Conor. "Sex and the Class of 2020: How Will Hookups Change?" *Atlantic*, October 18, 2014.

Friedman, Andrea. "'The Habitats of Sex-Crazed Perverts': Campaigns against Burlesque in Depression-Era New York City." *Journal of the History of Sexuality* 7, no. 2 (1996): 203–38.

————. "The Smearing of Joe McCarthy: The Lavender Scare, Gossip and Cold War Politics." *American Quarterly* 57, no. 4 (2005).

Frohmann, Lisa. "Discrediting Victims' Allegations of Sexual Assault: Prosecutorial Accounts of Case Rejections." *Social Problems* 38, no. 2 (May 1991): 213–26.

Fussell, Paul. *The Great War and Modern Memory*. New York: Oxford University Press, 1975.

Gage, Beverly. "What an Uncensored Letter to M.L.K. Reveals." *New York Times*, November 11, 2014.

Gamson, Joshua. "Rubber Wars: Struggles over the Condom in the United States." *Journal of the History of Sexuality* 1, no. 2 (1990): 262–82.

Ganim, Sara. "Gay Florida Teen Kaitlyn Hunt Pleads No Contest as Part of Deal." CNN, October 9, 2013.

Garbus, Martin. *Ready for the Defense*. New York: Farrar, Straus and Giroux, 1971.

Garrett, Lindsay R. "Repressed Memory Evidence in Civil Sexual Abuse Cases." *Bepress Legal Series*, March 23, 2006.

"Gay Rights Showdown in Miami." *Time*, June 13, 1977.

"Gays on the March." *Time*, September 8, 1975.

Gebhard, Paul H., John H. Gagnon, Wardell B. Pomeroy, and Cornelia V. Christenson. *Sex Offenders: An Analysis of Types*. New York: Bantam Books, 1967.

Geis, G. "Lord Hale, Witches, and Rape." *British Journal of Law and Society* 5, no. 1 (Summer 1978): 26–44.

"General Information Regarding Declarations of Family Court as to Sex to Be Shown on Birth Certificates." New Zealand Department of Internal Affairs, n.d.

"Germany to Become First European State to Allow 'Third Gender' Birth Certificates." *Russia Times*, August 18, 2013.

Gilbert, Neil. "Realities and Mythologies of Rape." *Society* 35, no. 2 (February 1998).

Giles, Geoffrey. "The Denial of Homosexuality: Same-Sex Incidents in Himmler's SS and Police." *Journal of the History of Sexuality* 11, no. 1 (2002).

Gilmore, Leigh. "Obscenity, Modernity, Identity: Legalizing 'The Well of Loneliness' and 'Nightwood.'" *Journal of the History of Sexuality* 4, no. 4 (April 1994).

Glaberson, William. "In Jogger Case, Once Viewed Starkly, Some Skeptics Side with Defendants." *New York Times*, August 8, 1990.

Gladwell, Malcom. "In Plain View." *New Yorker*, September 24, 2012.

Glassgold, Judith M., Lee Beckstead, Jack Drescher, Beverly Greene, Robin Lin Miller, and Roger L. Worthington. "Report of the American Psychological Association Task Force on Appropriate Therapeutic Responses to Sexual Orientation." American Psychological Association, 2009.

"The Global Divide on Homosexuality." *Pew Research Center: Global Attitudes Project*, June 4, 2013.

Godfrey, Phoebe. "Bayonets, Brainwashing, and Bathrooms: The Discourse of Race, Gender, and Sexuality in the Desegregation of Little Rock's Central High." *Arkansas Historical Quarterly* 62, no. 1 (2003): 42–67.

Goldman, Emma. *Living My Life*. New York: Alfred A. Knopf, 1931.

Goldstein, Joseph. "Housing Restrictions Keep Sex Offenders in Prison beyond Release Dates." *New York Times*, August 21, 2014.

Goldstein, Richard. "Queer on Death Row." *Village Voice*, March 13, 2001.

Gomstyn, Alice. "Wife Wins $9 Million From Husband's Alleged Mistress." ABC News, March 22, 2010.

Goodstein, Laurie, and Erik Eckholm. "Church Battles Efforts to Ease Sex Abuse Suits." *New York Times*, June 14, 2012.

Gordon, Linda, and Sara McLanahan. "Single Parenthood in 1900." *Journal of Family History* 16, no. 2 (1991): 97–116.

Gould, Joe. "Army Demotes General Two Grades; Will Retire as Lieutenant Colonel." *ArmyTimes*, June 20, 2014.

Grace, Francie. "N.C. Cohabitation Law Struck Down." CBS News, September 14, 2006.

Gradstein, Linda. "Nissim Yeshaya, Israeli Judge, Says 'Some Girls Enjoy Being Raped,' Resigns Amid Outcry." *World Post*, June 6, 2013.

Grant, Linda. *Sexing the Millennium*. New York: Grove Press, 1994.

Grant, Madison. *The Passing of the Great Race or the Racial Basis of European History*. Whitefish, MT: Kessinger Publishing, 2006.

Graves, Robert. *Goodbye to All That: An Autobiography*. New York: Doubleday Anchor, 1957.

———. "Recalling War." reprinted in *Guardian*, November 12, 2008.

Greenberg, Julie. "Legal Aspects of Gender Assignment." *Endocrinologist* 13, no. 3 (June 2003): 277–86.

Greenberg, Julie A. "Defining Male and Female: Intersexuality and the Collision between Law and Biology." *Arizona Law Review* 41 (1999): 265–328.

Greenhouse, Linda. "A Never-Ending Story." *New York Times*, September 5, 2012.

Grenier, Richard. "Colonel Redl: The Man behind the Screen Myth." *New York Times*, October 13, 1985.

Grinberg, Emanuella. "Report: Registry Does More Harm Than Good for Teen Sex Offenders." CNN, May 1, 2013.

Groer, Annie. "Indiana GOP Senate Hopeful Richard Mourdock Says God 'Intended' Rape Pregnancies." *Washington Post*, October 24, 2012.

Grosboll, Dick. "Sterilization Abuse: Current State of the Law and Remedies for Abuse." *Golden Gate University Law Review* 10 (1980): 1147–89.

Gross, Jane. "When the Biggest Firm Faces Sexual Harassment Suit." *New York Times*, July 29, 1994.

Gustafson, Kaaryn. "The Criminalization of Poverty." *Journal of Criminal Law and Criminology* 99, no. 3 (2009).

Guy, Donna J. *Sex and Danger in Buenos Aires: Prostitution, Family, and Nation in Argentina*. Lincoln: University of Nebraska Press, 1991.

Haas, Kate. "Who Will Make Room for the Intersexed?" *American Journal of Law and Medicine* 30, no. 1 (2004): 41–68.

Haberman, Clyde. "Baby M and the Question of Surrogate Motherhood." *New York Times*, March 23, 2014.

Hackett, Simon, S. Vosmer, and M. Callanan. "'Normal' and 'Inappropriate' Childhood Sexual Behaviours; Findings from a Delphi Study of Professionals in the United Kingdom." *Journal of Sexual Aggression* 15, no. 3 (2009): 275–88.

Haidt, Jonathan, and Matthew A. Hersh. "Sexual Morality: The Cultures and Emotions of Conservatives and Liberals." *Journal of Applied Social Psychology* 31, no. 1 (2001): 191–221.

Hall, Jacquelyn Dowd. *Revolt against Chivalry: Jessie Daniel Ames and the Women's Campaign against Lynching*. New York: Columbia University Press, 1993.

Hall, Radclyffe. *The Well of Loneliness*. London: Wordsworth Editions, 2005.

Ham, Julie. "Moving beyond 'Supply and Demand' Catchphrases: Assessing the Uses and Limitations of Demand-Based Approaches in Anti-Trafficking." Global Alliance Against Traffic in Women, 2011, footnotes 39–44.

———. "What's the Cost of a Rumour? A Guide to Sorting Out the Myths and the Facts about Sporting Events and Trafficking." Global Alliance Against Traffic in Women, 2011.

Hancock, Lynnell. "Coloring the Central Park Jogger Case." Alternet, January 15, 2003.

Hanna, Jason, Emanuella Grinberg, and Eliott C. McLaughlin. "55 Colleges under Investigation over Handling of Sexual Violence Complaints." CNN, May 2, 2014.

Hanna, Judith Lynne. *Naked Truth: Strip Clubs, Democracy, and a Christian Right*. Austin: University of Texas Press, 2012.

Hansen, Suzy. "Mixing It Up." *Salon*, March 8, 2001.

Harding, Kate. "Is Forced Sterilization Ever OK?" *Salon*, January 5, 2010.

Harris, A. J. R., and R. K. Hanson. "Clinical, Actuarial, and Dynamic Risk Assessment of Sexual Offenders: Why Do Things Keep Changing?" *Journal of Sexual Aggression* 16 (2010): 296–310.

"Harris Survey Shows Viewers Think Contraceptive Ads OK." *Broadcasting*, March 30, 1987.

Harwood, John. "A Sea Change in Less Than 50 Years as Gay Rights Gained Momentum." *New York Times*, March 25, 2013.

Hasday, Jill Elaine. "Contest and Consent: A Legal History of Marital Rape." *California Law Review* 88, no. 5 (2000).

Hatch, Orrin G. "Fighting the Pornification of America by Enforcing Obscenity Laws." *Stanford Law and Policy Review* 23, no. 1 (January 2012).

Heer, Jeet. "Sex, Economics, and Austerity." *American Prospect*, May 7, 2013.

Hegarty, Marilyn. *Victory Girls, Khaki-Wackies and Patriotutes*. New York: New York University Press, 2007.

Heins, Marjorie. *Sex, Sin, and Blasphemy: A Guide to America's Censorship Wars*. New York: New Press, 1993.

Heldman, Caroline, and Baillee Brown. "Why Schools—Not Law Enforcement—Should Investigate Campus Rapes." *Ms. Magazine*, October 17, 2014.

Hentoff, Nat. "Harassment by a Goya Painting?" *Reading Eagle*, January 4, 1992.

———. "Sexual Harassment by Francisco Goya." *Washington Post*, December 27, 1991.

Herbert, Hilary A. "The Race Problem at the South: Introductory Remarks." *Annals of the American Academy of Political and Social Science* 18, (July 1901): 95–101.

Hernandez, Sergio. "State-by-State: HIV Laws." *ProPublica*, December 1, 2013.

Herzer, Manfred. "Kertbeny and the Nameless Love." *Journal of Homosexuality* 12, no. 1 (1986).

Herzog, Dagmar. *Sexuality in Europe: A Twentieth-Century History*. Cambridge: Cambridge University Press, 2011.

Hicks, Nancy. "Sterilization of Black Mother of 3 Stirs Aiken, S.C." *New York Times*, August 1, 1973.

Hirschfeld, Magnus. *The Sexual History of the World War*. New York: Falstaff Press Inc., 1937.

Hitler, Adolf. *Mein Kampf*. Translated by James Murphy. London: Hurst and Blackett, 1942.

"HIV-Specific Criminal Laws." Centers for Disease Control and Prevention, n.d.

Hoare, Philip. *Oscar Wilde's Last Stand: Decadence, Conspiracy, and the Most Outrageous Trial of the Century.* New York: Arcade Publishing, 1997.

Hobsbawm, Eric. *The Age of Extremes: A History of the World, 1914–1991.* New York: Pantheon Books, 1991.

Hodes, Martha. *White Women, Black Men: Illicit Sex in the Nineteenth-Century South.* New Haven, CT: Yale University Press, 1997.

Hoffman, Allan M., John H. Schuh, and Robert H. Fenske. *Violence on Campus: Defining the Problems, Strategies for Action.* Gaithersburg, MD: Aspen Publishers, Inc., 1998.

Hollister, Gail D. "Parent-Child Immunity: A Doctrine in Search of Justification." *Fordham Law Review* 50, no. 4 (1982): 489–532.

"Homosexuality and Citizenship in Florida: A Report of the Florida Legislative Investigation Committee." Florida Legislative Investigation Committee, January 1964.

"Homosexuals: To Punish or to Pity." *Newsweek,* July 11, 1960.

"Houston Woman Wins $500,000 in 'Revenge Porn' Lawsuit." ABC News, February 27, 2014.

Hsu, Spencer S. "U.S. District Judge Drops Porn Charges against Video Producer John A. Stagliano." *Washington Post,* July 17, 2010.

Hughes, Donna M. *Best Practices to Address the Demand Side of Sex Trafficking.* Kingston: University of Rhode Island, 2004.

Hughes, Donna M., and Janice G. Raymond. "Sex Trafficking of Women in the United States: International and Domestic Trends." Coalition Against Trafficking in Women, March 2001.

Hunt, Alan. *Governing Morals: A Social History of Moral Regulation.* Cambridge: Cambridge University Press, 1999.

Hunter. "George Will Says Unmarried Black Women a Bigger Problem Than Any 'Absence of Rights.'" *Daily Kos,* August 26, 2013.

Hutchison, Courtney. "Sterilizing the Sick, Poor to Cut Welfare Costs: North Carolina's History of Eugenics." ABC News, August 4, 2011.

Hyde, Harford Montgomery. *The Trials of Oscar Wilde.* Courier Corporation, 1973.

ILO 2012 Global Estimage of Forced Labour Executive Summary. International Labour Organization, 2012.

"In 1972, Davis Blazed Party Trail on Gay Rights." NPR, September 5, 2012.

"International Covenant on Civil and Political Rights." United Nations: Human Rights Committee, April 23, 2014.

"An Interview with David K. Johnson, Author of The Lavender Scare: The Cold War Persecution of Gays and Lesbians in the Federal Government." Chicago: University of Chicago Press, 2004.

"Introducing the 2013 Soros Justice Fellows." Open Society Foundations, May 2013.

"Is Sexual Harassment Training Mandatory?" HRM Partners, n.d.

Jackman, Tom. "In 'Sexting' Case, Police Want to Take Photo of Teen's Erect Geneitalia, His Lawyer Says." *Washington Post*, July 9, 2014.

———. "Manassas City Police Say They Will Not Serve Search Warrant in Teen 'Sexting' Case." *Washington Post*, July 10, 2014.

Jeffreys, Sheila. *The Idea of Prostitution*. North Melbourne, Australia: Spinifex Press, 1997.

Jenkins, Philip. *Moral Panic: Changing Concepts of the Child Molester in Modern America*. New Haven, CT: Yale University Press, 1998.

"Jessica's Law, California Proposition 83 (2006)." Ballotpedia, n.d.

Joe-Cannon, Ilvi, ed. *Primer on the Male Demand for Prostitution*. Coalition Against Trafficking in Women, 2006.

Johnson. "Child Perpetrators—Children Who Molest Other Children: Preliminary Findings." *Child Abuse and Neglect* 12, no. 2 (1988): 219–29.

Johnson, David K. *The Lavender Scare: The Cold War Persecution of Gays and Lesbians in the Federal Government*. Chicago: University of Chicago Press, 2009.

Johnson, Dirk. "A Sexual Harassment Case to Test Academic Freedom." *New York Times*, May 11, 1994.

Johnson, Marcia K., Carol L. Raye, Karen J. Mitchell, and Elizabeth Ankudowich. "The Cognitive Neuroscience of True and False Memories." In *True and False Recovered Memories: Toward a Reconciliation of the Debate*, edited by Robert F. Belli. New York: Springer Science and Business Media, 2011.

Johnson, Toni Cavanagh. "Sexuality in Children: From Normal to Pathological." Paper presented at the Western Region, Los Angeles Chapter meeting of the Society for the Scientific Study of Sex. 1991.

———. *Understanding Children's Sexual Behaviors: What's Natural and Healthy*. Institute on Violence, 2013.

———. "Understanding the Sexual Behaviors of Young Children." Sexual Information and Education Council of the United States, 1991.

———. Female Child Perpetrators: Children Who Molest Other Children." *Child Abuse and Neglect* 13 (1989): 571–85.

Johnson, Toni Cavanagh, and Ronda Doonan. "Children Twelve and Younger with Sexual Behavior Problems: What We Know in 2005 That We Didn't Know in 1985." In *Current Perspectives: Working with Sexually Aggressive Youth and Youth with Sexual Behavior Problems*, edited by Robert E. Longo and David S. Prescott. Holyoke, MA: NEARI Press, 2006.

Johnson, Toni Cavanagh, Eliana Gil, and William N. Friedrich. *Sexualized Children: Assessment and Treatment of Sexualized Children and Children Who Molest*. Rockville, MD: Launch Press, 1993.

Jones, James. *The Thin Red Line.* New York: Delta, 1962.

Jones, James H. *Bad Blood: The Tuskegee Syphilis Experiment.* New York: Free Press, 1981.

Jones, Robert P., Daniel Cox, and Juhem Navarro-Rivera. "A Shifting Landscape: A Decade of Change in American Attitudes about Same-Sex Marriage and LGBT Issues." Public Religion Research Institute, 2013.

"Kaitlyn Hunt, Florida Teen, Faces Felony Charges over Same-Sex Relationship." *Huffington Post*, May 19, 2013.

"Kaitlyn Hunt, Gay Florida Teen Accused of Underage Sex, Loses Plea Deal." *Huffington Post*, August 19, 2013.

"Kaitlyn Hunt Refuses Plea Deal: Gay Teen Charged over Underage Relationship Will Appear in Court." *Huffington Post*, May 24, 2013.

Kalven, Harry, and Hans Zeisel. *The American Jury.* Boston: Little, Brown, 1966.

Kaminer, Ariel. "New Factor in Campus Sexual Assault Cases: Counsel for the Accused." *New York Times*, November 19, 2014.

Kapur, Sahil. "Judge Richard Posner Pokes Scalia in Major Decision for Gay Marriage." *Talking Points Memo*, September 4, 2014.

Kemp, David S. "The Failure of Criminal HIV Transmission Laws." *Verdict: Legal Analysis and Commentary from Justia*, September 10, 2012.

Kempf, Edward J. *Psychopathology.* St. Louis: C. V. Mosby Company, 1920.

Kempster, Norman. "Lying, Not Adultery, Is Female Pilot's Top Crime, AF Says." *Los Angeles Times*, May 22, 1997.

Kenworthy, Tom, and Patrick O'Driscoll. "Judge Dismisses Bryant Rape Case." *USA Today*, September 1, 2004.

Kessler, Suzanne J. *Lessons from the Intersexed.* New Brunswick, NJ: Rutgers University Press, 1998.

Kim, Ann S. "Police Name 21 Alleged Kennebunk 'Johns,' but Confusion Follows." CentralMaine.com, October 15, 2012.

Kincaid, James R. *Erotic Innocence: The Culture of Child Molesting.* Durham, NC: Duke University Press, 1998.

Kingkade, Tyler. "Fewer Than One-Third of Campus Sexual Assault Cases Result in Expulsion." *Huffington Post*, September 29, 2014.

———. "Yale Law Students: Professor's Campus Rape Op-Ed Gets It Wrong." *Huffington Post*, November 17, 2014.

Kinsey, Alfred Charles. *Sexual Behavior in the Human Female.* Bloomington: Indiana University Press, 1953.

Kirka, Danica, and Jim Gomez. "Operation Endeavor: Authorities Dismantle International Pedophile Ring That Live-Streamed Sex Abuse." *Huffington Post*, January 16, 2014.

Knezevic, Jovana. "Prostitutes as a Threat to National Honor in Habsburg-Occupied Serbia during the Great War." *Journal of the History of Sexuality* 20, no. 2 (2011).

Knowles, David. "Under Pressure, New Mexico Rep. Amends Bill That Would Have Charged Rape Victims Who Had Abortions with 'Tampering with Evidence.'" *New York Daily News*, January 25, 2013.

Kollontai, Aleksandra M. *Communism and the Family*. New York: Andrade's Bookshop, 1920.

Kon, Igor S. *The Sexual Revolution in Russia: From the Age of the Czars to Today*. New York: Free Press, 1995.

Kono, Yohei. "Statement by the Chief Cabinet Secretary Yohei Kono on the Result of the Study on the Issue of 'Comfort Women.'" Ministry of Foreign Affairs of Japan, August 4, 1993.

Koop, C. Everett. "Surgeon General's Report on Acquired Immune Deficiency Syndrome," Office of the Surgeon General, 1986.

Kornbluh, Felicia Ann. *The Battle for Welfare Rights: Politics and Poverty in Modern America*. Philadelphia: University of Pennsylvania Press, 2007.

Koshy, Susan. *Sexual Naturalization: Asian Americans and Miscegenation*. Stanford, CA: Stanford University Press, 2004.

Koss, Mary P., Christine A. Gidycz, and Nadine Wisniewski. "The Scope of Rape: Incidence and Prevalence of Sexual Aggression and Victimization in a National Sample of Higher Education Students." *Journal of Consulting and Clinical Psychology* 55, no. 2 (1987): 162–70.

Kotz, Pete. "The Super Bowl Prostitute Myth: 100,000 Hookers Won't Be Showing Up in Dallas." *Dallas Observer*, January 27, 2011.

Krafft-Ebing, R. von. *Psychopathia Sexualis*. Philadelphia: F. A. Davis Company, Publishers, 1894.

Kramer, Andrew E. "Pro-Government Ukrainians Take to Streets to Denounce European Social Values." *New York Times*, December 6, 2013.

Krebs, Albin. "Clarence Norris, Last Survivor of 'Scottsboro Boys,' Dies at 76." *New York Times*, January 26, 1989.

Krebs, Christopher P., Christine H. Lindquist, Tara D. Warner, Bonnie S. Fisher, and Sandra L. Martin. "The Campus Sexual Assault (CSA) Study." National Criminal Justice Reference Service, 2007.

Kristof, Nicholas D. "Back to the Brothel." *New York Times*, January 22, 2005.

———. *Half the Sky: Turning Oppression into Opportunity for Women Worldwide*. New York: Alfred A. Knopf, 2009.

Kuhl, Stefan. *The Nazi Connection: Eugenics, American Racism, and German National Socialism*. New York: Oxford University Press, 1994.

Kusch, Frank. *All American Boys: Draft Dodgers in Canada from the Vietnam War*. Santa Barbara, CA: Greenwood Publishing Group, 2001.

Kushner, David. "Casualty of Porn." *Rolling Stone*, December 5, 2005.

Kyle, Keegan, Tony Saavedra, and Denisse Salazar. "Where Are Sex Offenders? Jessica's Law Complicates Monitoring." *Orange County Register*, April 26, 2014.

Ladd-Taylor, Molly, and Lauri Umansky, eds. *"Bad" Mothers: The Politics of Blame in Twentieth-Century America.* New York: New York University Press, 1998.

Lancaster, Roger N. *Sex Panic and the Punitive State.* Berkeley: University of California Press, 2011.

"LAPD Chief Compares Gays, Lepers." *Advocate,* January 5, 1972.

Laqueur, Thomas W. *Solitary Sex: A Cultural History of Masturbation.* New York: Zone Books, 2003.

Larson, Edward J. *Sex, Race, and Science: Eugenics in the Deep South.* Baltimore: Johns Hopkins University Press, 1995.

Lave, Tamara Rice. "Only Yesterday: The Rise and Fall of Twentieth Century Sexual Psychopath Laws." *Louisiana Law Review* 69 (2009): 550–591.

Lawrence v. Texas, 539 U.S. 558 (2003).

Lee, Cynthia. "The Gay Panic Defense." *University of California, Davis Law Review* 42 (2008): 471–517.

———. "Masculinity on Trial: Gay Panic in the Criminal Courtroom." *Southwestern Law Review* 42 (2013): 817–31.

Lee, Jolie. "In Which States Is Cheating on Your Spouse Illegal?" *Detroit Free Press,* April 17, 2014.

Lee, Peter A., Christopher P. Houk, S. Faisal Ahmed, and Ieuan A. Hughes. "Consensus Statement on Management of Intersex Disorders." *Pediatrics* 118, no. 2 (2006): 488–500.

Lefkovitz, Alison. "Men in the House: Race, Welfare, and the Regulation of Men's Sexuality in the United States, 1961–1972." *Journal of the History of Sexuality* 20, no. 3 (September 2011): 594–614.

"Legal Issues Pertaining to Retractors." False Memory Syndrome Foundation, February 5, 2014.

Lehrman, Sally. "Gender Research." *Stanford Today Online,* 1997.

Lenhardt, R. A. "Beyond Analogy: Perez v. Sharp, Antimiscegenation Law, and the Fight for Same-Sex Marriage." *California Law Review* 96, no. 4 (August 2008).

Leon, Chrysanthi S. *Sex Fiends, Perverts, and Pedophiles: Understanding Sex Crime Policy in America.* New York: New York University Press, 2011.

"Let Them Eat Wedding Rings." Alternatives to Marriage Project, June 2007.

Levendowski, Amanda. "Arizona's Revenge Porn Law Isn't a Solution—It's a Different Kind of Problem." *Vice News,* September 29, 2014.

Levine, Judith. *Harmful to Minors: The Perils of Protecting Children from Sex.* New York: Thunder's Mouth Press, 2002.

Levin, Josh. "The Welfare Queen." *Slate,* December 19, 2013.

Levy, Ariel. "Trial by Twitter." *New Yorker,* August 5, 2013.

Lewis, Earl, and Heidi Ardizzone. *Love on Trial: An American Scandal in Black and White.* New York: W. W. Norton and Company, 2001.

Lewis, Fulton Jr. "Washington Report." *Reading Eagle*, June 20, 1966.

Lieb, Roxanne, and Scott Matson. "Sexual Predator Commitment Laws in the United States: 1998 Update." Washington State Institute for Public Policy, September 1998.

Liew, Jonathan. "All Men Watch Porn, Scientists Find." *Telegraph*, December 2, 2009.

Lighty, Todd, Stacy St. Clair, and Jodi S. Cohen. "Few Arrests, Convictions in Campus Sex Assault Cases." *Chicago Tribune*, June 16, 2011.

"The Link between Prostitution and Sex Trafficking." US Department of State, Bureau of Public Affairs, November 24, 2004.

Liptak, Adam. "Children Not Entitled to Dead Father's Benefits, Justices Rule." *New York Times*, May 21, 2012.

———. "Exhibit A for a Major Shift: Justices' Gay Clerks." *New York Times*, June 8, 2013.

Lithwick, Dahlia. "The Shield That Failed." *New York Times*, August 8, 2004.

Little, Rivka Gewirtz. "Rage before Race." *Village Voice*, October 15, 2002.

Lombardo, Paul A. "'The American Breed': Nazi Eugenics and the Origins of the Pioneer Fund." *Albany Law Review* 65, no. 3 (2002): 743–830.

———. "Miscegenation, Eugenics, and Racism: Historical Footnotes to Loving v. Virginia." *University of California, Davis Law Review* 21 (1988): 421–52.

"Lord Montagu on the Court Case Which Ended the Legal Persecution of Homosexuals." *Daily Mail Online*, July 17, 2007.

Loughery, John. *The Other Side of Silence: Men's Lives and Gay Identities, a Twentieth-Century History*. New York: Henry Holt, 1998.

"Louisiana: Calls for Resignation." *New York Times*, October 17, 2009.

Lounsbury, Kaitlin, Kimberly J. Mitchell, and David Finkelhor. "The True Prevalence of 'Sexting.'" Crimes Against Children Research Center, April 2011.

Lovett, Ian. "After 37 Years of Trying to Change People's Sexual Orientation, Group Is to Disband." *New York Times*, June 20, 2013.

———. "Neighborhoods Seek to Banish Sex Offenders by Building Parks." *New York Times*, March 9, 2013.

Lowrey, Annie. "Can Marriage Cure Poverty?" *New York Times*, February 4, 2014.

Luhan, Mabel Dodge. *Movers and Shakers*. Albuquerque: University of New Mexico Press, 1936.

Luibhéid, Eithne. *Entry Denied: Controlling Sexuality at the Border*. Minneapolis: University of Minnesota Press, 2002.

Lydon, Mary. "On Censorship: Staying Power." *SubStance* 12, no. 37/38: A special issue from the Center for Twentieth Century Studies (1983): 107–17.

"'M' Quotes." IMDB, n.d.

MacDonald, Heather. "The Campus Rape Myth." *City Journal*, Winter 2008.

Macfarlane, Peter Clark. "Diagnosis by Dreams." *Good Housekeeping*, February 1915.

MacKinnon, Catharine A. "Feminism, Marxism, Method, and the State: Toward Feminist Jurisprudence." *Signs* 8, no. 4 (Summer 1983): 635–58.

———. *Only Words*. Cambridge, MA: Harvard University Press, 1993.

———. *Sexual Harassment of Working Women*. New haven, CT: Yale University Press, 1979.

———. "Trafficking, Prostitution, and Inequality." *Harvard Civil Rights-Civil Liberties Law Review* (2011).

Maillard, Kevin Noble. "The Pocahontas Exception: American Indians and Exceptionalism in Virginia's Racial Integrity Act of 1924." *Michigan Journal of Race and Law* 12, no. 107 (2007).

"Map of Registered Sex Offenders in the United States." National Center for Missing and Exploited Children, n.d.

"The Marital Rape Exemption." *New York University Law Review* 52 (1977): 306–23.

"Martensville Scandal: Sold Out and Talked into Lovin' It." Injustice Busters, n.d.

Martin, Douglas. "Mildred Loving, Who Battled Ban on Mixed-Race Marriage, Dies at 68." *New York Times*, May 6, 2008.

Martinez Cantera, Angel L. "Nepal's 'Third Gender.'" Aljazeera, March 12, 2014.

Marvin v. Marvin, 18 Cal. 3rd 660 (1976).

Matard-Bonucci, Marie-Anne. "Italian Fascism's Ethiopian Conquest and the Dream of a Prescribed Sexuality." In *Brutality and Desire: War and Sexuality in Europe's Twentieth Century*, edited by Dagmar Herzog. London: Palgrave Macmillan, 2009.

Matthews, James. "Mixed Marriage 'More Accepted' in Britain." *Sky News*, December 11, 2012.

Mayer, Jane, and Jill Abramson. *Strange Justice: The Selling of Clarence Thomas*. New York: Houghton Mifflin Company, 1994.

McRobbie, Linda Rodriguez. "The Real Victims of Satanic Ritual Abuse." *Slate*, January 7, 2014.

Medina, Jennifer. "Warning: The Literary Canon Could Make Students Squirm." *New York Times*, May 17, 2014.

Memmott, Mark. "In Hawaii, Sex with a Prostitute May Be Legal for Undercover Cops." NPR, March 21, 2014.

Memon, Amina, and Mark Young. "Desperately Seeking Evidence: The Recovered Memory Debate." *Legal and Criminological Psychology* 2, no. 2 (1997): 131–54.

"Military Color Guard to March in Gay Pride Parade." *Military.com News*, June 7, 2014.

Miller, Daniel. "The Spectacular Rise and Surprising Exit of a Hollywood Executive." *Los Angeles Times*, August 23, 2013.

Miller, Neil. *Out of the Past: Gay and Lesbian History from 1869 to the Present.* New York: Alyson Books, 2006.

Miller, Rich. "Is Everybody Single? More Than Half the U.S. Now, up from 37% in '76." *Bloomberg*, September 8, 2014.

Milloy, Christin Scarlett. "Don't Let the Doctor Do This to Your Newborn." *Slate*, June 26, 2014.

Ministry of Justice. "New Law to Tackle Revenge Porn." Gov.uk, October 12, 2014.

"Mississippi Law Will Require Collection of Umbilical Blood from Babies Born to Young Mothers." *Huffington Post*, June 7, 2013.

"Mixed Blessings." *Guardian*, August 2, 2005.

Mogulescu, Kate. "The Super Bowl and Sex Trafficking." *New York Times*, January 31, 2014.

Mogul, Joey L., Andrea J. Ritchie, and Kay Whitlock. *Queer (In)justice: The Criminalization of LGBT People in the United States.* Boston: Beacon Press, 2011.

Moll, David. "U.S. Gives Thailand and Malaysia Lowest Grade on Human Trafficking." *New York Times*, June 20, 2014.

Money, John. *Love and Love Sickness: The Science of Sex, Gender Difference, and Pair-Bonding.* Baltimore: Johns Hopkins University Press, 1980.

Money, John, and Anke A. Ehrhardt. *Man and Woman, Boy and Girl: Gender Identity from Conception to Maturity.* Lanham, MD: Jason Aronson, 1996.

Money, John, and Patricia Tucker. *Sexual Signatures on Being a Man or a Woman.* Boston: Little, Brown and Company, 1975.

Montefiore, Simon Sebag. *Stalin: The Court of the Red Tsar.* London: Phoenix, 2003.

"Morals: The Second Sexual Revolution." *Time*, January 24, 1964.

Moran, Rachel F. *Interracial Intimacy: The Regulation of Race and Romance.* Chicago: University of Chicago Press, 2001.

Morgan. "We Welcome New Federal Guidelines on Sex and Gender Recognition." Organization Intersex International Australia, June 13, 2013.

Morris, A. T. "The Empirical, Historical and Legal Case against the Cautionary Instruction: A Call for Legislative Reform." *Duke Law Journal* 1988, no. 1 (1988): 154–73.

Murdoch, Joyce, and Deb Price. *Courting Justice: Gay Men and Lesbians V. The Supreme Court.* New York: Basic Books, 2001.

Murphy, Kim. "Palimony Suit against Liberace Settled." *Los Angeles Times*, December 30, 1986.

Murphy, Lawrence. "Cleaning Up Newport: The U.S. Navy's Persecution of Homosexuals after World War I." *Journal of American Culture* 7, no. 3 (1984): 57–64.

Murphy, Meghan. "Prostitution Is More Than a Labour Rights Issue." Aljazeera, August 7, 2014.

Murphy, Timothy F. "Brief History of a Recurring Nightmare." *Gay and Lesbian Review*, January 1, 2008.

Murray, Stephen O. *American Gay*. Chicago: University of Chicago Press, 1996.

Myrdal, Gunnar. *An American Dilemma: The Negro Problem and Modern Democracy*. New York: Harper and Brothers Publishers, 1944.

Nandi, Jacinta. "Germany Got It Right by Offering a Third Gender Option on Birth Certificates." *Guardian*, November 10, 2013.

Narayan, Chandrika. "Kansas Court Says Sperm Donor Must Pay Child Support." CNN, January 24, 2014.

Nathan, Debbie. "The New York Times, Kurt Eichenwald and the World of Justin Berry: Hysteria, Exploitation and Witch-Hunting in the Age of Internet Sex." *CounterPunch* 14, no. 7/8 (April 2007): 1–12.

"National HIV/AIDS Strategy for the United States." Whitehouse.gov, July 2010.

Neuhaus, John. "God Save This Vulnerable Court." *National Review*, August 15, 1986.

Nichols, James. "Dmitri Kisilev, Russian Official, Degrades Gays on National Television." *Huffington Post*, August 12, 2013.

Nietzsche, Friedrich. *Nietzsche: The Gay Science*. Cambridge: Cambridge University Press, 2001.

Noe, Eric. "Condom Ads Hit Network TV." ABC News, June 1, 2005.

Novkov, Julie. "Racial Constructions: The Legal Regulation of Miscegenation in Alabama, 1890–1934." *Law and History Review* 20, no. 2 (2002): 225–77.

"Number of Priests Accused of Sexually Abusing Children as Reported by the U.S. Conference of Catholic Bishops with Numbers of Persons Alleging Abuse." BishopAccountability.org, March 28, 2014.

Nussbaum, Martha C. *Hiding from Humanity: Disgust, Shame, and the Law*. Princeton, NJ: Princeton University Press, 2004.

Odem, Mary E. *Delinquent Daughters: Protecting and Policing Adolescent Female Sexuality in the United States, 1885–1920*. Chapel Hill: University of North Carolina Press, 1995.

Okami, Paul. "'Child Perpetrators of Sexual Abuse': The Emergence of a Problematic Deviant Category." *Journal of Sex Research* 29, no. 1 (February 1992): 109–30.

————. "Childhood Exposure to Parental Nudity, Parent-Child Co-Sleeping, and 'Primal Scenes': A Review of Clinical Opinion and Empirical Evidence." *Journal of Sex Research* 32, no. 1 (1995): 51–64.

Okami, Paul, and Amy Goldberg. "Personality Correlates of Pedophilia: Are They Reliable Indicators?" *Journal of Sex Research* 29, no. 3 (1992): 297–328.

Onwauchi-Willig, Angela. "The Return of the Ring: Welfare Reform's Marriage Cure as the Revival of Post-Bellum Control." *California Law Review* 93 (2005): 1647–96.

Oosterhuis, Harry. "Stepchildren of Nature: Krafft-Ebing, Psychiatry, and the Making of Sexual Identity (2000)." In *The History of Sexuality in Europe: A Sourcebook and Reader*, edited by Anna Clark. London: Routledge, 2011.

Oppel, Richard A. Jr. "Ohio Teenagers Guilty in Rape That Social Media Brought to Light." *New York Times*, March 17, 2013.

Ordover, Nancy. *American Eugenics: Race, Queer Anatomy, and the Science of Nationalism*. Minneapolis: University of Minnesota Press, 2003.

"Oregon Court Releases 20,000 Pages from Boy Scouts 'Perversion Files.'" *Daily News*, June 14, 2012.

Orenstein, Dara. "Void for Vagueness: Mexicans and the Collapse of Miscegenation Law in California." *Pacific Historical Review* 74, no. 3 (2005): 367–407.

Osumi, Megumi Dick. "Asians and California's Anti-Miscegenation Laws." Edited by Nobuya Tsuchida. *Asian and Pacific American Experiences: Women's Perspectives* 1 (1982).

Otterman, Sharon. "Abuse Verdict Topples a Hasidic Wall of Secrecy." *New York Times*, December 10, 2012.

Pai, Hsiao-Hung. *Invisible: Britain's Migrant Sex Workers*. London: Westbourne Press, 2013.

Pappas, Stephanie. "23andMe Genetic Test Reveals Disturbing Artificial Insemination Switch." *Fox News*, January 10, 2014.

Parenti, Christian. "Rape as a Disciplinary Tactic." *Salon*, August 23, 1999.

Parker, Ian. "The Story of a Suicide." *New Yorker*, February 6, 2013.

Parker, Kristin H. Berger. "Ambient Harassment under Title VII: Reconsidering the Workplace Environment." *Northwestern University Law Review* 102, no. 2 (2008): 945–86.

Pascoe, Peggy. "Miscegenation Law, Court Cases, and Ideologies of 'Race' in Twentieth-Century America." In *Interracialism: Black-White Intermarriage in American History, Literature, and Law*, edited by Werner Sollors. New York: Oxford University Press, 2000.

————. "Race, Gender, and Intercultural Relations: The Case of Interracial Marriage." *Frontiers: A Journal of Women Studies* 12, no. 1 (1991): 5–18.

Patton, Michael S. "Twentieth-Century Attitudes toward Masturbation." *Journal of Religion and Health* 25, no. 4 (Winter 1986): 291–302.

Payton, George T., and Michael Amaral. *Patrol Operations and Enforcement Tactics.* San Jose, CA: Criminal Justice Services, 1993.

Peckenpaugh, Jason. "Controlling Sex Offender Re-Entry: Jessica's Law Measures in California." *Journal of Offender Monitoring* 19, no. 1 (2006): 13–29.

Petchesky, Rosalind Pollack. *Abortion and Woman's Choice: The State, Sexuality, and Reproductive Freedom.* Boston: Northeastern University Press, 1990.

"Philippines Web Abuse Ring Smashed in UK-Led Operation." BBC News, January 15, 2014.

Pinker, Steven. *The Better Angels of Our Nature: Why Violence Has Declined.* Penguin Books, 2012.

Plato. "783a." In *Laws,* edited by Gregory R. Crane. Perseus Digital Project, Tufts University, n.d.

Pleck, Elizabeth H. *Not Just Roommates: Cohabitation after the Sexual Revolution.* Chicago: University of Chicago Press, 2012.

"A Pledge of Allegiance to Partisan Policy." *New York Times,* June 20, 2013.

Ploscowe, Morris. *Sex and the Law.* New York: Prentice-Hall, Inc., 1951.

———. *Sex and the Law.* New York: Ace Books, 1962.

———. "Sex Offenses: The American Legal Context." *Law and Contemporary Problems* 25 (Spring 1960): 217–24.

Pogrebin, Letty Cottin. "Sex Harassment." In *Debating Sexual Correctness: Pornography, Sexual Harassment, Date Rape and the Politics of Sexual Equality,* edited by Adele M. Stan. New York: Delta, 1995.

"Poland Ends Subsidies for Birth Control Pills." *New York Times,* May 9, 1991.

"Police Discretion and Judgment That a Crime Has Been Committed—Rape in Philadelphia." *University of Pennsylvania Law Review* 117, no. 2 (December 1968): 277–322.

"Police Uncover Sex Ring." *Hour,* July 5, 1999.

Pollini, Robin A., Estela Blanco, Carol Crump, and María Luisa Zúniga. "A Community-Based Study of Barriers to HIV Care Initiation." *AIDS Patient Care and STDs* 25, no. 10 (2011): 601–9.

"Porn Producer Invokes the Bush/Yoo Defense—Unsuccessfully." *Salon,* October 5, 2008.

"Porn Sites Get More Visitors Each Month Than Netflix, Amazon and Twitter Combined." *Huffington Post,* May 4, 2013.

Posner, Richard A. *Sex and Reason.* Cambridge, MA: Harvard University Press, 1992.

Posner, Richard A., and Katharine B. Silbaugh. *A Guide to America's Sex Laws*. Chicago: University of Chicago Press, 1996.

"Post Tailhook Punishment." PBS, n.d.

Potter, Claire Bond. "Queer Hoover: Sex, Lies, and Political History." *Journal of the History of Sexuality* 15, no. 3 (2006).

Poullard, Paul. "Judgments about Victims and Attackers in Depicted Rapes: A Review." *British Journal of Social Psychology* (1992): 307, 310.

Povoledo, Elisabetta. "Pope Francis to Meet Victims of Sexual Abuse." *New York Times*, May 27, 2014.

Powell, John. "Japanese Immigration." *Encyclopedia of North American Immigration*. New York: Infobase Publishing, 2009.

"PREA Data Collection Activities, 2014." US Department of Justice, Bureau of Justice Statistics, May 2014.

Prescott, J. J., and Jonah E. Ruckoff. "Do Sex Offender Registration and Notification Laws Affect Criminal Behavior?" *Journal of Law and Economics* 54, no. 1 (2011): 161–206.

"President George W. Bush's Address to the United Nations." White House Online, September 2003, http://www.johnstonsarchive.net/terrorism/bushiraq6.html.

"Press Release: ACLU of Florida Statement on Prosecution of 18-Year-Old Kaitlyn Hunt." American Civil Liberties Union of Florida, May 21, 2013.

"Press Release: MS GOP: Bryant for Gov., Barbour or Huckabee for Pres." Public Policy Polling, April 7, 2011.

Preston, Julia. "Obama Lifts a Ban on Entry into U.S. by H.I.V.-Positive People." *New York Times*, October 30, 2009.

"Prevention: Fighting Sex Trafficking by Curbing Demand for Prostitution." United States Department of State: Office to Monitor and Combat Trafficking in Persons, June 2011.

Prewitt, Shauna R. "Giving Birth to a 'Rapist's Child': A Discussion and Analysis of the Limited Legal Protections Afforded to Women Who Become Mothers through Rape." *Georgetown Law Journal* 98 (2010): 827–62.

Prosser, William L. *Handbook of the Law of Torts*. 4th ed. St. Paul, MN: West Publishing, 1971.

"Prostitution and Male Supremacy." *Michigan Journal of Gender and Law*, (1992).

"Public Health Crisis: The Impact of Using Condoms as Evidence of Prostitution in New York City." Sex Workers Project, April 2012.

Pugh, M. D. "Contributory Fault and Rape Convictions: Loglinear Models for Blaming the Victim." *Social Psychology Quarterly* 46, no. 3 (1983): 233–42.

Puhl, Jan. "Beyond the Church's Reach: Fleeing West from Poland's Restrictive Abortion Laws." *Spiegel Online International*, October 20, 2010.

Pullella, Philip. "Pope Francis Calls Clergy Sex Abuse 'A Leprosy,' Says 2 Percent of Priests Are Pedophiles in Eugenio Scalfari Interview." *Huffington Post*, July 13, 2014.

———. "Pope Says Gays Should Not Be Marginalized." *Reuters*, July 29, 2013.

Purdum, Todd S. "Registry Laws Tar Sex-Crime Convicts with Broad Brush." *New York Times*, July 1, 1997.

"Q&A Abortion in the Netherlands." *Ministry of Foreign Affairs*. August 2011.

Railey, John, and Kevin Begos. "Sign This or Else . . ." *Winston-Salem Journal*, March 19, 2013.

———. "Still Hiding." *Winston-Salem Journal*, March 19, 2013.

"Raised on the Registry: The Irreparable Harm of Placing Children on Sex Offender Registries in the US." Human Rights Watch, May 2013.

Ramakrishnan, Kavita B. "Inconsistent Legal Treatment of Unwanted Sexual Advances: A Study of the Homosexual Advance Defense, Street Harassment, and Sexual Harassment in the Workplace." *Berkeley Journal of Gender, Law and Justice* 26, no. 2 (September 2013): 291–355.

"Rape and Battery between Husband and Wife." *Stanford Law Review* 6, no. 4 (1954).

Reavy, Pat. "Inmate Once Raped by Prison Guard Found Dead in Cell." *Deseret News*, September 21, 2012.

Reich, Charles A. "Midnight Welfare Searches and the Social Security Act." *Yale Law Journal* 72, no. 7 (June 1963): 1347–60.

Reich, Wilhelm. *The Mass Psychology of Fascism*. New York: Orgone Institute Press, 1946.

———. *Selected Writings: An Introduction to Orgonomy*. New York: Macmillan, 2013.

Reid, T. R. "Rape Case against Bryant Is Dropped." *Washington Post*, September 2, 2004.

Reilly, Ryan J. "Seven Republican Governors Won't Comply with Anti-Rape Rules." *Huffington Post*, May 28, 2014.

"Remarks by the President in Apology for Study Done in Tuskegee." White House: Office of the Press Secretary, May 16, 1997.

Rembar, Charles. *The End of Obscenity: The Trials of Lady Chatterley, Tropic of Cancer, and Fanny Hill*. New York: Simon and Schuster, 1968.

Remnick, David. *Lenin's Tomb: The Last Days of the Soviet Empire*. New York: Vintage Books, 1994.

"A Report by Empower Chiang Mai on the Human Rights Violations Women Are Subjected to When 'Rescued' by Anti-Trafficking Groups Who Employ Methods Using Deception, Force and Coercion."

Empower Chiang Mai, n.d. http://www.nswp.org/sites/nswp.org/files/ RESCUE-REPORT.pdf.

Report on Activities to Combat Human Trafficking: Fiscal Years 2001– 2005. US Department of Justice, Civil Rights Division, 2006.

Reuters. "Secrets of Nazi Camp Brothels Emerge in German Exhibition." *Haaretz*, July 11, 2007.

Reverby, Susan M. "'Normal Exposure' and Inoculation Syphilis: A PHS 'Tuskegee' Doctor in Guatemala, 1946–1948." *Journal of Policy History* 23, no. 1 (2011): 6–28.

Reynolds, Dave. "Oregon Governor Apologizes for Eugenics 'Misdeeds.'" *Inclusion Daily Express*, December 2, 2002.

Richardson, Ted, Michelle Johnson, and Katherine Elkins. "Against Their Will: Elaine's Story." *Winston-Salem Journal*, March 21, 2013.

Rich, Camille Gear. "Innocence Interrupted: Reconstructing Fatherhood in the Shadow of Child Molestation Law." *California Law Review* 101, no. 3 (2013).

Rich, Frank. "Endpaper: Public Stages; Men in Uniform." *New York Times*, April 11, 1993.

———. "Journal; the Girl Next Door." *New York Times*, February 20, 1994.

———. "Mae West 'Sex' Capade!" *New York Magazine*, April 1, 2012.

Richtel, Matt. "What's Obscene? Google Could Have an Answer." *New York Times*, June 24, 2008.

Riddell, Kelly. "Shades of Shawshank: Guards, Staff Committed Half of All Prison Sex Assaults." *Washington Times*, January 23, 2014.

Robin, Corey. *The Reactionary Mind: Conservatism from Edmund Burke to Sarah Palin*. New York: Oxford University Press, 2011.

Rogin, Josh. "Exclusive: 'Hillary Clinton Took Me through Hell,' Rape Victim Says." *Daily Beast*, June 20, 2014.

Rosenfeld, Michael J. "Nontraditional Families and Childhood Progress through School." *Demography* 47, no. 3 (August 2010): 755–75.

Rosin, Hanna. "Why Kids Sext." *Atlantic*, October 14, 2014.

Roth, Martha T. *Law Collections from Mesopotamia and Asia Minor*. Atlanta: Scholars Press, 1997.

Roth, Philip. *The Human Stain*. New York: Vintage International, 2000.

"Royal College of Psychiatrists' Statement on Sexual Orientation." Royal College of Psychiatrists, April 2014.

Rubenfeld, Jed. "Mishandling Rape." *New York Times*, November 15, 2014.

Rudoren, Jodi. "Standoff at Western Wall over Praying by Women." *New York Times*, May 10, 2013.

Rush, Emma, and Andrea La Nauze. "Corporate Paedophilia: Sexualization of Children in Australia." Australia Institute, October 2006.

Russell, Diana E. H. *Rape in Marriage.* Bloomington: Indiana University Press, 1990.

"Russia's Putin Signs Law Limiting Adoption by Gays." Associated Press, July 3, 2014.

Ryan, Gail, Tom F. Leversee, and Sandy Lane. *Juvenile Sexual Offending: Causes, Consequences, and Correction.* Hoboken, NJ: Wiley, 2010.

Ryan, Rebecca. "The Sex Right: A Legal History of the Marital Rape Exemption." *Law and Social Inquiry* 20, no. 4 (1995).

"Same-Sex Ceremony Held at Fort Bragg's Chapel." *Military.com News,* December 23, 2013.

"Sample Interviews by Investigators with Former Students of the McMartin Preschool." University of Missouri–Kansas City School of Law, n.d.

Sanders, Holly. "Panpan: Streetwalking in Occupied Japan." *Pacific Historical Review* 81, no. 3 (August 2012).

Sanger, Margaret. "The Eugenic Value of Birth Control Propaganda." *Birth Control Review,* October 1921.

———. *Woman, Morality, and Birth Control.* American Birth Control League, 1922.

Sankoorikal, Teena-Ann V. "Using Scientific Advances to Conceive the Perfect Donor: The Pandora's Box of Creating Child Donors for the Purpose of Saving Ailing Family Members." *Seton Hall Law Review* 32, no. 3 (2011).

Sapien, Joaquin. "Efforts to End Rampant Prison Rape Stall Out—Again." *Salon,* May 20, 2014.

Saul, Josh. "Hasidic Counselor Nechemya Weberman Gets 103 Years in Child Sex-Abuse Case." *New York Post,* January 22, 2013.

Saul, Stephanie. "Building a Baby, with Few Ground Rules." *New York Times,* December 12, 2009.

Sayre, Gordon. "Native American Sexuality in the Eyes of the Beholder 1535–1710." In *Sex and Sexuality in Early America,* edited by Merril D. Smith. New York: New York University Press, 1998.

Scales-Trent, Judy. "Racial Purity Laws in the United States and Nazi Germany: The Targeting Process." *Human Rights Quarterly* 23, no. 2 (May 2001): 259–307.

Schanberg, Sydney H. "A Journey through the Tangled Case of the Central Park Jogger." *Village Voice,* November 19, 2002.

Scheller, Alissa. "48 States Still Allow This Ridiculous Thing, but California's Now Free to Ban It." *Huffington Post,* July 3, 2014.

Schmidt, Heike I. "Colonial Intimacy: The Rechenberg Scandal and Homosexuality in German East Africa." *Journal of the History of Sexuality* 17, no. 1 (January 2008): 25–59.

Schnur, James A. "Closet Crusaders: The Johns Committee and Homophobia, 1956–1965." In *Carryin' On in the Lesbian and Gay South*, edited by John Howard, 133–63. New York University Press, 1997.

Schoen, Johanna. *Choice and Coercion: Birth Control, Sterilization, and Abortion in Public Health and Welfare*. Chapel Hill: University of North Carolina Press, 2005.

Schultz, Vicki. "Reconceptualizing Sexual Harassment." *Yale Law Journal* 107 (1998): 1683–1805.

———. "The Sanitized Workplace." *Yale Law Journal* 112, no. 8 (2003).

Scolforo, Mark. "Graham Spanier Charged: Ex-Penn State President Facing Perjury Charge in Jerry Sandusky Case." *Huffington Post*, November 1, 2012.

———. "Penn State Will Pay Nearly $60 Million to 26 Sandusky Victims." *Huffington Post*, October 28, 2013.

Scott, Lisa. "Strip Clubs 'May Die Out' If New Lap-Dancing Laws Come into Place." *Metro*, March 7, 2010.

Scutt, Jocelynne A. *The Sexual Gerrymander: Women and the Economics of Power*. North Melbourne, Australia: Spinifex Press, 1994.

Sealander, Judith. *Private Wealth and Public Life: Foundation Philanthropy and the Reshaping of American Social Policy from the Progressive Era to the New Deal*. Baltimore: Johns Hopkins University Press, 1997.

Segal, David. "Does Porn Hurt Children?" *New York Times*, March 28, 2014.

Segal, Kim, and Greg Botelho. "Gay Florida Teen Kaitlyn Hunt Sent Back to Jail over Explicit Texts, Images." CNN, August 21, 2013.

"Sex Offender Fighting Eviction Due to Registry as 12-Year-Old." CBS DFW, October 2, 2012.

"Sexual Abuse by U.S. Catholic Clergy: Settlements and Monetary Awards in Civil Suits." BishopAccountability.org, n.d.

"Sexual Assault." Texas Department of Public Safety, 2012.

"Sexual Harassment." California Department of Fair Employment and Housing, n.d.

"Sexual Harassment at Six Years Old?" CNN, December 11, 2013.

"Sexual Harassment—California Compliant." HRM Consulting, n.d. Accessed December 5, 2014.

Sharp, Ingrid. "The Sexual Unification of Germany." *Journal of the History of Sexuality* 13, no. 3 (July 2004): 348–65.

Sheehan, Ruth. "Rapists Lose Facet of Power." *Raleigh News and Observer*. September 6, 2004.

Shevory, Thomas C. *Notorious H.I.V.: The Media Spectacle of Nushawn Williams*. Minneapolis: University of Minnesota Press, 2004.

Shik, Na'ama. "Sexual Abuse of Jewish Women in Auschwitz-Birkenau." In *Brutality and Desire: War and Sexuality in Europe's Twentieth Century*, edited by Dagmar Herzog. London: Palgrave Macmillan, 2009.

Shilts, Randy. *And the Band Played On: Politics, People, and the AIDS Epidemic*. New York: Macmillan, 2007.

————. *Conduct Unbecoming: Gays and Lesbians in the U.S. Military*. New York: Macmillan, 2005.

Shively, Michael, Kristina Kliorys, Kristin Wheeler, and Dana Hunt. "An Overview of Shaming Applied to Sex Buyers in the United States: Summary Based upon Research from the Study, 'A National Assessment of Prostitution and Sex Trafficking Demand Reduction Efforts.'" Abt Associates with support by the National Institute of Justice, January 7, 2012.

Sickles, Jason. "Retired Boy Scouts Executive Defends His Work as Keeper of Secret Sex Files." Yahoo News, November 5, 2012.

Sifakis, Carl. *The Encyclopedia of American Prisons*. New York: Checkmark Books, 2003.

Sigle-Rushton, Wendy, and Sara Mclanahan. "For Richer or Poorer? Marriage as an Anti-Poverty Strategy in the United States." *Population* 57, no. 3 (2002): 509–26.

Simmons, Christina. *Making Marriage Modern: Women's Sexuality from the Progressive Era to World War II*. New York: Oxford University Press, 2009.

Simon, Jonathan. *Governing through Crime: How the War on Crime Transformed American Democracy and Created a Culture of Fear*. New York: Oxford University Press, 2007.

Simpson, Craig. "'Scottsboro Boys'—New Tactics and Strategy for Civil Rights." *Washington Area Spark*, n.d.

Skenazy, Lenore. "I Saw a Man Get Arrested for a Sex Crime Because He Made a Scheduling Error." Reason.com, July 17, 2014.

"Slated Release of Gay Texas Inmate Further Reveals Death Penalty's Injustice, Merits Statewide Moratorium." American Civil Liberties Union, March 2, 2000.

Smith, J. Douglas. *Managing White Supremacy: Race, Politics, and Citizenship in Jim Crow Virginia*. Chapel Hill: University of North Carolina Press, 2002.

Smith, Oran P. *The Rise of Baptist Republicanism*. New York: New York University Press, 1997.

Smith, Rebecca. "British Man 'Fathered 600 Children' at Own Fertility Clinic." *Telegraph*, April 8, 2012.

Snyder, Howard N. "Sexual Assault of Young Children as Reported to Law Enforcement: Victim, Incident, and Offender Characteristics." US Department of Justice, Bureau of Justice Statistics, July 2000.

Soderlund, Gretchen. "Running from the Rescuers: New U.S. Crusades against Sex Trafficking and the Rhetoric of Abolition." *NWSA Journal* 17, no. 3 (2005): 64–87.

Sokolove, Michael. "The Trials of Graham Spanier, Penn State's Ousted President." *New York Times*, July 16, 2014.

Sollors, Werner, ed. *Interracialism: Black-White Intermarriage in American History, Literature, and Law*. New York: Oxford University Press, 2000.

Sommer, Robert. "Camp Brothels: Forced Sex Labour in Nazi Concentration Camps." In *Brutality and Desire: War and Sexuality in Europe's Twentieth Century*, edited by Dagmar Herzog, 169–70. London: Palgrave Macmillan, 2009.

Sommers, Christina Hoff. "True Blue: The Respectable Pornographer." *Weekend Australian*, March 13, 1999.

Sontag, Susan. *On Photography*. New York: Picador, 2001.

Sorvino, Mira. "Mira's Cambodia Journal—Day Two: Meeting Heroes and Survivors." CNN, December 12, 2013, sec. CNN Freedom Project: Ending Modern-Day Slavery.

Spohn, Cassia C., and Julie Horney. "The Impact of Rape Law Reform on the Processing of Simple and Aggravated Rape Cases." *Journal of Criminal Law and Criminology* 86, no. 3 (1996).

"Spotlight Investigation: Abuse in the Catholic Church." *Boston Globe*, n.d.

Stack, Liam. "Beheading in Syria Is Called a Mistake." *New York Times*, November 15, 2013.

Stanley, Lawrence A. "The Child Porn Myth." *Cardozo Arts and Entertainment Law Journal* 7 (1989): 295–358.

Starr, Kenneth W. "The Report." Office of the Independent Counsel, September 9, 1998.

"Statement by the Minister of Justice Regarding Legislation in Response to the Supreme Court of Canada Ruling in Attorney General of Canada v. Bedford et Al." Department of Justice Canada, June 4, 2014.

State v. Liberta, 64 N.Y. 2d 152 (N.Y. 1984).

Steakley, James D. "Iconography of a Scandal: Political Cartoons and the Eulenburg Affair in Wilhelmin Germany." In *Hidden from History: Reclaiming the Gay and Lesbian Past*, edited by Martin Duberman, Martha Vicinus, and George Chauncey Jr. New York: Meridian, 1989.

"Stephen Harper 'Sickened' by Alleged 'Sexual Criminal Activity' Linked to Rehtaeh Parsons Tragedy." *National Post*, April 11, 2013.

Stern, Mark Joseph. "Iowa's Reformed HIV Criminalization Law Is Still Pretty Terrible." *Slate*, June 16, 2014.

Strossen, Nadine. *Defending Pornography: Free Speech, Sex, and the Fight for Women's Rights*. New York: New York University Press, 1995.

Strub, Whitney. "Perversion for Profit: Citizens for Decent Literature and the Arousal of an Antiporn Public in the 1960s." *Journal of the History of Sexuality* 15, no. 2 (May 2006): 258–91.

Stuart, Elizabeth. "The Suicide of LeAnn Leutner." *Village Voice*, July 31, 2013.

"Student Handbook: School of Law Section: Sexual Relationships." Pepperdine University, n.d., http://law.pepperdine.edu/academics/student-handbook/law/studentlife.htm.

Stumhofer, Nancy. "Goya's Naked Maja and the Classroom Climate." *Democratic Culture*, Spring 1994.

Sullivan, Paul. "Fertility Treatments Produce Heirs Their Parents Never Knew." *New York Times*, August 30, 2013.

Sullivan, Timothy. *Unequal Verdicts: The Central Park Jogger Trials*. New York: Simon and Schuster, 1992.

Sullum, Jacob. "DOJ Shuts Down Obscenity Task Force." *Opposing Views*, April 18, 2011.

Sutherland, Edwin H. "The Diffusion of Sexual Psychopath Laws." *American Journal of Sociology* 56, no. 2 (1950).

Sweetingham, Lisa. "Women Drop Sexual Harassment Suit against Koko the Gorilla's Caretaker." Court TV, November 28, 2005.

Symonds, William C., Steve Hamm, and Gail DeGeorge. "The Lewinsky Effect: Business Takes a Closer Look at Executive Affairs." *Business Week*, February 16, 1998.

Szobar, Patricia. "Telling Sexual Stories in the Nazi Courts of Law: Race Defilement in Germany, 1933 to 1945." *Journal of the History of Sexuality* 11, no. 1/2 (April 2002): 131–63.

"Tailhook: Scandal Time." *Newsweek*, July 5, 1992.

Talmadge, Eric. "GIs Frequented Japan's 'Comfort Women.'" *Washington Post*, April 25, 2007.

Tanaka, Masakazu. "The Sexual Contact Zone in Occupied Japan: Discourses on Japanese Prostitutes or Panpan for U.S. Military Servicemen." *Intersections: Gender and Sexuality in Asia and the Pacific*, no. 31 (December 2012).

Tanaka, Yuki. *Japan's Comfort Women: Sexual Slavery and Prostitution during World War II and the US Occupation*. London: Routledge, 2002.

Taslitz, Andrew E. *Rape and the Culture of the Courtroom*. New York: New York University Press, 1999.

———. "Willfully Blinded: On Date Rape and Self-Deception." *Harvard Journal of Law and Gender* 28 (2005): 381–446.

Taylor, Leslie A. "'I Made Up My Mind to Get It': The American Trial of The Well of Loneliness, New York City, 1928–1929." *Journal of the History of Sexuality* 10, no. 2 (2001).

Taylor, Paul. "Marrying Out: One-in-Seven New U.S. Marriages Is Interracial or Interethnic." Pew Research Center, June 15, 2010.

"Teens, Sex and the Law: Genarlow Wilson." NPR, June 12, 2007.

Tewksbury, Richard, Wesley G. Jennings, and Kristen Zgoba. "Sex Offenders: Recidivism and Collateral Consequences." National Criminal Justice Reference Service, March 2012.

"Texts of Colombia Decisions." Intersex Society of North America, n.d.

Thomas, Susan L. "Race, Gender, and Welfare Reform: The Antinatalist Response." *Journal of Black Studies* 28, no. 4 (March 1998): 419–46.

Thompson, Wright. "Outrageous Injustice." ESPN, n.d.

Thrupkaew, Noy. "The Crusade against Sex Trafficking." *Nation*, September 16, 2009.

"Timeline: Anthony Walker Murder." *Guardian*, November 30, 2005.

Timm, Annette. "Sex with a Purpose: Prostitution, Venereal Disease, and Militarized Masculinity in the Third Reich." *Journal of the History of Sexuality* 11, no. 1/2 (April 2002).

Timmins, Annmarie. "Offer to Tape Sex Nullifies Conviction." *Concord Monitor*, December 5, 2008.

"Tracing One Package—The Case That Legalized Birth Control." Margaret Sanger Papers Project, Newsletter 59, Winter 2011.

"Trafficking in Persons Report." US Department of State, 2012.

"Trafficking in Persons Report." US Department of State, 2014.

Tragen, Irving G. "Statutory Prohibitions against Interracial Marriage." *California Law Review* 32, no. 3 (1944): 269–80.

"Transcript: 'Sex: Unknown.'" PBS, October 30, 2011.

"Treating Youth with Sexual Behavior Problems." Children's Institute, May 29, 2012.

Treichler, Paula A. "AIDS, Gender, and Biomedical Discourse." In *AIDS: The Burdens of History*, edited by Elizabeth Fee and Daniel M. Fox. Berkeley: University of California Press, 1988.

Tribe, Laurence H. "Lawrence v. Texas: The 'Fundamental Right' That Dare Not Speak Its Name." *Harvard Law Review* 117, no. 6 (April 2004).

Tritten, Travis J. "Gay, Lesbian Troops Perform in Drag at Fundraiser." *Military.com News*, March 3, 2014.

Trivits, and Reppucci. "Application of Megan's Law to Juveniles." *American Psychologist* 57, no. 9 (2002).

Turner, Christopher. *Adventures in the Orgasmatron: The Invention of Sex.* London: Fourth Estate, 2011.

———. "Wilhelm Reich: The Man Who Invented Free Love." *Guardian*, July 8, 2011.

Tyner, James, and Donna Houston. "Controlling Bodies: The Punishment of Multiracialized Sexual Relations." *Antipode* 32, no. 4 (2000): 387–409.

"Understanding Child Sexual Abuse: Education, Prevention, and Recovery." American Psychological Association, n.d.

"Understanding Juvenile Sexual Offending Behavior: Emerging Research, Treatment Approaches and Management Practices." US Department of Justice, Center for Sex Offender Management, December 1999.

United States v. One Package, 86 F.2d 737 (1936).

United States v. Soripada Lubis (E.D. Virginia 2009).

"UVA Suspends Fraternities Following Rolling Stone Campus Rape Investigation." *Rolling Stone*, November 22, 2014.

Vaas, Francis J. "Title VII: Legislative History." *Boston College Industrial and Commercial Law Review* 7, no. 3 (1966): 431–58.

Van Dam, Carla. *Identifying Child Molesters: Preventing Child Sexual Abuse by Recognizing the Patterns of the Offenders.* Binghamton, NY: Haworth Maltreatment and Trauma Press, 2001.

Vargo, Marc E. *Scandal: Infamous Gay Controversies of the Twentieth Century.* London: Routledge, 2013.

Vickers, Emma. "'The Good Fellow': Negotiation, Remembrance, and Recollection—Homosexuality in the British Armed Forces, 1939–1945." In *Brutality and Desire: War and Sexuality in Europe's Twentieth Century*, edited by Dagmar Herzog. London: Palgrave Macmillan, 2009.

"Virginia Law Takes Aim at Adults Who French Kiss Minors." Fox News, March 9, 2008.

Volokh, Eugene. "Freedom of Speech and Workplace Harassment." *UCLA Law Review* 39 (1992): 1791.

Von Krafft-Ebing, Richard. *Psychopathia Sexualis: With Especial Reference to the Antipathic Sexual Instinct, a Medico-Forensic Study.* Translated by Franklin S. Klaf. 12th ed. New York: Bell, 1965.

Vozzella, Laura. "Bill Would Legalize Cohabitation in Virginia." *Washington Post*, January 27, 2013.

Wacks, Jamie L. "Reading Race, Rhetoric, and the Female Body in the Rhinelander Case." In *Interracialism: Black–White Intermarriage in American History, Literature, and Law*, edited by Werner Sollors. New York: Oxford University Press, 2000.

Walker, Jesse. "The Death of David Reimer." Reason.com, May 24, 2004.

Wallenstein, Peter. "Race, Marriage, and the Supreme Court from Pace v. Alabama (1883) to Loving v. Virginia (1967)." *Journal of Supreme Court History* 23, no. 2 (1998): 65–86.

———. *Tell the Court I Love My Wife: Race, Marriage, and Law—An American History.* London: Palgrave Macmillan, 2002.

Waller, Mark. "LaBruzzo Considering Plan to Pay Poor Women $1,000 to Have Tubes Tied." NOLA.com, October 23, 2009.

Walters, Lawrence G. "How to Fix the Sexting Problem: An Analysis of the Legal and Policy Considerations for Sexting Legislation." *First Amendment Law Review* 9 (December 14, 2010): 98–144.

———. "Shooting the Messenger: An Analysis of Theories of Criminal Liability Used against Adult-Themed Online Service Providers." *Stanford Law and Policy Review* 23, no. 1 (2012).

Wang, Wendy. "The Rise of Intermarriage: Rates, Characteristics Vary by Race and Gender." Pew Research Center, February 16, 2012.

Warren, Earl. *The Memoirs of Earl Warren*. New York: Doubleday, 1977.

Washington, Mary Dejevsky. "Female B-52 Pilot Quits over Charges of Adultery." *Independent*, May 19, 1997.

Watson, Julie. "Rape Victim: Retaliation Prevalent in Military." Associated Press, May 31, 2013.

"'We're Not Prostitutes': The Sex Surrogates Helping Real Life 40-Year-Old Virgins Overcome Crippling Inexperience with One-on-One Coaching." *Daily Mail Online*, October 25, 2012.

Weber, Jill M. "'Needy Families' and 'Welfare Cheats': The Rhetoric of Family Values in the 1961–1962 Welfare Reform Debates." *Relevant Rhetoric* 4 (2013).

Weeks, Jeffrey. "Movements of Affirmation: Sexual Meanings and Homosexual Identities." In *Passion and Power: Sexuality in History*, edited by Kathy Peiss and Christina Simmons. Philadelphia: Temple University Press, 1989.

———. *Sex, Politics, and Society: The Regulation of Sexuality since 1800*. 2nd ed. Philadelphia: Trans-Atlantic Publications, 1989.

Weiner, Rachel, and Matt Zapotosky. "Air Force Colonel Acquitted in Assault Trial." *Washington Post*, November 13, 2013.

Weiser, Benjamin. "5 Exonerated in Central Park Jogger Case Agree to Settle Suit for $40 Million." *New York Times*, June 19, 2014.

Wheeler, Leigh Ann. *How Sex Became a Civil Liberty*. New York: Oxford University Press, 2013.

"Whipping and Castration as Punishments for Crime." *Yale Law Journal* 8, no. 9 (June 1899): 371–86.

"Who Was Ryan White?" US Department of Health and Human Services, Health Resources and Services Administration, HIV/AIDS Programs, n.d.

Wilgoren, Debbi. "Area Juvenile Sex Rings Targeted Using Anti-Trafficking Laws." *Washington Post*, March 6, 2006.

Will, George F. "Colleges Become the Victims of Progressivism." *Washington Post*, June 6, 2014.

Williams, Mary Elizabeth. "'Buttman's' Porn Obscenity Trial: Why It Matters." *Salon*, July 13, 2010.

Willis, Ellen. *No More Nice Girls: Countercultural Essays*. Minneapolis: University of Minnesota Press, 1992.

"Wilson Released after Two Years behind Bars for Teen Sex Conviction." CNN, October 27, 2007.

Winerip, Michael. "Revisiting the Military's Tailhook Scandal." *New York Times*, May 13, 2013.

Winston, George T. "The Relation of the Whites to the Negroes." *Annals of the American Academy of Political and Social Science* 18, (July 1901): 105–18.

"The Word—Truthiness." *Colbert Report*, October 17, 2005.

"Workplace Rights Policy." Coca-Cola Company, n.d.

"Workplace Romance: A Survey." Society for Human Resource Management, September 24, 2013.

Wright, Thomas. *Oscar's Books*. London: Chatto and Windus, 2008.

Yalom, Marilyn. *A History of the Wife*. New York: HarperCollins Publishers, 2001.

Young, Philip. "The Mother of Us All: Pocahontas Reconsidered." *Kenyon Review* 24, no. 3 (1962): 391–415.

———. "Pocahontas." In *Portraits of American Women: From Settlement to the Present*, edited by G. J. Barker-Benfield and Catherine Clinton. New York: St. Martin's Press, 1991.

Young, Saundra. "Imprisoned over HIV: One Man's Story." CNN, November 9, 2012.

Zabel, William D. "Interracial Marriage and the Law." In *Interracialism: Black–White Intermarriage in American History, Literature, and Law*, edited by Werner Sollors. New York: Oxford University Press, 2000.

Zengerle, Jason. "Wanna Be Veep? Okay, but This Is Going to Hurt." *GQ*, August 2012.

Zetter, Kim. "Court Slaps Prosecutor Who Threatened Child-Porn Charges over 'Sexting.'" *Wired*, March 18, 2010.

Zgoba, Kristen, Philip Witt, Melissa Dalessandro, and Bonita Veysey. "Megan's Law: Assessing the Practical and Monetary Efficacy." Office of Policy and Planning, New Jersey Department of Corrections, Research and Evaluation Unit, December 2008.

ENDNOTES

INTRODUCTION

p. 2, "Sex is always something: Jodi Rudoren, "Standoff at Western Wall over Praying by Women," *New York Times,* May 10, 2013.

p. 2, At both the left and right: Alan Hunt, *Governing Morals: A Social History of Moral Regulation* (Cambridge: Cambridge University Press, 1999), 200.

p. 2, the FBI wrote to him: Beverly Gage, "What an Uncensored Letter to MLK Reveals," *New York Times,* November 11, 2014.

p. 3, In 2010, Julian Assange: Nick Davies, "10 Days in Sweden: The Full Allegations against Julian Assange," *Guardian,* December 17, 2010.

p. 3, (This charge had already: Jeet Heer, "Sex, Economics, and Austerity," *American Prospect,* May 7, 2013.

p. 3, Economics is indeed a: Derek Thompson, "Why Economics Is Really Called the 'Dismal Science,'" *Atlantic,* December 17, 2013. This formulation is credited to Thomas Carlyle.

p. 3, *New York Times* columnist: Frank Rich, "Endpaper: Public Stages; Men in Uniform," *New York Times,* April 11, 1993; Claire Bond Potter, "Queer Hoover: Sex, Lies, and Political History," *Journal of the History of Sexuality* 15, no. 3 (2006): 355–381.

p. 3, As many of the legal screws: Eric Hobsbawm, *The Age of Extremes: A History of the World, 1914–1991* (New York: Pantheon Books, 1991), 334.

p. 4, The sexual urge still churns: "Plato, *Laws*," Perseus Digital Project, Tufts University, n.d. http://www.perseus.tufts.edu/hopper/text ?doc=Plat.+Laws+783a&fromdoc=Perseus%3Atext%3A1999.01.0166.

p. 5, When an Alabama court: J. C. Parris v. State, 190 So.2d 564, at 565 (1966).

p. 5, Once the law signs on: Rachel Aviv, "The Science of Sex Abuse," *New Yorker,* January 14, 2013, 36–45.

p. 5, One group of mental-health: Paul Okami, "Childhood Exposure to Parental Nudity, Parent–Child Co-Sleeping, and 'Primal Scenes': A Review of Clinical Opinion and Empirical Evidence," *Journal of Sex Research* 32, no. 1 (1995): 51–64.

p. 6, there is a well-founded argument: See, e.g., Rachel Aviv, "Science of Sex Abuse"; Amanda Y. Agan, "Sex Offender Registries: Fear without Function?" *Journal of Law and Economics* 54, no. 1 (February 2011): 208; Kristen

Zgoba et al., "Megan's Law: Assessing the Practical and Monetary Efficacy,"
Office of Policy and Planning, New Jersey Department of Corrections,
Research and Evaluation Unit, December 2008; J. J. Prescott and Jonah E.
Ruckoff, "Do Sex Offender Registration and Notification Laws Affect Crim-
inal Behavior?" *Journal of Law and Economics* 54, no. 1 (2011): 161–206;
Richard Tewksbury, Wesley G. Jennings, and Kristen Zgoba, "Sex Offend-
ers: Recidivism and Collateral Consequences," National Criminal Justice
Reference Service, March 2012. https://www.ncjrs.gov/pdffiles1/nij
/grants/238060.pdf; http://www.bjs.gov/content/pub/pdf/rsorp94.pdf.

p. 6, Driven by lawyers: See, generally, Lindsay R. Garrett, "Repressed Memory Evidence in Civil Sexual Abuse Cases," Bepress Legal Series, March
23, 2006. http://law.bepress.com/expresso/eps/1181/; Laurie Goodstein
and Erik Eckholm, "Church Battles Efforts to Ease Sex Abuse Suits," *New
York Times,* June 14, 2012; Gary M. Ernsdorff, "Let Sleeping Memories
Lie—Words of Caution about Tolling the Statute of Limitations in Cases
of Memory Repression," *Journal of Criminal Law and Criminology* 84, no. 1
(1993): 129–174.

p. 6, But as useful as repressed-memory: Amina Memon and Mark Young,
"Desperately Seeking Evidence: The Recovered Memory Debate," *Legal
and Criminological Psychology* 2, no. 2 (1997): 131–154; Garrett, "Re-
pressed Memory Evidence in Civil Sexual Abuse Cases"; Goodstein and
Eckholm, "Church Battles Efforts to Ease Sex Abuse Suits," 11–15; Faith
Brynie, "Brain Sense," *Psychology Today,* December 13, 2013; Marcia K.
Johnson et al., "The Cognitive Neuroscience of True and False Memories,"
in *True and False Recovered Memories: Toward a Reconciliation of the Debate,* ed.
Robert F. Belli (New York: Springer Science and Business Media, 2011);
Friedman v. Rehal, 618 F.3d 142 (2d Cir. 2010) (finding, in the context of
the satanic-ritual-abuse cases of the 1980s and 1990s, that "almost all—if
not all—of the recovered memories of horrific abuse" from children in
those cases "were false").

p. 6, Some people who claim: "About FMSF—Introduction," False Memory
Syndrome Foundation, November 26, 2013. http://www.falsememorysyn-
dromefoundationonline.org/index.php.

p. 6, (Interestingly, FMSF's website: "Legal Issues Pertaining to Retractors," False Memory Syndrome Foundation, February 5, 2014.
http://www.falsememorysyndromefoundationonline.org/index.
php?ginterest=RetractorLawsuits.

p. 7, The profound influence: John D'Emilio and Estelle Freedman, *Intimate
Matters: A History of Sexuality in America* (Chicago: University of Chicago
Press, 1988), 224.

p. 7, While Freud affirmed: Sigmund Freud, *"Civilized" Sexual Morality and
Modern Nervousness* (1908) (Aylesbury, UK: Chrysoma Associates, 2000), 4.
http://www.lightoftheimagination.com/Civilized%20Sexual%20Morality
%20and%20Modern%20Nervousness%20Freud.pdf.

p. 7, he criticized enforced abstinence: Ibid., 9.

p. 7, By 1930, one of the US's: US v. Dennett, 39 F.2d 534 (2d Cir. 1930).

p. 7, As recalled in 1936: Mabel Dodge Luhan, *Movers and Shakers* (Albuquerque: University of New Mexico Press, 1936), 70–71; Ellen Chesler, *Woman of Valor: Margaret Sanger and the Birth Control Movement in America* (New York: Simon and Schuster, 1992), 96.

p. 8, Greenwich Village eccentrics: Christopher Turner, *Adventures in the Orgasmatron: The Invention of Sex* (London: Fourth Estate, 2011), 4.

p. 8, One's well being: Wilhelm Reich, *Selected Writings: An Introduction to Orgonomy* (New York: Macmillan, 2013), 37 (italics in original).

p. 8, The nurturing of true: Turner, *Adventures in the Orgasmatron*, 5.

p. 8, "The formation of the authoritarian: Wilhelm Reich, *The Mass Psychology of Fascism* (New York: Orgone Institute Press, 1946), 25.

p. 8, By 1964, years after orgone boxes: "Morals: The Second Sexual Revolution," *Time*, January 24, 1964.

p. 9, In 1968, student revolutionaries: Christopher Turner, "Wilhelm Reich: The Man Who Invented Free Love," *Guardian*, July 8, 2011.

p. 9, According to *Time*: "Morals: The Second Sexual Revolution."

p. 9, "Birth control must lead: Margaret Sanger, *Woman, Morality, and Birth Control* (New York: American Birth Control League, 1922), 11.

p. 9, whose passion for eugenics: See, for example, Chesler's *Woman of Valor*, which barely mentions Sanger's extensive eugenic activities.

p. 9, "The most urgent problem: Margaret Sanger, "The Eugenic Value of Birth Control Propaganda," *Birth Control Review*, October 1921. http://www.nyu.edu/projects/sanger/webedition/app/documents/show.php?sangerDoc=238946.xml.

p. 9, Sanger didn't maintain: Angela Franks, *Margaret Sanger's Eugenic Legacy: The Control of Female Fertility* (Jefferson, NC: McFarland and Co., 2005), 40–46; Jane Carey, "The Racial Imperatives of Sex: Birth Control and Eugenics in Britain, the United States and Australia in the Interwar Years," *Women's History Review* 21, no. 5 (2012): 733–752.

p. 9, The Third Reich demonstrated: Planned Parenthood does have a page on its website concerning "opposition claims" about Margaret Sanger. See http://www.plannedparenthood.org/files/8013/9611/6937/Opposition_Claims_About_Margaret_Sanger.pdf.

p. 10, In 1962, Sherri Chessen Finkbine: Linda Greenhouse, "A Never-Ending Story," *New York Times*, September 5, 2012; Vern L. Bullough, *Sexual Variance in Society and History* (Chicago: University of Chicago Press, 1976), 657–658.

p. 10, As US abortion foes: See, e.g., Pam Belluck, "Complex Science at Issue in Politics of Fetal Pain," *New York Times*, September 16, 2013.

p. 10, In Britain, the abortion issue: Dagmar Herzog, *Sexuality in Europe: A Twentieth-Century History* (Cambridge: Cambridge University Press, 2011), 76.

p. 10, In light of the dangers: "Q&A Abortion in the Netherlands," Ministry of Foreign Affairs, August 2011. http://www.minbuza.nl/binaries /content/assets /minbuza/en/import/en/you_and_the_netherlands/about _the_netherlands /ethical_issues/qa-abortus-en-2011.pdf.

p. 11, The Soviet Union was: Malgorzata Fidelis, *Women, Communism, and Industrialization in Postwar Poland* (Cambridge: Cambridge University Press, 2010), 195–196.

p. 11, By the early 1990s: "Poland Ends Subsidies for Birth Control Pills," *New York Times,* May 9, 1991.

p. 11, However, that changed in 1990: Ibid.

p. 11, In 2010, *Der Spiegel:* Jan Puhl, "Beyond the Church's Reach: Fleeing West from Poland's Restrictive Abortion Laws," *Spiegel Online International,* October 20, 2010.

p. 11, While porn sites get: "Porn Sites Get More Visitors Each Month Than Netflix, Amazon and Twitter Combined," *Huffington Post,* May 4, 2013.

p. 11, what one Virginia girl called: Hanna Rosin, "Why Kids Sext," *Atlantic,* October 14, 2014.

p. 11, Sexting also may prime: Ibid.

p. 11, In any event, current law: Tom Jackman, "In 'Sexting' Case, Police Want to Take Photo of Teen's Erect Geneitalia, His Lawyer Says," *Washington Post,* July 9, 2014. After this story was made public, the prosecutors withdrew their request to photograph the boy's erect penis. Tom Jackman, "Manassas City Police Say They Will Not Serve Search Warrant in Teen 'Sexting' Case," *Washington Post,* July 10, 2014.

p. 12, This was the case with: Kurt Eichenwald, "Through His Webcam, a Boy Joins a Sordid Online World," *New York Times,* December 19, 2005.

p. 12, Gourlay asked the court: Michigan v. Gourlay, case no. 278214 (Mich. Ct. App. 2007); Lawrence G. Walters, "Shooting the Messenger: An Analysis of Theories of Criminal Liability Used against Adult-Themed Online Service Providers," *Stanford Law and Policy Review* 23, no. 1 (2012): 171, 187–188. The Berry story was the subject of a blockbuster series of articles in the *New York Times* in 2005. Subsequent to the release of these articles, reporter Kurt Eichenwald admitted to giving Berry $2,000 and to a series of other ethical lapses, as well as mistakes in reporting. See Kurt Eichenwald, "Making a Connection with Justin," *New York Times,* December 19, 2005; Debbie Nathan, "New York Times, Kurt Eichenwald and the World of Justin Berry: Hysteria, Exploitation and Witch-Hunting in the Age of Internet Sex," *CounterPunch* 14, no. 7/8 (April 2007): 1–12.

p. 12, In 2012, the hideous rape: Richard A. Oppel Jr., "Ohio Teenagers Guilty in Rape That Social Media Brought to Light," *New York Times,* March 17, 2013.

p. 13, The perpetrators in these cases: Ibid; Ariel Levy, "Trial by Twitter," *New Yorker,* August 5, 2013; Ian Parker, "The Story of a Suicide," *New Yorker,* February 6, 2013.

p. 13, In *On Photography,* Susan Sontag: Susan Sontag, *On Photography* (New York: Picador, 2001), 22.

CHAPTER 1

p. 16, as people form living arrangements: "UK Moves toward Making Babies from DNA of Three People," *Salt Lake Tribune*, February 2, 2015. rhttp://www .sltrib.com/lifestyle/faith/2136369-155/uk-moves-toward-making-babies -from.

p. 17, In 1920, for example: Dagmar Herzog, *Sexuality in Europe*, 55.

p. 17, In Florida in the 1970s: Gillian Frank, "'The Civil Rights of Parents': Race and Conservative Politics in Anita Bryant's Campaign against Gay Rights in 1970s Florida," *Journal of the History of Sexuality* 22, no. 1 (January 2013): 136–139.

p. 18, And while biblical injunctions: Vern L. Bullough, *Sexual Variance in Society and History* (Chicago: University of Chicago Press, 1976), 641–642.

p. 18, Saint Paul threatened those: English Standard Bible, 1 Corinthians 6.9–10.

p. 18, If women sought other sources: Jonathan Simon, *Governing through Crime: How the War on Crime Transformed American Democracy and Created a Culture of Fear* (New York: Oxford University Press, 2007), 180–181.

p. 19, "Public policy," the court explained: State v. Richard Oliver, 70 N.C. 60 (1874).

p. 19, unless a wife had been: Rebecca Ryan, "The Sex Right: A Legal History of the Marital Rape Exemption," *Law and Social Inquiry* 20, no. 4 (1995): 941, 946.

p. 19, When the State v. Oliver case: Middle Assyrian Law 59, cited in Martha T. Roth, *Law Collections from Mesopotamia and Asia Minor* (Atlanta: Scholars Press, 1997).

p. 19, However, given that Assyrian: Ibid., ix.

p. 19, Under principles reaching back: William Blackstone, Commentaries on the Laws of England, ed. George Sharswood (Philadelphia: J. B. Lippincott, 1890); see also, Ryan, "Sex Right," 943–944; William L. Prosser, *Handbook of the Law of Torts,* 4th ed. (West Publishing, 1971), 859–861.

p. 19, The idea of coverture: Ryan, "Sex Right," 948–950; Prosser, *Handbook of the Law of Torts,* 859–861.

p. 19, But the husband cannot: Quoted in Diana E. H. Russell, *Rape in Marriage* (Bloomington: Indiana University Press, 1990), 17.

p. 20, Brides never actually stated: "Rape and Battery between Husband and Wife," *Stanford Law Review* 6, no. 4 (1954).

p. 20, This rule is referred to: Susan Estrich, *Real Rape: How the Legal System Victimizes Women Who Say No* (Cambridge, MA: Harvard University Press, 1987), 73.

p. 20, The law wasn't even criticized: But see Jill Elaine Hasday, "Contest and Consent: A Legal History of Marital Rape," *California Law Review* 88, no. 5 (2000).

p. 20, rather than cut the: Richard A. Posner and Katharine B. Silbaugh, *A Guide to America's Sex Laws* (Chicago: University of Chicago Press, 1996), 35; Ryan, "Sex Right," 963; Estrich, *Real Rape,* 74.

p. 20, first showed a crack in 1949: R v. Miller 2 All ER 529 (1954).

p. 20, would not be definitively abolished: Regina v. R. [1991] UKHL 12.

p. 20, "a husband forcing sex: "The Marital Rape Exemption," *New York University Law Review* 52 (1977): 309.

p. 21, Rape was rape, the court held: State v. Liberta, 62 (N.Y. 1984).

p. 21, Florida representative Tom Bush: Russell, *Rape in Marriage,* 18.

p. 21, the Colorado Supreme Court: People v. Brown, 632 P.2d 1025 (Colo. 1981).

p. 21, California state senator Bob Wilson: Russell, *Rape in Marriage,* 18.

p. 21, While spousal rape is now: Ibid., 21–22; Hasday, "Contest and Consent" 1484–1485.

p. 21, "a legal monster": Commonwealth v. Mlinarich, 498 A.2d 395, 403 (Supreme Court of Pennsylvania 1985). Hasday, "Contest and Consent," 1484, 1487.

p. 22, A century ago, the: Prosser, *Handbook of the Law of Torts,* 865–866; Gail D. Hollister, "Parent-Child Immunity: A Doctrine in Search of Justification," *Fordham Law Review* 50, no. 4 (1982): 489–532.

p. 22, Parents were encouraged: Hollister, "Parent-Child Immunity," 491.

p. 22, highest court refused in 1886: Robert H. Bremner, ed., *Children and Youth in America: A Documentary History* (Washington, DC: American Public Health Association, 1971), 2:119.

p. 22, in 1905, one E. W. Roller: Roller v. Roller, 37 Wash. 242 (1905).

p. 23, Well into the twentieth century: Prosser, *Handbook of the Law of Torts,* 875.

p. 23, impotent husbands had: Ibid.

p. 23, unnamed wife of Frank W. Duffies: Duffies v. Duffies 76 Wis. 374, 383-384 (1890).

p. 24, Dr. Edward H. Clarke's enormously influential: Edward H. Clarke, *Sex in Education; or A Fair Chance for the Girls* (Boston: James R. Osgood and Company, 1873), 12.

p. 25, world exhibitions in London, Frankfurt: Aleksandra Djajic Horváth, "Of Female Chastity and Male Arms: The Balkan "Man-Woman" in the Age of the World Picture," *Journal of the History of Sexuality* 20, no. 2 (2011): 358–381.

p. 26, Anti-adultery laws remained: Jolie Lee, "In Which States Is Cheating on Your Spouse Illegal?" *Detroit Free Press,* April 17, 2014.

p. 26, In 1983, Judith Stowell: Commonwealth v. Judith Stowell, 389, 171 (Mass. 1983).

p. 26, North Carolina woman sued: Alice Gomstyn, "Wife Wins $9 Million from Husband's Alleged Mistress," ABC News, March 22, 2010.

p. 27, Former brigadier general Jeffrey Sinclair: Joe Gould, "Army Demotes General Two Grades; Will Retire as Lieutenant Colonel," *Army Times,* June 20, 2014; Jeffrey Collins and Michael Biesecker, "Army General Fined, Reprimanded in Sex Case," *Yahoo News,* March 20, 2014.

p. 27, The unmarried Kelly Flinn: Mary Dejevsky Washington, "Female B-52 Pilot Quits over Charges of Adultery," *Independent,* May 19, 1997; Norman

Kempster, "Lying, Not Adultery, Is Female Pilot's Top Crime, AF Says," *Los Angeles Times,* May 22, 1997.

p. 27, "irreversibility of some kind: Christina Simmons, *Making Marriage Modern: Women's Sexuality from the Progressive Era to World War II* (New York: Oxford University Press, 2009), 108.

p. 27, as many single working mothers: Linda Gordon and Sara McLanahan, "Single Parenthood in 1900," *Journal of Family History* 16, no. 2 (1991): 97–116.

p. 27, percentage of working married women: Simmons, *Making Marriage Modern,* 112.

p. 28, Nearly every state and the federal government: William H. Chafe, *The Paradox of Change: American Women in the 20th Century* (New York: Oxford University Press, 1991), 115–116; Marilyn Yalom, *A History of the Wife* (New York: HarperCollins Publishers, 2001), 312.

p. 28, birth control had incalculable effects: Yalom, *History of the Wife.*

p. 28, "self-propelling torpedo": Peter Clark Macfarlane, "Diagnosis by Dreams," *Good Housekeeping,* February 1915, 280.

p. 29, "chief and central function: D'Emilio and Freedman, *Intimate Matters,* 224.

p. 29, "I believe we are living: Emma Goldman, *Living My Life* (New York: Alfred A. Knopf, 1931).

p. 29, judge observed that "the trouble: D'Emilio and Freedman, *Intimate Matters,* 232.

p. 29, introduction of cheap latex condoms: Ibid., 245.

p. 29, contained 120 "rubber pessaries: "Tracing One Package—The Case That Legalized Birth Control," Margaret Sanger Papers Project, newsletter 59 (Winter 2011). http://www.nyu.edu/projects/sanger/articles/tracing_one_package.php.

p. 30, sold for "immoral purposes": United States v. One Package, 86 F.2d 737 (1936); Joshua Gamson, "Rubber Wars: Struggles over the Condom in the United States," *Journal of the History of Sexuality* 1, no. 2 (1990): 262–282.

p. 30, no fewer than fifteen manufacturers: Gamson, "Rubber Wars," 265.

p. 30, the American Medical Association: D'Emilio and Freedman, *Intimate Matters,* 244.

p. 30, nearly four-fifths of American women: Yalom, *History of the Wife,* 314.

p. 30, laws punishing domestic violence: Hollister, "Parent-Child Immunity."

p. 30, Far from ignoring a husband: See, e.g., Cal. Fam. Code § 6326; see also, Eric Berkowitz, "Desperate Hours: Legal Aid Attorney Protima Pandey Works against the Clock to Protect Battered Women," *California Lawyer,* August 2012.

p. 31, Mississippi has defined parental child abuse: Mississippi Senate Bill 2472 (2009) ("Mississippi Child Protection Act of 2009").

p. 31, Much closer to home: Okami, "Childhood Exposure to Parental Nudity," 51–64.

p. 31, scholar James Kincaid explains: Camille Gear Rich, "Innocence Interrupted: Reconstructing Fatherhood in the Shadow of Child Molestation

Law," *California Law Review* 101, no. 3 (2013): 626; James R. Kincaid, *Erotic Innocence: The Culture of Child Molesting* (Durham, NC: Duke University Press, 1998), 78.

p. 31, UCLA scholar Paul Okami observed: Okami, "Childhood Exposure to Parental Nudity," 51.

p. 32, Camille Gear Rich recently pointed out: Rich, "Innocence Interrupted," 633.

p. 32, A Utah father's rubbing of baby oil: State v. Emmett, 839 P.2d 783 (1992).

p. 32, woman's fiancé was charged with child molestation: Rich, "Innocence Interrupted," 646.

p. 32, Other fathers have been charged: Ibid., 625.

p. 33, a drunken football fan, Brian Downing: "Alabama Man Pleads Guilty to Obscenity for Sexually Taunting LSU Fan in Video after BCS Game," *Washington Post,* October 2, 2012.

p. 34, Bryant argued that the new law: Conservative columnist Patrick Buchanan echoed those sentiments when he wrote that society's health depends on the "right to discriminate" against "immoral" minorities; Frank, "'The Civil Rights of Parents'"; Patrick Buchanan, "Florida's Vote: Hopeful Symptom," *Reno Evening Gazette,* June 15, 1977.

p. 34, Soviet communism and sexual transgression: David K. Johnson, *The Lavender Scare: The Cold War Persecution of Gays and Lesbians in the Federal Government* (Chicago: University of Chicago Press, 2009), 22 et seq.

p. 34, A much-publicized 1950 report: "Employment of Homosexuals and Other Perverts in Government," Interim Report, Committee on Expenditures in the Executive Departments, Subcommittee on Investigations, 1950. https://ecf.cand.uscourts.gov/cand/09cv2292/evidence/PX2337.pdf.

p. 34, This was folded into American: Johnson, *Lavender Scare,* 124–125.

p. 35, According to Senator Joseph McCarthy: Ibid., 23.

p. 35, a State Department language specialist: Ibid., 145.

p. 35, Henry later noted that: Ibid., 136–137.

p. 36, During the same period: Simon Sebag Montefiore, *Stalin: The Court of the Red Tsar* (London: Phoenix, 2003), 246.

p. 36, information on sex, reproduction: Igor S. Kon, *The Sexual Revolution in Russia: From the Age of the Czars to Today* (New York: Free Press, 1995), 85.

p. 36, Observed Russian historian Igor S. Kon: Ibid., 2–3.

p. 36, an official Soviet journal warned: David Remnick, *Lenin's Tomb: The Last Days of the Soviet Empire* (New York: Vintage Books, 1994), 330.

p. 36, "The [capitalist] family deprives: Aleksandra M. Kollontai, *Communism and the Family* (New York: Andrade's Bookshop, 1920), 10; cited in H. Kent Geiger, *The Family in Soviet Russia* (Cambridge, MA: Harvard University Press, 1970), 51.

p. 37, in 1920, Soviet women enjoyed: Kon, *Sexual Revolution in Russia,* 55.

p. 37, Lenin understood the need: Ibid., 59.

p. 37, "Lack of restraint in: Ibid., 58.

p. 37, Simon Sebag Montefiore called "the triumph: Montefiore, *Stalin,* 245.

p. 38, The policy of promoting "traditional" marriage: "Defense of Marriage Act: Update to Prior Report, GAO-04-353R," US General Accounting Office, January 23, 2004; Diana Adams, "The Freedom Not to Marry: Separating Sexual Relationships from Economic Dependency," 1. Paper in author's files.

p. 38, The government has spent nearly $1 billion: Elizabeth H. Pleck, *Not Just Roommates: Cohabitation after the Sexual Revolution* (Chicago: University of Chicago Press, 2012), 66–70; "Let Them Eat Wedding Rings," Alternatives to Marriage Project, June 2007.

p. 38, Congress allocated $750 million: Pleck, *Not Just Roommates,* 69, footnote 57.

p. 38, 41 percent of US babies: Natalie Angier, "The Changing American Family," *New York Times,* November 25, 2013.

p. 38, percentage of Americans who disapprove: Pleck, *Not Just Roommates,* 2.

p. 38, Far from toeing the pro-marriage line: Aja Gabel, "The Marriage Crisis: How Marriage Has Changed in the Last 50 Years and Why It Continues to Decline," *Virginia,* Summer 2012. http://uvamagazine.org/articles/the_marriage_crisis; Sharon Jayson, "Nearly 40% Say Marriage Is Becoming Obsolete," *USA Today,* November 18, 2010. http://usatoday30.usatoday.com/yourlife/sex-relationships/marriage/2010-11-18-1Amarriage18_ST_N.htm.

p. 38, single people now make up: Rich Miller, "Is Everybody Single? More Than Half the US Now, up from 37% in '76," *Bloomberg,* September 8, 2014.

p. 39, As explained by researchers: Wendy Sigle-Rushton and Sara Mclanahan, "For Richer or Poorer? Marriage as an Anti-Poverty Strategy in the United States," *Population* 57, no. 3 (2002): 523; "Let Them Eat Wedding Rings"; Annie Lowrey, "Can Marriage Cure Poverty?" *New York Times,* February 4, 2014.

p. 39, as explained by Elizabeth H. Pleck: Pleck, *Not Just Roommates,* 95, footnote 6.

p. 39, Several dozen states required: Ibid., 94.

p. 39, One survey of about four hundred: Ibid., 99.

p. 39, The town of Sheboygan, Wisconsin: Ibid., 98.

p. 40, Barnard College student Linda LeClair: Ibid., 72; see also, Maggie Astor, "In Another Era, a Barnard Student Makes National Headlines after Moving in with Boyfriend," *Columbia Daily Spectator,* April 27, 2008.

p. 40, By the 1980s, most states: As of this writing, four states—Virginia, Michigan, Florida, and Mississippi—still have anti-cohabitation laws on the books. See, Laura Vozzella, "Bill Would Legalize Cohabitation in Virginia," *Washington Post,* January 27, 2013.

p. 40, Debora Hobbs, a police dispatcher: Francie Grace, "N.C. Cohabitation Law Struck Down," CBS News, September 14, 2006.

p. 40, Consider Jacqueline Jarrett: *Pleck, Not Just Roommates,* 169.

p. 41, In 1983, the Illinois Supreme Court: In re Marriage of Thompson, 449 N.E.2d 88 (1983).

p. 41, Anne Wellman, a divorced mother: In re Marriage of Wellman, 104 Cal. App. 3d 993 (1980).

p. 42, Anne Wellman received a sexual pass: Pleck, *Not Just Room-mates,* 182–183; In re Marriage of Wellman, 998.

p. 42, The issue starts with the: But see, Angela Onwauchi-Willig, "The Return of the Ring: Welfare Reform's Marriage Cure as the Revival of Post-Bellum Control," *California Law Review* 93 (2005): 1655, footnote 54.

p. 43, If black women were allowed to marry: Ibid., 1655.

p. 43, Despite the prohibitions: D'Emilio and Freedman, *Intimate Matters,* 99; some slave couples were also married in Christian ceremonies.

p. 43, only to see them ripped apart: Ibid., 99–100.

p. 43, The prohibition against African American marriages: Onwauchi-Willig, "Return of the Ring," footnote 58.

p. 43, Despite the fact that jobs: Ibid., 1655–1663.

p. 43, As one Confederate army officer proclaimed: Ibid., 1659, footnote 73.

p. 44, The beliefs that marriage cures: Ibid., 1663–1664; Susan L. Thomas, "Race, Gender, and Welfare Reform: The Antinatalist Response," *Journal of Black Studies* 28, no. 4 (March 1998): 419–424.

p. 44, talk-show perennial George Will: Onwauchi-Willig, "Return of the Ring," 1671; Hunter, "George Will Says Unmarried Black Women a Bigger Problem Than Any 'Absence of Rights,'" *Daily Kos,* August 26, 2013.

p. 44, in the words of Senator Robert Byrd: Pleck, *Not Just Roommates,* 54; Fulton Lewis Jr., "Washington Report," *Reading Eagle,* June 20, 1966; Jill M. Weber, "'Needy Families' and 'Welfare Cheats': The Rhetoric of Family Values in the 1961–1962 Welfare Reform Debates," *Relevant Rhetoric* 4 (2013).

p. 44, By the 1960s, the majority: Onwauchi-Willig, "Return of the Ring," 1688–1689.

p. 44, In 1961, the city manager: Weber, "'Needy Families' and 'Welfare Cheats,'" 8–9.

p. 44, That same year, a Gallup poll: Pleck, *Not Just Roommates,* 52.

p. 44, The result: 22,501 children: Alison Lefkovitz, "Men in the House: Race, Welfare, and the Regulation of Men's Sexuality in the United States, 1961–1972," *Journal of the History of Sexuality* 20, no. 3 (September 2011): 598.

p. 45, The main tools to find "men in the house": Kaaryn Gustafson, "The Criminalization of Poverty," *Journal of Criminal Law and Criminology* 99, no. 3 (2009); Lefkovitz, "Men in the House."

p. 45, Reuben K. King summarized the policy: Pleck, *Not Just Roommates,* 56; Lefkovitz, "Men in the House," 594.

p. 45, It took a lot of effort to net: See, generally, Charles A. Reich, "Midnight Welfare Searches and the Social Security Act," *Yale Law Journal* 72, no. 7 (June 1963): 1347–1360; Gustafson, "Criminalization of Poverty," 3.

p. 45, In an East Harlem housing project: Pleck, *Not Just Roommates.,* 51–52.

p. 45, Oakland's infamous "Operation Bedcheck": Benny Max Parrish v. The Civil Service Commission of the County of Alameda, 66 Cal.2d 260, 263

(1967); Felicia Ann Kornbluh, *The Battle for Welfare Rights: Politics and Poverty in Modern America* (Philadelphia: University of Pennsylvania Press, 2007), 29.

p. 45, Fraud investigators and social workers: Benny Max Parrish v. The Civil Service Commission of the County of Alameda, 66 Cal.2d 260, 264 (1967).

p. 46, The court decided that Parrish: Benny Max Parrish v. The Civil Service Commission of the County of Alameda, 66 Cal.2d 260, 264, 276 (1967).

p. 46, Sylvester Smith, a widowed African American: Martin Garbus, *Ready for the Defense* (New York: Farrar, Straus, and Giroux, 1971), 144.

p. 47, Reuben King, for example, testified that: Ibid., 157–158.

p. 47, Garbus met with Mary Lee Stapp: Ibid., 189.

p. 48, Wrote Chief Justice Earl Warren: Ibid., 207; Pleck, *Not Just Roommates*, 58; Gustafson, "Criminalization of Poverty," 651; King v. Smith, 392, US 309 (1968). http://caselaw.lp.findlaw.com/scripts/getcase.pl?navby=CASE&court=US&vol=392&page=309.

p. 48, The *Smith* decision: Onwauchi-Willig, "Return of the Ring," 1672–1773; Thomas, "Race, Gender, and Welfare Reform."

p. 48, *New York Times* praising it: Garbus, *Ready for the Defense*, 203.

p. 48, One Michigan legislator declared: Ibid., 204.

p. 48, Roger Freeman testified that: Lefkovitz, "Men in the House," 606–607.

p. 48, words of President Richard Nixon: Ibid., 608.

p. 48, During his 1976 presidential campaign: John Blake, "Return of the 'Welfare Queen,'" CNN, January 23, 2012; but see Josh Levin, "The Welfare Queen," *Slate,* December 19, 2013.

p. 49, In 1996, President Bill Clinton: Onwauchi-Willig, "Return of the Ring," 1675–1676.

p. 49, John Mica put it more candidly: Gustafson, "Criminalization of Poverty," 7; 141 Cong. Rec. 9194 (1995) (statement of Representative Mica).

p. 49, Under PRWORA and the raft: Pleck, *Not Just Roommates*, 65–67; Gustafson, "Criminalization of Poverty," 1–8.

p. 49, In San Diego County, where: Pleck, *Not Just Roommates*, 66.

p. 49, political journalist Annie Lowrey observed: Lowrey, "Can Marriage Cure Poverty?" *New York Times,* February 9, 2014. http://www.nytimes.com/2014/02/09/magazine/can-marriage-cure-poverty.html?_r=0.

p. 49, For about sixty years: "Eugenics: Three Generations, No Imbeciles; Virginia, Eugenics and Buck v. Bell: Carrie Buck Revisited and Virginia's Apology for Eugenics," University of Virginia, Historical Collections at the Claude Moore Health Sciences Library, 2007. http://exhibits.hsl.virginia.edu/eugenics/5-epilogue/.

p. 50, a 1927 case, *Buck v. Bell:* "Eugenics: Three Generations, No Imbeciles; Virginia, Eugenics and Buck v. Bell: Buck v. Bell: The Test Case for Virginia's Eugenical Sterilization Act," University of Virginia, Historical Collections at the Claude Moore Health Sciences Library, 2007. http://exhibits.hsl.virginia.edu/eugenics/3-buckvbell/.

p. 50, per Justice Oliver Wendell Holmes: Buck v. Bell, 274 US 200 (1927).

p. 51, The most notorious proponent of eugenics: Stefan Kuhl, *The Nazi Connection: Eugenics, American Racism, and German National Socialism* (New York: Oxford University Press, 1994); Edwin Black, *War against the Weak: Eugenics and America's Campaign to Create a Master Race* (New York: Four Walls Eight Windows, 2003).

p. 51, By the time the procedures: Johanna Schoen, *Choice and Coercion: Birth Control, Sterilization, and Abortion in Public Health and Welfare* (Chapel Hill: University of North Carolina Press, 2005), 80.

p. 51, Said Mississippi legislator David Glass: Onwauchi-Willig, "Return of the Ring," 1670; Thomas, "Race, Gender, and Welfare Reform," 423–426.

p. 52, Half of the purportedly: Schoen, *Choice and Coercion,* 76; Kevin Begos, "Lifting the Curtain on a Shameful Era," *Winston-Salem Journal,* March 18, 2013.

p. 52, Most of them were African Americans: Lutz Kaelber, "Eugenics/Sexual Sterilizations in North Carolina," University of Vermont, 2014, 3, http://www.uvm.edu/~lkaelber/eugenics/NC/NC.html.

p. 52, suspected of using babies: Schoen, *Choice and Coercion,* 91.

p. 52, As in most other states: Ibid., 93–110.

p. 52, Given the stereotypes that: Ibid., 94–95; John Railey and Kevin Begos, "Sign This or Else . . . " *Winston-Salem Journal,* March 19, 2013.

p. 52, the following summary of the girl's life: John Railey and Kevin Begos, "Still Hiding," *Winston-Salem Journal,* March 19, 2013 (italics added).

p. 53, which approved about 90 percent: Courtney Hutchison, "Sterilizing the Sick, Poor to Cut Welfare Costs: North Carolina's History of Eugenics," ABC News, August 4, 2011; Railey and Begos, "Still Hiding."

p. 53, When Riddick went to the hospital: Ted Richardson, Michelle Johnson, and Katherine Elkins, "Against Their Will: Elaine's Story," *Winston-Salem Journal,* March 21, 2013; Hutchison, "Sterilizing the Sick"; Railey and Begos, "Still Hiding."

p. 53, one of the board members, Jacob Koomen: Railey and Begos, "Still Hiding."

p. 53, eighteen-year-old Nial Cox: Railey and Begos, "Sign This or Else . . . "

p. 54, Not long after Cox's daughter: Ibid.

p. 54, Cox was sterilized: Ibid; Schoen, *Choice and Coercion,* 241.

p. 54, The last sterilization in North Carolina: D'Emilio and Freedman, *Intimate Matters,* 315.

p. 54, Clovis H. Pierce, was the only: Edward Larson, *Sex, Race, and Science: Eugenics in the Deep South* (Baltimore: Johns Hopkins University Press, 1995), 162–163.

p. 54, Pierce defended the practice: Nancy Hicks, "Sterilization of Black Mother of 3 Stirs Aiken, S.C.," *New York Times,* August 1, 1973.

p. 54, federal judge in South Carolina: Dick Grosboll, "Sterilization Abuse: Current State of the Law and Remedies for Abuse," *Golden Gate University Law Review* 10 (1980): 1147–1189.

p. 54, By 1978, new regulations: D'Emilio and Freedman, *Intimate Matters,*

315.

p. 54, the last legally compulsory: Kate Harding, "Is Forced Sterilization Ever OK?" *Salon,* January 5, 2010.

p. 54, the *Winston-Salem Journal* published: "Editorial: State Must Move ahead on Compensation Process," *Winston-Salem Journal,* August 23, 2013.

p. 55, governor of Oregon also apologized: Dave Reynolds, "Oregon Governor Apologizes for Eugenics 'Misdeeds,'" *Inclusion Daily Express,* December 2, 2002.

p. 55, Despite these apologies: Rosalind Pollack Petchesky, *Abortion and Woman's Choice: The State, Sexuality, and Reproductive Freedom* (Boston: Northeastern University Press, 1990), 179.

p. 55, Charles Murray, that births: Charles Murray, "The Coming White Underclass," *Wall Street Journal,* September 29, 1993, A14 (italics added).

p. 55, John LeBruzzo, proposed paying: Mark Waller, "LaBruzzo Considering Plan to Pay Poor Women $1,000 to Have Tubes Tied," NOLA.com, October 23, 2009.

p. 55, law professor Linda Fentiman: Constantino Diaz-Duran, "Sterilized for Being Poor?" *Daily Beast,* January 16, 2010.

p. 55, This happened in 1973: D'Emilio and Freedman, *Intimate Matters,* 315; Petchesky, *Abortion and Woman's Choice,* 179–180.

p. 55, the 1977 Hyde amendment: D'Emilio and Freedman, *Intimate Matters,* 348.

p. 55, Medicaid and most insurance plans: Petchesky, *Abortion and Woman's Choice,* 180.

p. 55, The family these days: Michael J. Rosenfeld, "Nontraditional Families and Childhood Progress through School," *Demography* 47, no. 3 (August 2010): 755–775.

p. 56, the rate of interracial marriages: Wendy Wang, "The Rise of Intermarriage: Rates, Characteristics Vary by Race and Gender," Pew Research Center, February 16, 2012.

p. 56, More than $70 billion: Angier, "Changing American Family."

p. 56, a child in 2003: In Re Bobbijean, 46 AD3d 12 (2007).

p. 56, courts are split on whether: Carter Dillard, "Future Children as Property," *Duke Journal of Gender Law and Policy* 17 (2010): 47, 49–50.

p. 56, two parents created a baby: Teena-Ann V. Sankoorikal, "Using Scientific Advances to Conceive the Perfect Donor: The Pandora's Box of Creating Child Donors for the Purpose of Saving Ailing Family Members," *Seton Hall Law Review* 32, no. 3 (2011).

p. 56, As science advances: Ibid., 601–602.

p. 56, the *Baby M* case: Clyde Haberman, "Baby M and the Question of Surrogate Motherhood," *New York Times,* March 23, 2014.

p. 56, In Kansas, a man who: Chandrika Narayan, "Kansas Court Says Sperm Donor Must Pay Child Support," CNN, January 24, 2014.

p. 57, In 2009, Amy and Scott Kehoe: Stephanie Saul, "Building a Baby, with Few Ground Rules," *New York Times,* December 12, 2009.

p. 57, In New York, an unmarried couple: Elizabeth Stuart, "The Suicide of LeAnn Leutner," *Village Voice,* July 31, 2013.

p. 57, In London, a fertility clinic: Rebecca Smith, "British Man 'Fathered 600 Children' at Own Fertility Clinic," *Telegraph,* April 8, 2012.

p. 57, in Utah, a fertility clinic: Stephanie Pappas, "23andMe Genetic Test Reveals Disturbing Artificial Insemination Switch," Fox News, January 10, 2014.

p. 57, The US Supreme Court ruled: Adam Liptak, "Children Not Entitled to Dead Father's Benefits, Justices Rule," *New York Times,* May 21, 2012.

p. 57, New York court ruled in 2007: Paul Sullivan, "Fertility Treatments Produce Heirs Their Parents Never Knew," *New York Times,* August 30, 2013.

CHAPTER 2

p. 59, In 2013, Ukraine was: Andrew E. Kramer, "Pro-Government Ukrainians Take to Streets to Denounce European Social Values," *New York Times,* December 6, 2013.

p. 59, in Syria, Sunni Muslim fighters: Liam Stack, "Beheading in Syria Is Called a Mistake," *New York Times,* November 15, 2013.

p. 59, a Boise, Idaho, judge: William N. Eskridge Jr., *Dishonorable Passions: Sodomy Laws in America, 1861–2003* (New York: Penguin Books, 2008), 87–88.

p. 59, William Rehnquist, compared the: Ratchford v. Gay Lib, 434 US 1080, 1084 (1978) (Rehnquist, C.J. dissenting); Joyce Murdoch and Deb Price, *Courting Justice: Gay Men and Lesbians v. The Supreme Court* (New York: Basic Books, 2001), 203. ("To Rehnquist, homosexuality apparently was not merely an illness but a contagion.")

p. 60, The fear of gay: McCarran-Walter Act of 1952, §212(a)(4); Immigration Act of 1990, Pub. L. 101-649, 104 Stat. 4978 (withdrew exclusion of homosexuals as "deviants").

p. 60, The Ukrainian protesters' horror: James Nichols, "Dmitri Kisilev, Russian Official, Degrades Gays on National Television," *Huffington Post,* August 12, 2013.

p. 60, a little girl in Miami: Fred Fejes, "Murder, Perversion, and Moral Panic: The 1954 Media Campaign against Miami's Homosexuals and the Discourse of Civic Betterment," *Journal of the History of Sexuality* 9, no. 3 (2000): 305–347.

p. 60, law professor Martha Nussbaum: Martha C. Nussbaum, *Hiding from Humanity: Disgust, Shame, and the Law* (Princeton, NJ: Princeton University Press, 2004), 30–31 (italics added).

p. 61, This is why participants: Jonathan Haidt and Matthew A. Hersh, "Sexual Morality: The Cultures and Emotions of Conservatives and Liberals," *Journal of Applied Social Psychology* 31, no. 1 (2001): 203.

p. 61, some of the literature supporting: Nussbaum, *Hiding from Humanity,* 101.

p. 61, The words "homosexual" and: Manfred Herzer, "Kertbeny and the

Nameless Love," *Journal of Homosexuality* 12, no. 1 (1986). Another decade would pass before the words entered English usage. Jeffrey Weeks, "Movements of Affirmation: Sexual Meanings and Homosexual Identities," in *Passion and Power: Sexuality in History,* ed. Kathy Peiss and Christina Simmons (Philadelphia: Temple University Press, 1989), 70–71.

p. 61, wrote that homosexuals were: Vern L. Bullough, *Sexual Variance in Society and History* (Chicago: University of Chicago Press, 1976), 637.

p. 61, as the historian Dagmar Herzog: Herzog, *Sexuality in Europe,* 35.

p. 62, At the turn of the twentieth century: Ibid., 37.

p. 62, The law's hostility was not: Weeks, "Movements of Affirmation," 74.

p. 62, In some quarters, the term: Herzog, *Sexuality in Europe,* 32.

p. 62, That said, no one regarded: Bullough, *Sexual Variance,* 639–644.

p. 62, Inversion, for example, was: Lisa Carstens, "Unbecoming Women: Sex Reversal in the Scientific Discourse of Female Deviance in Britain, 1880–1920," *Journal of the History of Sexuality* 20, no. 1 (2011): 80–82.

p. 62, Another theory pegged: Bullough, *Sexual Variance,* 639.

p. 62, American researchers added: Eskridge Jr., *Dishonorable Passions,* 48.

p. 62, the German Richard von Krafft-Ebing: Richard von Krafft-Ebing, *Psychopathia Sexualis: With Especial Reference to the Antipathic Sexual Instinct, a Medico-Forensic Study,* trans. Franklin S. Klaf, 12th ed. (New York: Bell, 1965), 321, 324. See also Richard von Krafft-Ebing, *Psychopathia Sexualis: With Especial Reference to the Antipathic Sexual Instinct, a Medico-Forensic Study,* trans. Charles Chaddock, (London: F. A. Davis, 1894), 273–275.

p. 63, medical researchers sought to: Weeks, "Movements of Affirmation," 74.

p. 63, Krafft-Ebing's calls to eliminate: Ibid., 80.

p. 63, One of Krafft-Ebing's correspondents: Harry Oosterhuis, "Stepchildren of Nature: Krafft-Ebing, Psychiatry, and the Making of Sexual Identity," in *The History of Sexuality in Europe: A Sourcebook and Reader,* ed. Anna Clark (London: Routledge, 2011), 189.

p. 63, Irish nationalist Roger Casement: Weeks, "Movements of Affirmation," 80.

p. 64, Wilde's response: "I don't know: Thomas Wright, *Oscar's Books* (London: Chatto and Windus, 2008), 227.

p. 64, response of the *London Evening News:* Harford Montgomery Hyde, The Trials of Oscar Wilde (Minneola, NY: Dover, 1973), 18 (italics added).

p. 64, the later words of an English judge: Jeffrey Weeks, *Sex, Politics, and Society: The Regulation of Sexuality since 1800,* 2nd ed. (Philadelphia: Trans-Atlantic Publications, 1989), 100.

p. 64, As Michel Foucault observed: Michel Foucault, *The History of Sexuality, Vol. 1: An Introduction* trans. Robert Hurley (New York: Pantheon Books, 1978), 43.

p. 64, The Wilde trials were: Weeks, "Movements of Affirmation," 80–81.

p. 65, The steel heir Friedrich Krupp: Marc E. Vargo, *Scandal: Infamous Gay Controversies of the Twentieth Century* (London: Routledge, 2003), 155–156.

p. 65, on a private Black Forest estate: James D. Steakley, "Iconography of a Scandal:

Political Cartoons and the Eulenburg Affair in Wilhelmin Germany," in *Hidden from History: Reclaiming the Gay and Lesbian Past,* ed. Martin Duberman, Martha Vicinus, and George Chauncey Jr. (New York: Meridian, 1989), 324.

p. 65, In Europe, gay sex: Philip Hoare, *Oscar Wilde's Last Stand: Decadence, Conspiracy, and the Most Outrageous Trial of the Century* (New York: Arcade Publishing, 1997), 43.

p. 65, In articles published in 1906 and 1907: Ibid., 42.

p. 66, The Eulenburg affair: Steakley, "Iconography of a Scandal"; Vargo, *Scandal,* 155–176.

p. 66, at least six unrelated military figures: Vargo, *Scandal,* 165.

p. 66, The kaiser, stung by: Hoare, *Oscar Wilde's Last Stand,* 42.

p. 66, Harden later said that: Vargo, *Scandal,* 175.

p. 66, The connection between gay sex: Richard Grenier, "Colonel Redl: The Man behind the Screen Myth," *New York Times,* October 13, 1985.

p. 67, In his fascinating 1937 book: Magnus Hirschfeld, *The Sexual History of the World War* (New York: Falstaff Press, 1937), 263.

p. 67, (This logic would be reversed: "Employment of Homosexuals and Other Perverts in Government," 4–6.

p. 68, Hirschfeld also sifted through: Hirschfeld, *Sexual History of the World War,* 136–137.

p. 68, Hirschfeld noted another aspect: Ibid., 143–144.

p. 68, According to Paul Fussell: Paul Fussell, *The Great War and Modern Memory* (London: Oxford University Press, 1975), 272.

p. 69, "Could it be," asks a character: James Jones, *The Thin Red Line* (New York: Delta, 1962), 286.

p. 69, Robert Graves's description: Robert Graves, "Recalling War," *Guardian,* November 12, 2008.

p. 69, As Hirschfeld observed: Hirschfeld, *Sexual History,* 34.

p. 70, As the writer John Loughery put it: John Loughery, *The Other Side of Silence: Men's Lives and Gay Identities, a Twentieth-Century History* (New York: Henry Holt, 1998), 4. http://www.nytimes.com/books/first/l/loughery-silence.html.

p. 70, Chief Machinist's Mate Ervin Arnold: B. R. Burg, *Gay Warriors: A Documentary History from the Ancient World to the Present* (New York University Press, 2001), 193.

p. 70, Following on Roosevelt's superb: Loughery, *Other Side of Silence,* 5.

p. 70, Arnold made sure that: Burg, *Gay Warriors,* 193.

p. 70, "I entered the room with: Lawrence Murphy, "Cleaning Up Newport: The US Navy's Persecution of Homosexuals after World War I," *Journal of American Culture* 7, no. 3 (1984): 57–64.

p. 70, "Surely," wrote historian: Burg, *Gay Warriors,* 194.

p. 71, *New York Times* headline: "Lay Navy Scandal to F. D. Roosevelt," *New York Times,* July 20, 1921.

p. 71, "Perversion is not a crime": Loughery, *Other Side of Silence,* 8; Aaron Belkin, "A Sting He Didn't Deserve," *Washington Post,* September 1, 2007.

p. 71, Until the Second World War: Allan Bérubé, *Coming Out under Fire: The History of Gay Men and Women in World War Two* (New York: Free Press, 1990), 33.

p. 71, Among the list of "deviations": Ibid., 12.

p. 72, By 1942, new directives stated: Ibid., 19.

p. 72, The next year, another checklist: Ibid., 20.

p. 72, As historian Allan Bérubé noted: Ibid., 28.

p. 72, In 1945, Pat Bond went: Ibid., 32.

p. 72, Once Bond was in the WAC: D'Emilio and Freedman, *Intimate Matters*, 289–290.

p. 73, Getting into the American armed forces: Bérubé, *Coming Out under Fire*, 201.

p. 73, Interrogators wanted detailed confessions: Ibid., 204.

p. 73, "A single rumor that someone": Ibid., 214.

p. 73, "The guards were all getting": Ibid., 220–221.

p. 73, From 1941 until 2011: Matthew M. Burke, "Senate Bill Would Provide Clean Service Records for Discharged Gay, Lesbian Troops," *Stars and Stripes,* February 12, 2014.

p. 73, Some straight men avoided: Frank Kusch, *All American Boys: Draft Dodgers in Canada from the Vietnam War* (Santa Barbara, CA: Greenwood Publishing Group, 2001), 71.

p. 74, Male homosexuality was also: Emma Vickers, "'The Good Fellow': Negotiation, Remembrance, and Recollection—Homosexuality in the British Armed Forces, 1939–1945," in *Brutality and Desire: War and Sexuality in Europe's Twentieth Century,* ed. Dagmar Herzog (London: Palgrave Macmillan, 2009), 127.

p. 74, Of the estimated 250,000 to: Ibid., 115–116.

p. 74, a respected soldier, Crank Dyer: Ibid., 118, 123.

p. 74, One gay soldier, Dennis Campbell: Ibid., 125–126.

p. 74, The Nazi hostility toward homosexuals: Herzog, *Sexuality in Europe*, 73–74.

p. 75, The Röhm, Eulenburg, and Redl: Geoffrey Giles, "The Denial of Homosexuality: Same-Sex Incidents in Himmler's SS and Police," *Journal of the History of Sexuality* 11, no. 1 (2002): 267.

p. 75, The elite Schutzstaffel (SS): Ibid., 263–270.

p. 75, a gay Waffen [Armed]-SS man: Ibid., 271.

p. 76, The judges were unmoved by G.'s defense: Ibid., 273–278.

p. 77, One woman who read it: Herzog, *Sexuality in Europe*, 57.

p. 77, From a book with little kissing: Radclyffe Hall, *The Well of Loneliness* (London: Wordsworth Editions, 2005), 179.

p. 77, Hall was the child of: Vargo, *Scandal*, 64.

p. 77, Hall took it upon herself to: Leslie A. Taylor, "'I Made Up My Mind to Get It': The American Trial of The Well of Loneliness, New York City, 1928–1929," *Journal of the History of Sexuality* 10, no. 2 (2001): 250, 253.

p. 77, In 1927, at age forty-seven: Vargo, *Scandal*, 66.

p. 78, With both relief and vexation, she declares: Hall, *Well of Loneliness,* 186.

p. 78, *The Well* drew a mixed: Vargo, *Scandal,* 72.

p. 78, Given the events in London: Taylor, "'I Made Up My Mind to Get It,'" 261.

p. 79, Covici-Friede turned to Morris Ernst: Ibid., 250, 259.

p. 79, Buoyed by this victory and: Ibid., 260.

p. 79, To prepare for the legal contest: Ibid., 262.

p. 79, As his private notes reflect: Ibid., 264.

p. 79, When the trial began in 1929: Vargo, *Scandal,* 78.

p. 79, First, he argued that: Taylor, "'I Made Up My Mind to Get It,'" 272–275.

p. 79, Unlike *Maupin,* he argued: Ibid., 275.

p. 79, To scholar Leslie Taylor: Ibid., 277.

p. 80, In 1915, a California court: People v. Camp, 26 Cal.App. 385, 388 (1915).

p. 80, Building on the medical diagnosis: Estelle Freedman, "'Uncontrolled Desires': The Response to the Sexual Psychopath, 1920–1960," *Journal of American History* 74, no. 1 (June 1987): 83, 103.

p. 80, Along the way, homosexuals: Lisa Bennett, "The Perpetuation of Prejudice in Reporting on Gays and Lesbians: Time and Newsweek: The First Fifty Years," Joan Shorenstein Center on the Press, Politics and Public Policy, September 1998, 3–4. http://shorensteincenter.org/wp-content/uploads/2012/03/r21_bennett.pdf.

p. 80, To give police maximum latitude: Eskridge Jr., *Dishonorable Passions,* 51–52.

p. 80, In response to a man's: Ibid., 91.

p. 80, Sodomy laws were also: Ibid., 56–57, 77, 173.

p. 81, law professor William Eskridge: Ibid., 77.

p. 81, Many of those caught having: Todd S. Purdum, "Registry Laws Tar Sex-Crime Convicts with Broad Brush," *New York Times,* July 1, 1997; Eskridge Jr., *Dishonorable Passions,* 92–93.

p. 81, With a 1960 *Newsweek* headline: "Homosexuals: To Punish or to Pity," *Newsweek,* July 11, 1960.

p. 81, with *Time* magazine in 1966: "The Homosexual in America," *Time,* January 21, 1966.

p. 81, The methods used to ensnare: William N. Eskridge Jr., "Privacy Jurisprudence and the Apartheid of the Closet, 1946–1961," *Florida State University Law Review* 24, no. 703 (1997): 719.

p. 81, Thomas Earl, a white man: People v. Earl, 216 Cal.App.2d 608 (1963).

p. 82, By the 1950s, mass raids: Eskridge Jr., "Privacy Jurisprudence," 721–722.

p. 82, in 1969, at the Stonewall Inn: Joey L. Mogul, Andrea J. Ritchie, and Kay Whitlock, *Queer (In)justice: The Criminalization of LGBT People in the United States* (Boston: Beacon Press, 2011), 46–47.

p. 82, The vast majority of the: Eskridge Jr., "Privacy Jurisprudence," 703, 710.

p. 82, The arrests would often be: William N. Eskridge, *Gaylaw: Challenging the Apartheid of the Closet* (Cambridge, MA: Harvard University Press 2009), 27.

p. 82, In Toledo, Ohio, it was: Mogul, Ritchie, and Whitlock, *Queer (In)justice,* 64–67.

p. 82, Some of the more oblique: I. Bennett Capers, "Cross Dressing and the Criminal," *Yale Journal of Law and the Humanities* 20, no. 1 (2008): 8–9.

p. 82, Butch lesbians took the brunt: Katherine M. Franke, "The Central Mistake of Sex Discrimination Law: The Disaggregation of Sex from Gender," *University of Pennsylvania Law Review* 144 (1995): 63.

p. 82, In 1960, as Sara Quiroz: This impression was supplemented in deportation proceedings by her employer's observation that she often "wore trousers and a shirt when she came to work, and that her hair was cut shorter than some other women's." Eithne Luibhéid, *Entry Denied: Controlling Sexuality at the Border* (Minneapolis: University of Minnesota Press, 2002), 77, 81.

p. 82, Investigators drilled her on: Ibid., 89–90.

p. 83, (While psychopaths and those: Ibid., 78.

p. 83, Quiroz later recanted her: Ibid., 92–94.

p. 83, Michel Foucault famously wrote: Foucault, *History of Sexuality,* 103.

p. 84, "homosexual panic" murder defense in courts: See, generally, Cynthia Lee, "The Gay Panic Defense," *University of California, Davis Law Review* 42 (2008): 471–517.

p. 84, The idea of homosexual panic was: Edward J. Kempf, *Psychopathology* (St. Louis: C. V. Mosby Company, 1920), 477–515; Christina Pei-Lin Chen, "Provocation's Privileged Desire: The Provocation Doctrine, 'Homosexual Panic,' and the Non-Violent Unwanted Sexual Advance Defense," *Cornell Journal of Law and Public Policy* 10 (2000): 199–200.

p. 84, In 1952, "homosexual panic" was included: Lee, "Gay Panic Defense," 483.

p. 84, In criminal courtrooms, however: Chen, "Provocation's Privileged Desire," 202; Kavita B. Ramakrishnan, "Inconsistent Legal Treatment of Unwanted Sexual Advances: A Study of the Homosexual Advance Defense, Street Harassment, and Sexual Harassment in the Workplace," *Berkeley Journal of Gender, Law and Justice* 26, no. 2 (September 2013): 305–306.

p. 84, When Nathan "Babe" Leopold: "Famous American Trials: Illinois v. Nathan Leopold and Richard Loeb, 1924: Excerpts from the Psychiatric ('Alienist') Testimony in the Leopold and Loeb Hearing (August 18–August 19, 1924)," University of Missouri–Kansas City School of Law, n.d. http://law2.umkc.edu/faculty/projects/ftrials/leoploeb/psychiatrictestimony.html.

p. 84, referred to them as "perverts": Mogul, Ritchie, and Whitlock, *Queer (In) justice,* 21.

p. 84, Their attorney, the famed Clarence Darrow: Ibid., 22.

p. 85, Homosexual panic–related defenses: Ramakrishnan, "Inconsistent Legal Treatment," 304; Lee, "Gay Panic Defense," 491–499.

p. 85, For example, in 1972, John Parisie: People v. Parisie, 287 N.E.2d 310 (1972); Lee, "Gay Panic Defense," 492–493.

p. 85, Three years later, while two male neighbors: State v. Thornton, 532 S.W.2d 37 (Mo. Ct. App. 1975).

p. 85, In 1995 a heterosexual man, Jonathan Schmitz: Lee, "Gay Panic Defense," 495–496; People v. Schmitz, 586 N.W.2d 766, 768 (Mich. Ct. App. 1998).

p. 85, In 1978, for example, David Mills: Mills v. Shepherd, 445 F.Supp. 1231 (1978).

p. 86, In 1991 another young man, Timothy Schick: Schick v. State, 570 N.E.2d 918 (1991).

p. 86, came in 1998, after Matthew Shepard: Cynthia Lee, "Masculinity on Trial: Gay Panic in the Criminal Courtroom," *Southwestern Law Review* 42 (2013): 823.

p. 86, The other, Aaron McKinney, took: Lee, "Gay Panic Defense," 524.

p. 87, The judge first attempted to shut: Ibid., 527.

p. 87, the so-called trans-panic defense: Ramakrishnan, "Inconsistent Legal Treatment," 316–317.

p. 87, seventeen-year-old Gwen (born Eddie) Araujo: Lee, "Masculinity on Trial," 817, 828.

p. 87, While defenses related to homosexual panic: Lee, "Gay Panic Defense," 475; Ramakrishnan, "Inconsistent Legal Treatment," 341.

p. 88, as scholar Cynthia Lee has written: Lee, "Gay Panic Defense," 510–511.

p. 88, When women are subjected to: Ramakrishnan, "Inconsistent Legal Treatment," 321–325.

p. 88, In one 1976 case a woman: Commonwealth v. Duncan, 239 Pa.Super. 539, footnote 4 (1976).

p. 88, The appellate judges reasoned that: Brooks v. City of San Mateo, 229 F.3d 917, 926-927 (9th Cir. 2000).

p. 88, supervisor in Louisiana told his male employee: La Day v. Catalyst Technology Inc., 302 F.3d 474 (2002).

p. 88, Another case at about the same time: Gerd v. United Parcel Service, Inc., 934 F.Supp. 357 (1996).

p. 89, Aside from these horrors: Herzog, *Sexuality in Europe,* 96–97.

p. 90, In Germany and Austria, men: Ibid., 117–119.

p. 90, In 1957, a government committee: "Lord Montagu on the Court Case Which Ended the Legal Persecution of Homosexuals," *Daily Mail Online,* July 17, 2007.

p. 90, (Prosecutions for gay sex among minors: Herzog, *Sexuality in Europe,* 125.

p. 90, In 2001, the Netherlands became: "The Global Divide on Homosexuality," Pew Research Center, June 4, 2013. http://www.pewglobal.org/2013/06/04/the-global-divide-on-homosexuality/.

p. 91, That same year, Russia also forbade: "Russia's Putin Signs Law Limiting Adoption by Gays," Associated Press, July 3, 2014.

p. 91, Soon after Lyndon Johnson's 1964: Matt Apuzzo, "Uncovered Papers Show Past Government Efforts to Drive Gays from Jobs," *New York Times,* May 20, 2014.

p. 91, The response, by personnel officer John W. Steele: Memo from John W. Steele to O. Glenn Stahl, "Homosexuality and Government Employment,"

November 17, 1964. http://s3.documentcloud.org/documents/1164936/
original-memo-from-1964.pdf.

p. 91, "Commies" and "queers" were not: Johnson, *Lavender Scare,* 31.

p. 91, The "purge of the perverts": "An Interview with David K. Johnson,"
University of Chicago Press, 2004. http://press.uchicago.edu/Misc/
Chicago/404811in.html.

p. 92, While Hoover had been stockpiling: Douglas M. Charles, *The FBI's Obscene
File: J. Edgar Hoover and the Bureau's Crusade against Smut* (Lawrence: University Press of Kansas, 2012), 43; Eskridge Jr., "Privacy Jurisprudence," 719.

p. 92, Starting in 1943, Hoover had FBI agents: Claire Bond Potter, "Queer
Hoover: Sex, Lies, and Political History," *Journal of the History of Sexuality*
15, no. 3 (2006): 355, 377.

p. 92, As the postwar government came: Eskridge Jr., "Privacy Jurisprudence,"
754–755.

p. 92, As late as the 1960s, FBI agents would: John D'Emilio, *Sexual Politics,
Sexual Communities: The Making of a Homosexual Minority in the United
States, 1940–1970* (Chicago: University of Chicago Press, 1998), 47.

p. 92, However, when Welles was caught: Eskridge Jr., "Privacy Jurisprudence," 703–704, 754.

p. 93, More importantly, the State Department: Johnson, *Lavender Scare,* 70.

p. 93, After the war, Congressional Republicans: Ibid., 21.

p. 93, the government investigated about two hundred employees: Ibid., 88.

p. 93, In 1950, one week after Senator Joseph McCarthy: Ibid., 19.

p. 93, The fear of pervasive homosexuality: Ibid., 31.

p. 94, conservative North Carolina Democrat Clyde Hoey: Corey Robin, *The Reactionary Mind: Conservatism from Edmund Burke to Sarah Palin* (New York:
Oxford University Press, 2011), 202.

p. 94, Instead, the subcommittee dredged up: "Employment of Homosexuals
and Other Perverts in Government," 5.

p. 94, The report also stated: Ibid., 5

p. 94, concluded that "Persons who indulge: Ibid., 19

p. 94, The Hoey report was covered: Ibid., 4

p. 94, The subcommittee castigated the: Ibid., 12, 20.

p. 94, "To pussyfoot or to take: Ibid., 21.

p. 94, With the Hoey investigation: Eskridge Jr., *Dishonorable Passions* 101.

p. 94, In 1952, homosexuals, as "persons: McCarran-Walter Act of 1952, sec.
212 (a)(4).

p. 94, The most important anti-gay measure: "Executive Order 10450—Security
Requirements for Government Employment," National Archives, n.d. http://
www.archives.gov/federal-register/codification/executive-order/10450.html.

p. 95, In 1953, a State Department clerical worker: Johnson, *Lavender Scare,*
148–149.

p. 95, McCoy's and Tress's experiences: Ibid., 152.

p. 95, a federal employee was fired for: Scott v. Macy, 349 F.2d 182 (D.C. Cir. 1965).

p. 95, The Lavender Scare also struck: Neil Miller, *Out of the Past: Gay and*

Lesbian History from 1869 to the Present (New York: Alyson Books, 2006), 271.

p. 96, Yet gay smears also boomeranged: Andrea Friedman, "The Smearing of Joe McCarthy: The Lavender Scare, Gossip and Cold War Politics," *American Quarterly* 57, no. 4 (2005): 1105, 1114.

p. 96, The resulting Army-McCarthy hearings: Congressional Record, 83rd Cong., 2d sess., June 1, 1954, 7389-90.

p. 96, Joseph Welch demanded of McCarthy: Friedman, "Smearing of Joe McCarthy," 1122–1123.

p. 97, Unless there was a rational connection: Clifford L. Norton v. John Macy, 417 F.2d 1161 (D.C. Cir. 1969).

p. 97, A 1975 *Time* magazine cover story: "Gays on the March," *Time,* September 8, 1975, 43.

p. 98, Next to a passage about: Ibid., 32–43.

p. 98, The APA's 1973 vote: Ibid., 36.

p. 98, On the law-enforcement side: "LAPD Chief Compares Gays, Lepers," *Advocate,* January 5, 1972, 7.

p. 98, Chief Justice Rehnquist likened: Ratchford v. Gay Lib, 434 US 1080, 1084 (1978) (Rehnquist, C.J. dissenting).

p. 98, And in a bizarre twist of logic: "Slated Release of Gay Texas Inmate Further Reveals Death Penalty's Injustice, Merits Statewide Moratorium," American Civil Liberties Union, March 2, 2000; Richard Goldstein, "Queer on Death Row," *Village Voice,* March 13, 2001. Burdine's conviction was later overturned.

p. 98, there were at least three dozen: D'Emilio and Freedman, *Intimate Matters,* 346.

p. 98, From 1956 to 1964, the "Johns Committee": James A. Schnur, "Closet Crusaders: The Johns Committee and Homophobia, 1956–1965," in *Carryin' On in the Lesbian and Gay South,* ed. John Howard (New York: New York University Press, 1997), 133–163.

p. 99, Dozens of people were dismissed: Eskridge Jr., *Dishonorable Passions,* 103.

p. 99, known as the Purple Report: "Homosexuality and Citizenship in Florida: A Report of the Florida Legislative Investigation Committee," Florida Legislative Investigation Committee, January 1964, 14. http://ufdc.ufl.edu/UF00004805/00001/14x.

p. 99, Bryant adopted this rhetoric: "Anita Bryant vs. the Homosexuals," *Newsweek,* June 6, 1977, 22.

p. 99, According to one Save Our Children ad: Eskridge Jr., *Dishonorable Passions,* 211.

p. 99, another Save Our Children ad: "Gay Rights Showdown in Miami," *Time,* June 13, 1977.

p. 100, In 1979, almost 90 percent of Americans: Eskridge Jr., *Dishonorable Passions,* 201–202.

p. 100, *Time* magazine, for example, reported: "Gays on the March," 34.

p. 100, Once the AIDS outbreak began: Bennett, "Perpetuation of Prejudice," 8–10; D'Emilio and Freedman, *Intimate Matters,* 355.

p. 100, pointing to its spread in "hotbeds: Stephen O. Murray, *American Gay* (Chicago: University of Chicago Press, 1996), 104.

p. 101, Ever the opportunist, Falwell: D'Emilio and Freedman, *Intimate Matters,* 354.

p. 101, "You get heterosexual doctors: Murray, *American Gay,* 104.

p. 101, The CDC, which was the: Ibid.

p. 101, The New Right saw the outbreak: Eskridge Jr., *Dishonorable Passions,* 218.

p. 101, The Southern Baptist Convention: Oran P. Smith, *The Rise of Baptist Republicanism* (New York: New York University Press, 1997), 218–231.

p. 101, Patrick Buchanan wrote: Patrick Buchanan, "Nature's Retribution," *New York Post,* February 24, 1983.

p. 101, when AIDS cases already exceeded: D'Emilio and Freedman, *Intimate Matters,* 354.

p. 101, the White House started to pay attention: Jennifer Brier, *Infectious Ideas: US Political Responses to the AIDS Crisis* (Chapel Hill: University of North Carolina Press, 2009), 83.

p. 101, Health and Human Services chief Margaret Heckler: Randy Shilts, *And the Band Played On: Politics, People, and the AIDS Epidemic* (New York: Macmillan, 2007), 554.

p. 102, Reagan's surgeon general, C. Everett Koop: C. Everett Koop, "Surgeon General's Report on Acquired Immune Deficiency Syndrome," 1986, 4. http://profiles.nlm.nih.gov/ps/access/NNBBVN.pdf.

p. 102, Instead of avoiding the subject: Ibid., 6.

p. 102, who saw Koop's position as: Brier, *Infectious Ideas,* 90.

p. 102, In the end, Koop lost: Ibid., 92.

p. 102, Fire officials refused to resuscitate: Allan M. Brandt, "AIDS: From Social History to Social Policy," in *AIDS: The Burdens of History,* ed. Elizabeth Fee and Daniel M. Fox (Berkeley: University of California Press, 1988), 154.

p. 102, Utah passed a law in 1987: Weeks v. State, 834 S.W.2d 559 (1992).

p. 102, It was punishable in some cases: Cooper v. State, 539 So. 2d 508 (Fla. Dist. Ct. App. 1989).

p. 102, thirteen-year-old Ryan White: "Who Was Ryan White?" US Department of Health and Human Services, Health Resources and Services Administration, HIV/AIDS Programs, n.d. http://hab.hrsa.gov/abouthab/ryanwhite.html.

p. 102, In 1990, not long after: Ryan White Comprehensive AIDS Resources Emergency Act of 1990, Pub. L. No. 101-381, 104 Stat. 576 (1990).

p. 102, However, the law gave: Posner and Silbaugh, *Guide to America's Sex Laws,* 72.

p. 103, One such law was passed: David S. Kemp, "The Failure of Criminal HIV Transmission Laws," *Verdict: Legal Analysis and Commentary from Justia,* September 10, 2012.

p. 103, When Plendl learned that Rhoades: Saundra Young, "Imprisoned over HIV: One Man's Story," CNN, November 9, 2012; Kemp, "Failure of Criminal HIV Transmission Laws."

p. 103, Rhoades's conviction was finally: Mark Joseph Stern, "Iowa's Reformed HIV Criminalization Law Is Still Pretty Terrible," *Slate*, June 16, 2014.

p. 103, the Ryan White Act no longer: "HIV-Specific Criminal Laws," Centers for Disease Control and Prevention, n.d. http://www.cdc.gov/hiv/policies/ law/states/exposure.html; Sergio Hernandez, "State-by-State: HIV Laws," ProPublica, December 1, 2013.

p. 103, In 1986, a spate of news stories: Paula A. Treichler, "AIDS, Gender, and Biomedical Discourse," in Fee and Fox, *AIDS*, 212.

p. 103, the stock price of Carter-Wallace: Gamson, "Rubber Wars," 262, 271.

p. 103, By the end of 1986, magazines: Ibid., 262, 272–273.

p. 103, In 1987, a Harris poll showed: "Harris Survey Shows Viewers Think Contraceptive Ads OK," *Broadcasting*, March 30, 1987, 178.

p. 103, The first prime-time condom ads: Eric Noe, "Condom Ads Hit Network TV," ABC News, June 1, 2005.

p. 103, In 2009, President Barack Obama: Julia Preston, "Obama Lifts a Ban on Entry into US by HIV-Positive People," *New York Times*, October 30, 2009; see also "National HIV/AIDS Strategy for the United States," Whitehouse.gov, July 2010, vii. http://www.whitehouse.gov/sites/default/ files/uploads/NHAS.pdf (outlining a "vision" for the US becoming a place where "every person, regardless of . . . sexual orientation . . . will have unfettered access to high quality, life-extending care, free from stigma and discrimination").

p. 103, The percentage of people in: "2009 Survey of Americans on HIV/ AIDS: Summary of Findings on the Domestic Epidemic," Kaiser Family Foundation, April 2009. http://kaiserfamilyfoundation.files.wordpress. com/2013/01/7889.pdf.

p. 103, With HIV/AIDS still closely: Robin A. Pollini et al., "A Community-Based Study of Barriers to HIV Care Initiation," *AIDS Patient Care and STDs* 25, no. 10 (2011): 601–609.

p. 104, Not only may homosexuals: "Military Color Guard to March in Gay Pride Parade," *Military.com News*, June 7, 2014.

p. 104, a general attended a same-sex: "Same-Sex Ceremony Held at Fort Bragg's Chapel," *Military.com News*, December 23, 2013.

p. 104, and gays and lesbians performed: Travis J. Tritten, "Gay, Lesbian Troops Perform in Drag at Fundraiser," *Military.com News*, March 3, 2014.

p. 104, In 2014, thirty-five years after: Matthew M. Burke, "Senate Bill Would Provide Clean Service Records for Discharged Gay, Lesbian Troops," *Stars and Stripes*, February 12, 2014.

p. 104, won her fight to have: Randy Ellis, "Gay Soldier's Discharge Upgraded to Honorable," *Military.com News* (via the *Daily Oklahoman*), June 16, 2014.

p. 104, Even the pope: Philip Pullella, "Pope Says Gays Should Not Be Marginalized," Reuters, July 29, 2013.

p. 104, the 1972 Democratic National Convention: "In 1972, Davis Blazed Party Trail on Gay Rights," NPR, September 5, 2012.

p. 104, and on to presidential candidate: Randy Shilts, *Conduct Unbecoming: Gays and Lesbians in the US Military* (New York: Macmillan, 2005), 274.

p. 104, It exploded in the 1980s: John Harwood, "A Sea Change in Less Than 50 Years as Gay Rights Gained Momentum," *New York Times,* March 25, 2013.

p. 105, By 2002–2003, 58 percent: Eskridge Jr., *Dishonorable Passions,* 267.

p. 105, (This oft-repeated anecdote: Adam Liptak, "Exhibit A for a Major Shift: Justices' Gay Clerks," *New York Times,* June 8, 2013.

p. 105, whom he said were addicted: Eskridge Jr., *Dishonorable Passions.* 245.

p. 105, The very idea seemed: Laurence H. Tribe, "Lawrence v. Texas: The 'Fundamental Right' That Dare Not Speak Its Name," *Harvard Law Review* 117, no. 6 (April 2004): 1893, 1953–1954.

p. 105, For gay-rights attorneys: Eskridge Jr., *Dishonorable Passions,* 235.

p. 106, Hardwick had been caught giving: GA. CODE ANN. § 26-2002 (1983).

p. 106, When the case reached the Supreme Court: Bowers v. Hardwick, 478 US 186, 191 (1986).

p. 106, Georgia's lawyers encouraged: Tribe, "Lawrence v. Texas," 1893, 1900–1901.

p. 106, Chief Justice Warren Burger added: Bowers v. Hardwick, 478 US 186, 200 (1986).

p. 107, When Falwell congratulated the court: John Neuhaus, "God Save This Vulnerable Court," *National Review,* August 15, 1986.

p. 107, The American Center for Law and Justice claimed: Dale Carpenter, *Flagrant Conduct: The Story of Lawrence v. Texas* (New York: W. W. Norton and Company, 2012), 203–206.

p. 108, Going further, the court corrected: Lawrence v. Texas, 539 US 558, 578 (2003).

p. 108, Gay-rights activists wept while: Lawrence v. Texas, 539 US 558, 586-600 (2003).

p. 108, Most horrifying to Scalia: United States v. Windsor, 570 US ___ (2013). In his dissent, Scalia seethed, "By formally declaring anyone opposed to same-sex marriage an enemy of human decency, the majority arms well every challenger to a state law restricting marriage to its traditional definition. . . . It is just a matter of listening and waiting for the other shoe [to drop.]"

p. 109, would be cited in many: Sahil Kapur, "Judge Richard Posner Pokes Scalia in Major Decision for Gay Marriage," *Talking Points Memo,* September 4, 2014; Jonathan Capehart, "Gays and Lesbians Owe Thanks to President George W. Bush and Justice Scalia," *Washington Post,* October 20, 2014; Garrett Epps, "The Twilight of Antonin Scalia," *Atlantic,* August 21, 2014.

p. 109, In one representative passage: Obergefell v. Kasich, case no. 1:13-cv-501 (S.D. Ohio 2013).

p. 109, close its ruling with the following observation: Bostic v. Schaefer, 760 F.3d 352 (2014).

p. 109, As of October 2014, a majority: Robert Barnes, "Supreme Court Declines to Review Same-Sex Marriage Cases, Allowing Unions in 5 States," *Washington Post,* October 6, 2014.

p. 109, five states where it is legal: Jonathan Capehart, "Gay Marriage Victories Only Go So Far," *Washington Post,* October 13, 2014.

p. 110, 2014 study by the Public Religion Research Institute: Robert P. Jones, Daniel Cox, and Juhem Navarro-Rivera, "A Shifting Landscape: A Decade of Change in American Attitudes about Same-Sex Marriage and LGBT Issues," Public Religion Research Institute, 2013, 12, 42–43.

p. 110, In 1894, Krafft-Ebing wrote: Krafft-Ebing, *Psychopathia Sexualis,* 324.

p. 110, Graeme Hammond, a neurologist, suggested: Timothy F. Murphy, "Brief History of a Recurring Nightmare," *Gay and Lesbian Review,* January 1, 2008.

p. 110, The pioneering British computer: Emma G. Fitzsimmons, "Alan Turing, Enigma Code-Breaker and Computer Pioneer, Wins Royal Pardon," *New York Times,* December 24, 2013.

p. 110, At California's Atascadero State Hospital: Nancy Ordover, *American Eugenics: Race, Queer Anatomy, and the Science of Nationalism* (Minneapolis: University of Minnesota Press, 2003), 114.

p. 110, When the singer Lou Reed: Chris Colin, "Lou Reed," *Salon,* May 16, 2000.

p. 110, British psychologist I. Oswald: Murphy, "Brief History of a Recurring Nightmare."

p. 111, While reputable medical organizations: See, e.g., the American Medical Association's position at http://www.ama-assn.org/ama/pub/about-ama/our-people/member-groups-sections/glbt-advisory-committee/ama-policy-regarding-sexual-orientation.page: "[The AMA] opposes, the use of "reparative" or "conversion" therapy that is based upon the assumption that homosexuality per se is a mental disorder or based upon the a priori assumption that the patient should change his/her homosexual orientation" (section H-160.991). See also "Royal College of Psychiatrists' Statement on Sexual Orientation," Royal College of Psychiatrists, April 2014. http://www.rcpsych.ac.uk/pdf/PS02_2014.pdf: "There is no sound scientific evidence that sexual orientation can be changed. . . . Furthermore, so-called treatments of homosexuality can create a setting in which prejudice and discrimination flourish, and there is evidence that they are potentially harmful." See also Judith M. Glassgold et al., "Report of the American Psychological Association Task Force on Appropriate Therapeutic Responses to Sexual Orientation," American Psychological Association, 2009. http://www.apa.org/pi/lgbt/resources/therapeutic-response.pdf.

p. 111, an American court held that the Russian: Pitcherskaia v. INS, 118 F.3d 641 (9th Cir. 1997).

p. 111, California and New Jersey have barred: Alissa Scheller, "48 States Still Allow This Ridiculous Thing, but California's Now Free to Ban It," *Huffington Post,* July 3, 2014.

p. 111, while other states are considering: Paige Lavender, "Some States Are Taking a Stand against Controversial Gay Conversion Therapy," *Huffington Post,* February 24, 2015.

p. 111, In 2013 a leading US gay-cure group: Ian Lovett, "After 37 Years of

Trying to Change People's Sexual Orientation, Group Is to Disband," *New York Times*, June 20, 2013.

p. 111, So far these arguments have not: Burwell v. Hobby Lobby Stores, Inc., 573 US ___, 134 S.Ct. 2751 (2014).

CHAPTER 3

p. 113, In Scotland, among other places: Roger Davidson, "'This Pernicious Delusion': Law, Medicine, and Child Abuse in Early-Twentieth-Century Scotland," *Journal of the History of Sexuality* 10, no. 1 (2001): 62–63.

p. 113, A Child Outrage Committee: Ibid., 66.

p. 113, In 1913, after one Jessie B.: Ibid., 69, 73.

p. 115, However, for the 1 to 4 percent: Julie A. Greenberg, "Defining Male and Female: Intersexuality and the Collision between Law and Biology," *Arizona Law Review* 41 (1999): 267.

p. 115, born with atypical reproductive equipment: Peter A. Lee et al., "Consensus Statement on Management of Intersex Disorders," *Pediatrics* 118, no. 2 (2006): 488–500.

p. 115, Linda Shortliffe, explained that: Sally Lehrman, "Gender Research," *Stanford Today Online*, 1997.

p. 116, what bioethicist Alice Dreger calls: Alice Domurat Dreger, *Hermaphrodites and the Medical Invention of Sex* (Cambridge, MA: Harvard University Press, 1998).

p. 116, Those with testicular tissue: Alice Domurat Dreger, "'Ambiguous Sex'—or Ambivalent Medicine? Ethical Issues in the Treatment of Intersexuality," *Hastings Center Report* 28, no. 3 (1998): 24–35.

p. 116, developed mainly by John Money: Alice Dreger, "Ethical Problems in Intersex Treatment," *Medical Humanities Report* 19, no. 1 (1997).

p. 116, As maleness is widely considered: Kishka-Kamari Ford, "'First, Do No Harm'—The Fiction of Legal Parental Consent to Genital-Normalizing Surgery on Intersexed Infants," *Yale Law and Policy Review* 19, no. 2 (2001): 471; Julie Greenberg, "Legal Aspects of Gender Assignment," *Endocrinologist* 13, no. 3 (June 2003): 277–286.

p. 117, These decisions are usually made: See, e.g., Christin Scarlett Milloy, "Don't Let the Doctor Do This to Your Newborn," *Slate*, June 26, 2014; Dreger, *Hermaphrodites*, Kindle location 2353.

p. 117, In 1995, a medical student: Dreger, *Hermaphrodites*, Kindle locations 2355, 2361.

p. 117, As Dreger observed in 2000: Ibid., Kindle location 2355–2356.

p. 117, To the parents of young Bruce Reimer: John Colapinto, *As Nature Made Him: The Boy Who Was Raised as a Girl* (New York: Perennial, 2000), 32–33.

p. 117, When the Reimers saw the handsome: John Colapinto, "The Case of Joan/John," *Rolling Stone*, December 11, 1997.

p. 118, Money was eager to get started: Ibid; Colapinto, *As Nature Made Him*, 54.

p. 118, Money always had a lot to say: Colapinto, "The Case of Joan/John."

p. 118, None of this went unnoticed at school: Colapinto, *As Nature Made Him,* 165.

p. 118, To reinforce gender and identity roles: Ibid., 86.

p. 118, He also had the twins inspect: Ibid., 86–87.

p. 119, In 1972,: John Money and Anke A. Ehrhardt, *Man and Woman, Boy and Girl: Gender Identity from Conception to Maturity* (Lanham, MD: Jason Aronson, 1996); John Money and Patricia Tucker, *Sexual Signatures on Being a Man or a Woman* (Boston: Little, Brown and Company, 1975), 91–98.

p. 119, Money was lionized in *Time* magazine: [name of article] *Time,* January 8, 1973.

p. 119, The experiment's purported success: Colapinto, *As Nature Made Him,* 69–70.

p. 119, Brown University's Anne Fausto-Sterling: "Transcript: 'Sex: Unknown,'" PBS, October 30, 2011.

p. 119, "all of a sudden everything clicked: Ford, "'First, Do No Harm,'" 473.

p. 120, His marriage failed and in 2004: John Colapinto, "Gender Gap: What Were the Real Reasons behind David Reimer's Suicide?" *Slate,* June 3, 2004.

p. 120, "There are people who are going: Colapinto, *As Nature Made Him*; Colapinto, "The Case of Joan/John."

p. 120, Articles about his case appeared: Jesse Walker, "The Death of David Reimer," Reason.com, May 24, 2004.

p. 120, At least until 2006, the birth: Greenberg, "Legal Aspects of Gender Assignment," 279; Ford, "'First, Do No Harm.'"

p. 120, That year, the American Academy of Pediatrics: Lee et al., "Consensus Statement on Management of Intersex Disorders."

p. 120, Yet no law in the United States: Greenberg, "Legal Aspects of Gender Assignment," 279; Ford, "'First, Do No Harm,'" Milloy, "Don't Let the Doctor Do This to Your Newborn"; Kate Haas, "Who Will Make Room for the Intersexed?" *American Journal of Law and Medicine* 30, no. 1 (2004): 41–68.

p. 120, Colombia has led the way: "Colombia's Highest Court Restricts Surgery on Intersex Children," Intersex Society of North America, http://www.isna.org/colombia, n.d.; "Texts of Colombia Decisions," Intersex Society of North America, http://www.isna.org/node/516, n.d.

p. 121, In 2013, Germany became the first: Jacinta Nandi, "Germany Got It Right by Offering a Third Gender Option on Birth Certificates," *Guardian,* November 10, 2013.

p. 121, Argentine law now permits: Morgan Carpenter, "Australia Can Lead the Way for Intersex People," *Guardian,* June 17, 2013; "We Welcome New Federal Guidelines on Sex and Gender Recognition," Organization Intersex International Australia, June 13, 2013.

p. 121, as do Nepal: Angel L. Martinez Cantera, "Nepal's 'Third Gender,'" Aljazeera, March 12, 2014.

p. 121, and New Zealand: "General Information Regarding Declarations of Family Court as to Sex to Be Shown on Birth Certificates," Internal Affairs

(New Zealand), n.d. http://www.dia.govt.nz/diawebsite.nsf/Files/Geninfo-DeclarationsofFamilyCourt/$file/GeninfoDeclarationsofFamilyCourt.pdf.

p. 121, While other countries make strides: P. Solomon Banda and Nicholas Riccardi, "Coy Mathis Case: Colorado Civil Rights Division Rules in Favor of Transgender 6-Year-Old in Bathroom Dispute," *Huffington Post,* June 24, 2013; California Education Code § 221.5 (2014).

p. 121, For its part, Facebook permits: Aimee Lee Ball, "Who Are You on Facebook Now?" *New York Times,* April 4, 2014.

p. 122, At least as late as the year 2000: Greenberg, "Legal Aspects of Gender Assignment," 279; Ford, "'First, Do No Harm.'"

p. 122, Six years later the AAP took: Lee et al., "Consensus Statement on Management of Intersex Disorders."

p. 122, In her 1998 book *Lessons from the Intersexed:* Suzanne J. Kessler, *Lessons from the Intersexed* (New Brunswick, NJ: Rutgers University Press, 1998), 136.

p. 122, As Johns Hopkins surgeon William Reiner said: "Transcript: 'Sex: Unknown.'"

p. 122, Money's ideas also "dovetailed: Ibid.

p. 122, for which Money provided scientific proof: Colapinto, *As Nature Made Him,* 69–70.

p. 123, Had intersex people enjoyed: Ibid., 88–90; John Money, *Love and Love Sickness: The Science of Sex, Gender Difference, and Pair-Bonding* (Baltimore: Johns Hopkins University Press, 1980), 51–56.

p. 123, He told *Time* magazine in 1980: "Attacking the Last Taboo," *Time,* April 14, 1980.

p. 123, In his book of the same year: Money, *Love and Love Sickness,* 53.

p. 123, sex researcher Alfred Kinsey, who wrote: Alfred Charles Kinsey, *Sexual Behavior in the Human Female* (Bloomington: Indiana University Press, 1953), 121.

p. 123, Kinsey echoed Wilhelm Reich: Turner, *Adventures in the Orgasmatron;* Wilhelm Reich, *The Sexual Revolution: Toward a Self-Regulating Character Structure* (New York: Macmillan 1963).

p. 124, evangelical Josephine Butler, contended that: Eric Berkowitz, *Sex and Punishment: Four Thousand Years of Judging Desire* (Berkeley, CA: Counterpoint Press, 2012), 331.

p. 124, newspaperman W. T. Stead caused riots: Ibid., 334.

p. 125, what Stephen Colbert would call "truthiness": "The Word—Truthiness," *Colbert Report,* October 17, 2005. http://thecolbertreport.cc.com/videos/63ite2/the-word---truthiness.

p. 125, Stead became a worldwide hero: Carolyn Cocca, *Jailbait: The Politics of Statutory Rape Laws in the United States* (Albany: State University of New York Press, 2004), 3–4; Mary E. Odem, *Delinquent Daughters: Protecting and Policing Adolescent Female Sexuality in the United States, 1885–1920* (Chapel Hill: University of North Carolina Press, 1995), 9–13.

p. 125, Within a few decades, it was illegal: Odem, *Delinquent Daughters,* 14.

p. 125, To justify the new laws: Ibid., 16–18; Cocca, *Jailbait,* 3–6.

p. 125, A young woman's virtue: Odem, *Delinquent Daughters*, 24–25.

p. 126, As the laws were written: Cocca, *Jailbait*, 2–3.

p. 126, The "chaste character" exception: Ibid., 3–4.

p. 126, Lawmakers and courts were also: Odem, *Delinquent Daughters*, 31.

p. 126, One medical journal, *Medical Age:* Ibid.

p. 126, To the extent they were victimized sexually: Ibid., 58.

p. 127, In 1915, police in Oakland: Ibid., 63–64.

p. 127, In one 1910 case, the judge: Ibid., 69.

p. 128, According to historian Mary Odem: Ibid., 144–147.

p. 128, On one hand, the laws helped: "Spotlight Investigation: Abuse in the Catholic Church," *Boston Globe,* n.d. http://www.boston.com/globe/spotlight/abuse/geoghan/.

p. 128, Take Kevin Gillson, who at eighteen: Jeff Cole, "Young Expectant Father Gets Probation," *Milwaukee Journal Sentinel,* June 25, 1997; Catherine Elton, "Jail Baiting: Statutory Rape's Dubious Comeback," *New Republic* 217, no. 16 (1997): 12–14.

p. 129, known as Romeo and Juliet exceptions: Cocca, *Jailbait*, 25–28.

p. 129, For example, Nushawn Williams, twenty: Ibid., 50–51; Thomas C. Shevory, *Notorious HIV: The Media Spectacle of Nushawn Williams* (Minneapolis: University of Minnesota Press, 2004).

p. 129, Another sexual encounter that slipped: Shaila Dewan, "Georgia Man Fights Conviction as Molester," *New York Times,* December 19, 2006.

p. 129, Wilson had been offered: Wright Thompson, "Outrageous Injustice," ESPN, n.d. http://sports.espn.go.com/espn/eticket/story?page=wilson.

p. 129, The case drew widespread attention: "Teens, Sex and the Law: Genarlow Wilson," NPR, June 12, 2007.

p. 129, Ugly litigation ensued and: "Wilson Released after Two Years behind Bars for Teen Sex Conviction," CNN, October 27, 2007; Roger N. Lancaster, *Sex Panic and the Punitive State* (Berkeley: University of California Press, 2011), 66.

p. 130, In 1996, President Bill Clinton signed: Judith Levine, *Harmful to Minors: The Perils of Protecting Children from Sex* (New York: Thunder's Mouth Press, 2002), 79–80; Cocca, *Jailbait*, 93–95; Pub.L. 104-193 (1996).

p. 130, Mississippi went further by requiring: "Mississippi Law Will Require Collection of Umbilical Blood from Babies Born to Young Mothers," *Huffington Post,* June 7, 2013.

p. 130, eighteen-year-old Kaitlyn Hunt: "Kaitlyn Hunt, Florida Teen, Faces Felony Charges over Same-Sex Relationship," *Huffington Post,* May 19, 2013.

p. 130, Florida prosecutors offered Hunt: "Kaitlyn Hunt Refuses Plea Deal: Gay Teen Charged over Underage Relationship Will Appear in Court," *Huffington Post,* May 24, 2013.

p. 130, Hunt was jailed after it was discovered: "Kaitlyn Hunt, Gay Florida Teen Accused of Underage Sex, Loses Plea Deal," *Huffington Post,* August 19, 2013; Kim Segal and Greg Botelho, "Gay Florida Teen Kaitlyn Hunt Sent back to Jail over Explicit Texts, Images," CNN, August 21, 2013.

p. 130, Hunt was also charged with: Segal and Botelho, "Gay Florida Teen."

p. 130, She finally pled guilty: Sara Ganim, "Gay Florida Teen Kaitlyn Hunt Pleads No Contest as Part of Deal," CNN, October 9, 2013.

p. 130, served several more months in jail: Joseph Diaz, Jenner Smith, and Alexa Valiente, "Fla. Teen Jailed for Same-Sex Relationship with Underage Girlfriend Ready to 'Move On,'" ABC News, February 14, 2014.

p. 130, To the parents of the young girlfriend: Ibid.

p. 130, To the ACLU, Hunt's ordeal: "Press Release: ACLU of Florida Statement on Prosecution of 18-Year-Old Kaitlyn Hunt," American Civil Liberties Union of Florida, May 21, 2013.

p. 130, To Hunt, her girlfriend was a joy: Diaz, Smith, and Valiente, "Fla. Teen Jailed for Same-Sex Relationship."

p. 131, In 1989, when Josh Gravens: "Sex Offender Fighting Eviction Due to Registry as 12-Year-Old," CBS DFW, October 2, 2012.

p. 132, Because of his status as a sex offender: Lenore Skenazy, "I Saw a Man Get Arrested for a Sex Crime Because He Made a Scheduling Error," Reason.com, July 17, 2014.

p. 132, Taking his kids to school: Emanuella Grinberg, "Report: Registry Does More Harm Than Good for Teen Sex Offenders," CNN, May 1, 2013.

p. 132, After a lengthy and sympathetic: Emily DePrang, "Life on the List," *Texas Observer,* May 31, 2012.

p. 132, Gravens was able to persuade: Emily DePrang, "Josh Gravens, Subject of Observer Feature, Removed from Sex Offender Registry," *Texas Observer,* December 7, 2012.

p. 132, He was also awarded a fellowship: "Introducing the 2013 Soros Justice Fellows," Open Society Foundations, May 2013.

p. 132, According to a 2009 Justice Department: David Finkelhor, Richard Ormrod, and Mark Chaffin, "Juveniles Who Commit Sex Offenses against Minors," US Department of Justice, Office of Juvenile Justice and Delinquency Prevention, December 2009.

p. 132, Of the 17,835 sexual assault: "Sexual Assault," Texas Department of Public Safety, 2012. http://www.txdps.state.tx.us/crimereports/12/citCh7.pdf.

p. 133, The answer to the last question: Gail Ryan, Tom F. Leversee, and Sandy Lane, *Juvenile Sexual Offending: Causes, Consequences, and Correction* (Hoboken, NJ: Wiley, 2010), 267; Michael F. Caldwell, Mitchell H. Ziemke, and Michael J. Vitacco, "An Examination of the Sex Offender Registration and Notification Act as Applied to Juveniles: Evaluation the Ability to Predict Sexual Recidivism," *Psychology, Public Policy, and Law* 14, no. 2 (2008): 91.

p. 133, and when a vocal group of: See, generally, Howard S. Becker, *Outsiders: Studies in the Sociology of Deviance* (New York: Free Press, 1963), 147–163.

p. 133, This was the time when hundreds: Nadine Brozan, "Witness Says She Fears 'Child Predator' Network," *New York Times,* September 18, 1984; see also comments by Donald Wildmon from 1986: "Each year 50,000 missing children are victims of pornography. Most are kidnapped, raped, abused, filmed for porno magazines and movies and finally, more often than not, murdered"; in Joel Best, *Threatened Children: Rhetoric and Concern about Child-Victims* (Chicago: University of Chicago Press, 1990), 47.

p. 133, It was when missing kids: Kenneth R. Clark, "Sen. Paula Hawkins: Sexual Abuse Happens Everywhere to So Many," *Chicago Tribune,* November 2, 1986.

p. 133, The late 1980s was also: Lancaster, *Sex Panic and the Punitive State,* 59.

p. 133, Driven by the new institutional apparatus: Ibid.

p. 133, A Chicago television station circulated: Best, *Threatened Children,* 30.

p. 133, In Congress, it was announced: Ibid.

p. 133, The Sharper Image catalog: Ibid., 22.

p. 133, What sociologist Joel Best called: Ibid., 179.

p. 134, In this heated environment: Ibid., 75–77.

p. 134, Parents who appeared nude: Okami, "Childhood Exposure to Parental Nudity," 51–64.

p. 134, For example, in a 1988 paper: Hendrika B. Cantwell, "Child Sexual Abuse: Very Young Perpetrators," *Child Abuse and Neglect* 12, no. 4 (1988): 579–582.

p. 134, Cantwell's article came at the: From 1985 to 1990, Johnson worked with MacFarlane at SPARK, a project at MacFarlane's Children's Institute International, the stated mission of which is to provide services to children thirteen and under who have "committed sexual offenses against other children." SPARK continues to receive considerable public money for its work. Since leaving SPARK, Johnson has built a substantial therapy and consulting practice specializing in "children with sexual behavior problems."

p. 135, In these articles, Johnson coined: Toni Cavanagh Johnson, "Child Perpetrators—Children Who Molest Other Children: Preliminary Findings," *Child Abuse and Neglect* 12, no. 2 (1988): 219–229.

p. 135, Among other horrors, her articles: T. C. Johnson, "Understanding the Sexual Behaviors of Young Children," *SIECUS Reports,* 1991, 8–15; T. C. Johnson, "Sexuality in Children: From Normal to Pathological," paper presented at the Western Region, Los Angeles Chapter meeting of the Society for the Scientific Study of Sex, 1991.

p. 135, In a 1989 article discussing female: Toni Cavanagh Johnson, "Female Child Perpetrators: Children Who Molest Other Children," *Child Abuse and Neglect* 13 (1989): 571–585.

p. 135, While Johnson had admitted earlier: Johnson, "Child Perpetrators," 221.

p. 135, she nevertheless called the girls: Johnson, "Female Child Perpetrators," 571–573. See also, Simon Hackett, S. Vosmer, and M. Callanan, "'Normal' and 'Inappropriate' Childhood Sexual Behaviours; Findings from a Delphi Study of Professionals in the United Kingdom," *Journal of Sexual Aggression* 15, no. 3 (2009): 275, 276.

p. 135, Perhaps sensing the trouble inherent: Paul Okami, "'Child Perpetrators of Sexual Abuse': The Emergence of a Problematic Deviant Category," *Journal of Sex Research* 29, no. 1 (February 1992): 112–113; Toni Cavanagh Johnson, Eliana Gil, and William N. Friedrich, *Sexualized Children: Assessment and*

Treatment of Sexualized Children and Children Who Molest (Rockville, MD: Launch Press, 1993); T. C. Johnson, *Understanding Children's Sexual Behaviors: What's Natural and Healthy* (San Diego: Institute on Violence, 2013).

p. 135, in her own therapy and child-sexuality: "Assessment," Toni Cavanagh Johnson, Ph.D., n.d. http://www.tcavjohn.com/products.php#Assessment.

p. 135, (which she later admitted were: Toni Cavanagh Johnson and Ronda Doonan, "Children Twelve and Younger with Sexual Behavior Problems: What We Know in 2005 That We Didn't Know in 1985," in *Current Perspectives: Working with Sexually Aggressive Youth and Youth with Sexual Behavior Problems,* ed. Robert E. Longo and David S. Prescott (Holyoke, MA: NEARI Press, 2006), 79.

p. 135, Among the behaviors of kindergarteners: Johnson, *Understanding Children's Sexual Behaviors,* 13–18.

p. 136, In criticizing this willy-nilly: Okami, "'Child Perpetrators of Sexual Abuse,'" 114.

p. 136, Okami also pointed to the self-interest: Ibid., 121; see also, Levine, *Harmful to Minors,* 52–53.

p. 136, When, for example, Johnson demanded: Johnson, "Child Perpetrators," 219.

p. 136, The Justice Department noted that there: Finkelhor, Ormrod, and Chaffin, "Juveniles Who Commit Sex Offenses against Minors."

p. 136, Woven through all of this: Caldwell, Ziemke, and Vitacco, "An Examination of the Sex Offender Registration and Notification Act," 91; Ryan, Leversee, and Lane, *Juvenile Sexual Offending,* 272.

p. 136, By the mid-1990s, despite the fact: Lisa C. Trivits and N. Dickon Reppucci, "Application of Megan's Law to Juveniles," *American Psychologist* 57, no. 9 (2002): 690, 695.

p. 136, In 1994, in the Princeton journal: Judith V. Becker, "Offenders: Characteristics and Treatment," *Future of Children* 4, no. 2 (1994): 179.

p. 136, The results of this movement: Ryan, Leversee, and Lane, *Juvenile Sexual Offending,* 267–271.

p. 137, By 2009, thirty-six states had laws: Ibid., 267–270; Caldwell, Ziemke, and Vitacco, "An Examination of the Sex Offender Registration and Notification Act."

p. 137, In 1996, a neurologically impaired: Levine, *Harmful to Minors,* 47.

p. 137, In 1999, police busted a child: "Police Uncover Sex Ring," *Hour,* July 5, 1999, B13.

p. 137, In 2001, an eleven-year-old Minnesota boy: In Re Welfare of J.R.Z., 648 N.W.2d 241 (Minn. Ct. App. 2002).

p. 137, that same year, a twelve-year-old: In Re J.W., docket no. 92116 (Ill. S. Ct. 2002).

p. 137, In 1993, after spending two years: Levine, *Harmful to Minors,* 47.

p. 137, In Texas, a twelve-year-old boy: Trivits and Reppucci, "Application of Megan's Law to Juveniles," 690, 692.

p. 138, In 1996, an eleven-year-old boy: Johnson and Doonan, "Children Twelve and Younger with Sexual Behavior Problems," 89.

p. 138, In 2000, in New Jersey, a twelve-year-old boy: "Raised on the Registry: The Irreparable Harm of Placing Children on Sex Offender Registries in the US," Human Rights Watch, May 2013, 35–36.

p. 138, Dominic G. was charged in 2006: Ibid., section 5.

p. 138, At least six countries besides the US: Ibid., 94.

p. 138, If, for example, a child offender: "Understanding Juvenile Sexual Offending Behavior: Emerging Research, Treatment Approaches and Management Practices," Center for Sex Offender Management, US Department of Justice, December 1999, 10.

p. 138, Moreover, if a therapist keeps: Ibid.

p. 138, sex-offender specialist Christopher Lobanov-Rostovsky: Ryan, Leversee, and Lane, *Juvenile Sexual Offending,* 270.

p. 138, Moreover, in the short time since: Ibid., 271–274; Caldwell, Ziemke, and Vitacco, "An Examination of the Sex Offender Registration and Notification Act," Johnson and Doonan, "Children Twelve and Younger with Sexual Behavior Problems," 94, 96–97.

p. 139, In 2013, Human Rights Watch: "Raised on the Registry."

p. 139, Johnson, for one, has stepped back: Johnson and Doonan, "Children Twelve and Younger with Sexual Behavior Problems," 79–90.

p. 139, Johnson reaffirmed this position: Johnson, *Understanding Children's Sexual Behaviors,* 23.

p. 140, After killing eight girls, Beckert: "'M' Quotes," IMDB, n.d.

p. 140, The laws, mostly written by: Freedman, "'Uncontrolled Desires,'" 84.

p. 140, As with the other bogeymen: Ibid., 94.

p. 141, Hoover could take credit: Chrysanthi S. Leon, *Sex Fiends, Perverts, and Pedophiles: Understanding Sex Crime Policy in America* (New York: New York University Press, 2011), 40.

p. 141, The sexual-psychopath panics of: Freedman, "'Uncontrolled Desires,'" 84, footnote 3.

p. 141, Arrests for sexual offenses always: Lancaster, *Sex Panic and the Punitive State,* 35.

p. 141, as observed by sociologist Edward Sutherland: Edwin H. Sutherland, "The Diffusion of Sexual Psychopath Laws," *American Journal of Sociology* 56, no. 2 (1950): 145.

p. 141, In New York in 1937: Ibid., 143.

p. 141, a shock repeated the same year in California: Freedman, "'Uncontrolled Desires,'" 93.

p. 141, In 1949, during a frenzied week: Sutherland, "Diffusion of Sexual Psychopath Laws," 143.

p. 141, while the *Saturday Evening Post* reported: Tamara Rice Lave, "Only Yesterday: The Rise and Fall of Twentieth Century Sexual Psychopath Laws," *Louisiana Law Review* 69 (2009): 550–551.

p. 141, During the 1930s panic, five states: Lancaster, *Sex Panic and the Punitive State,* 34.

p. 142, A common feature of the sexual-psychopath laws: Freedman, "'Uncontrolled Desires,'" 98.

p. 142, Some states didn't require a conviction: Lave, "Only Yesterday," 572–574.

p. 142, Observed Sutherland in 1950: Sutherland, "Diffusion of Sexual Psychopath Laws," 145.

p. 142, Illinois's sexual-psychopath law: Ibid; Becker, *Outsiders*, 149–152. Not all psychiatrists were gung-ho on passing sexual psychopath laws. Many were in fact skeptical. Freedman, "'Uncontrolled Desires,'" 84, 97.

p. 142, In 1934, Ohio psychiatrists: Freedman, "'Uncontrolled Desires,'" 96.

p. 142, the *Saturday Evening Post* opined: Lave, "Only Yesterday," 569.

p. 142, Immediately following the Stroble drama: Leon, *Sex Fiends, Perverts, and Pedophiles*, 38.

p. 142, The laws also sparked a construction boom: Freedman, "'Uncontrolled Desires,'" 99.

p. 143, By the 1960s, what had begun: Philip Jenkins, *Moral Panic: Changing Concepts of the Child Molester in Modern America* (New Haven, CT: Yale University Press, 1998), 75–93.

p. 143, New Jersey's law in 1950: Lave, "Only Yesterday," 572, footnote 109.

p. 143, In 1952, a young District of Columbia man: Cross v. Harris, 418 F.2d 1095 (D.C. Cir. 1969).

p. 143, Soon after New Jersey's law: Lave, "Only Yesterday," 583.

p. 143, A New Jersey black man: Ibid., 582–583.

p. 143, In 1943, a Minnesota father: Dittrich v. Brown County, 9 N.W.2d 510 (Minn. 1943).

p. 144, In his influential 1962 book: Morris Ploscowe, *Sex and the Law* (New York: Ace Books, 1962), 212.

p. 144, The Group for the Advancement of Psychiatry: Lave, "Only Yesterday," 582, footnote 159.

p. 144, In 1977 the group went even further: W. Lawrence Fitch and Richard James Ortega, "Law and the Confinement of Psychopaths," *Behavioral Sciences and the Law* 18, no. 5 (2000): 666 (quoting the 1977 plea for repeal of the special commitment laws by the Group for the Advancement of Psychiatry).

p. 144, In truth, opined a prominent appellate judge: Cross v. Harris, 418 F.2d 1095 (D.C. Cir. 1969); see also, Sprecht v. Patterson, 368 US 605 (1967).

p. 144, The following year Michigan, which: Freedman, "'Uncontrolled Desires,'" 100.

p. 144, The laws fell into disuse: Roxanne Lieb and Scott Matson, "Sexual Predator Commitment Laws in the United States: 1998 Update," Washington State Institute for Public Policy, September 1998, 1–2.

p. 145, In 1984, the newly created: "Congressional Authorization," National Center for Missing and Exploited Children, n.d.

p. 145, in the process became a dominant force: Jenkins, *Moral Panic*, 128–129.

p. 145, That same year, the Justice Department: Ibid., 118.

p. 145, The NCMEC was formed in response: In fact, a drifter and convicted serial killer named Ottis Toole confessed in 1983 to the killing of Walsh.

Yolanne Almanzar, "27 Years Later, Case Is Closed in Slaying of Abducted Child, *New York Times,* December 16, 2008.

p. 145, Nevertheless, Walsh's father (later to become: Levine, *Harmful to Minors,* 24.

p. 145, In 2006, Adam Walsh's name: Adam Walsh Child Protection and Safety Act of 2006, H.R. 4472, 109th Cong. (2006).

p. 146, In 1988, Margaret Kelly Michaels: Seth Faison, "Child-Abuse Conviction of Woman Is Overturned," *New York Times,* March 27, 1993.

p. 146, At the Little Rascals Day Care Center: "Settlement Reached in Martensville Sex-Abuse Case," CBC News, November 18, 2004; see also articles collected in "Martensville Scandal," Injustice Busters, n.d. http://injusticebusters.org/04/Sterlings_settlement.shtml.

p. 146, In 2014, day-care center operators: Linda Rodriguez McRobbie, "The Real Victims of Satanic Ritual Abuse," *Slate,* January 7, 2014.

p. 147, In 1983, Judy Johnson: "Chronology of the McMartin Preschool Abuse Trials," University of Missouri–Kansas City School of Law, n.d. http://law2.umkc.edu/faculty/projects/ftrials/mcmartin/mcmartinchrono.html.

p. 147, MacFarlane's methods of interviewing: Douglas Linder, "Sample Interviews by Investigators with Former Students of the McMartin Preschool," University of Missouri–Kansas City School of Law, n.d. http://law2.umkc.edu/faculty/projects/ftrials/mcmartin/victiminterviews.html.

p. 147, She also said that the McMartin Preschool: Brozan, "Witness Says She Fears 'Child Predator' Network."

p. 147, By the time the Buckeys were indicted: McRobbie, "The Real Victims of Satanic Ritual Abuse."

p. 147, MacFarlane and several confused kids: Lancaster, *Sex Panic and the Punitive State,* 55.

p. 148, In 1990, the jury deadlocked: Douglas Linder, "Chronology of the McMartin Preschool Abuse Trials," University of Missouri–Kansas City School of Law, n.d. http://law2.umkc.edu/faculty/projects/ftrials/mcmartin/mcmartinchrono.html.

p. 148, While killers like Gacy fit: Jenkins, *Moral Panic.*

p. 148, (For his part, Malcolm Gladwell: Malcom Gladwell, "In Plain View," *New Yorker,* September 24, 2012, 87.

p. 148, Without a working profile of a pedophile: Paul Okami and Amy Goldberg, "Personality Correlates of Pedophilia: Are They Reliable Indicators?" *Journal of Sex Research* 29, no. 3 (1992): 297, 302.

p. 148, Depending on whom one listened to: Ibid., 302.

p. 148, one who has had contact with: David Finkelhor, *A Sourcebook on Child Sexual Abuse* (Thousand Oaks, CA: Sage Publications, 1986), 24.

p. 148, one who desires sex with people: Okami and Goldberg, "Personality Correlates of Pedophilia," 302.

p. 148, one who makes verbal propositions: Finkelhor, *A Sourcebook on Child Sexual Abuse,* 24.

p. 148, one who "watches" children: Carla Van Dam, *Identifying Child Molesters: Preventing Child Sexual Abuse by Recognizing the Patterns of the Offenders*

(Binghamton, NY: Haworth Maltreatment and Trauma Press, 2001), 49–50.

p. 148, a minor who has sex: Ibid., 44.

p. 148, There is even something called corporate paedophilia: Emma Rush and Andrea La Nauze, "Corporate Paedophilia: Sexualization of Children in Australia," Australia Institute, October 2006, 1.

p. 148, as has been true in Virginia since 2008: VA stats § 18.2-370.6. (2008); "Virginia Law Takes Aim at Adults Who French Kiss Minors," Fox News, March 9, 2008; "AP: Adults Who French Kiss Minors Must Register as Sex Offenders," NBC News, March 8, 2008.

p. 149, According to two Canadian experts: A. J. R. Harris and R. K. Hanson, "Clinical, Actuarial, and Dynamic Risk Assessment of Sexual Offenders: Why Do Things Keep Changing?" *Journal of Sexual Aggression* 16 (2010): 298.

p. 149, Between 2003 and 2008, an average: Ibid., 297.

p. 149, a 2013 article titled "The Science of Sex Abuse": Aviv, "Science of Sex Abuse," 40.

p. 149, In fact, as a prominent psychiatrist told Aviv: Ibid., 41.

p. 150, the registries have now ensnared more: "Map of Registered Sex Offenders in the United States," National Center for Missing and Exploited Children, n.d. http://www.missingkids.com/en_US/documents/Sex_Offenders_Map .pdf#page=1.

p. 150, Sex-offender registries were created: Lave, "Only Yesterday," 565–566.

p. 150, Chicago did the same, as did: Ibid., 566.

p. 150, California was first to set up: Catherine L. Carpenter and Amy E. Beverlin, "The Evolution of Unconstitutionality in Sex Offender Registration Laws," *Hastings Law Journal* 63 (May 2012): 1077.

p. 150, a Minnesota boy, Jacob Wetterling: To this day, the fate of Jacob Wetterling is unknown.

p. 150, The Wetterling Act established: Jacob Wetterling Crimes Against Children and Sexually Violent Offender Registration Act, Pub. L. No. 103-322 tit. XVII, subtit.A, 108 Stat. 2038-2042 (1994). Title XVII of the Violent Crime Control and Law Enforcement Act of 1994, 42 USC. 14071 et seq.

p. 150, By the end of the decade: Agan, "Sex Offender Registries," 207, 210.

p. 150, In 1996, in response to the abduction: Ibid., 210.

p. 150, That same year saw the passage: "Raised on the Registry," 20.

p. 150, California voters, for example: "Jessica's Law, California Proposition 83 (2006)," Ballotpedia, n.d. http://ballotpedia.org/Jessica's_Law,_California_Proposition_83_(2006)#Retroactivity_challenged.

p. 150, This law requires that felony sex offenders: Ibid.

p. 151, These restrictions have been widely duplicated: Lancaster, *Sex Panic and the Punitive State,* 100–102.

p. 151, Many cities are also building "pocket parks": Ian Lovett, "Neighborhoods Seek to Banish Sex Offenders by Building Parks," *New York Times,* March 9, 2013.

p. 151, If the laws were tailored to keep: Tewksbury, Jennings, and Zgoba, "Sex Offenders."

p. 151, In 1986, in Massachusetts: Lancaster, *Sex Panic and the Punitive State,* 101.

p. 151, In Miami, where sex offenders: Joseph Goldstein, "Housing Restrictions Keep Sex Offenders in Prison beyond Release Dates," *New York Times,* August 21, 2014.

p. 152, As of 2010, anyone who robs: Rainer v. State of Georgia, 690 S.E.2d 827 (2010).

p. 152, In Illinois, in 2002, a man: People v. Johnson, 225 Ill.2d 573 (2007).

p. 152, With variations depending on where: See, generally, Carpenter and Beverlin, "The Evolution of Unconstitutionality."

p. 152, After an exhaustive 2011 study: Agan, "Sex Offender Registries," 208.

p. 152, Other studies have shown similar results: Zgoba et al., "Megan's Law."

p. 153, In another major study, in 2011: J. J. Prescott and Jonah E. Ruckoff, "Do Sex Offender Registration and Notification Laws Affect Criminal Behavior?" *Journal of Law and Economics* 54, no. 1 (2011): 161–206.

p. 153, a "race to the harshest": Carpenter and Beverlin, "Evolution of Unconstitutionality," 1071, 1076.

p. 153, When, for example, Patti O'Connell: "Jessica's Law, California Proposition 83 (2006)."

p. 153, Jessica had been attacked by a convicted: Keegan Kyle, Tony Saavedra, and Denisse Salazar, "Where Are Sex Offenders? Jessica's Law Complicates Monitoring," *Orange County Register,* April 26, 2014.

p. 153, "There's not a shred of research: Ibid.

p. 153, In voicing support for Jessica's Law: Jason Peckenpaugh, "Controlling Sex Offender Re-Entry: Jessica's Law Measures in California," *Journal of Offender Monitoring* 19, no. 1 (2006): 13–29.

p. 153, So long as our inquiries stop: Fortunately, in 2015 the California Supreme Court took a first step toward undoing some of the injustices done to sex offenders by unanimously declaring that San Diego's blanket enforcement of Jessica's Law's residency restrictions is unconstitutional. According to the court, the restrictions have "result[ed] in large groups of parolees having to sleep in alleys and riverbeds, a circumstance that did not exist prior to Jessica's Law," and "the increased incidence of homelessness has in turn hampered the surveillance and supervision of such parolees, thereby thwarting the legitimate governmental objective [. . . of] protecting the public from sex offenders." Hopefully, this decision will encourage other locales to reexamine their own residency restrictions. In Re William Taylor, Cal.Sup.Ct. case no. S206143 (March 2, 2015).

p. 154, More than 90 percent of child sexual abuse: According to the Justice Department, 93 percent of sexually abused children are molested by family members, close friends, or acquaintances. Howard N. Snyder, "Sexual Assault of Young Children as Reported to Law Enforcement: Victim, Incident, and Offender Characteristics," US Department of Justice, Bureau of Justice Statistics, July 2000.

p. 154, The Catholic sex-abuse cases: "Number of Priests Accused of Sexually Abusing Children as Reported by the US Conference of Catholic Bishops with Numbers of Persons Alleging Abuse," BishopAccountability.org, March 28, 2014. This data does not include cases from 2003.

p. 154, Litigation has already been going on: "Sexual Abuse by US Catholic Clergy: Settlements and Monetary Awards in Civil Suits," BishopAccountability.org, n.d. http://www.bishop-accountability.org/settlements/#largest_settlements.

p. 154, Despite Pope Francis's gestures: See, e.g., Elisabetta Povoledo, "Pope Francis to Meet Victims of Sexual Abuse," *New York Times,* May 27, 2014; Sandro Contenta, "Pope Francis Names Sex Abuse Victim as Adviser," *Star,* March 31, 2014; Philip Pullella, "Pope Francis Calls Clergy Sex Abuse 'A Leprosy,' Says 2 Percent of Priests Are Pedophiles in Eugenio Scalfari Interview," *Huffington Post,* July 13, 2014.

p. 154, Nor will the church purge itself: "Convention on the Rights of the Child," United Nations, February 25, 2014; Lizzy Davies, "UN Committee Against Torture Criticises Vatican Handling of Sex Abuse," *Guardian,* May 23, 2014.

p. 154, The full scope and implications: "Database of Publicly Accused Priests in the United States," BishopAccountability.org, n.d. http://bishop-accountability.org/priestdb/PriestDBbylastName-A.html.

p. 154, but others—whose cases haven't gone: Michelle Boorstein and William Wan, "After Child Abuse Accusations, Catholic Priests Often Simply Vanish," *Washington Post,* December 4, 2010.

p. 155, As observed by the UN Committee: "Convention on the Rights of the Child," 9.

p. 155, Penn State University allegedly covered up: Mark Scolforo, "Graham Spanier Charged: Ex-Penn State President Facing Perjury Charge in Jerry Sandusky Case," *Huffington Post,* November 1, 2012; Michael Sokolove, "The Trials of Graham Spanier, Penn State's Ousted President," *New York Times,* July 16, 2014.

p. 155, before the school agreed to pay $60 million: Mark Scolforo, "Penn State Will Pay Nearly $60 Million to 26 Sandusky Victims," *Huffington Post,* October 28, 2013.

p. 155, Given that Penn State's annual budget: Sokolove, "Trials of Graham Spanier."

p. 155, Starting in about 1920, the Boy Scouts of America: "Boy Scouts Ordered to Pay Oregon Man Kerry Lewis $18.5M in Sex Abuse Case," *Daily News,* April 24, 2010.

p. 155, The perversion files contain multiple: Jason Sickles, "Retired Boy Scouts Executive Defends His Work as Keeper of Secret Sex Files," *Yahoo News,* November 5, 2012.

p. 155, Some of the perversion files were released: "Oregon Court Releases 20,000 Pages from Boy Scouts 'Perversion Files,'" *Daily News,* June 14, 2012.

p. 155, While Judaism, like Islam, has no "church": Sharon Otterman, "Abuse Verdict Topples a Hasidic Wall of Secrecy," *New York Times,* December 10, 2012.

p. 155, A 2012 trial was the first to crack: Josh Saul, "Hasidic Counselor Nechemya Weberman Gets 103 Years in Child Sex-Abuse Case," *New York Post,* January 22, 2013.

p. 156, Her fears were well-founded: Ibid.

p. 156, In 2012, UK police paid a visit: Danica Kirka and Jim Gomez, "Operation Endeavor: Authorities Dismantle International Pedophile Ring That Live-Streamed Sex Abuse," *Huffington Post,* January 16, 2014; "Philippines Web Abuse Ring Smashed in UK-Led Operation," BBC News, January 15, 2014.

p. 157, In 1977, child psychiatrist Judianne Densen-Gerber: Lawrence A. Stanley, "The Child Porn Myth," *Cardozo Arts and Entertainment Law Journal* 7 (1989): 311–315.

p. 157, the Protection of Children Against Sexual Exploitation Act: Ibid., 302–303.

p. 157, With these and other laws in place: Ibid., 315.

p. 157, Two years later, after searching under: Ibid.

p. 157, With little to do in this regard: Levine, *Harmful to Minors,* 37.

p. 158, One of the first casualties was a sex-education book: Okami, "'Child Perpetrators of Sexual Abuse,'" 117.

p. 158, Following that auspicious beginning came: Levine, *Harmful to Minors,* 40–41.

p. 158, the San Francisco art photographer Jock Sturges: Marjorie Heins, *Sex, Sin, and Blasphemy: A Guide to America's Censorship Wars* (New York: New Press, 1993), 110–111.

p. 158, Sturges was arrested just before: Meredith Dank et al., "Estimating the Size and Structure of the Underground Commercial Sex Economy in Eight Major US Cities," Urban Institute, March 2014, 252–253.

p. 159, Nevertheless, as Operation Endeavor: Aviv, "Science of Sex Abuse," 38.

p. 159, After four years in prison, John was released: Ibid., 36–46.

p. 160, the American Psychological Association has already come out: Ibid., 41.

CHAPTER 4

p. 161, Gratuitous hard-core passages in popular books: Mario Puzo, *The Godfather* (New York: Penguin, New York, 1969).

p. 161, At least forty million Americans: Jonathan Liew, "All Men Watch Porn, Scientists Find," *Telegraph,* December 2, 2009.

p. 161, and while estimates differ as to: Charlie Warzel, "The Internet's Dirty Secret: Nobody Knows How Much Porn There Is," Buzzfeed, May 15, 2013.

p. 161, Feminist activist Andrea Dworkin warned: "Anti-Porn Crusader Dworkin Dies," BBC News, April 13, 2005.

p. 162, After describing the grisly rape: Catharine A. MacKinnon, *Only Words* (Cambridge, MA: Harvard University Press, 1993), 19; "Attorney General's Commission on Pornography: Final Report ('The Meese Report')," 1986, 299–352, http://www.porn-report.com/; Orrin G. Hatch, "Fighting the Pornification of America by Enforcing Obscenity Laws," *Stanford Law and Policy Review* 23, no. 1 (January 2012). (Hatch vigorously argues that pornography causes sexual aggression.)

p. 162, According to British journalist Linda Grant: Linda Grant, *Sexing the Millennium* (New York: Grove Press, 1994), 5.

p. 162, As for judges who hesitate to send: MacKinnon, *Only Words,* 19.

p. 162, a high-level government commission in 1986: "The Meese Report," 1573, 1578.

p. 162, Are female "ejaculation": Frankie Mullin, "British BDSM Enthusiasts, Say Goodbye to Your Favourite Homegrown Porn," *Vice,* December 1, 2014. http://www.vice.com/en_uk/read/the-end-of-uk-bdsm-282. For an account of the UK's long-standing uneasy relationship with depictions of female ejaculation, see Tracy Clark-Flory, "The Orgasm Police: Why Female Ejaculation Is One of the Last Porn Taboos, *Salon,* December 16, 2014. Apparently, the issue turns on whether the film involves "urolangia" (the eroticism of urination), in which case censorship is allowed.

p. 163, In 1873, in support of a sweeping: Berkowitz, *Sex and Punishment,* 368.

p. 163, As eminent judge Richard A. Posner: Richard A. Posner, *Sex and Reason* (Cambridge, MA: Harvard University Press, 1992), 2.

p. 163, The case to which Posner was referring: Barnes v. Glen Theatre, 501 US 560 (1991).

p. 163, After Posner's Chicago-based court: Ibid.; Heins, *Sex, Sin, and Blasphemy,* 97–98.

p. 163, the alleged obscenity of James Joyce's Ulysses: Leigh Gilmore, "Obscenity, Modernity, Identity: Legalizing 'The Well of Loneliness' and 'Nightwood,'" *Journal of the History of Sexuality* 4, no. 4 (April 1994): 603, 622; Edward De Grazia, *Girls Lean back Everywhere: The Law of Obscenity and the Assault on Genius* (New York: Vintage Books, 1993), xi–xii; Kevin Birmingham, *The Most Dangerous Book: The Battle for James Joyce's Ulysses* (New York: Penguin Press, 2014), 327.

p. 163, Fortunately for subsequent generations: United States v. One Book Called "Ulysses," 5 F.Supp. 182 (1933); Morris L. Ernst, "Reflections on the Ulysses Trial and Censorship," *James Joyce Quarterly* 3, no. 1 (1965).

p. 164, Had Woolsey's erection test produced: Mary Lydon, "On Censorship: Staying Power," *SubStance* 12, no. 37/38: A special issue from the Center for Twentieth Century Studies (1983): 107.

p. 164, courtroom experts such as Judith Lynne Hanna: Judith Lynne Hanna, *Naked Truth: Strip Clubs, Democracy, and a Christian Right* (Austin: University of Texas Press, 2012), 105–106.

p. 164, or when cities impose a four-foot distance: Ibid., 38.

p. 164, In the hundreds of laws and court decisions: Here, in no particular order, is a partial list of iconic books (to say nothing of films, visual images, audio recordings, or sculptures) that have been banned, confiscated, or otherwise restricted from circulation for sexual content in the United States, Europe, or the British Commonwealth during the twentieth century: Voltaire's *Candide;* Aristophanes's *Lysistrata;* Geoffrey Chaucer's *Canterbury*

Tales; Boccaccio's *Decameron;* Daniel Defoe's *Moll Flanders; The Arabian Nights;* Jean-Jacques Rousseau's *Confessions;* Mary Shelley's *Frankenstein;* D. H. Lawrence's *Lady Chatterly's Lover;* Shakespeare's *Hamlet, Macbeth, King Lear,* and *Twelfth Night* (pulled from school curriculum for promoting an "alternate lifestyle"); William Styron's *Sophie's Choice;* Henry Miller's *Tropic of Cancer* and *Sexus;* Allen Ginsburg's *Howl;* various of Samuel Beckett's works, Maya Angelou's *I Know Why the Caged Bird Sings;* Radclyffe Hall's *The Well of Loneliness;* William Burroughs's *Naked Lunch;* Aldous Huxley's *Brave New World;* Vladimir Nabokov's *Lolita;* Norman Mailer's *The Naked and the Dead;* Toni Morrison's *Beloved;* and Richard Wright's *Native Son.*

p. 164, (rather than his or her "good, old fashioned: See, e.g., Brockett v. Spokane Arcades, Inc., 472 US 491 (1985).

p. 164, then it can be outlawed as obscene: This is drawn from Miller v. California, 413 US 15, 21 (1973), which phrases the standard as follows: "The basic guidelines for the trier of fact must be: (a) whether 'the average person, applying contemporary community standards' would find that the work, taken as a whole, appeals to the prurient interest, (b) whether the work depicts or describes, in a patently offensive way, sexual conduct specifically defined by the applicable state law; and (c) whether the work, taken as a whole, lacks serious literary, artistic, political, or scientific value." The quoted distinction between "good, old-fashioned, healthy" sexual appetites and prurient or morbid sexual ones comes from Brokett v. Spokane Arcades, Inc., 472 US 491 (1985).

p. 164, Since at least the 1920s, commercial enterprises: D'Emilio and Freedman, *Intimate Matters,* 279.

p. 165, During the same period, a commission headed: Penthouse International, Ltd. v. Edwin A. Meese, 939 F.2d 1011 (1991).

p. 165, porn producer and director Harold Freeman: People v. Freeman, 46 Cal.3d 419 (1988).

p. 166, Eleven years after *Freeman,* a restless: Annmarie Timmins, "Offer to Tape Sex Nullifies Conviction," *Concord Monitor,* December 5, 2008.

p. 166, While both Shevon and Saint: Daniel Miller, "The Spectacular Rise and Surprising Exit of a Hollywood Executive," *Los Angeles Times,* August 23, 2013.

p. 167, It should be noted that the state of Utah: Benjamin Edelman, "Red Light States: Who Buys Online Adult Entertainment?" *Journal of Economic Perspectives* 23, no. 1 (2009): 209, 215.

p. 168, For innovators such as Isadora Duncan: Edward Ross Dickinson, "'Must We Dance Naked?' Art, Beauty, and Law in Munich and Paris, 1911–1913," *Journal of the History of Sexuality* 20, no. 1 (2011): 99.

p. 168, The American performer Maud Allan: Ibid., 103.

p. 168, the Dutch dancer/prostitute/spy: Hirschfeld, *Sexual History of the World War,* 284.

p. 168, The minor French danseuse Adorée Villany: Dickinson, "'Must We Dance Naked?'" 122.

p. 168, The core of the controversy was Villany's body: Ibid., 127.

p. 169, In 1907, at the famed Moulin Rouge: Nicole Albert, "Books on Trial:

Prosecutions for Representing Sapphism in Fin-de-Siècle France," in *Disorder in the Court: Trials and Sexual Conflict at the Turn of the Century*, ed. George Robb and Nancy Erber (New York: New York University Press, 1999).

p. 169, In 1907, the city of Chicago: D'Emilio and Freedman, *Intimate Matters*, 281–282.

p. 169, For example, in 1972: Jenkins v. Georgia, 418 US 153 (1974).

p. 170, On the battlefronts and in the cities: Hirschfeld, *Sexual History of the World War*, 30, 34.

p. 170, Everywhere, Hirschfeld observed, "the pleasure: Ibid., 210–211.

p. 170, When prostitutes were unavailable: Ibid., 83.

p. 170, They had sex with each other: Ibid., 94–95.

p. 170, Reviews had praised her "animal-like and carnal": Hoare, *Oscar Wilde's Last Stand*, 76–77.

p. 171, Proto-fascist politicians such as: Ibid., 1.

p. 172, In the months to come, Douglas worked: Ibid., 152.

p. 172, Six days after the advert for *Salome* appeared: Ibid., 126.

p. 173, but the real crowd-pleaser: Frank Rich, "Mae West 'Sex' Capade!" *New York Magazine*, April 1, 2012.

p. 174, The issue often arose in the context: Andrea Friedman, "'The Habitats of Sex-Crazed Perverts': Campaigns against Burlesque in Depression-Era New York City," *Journal of the History of Sexuality* 7, no. 2 (1996): 216.

p. 174, As observed by historian Andrea Friedman: Ibid., 227.

p. 175, Nudity itself has long been the stuff: Hanna, *Naked Truth*, 106.

p. 175, When Martha Graham integrated: Ibid., 139.

p. 175, when the Washington Shakespeare Company: Glen Weldon, "Macbeth," *Washington Citypaper*, June 29, 2007.

p. 175, a hydrogen bomb: See, e.g., United States of America v. Progressive, Inc., Erwin Knoll, Samuel Day Jr., and Howard Morland, 467 F. Supp. 990 (W.D. Wis. 1979).

p. 175, In fact, five years before Keating: Freedman v. Maryland, 380 US 51 (1965).

p. 176, However, in 1970, the prospect of naked: Douglas M. Charles, *FBI's Obscene File*, 84.

p. 176, opining that the play's advocacy: Heins, *Sex, Sin, and Blasphemy*, 105–106.

p. 176, As of 2012, there were about four thousand: Hanna, *Naked Truth*, 2.

p. 176, Two strip club companies: Lisa Scott, "Strip Clubs 'May Die Out' If New Lap-Dancing Laws Come into Place," *Metro*, March 7, 2010.

p. 177, Most strip clubs are zoned: Hanna, *Naked Truth*, 67.

p. 177, Maryland club called Showcase: Ibid., 142.

p. 177, (While arresting Lenny Bruce: Lenny Bruce, "The People of the State of California vs. Lenny Bruce (from How to Talk Dirty and Influence People, 1965)," in *Sexual Revolution*, ed. Jeffery Escoffier (New York: Thunder's Mouth Press, 2003).

p. 177, Public nudity was barred: NY v. Craft, 564 NY S2d 695 (1991).

p. 178, exposed their breasts in other "noncommercial" ways: The People v.

Ramona Santorelli and Mary Lou Schloss, 80 N.Y.2d 875, 600 N.E.2d 232 (1992).

p. 178, Nude sunbathing is allowed: See, e.g., In re Smith, 7 Cal. 3d 362 (1972).

p. 178, Nude dancing can be protected: Posner and Silbaugh, *Guide to America's Sex Laws*, 85.

p. 178, Since 1957, the question of whether: Miller v. California, 413 US 15, 32 (1973).

p. 178, In 2008, the George W. Bush administration: Spencer S. Hsu, "US District Judge Drops Porn Charges against Video Producer John A. Stagliano," *Washington Post,* July 17, 2010.

p. 179, One of the task force's victories: United States v. Paul F. Little, No. 08-15964 (11th Cir., 2010); "Porn Producer Invokes the Bush/Yoo Defense—Unsuccessfully," *Salon,* October 5, 2008.

p. 179, According to a *Rolling Stone* source: David Kushner, "Casualty of Porn," *Rolling Stone,* December 5, 2005.

p. 180, John Stagliano, known as Buttman: Mary Elizabeth Williams, "'Buttman's' Porn Obscenity Trial: Why It Matters," *Salon,* July 13, 2010; Hsu, "US District Judge Drops Porn Charges"; US v. Stagliano, 729 F. Supp.2d 222 (D.D.C. 2010).

p. 180, Not long afterward, the Obama administration: Jacob Sullum, "DOJ Shuts down Obscenity Task Force," *Opposing Views,* April 18, 2011.

p. 180, a savvy Florida lawyer, Lawrence Walters: Matt Richtel, "What's Obscene? Google Could Have an Answer," *New York Times,* June 24, 2008.

p. 181, Take the advent of sexting: Kaitlin Lounsbury, Kimberly J. Mitchell, and David Finkelhor, "The True Prevalence of 'Sexting,'" Crimes Against Children Research Center, University of New Hampshire, April 2011.

p. 181, sexting is emerging as a common: Rosin, "Why Kids Sext."

p. 181, Adults can generally sext without penalty: Lawrence G. Walters, "How to Fix the Sexting Problem: An Analysis of the Legal and Policy Considerations for Sexting Legislation," *First Amendment Law Review* 9 (December 14, 2010): 109.

p. 181, the court offered the following wisdom: A.H. v. State of Florida, case no. 1D06-0162 (DCA Fla. 2007).

p. 182, female high school students in Pennsylvania: Walters, "How to Fix the Sexting Problem," 103–105; Kim Zetter, "Court Slaps Prosecutor Who Threatened Child-Porn Charges over 'Sexting,'" *Wired,* March 18, 2010; Miller v Skumanick, 605 F.Supp.2d 634 (2009).

p. 182, In one recent Virginia case: Rosin, "Why Kids Sext."

p. 183, This is especially true given: Emily Bazelon, "Another Sexting Tragedy," *Slate,* April 12, 2013.

p. 183, Audrie Pott, fifteen, hanged herself: "Audrie Pott Suicide: Three Teens Arrested for Alleged Sexual Assault of Calif. Girl Who Committed Suicide," CBS News, April 12, 2013.

p. 183, high school girl named Rehtaeh Parsons: "Stephen Harper 'Sickened' by

Alleged 'Sexual Criminal Activity' Linked to Rehtaeh Parsons Tragedy,"
National Post, April 11, 2013.

p. 183, the boy who photographed Parsons: Steve Bruce, "Young Man Enters
Guilty Plea in High-Profile Nova Scotia Child Porn Case," *Chronicle Herald,* September 22, 2014.

p. 183, Consider the Maryland man who: Annmarie Chiarini, "I Was a Victim
of Revenge Porn—I Don't Want Anyone Else to Face It," Alternet, November 19, 2013.

p. 183, There is also the woman who runs: Louise Boyle, "Meet the Mom Who
Runs a Revenge Porn Website Filled with Explicit Pictures of 'Home
Wrecking Mistresses' (but NOT the Cheating Husbands)," *Daily Mail
Online,* December 13, 2013.

p. 183, and the fraternity brothers who amused: Terrence McCoy, "Penn State
Frat Boys Sure Enjoyed Posting Facebook Pics of Nude, Passed out
Women," *Washington Post,* March 18, 2015.

p. 183, Then there is the worst of the worst: Samantha Payne, "'Revenge Porn'
Website Owner Kevin Bollaert Faces Trial over Explicit Images," *International Business Times,* June 18, 2014, Bollaert was convicted on multiple
counts of extortion and identity theft. David Wagner, "San Diego Man
Found Guilty in Revenge Porn Trial," KPBS, February 2, 2015.

p. 184, According to one 2013 study: See Robert Siciliano, "Do You Share Passwords with Your Partner?" February 4, 2013, https://blogs.mcafee.com/
consumer/love-relationships-technology-survey.

p. 184, In 2014, the UK passed a law: Ministry of Justice, "New Law to Tackle
Revenge Porn," Gov.uk, October 12, 2014.

p. 184, Israel also classifies revenge porn: House Bill 2515, Arizona (2014).
http://www.azleg.gov/legtext/51leg/2r/bills/hb2515s.pdf.

p. 184, Arizona's law, for example,: Amanda Levendowski, "Arizona's Revenge
Porn Law Isn't a Solution—It's a Different Kind of Problem," *Vice News,*
September 29, 2014.

p. 184, other laws are also quite broad: Ibid.: In 2014, the ACLU, representing the
National Press Photographers Association and others, challenged Arizona's
revenge porn law, claiming, among other things, that it criminalizes a news
organization's publication of images of nude victims of crimes, such as the
unclothed subjects of abuses at the Abu Ghraib prison during the Iraq War.

p. 184, Even with no specific revenge-porn law: "Houston Woman Wins
$500,000 in 'Revenge Porn' Lawsuit," ABC News, February 27, 2014.

p. 184, And no revenge-porn law: US v. Hunter Moore, et al., case no. CR 13-
0917 (CD, CA, 2013), grand jury indictment.

p. 184, Increasingly, couples who sign prenuptial: Lauren Effron, "I Love You,
You're Perfect, but Watch What You Facebook: Social Media Prenups,"
ABC News, June 3, 2014.

p. 185, Doyle R. Paroline, who was found guilty: Paroline v. United States, 572
US_(2014).

p. 185, In response to the decision, Amy: Paul Cassell, "The Crime Victim's

Reaction to Today's Supreme Court Decision," *Washington Post,* April 23, 2014.

p. 185, The issue of compensating victims: Heins, *Sex, Sin, and Blasphemy,* 159–161.

p. 186, a grieving mother sued *Penthouse* magazine: Ibid., 9–10.

p. 186, When the elites of Renaissance Europe: Paula Findlen, "Humanism, Politics and Pornography in Renaissance Italy," in *The Invention of Pornography: Obscenity and the Origins of Modernity, 1500–1800* (New York: Zone Books, 1993), 49–108.

p. 187, A federal law from 1873 banned: Berkowitz, *Sex and Punishment,* 364.

p. 188, In the words of one proud: Ibid., 371.

p. 188, Morals advocates such as Comstock: Herzog, *Sexuality in Europe,* 129; Vern L. Bullough, "Masturbation: A Historical Overview," *Journal of Psychology and Human Sexuality* 14, no. 2/3 (2002): 17–33.

p. 188, and a source of weakness in societies: Herzog, *Sexuality in Europe,* 29.

p. 188, Even Sigmund Freud and his followers: Thomas W. Laqueur, *Solitary Sex: A Cultural History of Masturbation* (New York: Zone Books, 2003), 365; Michael S. Patton, "Twentieth-Century Attitudes toward Masturbation," *Journal of Religion and Health* 25, no. 4 (Winter 1986): 291–302.

p. 188, As Comstock thundered in his manifesto: Anthony Comstock, *Traps for the Young* (New York: Funk and Wagnalls, 1883).

p. 189, In 2012, Wisconsin Governor Scott Walker: Wisconsin Senate Bill 237 (passed 2012).

p. 190, Nowhere was this more the case: Prior to 1935, when the FBI was formally named the Federal Bureau of Investigation, it had various other names, including the United States Bureau of Investigation.

p. 190, Aside from the incriminating material: Charles, *The FBI's Obscene File,* 95.

p. 190, Former assistant director William Sullivan wrote: Ibid., 62.

p. 191, two agents were dispatched to a San Francisco film festival: Ibid., 66.

p. 191, Keating himself was a mixed bag: Whitney Strub, "Perversion for Profit: Citizens for Decent Literature and the Arousal of an Antiporn Public in the 1960s," *Journal of the History of Sexuality* 15, no. 2 (May 2006): 259.

p. 191, In 1962, as the CDL cheered on: Ibid., 279.

p. 192, In 1965, at a CDL conference: Strub, "Perversion for Profit," 280–284.

p. 192, the CDL and Senator Strom Thurmond: De Grazia, *Girls Lean back Everywhere,* 538–539.

p. 192, Even the strident and influential 1993 book: MacKinnon, *Only Words,* 3.

p. 193, "I've got no problem wanting: Christina Hoff Sommers, "True Blue: The Respectable Pornographer," *Weekend Australian,* March 13, 1999.

p. 193, Philip Roth called "an enormous piety binge": Philip Roth, *The Human Stain* (New York: Vintage International, 2000), 2–3.

p. 193, The findings of Starr's investigation: Kenneth W. Starr, "The Report," Office of the Independent Counsel, September 9, 1998.

p. 194, However, the *Starr Report* stands on its own: Ibid., 17.

p. 194, Five years after Starr finished smearing Clinton: "Student Handbook:

School of Law Section: Sexual Relationships," Pepperdine University, n.d., http://law.pepperdine.edu/academics/student-handbook/law/studentlife.htm.

p. 194, As one reporter for *GQ* magazine discovered: Jason Zengerle, "Wanna Be Veep? Okay, but This Is Going to Hurt," *GQ,* August 2012.

p. 195, One law school friend, Henry Terry: Jane Mayer and Jill Abramson, *Strange Justice: The Selling of Clarence Thomas* (New York: Houghton Mifflin Company, 1994), 57.

p. 195, Thomas's key supporter in the Senate: Ibid., 271, 334.

p. 195, If that happened, Danforth threatened: Ibid., 334.

p. 196, He was on the court for life: Ibid., 350.

p. 196, Had the whole truth emerged: Ibid., 337. Biden agreed that Thomas would have been "decimated" by the exposure of his pornography rentals.

p. 196, sexual-harassment law can allow an "end run": Eugene Volokh, "Freedom of Speech and Workplace Harassment," *UCLA Law Review* 39 (1992): 1791.

p. 197, Not only was the professor, Nancy Stumhofer: Nancy Stumhofer, "Goya's Naked Maja and the Classroom Climate," *Democratic Culture* (Spring 1994).

p. 197, They also offered to remove: Nat Hentoff, "Harassment by a Goya Painting?" *Reading Eagle,* January 4, 1992.

p. 197, The painting constituted sexual harassment: Nat Hentoff, "Sexual Harassment by Francisco Goya," *Washington Post,* December 27, 1991; Volokh, "Freedom of Speech and Workplace Harassment."

p. 198, In 1993, the University of Nebraska: Nadine Strossen, *Defending Pornography: Free Speech, Sex, and the Fight for Women's Rights* (New York: New York University Press, 1995), 127.

p. 198, In another incident a few years later: Henderson v. City of Murfreesboro, Tenn., 960 F.Supp. 1292 (1997).

p. 198, about a year after the Hill–Thomas hearings: Kristin H. Berger Parker, "Ambient Harassment under Title VII: Reconsidering the Workplace Environment," *Northwestern University Law Review* 102, no. 2 (2008): 951–952.

p. 199, Yet in California's Coalinga State Hospital: Tom McNichol, "Trapped in the Treatment Mall," *California Lawyer,* September 2008; Louis Theroux, "Where They Keep the Paedophiles," BBC News, April 17, 2009; "Controversial Sex Offender Hospital Costs Taxpayers," Inside Edition, September 27, 2010.

p. 199, "Although Men's Health magazine: In Re Johnson, 176 Cal.App.4th 290 (2009).

p. 199, However, in 2013, another California court: In re Andres Martinez, case no. A134400 (CA. App., 2013).

p. 200, Connecticut recently banned all: Pat Eaton-Robb, "Connecticut Prisoners Express Anger over Porn Ban," CBS Connecticut, October 8, 2011.

p. 200, noted First Amendment lawyer Charles Rembar: Charles Rembar, *The End of Obscenity: The Trials of Lady Chatterley, Tropic of Cancer, and Fanny Hill* (New York: Simon and Schuster, 1968), 492.

p. 200, the regions with the most restrictive obscenity laws: Edelman, "Red Light States," 209–220.

p. 200, New York governor Mario Cuomo observed: Mario Cuomo, *Reason to Believe* (New York: Simon and Schuster, 1995), 154.

p. 201, Recently, British Internet providers made: David Segal, "Does Porn Hurt Children?" *New York Times,* March 28, 2014.

p. 201, So long as sex remains (in the words: Roth v. United States, 354 US 476, 487 (1957).

CHAPTER 5

p. 203, In 1961, a sixty-year-old: Jenkins, *Moral Panic,* 26.

p. 203, Fourteen years later, an English man: Director of Public Prosecutions v. Morgan (1976) AC 182, (1975) 2 All ER 347.

p. 203, In 2013, an Israeli judge: Linda Gradstein, "Nissim Yeshaya, Israeli Judge, Says 'Some Girls Enjoy Being Raped,' Resigns amid Outcry," *World Post,* June 6, 2013.

p. 203, A rape counselor at a major: Heather MacDonald, "The Campus Rape Myth," *City Journal,* Winter 2008.

p. 204, In 2014, for example, a Texas judge: Jennifer Emily, "Judge Says Sexually Assaulted 14-Year-Old 'Wasn't the Victim She Claimed to Be,'" *Dallas News,* May 1, 2014.

p. 204, The men who gang-raped: The court upheld the convictions on the ground that a jury could never have decided that the men honestly believed that she had consented.

p. 204, British law soon changed to require: Regina v. Cogan and Leek, 3 WLR 316 (1975).

p. 204, Rape has come to be seen: Vicki Shultz, "Reconceptualizing Sexual Harassment," *Yale Law Journal* 107 (1998): 1698; Ellen Willis, *No More Nice Girls: Countercultural Essays* (Minneapolis: University of Minnesota Press, 1992), 143–144.

p. 205, Approximately half the females who accused: Berkowitz, *Sex and Punishment,* 141–142.

p. 205, In 1320, a ten-year-old London girl: Ibid., 142–143.

p. 205, Hale warned that rape was: G. Geis, "Lord Hale, Witches, and Rape," *British Journal of Law and Society* 5, no. 1 (Summer 1978): 26–44.

p. 205, Lord Hale was a Puritan prig: Ibid., 29.

p. 205, When he wrote that husbands could: Ibid., 29–30.

p. 206, Hale's positions on rape: Jocelynne A. Scutt, *The Sexual Gerrymander: Women and the Economics of Power* (North Melbourne, Australia: Spinifex Press, 1994), 139–160.

p. 206, Judges routinely cautioned juries: A. T. Morris, "The Empirical, Historical and Legal Case against the Cautionary Instruction: A Call for Legislative Reform," *Duke Law Journal* 1988, no. 1 (1988): 154–157; Vivian Berger, "Man's Trial, Woman's Tribulation: Rape Cases in the Courtroom," *Columbia Law Review* 77, no. 1 (January 1977): 10; Scutt, *Sexual Gerrymander,* 148.

p. 206, a 60 percent chance of being charged: Berger, "Man's Trial, Woman's Tribulation," 6.

p. 206, John Wigmore, a major legal authority: John Wigmore, *Wigmore on Evidence*, vol. 1, at 683 (1940 edition).

p. 206, When he wrote that women fantasized: Scutt, *Sexual Gerrymander*, 137; Estelle B. Freedman, *Redefining Rape* (Cambridge, MA: Harvard University Press, 2013), 273–274; Berger, "Man's Trial, Woman's Tribulation," 21–22; Susan Brownmiller, *Against Our Will: Men, Women, and Rape* (New York: Fawcett Columbine, 1975), 315, et seq.

p. 207, And when he wrote that rape trials: John Wigmore, *Wigmore on Evidence*, vol. 3A, sec. 924.

p. 207, In its 1970 edition, Wigmore's treatise: Berger, "Man's Trial, Woman's Tribulation," 27, footnote 168.

p. 207, An influential *Yale Law Journal* article: "Forcible and Statutory Rape: An Exploration of the Operation and Objectives of the Consent Standard," *Yale Law Journal* 62, no. 1 (1952): 55.

p. 207, When [the accuser's] behavior looks: Ibid., 67–68 (italics added); cf. Sigmund Freud, "The Economic Problem in Masochism," in *Freud on Women: A Reader* (New York: W. W. Norton and Company, 1990), 283, et seq.

p. 208, the *Stanford Law Review* weighed in: Roger B. Dworkin, "The Resistance Standard in Rape Legislation," *Stanford Law Review* 18 (1966): 682 (internal citations omitted); Scutt, *Sexual Gerrymander*, 137, quoting an Australian judge who observed that in his legal experience, no did not always mean no.

p. 208, In 1971, Menachem Amir, a prominent: Menachem Amir, *Patterns in Forcible Rape* (Chicago: University of Chicago Press, 1971).

p. 208, Amir echoed Morris Ploscowe: Morris Ploscowe, "Sex Offenses: The American Legal Context," *Law and Contemporary Problems* 25 (Spring 1960): 217–224; see, generally, Morris Ploscowe, *Sex and the Law* (New York: Prentice-Hall, 1951), 187–190.

p. 209, none other than Alfred C. Kinsey: Paul H. Gebhard et al., *Sex Offenders: An Analysis of Types* (New York: Bantam Books, 1967), 178.

p. 209, Lord Hale's observation that: Morris, "Empirical, Historical and Legal Case against the Cautionary Instruction," 160, et seq.

p. 209, In other violent crime cases: See, generally, "The Corroboration Rule and Crimes Accompanying Rape," *University of Pennsylvania Law Review* 118 (January 1970): 458–472.

p. 209, A 1970s edition of the popular police manual: George T. Payton and Michael Amaral, *Patrol Operations and Enforcement Tactics* (San Jose, CA: Criminal Justice Services, 1993), 290. Quoted in Brownmiller, *Against Our Will*, 364. The opening line of the 1993 edition of *Patrol Operations and Enforcement Tactics* was amended to say, "Forcible rape is sometimes falsely reported."

p. 210, In her landmark 1975 book: Brownmiller, *Against Our Will*, 365.

p. 210, In one account, a woman arrives: Ibid., 365–366.

p. 210, Prostitutes stood at the far end: Michelle J. Anderson, "Chastity Requirement to Sexuality License: Sexual Consent and a New Rape Shield Law," *George Washington Law Review* 70, no. 1 (2002): 51–162.

p. 210, Here is the official statement: Berger, "Man's Trial, Woman's Tribulation," 15.

p. 210, Knowing this, it is not surprising: Sergeant Joanne Archambault and Kimberly A. Lonsway, "Clearance Methods for Sexual Assault Cases," End Violence Against Women International, July 2007, 16, 21.

p. 210, or that the Philadelphia police would: "Police Discretion and Judgment That a Crime Has Been Committed—Rape in Philadelphia," *University of Pennsylvania Law Review* 117, no. 2 (December 1968): 291.

p. 210, In a fascinating study conducted: Lisa Frohmann, "Discrediting Victims' Allegations of Sexual Assault: Prosecutorial Accounts of Case Rejections," *Social Problems* 38, no. 2 (May 1991): 213–226.

p. 210, One such prosecutor rejected: Ibid., 217–218.

p. 211, In another of Frohman's examples: Ibid., 223.

p. 211, Other studies, conducted in the: Susan Estrich, *Real Rape*, 17–18.

p. 211, Actual examples of questions posed: Anderson, "Chastity Requirement to Sexuality License," 51, 54, and cases cited therein.

p. 212, As one court held in 1955: Frady v. State, 90 S.E.2d 664 (1955).

p. 212, If the victim was humiliated: Roper v. State, 375 S.W.2d 454 (1964).

p. 212, In a San Francisco rape case: Berger, "Man's Trial, Woman's Tribulation," 14–15.

p. 212, In 1975, a hotshot young: See July 28, 1975 affidavit of Hilary Rodham filed in State of Arkansas v. Thomas Alfred Taylor, Circuit Court of Washington County, Arkansas, Case no. CR-75-203.

p. 212, Clinton (through a spokesperson): Josh Rogin, "Exclusive: 'Hillary Clinton Took Me Through Hell,' Rape Victim Says," *Daily Beast,* June 20, 2014.

p. 212, Arguably, the most formidable barrier: Morris, "Empirical, Historical and Legal Case against the Cautionary Instruction," 161–163.

p. 212, A widely published 1966 study: Harry Kalven and Hans Zeisel, *The American Jury* (Boston: Little, Brown, 1966), 248–255.

p. 213, Typical is a case from North Dakota: Packineau v. United States, 202 F.2d 681, 686 (1953).

p. 213, This helps to explain the troubling result: State v. Alston, 312 S.E. 2d 470 (1984).

p. 214, The trial judge found the man guilty: Gonzales v. State, 516 P.2d 592, 595 (Wyo. 1973).

p. 215, In all, the court found the situation: Ibid.

p. 215, what Andrew Taslitz defined in 2005: Andrew E. Taslitz, "Willfully Blinded: On Date Rape and Self-Deception," *Harvard Journal of Law and Gender* 28 (2005): 385.

p. 215, The requirement that rape victims: Berger, "Man's Trial, Woman's Tribulation," 11; Dworkin, "The Resistance Standard in Rape Legislation."

p. 215, The many reasons for this go beyond: Martha Hodes, *White Women,*

Black Men: Illicit Sex in the Nineteenth-Century South (New Haven, CT: Yale University Press, 1997), 210.

p. 216, For instance, in 1872, a Rochester: Estelle B. Freedman, "'Crimes Which Startle and Horrify': Gender, Age, and the Racialization of Sexual Violence in White American Newspapers, 1870–1900," *Journal of the History of Sexuality* 20, no. 3 (2011): 479–480.

p. 216, Northern newspapers affirmed that rape: Ibid., 481, footnote 41.

p. 216, In 1892, the *New York Times* reported: Freedman, *Redefining Rape,* 98–99.

p. 216, Between 1930 and 1977 (when capital punishment: Berger, "Man's Trial, Woman's Tribulation," 4.

p. 216, Twice the US Supreme Court reversed: Powell v. Alabama, 287 US 45 (1932).

p. 217, no African Americans on the jury rolls: Norris v. Alabama, 294 US 587 (1935).

p. 217, One of the judges told jurors: Freedman, *Redefining Rape,* 261.

p. 217, Most importantly, after the Scottsboro cases: Ibid., 269.

p. 217, In 1989, the last surviving Scottsboro Boy: Albin Krebs, "Clarence Norris, the Last Survivor of 'Scottsboro Boys,' Dies at 76," *New York Times,* January 26, 1989.

p. 217, Three months later, another racially suffused: Sarah Burns, *The Central Park Five: The Untold Story behind One of New York City's Most Infamous Crimes* (New York: Vintage Books, 2011), 31–36.

p. 217, That Meili survived was miraculous: Sydney H. Schanberg, "A Journey through the Tangled Case of the Central Park Jogger," *Village Voice,* November 19, 2002.

p. 217, The *New York Post*'s Pete Hamill: Lynnell Hancock, "Coloring the Central Park Jogger Case," Alternet, January 15, 2003.

p. 218, The fallout from the attacks: Ibid.

p. 218, Donald Trump ran full-page ads: Timothy Sullivan, *Unequal Verdicts: The Central Park Jogger Trials* (New York: Simon and Schuster, 1992), 57.

p. 218, "If we don't get a rape: Ibid., 296.

p. 218, The real attacker, Matias Reyes: Benjamin Weiser, "5 Exonerated in Central Park Jogger Case Agree to Settle Suit for $40 Million," *New York Times,* June 19, 2014.

p. 219, In 1901, : *America's Race Problems: Addresses at the Annual Meeting of the American Academy of Political and Social Science, Philadelphia, April Twelfth and Thirteenth* (New York: McClure, Phillips and Co., 1901).

p. 219, journalist Bob Herbert attacked the boys: William Glaberson, "In Jogger Case, Once Viewed Starkly, Some Skeptics Side with Defendants," *New York Times,* August 8, 1990.

p. 219, The fact is that Winston's stereotype: Rivka Gewirtz Little, "Rage before Race," *Village Voice,* October 15, 2002.

p. 219, While some at the time noted: Glaberson, "In Jogger Case."

p. 219, In May 1933, some four thousand people: Craig Simpson, "'Scottsboro Boys'—New Tactics and Strategy for Civil Rights," *Washington*

Area Spark, n.d. http://washingtonspark.wordpress.com/2013/02/19/
scottsboro-boys-a-new-type-of-march-on-washington-1933/.

p. 220, Is rape a natural result of: People v. Flanagan, 342 N.W.2d 609 (Mich.
Ct. App. 1983).

p. 220, ("The thrusting is persistent invasion: Andrea Dworkin, *Intercourse: The
Twentieth Anniversary Edition* (New York: Basic Books, 1987), 154.

p. 220, It also sparked: Brownmiller, *Against Our Will,* 301–302.

p. 220, Catharine MacKinnon's suggestions that rapists: Catharine A. MacKinnon, "Feminism, Marxism, Method, and the State: Toward Feminist Jurisprudence," *Signs* 8, no. 4 (Summer 1983): 643–647 (italics in original).

p. 221, As usual, MacKinnon framed: MacKinnon, Ibid. 649.

p. 221, In 2012, the FBI also announced: "Attorney General Eric Holder
Announces Revisions to the Uniform Crime Report's Definition of Rape,"
Department of Justice, Office of Public Affairs, January 6, 2012. http://
www.justice.gov/opa/pr/attorney-general-eric-holder-announces-revi-
sions-uniform-crime-report-s-definition-rape.

p. 221, Equally overdue have been efforts: Anderson, "Chastity Requirement to
Sexuality License," 2; Berger, "Man's Trial, Woman's Tribulation," 69 et
seq.

p. 222, It is debatable whether such laws: Steven Pinker, *The Better Angels of Our
Nature: Why Violence Has Declined* (New York: Penguin Books, 2012), 403.

p. 222, When President Jimmy Carter signed: Anderson, "Chastity Requirement to Sexuality License," 93.

p. 222, Another ACLU board member, Lawrence Herman: Leigh Ann Wheeler,
How Sex Became a Civil Liberty (New York: Oxford University Press, 2013),
200–202.

p. 222, The laws are so riddled with: Anderson, "Chastity Requirement to
Sexuality License," 113.

p. 222, In a 1982 study, mock jurors: David P. Bryden, "Rape in the Criminal
Justice System," *Journal of Criminal Law and Criminology* 87, no. 4 (1997):
1272.

p. 223, In a 1983 study, mock jurors: M. D. Pugh, "Contributory Fault and
Rape Convictions: Loglinear Models for Blaming the Victim," *Social
Psychology Quarterly* 46, no. 3 (1983): 233–42, quoted in Paul Poullard,
"Judgments about Victims and Attackers in Depicted Rapes: A Review,"
British Journal of Social Psychology (1992): 307, 310.

p. 223, Many appellate judges also cannot: Baker v. State of Missouri, 403
SW3d 91 (2013).

p. 223, In 1994, an army sergeant: United States v. Gray, 40 M.J. 77, 80
(C.M.A. 1994).

p. 223, According to Judge David Souter: State v. Colbath, 130 N.H. 316
(1988).

p. 223, putting her through this kind of questioning: Andrew E. Taslitz, *Rape
and the Culture of the Courtroom* (New York: New York University Press,
1999), 86.

p. 224, When basketball star Kobe Bryant: Tom Kenworthy and Patrick O'Driscoll, "Judge Dismisses Bryant Rape Case," *USA Today,* September 1, 2004.

p. 224, [They have] led to two unappealing alternatives: Dahlia Lithwick, "The Shield That Failed," *New York Times,* August 8, 2004.

p. 225, "Although I truly believe: T. R. Reid, "Rape Case against Bryant Is Dropped," *Washington Post,* September 2, 2004.

p. 225, Rape-shield laws are supposed: Freedman, *Redefining Rape,* 284; Cassia C. Spohn and Julie Horney, "The Impact of Rape Law Reform on the Processing of Simple and Aggravated Rape Cases," *Journal of Criminal Law and Criminology* 86, no. 3 (1996).

p. 226, In 1987, *Ms.* magazine published: Mary P. Koss, Christine A. Gidycz, and Nadine Wisniewski, "The Scope of Rape: Incidence and Prevalence of Sexual Aggression and Victimization in a National Sample of Higher Education Students," *Journal of Consulting and Clinical Psychology* 55, no. 2 (1987): 162–170; Allan M. Hoffman, John H. Schuh, and Robert H. Fenske, *Violence on Campus: Defining the Problems, Strategies for Action* (Gaithersburg, MD: Aspen Publishers, 1998), 152.

p. 226, The rapists weren't always creeps: Bonnie S. Fisher, "Measuring Rape against Women: The Significance of Survey Questions," 2004. https://www.ncjrs.gov/pdffiles1/nij/199705.pdf.

p. 226, Applying the conclusions of this study: Neil Gilbert, "Realities and Mythologies of Rape," *Society* 35, no. 2 (February 1998).

p. 226, According to a widely cited 2007: Christopher P. Krebs et al., "The Campus Sexual Assault (CSA) Study," National Criminal Justice Reference Service, 2007.

p. 226, The study only summarized: Ibid., 3-14, A-1.

p. 226, but the "one-in-five" figure: Jake New, "Critics, Advocates Doubt Oft-Cited Sexual Assault Statistic," *Inside Higher Ed,* December 15, 2014.

p. 226, Undeniable is the fact that: Jed Rubenfeld, "Mishandling Rape," *New York Times,* November 15, 2014.

p. 226, some still say the myth: MacDonald, "Campus Rape Myth"; George F. Will, "Colleges Become the Victims of Progressivism," *Washington Post,* June 6, 2014; A. J. Delgado, "Crying Rape," *National Review Online,* May 19, 2014.

p. 227, rape is said to result unless "affirmative": Cal. Education Code § 67386 (a)(1)(2014).

p. 227, As Yale law professor Jed Rubenfeld: Rubenfeld, "Mishandling Rape."

p. 227, Proponents say that the new rules: See, e.g., the response of some Yale students to Rubenfeld's opinions: Tyler Kingkade, "Yale Law Students: Professor's Campus Rape Op-Ed Gets It Wrong," *Huffington Post,* November 17, 2014. ("What the affirmative consent standard does is respond to a long-standing problem faced by gender-based violence victims. The old complicated standards required a debate over whether the sex or other offending behavior was or wasn't "wanted" by the victim, or whether the victim fought back. Under affirmative consent, the question is simply whether both parties expressed a desire to proceed.")

p. 227, such as journalist Heather MacDonald: Conor Friedersdorf, "Sex and the Class of 2020: How Will Hookups Change?" *Atlantic,* October 18, 2014.

p. 227, According to a group of twenty-eight: "Rethink Harvard's Sexual Harassment Policy," *Boston Globe,* October 15, 2014.

p. 228, Since 2011, the federal government: "Dear Colleague Letter: Sexual Violence," United States Department of Education, Office for Civil Rights, April 4, 2011. http://www.whitehouse.gov/sites/default/files/dear_colleague_sexual_violence.pdf.

p. 228, Repeatedly, we read of botched: See, for example, Ariel Kaminer, "New Factor in Campus Sexual Assault Cases: Counsel for the Accused," *New York Times,* November 19, 2014. See also the powerful 2014 documentary film *The Hunting Ground,* which examines the resistance of universities to sexual assault cases.

p. 228, Returning to Harvard, the twenty-eight: "Rethink Harvard's Sexual Harassment Policy."

p. 228, The government now requires that rape: "Dear Colleague Letter: Sexual Violence," 10.

p. 229, At the center of the controversy: See, e.g., Todd Lighty, Stacy St. Clair, and Jodi S. Cohen, "Few Arrests, Convictions in Campus Sex Assault Cases," *Chicago Tribune,* June 16, 2011.

p. 229, the majority choose the college: Caroline Heldman and Baillee Brown, "Why Schools— Not Law Enforcement—Should Investigate Campus Rapes," *Ms.,* October 17, 2014; Walt Bogdanich, "Reporting Rape, and Wishing She Hadn't," *New York Times,* July 12, 2014.

p. 229, Yet they often walk away: Tyler Kingkade, "Fewer Than One-Third of Campus Sexual Assault Cases Result in Expulsion," *Huffington Post,* September 29, 2014.

p. 229, By January 2015, ninety-five: Tara Culp-Ressler, "These Are the Colleges and Universities Now under Federal Investigation for Botching Rape Cases," Think Progress, January 13, 2015. http://thinkprogress.org/health/2015/01/13/3610865/title-ix-investigations/.

p. 229, A recent American University study: Callie Marie Rennison, "Privilege, among Rape Victims," *New York Times,* December 12, 2014.

p. 230, Planes that operate off aircraft carriers: Kingsley R. Browne, "Military Sex Scandals from Tailhook to the Present: The Cure Can Be Worse Than the Disease," *Duke Journal of Gender Law and Policy* 14 (2007).

p. 230, More than eighty women claimed: Michael Winerip, "Revisiting the Military's Tailhook Scandal," *New York Times,* May 13, 2013; "Tailhook: Scandal Time," *Newsweek,* July 5, 1992; Browne, "Military Sex Scandals from Tailhook to the Present," 750–751.

p. 230, In the coming months, the Tailhook scandal: "Post Tailhook Punishment," PBS, n.d. http://www.pbs.org/wgbh/pages/frontline/shows/navy/tailhook/disc.html.

p. 230, Additionally, the promotions of about: Browne, "Military Sex Scandals from Tailhook to the Present," 752.

p. 230, Frank Rich of the *New York Times:* Frank Rich, "Journal; The Girl Next Door," *New York Times,* February 20, 1994.

p. 231, In a scathing commentary: Browne, "Military Sex Scandals from Tailhook to the Present," 789.

p. 231, To show how the military: Mona Charen, "The General's Protracted Charge," *Washington Times,* April 10, 2000, quoted in Browne, "Military Sex Scandals from Tailhook to the Present," 777.

p. 231, Browne's commentary came in 2007: David Alexander, "Pentagon Report Shows Big Jump in Sex Crimes in Military," Reuters, May 7, 2013. Krusinski [The text doesn't mention Krusinski] was later acquitted. See Rachel Weiner and Matt Zapotosky, "Air Force Colonel Acquitted in Assault Trial," *Washington Post,* November 13, 2013.

p. 231, For the few brave souls: Julie Watson, "Rape Victim: Retaliation Prevalent in Military," Associated Press, May 31, 2013.

p. 231, So far, the efforts to address: Dana Ford, "Representatives Knock Sen. Saxby Chambliss' Comments on Sexual Assault," CNN, June 5, 2013.

p. 231, or when the army's top sex-crimes prosecutor: Robert Draper, "The Military's Rough Justice on Sexual Assault," *New York Times,* November 26, 2014.

p. 231, or when military commanders still: Ibid.

p. 231, or when more than half of the estimated: James Dao, "In Debate over Military Sexual Assault, Men Are Overlooked Victims," *New York Times,* June 23, 2013.

p. 232, To be raped in prison is to: Christian Parenti, "Rape as a Disciplinary Tactic," *Salon,* August 23, 1999.

p. 232, As a Louisiana prison guard described: Carl Sifakis, *The Encyclopedia of American Prisons* (New York: Checkmark Books, 2003), 214.

p. 232, A heart-rending 1999 exposé: Parenti, "Rape as a Disciplinary Tactic."

p. 232, In 1994, the US Supreme Court: Farmer v. Brennan, 511 US 825 (1994).

p. 232, Twenty years later, rape levels: "PREA Data Collection Activities, 2014," US Department of Justice, Bureau of Justice Statistics, May 2014. http://www.bjs.gov/content/pub/pdf/pdca14.pdf.

p. 232, and despite legislation requiring prisons: See the 2003 Prison Rape Elimination Act, Public Law 108–79, September 4, 2003, http://www.gpo.gov/fdsys/pkg/PLAW-108publ79/pdf/PLAW-108publ79.pdf.

p. 232, little has been accomplished: Joaquin Sapien, "Efforts to End Rampant Prison Rape Stall Out—Again," *Salon,* May 20, 2014.

p. 232, seven Republican governors had refused: Ryan J. Reilly, "Seven Republican Governors Won't Comply with Anti-Rape Rules," *Huffington Post,* May 28, 2014.

p. 232, One reason for the lack: Kelly Riddell, "Shades of Shawshank: Guards, Staff Committed Half of All Prison Sex Assaults," *Washington Times,* January 23, 2014.

p. 232, (About one-fifth of youth victims: "PREA Data Collection Activities, 2014," 1–2.

p. 233, "An inmate is just as threatened: Riddell, "Shades of Shawshank."

p. 233, In 2012, a female prisoner in Utah: Pat Reavy, "Inmate Once Raped by Prison Guard Found Dead in Cell," *Deseret News,* September 21, 2012.

p. 233, In about half the US states: Shauna R. Prewitt, "Giving Birth to a 'Rapist's Child': A Discussion and Analysis of the Limited Legal Protections Afforded to Women Who Become Mothers through Rape," *Georgetown Law Journal* 98 (2010): 831. Even if a man has sexually abused his own child, courts may still allow him visitation rights. See Kara N. Bitar, "Parental Rights of Rapists," *Duke Journal of Gender Law and Policy* 19 (2012): 275, 276.

p. 233, I was raped in [North Carolina]: Prewitt, "Giving Birth to a 'Rapist's Child,'" 831.

p. 233, In 2009, the child of a Pennsylvania rape victim: Bitar, "Parental Rights of Rapists," 294.

p. 233, In 2004, for example, a rape victim: Ruth Sheehan, "Rapists Lose Facet of Power," *Raleigh News and Observer,* September 6, 2004.

p. 234, about twenty-five thousand rape-related pregnancies: Prewitt, "Giving Birth to a 'Rapist's Child,'" 828–829.

p. 234, While about half of the states: A federal bill introduced in 2013 to address the problem, sponsored by Representative Debbie Wasserman Schultz, never even came up for a vote.

p. 234, Some require that the father: Bitar, "Parental Rights of Rapists," 289–290.

p. 234, Some laws go too far in the other: Ibid., 294–295.

p. 234, In the years before 1973: Rosalind Pollack Petchesky, *Abortion and Woman's Choice: The State, Sexuality, and Reproductive Freedom* (Boston: Northeastern University Press, 1990), 126.

p. 234, In the 1960s, pro-choice advocates: Prewitt, "Giving Birth to a 'Rapist's Child,'" 840–841.

p. 235, The rape exception continues to be: Ibid., 843.

p. 235, Think. Rape is someone grabbing you: Ibid., 844.

p. 235, Indiana Senate candidate Richard Mourdock: Annie Groer, "Indiana GOP Senate Hopeful Richard Mourdock Says God 'Intended' Rape Pregnancies," *Washington Post,* October 24, 2012.

p. 235, A few months later, the antiabortion Republican: Laura Bassett, "New Mexico Bill Would Criminalize Abortions after Rape as 'Tampering with Evidence,'" *Huffington Post,* January 24, 2013.

p. 236, The definitions of rape, and the: Arthur S. Brisbane, "Confusing Sex and Rape," *New York Times,* November 19, 2011.

p. 236, The lawyer and law professor Alan Dershowitz: Alan M. Dershowitz, *The Abuse Excuse: And Other Cop-Outs, Sob Stories, and Evasions of Responsibility* (New York: Back Bay Books, 1995), 275–277 (italics added).

p. 236, Was Steven Pinker correct when: Pinker, *The Better Angels of Our Nature,* 401–403.

p. 236, Going beyond the statistics: MacKinnon, "Feminism, Marxism, Method, and the State," 646.

p. 236, When told in 1945 that some people: Montefiore, *Stalin,* 489.

p. 236, It is no accident that it was MacKinnon: The term was coined in 1976 by Letty Cottin Pogrebin, a founding editor of *Ms.* magazine. See Letty Cottin Pogrebin, "Sex Harassment," in *Debating Sexual Correctness: Pornography, Sexual Harassment, Date Rape and the Politics of Sexual Equality* (New York: Delta, 1995), 3–9.

p. 236, Thus the "imposition of sexual requirements": Catharine A. MacKinnon, *Sexual Harassment of Working Women* (New Haven, CT: Yale University Press, 1979), 1.

p. 237, On the first page of her: Ibid., 1–2.

p. 237, In other situations, the concept: Memorandum Opinion and Order, Paula Corbin Jones v. William Jefferson Clinton, U.S.D.C., E. Dist. Ark., Case no. LR-C-94-290, April 1, 1998, 31–32.

p. 237, In many respects, the rules: Susan Estrich, "Sex at Work," *Stanford Law Review* 43 (1991): 815. ("The rules and prejudices have been borrowed almost wholesale from traditional rape law.")

p. 237, Knight's wife discovered the texts: Nelson v. Knight, No. 11-1857 (Iowa S.Ct. 2013).

p. 238, The case ended up before: Ibid., 15

p. 238, Even if Nelson had expressed: See, e.g., Walter v. KFGO Radio, 518 F. Supp. 1309, 1315-16 (D.N.D. 1981).

p. 238, or even forced intercourse: Staton v. Maries County, 868 F.2d 996, 998 (8th Cir. 1989).

p. 238, As the lawyer and commentator Susan Estrich: Estrich, "Sex at Work," 845.

p. 238, Rather than protect Nelson from Knight's: Vicki Schultz, "The Sanitized Workplace," *Yale Law Journal* 112, no. 8 (2003): 2075.

p. 238, The bar against job discrimination: Estrich, "Sex at Work," 816–817.

p. 239, In a speech, Smith read from: Francis J. Vaas, "Title VII: Legislative History," *Boston College Industrial and Commercial Law Review* 7, no. 3 (1966): 439, 441–442.

p. 239, Sexual-discrimination complaints started: Ibid., 442.

p. 239, two female clerical workers at Bausch and Lomb: Corne v. Bausch and Lomb, Inc., 390 F.Supp. 161 (1975).

p. 239, Two years later, a female government employee: Barnes v. M Costle, 561 F.2d 983 (1977).

p. 239, It is conceivable . . . that flirtations: Miller v. Bank of America, 418 F.Supp 233, 236 (N.D. Cal. 1976).

p. 239, Federal guidelines coming out that year: 29 C.F.R. § 1604.11(a) (2014): "Harassment on the basis of sex is a violation of section 703 of title VII. Unwelcome sexual advances, requests for sexual favors, and other verbal or physical conduct of a sexual nature constitute sexual harassment when (1) submission to such conduct is made either explicitly or implicitly a term or condition of an individual's employment, (2) submission to or rejection of such conduct by an individual is used as the basis for employment decisions affecting such individual, or (3) such conduct has the purpose or effect of unreasonably interfering with an individual's work performance or creating an intimidating, hostile, or offensive working environment."

p. 240, In 1986, the growing sexual harassment: Meritor Savings Bank v. Vinson, 477 US 57 (1986).

p. 240, The Supreme Court chose a rather: Ibid.

p. 241, Even with its limitations, the *Vinson:* Lynn Evans, "Confusion in the Court: Sexual Harassment Law, Employer Liability, and Statutory Purpose," *Loyola of Los Angeles International and Comparative Law Review* 21 (1999): 525.

p. 241, Nancy Fraser called a "national teach-in": Nancy Fraser, "Sex, Lies, and the Public Sphere: Some Reflections on the Confirmation of Clarence Thomas," *Critical Inquiry* 18, no. 3 (1992): 596.

p. 241, The accused harasser was a young: Mayer and Abramson, *Strange Justice,* 235.

p. 241, The more disquiet she showed: Ibid., 96.

p. 241, Hill said she found Thomas's patter: Ibid., 90–91.

p. 242, "I was really upset," she later explained: Ibid., 100.

p. 242, This was still the case in 1982: Ibid., 111.

p. 242, Hill never complained . . . because: Susan Estrich, "It's a Case of the Powerless versus the Powerful," in *Debating Sexual Correctness: Pornography, Sexual Harassment, Date Rape and the Politics of Sexual Equality* (New York: Delta, 1995), 78–82.

p. 242, at the EEOC, Thomas told her: Mayer and Abramson, *Strange Justice,* 114.

p. 242, Alan Simpson of Wyoming said: Fraser, "Sex, Lies, and the Public Sphere," 599.

p. 243, And I have to tell you this: "Hearings before the Committee on the Judiciary." US Senate, 102nd Congress, first session, October 11, 12, and 13, 1991, 4:184.

p. 243, Even Simpson, who later admitted: Tara Culp-Ressler, "23 Years Later, Senator Who Interrogated Anita Hill Still Doesn't Understand Sexual Harassment," Think Progress, May 7, 2014.

p. 243, Rather, he attacked Hill as untruthful: Mayer and Abramson, *Strange Justice,* 308.

p. 244, Between 1980 and 1985, sixteen: Kristin H. Berger Parker, "Ambient Harassment under Title VII: Reconsidering the Workplace Environment," *Northwestern University Law Review* 102, no. 2 (2008): 953–955.

p. 244, Clinton was forced to testify about: Starr, "The Report," 14.

p. 244, "If it can happen to me: "Nomination of Judge Clarence Thomas to be Associate Justice of the Supreme Court of the United States," US Senate Judiciary Committee Hearings, Oct. 11, 12 and 13, 1991, Pt. 4, p. 185. http://www.loc.gov/law/find/nominations/thomas/hearing-pt4.pdf.

p. 245, As later confessed by David Brock: David Brock, "The Fire This Time," *Esquire,* April 1998; David Brock, "Confessions of a Right-Wing Hit Man," *Esquire,* July 1997.

p. 245, Brock had gained national notice: David Brock, *The Real Anita Hill: The Untold Story* (New York: Free Press, 1993).

p. 245, Eight months later, Brock launched: David Brock, "Living with the Clintons," *American Spectator,* December 1993.

p. 245, In what Brock later called an oversight: Ibid.

p. 245, The Paula, of course, was: Memorandum Opinion and Order, Paula Corbin Jones v. William Jefferson Clinton, 5.

p. 245, She refused and soon left: Ibid., 6.

p. 245, firebrand Ann Coulter to lament: Ann Coulter, "Clinton Sure Can Pick 'Em," *Jewish World Review,* October 30, 2000.

p. 246, The hoopla over Clinton: Oncale v. Sundowner Offshore Services, 523 US 75 (1998).

p. 246, For a court that still blessed: Bowers v. Hardwick, 478 US 186, 191 (1986).

p. 246, If sexual harassment is to be forbidden: Oncale v. Sundowner Offshore Services, 523 US 75, 80 (1998).

p. 246, Consider the gay Coca-Cola employee: Bibby v. Coca-Cola, et al., 260 F.3d 257 (3d Cir. 2001).

p. 247, Coca-Cola has cleaned up: "Workplace Rights Policy," Coca-Cola Company, n.d. http://assets.coca-colacompany.com/65/e0/36fa-0f6e4aa9bae055a644ad15d6/workplace_rights_policy.pdf.

p. 247, about half the Fortune 500: "Corporate Equality Index 2015," Human Right Campaign, 2015, 6. http://www.ct.gov/shp/lib/shp/pdf/CEI-2015 .pdf.

p. 247, Several states now require large employers: So far, it's California, Maine, and Connecticut.

p. 247, This requirement, plus a stream: Schultz, "Sanitized Workplace," 2083.

p. 247, One such service, HRM Consulting: "Sexual Harassment—California Compliant," HRM Consulting, December 5, 2014. http://www .hrmconsulting.com/hr-training/sexual-harrasment/.

p. 247, In 1994, Rena Weeks, a secretary: Jane Gross, "When the Biggest Firm Faces Sexual Harassment Suit," *New York Times,* July 29, 1994; Jane Meredith Adams, "$7.1 Million Award for Sexual Harassment," *Chicago Tribune,* September 2, 1994.

p. 248, In workplaces everywhere, these policies: Schultz, "Sanitized Workplace."

p. 248, In 2004, for example, the California: "Administrative Bulletin: Discrimination, Harassment and Retaliation Complaint Procedures," California Department of Justice, August, 11, 2004. http://ag.ca.gov/eeo/ publications/04-09ac.pdf?q=administrative-bulletin.

p. 248, Two years later, a Web publication: Bob Brady, "8 Elements Your Sexual Harassment Policy Must Have . . . and Why Just Having a Strong Policy Isn't Enough," *HR Daily Advisor,* June 18, 2006.

p. 248, In one 1994 incident, a Chicago: Dirk Johnson, "A Sexual Harassment Case to Test Academic Freedom," *New York Times,* May 11, 1994.

p. 248, Also in 1994, several female bank: Schultz, "Sanitized Workplace," 2106.

p. 248, The following year, a low-level "leadman": In Re Am Mail-Well Envelope, 105 Lab. Arb. Rep. (BNA) 1209 (1995).

p. 249, According to a 2013 survey: "Workplace Romance: A Survey," Society for Human Resource Management, September 24, 2013.

p. 249, One such contract, written by a lawyer: William C. Symonds, Steve Hamm, and Gail DeGeorge, "The Lewinsky Effect: Business Takes a Closer Look at Executive Affairs," *Business Week,* February 16, 1998, 30–31.

p. 250, With college students demanding: Jennifer Medina, "Warning: The Literary Canon Could Make Students Squirm," *New York Times,* May 17, 2014.

p. 250, with animal keepers suing: Lisa Sweetingham, "Women Drop Sexual Harassment Suit against Koko the Gorilla's Caretaker," Court TV, November 28, 2005. They claimed that their supervisor pressured them to comply with the gorilla's demand. The case was settled out of court.

p. 250, and when a six-year-old boy: "Sexual Harassment at Six Years Old?" CNN, December 11, 2013.

CHAPTER 6

p. 251, Another has Constantinople's prostitutes: James Brundage, *Law, Sex, and Christian Society in Medieval Europe* (Chicago: University of Chicago Press, 1990), 105–106, 120–121.

p. 252, Under the banner of saving: Melissa Ditmore, "The Use of Raids to Fight Trafficking in Persons," Urban Justice Center, 2009.

p. 252, For the radical feminist Andrea Dworkin: Andrea Dworkin, "Prostitution and Male Supremacy," speech presented at the University of Michigan Law School, 1992.

p. 252, Do women who return to prostitution: Janie A. Chuang, "Rescuing Trafficking from Ideological Capture: Prostitution Reform and Anti-Trafficking Law and Policy," *University of Pennsylvania Law Review* 158, no. 6 (2010): 1655–1656.

p. 252, Are they, as the journalist Nicholas Kristof: Nicholas D. Kristof, "Back to the Brothel," *New York Times,* January 22, 2005, A15.

p. 253, The plight of imprisoned maids: See Chuang, "Rescuing Trafficking," 1697, footnote 171.

p. 253, By the same token, when actress: Mira Sorvino, "Mira's Cambodia Journal—Day Two: Meeting Heroes and Survivors," CNN, December 12, 2013, sec. CNN Freedom Project: Ending Modern-Day Slavery.

p. 253, And when the actress Demi Moore: Neil Curry, "Demi Moore Sees Plight of Sex Slaves," CNN, June 23, 2011, sec. CNN Freedom Project: Ending Modern-Day Slavery.

p. 255, In its landmark opinion in *Marvin v. Marvin:* Marvin v. Marvin, 18 Cal. 3rd 660 (1976).

p. 256, involved the flamboyant entertainer Liberace: Kim Murphy, "Palimony Suit against Liberace Settled," *Los Angeles Times,* December 30, 1986.

p. 256, In 1981, tennis champion Billie Jean King: Linda Deutsch, "Billie Jean King Wins 'Palimony' Suit," *Telegraph,* November 20, 1982.

p. 256, From 1972 until 2014, vice cops: Hawaii Statutes and Codes & 712-1200 (2014).

p. 256, gave police the "flexibility": Mark Memmott, "In Hawaii, Sex with a Prostitute May Be Legal for Undercover Cops," NPR, March 21, 2014.

p. 256, In the eighteenth century, Parisian: Vern Bullough and Bonnie Bullough, *Women and Prostitution: A Social History* (Amherst, NY: Prometheus Books, 1987), 172.

p. 256, Following the Second World War: One young man, Dale Jennings, claimed in 1952 that a vice cop followed him home from a public toilet in Los Angeles, forced his way into his apartment, and "grabbed my hand and tried to force it down the front of his trousers." See William Eskridge Jr., "Privacy Jurisprudence," 721.

p. 257, Present-day sex-worker advocates: Sam Eifling, "Police Lobby to Remain Exempt from Law against Prostitution," *Honolulu Star Advertiser,* March 21, 2014.

p. 257, But only in the Aloha State: Eliana Dockterman, "Hawaii Police Won't Get to Have Sex with Prostitutes Anymore," *Time,* March 26, 2014.

p. 257, A more serious and legally ambiguous: Sherry Colb, "Sexual Surrogacy: Better Than Prostitution?" *Verdict: Legal Analysis and Commentary from Justia,* July 24, 2013, sec. Health Law.

p. 257, Said one criminal-defense lawyer: "'We're Not Prostitutes': The Sex Surrogates Helping Real Life 40-Year-Old Virgins Overcome Crippling Inexperience with One-on-One Coaching," *Daily Mail Online,* October 25, 2012.

p. 257, The French National Ethics Committee: Maia de la Baume, "Disabled People Say They, Too, Want a Sex Life, and Seek Help in Attaining It," *New York Times,* July 4, 2013.

p. 258, There are advocates for a clear exemption: See Colb, "Sexual Surrogacy."

p. 258, "Sex helps the disabled reincarnate: Ibid.

p. 260, In 2011, Louisiana finally: See "Crimes Against Nature by Solicitation (CANS) Litigation," Center for Constitutional Rights, n.d., http://ccrjustice.org/crime-against-nature#files.

p. 260, In 2013, male undercover police: Lawrence v. Texas, 539 US 558 (2003).

p. 260, After protests about these arrests: Meredith Bennett-Smith, "Louisiana Police Sting Targets, Arrests Gay Men for Sex Using Unconstitutional Anti-Sodomy Law," *Huffington Post,* July 29, 2013, sec. Huffpost Gay Voices.

p. 260, [Prostitutes] are in hostility to the idea: United States v. Bitty, 208 US 393, 401 (1908) (internal citation omitted).

p. 261, During the "white slavery" panic: D'Emilio and Freedman, *Intimate Matters,* 209–210.

p. 261, One 1912 study found that: Ibid., 210.

p. 262, American psychiatrists in the 1920s and 1930s: Freedman, "'Uncontrolled Desires,'" 87–89.

p. 262, Providing intellectual heft to this: Judith Sealander, *Private Wealth and Public Life: Foundation Philanthropy and the Reshaping of American Social Policy from the Progressive Era to the New Deal* (Baltimore: Johns Hopkins University Press, 1997); Freedman, "'Uncontrolled Desires,'" 89.

p. 262, a 1919 "mental hygiene" survey: Larson, *Sex, Race, and Science.*

p. 262, Prostitutes thus became prime targets: Melissa Ditmore, ed., *Encyclopedia of Prostitution and Sex Work* (Westport, CT: Greenwood Press, 2006), 147.

p. 262, Margaret Sanger, the founder of: Margaret Sanger, "My Way to Peace," Margaret Sanger Project, 2003, http://www.nyu.edu/projects/sanger/webedition/app/documents/show.php?sangerDoc=129037.xml.

p. 262, In Sweden, some sixty thousand: Ditmore, *Encyclopedia of Prostitution and Sex Work,* 147.

p. 263, In 1993, in what became known: Yohei Kono, "Statement by the Chief Cabinet Secretary Yohei Kono on the Result of the Study on the Issue of 'Comfort Women,'" Ministry of Foreign Affairs of Japan, August 4, 1993.

p. 263, In 2007, Prime Minister Shinzo Abe's: Mindy Kotler, "The Comfort Women and Japan's War on Truth," *New York Times,* November 16, 2014.

p. 263, Only after Abe, at the US's urging: Martin Fackler, "Japan Stands by Apology to Its Wartime Sex Slaves," *New York Times,* March 14, 2014; Martin Fackler, "US Emerges as Central Stage in Asian Rivalry," *New York Times,* March 22, 2014; Martin Fackler, "Japan's Foreign Minister Says Apologies to Wartime Victims Will Be Upheld," *New York Times,* April 8, 2014.

p. 263, Soldiers were also told that: D'Emilio and Freedman, *Intimate Matters,* 211–212.

p. 263, A pamphlet distributed to troops: Ibid., 212; see also Mark Thomas Connelly, *The Response to Prostitution in the Progressive Era* (Chapel Hill: University of North Carolina Press, 2011).

p. 264, For European participants in the Great War: Hirschfeld, *Sexual History of the World War,* 101–102.

p. 264, The Belgians, for example, informed: Ibid., 268

p. 264, "The best women spies were: Ibid., 259.

p. 265, Another prostitute-spy prevailed: Ibid., 278.

p. 265, The best known of the seductress-spies: Ibid., 283.

p. 265, The British poet Robert Graves: Robert Graves, *Goodbye to All That: An Autobiography* (New York: Doubleday Anchor, 1957), 122.

p. 265, When Graves describes being greeted: Ibid., 91.

p. 266, In one instance a landlord went: Jovana Knezevic, "Prostitutes as a Threat to National Honor in Habsburg-Occupied Serbia during the Great War," *Journal of the History of Sexuality* 20, no. 2 (2011).

p. 267, While prostitutes (and other "deviants"): Annette Timm, "Sex with a Purpose: Prostitution, Venereal Disease, and Militarized Masculinity in the Third Reich," *Journal of the History of Sexuality* 11, no. 1/2 (April 2002): 224.

p. 267, While the "sanitation of the street scene": Ibid., 234.

p. 267, The subject of prostitution during the Third Reich: Robert Sommer, "Camp Brothels: Forced Sex Labour in Nazi Concentration Camps," in Herzog, *Brutality and Desire,* 169–170.

p. 267, Himmler's sex-incentive plan conformed: Ibid., 183.

p. 268, "The main thing was that: Mareike Fallet and Simone Kaiser, "Concentration Camp Bordellos: 'The Main Thing Was to Survive at All,'" *Spiegel Online International,* June 25, 2009.

p. 268, Magdalena Walter, a German, was selected: Sommer, "Camp Brothels," 174.

p. 268, (Some prisoners masturbated from time to time: Ibid., 184.

p. 269, The doors to the little sex chambers: Ibid., 178; see also "Secrets of Nazi Camp Brothels Emerge in German Exhibition," *Haaretz,* July 11, 2007.

p. 270, "Since time began," boasted one: Na'ama Shik, "Sexual Abuse of Jewish Women in Auschwitz-Birkenau," in Herzog, *Brutality and Desire,* 235.

p. 270, I stopped beside him. . . . He looked: Ibid., 236.

p. 270, "I was only a shadow: Ibid., 241.

p. 270, Nearly fifteen thousand babies were born: Herzog, *Sexuality in Europe,* 89.

p. 270, The one constant was that: Ibid., 90.

p. 271, One showed a grinning American officer: Yuki Tanaka, *Japan's Comfort Women: Sexual Slavery and Prostitution during World War II and the US Occupation* (London: Routledge, 2002), 105.

p. 271, The long-standing assumptions about: Herzog, *Sexuality in Europe,* 91.

p. 271, Returning, war-weary soldiers were: Antony Beevor, "An Ugly Carnival," *Guardian,* June 4, 2009.

p. 272, With the intensification of Japan's colonization: Tanaka, *Japan's Comfort Women,* 15.

p. 272, It is impossible to know how many women: Ibid., 78–79; see also, Kotler, "The Comfort Women and Japan's War on Truth."

p. 272, There were many times when I was almost killed: Tanaka, *Japan's Comfort Women,* 56.

p. 273, Mun P'ilgi also described being beaten: Ibid., 49.

p. 273, The comfort-women system did not: Ibid., 110–112.

p. 273, To create a sexual "breakwater": Ibid., 134–166; see also: Masakazu Tanaka, "The Sexual Contact Zone in Occupied Japan: Discourses on Japanese Prostitutes or Panpan for US Military Servicemen," *Intersections: Gender and Sexuality in Asia and the Pacific,* no. 31 (December 2012).

p. 273, Within one day of the first: Eric Talmadge, "GIs Frequented Japan's 'Comfort Women,'" *Washington Post,* April 25, 2007.

p. 273, but it was low on their list: In the two-year reckoning known as the International Military Tribunal for the Far East, convened at American instigation to try the leaders of Japan for a long list of war crimes, the issue of comfort women was never even addressed.

p. 274, A memorandum dated December 6: Talmadge, "GIs Frequented Japan's 'Comfort Women.'"

p. 274, Moreover, as historian Yuki Tanaka: Tanaka, *Japan's Comfort Women,* 147.

p. 274, American troops were also known: Ibid., 148.

p. 274, Just as suddenly as the comfort stations: Most of them continued to serve the Americans illegally, joining the vast legions of "panpan" girls who sold sex on the streets and in other brothels. See also: Holly Sanders, "Panpan: Streetwalking in Occupied Japan," *Pacific Historical Review* 81, no. 3 (August 2012): 404–431.

p. 274, In a 1949 survey of five hundred: Tanaka, *Japan's Comfort Women,* 149.

p. 275, In San Bernardino, California, for example: Marilyn Hegarty, *Victory Girls, Khaki-Wackies and Patriotutes* (New York: New York University Press, 2007), 104.

p. 275, It was better for men to go: Ibid., 111–112.

p. 275, While the libidinous "tendencies": Ibid., 14.

p. 275, One article in the magazine *Coronet:* Ibid., 133.

p. 275, The campaign against traditional prostitutes: Ibid., 144.

p. 275, According to the SPD, such a type: D'Emilio and Freedman, *Intimate Matters,* 261.

p. 276, Soon, all women became potential prostitutes: Hegarty, *Victory Girls, Khaki-Wackies and Patriotutes,* 130.

p. 276, They were supposedly everywhere: Ibid., 120.

p. 276, prostitution arrests rose about 20 percent: D'Emilio and Freedman, *Intimate Matters,* 261.

p. 276, The idea that good girls did war duty: D'ann Campbell, *Women at War with America: Private Lives in a Patriotic Era* (Cambridge: Cambridge University Press, 1984), 208.

p. 277, In response to their complaints: Jennifer Evans, "Bahnhof Boys: Policing Male Prostitution in Post-Nazi Berlin," *Journal of the History of Sexuality* 12, no. 4 (October 2003): 617–618.

p. 278, The infamous Paragraph 175: Ibid., 610–615.

p. 278, Consider Otto N., a forty-nine-year-old: Ibid., 605–607.

p. 278, In yet another encounter beginning: Ibid., 623–624.

p. 279, When a middle-aged laborer: Ibid., 636.

p. 279, By the time Germany unified: Ingrid Sharp, "The Sexual Unification of Germany," *Journal of the History of Sexuality* 13, no. 3 (July 2004): 352.

p. 280, As noted by Kate Mogulescu: Kate Mogulescu, "The Super Bowl and Sex Trafficking," *New York Times,* January 31, 2014.

p. 280, This was the case with the 2010 World Cup: Julie Ham, What's the Cost of a Rumour? A Guide to Sorting out the Myths and the Facts about Sporting Events and Trafficking, Global Alliance against Traffic in Women, 2011.

p. 280, "I don't know if the increased: Nina Burleigh, "Super Bowl Prostitution Crackdown: Inside the NYPD's New Strategy," *Time,* January 31, 2014.

p. 281, The routine is the same in every Super Bowl city: Pete Kotz, "The Super Bowl Prostitute Myth: 100,000 Hookers Won't Be Showing up in Dallas," *Dallas Observer,* January 27, 2011.

p. 281, What of Hanna Morris, who ran: Hsiao-Hung Pai, *Invisible: Britain's*

Migrant Sex Workers (London: Westbourne Press, 2013), 111–112; see also "Couple Given Six Months to Pay back Brothel's Money," *GetSurry,* October 7, 2011.

p. 281, Cases such as this one lead: Pai, *Invisible,* 111.

p. 282, "[I have] never seen an issue: Gretchen Soderlund, "Running from the Rescuers: New US Crusades against Sex Trafficking and the Rhetoric of Abolition," *NWSA Journal* 17, no. 3 (2005): 66.

p. 282, That same year, a US-funded: "A Report by Empower Chiang Mai on the Human Rights Violations Women Are Subjected to When 'Rescued' by Anti-Trafficking Groups Who Employ Methods Using Deception, Force and Coercion," Empower Chiang Mai, n.d. http://www.nswp.org/sites/nswp.org/files/RESCUE-REPORT.pdf.

p. 284, The roots of the modern anti-sex-trafficking: Chuang, "Rescuing Trafficking," 1666; see also Elizabeth Bernstein, "The Sexual Politics of the 'New Abolitionism,'" *Differences: A Journal of Feminist Cultural Studies* 18, no. 3 (2007): 132.

p. 284, While it succeeded in closing dozens: Bernstein, "Sexual Politics," 133.

p. 284, In the late 1990s, a similar effort: See "Global Estimate of Forced Labour Executive Summary," International Labour Organization, 2012; see also Chuang, "Rescuing Trafficking," 1696.

p. 285, Between 2000 and 2005, the number: "Report on Activities to Combat Human Trafficking: Fiscal Years 2001–2005," US Department of Justice, Civil Rights Division, 2006, 25, 27.

p. 285, Since then, the volume of sex-trafficking: "Attorney General's Annual Report to Congress and Assessment of US Government Activities to Combat Trafficking in Persons: Fiscal Year 2010," US Department of Justice, Office of Legal Policy, 2011, 62.

p. 285, from 2000 to 2008, an Indonesian man: Chuang, "Rescuing Trafficking," 1698; see also Janie A. Chuang, "Achieving Accountability for Migrant Domestic Worker Abuse," *North Carolina Law Review* 88 (2010): 1636–1637; see also United States v. Soripada Lubis (E.D. Virginia 2009).

p. 285, Renowned anti-trafficking activist Donna Hughes: Bernstein, "Sexual Politics," 245–246; see also Donna M. Hughes and Janice G. Raymond, "Sex Trafficking of Women in the United States: International and Domestic Trends," Coalition Against Trafficking in Women, March 2001, 2–3.

p. 286, Others blamed "TV commercials: Bernstein, "Sexual Politics," 246.

p. 286, Add to that the advent of: Dennis Altman, *Global Sex* (Chicago: University of Chicago Press, 2001), 107.

p. 286, As explained by feminist activist: Sheila Jeffreys, *The Idea of Prostitution* (North Melbourne, Australia: Spinifex Press, 1997), 239, 319.

p. 286, A whole consortium from the farthest: Elizabeth Bernstein, "Carceral Politics as Gender Justice? The 'Traffic in Women' and Neoliberal Circuits of Crime, Sex, and Rights," *Theory and Society* 41, no. 3 (2012): 246.

p. 286, In addition, established feminist groups: Bernstein, "Sexual Politics," 133–134.

p. 286, With the backing of faith-based: Chuang, "Rescuing Trafficking," 1672–1677; see also Stephanie M. Berger, "No End in Sight: Why the 'End Demand' Movement Is the Wrong Focus for Efforts to Eliminate Human Trafficking," *Harvard Journal of Law and Gender* 35 (2012): 534 et seq.

p. 287, The Trafficking Victims Protection Act: Soderlund, "Running from the Rescuers" Bernstein, "Sexual Politics," 130.

p. 287, The breadth of the TVPA is matched: See Elizabeth Bernstein and Laurie Schaffner, eds., *Regulating Sex: The Politics of Intimacy and Identity* (New York: Routledge, 2004), 51, 53.

p. 287, This assertion was echoed: Ibid.

p. 287, Even when focusing exclusively: Berger, "No End in Sight," 525; see also "Estimating the Numbers," PBS, February 7, 2006, sec. Frontline.

p. 287, *New York Times* columnist and anti-sex-trafficking: Nicholas D. Kristof and Sheryl WuDunn, *Half the Sky: Turning Oppression into Opportunity for Women Worldwide* (New York: Alfred A. Knopf, 2009), 10.

p. 287, People use the numbers that suit: Chuang, "Rescuing Trafficking," 1707.

p. 287, In a 2003 speech at the UN: "President George W. Bush's Address to the United Nations," White House Online, September 2003, http://www. johnstonsarchive.net/terrorism/bushiraq6.html.

p. 288, Bush issued a national security directive: "National Security Presidential Directive 22," December 16, 2002. http://www.combat-trafficking.army.mil/ documents/policy/NSPD-22.pdf; Chuang, "Rescuing Trafficking," 1680.

p. 288, The neo-abolitionist community hailed: Ibid., 1681.

p. 288, the Bush administration issued a "fact sheet": "The Link between Prostitution and Sex Trafficking," Bureau of Public Affairs, US Department of State, 2004. http://2001-2009. state.gov/r/pa/ei/rls/38790.htm.

p. 288, The Bush and Obama administrations: Soderlund, "Running from the Rescuers," 75–76.

p. 288, Under the rules, pimps can: Bernstein, "Sexual Politics," 141–143.

p. 288, For some bad actors—e.g., pimps: See, Debbi Wilgoren, "Area Juvenile Sex Rings Targeted Using Anti-Trafficking Laws," *Washington Post,* March 6, 2006.

p. 288, There were so many policemen; the whole house: Ditmore, "Use of Raids," 8.

p. 289, Events such as this exemplify: Bernstein, "Carceral Politics as Gender Justice?" 253.

p. 289, the UN Human Rights Committee urged: "International Covenant on Civil and Political Rights," United Nations, Human Rights Committee, April 23, 2014.

p. 289, As with the global war on terrorism: Soderlund, "Running from the Rescuers," 76.

p. 289, In this way, the TVPA: Agency for International Development v. Alliance for Open Society International, Inc., 570 US __(2013).

p. 289, The foreign rescue missions have: Chuang, "Rescuing Trafficking," 1715; see also Form 990 Tax Returns, International Justice Mission, 2011–2012. http://ijm.org/sites/default/files/download/2011-IRS-990.pdf; http://ijm.org/sites/default/files/download/2012-IRS-990.pdf.

p. 289, (That year, its president, Gary Haugen: Form 990 Tax Return, International Justice Mission, 2012, http://ijm.org/sites/default/files/download/2012-IRS-990.pdf.

p. 290, (for some, the choice amounts to: Chuang, "Rescuing Trafficking," footnote 243.

p. 290, or confinement in dangerous shelters: Ibid., 1716.

p. 290, In a series of raids: Soderlund, "Running from the Rescuers," 66.

p. 290, Some of those caught in the rescue operation: Noy Thrupkaew, "The Crusade against Sex Trafficking," *Nation,* September 16, 2009.

p. 290, After the raid, the number of child prostitutes: Ibid.

p. 290, When Nicholas Kristof came to Svay Pak: Kristof and WuDunn, *Half the Sky,* 33–34.

p. 290, Do women who flee their rescues: Chuang, "Rescuing Trafficking," 1664–1665.

p. 290, Kristof himself answered the question: Kristof and WuDunn, *Half the Sky,* 39.

p. 290, So long as the brute law-enforcement: Altman, *Global Sex,* 113.

p. 291, When she was named a *Time* magazine: Angelina Jolie, "Somaly Mam," *Time,* April 30, 2009.

p. 291, One of Mam's early advisors: Gerry Mullany, "Activist Resigns amid Charges of Fabrication," *New York Times,* May 30, 2014.

p. 291, By 2012, Somaly Mam's foundation: Form 990 Tax Return, Somaly Man Foundation, 2012. http://www.guidestar.org/FinDocuments/2012/26 0/392/2012-260392207-09dc1f55-9.pdf.

p. 291, However, in 2014, the foundation closed: Taylor Wofford, "Somaly Mam Foundation Closes," *Newsweek,* October 20, 2014. Mam denies that she fabricated any stories about herself or others. Abigail Pesta, "Somaly Mam's Story: 'I Didn't Lie,'" *Marie Claire,* September 16, 2014.

p. 291, "She used the system, and she: Gerry Mullany, "Activist Resigns."

p. 291, Besides funding rescue efforts, the US: "Trafficking in Persons Report," US Department of State, 2012, 51.

p. 291, The cost of a Tier 3 ranking: Ibid., 44.

p. 291, While a 2004 State Department: "The Link between Prostitution and Sex Trafficking," US Department of State, Bureau of Public Affairs, November 24, 2004.

p. 292, For example, Germany, New Zealand: "Trafficking in Persons Report," 52.

p. 292, A Tier 3 status, on the other hand: Soderlund, "Running from the Rescuers," 76.

p. 292, As a center of sex tourism, Thailand's: "Empower Writes to Thai PM Re

'Anti-Trafficking' Raids," NSWP: Global Network of Sex Work Projects, June 8, 2012.

p. 292, Added EMPOWER's director, Chantawipa Apisuk: Subhatra Bhumip-rabhas, "Sex 'Trade,' Not 'Traffic,'" *Nation,* March 6, 2012.

p. 292, The Thai government's efforts have: "Trafficking in Persons Report," US Department of State 2014; see also, "Trafficking in Persons Report," 2012.

p. 292, The last and perhaps most ludicrous: Ilvi Joe-Cannon, ed., *Primer on the Male Demand for Prostitution* (North Amherst, MA: Coalition Against Trafficking in Women, 2006), 15–16.

p. 292, "End Demand" policies have been: Donna M. Hughes, *Best Practices to Address the Demand Side of Sex Trafficking* (Kingston: University of Rhode Island, 2004), 42–43; see also Jordan Carleo-Evangelist, "Police Sign of Shame Set for Its First John," *Times Union,* October 3, 2009; see also Michael Shively et al., "An Overview of Shaming Applied to Sex Buyers in the United States: Summary Based upon Research from the Study, 'A National Assessment of Prostitution and Sex Trafficking Demand Reduction Efforts,'" Abt Associates, January 7, 2012.

p. 293, In the US, these efforts have: Berger, "No End in Sight," 554–555.

p. 293, "If there were no demand for commercial sex: "Prevention: Fighting Sex Trafficking by Curbing Demand for Prostitution," United States Department of State, Office to Monitor and Combat Trafficking in Persons, June 2011.

p. 293, Advocates of End Demand policies: Berger, "No End in Sight," 539–540.

p. 293, The truth is that men of all ages: Julie Ham, "Moving beyond 'Supply and Demand' Catchphrases: Assessing the Uses and Limitations of Demand-Based Approaches in Anti-Trafficking," Global Alliance Against Traffic in Women, 2011, footnotes 39–44.

p. 293, Moreover, the idea that johns "drive": Bridget Anderson and Julia O'Connell, "Is Trafficking in Human Beings Demand Driven? A Multi-Country Pilot Study," International Organization for Migration, 2003.

p. 293, For neo-abolitionists, the most alarming: Ibid., 41.

p. 294, If the law's goal is the safety: See Joe-Cannon, *Primer on the Male Demand for Prostitution;* see also, Catharine A. MacKinnon, "Trafficking, Prostitution, and Inequality," *Harvard Civil Rights-Civil Liberties Law Review* (2011): 276. ("In a growing list of jurisdictions, the Swedish model is one initiative that, having shown promise, is increasingly favored by abolitionists at the principled and practical forefront of this movement.")

p. 294, In a thorough study of the impact: Susanne Dodillet and Petra Ostergren, "The Swedish Sex Purchase Act: Claimed Success and Documented Effects," presented at the workshop Decriminalizing Prostitution and Beyond: Practical Experiences and Challenges, The Hague, 2011, 3 (italics in original).

p. 294, Street prostitution in Sweden dipped: Ibid., 14–16.

p. 294, Most importantly, with increased risk: Ibid., 22–23; see also, Elizabeth Bernstein, "Temporarily Yours: Intimacy, Authenticity, and the Commerce of Sex (2007)," in *The History of Sexuality in Europe: A Sourcebook and Reader* (London: Routledge, 2011), 342–343.

p. 295, Finally, the Swedish law's motives: Bernstein, "Temporarily Yours," 341–343.

p. 295, In Kennebunk, Maine,: Ann S. Kim, "Police Name 21 Alleged Kennebunk 'Johns,' but Confusion Follows," CentralMaine.com, October 15, 2012.

p. 295, Some cities that are strongly committed: Shively et al., "An Overview of Shaming," 4.

p. 295, In 2013, the Canadian Supreme Court: Canada (Attorney General) v. Bedford, 2013 SCC 72.

p. 295, on the Swedish End Demand model: Meghan Murphy, "Prostitution Is More Than a Labour Rights Issue," Aljazeera, August 7, 2014; see also "Statement by the Minister of Justice Regarding Legislation in Response to the Supreme Court of Canada Ruling in Attorney General of Canada v. Bedford et Al," Department of Justice Canada, June 4, 2014.

p. 295, Meanwhile, in New York City, where: See "Public Health Crisis: The Impact of Using Condoms as Evidence of Prostitution in New York City," Sex Workers Project, April 2012.

p. 296, Hopefully, the judges in the city's: "A Bold Plan to Aid Sex-Trafficking Victims," *New York Times,* September 25, 2013.

p. 296, "Most women won't be doing: Imogen Foulkes, "Zurich Introduces 'Drive-in' Sex," BBC News, August 26, 2013.

p. 296, In 2013, the French National Assembly: Taina Bien-Aime, "France Takes First Steps towards Abolition of Prostitution," *World Post,* April 15, 2014; see also "France's New Approach to Curbing Prostitution," *New York Times,* December 8, 2013.

CHAPTER 7

p. 297, Marie Antoinette Monks's fingernails: Peggy Pascoe, "Miscegenation Law, Court Cases, and Ideologies of 'Race' in Twentieth-Century America," in *Interracialism: Black–White Intermarriage in American History, Literature, and Law,* ed. Werner Sollors (New York: Oxford University Press, 2000), 192.

p. 297, The judge ruled that Allan's will: Estate of Monks, 48 Cal.App.2d 603 (1941).

p. 297, In the mid-twentieth-century US: Gunnar Myrdal, *An American Dilemma: The Negro Problem and Modern Democracy* (New York: Harper and Brothers, 1944), 108; Earl Lewis and Heidi Ardizzone, *Love on Trial: An American Scandal in Black and White* (New York: W. W. Norton and Company, Inc., 2001), 57.

p. 298, but it could have played out: Irving G. Tragen, "Statutory Prohibitions against Interracial Marriage," *California Law Review* 32, no. 3 (1944): 269–280. Note that California did not criminalize miscegenation, but all other states did.

p. 298, These laws were part of a larger matrix: Ibid., 271.

p. 298, In Arizona, people of mixed ancestry: William D. Zabel, "Interracial Marriage and the Law," in Sollors, *Interracialism,* 57.

p. 299, When Calvin Coolidge wrote that: Kevin Noble Maillard, "The Pocahontas Exception: American Indians and Exceptionalism in Virginia's Racial Integrity Act of 1924," *Michigan Journal of Race and Law* 12, no. 107 (2007): 23, footnote 131.

p. 299, he was more politic than Harry Truman: Werner Sollors, ed., *Interracialism: Black–White Intermarriage in American History, Literature, and Law* (New York: Oxford University Press, 2000), 13.

p. 299, but no less racist than Dwight D. Eisenhower: Earl Warren, *The Memoirs of Earl Warren* (New York: Doubleday, 1977), 291.

p. 299, Foucault's critical observation about sexuality: Foucault, *History of Sexuality,* 103.

p. 299, South Africa, of course, also used: Rita M. Byrnes, ed. "South Africa: A Country Study," Library of Congress, 1996.

p. 299, In Europe, where eugenics theories: See, e.g., Sholto Byrnes, "Mixed Blessings," *Guardian,* January 20, 2009.

p. 299, More than a little sex took place: Richard S. Fogarty, "Race and Sex, Fear and Loathing in France during the Great War," in Herzog, *Brutality and Desire,* footnotes 5–7.

p. 300, As colonial troops and workers: Ibid., 66.

p. 300, Colonial soldiers not only bragged: Ibid., 68–69, 77.

p. 300, Other efforts to halt interracial relationships: Ibid., 71.

p. 301, One young man was said to have "bought": Marie-Anne Matard-Bonucci, "Italian Fascism's Ethiopian Conquest and the Dream of a Prescribed Sexuality," in Herzog, *Brutality and Desire,* 95.

p. 301, Cohabitation arrangements between whites: Ibid., 94.

p. 301, If, however, the relations assumed: Ibid., 98.

p. 302, Domestic servants, for example, were forbidden: Heike I. Schmidt, "Colonial Intimacy: The Rechenberg Scandal and Homosexuality in German East Africa," *Journal of the History of Sexuality* 17, no. 1 (January 2008): 30.

p. 302, According to historian Heike I. Schmidt: Ibid., 54.

p. 303, The first result of the Nuremberg Laws: Patricia Szobar, "Telling Sexual Stories in the Nazi Courts of Law: Race Defilement in Germany, 1933 to 1945," *Journal of the History of Sexuality* 11, no. 1/2 (April 2002): 137.

p. 303, For Jews convicted under the laws: Ibid., 140.

p. 304, (those who had at least three: Ibid., 144.

p. 305, Another case file recorded that the accused: Ibid., 156.

p. 305, In 1938, the Jewish Leo Wallach: Ibid., 161.

p. 305, In April 1901, Colonel Hilary A. Herbert: *America's Race Problems.*

p. 305, The symposium covered Cuba: Hilary A. Herbert, "The Race Problem at the South: Introductory Remarks," *Annals of the American Academy of Political and Social Science* 18 (July 1901): 99.

p. 305, Expanding on the Negro Question: George T. Winston, "The Relation of the Whites to the Negroes," *Annals of the American Academy of Political and Social Science* 18 (July 1901): 108.

p. 306, However, Winston's idyll had been lost: Ibid., 108–109.

p. 306, In the South and border states: D'Emilio and Freedman, *Intimate Matters*, 217.

p. 306, Critical to the wave of lynchings: Ibid., 220.

p. 307, The swirl of lurid accusations: Jacquelyn Dowd Hall, *Revolt against Chivalry: Jessie Daniel Ames and the Women's Campaign against Lynching* (New York: Columbia University Press, 1993), 150.

p. 307, "We will hang two, three, or four: Freedman, *Redefining Rape*, 101.

p. 307, The true crime, according to Graves: James Tyner and Donna Houston, "Controlling Bodies: The Punishment of Multiracialized Sexual Relations," *Antipode* 32, no. 4 (2000): 401.

p. 307, "No law of God or man can hold: Freedman, *Redefining Rape*, 101.

p. 307, In 1899. during the depths: "Whipping and Castration as Punishments for Crime," *Yale Law Journal* 8, no. 9 (June 1899): 380.

p. 307, The solution, the anonymous author: Ibid., 382.

p. 308, As historian Catherine Cocks observed: Catherine Cocks, "Rethinking Sexuality in the Progressive Era," *Journal of Gilded Age and Progressive Era* 5, no. 2 (April 2006): 93, 105.

p. 308, During the same decade that George T. Winston: Donna J. Guy, *Sex and Danger in Buenos Aires: Prostitution, Family, and Nation in Argentina* (Lincoln: University of Nebraska Press, 1991), 34–35.

p. 308, Soon, President William Howard Taft: Freedman and D'Emilio, *Intimate Matters*, 209.

p. 308, The main legislative result: 18 USCA. § 2421 et seq.

p. 309, He returned in 1920 to serve: Berkowitz, *Sex and Punishment*, 356; D'Emilio and Freedman, *Intimate Matters*, 202–203; Gerald Early, "Rebel of the Progressive Era," PBS, n.d. http://www.pbs.org/unforgivableblackness/rebel/.

p. 309, Medical research was identifying the organisms: Allan M. Brandt, "AIDS: From Social History to Social Policy," in Fee and Fox, *AIDS*, 148.

p. 310, "The tide [of venereal disease] has been rising: Elizabeth Fee, "Sin versus Science: Venereal Disease in Twentieth-Century Baltimore," in Fee and Fox, *AIDS*, 127.

p. 310, and red-light districts (populated mainly: Brandt, "AIDS: From Social History to Social Policy," 149.

p. 310, Ignoring that the majority of prostitutes: John C. Burnham, "The Progressive Era Revolution in American Attitudes toward Sex," *Journal of American History* 59, no. 4 (March 1973): 901.

p. 310, launched attacks on brothels: Brandt, "AIDS: From Social History to Social Policy," 151.

p. 310, In what medical historian Alan Brandt: Ibid.

p. 310, By the mid-1940s, penicillin: Fee, "Sin versus Science," 139–140.

p. 311, The association of syphilis with African Americans: James H. Jones,

Bad Blood: The Tuskegee Syphilis Experiment (New York: Free Press, 1981), 8–9, 177–178.

p. 311, Such trivialities as medical ethics: Ibid., 132.

p. 311, "The success of the experiment turned: Ibid., 145.

p. 311, As one health official concluded: "Nothing: Ibid., 196–202.

p. 311, But then there's Guatemala: Susan M. Reverby, "'Normal Exposure' and Inoculation Syphilis: A PHS 'Tuskegee' Doctor in Guatemala, 1946–1948," *Journal of Policy History* 23, no. 1 (2011): 6–28; Arthur Caplan, "Past Horrific Human Experiments Stir Concerns of Today," NBC News, October 1, 2010; Robert Bazell, "US Apologizes for STD Experiments in Guatemala," NBC News, October 1, 2010.

p. 312, "The American people are sorry: "Remarks by the President in Apology for Study Done in Tuskegee," White House, Office of the Press Secretary, May 16, 1997. http://clinton4.nara.gov/New/Remarks/Fri/19970516-898.html.

p. 312, Like more than two dozen other states: Julie Novkov, "Racial Constructions: The Legal Regulation of Miscegenation in Alabama, 1890–1934," *Law and History Review* 20, no. 2 (2002): 225–277.

p. 313, It must be borne in mind that: Madison Grant, *The Passing of the Great Race or the Racial Basis of European History* (Whitefish, MT: Kessinger Publishing, 2006), 17–18.

p. 313, Adolf Hitler, an enthusiastic student: Paul A. Lombardo, "'The American Breed': Nazi Eugenics and the Origins of the Pioneer Fund," *Albany Law Review* 65, no. 3 (2002): 743, 759.

p. 313, argued that nonwhites were a "poison: Adolf Hitler, *Mein Kampf,* trans. James Murphy (London: Hurst and Blackett, 1942), 192, 225.

p. 314, The law's main booster was John Powell: Paul A. Lombardo, "Miscegenation, Eugenics, and Racism: Historical Footnotes to Loving v. Virginia," *University of California, Davis Law Review* 21 (1988): 429.

p. 314, Madison Grant gave his "unqualified: Ibid., 432.

p. 314, This view was echoed by Lothrop Stoddard: Ibid., 423.

p. 314, Plecker later praised the law as: Ibid., 435–439.

p. 314, The pedigree of, for example, the Jefferson: Philip Young, "The Mother of Us All: Pocahontas Reconsidered," *Kenyon Review* 24, no 3 (1962), 394.

p. 314, would have forever been sullied: Maillard, "Pocahontas Exception"; Lombardo, "Miscegenation, Eugenics, and Racism," 434.

p. 314, The idea of an entire social class: Philip Young, "Pocahontas," in *Portraits of American Women: From Settlement to the Present,* ed. G. J Barker-Benfield and Catherine Clinton (New York; St. Martin's Press, 1991), 16–19.

p. 315, Soon after the Jamestown settlers: Gordon Sayre, "Native American Sexuality in the Eyes of the Beholder 1535–1710," in *Sex and Sexuality in Early America,* ed. Merril D. Smith (New York: New York University Press, 1998), 38–39.

p. 315, In his 1952 novel of race and identity: Ralph Ellison, *Invisible Man* (New York: Vintage International, 1947), 202.

p. 315, Literary irony was absent in Virginia's: Maillard, "Pocahontas Exception," 26.

p. 315, (No doubt Powell would have: Judy Scales-Trent, "Racial Purity Laws in the United States and Nazi Germany: The Targeting Process," *Human Rights Quarterly* 23, no. 2 (May 2001): 269.

p. 316, In twenty-five generations one has: Lombardo, "Miscegenation, Eugenics, and Racism," 441–442.

p. 316, Powell and Plecker were apoplectic: Ibid., 449.

p. 316, In 1928, for example, Mary Hall: J. Douglas Smith, *Managing White Supremacy: Race, Politics, and Citizenship in Jim Crow Virginia* (Chapel Hill: University of North Carolina Press, 2002), 220–221.

p. 317, Plecker also instituted a system: Lombardo, "Miscegenation, Eugenics, and Racism," 448.

p. 317, Just as racial definitions shifted in Virginia: Zabel, "Interracial Marriage and the Law"; Scales-Trent, "Racial Purity Laws," 283–284.

p. 317, The Motion Picture Production Code of 1934: Susan Courtney, *Hollywood Fantasies of Miscegenation: Spectacular Narratives of Gender and Race, 1903–1967* (Princeton, NJ: Princeton University Press, 2005), 114–116.

p. 318, One of the most dramatic examples: Jamie L. Wacks, "Reading Race, Rhetoric, and the Female Body in the Rhinelander Case," in Sollors, *Interracialism,* 166.

p. 319, In a surprise move, Jones's lawyer: Lewis and Ardizzone, *Love on Trial,* 69.

p. 319, [Jones and her mother] then withdrew in to the lavatory: Wacks, "Reading Race," 164–165.

p. 320, To save his client from being adjudged: Lewis and Ardizzone, *Love on Trial,* 168.

p. 320, One of the main civil rights battlefields: Phoebe Godfrey, "Bayonets, Brainwashing, and Bathrooms: The Discourse of Race, Gender, and Sexuality in the Desegregation of Little Rock's Central High," *Arkansas Historical Quarterly* 62, no. 1 (2003): 42–67.

p. 321, "My daughter's in there with those: Ibid., 46–47.

p. 321, The caption asked: "Is this YOUR: Ibid., 60–61.

p. 323, The court held that Ophelia's: In Re Estate of Fred Paquet, 200 Pac. 911 (1921).

p. 323, Matters were more complicated with Filipinos: Susan Koshy, *Sexual Naturalization: Asian Americans and Miscegenation* (Stanford, CA: Stanford University Press, 2004), 96.

p. 323, In 1936, commenting on sexual relationships: Ibid., 100–101.

p. 324, Fortunately for Salvador Roldan: Roldan v. Los Angeles County, 129 Cal. App. 267 (1933).

p. 324, To put it mildly, the *Roldan* court: Koshy, *Sexual Naturalization,* 98–100.

p. 324, The anti-Filipino race rioters: Rachel F. Moran, *Interracial Intimacy: The Regulation of Race and Romance* (Chicago: University of Chicago Press, 2001), 39.

p. 325, For their part, Chinese women: Berkowitz, *Sex and Punishment,* 345–355.

p. 325, Out of 39,579 Chinese people: Kerry Abrams, "Polygamy, Prostitution, and the Federalization of Immigration Law," *Columbia Law Review* 105 (2005): 641–646.

p. 325, Were the Chinese to amalgamate at all: Moran, *Interracial Intimacy,* 31.

p. 325, "Permitted neither to procreate: Moran, *Interracial Intimacy,* 32; Megumi Dick Osumi, "Asians and California's Anti-Miscegenation Laws," ed. Nobuya Tsuchida, *Asian and Pacific American Experiences: Women's Perspectives* 1 (1982): 8.

p. 325, The first real measure of respite: Berkowitz, *Sex and Punishment,* 355; Moran, *Interracial Intimacy,* 34.

p. 326, By 1900 there were about thirty thousand: John Powell, "Japanese Immigration," *Encyclopedia of North American Immigration* (New York: Infobase Publishing, 2009), 160.

p. 326, In 1900, there were almost five: Moran, *Interracial Intimacy,* 35.

p. 326, California's 1905 anti-miscegenation law: Ibid., 31–32; Koshy, *Sexual Naturalization.*

p. 326, Given such boundless hostility toward: Not all encounters between Americans and Japanese were romantic. See Chapter 6 for a discussion of Japanese females being provided as "comfort women" to occupying American troops in an effort to establish a "breakwater" against expected sexual violence.

p. 327, about 80 percent of the forty-five thousand: Koshy, *Sexual Naturalization,* 11.

p. 327, The war fought a century earlier: Dara Orenstein, "Void for Vagueness: Mexicans and the Collapse of Miscegenation Law in California," *Pacific Historical Review* 74, no. 3 (2005): 375, footnote 17.

p. 328, Most importantly, none of these groups: Ibid., 391–392.

p. 328, TRAYNOR: What is a Negro? Ibid., 395–396 (italics added).

p. 329, In short, in a world in which races: Ibid.; Moran, *Interracial Intimacy,* 84–88; R. A. Lenhardt, "Beyond Analogy: Perez v. Sharp, Antimiscegenation Law, and the Fight for Same-Sex Marriage," *California Law Review* 96, no. 4 (August 2008): 839–844; Perez v. Sharp, 32 Cal.2d 711 (1948).

p. 329, Traynor did not have the support: Perez v. Sharp.

p. 330, *Pérez v. Sharp,* as the case was known: Peter Wallenstein, *Tell the Court I Love My Wife: Race, Marriage, and Law—An American History* (London: Palgrave Macmillan, 2002), 199.

p. 331, Within a week, Hoffman and McLaughlin: Elizabeth H. Pleck, *Not Just Roommates,* 23, et seq. Florida law also forbade black women from cohabiting with white men. Moran, *Interracial Intimacy*; Peter Wallenstein, "Race, Marriage, and the Supreme Court from Pace v. Alabama (1883) to Loving v. Virginia (1967)," *Journal of Supreme Court History* 23, no. 2 (1998): 77.

p. 331, Seven other states as well as Houston: Pleck, *Not Just Roommates,* 32.

p. 331, Florida's law dated to the slave era: Ibid., 249.

p. 331, The US Supreme Court had blessed: Pace v. Alabama, 106 US 583 (1883); Wallenstein, "Race, Marriage, and the Supreme Court," 69–72.

p. 331, After their arrests, Hoffman and McLaughlin: McLaughlin v. State, 153 So.2d 1 (1963).

p. 331, However, everything changed once: McLaughlin v. Florida, 379 US 184 (1964).

p. 332, The *Pérez* and *McLaughlin* decisions: On these two cases, see, Wallenstein, "Race, Marriage, and the Supreme Court," 205–206, 213–214; Jones v. Lorenzen, 441 P.2d 986 (Okla. 1965).

p. 332, There, in 1958, Mildred Jeter: Douglas Martin, "Mildred Loving, Who Battled Ban on Mixed-Race Marriage, Dies at 68," *New York Times,* May 6, 2008.

p. 333, The two were hauled off to jail: They were told that they would serve the one-year sentence if they returned within twenty-five years. If they returned, they would still be subject to prosecution. See Wallenstein, "Race, Marriage, and the Supreme Court"; Wallenstein, *Tell the Court I Love My Wife,* 217.

p. 333, Almighty God created the races white: Lombardo, "Miscegenation, Eugenics, and Racism," 450.

p. 333, Had Judge Bazile spent much time: Moran, *Interracial Intimacy,* 95.

p. 334, Virginia countered with evidence: Ibid., 96.

p. 334, They told the justices that families: Ibid., 97.

p. 334, Not one of Virginia's arguments passed muster: Loving v. Virginia, 388 US 1 (1967).

p. 334, *Loving v. Virginia* marked a sea change: Peggy Pascoe, "Race, Gender, and Intercultural Relations: The Case of Interracial Marriage," *Frontiers: A Journal of Womens Studies* 12, no. 1 (1991): 11.

p. 335, Alabama didn't formally repeal its anti-miscegenation: Suzy Hansen, "Mixing It Up," *Salon,* March 8, 2001.

p. 335, In 2009, a Louisiana justice of the peace: "Louisiana: Calls for Resignation," *New York Times,* October 17, 2009; Don Elizey, "JP Refuses to Marry Couple," *Daily Star,* October 15, 2009.

p. 335, In 2011, Republican Party primary voters: "Press Release: MS GOP: Bryant for Gov., Barbour or Huckabee for Pres.," Public Policy Polling, April 7, 2011. http://www.publicpolicypolling.com/pdf/PPP_Release_MS_0407915.pdf.

p. 335, For example, in 1966—just before: Thomas L. Brayboy, "Interracial Sexuality as an Expression of Neurotic Conflict," *Journal of Sex Research* 2, no. 3 (1966): 179–184.

p. 335, None of the people Brayboy described: Molly Ladd-Taylor and Lauri Umansky, eds., *"Bad" Mothers: The Politics of Blame in Twentieth-Century America* (New York: New York University Press, 1998), 231.

p. 336, In 1978, the supreme court of Louisiana: Schexnayder v. Schexnayder, 371 So.2d 769 (1979).

p. 336, In 1981, an Iowa court held: In Re Marriage of Kramer, 297 N.W.2d 359 (1980).

p. 336, A few years later, the US Supreme Court: Palmore v. Sidoti, 466 US 429 (1984).

p. 336, As of 2010, one in seven new: Paul Taylor et al., "Marrying Out: One-in-Seven New US Marriages Is Interracial or Interethnic," Pew Research Center, June 15, 2010.

p. 336, In 2011, one in ten people in England: John Bingham, "Love across the Divide: Interracial Relationships Growing in Britain," *Telegraph,* July 3, 2014.

p. 336, In 1986, half of the British public: James Matthews, "Mixed Marriage 'More Accepted' in Britain," *Sky News,* December 11, 2012.

p. 336, In 2013, for example, in Greenwich Village: Caroline Bankoff, "White Guy Punched out after Yelling Racist Crap," *New York Magazine,* July 13, 2013.

p. 336, Would Anthony Walker—a young black man: "Timeline: Anthony Walker Murder," *Guardian,* November 30, 2005.

CONCLUSION

p. 339, The rising "autonomy of individual desire": Hobsbawm, *Age of Extremes,* 334.

p. 340, accompanied by what Wendell Berry: Wendell Berry, *Our Only World: Ten Essays* (Berkeley, CA: Counterpoint Press, 2015).

p. 340, an abstract form of judgment Berry calls: Ibid., 94.

p. 340, The 570 men across the US: Kim Bellware, "Hundreds of Johns Arrested in Sex Trafficking Sting That Culminated in Super Bowl Sunday," *Huffington Post,* February 2, 2015.

p. 340, And while gay and lesbian: Jane C. Timm, "Kansas Gov. Sam Brownback Rescinds States LGBT Protections," MSNBC, February 11, 2015.

p. 340, Meanwhile, many of those branded: Samuel R. Gross, "Exonerations in the United States 1989 through 2003," *Journal of Criminal Law and Criminology* 95, no. 2 (2005), 523–560; Jessie Wegman, "After a Guilty Plea, a Prison Term, and a Movie, a Sex Abuse Case Returns," *New York Times,* February 9, 2015; Friedman v. Rehal, 618 F.3d 142, 151-158 (2d Cir. 2010).

p. 341, In November 2014, as the panic: Colin Downes, "Greek Gangs," *Slate,* December 5, 2014.

p. 341, But the case unraveled before formal: Tyler Kingkade, "Police Find No Evidence to Support Alleged UVA Gang Rape," *Huffington Post,* March 23, 2015.

p. 341, Even before this, the *New York Times* called: Confusion of College Sexual Assault," *New York Times,* February 7, 2015.

p. 341, and voices were raised questioning: See, e.g., Judith Shulevitz, "The Best Way to Address Campus Rape," *New York Times,* February 8, 2015.

p. 341, In the case of one falsely accused: Wegman, "After a Guilty Plea."

p. 342, the "autoerotic pleasure: Berry, *Our Only World,* 96.

INDEX